D0843047

150

JOSIAH TUCKER

A SELECTION *from* HIS
ECONOMIC *and* POLITICAL WRITINGS

Josiah Tucker.

JOSIAH TUCKER

1713 f
II

A SELECTION *from* HIS
ECONOMIC *and* POLITICAL WRITINGS

WITH AN

INTRODUCTION

BY

ROBERT LIVINGSTON SCHUYLER

PROFESSOR OF HISTORY IN COLUMBIA UNIVERSITY

NEW YORK
COLUMBIA UNIVERSITY PRESS
1931

Copyright 1931
COLUMBIA UNIVERSITY PRESS

Published October, 1931

Printed in the United States of America
WAVERLY PRESS, INC.
Baltimore, Md.

IN MEMORY OF

WILLIAM ARCHIBALD DUNNING

NON OMNIS MORTUUS EST

04627

THE WILLIAM A. DUNNING FUND

The preparation and publication of this volume were made possible by assistance from the fund for the encouragement of historical studies bequeathed to Columbia University by Professor William A. Dunning.

PREFACE

The selection from the writings of Dean Tucker contained in this volume is published in the hope that it may be found useful to students of eighteenth-century thought, especially to those who are interested in the history of economics, political theory or Anglo-American relations. To the historically minded no man who seemed of consequence in his own day deserves oblivion, however much the distorting medium created by the prepossessions and standards of later times may have affected his subsequent reputation. In the judgment of his contemporaries Tucker was a thinker to be reckoned with. His publications, however, have been accessible in only a few libraries, and his most systematic work on economics is now published for the first time.

Except for the omission of some footnotes and of Part III of the *Treatise concerning Civil Government*, which adds nothing essential to the author's argument, and for the correction of some misprints, the writings are reprinted without alteration. They constitute but a small part of Tucker's total output. Of others something is said in the Introduction, and the titles listed in the Bibliography, though it is not complete, will serve, in some sort, as an index of the wide range of his interests.

I am deeply appreciative of the action of my colleagues in the History Department of Columbia University and of the Trustees of the University in awarding to me the income for the year 1929–30 of the William A. Dunning Fund, and thus making this publication possible. For procuring photostats of manuscript letters of Tucker in the Library of the British Museum and the Gloucester Public Library, and for other good offices, I am under obligation to Mr. Roger Howson, Librarian of the University, and to other members of the Library staff. The photograph which is reproduced as the frontispiece of this volume was generously presented by the Very Reverend Henry Gee, Dean of Gloucester; the portrait of his predecessor from which it was made now hangs in the Deanery. With the consent of the editors of the *Political Science Quarterly* I have incorporated in the Introduction a few paragraphs of an article, "The Rise of Anti-imperialism in England," which I contributed to the September, 1922, issue of that journal. Mr. William B. Fitzgerald has assisted me in reading proof.

R. L. S.

COLUMBIA UNIVERSITY
August 19, 1931

CONTENTS

INTRODUCTION

INTRODUCTION

In the golden age of English polemical pamphleteering, Josiah Tucker won distinction as a great controversialist, original in thought, independent in judgment and fearless in expression. His long life (1713–1799) nearly spanned the eighteenth century, and his career as a writer extended over almost fifty years, during which he gave to the public his thoughts on a wide range of subjects, economic, political and religious. "Almost all public events bring him forth," an unfriendly critic once wrote. Many of his ideas ran counter to public opinion and prejudice and evoked intense opposition. He was much given to prognostication and complained that his fate was like Cassandra's—none would believe him till it was too late. But he accepted his lot, which was perhaps not wholly distasteful to him, with resignation and contributed letters and articles to newspapers over the signature of the unheeded prophetess. When some of his predictions were fulfilled, he acquired a reputation for profound insight and uncanny prescience. The editor of a collection of anecdotes of celebrities, published shortly before Tucker's death, introduced only one living character. "In this," he said in explanation, "perhaps the compiler but anticipates the wishes of the reader, who may think that a man like Dr. Tucker *omni major eulogia* should be also *omni exceptione major*."[1] In an obituary notice in the *Annual Register* it was predicted that Tucker would rank "among the ablest divines and most distinguished polemical writers of his age and country."

But fortune has not been kind to his memory, and very few persons today are acquainted with any of his writings. The *Encyclopædia Britannica* has never been accused of hiding British light under a bushel, yet in the eleventh edition it devotes but a paltry paragraph to Tucker, giving, inaccurately, the title of only one of his many publications, and in the last edition his name does not appear. "Of all the pamphleteers on Anglo-American subjects in the eighteenth century," says Paul Leicester Ford, "Josiah Tucker, considering his ability and the number of his writings, is least remembered."[2] It was unfortunate for the survival of Tucker's reputation that his most scientific and least controversial economic work was not published but only privately printed, and that

---

[1] H. Seward, *Anecdotes of Distinguished Persons*, I, iv.
[2] *The Journal of Political Economy*, II, 330.

most of his published pamphlets were occasional in character, inspired by current events and, though full of original and constructive ideas, bound to lose savor with the passing of the controversies that gave them birth. He was logical in thought and vigorous in expression, but his style, formed in the rough-and-tumble of the arena of ephemeral disputation, lacks "the charm that conquers time." Even his most careful writing has little of the preserving salt of literary excellence that has saved some polemic works from oblivion. By his own confession he was deficient in critical appreciation of the fine arts, and though widely read in many subjects he was not a man of letters.

More than twenty years before Adam Smith published his masterpiece Tucker planned a comprehensive treatise on economics, the outline of which is published in this volume.[3] Had this been completed, it could scarcely have failed to give him an important place in the history of economic thought. But with no *opus magnum* to his credit as an economist, his contemporary reputation, as Professor Seligman has said, was subsequently "unduly dimmed by the lustre of his more famous successors." He wrote many tracts on the subject of the American colonies and their uselessness to the mother country, but he never developed his anti-imperial ideas in a systematic treatise. His interest in contemporary issues and movements led him to the study of political theory. The most comprehensive of his writings on this subject, and the longest of all his publications, *A Treatise concerning Civil Government*, caused considerable stir and elicited several replies; it was quoted and praised by Lord Mansfield in the House of Lords. As an early attack upon the doctrines of the natural-rights school it deserves more consideration than it has received from historians of political philosophy. But it is discursive and extremely controversial, and it made but a passing impression on the public. Hannah More, though she was Tucker's junior by more than thirty years, had a genuine affection for him and playfully spoke of him as one of her beaux. With a genius for friendship, she was a keen observer of her friends' traits. Referring to a presentation copy of the *Treatise*, which the author had sent her, she wrote in a private letter: "I am afraid it will draw upon him a number of enemies and answers, which at his time of life cannot be very agreeable. I believe where the spirit of controversy has once possessed the mind, no time can weaken it."[4]

Materials for the story of Tucker's career, apart from his writings, are scanty and fragmentary. His extant private letters contain some auto-

---

[3] Below, 214 ff.   [4] Annette M. B. Meakin, *Hannah More*, 146.

biographical data, brief sketches of his life can be found in various bio-graphical dictionaries and encyclopedias,[5] and obituary notices appeared in English newspapers and magazines immediately after his death.[6] The article in the *Dictionary of National Biography* is from the pen of Sir Leslie Stephen, who had previously paid some attention to Tucker in his *History of English Thought in the Eighteenth Century*. By far the most reliable account of Tucker's life is that given by Walter Ernest Clark in his admirable monograph, *Josiah Tucker: Economist*. In these intro-ductory pages no attempt will be made to write a formal biography, but it may be worth while to give some indication of the historical and bio-graphical setting of Tucker's writings, and to call attention to what seems most significant in his thought as an economist, an anti-imperialist and a political theorist.

Tucker came of Welsh peasant stock and was born in Laugharne, Carmarthenshire, in the year 1713.[7] He took no interest in his ancestry and tells us nothing about it. When he was a boy a maiden aunt gave him such a surfeit of genealogical lore that he took a lasting distaste for the subject. His father, a farmer, inherited a small estate near Aberyst-with, in Cardiganshire, to which he removed some time after his son's birth. Tucker makes little reference to his boyhood in his published writings or in the odds and ends of his correspondence that have survived. He must have grown up in an atmosphere of acute political contention, for the inhabitants of Aberystwith were divided into partisans of the House of Stuart and of the House of Hanover, and the hostility to Jacobitism which he often expressed in after years may well have had its origin in youthful experiences. He went to school in Ruthin, Denbigh-shire, where he made progress in the classics, and he was matriculated at

---

[5] In the following, among others: *The General Biographical Dictionary*, new ed., revised and enlarged, by Alexander Chalmers, XXX, 59–63; *Dictionary of Political Econ-omy*, ed. by R. H. I. Palgrave, III, 588–89; Joseph Stratford, *Gloucestershire Bio-graphical Notes*, 129–36.

[6] Of the obituary notices the most useful is a memoir in *Public Characters of 1798–9*, 3d ed. (London, 1801), 168–80. Others can be found in *The European Magazine, and London Review*, XXXVI, 291–93 (Nov., 1799), continued in *ibid.*, XXXVI, 377–79 (Dec., 1799) and concluded in *ibid.*, XXXVII, 18–22 (Jan., 1800); *The Gentleman's Magazine*, LXIX, 1000–1003 (1799).

[7] In a letter written in November, 1776, Tucker says that he will complete his "grand climacteric," i.e., his sixty-third year, on the 28th day of that month. Tucker to Dr. Adams, Nov. 14, 1776, Gloucester Public Library. Most of the biographical sketches and obituary notices erroneously give 1712 as the year of his birth.

St. John's College, Oxford, in January, 1733. He must have been endowed with a sturdy constitution and much physical endurance, as well as filial piety, for an anonymous writer, to whom he gave some information regarding his career, relates that he used to walk from his home in Wales to Oxford, a distance of more than one hundred and fifty miles. His father, desiring him to make a better appearance, gave him the use of his only horse, but the young man decided that this was not a seemly arrangement. "The horse was accordingly returned; and our student, for the remainder of the time he continued at the University, actually trudged backwards and forwards, with his baggage at his back!"[8] He continued long to be blessed with good health, and on a tablet erected to his memory in Gloucester Cathedral it is recorded that during the more than forty years that he served as its dean he "was never once obliged by sickness or induced by inclination to omit or abridge a single residence." In after life he had some symptoms of a "flying gout," and often found it advisable to take the cure at Bath, but this did not interfere with the discharge of his clerical duties.

It is recorded in the *Alumni Oxonienses* that he received the degree of Bachelor of Arts in 1736, Master of Arts in 1739, and Doctor of Divinity in 1755, but beyond this little can be said of his university career. The century following the Revolution of 1688 has been called the dark age in English academic history. The system of higher education, if such it can properly be called, had little to offer to an alert and inquiring mind. Joseph Butler, with whom Tucker was later to be thrown into close association, was a student at Oriel College, Oxford, in the second decade of the eighteenth century and found the teaching there lifeless and unintelligent. Adam Smith, who entered Balliol College in 1740, wrote in *The Wealth of Nations*: "In the University of Oxford the greater part of the public professors have, for these many years, given up altogether even the pretence of teaching." Gibbon left on record his opinion that the months he spent in residence at Magdalen, some twenty years after Tucker entered St. John's, were the most idle and unprofitable of his whole life. The subjects taught were taught badly, and the curriculum was sadly out of date. Such studies as Tucker may have engaged in could have had little relation to the political and economic inquiries of his later years. In after life he became convinced that the universities were not preparing their students to be public spirited citizens and believed that encouragement ought to be given to the study of subjects of current

---

[8] *Public Characters of 1798–9*, 3d ed., 168–69.

interest and importance. In 1784 he proposed that a fund be raised by annual subscription for the award of prizes to graduate students for dissertations upon such subjects, suggested a list of topics, predominantly economic in character, as suitable for investigation, and pledged himself to subscribe twenty pounds and to continue this contribution annually during his lifetime if the project proved successful.[9]

Tucker could not have been wholly unaffected, of course, by his academic surroundings. A disposition to controversy may well have been strengthened by his Oxford experiences. Perhaps it was at the university that his serious interest in political theory was first aroused. Oxford had been a hotbed of Jacobitism, and the embers of that lost cause were still smoldering. Our undergraduate was later to wield a forceful pen against the Pretender, and it may not be unduly fanciful to picture him engaged in private disputation at St. John's with unrepentant champions of indefeasible hereditary right. And in view of his later antipathy to the Methodists, one is tempted to wonder whether he had any acquaintance with John Wesley, who was then a tutor at Lincoln College, and whether he knew anything of those momentous religious meetings in Wesley's rooms.

Having taken holy orders, Tucker served for a short time as curate of a rural parish in Gloucestershire and in 1737 became curate of St. Stephen's Church in Bristol and a minor canon of Bristol Cathedral. In the following year the famous divine and theologian Joseph Butler was appointed bishop of Bristol. His *Analogy of Religion*, written to counteract the influence of the deists and freethinkers, and perhaps the most important English theological work of the eighteenth century, had recently been published and had given him a commanding position in the Church of England. Some years later he was offered the Primacy but declined it. The bishop formed a high regard for the curate and selected him as his private chaplain. There is no doubt that Tucker was greatly influenced by Butler, especially in matters of religious opinion. In a tract written years after the latter's death he alluded to him as "a very great man" and "an original genius in the learned world." For a time the two were much together and frequently conversed on metaphysical and theological questions. On these occasions the bishop often fell to musing, and once, emerging from his revery, propounded a query to which the younger man attached no great significance at the time, but which he often recalled in later years. The question was whether whole communities might not, like individuals, be deprived of the faculty of reason by some species of

---

[9] *Reflections on the Present Matters in Dispute between Great Britain and Ireland*, 35 ff.; also Tucker to Dr. Adams, Nov. 4, 1784, Gloucester Public Library.

collective insanity.[10]   Many years afterwards Tucker, reflecting upon war mentality, declared that some such supposition was necessary to account for the behavior of nations toward one another.[11]   There are many passages in his writings that give evidence of his interest in questions of social psychology.

It was while Tucker was curate of St. Stephen's that George Whitefield, who had lately returned from his missionary journey to America, began evangelizing activities in Bristol.   He was soon joined there by John Wesley, whose famous "conversion" took place in 1738, and Bristol became a stronghold of early Methodism.   Bishop Butler, though he deplored the low state of religious life in the Church of England at the time, was wholly out of sympathy with anything savoring of religious "enthusiasm" and objected especially to the Methodists' claim to extraordinary intercourse with the Deity.   He asked Wesley to desist from preaching in his diocese and in a personal interview admonished him that "the pretending to extraordinary revelation and gifts of the Holy Ghost is a horrid thing, a very horrid thing."   But notwithstanding, the evangelists made great headway, harangued large crowds outside the churches and won immense popularity with the masses.   Tucker, who was appointed vicar of All Saints' Church, Bristol, in 1739, preached against the "epidemical enthusiasm," thinking it his duty to do what he could to check the spread of ideas and practices that tended, in his opinion, to degrade and undermine all religion.

The first of his publications was a short series of Queries addressed to Whitefield respecting the Methodist tenet of "regeneration" and the "new birth."   The evangelist's influence, according to Tucker, was sufficient to prevent the *Bristol Journal* from publishing them, but copies were printed, and the Queries presently appeared in the press.   Whitefield, with great hauteur, if we may accept Tucker's statement, not only refused to reply but referred pointedly to his questioner in prayers and sermons, and even declared flatly that he despaired of meeting him in the future life.   The Bristol populace, presumably sharing this amiable and Christian view, insulted Tucker in the streets.   An answer to the Queries by an adherent of Whitefield's was published in *The General Evening Post*, and to this Tucker replied in a letter published in the same newspaper.[12]   His knowledge of Methodism evidently impressed Bishop

---

[10] Tucker, *An Humble Address and Earnest Appeal*, 20–21, footnote.
[11] *Cui Bono?*, 80–82.
[12] *The London Magazine: and Monthly Chronologer* (1739), 342–43.

Butler, for when the archbishop of Armagh asked for an authentic account of the division among the Methodists over the theological doctrine of election, Butler suggested that Tucker was a person well qualified to prepare it. The archbishop deemed the young clergyman's performance worthy of publication, and it appeared in 1742, with the title *A Brief History of the Principles of Methodism*. This earliest of Tucker's pamphlets elicited a reply from no less a personage than John Wesley.[13]

Tucker made his debut as a political pamphleteer in support of the Hanoverian dynasty during the Jacobite Rebellion of 1745. The astonishing though shortlived success of the Young Pretender in Scotland was followed by a raid into England that brought him and his Highland followers within a hundred and fifty miles of London and caused a panic in the capital, while preparations were making at Dunkirk for the dispatch of a supporting French expeditionary force to land in the south of England. The Pretender's military resources were never formidable in themselves, but if his incursion had been accompanied by a rising of the English Jacobites and a French invasion, he might have succeeded in his attempt to win the throne. There was a good deal of disaffection to the government, the nation was not inspired by any ardent loyalty to its foreign king, who had never been personally popular with his subjects, a large part of the British army was campaigning on the Continent, and a distracted administration was slow in providing for the defense of the realm. The collapse of the Pretender's cause was by no means a foregone conclusion when Tucker wrote *A Calm Address to All Parties in Religion, concerning Disaffection to the Present Government*.[14] At the advice of Sir Michael Foster, who was then recorder of Bristol and afterwards a justice of the Court of King's Bench, it was printed and given away in large numbers, and the government caused it to be reprinted and circulated throughout the country.[15]

In this pamphlet Tucker undertook to show that both interest and duty required the people of England to resist the Pretender's claims. A noticeable feature of the tract is the extent to which economic considerations are emphasized. The writer depicts in the darkest colors the economic results that might be expected to follow a Stuart restoration.

---

[13] *The Principles of a Methodist . . . occasioned by a late Pamphlet, intitled, A Brief History of the Principles of Methodism.*

[14] A new edition was published in 1752 as an Appendix to Part II of Tucker's *Reflections on the Expediency of a Law for the Naturalization of Foreign Protestants.*

[15] Tucker, *A Series of Answers*, 94–95, footnote.

The Pretender, owing his throne to the King of France and depending upon his patron for continued possession of it, would be obliged by honor and gratitude, as well as by prudence, to sacrifice the interests of Great Britain to those of her traditional enemy. Duties on imports from France would be lowered, to the ruin of British manufactures, and the Pretender could not decently or safely refuse French demands for territorial acquisitions at the expense of Great Britain in America or elsewhere. France would foment domestic strife in England in order to keep the restored Stuart monarchy in a state of dependence upon herself. In short, Tucker concludes, "the Chevalier would be little better than a Vice-Roy . . . under the Grand Monarch," and the British people would be actually in a worse condition than if they were ruled directly by France. The fear he expresses that the establishment of a Jacobite monarchy would be followed by a repudiation of the national debt was shared by the monied interests; nor was it by any means groundless, since the debt had been contracted in large part to prevent a Stuart restoration. There was equally good reason for the prediction that the Pretender would be compelled to maintain at public expense a large standing army as a prop to an insecure throne. The patriotic character of Tucker's arguments, his appeal to traditional English enmity toward France and his acceptance of current mercantile opinions regarding trade and the value of colonial possessions, are in striking contrast to the tone of his later writings. It is more in keeping with it, that he refrains from appealing to religious passions and does not so much as mention the Pretender's faith. Apart from considerations of interest and expediency, he maintains that the English people are in duty bound to support the reigning monarch, rejecting the Jacobite doctrine of indefeasible hereditary right as emphatically as he afterwards inveighed against the doctrine of the rights of man. But his arguments here belong to the domain of political theory and are reserved for later consideration.

Tucker's interest in economic questions is doubtless to be accounted for in large part by his environment. Bristol, during the years of his residence there, was, next to London, the largest city and the most important center of commerce in Great Britain. It far outshone Liverpool and Glasgow. Defoe described it in 1753 as "the greatest, the richest and the best Port of Trade in Great Britain, London alone excepted"; and the tone of its life was more distinctively commercial even than that of the capital, for its importance, unlike London's, was owing entirely to economic factors. It was not a county town or an important ecclesiastical center. It was in close commercial contact with the inland area of England drained by the Severn and its tributaries, with South Wales and with Ireland, and ever since the days of the Cabots its merchants had been interested in oversea trade. Bristol vessels voyaged to the British colonies in North America and the West Indies and engaged in the African slave trade. In manufacturing also the city was a scene of great activity. Bristol, to quote Professor Walter Ernest Clark, "epitomized eighteenth century Great Britain in manufactures and in commerce." Among Tucker's parishioners in All Saints' and in St. Stephen's, of which he became rector in 1749, there were many merchants and master manufacturers, and there is good reason to believe that his conversation with them was not confined to spiritual matters.

The first of Tucker's distinctly economic writings, his *Essay on Trade*, was published in 1749 and went through a number of editions within the next few years. In an introduction he advanced several ideas which he subsequently developed more fully and which will be discussed later. In the body of the pamphlet he examined the principal commercial advantages and disadvantages of France and Great Britain, and to the third edition, published in 1753, he added a series of constructive proposals for increasing the trade and improving the commercial position of Great Britain, some of which involved far-reaching political changes.

The *Essay on Trade* won for him a reputation as a well informed and thoughtful student of commerce, and a paraphrase of it, which was published in French in 1754, is known to have had some influence upon Quesnay and the physiocratic school.[16] Dr. Thomas Hayter, bishop of Norwich and tutor of the Prince of Wales, afterwards George III, was desirous of procuring a comprehensive treatise on national commerce for the instruction of his royal pupil, and Dr. John Conybeare, who succeeded Butler as bishop of Bristol in 1750, suggested Tucker as an authority on the subject. The work was begun at least as early as 1752,[17] but it was never completed. A substantial part of it was privately printed, though not published, in 1755, with the title *The Elements of Commerce and Theory of Taxes*, to which was appended an outline of the entire work

---

[16] Clark, *op. cit.*, 227. Henry Higgs, *The Physiocrats*, 31–32, footnote. The French paraphrase was by Plumard d'Angeul, writing under the assumed name of "Sir John Nicholls," and was entitled *Remarques sur les avantages et les désavantages de la France et de la Grande Bretagne par rapport au commerce . . .* See Tucker, *Instructions for Travellers*, below, 229 f.

[17] Tucker to Lord Townshend, April 5, 1752. *The Manuscripts of the Marquess Townshend*, Hist. MSS. Comm., Eleventh Report, Appendix, Part IV, 374.

as then planned.   This outline was published by Professor Clark in an
appendix to his monograph, but the *Elements* is published for the first
time in the present volume.   It is the most systematic and the best of
Tucker's economic writings.   It was, moreover, a pioneer work, written
before the publication of any of the important products of the French
physiocrats and more than twenty years before the appearance of *The
Wealth of Nations*.   But as it was not published it did not influence the
subsequent course of economic thought.   Tucker distributed copies of it
among his friends for criticism, but only three of these copies are known
to be in existence.   It justifies the opinion that if the larger treatise had
been completed, the author would have gained a position of eminence
in the history of economics.   One of the topics included in the outline
Tucker developed in his *Instructions for Travellers*.   In this he shows himself to be a keen and philosophically minded observer and thinker and
gives his opinions and reflections upon a wide range of subjects, political
and religious as well as economic.   Much of what he has to say in this
tract will be of interest to the student of English society in the mid-
eighteenth century.   Copies were struck off in 1757 and sent by the
author to his friends for criticism, and the work was published in Dublin
in the following year, but it is now very rare.   For this reason, as well as
on account of its intrinsic interest, it seemed desirable to reprint it.[18]
Another fragment of his projected treatise, *The Case of Going to War for
the Sake of Procuring, Enlarging, or Securing of Trade, Considered in a New
Light*, was published in 1763.[19]   In a letter written in the following year
Tucker intimated that his exacting duties as dean of Gloucester, which
he had then been performing for several years, were responsible for the
delay in the completion of his "great work,"[20] but he eventually came to
the conclusion that such a treatise as he had in mind would run counter
to cherished popular prejudices and delusions and arouse strong opposition, and that therefore it ought not to appear under royal patronage.
The project was accordingly laid aside and was never resumed.[21]

It is unnecessary to attempt here anything more than a summary of
certain phases of Tucker's economic thought.   Many of his leading
ideas will be found in his *Elements*, and Professor Clark gives a careful

---

[18] An extract from this was included by Leopold Berchtold in *An Essay to Direct
and Extend the Inquiries of Patriotic Travellers*, 520–26.

[19] Republished as Tract II of *Four Tracts* (Gloucester, 1774).

[20] Tucker to Lord Kames, Feb. 15, 1764, *Memoirs of the Life and Writings of the
Honourable Henry Home of Kames*, III, 174.

[21] Preface to *Four Tracts*.

analysis of his economic theory as a whole. To begin with, Tucker was one of the first, if not the very first, to envisage the whole range of economic life as a proper and worthy subject of scientific inquiry, and he believed that it ought to be cultivated as such, especially by statesmen and legislators. This opinion he expressed as early as 1749, before anybody had produced a systematic treatise on economics, and this alone entitles him to honorable mention in the history of the science. He used the word "commerce," it should be noted, to include not trade alone, but economic activity in general. "The elements of commerce," in his phraseology, meant, therefore, "the elements of economics."

Like the classical economists of later days Tucker regarded self-interest as the psychological basis of economics. Since human happiness seems to result from "the enjoyment of superior wealth, power, honor, pleasure or preferment, self-love, the great mover of created beings, determines each individual to aspire after these social goods, and to use the most probable means of obtaining them."[22] He recognized such a thing as a social impulse to benevolence, but he believed it to be much weaker than the self-regarding instinct. Reason must be called to the aid of benevolence to the end that self-interest might be so directed as to promote the public interest by pursuing its own. But unlike the classical economists he did not accept the view that private and public interest necessarily harmonize. The two, in his opinion, might, and often did, conflict, and he always maintained that it was the business of government to regulate the operation of self-interest so that it would conduce to the general welfare. "The great view of the divinely inspired legislator, Moses, seems to have been, to turn the principle of self-love into such a channel that it should always operate for the public good. And, indeed, this ought to be the sole aim of every government, if either good morals or national prosperity are expected."[23]

One who took this view could not advocate a policy of *laissez-faire*, and in this respect Tucker is to be classed with the mercantilists rather than with the French physiocrats or the British classical economists. It is true that there are passages in his writings which, if read apart from their context, might be taken to indicate that he favored complete freedom of trade between nations, but they really mean no more than that he was opposed to exclusive, monopolistic privileges, and desired the conditions of trade to be the same for all who engaged in it. Any trade

[22] *Elements*, below, 58.
[23] *A Second Letter to a Friend concerning Naturalizations*, 37, footnote.

he considered to be "free" in which any person might take part if he desired to do so, and it is in this sense only that he was an advocate of "free trade." His opinion as to the rôle which government ought to play in molding the economic life of a nation is shown clearly in his discussions of taxation. He was a strong supporter of the use of taxation as an instrument for the advancement of national prosperity, defining a good tax as one which tended "to prevent idleness, check extravagance and promote industry." In his *Instructions for Travellers* he writes: "That state or kingdom which by means of proper taxes converts drones into bees will be rich: But every community which turns bees into drones must be poor."[24] That he had no objection to a high degree of paternalism is shown by the discriminations which he proposes in the *Elements* in favor of married men and against bachelors.[25]

But though he agreed with the mercantilists as to the propriety and the efficacy of governmental action to promote national prosperity, he dissented vigorously from their theory of national prosperity. He denied that wealth consists in the precious metals. In a striking passage in the *Elements*, he definitely rejects what Adam Smith was later to refute as the basic economic doctrine of the mercantile system.[26] Like Smith, too, he regarded labor as the foundation of wealth, as is evident from many passages in his writings. In *Instructions for Travellers*, as an instance, he argues in favor of high import duties on foreign manufactures, not, however, for the mercantile object of securing a favorable balance of trade, but as a means of fostering national industry and labor, "because these are the only riches of a kingdom."[27] Elsewhere he writes, "Industry and labor are the only riches, money being merely the ticket or sign belonging to them."

---

[24] Below, 230.   [25] Below, 67 ff.

[26] Tucker was not the first to repudiate this cardinal mercantile dogma. That wealth consists exclusively of the precious metals was denied by Nicholas Barbon in *A Discourse of Trade* (1690) and by Sir Dudley North in his *Discourses upon Trade* (1691), both reprinted in *A Reprint of Economic Tracts*, ed. by J. H. Hollander. These writings, however, fell promptly into oblivion. Bishop Berkeley in *The Querist*, a series of queries proposed for public consideration, which appeared in 1737 and 1738 and were published collectively in 1740, challenged the precious-metals theory of wealth, as did David Hume in his essays, "Of Money" and "Of the Balance of Trade," in Part II of his *Essays, Moral, Political, and Literary*, published in 1752. It is probable that Tucker owed a good deal to Hume, with whom he corresponded for several years. Two of his letters to Hume have been published. See Clark, *Josiah Tucker*, 207–8, 255.

[27] Below, 258.

He was a staunch opponent of commercial monopolies of all kinds. Under certain circumstances, he admitted, they might serve a useful purpose, but he argued that under existing conditions they were detrimental to the public. In the *Essay on Trade*, in the *Elements* and elsewhere he attacked unsparingly those great English monopolistic organizations, the East India Company, the Turkey Company and the Hudson's Bay Company. Their effect, he contended, was to injure the many for the benefit of the favored few. His *Reflections on the Expediency of Opening the Trade to Turkey*, published in 1753, probably had some influence upon Parliament, which passed an act in the same year providing that any British subject should be admitted to the Company upon payment of twenty pounds.

Tucker shared the opinion, prevalent in his day, that Great Britain was underpopulated. He devoted the first part of the *Elements* to "polities for increasing the number of people," and in this he analyzed the disadvantages of a scanty population and argued at length in favor of the encouragement of marriage and immigration. The movement of population from country to town he deprecated as a menace to the nation, for he looked upon great cities as "the bane of mankind in every sense," nurseries of corruption, demoralization and vice, and upon the masses in English cities as "the most abandoned and licentious wretches on earth." As an economist he was naturally interested in the problem of poverty, and in *The Manifold Causes of the Increase of the Poor* he examined existing defects in the system of poor relief and advanced constructive proposals for its reform.

Most of his economic works were written on the eve of the Industrial Revolution, during the decade 1749–59. But English manufacturing industry, compared with that of other countries, was already marked by its employment of machinery. In an interesting passage in *Instructions for Travellers* he refers to the extensive use of new mechanical inventions and discusses its results. He derides "the mistaken notions of the infatuated populace, who, not being able to see farther than the first link of the chain, consider all such inventions as taking the bread out of their mouths, and therefore never fail to break out into riots and insurrections whenever such things are proposed"; and he denies that labor-saving inventions result in permanent unemployment, arguing that in lowering prices and increasing demand their effect, in the long run, is to create new employment.[28] Yet he was not in favor of the primitive factory system

---

[28] Below, 241.

of his own day.   The domestic system in the woolen manufacture, which prevailed in Yorkshire, seemed to him far preferable to the system in Gloucestershire and other counties, where master clothiers employed hundreds of persons working together in the same shops.   Under such conditions, says Tucker, the master was inclined to consider his employees as "the scum of the earth, whom he has a right to squeeze whenever he can," and they, in turn, looked upon him as their common enemy.[29]

Tucker was not a utilitarian in the Benthamite sense; he never adopted a hedonistic conception of goodness or discarded the absolutist conception of morality.   But he frequently gave expression to the view that there could be no conflict between sound economics and sound ethics, since God was the author of the laws of both.   Thus in his *Seventeen Sermons*, published in 1776, he declares that there is "no real and lasting opposition between the laws of sound morality and those of sound policy, whatever crude opinions may be entertained to the contrary"; and in his *Letter to Edmund Burke* he professes the conviction that "the laws of commerce, when rightly understood, do perfectly coincide with the laws of morality, both originating from the same Being, whose mercies are over all His works."   It would be going too far to say that Tucker treated economics as a branch of ethics or that his dominant interest in economic studies was ethical, but it would have been surprising if a clergyman had regarded the two subjects as unrelated.

The similarity of some of the basic economic ideas expounded in *The Wealth of Nations* to those which Tucker had previously set forth would make it reasonable to suppose that Adam Smith was influenced by his older contemporary, even if it were not known that he had a copy of Tucker's *Essay on Trade* in his library.[30]   It has been clearly established, moreover, that Smith owed much to the French economists, some of whom were undoubtedly influenced by Tucker.[31]   One of the latter's distinguished correspondents was Turgot, who translated two of his pamphlets into French and expressed high admiration for his economic ideas.[32]   The two men never met, but they exchanged copies of their writings, and their correspondence was continued while Turgot was

---

[29] Below, 245.

[30] James Bonar, *A Catalogue of the Library of Adam Smith*, 115.   I am indebted to Mr. Eli Ginzberg for this reference.

[31] Clark, *Josiah Tucker*, 226–28.

[32] Two of Turgot's letters to Tucker are published in *Œuvres de M. Turgot*, IX (Paris, 1810), 366 ff.   For evidence of later correspondence between them see *Cui Bono?*, 4.

finance minister and afterwards. Tucker's arguments against monopolistic restrictions on trade Turgot found especially admirable.

Tucker's interest in economic questions exposed him to adverse criticism on the ground that it was not becoming in a clergyman to concern
himself with the affairs of the market place. He was very sensitive to
such censures and more than once felt called upon to justify himself. In
the preface to a tract published in 1751[33] he denied that his economic
inquiries had led to any neglect of his clerical duties and intimated that
they had been prompted by ethical and religious motives. But he
did not succeed in silencing his critics, and the reputation of being a
"commercial clergyman" long clung to him. It afforded a celebrated
divine the opportunity for an epigram. William Warburton, who was
dean of Bristol before he became bishop of Gloucester, speaking of two
clergymen, a certain Dr. Squire and Tucker, remarked that "the one
made religion his trade, and the other, trade his religion."[34] It is evident
that this witticism rankled in Tucker's mind. "The bishop," he said,
"affects to consider me with contempt; to which I say nothing. He has
sometimes spoken coarsely of me; to which I replied nothing. He has
said that religion is my trade, and trade is my religion. Commerce and
its connections have, it is true, been favourite objects of my attention,
and where is the crime? And as for religion, I have attended carefully to
the duties of my parish, nor have I neglected my cathedral. The world
knows something of me as a writer on religious subjects; and I will add,
which the world does not know, that I have written near three hundred
sermons, and preached them all, again and again."[35] Warburton was
certainly not unbiased in his judgment of Tucker, for though the two
men were associated professionally for years, the one as bishop and the
other as dean of Gloucester, no love was lost between them. Bishop
Newton of Bristol lamented that their relations were not marked by the
harmony and friendship that should always exist between the bishop
and the dean of the same cathedral, and regretted that Tucker did
not have that respect for Warburton to which the latter was entitled.[36]

The evidence all goes to show that Tucker was conscientious in the
discharge of his clerical duties. In a private letter written a few years
after he became dean of Gloucester he explained why he had not made

---

[33] *Reflections on the Expediency of a Law for the Naturalization of Foreign Protestants*,
Part I.

[34] John Selby Watson, *The Life of William Warburton*, 496.

[35] *The English Nation*, ed. by George Godfrey Cunningham, IV, 158.

[36] John Nichols, *Illustrations of the Literary History of the Eighteenth Century*, II, 838.

more progress with his *opus magnum*. "The avocations belonging to my
new office of Dean are very many and are too important to be omitted.
I came into a house which wanted to be almost rebuilt and into a chapter
where many disorders required to be rectified; and I have a cathedral and
cloisters to examine and repair, which, in some respects, are the finest
Gothic structures in the world, and which are now perhaps the best kept.
. . . I will not put it in the power of any one to say that I neglected the
proper business of my function and station upon any pretences of serving
the Public."[37]   The constant interest which he took in the fabric of the
cathedral is recorded in the inscription on the tablet erected to his memory, and the writer of an obituary notice went so far as to say that there
was no chapter in the kingdom "whose discipline has been better maintained, whose revenues have been more wisely managed, and whose
patronage more properly bestowed, than that of Gloucester."[38]

Tucker's interest in immigration led him to favor a more liberal naturalization policy.   Foreigners had normally obtained the privileges of
British citizenship by means of private acts of Parliament, and before the
reign of James I it had been possible for Parliament to naturalize any
foreigner, irrespective of his religious belief.   But in 1610, at a time when
public opinion was aroused against Catholics on account of the Gunpowder Plot, a religious test was established.   It was provided by
statute that no person should be naturalized unless he had received
Communion, as administered in the Church of England, within the
month immediately preceding the introduction into Parliament of the
bill for his naturalization.[39]   In 1708, in order to encourage the immigration of Protestants from the Continent, an act was passed providing that
all persons who should take certain oaths, subscribe a declaration
against Transubstantiation and receive the Sacrament in any Protestant
church should be deemed natural-born subjects.[40]   This was followed
by a considerable influx of foreign Protestants, many of them fleeing from
Catholic persecution on the Continent, and the national prejudice
against foreigners was aroused to such an extent that the act was repealed
in 1711.[41]   In 1751 a measure similar to the act of 1708 was introduced in
Parliament, but various interests instigated such popular clamor that it
was withdrawn, though it had ministerial support.

---

[37] Tucker to Kames, Feb. 15, 1764, *Memoirs of the Life and Writings of the Honourable Henry Home of Kames*, III, 174–75.

[38] *The Gentleman's Magazine*, LXIX, 1002.

[39] 7 Jac. I, c. 2.   [40] 7 Anne, c. 5.   [41] 10 Anne, c. 5.

Tucker looked upon the inveterate national antipathy to foreigners as not only irrational but as distinctly injurious to British interests, and he set himself to combat it in a tract, published in two parts, entitled *Reflections on the Expediency of a Law for the Naturalization of Foreign Protestants*. In the first part of this pamphlet, published shortly after the withdrawal of the bill, he sketches the policy of the government toward aliens from the Middle Age to the early eighteenth century, showing how narrow commercial and sectarian interests had played upon the traditional national prejudice against foreigners, which he calls "the epidemical disorder of the country." He contrasts the illiberal naturalization policy of England with the more enlightened policies of other countries, especially Holland and Prussia, and ridicules the fears of High Churchmen that the immigration of Lutherans and Calvinists would imperil the Established Church. In the second part of the tract, published in 1752, he sets forth his views on many subjects that had been raised by the discussions on the naturalization bill, presenting his arguments by means of queries. The bill had been opposed almost exclusively because of its anticipated effects in encouraging immigration, and it was as a measure calculated to promote immigration that Tucker defended it. He argues that unemployment, of which there was complaint at the time, is caused not by overpopulation but by impediments to the circulation of labor, and that labor cannot be circulated so well in a sparsely inhabited as in a populous country. Since opposition to the bill had been stirred up in large part by the landed interest, he takes pains to show that improvements in the land and increase of rents depend upon increase of population. To the prophecy that immigration will corrupt British morals he replies by asking, "Whether the manufacturing poor in any country are so debauched and immoral as in England? Is there not therefore a greater danger that the English should corrupt the foreigners than be corrupted by them?" He ridicules the notion that the coming of foreigners would be a menace to the constituiton and urges that it is contrary to the dictates of humanity and the principles of Christianity to deny a refuge to the persecuted and distressed of other lands.

The act of James I referred to above, though originally aimed at Catholics, made it impossible for Jews to secure naturalization by private bills. They might, it is true, obtain the benefits of British citizenship, under an act of Charles II's reign, by working for three years in England at certain manual trades and taking the oaths of allegiance and supremacy,[42] or,

---

[42] 15 Car. II, c. 7.

under an act of 1739, by residing for seven years in any British colony in America and taking certain oaths.[43]   But very few Jews, and those of the poorer sort only, were actually naturalized in either of these ways.   In the middle of the eighteenth century there were less than ten thousand persons of the Jewish faith, all told, in England, and a majority of these were native born.   Those of foreign birth, in common with other aliens, were subject to various economic and political disabilities.   They could not, for example, own land or ships, or trade with the British colonies, or hold office, or sit in Parliament.[44]   In order to encourage rich foreign Jews to take up their residence in England an act was passed in 1753 providing that Jews, upon application to Parliament, might be naturalized by private bills, subject to certain conditions, without having received the Sacrament.[45]   It did not provide for the naturalization of foreign Jews in general but left it to Parliament to decide in each case whether the individual application should be granted or not.   Since the expense of private-bill legislation was great, only well-to-do Jews would be able to take advantage of the act;[46] and moreover, such as were successful in securing naturalization could not hold office or sit in Parliament, nor could their descendants do so as long as they adhered to the Jewish faith.[47]

The bill encountered strong opposition in the House of Commons, where the ominous note of religious fanaticism was sounded,[48] and out of doors the clamor of bigotry reached extraordinary intensity.   Pamphlets were published inveighing against the law on religious and economic grounds and spreading misunderstanding of its real meaning and intent. The direst calamities were predicted as a result of the measure—the destruction of the Christian religion in England, the corruption of morals, the ruin of trade and manufactures and the overthrow of the constitution. The gallant Admiral Vernon, a member of the House of Commons, predicted compulsory circumcision as one of the speedy consequences of the new law.[49]   In view of the state of public opinion no Jew ventured to apply for naturalization.[50]   The law did not lack defenders, but the voice of reason was powerless to calm the tempest of passion that had

[43] 13 Geo. II, c. 7.

[44] G. B. Hertz, *British Imperialism in the Eighteenth Century*, 63–64.

[45] 26 Geo. II, c. 26.

[46] *Parliamentary History*, XIV, 1375.

[47] 12 & 13 Gul. III, c. 2.   *Parl. Hist.*, XIV, 1396.

[48] *Parl. Hist.*, XIV, 1379–81.

[49] *Parl. Hist.*, XV, 161.

[50] Philip C. Yorke, *The Life and Correspondence of Philip Yorke, Earl of Hardwicke*, II, 56.

been aroused. Opponents of the ministry encouraged the popular clamor, and as a general election was approaching, the government decided on prudential grounds to repeal the law. This was done in the following session of Parliament.[51] "We should treat the people," said Lord Chan-cellor Hardwicke, the ablest member of the ministry, "as a skilful and humane physician would treat his patient: if they nauseate the salutary draught we have prescribed, we should think of some other remedy, or we should delay administering the prescription till time or a change of circumstances has removed the nausea."[52] To the aristocratic statesmen of the eighteenth century *vox populi* was never confused with *vox Dei*, but it had to be listened to, no matter how irrational, if it was loud enough.

Tucker was prominent among those who supported the act of 1753 and sought to dispel popular misunderstanding of it. In *A Letter to a Friend concerning Naturalizations* he undertook to show that there was no justi-fication whatever, religious, political or economic, for the outcry against the law, that many of the privileges popularly associated with naturaliza-tion were not, in fact, conferred by it, and that some of them could be acquired by foreigners without naturalization. He derided the notion, sedulously propagated, that the interests of Christianity were at stake and that British morals would be corrupted by Jewish influence and ex-ample, and he showed that the act was not calculated to result in any large Jewish immigration. During the course of the controversy the view had been expressed, inside as well as outside Parliament, that Jews, even though born in England, were not entitled to all the civil rights of British subjects, especially the right to purchase or own land. In *A Second Letter to a Friend concerning Naturalizations,* in which he sketched the history of the Jews in England, Tucker showed that this view was erroneous and contrary to the best legal opinion.

Tucker's interest in politics was by no means wholly academic. While he was rector of St. Stephen's he took an active part in political cam-paigns and acquired extensive personal knowledge of electioneering methods and procedure. His influence in his large and wealthy parish made him a power to be reckoned with, and for several years he acted as adviser of the local Whig organization, the Union Club, which, with its Tory rival, the Steadfast Society, commonly known as the White Lion Club, managed the politics of the city. Like all English boroughs Bristol

---

[51] 27 Geo. II, c. 1.   [52] *Parl. Hist.*, XV, 102.

was represented in the House of Commons by two members, and for some years both of them had been Tories.

On the eve of the general election of 1754 the Whigs proposed that the two parties should coöperate to elect representatives who would serve the city's best interests, and that to this end each party should nominate only one candidate and support both in the election. But the Tories rejected this proposal and insisted upon putting up two candidates of their own, Sir John Phillips and Richard Beckford. The Whigs named only one, Robert Nugent (afterwards Viscount Clare and Earl Nugent in the Irish peerage), a gentleman of large fortune and proprietor of the Cornish borough of St. Maws, for which he had sat in the House of Commons since 1741. He was known as a liberal in economic questions, having advocated the naturalization of foreign Protestants and supported bills for opening the Levant and African trades. In a letter written two years after the election Tucker claimed credit for having persuaded the Whigs not to nominate more than one candidate.[53]

Party passion ran high in Bristol, and the campaign was exciting. "The mob is all of our side, great numbers of the low and middling tradesmen of theirs," Tucker wrote to his friend the Reverend Dr. Birch, a strong Whig who enjoyed the favor of Lord Hardwicke.[54] He busied himself in composing election tracts and newspaper articles in behalf of Nugent and arranged a great procession, which "was a full hour in passing by," in honor of the candidate.[55] In a letter to Lord Hardwicke he referred to himself as "the principal agent" in the election.[56] The Whigs succeeded in electing Nugent, who continued to represent Bristol for the next twenty years. In the campaign they stirred up public sentiment against Sir John Phillips by alleging that he was an impenitent Jacobite, but they made no objection to Beckford, the other Tory candidate, who was elected with Nugent. According to Tucker, nothing except the objections to Phillips contributed so much to the success of the Whigs as their "continual insisting upon the ill behaviour of the Tories in rejecting a compromise."[57] Since they had named only one

---

[53] Tucker to Dr. Birch, May 19, 1756, Birch MSS., British Museum, Add. MSS., 4319, XX, f. 255.

[54] Same to same, March 30, 1754, ibid., f. 229.

[55] Same to same, April 13, 1754, ibid., f. 231. A number of election tracts sent by Tucker to Birch are preserved in the Birch MSS.

[56] Tucker to Hardwicke, March 13, 1756, Hardwicke MSS., British Museum, Add. MSS., 35692, f. 130–31.

[57] Ibid.

candidate the Whigs were in a position to declare that they were not seeking for ascendancy but merely for equality, and that the Tories, therefore, were responsible for all the bitterness and the disturbances that attended the campaign, an argument of which Tucker made effective use both in conversation and in print.[58] But though he proved himself to be an adroit politician, he found much in practical politics that was not to his liking. "My present situation," he wrote in the midst of the campaign, "grows irksome to me, as I find myself connected with a set of men, who have neither ideals, nor hearts."[59]

Beckford's seat was vacated by his death in 1756, and a by-election was held to choose his successor. In anticipation of this, Nugent urged Tucker to use his best endeavors to bring about a compromise that would prevent a contested election, and other prominent Whig politicians, including the Duke of Newcastle, expressed themselves to like effect. Tucker accordingly drew up an agreement, which was signed by Nugent and a few of his friends and by some of the leading Tories connected with Bristol. The signers pledged themselves to support the candidate nominated by the local Tory organization to fill Beckford's seat, and, if Nugent's seat should be vacated before the next general election, to support the Whig candidate, because "these mutual concessions and engagements appear to be the only effectual means of producing a lasting peace, of promoting the real interest and welfare of the city and extending its trade, and preventing feuds and animosities for the future."[60] The Bristol Tories were in favor of the compromise, but a faction of the Whigs, "a club of low tradesmen among the Dissenters," Tucker called them, who were also members of the Union Club, refused to accept it, and the city was thrown into an uproar worse even than that of 1754. The tables were turned, however, for the Whigs were now blamed for forcing a contested election. "Our mob's becoming every hour more and more outrageous," wrote Tucker. "But the Tory mob is by much the stronger at present. For the people in general are for peace, and are exasperated to a degree of fury against the disturbers of it."[61] Despite great pressure he

---

[58] *Ibid.*

[59] Tucker to Birch, April 2, 1754, British Museum, Add. MSS. 4319, XX, f. 230. For the Bristol election of 1754, see Tucker, *A Review of Lord Vis. Clare's Conduct as Representative of Bristol*, 1–5, and L. B. Namier, *The Structure of Politics at the Accession of George III*, I, 110 ff.

[60] Tucker to Dr. Forster, Feb. 25, 1756, Forster MSS., British Museum, Add. MSS., 11275, f. 147–49. Copies of this agreement are in Add. MSS, 35692, f. 132 and 11275, f. 151–52.

[61] Tucker to Forster, Feb. 25, 1756, Add. MSS., 11275, f. 147–49.

remained neutral in the campaign, though it is evident that the defeat of
the Whig candidate gave him no little satisfaction.[62]   At this time of life
he was not devoid of personal amibiton, and no doubt he hoped for some
reward for his past services to the Whig cause.   In a letter to Lord Hardwicke he took pains to explain his neutrality in the 1756 campaign and to
profess his continued devotion to "true Whig principles."[63]   It was probably with his Bristol election experiences in mind that he wrote the
passage in his *Instructions for Travellers* on the effects of the English
system of government upon the character and conduct of the people.[64]

The Whigs and Tories of Bristol now came to an understanding that
for three successive Parliaments each party would name only one candidate and support both.   Pursuant to this agreement Nugent was re-
elected without opposition five times, at general elections and by-elec-
tions.   It had not yet expired when, at the general election of 1774, the
Whigs, to quote Tucker, "departed from their engagement, and, naming
at first two candidates, named a third upon Lord Clare's withdrawing
from a contest in which he was sure of success."   His motives, Tucker
adds, "require no explanation."[65]   One of the Whig candidates was
Edmund Burke; who represented Bristol in the House of Commons from
1774 to 1780, while Nugent again sat for his pocket borough of St. Maws.
In a pamphlet published in 1775 and dedicated to Nugent, *A Review of
Lord Vis. Clare's Conduct as Representative of Bristol,* Tucker gave him
the highest praise for his parliamentary services to Bristol and to the
nation.

In the eighteenth century it was not at all unusual for clergymen to
take an active part in politics, and they were often rewarded for political
services by ecclesiastical advancement.   Tucker's friend Dr. Thomas
Birch, for example, basked in the favor of Lord Hardwicke, who secured
numerous preferments in the Church for him.   Nugent was naturally
grateful to Tucker, and shortly after the election of 1754 he used his influence with the Duke of Newcastle to procure some profitable advancement
for him, but without immediate result.[66]   In 1756, however, through the
favor of Nugent and Lord Hardwicke, Tucker received a prebendal

---

[62] *A Review of Lord Vis. Clare's Conduct,* 5.
[63] Tucker to Hardwicke, March 13, 1756, Add. MSS., 35692, f. 130–31.
[64] Below, 261 ff.
[65] *A Review of Lord Vis. Clare's Conduct,* 6.
[66] Tucker to Forster, Dec. 31, 1755, and Jan. 24, 1756, Forster MSS., Add. MSS.,
11275, f. 142, 144.

stall in the Cathedral of Bristol,[67] and in 1758 he was advanced to the deanery of Gloucester, which he held till his death.[68] In a list of the ecclesiastical dignities in the King's gift, which was compiled in 1762 and is in the Papers of George III at Windsor Castle, the value of the deanery of Gloucester is set down as £450 a year.[69] The new dean found, however, that his promotion was not immediately profitable. In a private letter written in 1758 he complained that his "usual ill luck" still pursued him. "For the present year," he wrote, "will be one of the poorest that ever was known, the last having proved an extraordinary good one. So that the Preb. of Bristol bids fair, for the next ensuing twelve months, to be near double in value to the deanery of Gloucester."[70] He retained the rectory of St. Stephen's until 1793, when he resigned it in favor of his curate, and for years he divided his time between Gloucester and Bristol. In Gloucester he encountered some prejudice for a time, but it did not last long. In 1760 he wrote to Lord Hardwicke that the people had been made to believe that he was "a monster made up of the vilest parts of Whigism and Judaism," but that their sentiments had changed and he had become popular.[71] His active interest in politics continued for a time, and he urged moderation and compromise at Gloucester as he had done at Bristol.[72]

Burke once intimated that Tucker was seeking a bishopric. In one of his pamphlets the dean expressed the view that the opposition to the Stamp Act in England had encouraged the American colonists to resist it, an opinion that was widely held in English political circles. For this, Burke in his speech on American taxation, delivered in the House of Commons on April 19, 1774, classed Tucker with the "vermin of court reporters." "This Dr. Tucker," he said, "is already a dean, and his earnest labors in this vineyard will, I suppose, raise him to a bishopric."[73] Nothing could have been more unfair than this sneer, which aroused the ire of even the gentle Hannah More, who wrote to her sisters that she

---

[67] Same to same, ibid., f. 167.

[68] Tucker to the Duke of Newcastle, June 25, 1758, Newcastle MSS., British Museum, Add. MSS., 32881, f. 74.

[69] The Correspondence of King George III, ed. by Sir John Fortescue, I, 37.

[70] Tucker to Birch, July 22, 1758, Birch MSS., Add. MSS., 4319, XX, f. 268.

[71] Hardwicke MSS., Add MSS., 35692, f. 143.

[72] Ibid., f. 143–44.

[73] The Works of the Right Honorable Edmund Burke (Boston, 1869), II, 57. The author of one biographical sketch of Tucker says that he was offered a bishopric and declined it, but no evidence has been found to confirm this statement. Clark, Josiah Tucker, 25.

was very angry with Burke. "They seem to think," she said, "that the man and the politician are different things; but I do not see why a person should not be bound to speak truth in the House of Commons as much as in his own house."[74] It is true that Tucker had no high opinion of Burke or of the other Whig opponents of Lord North's ministry. He regarded them as a factious band of "mock-patriots," inspired by no loftier motive than a desire for office, and he deemed the ministers to be at least as able and as honest as the best of those who were trying to supplant them.[75] But nobody who was aiming at court or ministerial favor would have come out boldly for giving up the colonies, as Tucker did in a remarkable pamphlet published in 1774.[76] In this he distinctly gave it as his conviction that under existing conditions no minister would dare to adopt his plan of renouncing all authority over the colonies and recognizing their independence; and in a tract issued in the following year he said that ministers, being "subject to many unhappy biasses," could not be expected to take a disinterested view of his proposal.[77] In his opinion "an honest man" was as far removed from "a ministerial sycophant" as from "a seditious republican."[78] In a letter written in 1782, shortly after the Whigs had come to power, he said that when he had first proposed separation from the colonies he had stood alone and "had the honour to be treated by the late Ministry as a fool, and by the present, then in opposition, as a knave."[79] In his *Letter to Edmund Burke*, elicited by Burke's speech on conciliation with America, he declared that he was indifferent to the orator's opinion of him. "As you have been pleased to bestow much abuse and scurrility on me in your public speech of the 19th of April, 1774, and also many commendations in private both before and since that publication, I shall take no other notice of either than just to assure you that I am neither elated by your praises nor chagrined at your censures, and that I hold myself indifferent in respect to both." But it is evident that Burke's taunt hurt him, for in several of his writings he took pains to profess complete satisfaction with his position as dean of Gloucester. In *A Series of Answers* (1776) he went so far as to declare most

---

[74] Annette M. B. Meakin, *Hannah More*, 45.

[75] For Tucker's opinion of the Whig opposition to Lord North's government, see *Four Tracts* (1774), 213; *An Humble Address and Earnest Appeal*, 6–9; *A Letter to Edmund Burke*, 57–58; *Four Letters on Important National Subjects*, 28 ff.

[76] Below, 331 ff.

[77] *An Humble Address*, 8–9.

[78] "Thoughts on the Present Posture of Affairs," July 24, 1779, published in Woodfall's *Public Advertiser*.

[79] *Memoirs of the Life and Writings of the Honourable Henry Home of Kames*, III, 181.

solemnly that he would never accept advancement: "As a clergyman it is often objected to me that I am a mercenary wretch (or as Mr. Burke was pleased to phrase it, a court vermin) writing for preferment. This is very hard and cruel after so many solemn declarations to the contrary. Let it therefore be observed that whereas I had often said before I would never directly or indirectly *seek* for preferment, I will here add, once for all, that I will never *accept* of any, even tho' offered to and pressed upon me. SO HELP ME GOD."

Some years after Tucker went to Gloucester a serious ecclesiastical controversy arose over the question of subscription to the Thirty-Nine Articles and the liturgy of the Church of England. The clergy and certain other classes of persons were required by law to acknowledge that the Articles, as well as the forms of public worship prescribed in the Prayer Book, were agreeable to the Word of God. To some clergymen, especially those of Latitudinarian persuasion, it seemed to be inconsistent with the right of private judgment and contrary to the true interests of the Church to require of the clergy acceptance of the opinions of the fallible authors of the Articles and the Prayer Book as to the meaning of the Bible. Archdeacon Francis Blackburne was one of those who advocated the abolition of subscription, and his *Confessional*, published in 1766, aroused much discussion of the subject. A later publication of his, *Proposals for an Application to Parliament for Relief in the Matter of Subscription to the Liturgy and Thirty-Nine Articles* (1771), led to the formation of an association which sent a petition to the House of Commons. A majority of the two hundred and fifty signers were clergymen; the others were lawyers and physicians who objected to imposing subscription upon students at the universities. The petitioners set forth what they regarded as the evil results of compulsory subscription, which they declared to be a violation of the right of private judgment and the original principles of the Reformation, and asked to be restored to their "undoubted rights as Protestants of interpreting Scripture for themselves." A motion for leave to present the petition led to a long and animated debate in the House of Commons on February 6, 1772.[80] The King was known to be strongly opposed to any change in the law relating to subscription, and the governing classes were averse to anything that seemed likely to cause discussion and excitement within the Church.

---

[80] For the petition and the debate, see *The Parliamentary History of England* (Hansard), XVII, 245, 295.

Lord North pointed out that all kinds of "absurd and monstrous doctrines" had been derived from Scripture and predicted that if the petition should be granted the result would be endless theological controversy and utter religious confusion. Burke took the same view. "If we would preserve in the church any order, any decorum, any peace, we must have some criterion of faith more brief, more precise and definite than the Scripture for the regulation of the priesthood." By a vote of 217 to 71 the House voted to reject the petition.

Tucker's *Apology for the Present Church of England as by Law Established* was published in 1772 in the form of a letter to one of the petitioners. In it and in his *Letters to Dr. Kippis*, which appeared in the following year, he not only gave evidence of theological learning but showed that he had reflected upon questions of the highest import in the religious life of the individual and of the community. His defense of the principle of an established church is not convincing, for it is based upon an unwarranted analogy between the individual and the state. "The magistrate," he says, "hath undoubtedly a right to encourage that system of religion which he esteems the most orthodox and the best, because every individual has the same right."[81] This overlooks the fact that the support which the Church of England received from the state and that which it, or any other religious denomination, received from its own adherents were very different in kind, for the state gave the church legal privileges which were not enjoyed by other sects. Moreover, "the magistrate" was not in a position to take an impartial view of the relative merits of the beliefs and practices of different denominations, since office-holding was restricted by law to members of a single church. Tucker failed to distinguish between support given to a church by the magistrate in his private and official capacities. His justification of religious establishments is not difficult to understand, but it sounds perfunctory when compared with his stalwart championship of freedom of conscience and religious toleration. He stood squarely and emphatically for "the unalienable right of private judgment, and the liberty of following the dictates of conscience in every case whatever, if really consistent with good morals and the just rights of other men."[82] He held it to be the duty of the magistrate to tolerate and protect all religious societies, "as far as a regard to good morals and the safety of the state can possibly admit," and the magistrate should be slow to deduce dangerous conse-

---

[81] *Letters to Dr. Kippis*, 65. *Apology* (2d ed.), 13.
[82] *Letters to Dr. Kippis*, 5.

quences from the irrational tenets of any sect, "for few sectaries, if any, will allow, or even believe, that such dangerous conclusions can be drawn from their principles as others draw."[83]

But Tucker saw no conflict between the individual's right of private judgment and the right of collections of individuals, or societies, to make regulations for their own members and officers, and he held that some sort of creed was implicit in every religious society. He was quite willing to see subscription abolished in the case of matriculants at the universities and of candidates for graduation, except those in divinity, and he thought that Dissenting ministers, who were required to subscribe to some of the Thirty-Nine Articles, ought to be freed from this obligation.[84] But he perceived that those who were agitating for the abolition of subscription by the clergy of the Church of England were really cutting at the roots of all organized religion, and he joined issue with them on this ground. He had no sympathy with the opinion that a clergyman had the right to remain in a church if he dissented from its teaching, though he freely conceded his right to join another religious society, or to found a new one of his own.[85]

He did not claim perfection for any church, not even for his own. He thought that some improvement might be made in the doctrinal system of Anglicanism. The Athanasian Creed he regarded as superfluous, and he did not consider the Thirty-Nine Articles altogether satisfactory.[86] He saw room for considerable improvement in the Book of Common Prayer, and it was his intention, at one time, to issue as his final publication a treatise in which various alterations would be proposed. Among other changes which he favored were the adoption of a new set of First Lessons, from which the less instructive parts of the Old Testament would be omitted, a new set of Collects, an abridgment of all the services to render them "more suitable to the circumstances of a public congregation," and the excision of "some offensive passages and incautious expressions."[87] It is evident that he gave much thought to a revision of the liturgy, but his projected work was never published and probably never written. "I do not hold forth the National Church as a model of all

[83] *Apology*, 13–14. In his *Essay on Trade* (3d ed., 33–34) he referred to the disabilities under which Roman Catholics in England still labored, but these had been placed upon them, he said, as a political, not as a religious, sect.

[84] *Apology*, 64.

[85] *Apology*, 16 ff. *Letters to Dr. Kippis*, 6–9, 14–15.

[86] *Apology*, 58 ff.

[87] Advertisement appended to *A Series of Answers*.

perfection," he confessed, "and yet I most sincerely declare that according to the most impartial judgment which I can form, I do not know a better, nor any one so good.   But penetrated as I am with this persuasion, I am still as willing that others should think differently, as I am desirous of thinking for myself."[88]

Tucker's anti-imperialism is to be accounted for in large part by his economic ideas.   His doctrine of self-interest explains the opinion which he expressed in his colonial tracts that it was impossible effectively to regulate the trade of the colonies, and his dissent from the mercantile theory of national prosperity, a theory that was closely related to the colonial system, led naturally to a questioning of the economic value of colonies to the mother country.

In his earlier economic writings, however, he did not take an antiimperial position; he was not opposed to the possession of colonies.   He did, indeed, predict as early as 1749 that the British colonies in America would revolt if the time should come when they felt themselves economically self-sufficient,[89] but he did not as yet reject the mercantile dogma that colonies were beneficial to their mother country as markets and as sources of supply.   He thought it important, for example, that the North American colonies should be encouraged to produce naval stores so as to free Great Britain from dependence for those commodities upon trade with the Baltic countries.[90]   The outline of his projected comprehensive treatise on economics shows that when he prepared it he regarded the extension of trade between the colonies and the mother country as a suitable means of developing British manufactures; and in *The Elements of Commerce* he advocated the establishment of a colony in the Hudson's Bay Territory.[91]   Before long, however, he became skeptical of the value of distant colonial possessions, and when Lord Shelburne asked his advice regarding the administration of the West Indian islands which had been acquired from France in 1763 he expressed doubt whether they were worth the cost of governing them.[92]   It appears to have been the dispute over the Stamp Act that turned his thoughts seriously to the question of the separation of the colonies from the mother country.[93]

Mercantilism was the economic phase of nationalism.   The age that

---

[88] *Letters to Dr. Kippis*, 66.   [89] *Essay on Trade* (3d ed.), 95–96.
[90] *Ibid.*, 93–94.   [91] Below, 172 ff.
[92] *Four Letters on Important National Subjects* (2d ed.), 2.
[93] *Four Tracts*, ix–xi, 135 ff.

witnessed its rise was one of bitter international rivalry and arrogant national egoism. Wars and rumors of war were incessant. The cosmopolitan ideal of the Middle Age faded before harsh realities; the Universal Church became a pretense and the Universal Empire a mockery. Statesmen in all countries put the first emphasis upon national defense and national economic self-sufficiency as a means thereto. In his views on nationalism, war and international relations Tucker was wholly at variance with the mercantilists, and his opinions on these subjects undoubtedly had a good deal to do with his attitude toward the controversy between Great Britain and her colonies.

During the Seven Years' War he was entirely out of sympathy with the patriotic fervor with which Pitt and victory inspired the English people. He was a disciple of Walpole in more respects than one, but in none more truly than in his desire for peace. His economic studies led him to a consideration of the prevention of wars as a means of increasing population and convinced him that war was necessarily injurious economically to the victor as well as to the vanquished. He held the "mock patriots" responsible for plunging the country into the war and believed that their motive was nothing higher than the desire for office.[94] While the war was in progress he wrote in a private letter: "It is a pity that peace could not have been made on such terms as the French were willing to accept. . . . the continuance of the war for every year longer will necessarily show that they are growing the stronger by their losses, and we the weaker by our acquisitions. But this is a paradox which the multitude will not believe till dear-bought experience has convinced them of it."[95]

In 1763, just after the close of the war, he published, as a fragment of his contemplated *opus magnum*, an anonymous tract, *The Case of Going to War for the Sake of Procuring, Enlarging, or Securing of Trade, Considered in a New Light*.[96] In this he undertook to show that no country could gain from the destruction or impoverishment of its neighbors, that neither princes nor peoples could be benefitted by the most successful war, that trade would inevitably make its way to the country where goods were manufactured best and most cheaply, and that conquering nations could not manufacture cheaply. The mob understood fighting the foreigner, but it did not understand trading with him so that both countries might prosper the more. The pamphlet contains a striking analysis of

[94] Tucker to Birch, Nov. 15, 1756, Add. MSS., 4319, XX, f. 259.
[95] Same to same, Nov. 2, 1761, *ibid.*, f. 271.
[96] Below, 281ff.

the forces and classes in the community making for war; it might have been written, *mutatis mutandis*, by Richard Cobden or by Norman Angell. It attracted little attention at the time in England, a fact which Tucker attributed to the bellicose disposition of "the mob and the news-writers," but it won some approval abroad, and was translated into French by Turgot.[97]   Jeremy Bentham appears to have been acquainted with it, for in his *Principles of International Law* he refers to Tucker as an "original writer," whose object was "to persuade the world of the inutility of war, but more particularly of the war then raging when he wrote."[98] The pamphlet was reprinted as Tract II of *Four Tracts*, published in 1774.   In a later tract, elicited by the controversy over the Stamp Act, Tucker pointed out that a shopkeeper could never increase his trade by beating his customers, and that what was true of a shopkeeper was equally true of a shopkeeping nation.[99]   The same thought is expressed in *Cui Bono?*, a tract consisting of a series of letters addressed to Necker and published in 1781, in which he wrote: "It is as much the real interest of Great Britian that France should be a rich country, and not a poor one, as I have already proved that the great riches of England are beneficial to France."[100]   In the *Treatise concerning Civil Government* he expressed astonishment that a commercial nation "should entertain that fondness for war, and should espouse so many quarrels as the English have eagerly done for almost half a century last past."[101]

He did not underrate the tenacity with which men cling to cherished ideas, and he harbored no vain expectation that the fallacious arguments for war would soon be discarded, but he hoped that the time would come when going to war for the sake of trade and dominion would be looked upon in the same light that men then regarded the madness of their ancestors "in fighting under the banner of the peaceful Cross, to recover the Holy Land."   In the midst of the Seven Years' War he wrote in a private letter: "War, conquests and colonies are our present system, and mine is just the opposite. . . . I look upon the nation at present to be frantic with military glory and therefore no more to be argued with than a person in a raving fit of a high fever."[102]   And twenty years later, toward the close of the War of the American Revolution, when the military and imperial

---

[97] *Four Tracts*, vi.   *Memoirs of the Life and Writings of the Honourable Henry Home of Kames*, III, 168.   *Œuvres de M. Turgot*, IX, 366.

[98] *The Works of Jeremy Bentham*, ed. by John Bowring, II, 546.

[99] *Four Tracts*, 132.   [100] *Cui Bono?*, Letter ii.   [101] Below, 524.

[102] *Memoirs of the Life and Writings of the Honourable Henry Home of Kames*, III, 163–64.

fortunes of Great Britain had reached the nadir, he recorded this opinion: "Among the various errors which have disturbed the intellects and perverted the judgment of a great part of mankind, none have been more fatal to the peace and happiness of the world than the Glory of Conquest and the Jealousy of Trade."[103] His pacifism, cosmopolitanism and hatred of jingoistic patriotism are exhibited in the following extract from one of his published sermons:

The love of country hath no place in the catalogue of Christian virtues. The love of country is, in fact, a local affection and a partial attachment; but the Christian covenant is general, comprehending all mankind within its embraces. Judge, therefore, with what propriety such a narrow, contracted passion can have any place in the diffusive, benevolent scheme of Christianity—a passion, however glittering and glorious in appearance, which hath been productive of more injustice, barbarity and bloodshed in the world than any other disgrace of human nature—a passion, in short, fit only for the enthusiastic rage of an old Roman robber, when cruelly exulting over the unhappy victims of his lust of power and dominion—but altogether unworthy of the breast of a Christian, who is commanded to regard all mankind not only as his countrymen, but as his brethren, doing to others as he would be done by, and helping and assisting even his enemies in distress. Indeed, so far as the love of country means no more than a principle of self-defense against invaders, so far it is justifiable, and so far hath Christianity provided for due exertion of it, by inculcating obedience to the respective powers set over us. But as to the ideas of honor and glory and conquest and dominion and the other fine things usually implied in the love of country, they are so foreign to the Christian plan that in this sense the love of country neither is, nor ought to be, a part of the Christian scheme of universal love and benevolence. And let the infidels make what uses they please of the concession.[104]

It is noteworthy that Tucker's cosmopolitanism was the result of his study of international trade, of reading and of reflection, rather than of wide personal acquaintance with foreign countries and civilizations. It is known that he visited France, as well as Scotland and Ireland, but from early manhood his residence was always in Gloucestershire, and it is probable that he left the county very seldom for any great length of time. His *Instructions for Travellers* makes it clear enough that he had a lively appreciation of the educational advantages of foreign travel, but he indulged in it very little himself.

The ill-will of European neighbors toward Great Britain was made manifest when the revolt of her colonies developed into a world war.

[103] *Cui Bono?*, Letter iii.   [104] *Seventeen Sermons*, 285–86.

France, Spain and Holland became her open enemies, and the northern powers of Europe leagued in armed neutrality in defense of their rights against the Mistress of the Seas. Tucker maintained that British maritime pretensions were unwarranted and arrogant,[105] and it was his intention at one time to propose a plan "for rendering the English nation more beloved and less hated abroad than it is at present," in which it would be shown that "the Gospel maxim of cultivating peace on earth and goodwill towards men (instead of insisting that all nations should bow down before us and do obeissance at sea) is the best rule for national politics."[106] The contempt for "the people," which he often expressed in his writings, was based in no small part upon their belligerent propensities and intemperate zeal for national aggrandizement and colonial conquests.

Long before the revolt of the American colonies Tucker declared that only self-interest bound them to their mother country. In the earliest of his American tracts he asserted that the British conquest of Canada, in freeing the colonies from the danger of French conquest, broke the tie of self-interest by releasing them from dependence upon Great Britain. This was the opinion of Turgot and other contemporaries, and it is regarded by historians as sound. It was in the nature of colonies, according to Tucker, "to aspire after independence, and to set up for themselves as soon as ever they find that they are able to subsist without being beholden to the mother country."[107] That the British colonies were the first to revolt he attributed to that "bold free Constitution, which is the prerogative and boast of us all."[108] He ridiculed the notion, widely held in England at the time, that taxation of the colonies by Parliament was the original cause of their quarrel with the mother country, and referred to British statutes to show that from the seventeenth century there had been "mutual discontents, mutual animosities and reproaches."[109] In A Letter from a Merchant in London to His Nephew in America, published in 1766, he ascribed colonial opposition to the Stamp Act not to that measure itself but rather to the colonists' hostility to the commercial regulations of the colonial system, which the British Government was trying to enforce.[110] In another pamphlet, written before the

---

[105] Below, 524. Reflections on the Present Matters in Dispute between Great Britain and Ireland, 2–3.

[106] Advertisement prefixed to Four Letters on Important National Subjects.

[107] Four Tracts, 153–54.   [108] Ibid., 154.   [109] Ibid., 143 ff.

[110] Like Tucker, the classical economists of the early nineteenth century regarded commercial restriction as the basic cause of the Revolution and believed that taxation merely hastened a crisis that was inevitable. See, e.g., an article on colonial policy by J. R. McCulloch in The Edinburgh Review, XLII, 282.

outbreak of military hostilities in America, he predicted the eventual independence of Canada.[111]

Tucker's anti-imperialism was not caused by any sympathy on his part for the cause of the colonists. His writings are full of contempt for those "most ungrateful, ungovernable and rebellious people,"[112] and one of his most unfortunate predictions was that they would remain, if they should gain their independence, a quarrelsome and disunited people to the end of time.[113] Unlike his radical contemporaries in England, he accepted the doctrine that the Americans were virtually represented in Parliament,[114] and he never doubted its right to tax them. At the time of the dispute over the Stamp Act he argued in the strongest terms for the unlimited sovereignty of Parliament throughout the Empire.[115] His anti-imperialism was based wholly upon British interests, not at all upon American rights.

In contending that colonial trade could not be controlled effectively in the interest of the mother country, Tucker struck at the whole elaborate scheme of commercial regulation that went to make up the old British colonial system. His conclusions on this point followed from his doctrine of self-interest and were supported by his study of the history of colonial trade. In the *Treatise concerning Civil Government* he asserted that it was "impossible to compel distant settlements to trade with the parent state to any great degree beyond what their own interest would prompt them to."[116] In *Four Letters on Important National Subjects* he said that trade depended on interest alone. "Nor was it in our power, even when we were strongest, and they in the weakest stage of their existence (as appears from their whole history) to compel them to trade with us to their own loss. Mutual interest was the only tie between America and Great Britain at all times and seasons. . . . As to the planting of colonies for the sake of a monopolizing or exclusive trade, it is the arrantest cheat and self-deception which poor, short-sighted mortals ever put upon themselves."

The doctrine of self-interest explains, moreover, Tucker's confident and happy prediction that the loss of the colonies would not result in a

---

[111] *The Respective Pleas and Arguments of the Mother Country and of the Colonies* (2d ed., 1776), vii.

[112] Below, 445. [113] *Cui Bono?*, 117–18.

[114] *An Humble Address and Earnest Appeal*, 90–92.

[115] *A Letter from a Merchant in London to His Nephew in America*, below, 307 ff. Also *The Respective Pleas*, sec. i.

[116] Below, 533.

decline of British trade.   The Americans, he said, could get better prices
for most of their products in the British market than in any other, and
could buy most of what they needed more cheaply there than elsewhere.
"The colonies, we know by experience," he wrote in 1774, "will trade with
any people, even with their bitterest enemies . . . provided they shall find
it their interest to do so. . . . Were the whole trade of North America to
be divided into two branches, *viz.*, the *voluntary*, resulting from a free
choice of the Americans themselves, pursuing their own interest, and
the *involuntary*, in consequence of compulsory acts of the British Parliament, this latter would appear so very small and inconsiderable as hardly
to deserve a name in an estimate of national commerce."[117]

Like later anti-imperialists, Tucker called attention to the heavy
burdens which the possession of colonies imposed upon the mother
country.   America, he said in 1783, "ever was a millstone hanging about
the neck of this country, to weigh it down; and as we ourselves had not
the wisdom to cut the rope and to let the burden fall off, the Americans
have kindly done it for us."[118]   In the *Treatise concerning Civil Government* he voiced the hope that Jamaica and the Leeward Islands would
become independent and declared that colonies were always an encum-
brance to their mother countries, "requiring perpetual and expensive
nursing in their infancy, and becoming headstrong and ungovernable in
proportion as they grow up, and never failing to revolt as soon as they
shall find that they do not want our assistance."[119]   Nor, in his opinion,
were the bad results of imperialism solely economic.   To it he attributed
in great part the political evils of the day in England, especially the
increasing influence of the Crown.   Neither ministerialists nor their
opponents dared to tell the truth on this subject, he said, for fear of the
effect on their own political fortunes.   Alluding to Burke's scheme for
economical reform, he asserted that the abandonment of the colonies
would be worth a thousand of the petty economies which reforming
politicians were proposing.[120]

Before the outbreak of the American Revolution many Americans and
some of their friends in England took the ground that Parliament had no
lawful authority over the colonies.   They claimed for the latter a status
of constitutional equality with Great Britain and proposed that the Em-

---

[117] *Four Tracts*, 195–201.
[118] *Four Letters on Important National Subjects* (2d ed.), 7.
[119] Below, 533.   [120] Below, 534.

pire should be reorganized on this basis.[121] Tucker discussed this "scheme of independency respecting the Parliament, but not respecting the King," and pronounced it to be inadmissible from every point of view.[122]

His arguments in favor of the total separation of the American colonies from Great Britain need not be followed here in detail. His proposal was stated clearly and boldly in *The True Interest of Great Britain Set Forth in Regard to the Colonies*, published in 1774, at a time when scarcely anyone else, even in the colonies, had ventured to suggest secession from the Empire. It was "to separate entirely from the North American colonies, by declaring them to be a free and independent people, over whom we lay no claim," and then to offer "to guarantee this freedom and independence against all foreign invaders whatever." This proposal was warmly praised by Major John Cartwright, the radical parliamentary reformer and friend of America, although his prescription for solving the imperial problem was different from Tucker's,[123] and it received respectful consideration in some of the English newspapers and reviews.[124] In another of his American tracts, published in 1775, Tucker urged that all colonies in revolt at a certain date be cut off from the Empire by act of Parliament.[125] He knew that it would not be easy to persuade the English people that separation from the colonies was desirable. "Prejudices and prepossessions are stubborn things in all cases, but in none more peculiarly obstinate than in relinquishing detached parts of an unwieldly, extended Empire; there not being, I believe, a single instance in all history of any nation surrendering a distant province voluntarily and of free choice, notwithstanding it was greatly their interest to have done it." This sentence occurs in a pamphlet of Tucker's published in 1775.[126] It is interesting to compare with it a rather well known observation made by Adam Smith in *The Wealth of Nations*, published in the following year: "No nation ever voluntarily gave up the dominion of any province, how troublesome soever it might be to govern it, and how small soever the revenue which it afforded might be in proportion to the expense which it occasioned."

---

[121] For example, John Cartwright, *American Independence the Interest and Glory of Great Britain.*

[122] *A Series of Answers*, 53 ff.

[123] Cartwright, *op. cit.* (new ed., 1775), Letter ix.

[124] Fred J. Hinkhouse, *The Preliminaries of the American Revolution as seen in the English Press*, 114–15.

[125] *An Humble Address and Earnest Appeal*, 23–25.

[126] *Ibid.*, 69.

When the War of Independence broke out Tucker was strongly opposed to the conquest and recovery of the rebellious colonies, and he remained of this mind throughout the course of the struggle.   Upon learning of the British occupation of New York in 1776 he wrote: "The only proper inference to be drawn from our present success is to terminate the war with more speed and with greater reputation."[127] Having been informed that a public fast had been appointed for December 13, 1776, he wrote to a friend that he could not conscientiously preach a sermon suitable to the occasion or pray for the success of His Majesty's arms.[128]   Upon learning of Cornwallis's surrender he did not attempt to conceal his satisfaction. "To congratulate my country on being defeated is contrary to that decency which is due to the public.   And yet, if this defeat should terminate in a total separation from America, it would be one of the happiest events that hath ever happened to Great Britain."[129]   After the fall of Lord North's ministry, when it was clear that the independence of the colonies was assured, he thus summed up his views on the American question in a letter to Lord Kames:

I look upon it to have been a very *imprudent* act to have settled any distant colonies at all whilst there remained an inch of land in Great Britain capable of further cultivation; afterwards, to have been very *foolish and absurd* to have engaged in their disputes either with the French or Spaniards, and to have espoused their quarrels; and lastly, to have been the *height of madness* to have endeavored to conquer them after they had broken out in open rebellion.   They were always, from first to last, a heavy weight upon us, a weight which we ourselves ought to have thrown off if they had not done it for us.[130]

The achievement of American independence naturally confirmed Tucker in his opinion that oversea dependencies could not be held permanently against their wishes.   Shortly after the defeat of Fox's India Bill in the House of Lords and the consequent fall of the Fox-North Ministry (December, 1783), at a time when the East India Company and its affairs were in the forefront of political discussion, he contributed an article to the *Bristol Journal*, in which the overthrow of British rule in Bengal was predicted.[131]   If Great Britain had been unable to maintain

---

[127] *A Series of Answers*, Postscript, 107–8.

[128] Tucker to Dr. Adams, Nov. 4 and 14, 1776, Gloucester Public Library.

[129] *Cui Bono?*, 140.

[130] *Memoirs of the Life and Writings of the Honourable Henry Home of Kames*, III, 181.

[131] "Cassandra's Short Method for Terminating the Disputes concerning the East India Company," *Bristol Journal*, Jan. 3, 1784.   An extract from this is reprinted by James M. Holzman, *The Nabobs in England*, 60.

her authority over a couple of million people at a distance of only three thousand miles, he was at a loss to understand how men could be so "infatuated with party rage" or "blinded with the hopes of filthy lucre" as not to realize that a handful of proprietors and directors could not continue their "detested usurpations over the lives, liberties and properties of thirty millions at the distance of 10,000 miles." He believed that the people of India, unlike the American colonists, had right on their side, and he was confident that they would recover their "original and native independence."

With the radical democratic movement that began in England when Tucker was in middle life, and with the political theory to which it appealed, he was wholly out of sympathy. What he had seen of the influence of "the mob" in politics seemed to him, as it seemed to so many of his contemporaries, the best of reasons for not increasing that influence. In eighteenth-century England the masses were, as a rule, content to leave the molding of governmental policies to their "betters," but they made some conspicuous appearances on the political scene, and when they did so it was almost invariably to exhibit ignorance and prejudice. Their riotous zeal for "Wilkes and Liberty" should perhaps be counted to them for righteousness, though Tucker, who detested Wilkes,[132] would certainly not have made this concession. It is not difficult to understand why a man who had witnessed the popular outcry against Walpole's Excise Bill, the stupid clamor against the reform of the calendar, the anti-Semitic frenzy of 1753, the anti-Catholic hysteria of the Gordon Riots, the brutal amusements of the lower classes and the disastrous effects of their addiction to the use of gin, should have looked with no favor upon proposals to extend the electoral franchise. To Tucker the common people seemed to be invincibly ignorant, wrong-headed, intolerant and truculent, and as a man of reason, tolerance and peace he believed that their active participation in politics would have deplorable results. His personal knowledge of the masses, moreover, was acquired mainly in Bristol, and of all English "mobs" that of Bristol had the reputation of being the most ruffianly.[133] In a footnote in his *Civil Government* he summed up his impressions of the people, based on half a century's observation, and declared that he had scarcely ever known a popular measure that was beneficial, or an unpopular one that was unwise. He recalled

---

[132] *An Humble Address and Earnest Appeal*, 85.
[133] J. F. Nicholls and John Taylor, *Bristol, Past and Present*, III, 167.

that in matters of internal improvement and reform the masses had shown themselves to be stupidly conservative, and in external affairs incorrigibly imperialistic and bellicose.[134]   *Vox populi, vox Dei* was, to him, a blasphemous motto. It would not be strange if something of personal animus entered into his attitude toward what Fielding called the "fourth estate."   He had had experience of popular hysteria at unpleasantly close range. One of the few scenes that can be reconstructed vividly from the fragmentary record of his life is that of the Bristol mob burning the rector of St. Stephen's in effigy because he had ventured to combat public prejudice against the Jews.[135]   Perhaps, as Bagehot says of Gibbon, Tucker concluded that he was the sort of person mobs kill.

In the course of some suggestive observations upon the difference between wise legislation and popular legislation, Dicey remarks that "faith in the voice of the people is closely connected with the doctrine of 'natural rights.' "[136]   In their political theory the leaders of the democratic movement of Tucker's day, such men as Joseph Priestley, John Cartwright and Richard Price, were whole-hearted disciples of John Locke, taking as self-evident truths the master's assumptions respecting the inherent and unalienable rights of the individual and the origin, nature and purposes of government. Tucker's distrust of the people naturally predisposed him to question the postulates of the natural-rights school, but it appears to have been his reflection upon the course of events in America that convinced him that such assumptions were a menace to civilization. The fact that the political radicalism of the time was in great part a product of religious Dissent did not tend to make it the more acceptable to a clergyman of the Established Church.[137]

Though Tucker in his early life had shared the general belief in the soundness of Locke's theory of government, he later came to the conclusion that it was not only invalid as an explanation of the origin of the state, but a source of danger to all established governments and a menace to the peace and happiness of the world.[138] Nor did he wait until radical political theories had borne their full fruit in France to warn against their incendiary tendencies. He believed, as we have seen, that the separation of the American colonies from Great Britain would be greatly to her interest, and he was strongly opposed to holding them

[134] Below, 515.

[135] *Public Characters of 1798–9* (3d ed.), 171.

[136] *Introduction to the Study of the Law of the Constitution* (8th ed.), lxii.

[137] *A Series of Answers*, 69, footnote.

[138] *Four Letters on Important National Subjects*, 109.

within the Empire by force, but the appeal made by the Americans to Locke's "right of revolution" and the writings of Locke's English disciples, most of whom sympathized warmly with the Americans, and of "honest, undissembling Rousseau," who "never boggled at consequences, however extravagant or absurd,"—all this filled him with anxious forebodings. In 1775 he declared that Locke's principles of government, if carried out as the Americans construed them, would destroy every government on earth.[139] Toward "the consent of the governed" he felt very much as Robert Lansing did toward Woodrow Wilson's "self-determination,"—that the phrase was loaded with dynamite.

In 1778 Tucker caused to be privately printed and circulated among his friends for criticism a study that he had made of the theories of Locke and his disciples,[140] which he utilized in the preparation of his *Treatise concerning Civil Government*, published in 1781. In this work he assailed the "Lockians" root and branch. Their writings, he said, had laid a foundation for "such disturbances, such mutual jealousies and animosities, as ages to come will not be able to settle or compose."[141] He dwelt upon their intolerance of all forms of government not based upon compact and consent, to "that dreadful notion, propagated by them with a kind of enthusiastic ardor, that *their* system of government is the only true one, in the nature of things," and that all others are "detestable robberies and barefaced usurpations of the unalienable Rights of Mankind."[142] He saw clearly, and years before the French Revolution made it apparent to the whole world, that the theory of Natural Rights was as much a religion as ever the Divine Right of Kings had been. If the Jacobites had insisted that the heir to the throne could not lawfully be barred from his inheritance, no matter how long a usurping dynasty had been in actual possession, the apostles of Liberty, Equality and Fraternity were to proclaim that those who ruled without popular consent were usurpers, be their government never so ancient. A dozen years before the French Republic launched its crusade against the monarchies of Europe Tucker asserted that Locke's disciples were in fact "proclaiming war against all the governments upon earth and exciting their subjects to rebel."[143] In *Cui Bono?* (1781) he gave prophetic warning that the Bourbon Monarchy was playing with fire in coquetting with American republicanism based upon Locke's doctrine of consent.[144]

---

[139] Below, 378.
[140] *The Notions of Mr. Locke and His Followers . . . Considered and Examined.*
[141] Below, 421.   [142] Below, 450.   [143] Below, 450.   [144] Letter ii.

Tucker was in his seventy-sixth year when the French Revolution began, and though he lived for another ten years, his career as a publicist had drawn to its close.   Such of his private letters as are accessible—in print, in the British Museum or in the Gloucester Public Library—do not throw light upon his thought during the last decade of his life.   He must have followed with grave concern the course of events across the Channel; he had been posting danger signals for fifteen years, and now his worst fears were realized.   A people more terrible in their "enthusiastic ardor" than the Americans were tearing down the old Europe in the name of the Rights of Man.

Political theories, generally speaking, have been born of political conflicts and have been controversial rather than scientific in aim. They have been the result not of disinterested curiosity concerning political phenomena but of the desire of partisans to defend and justify, or to attack and discredit, particular political ideas or institutions. The writings in which they are expounded, even when cast in the form of general treatises, are essentially polemics, as is apparent when they are viewed in their historical setting.   Tucker entered the eminently contentious field of political theory at a moment of crisis, during the Jacobite Rebellion of 1745, with his *Calm Address*, to which reference has already been made.   In this he undertook to show that the reigning sovereign was entitled to the continued allegiance of the English people and that the claims of the Pretender were invalid.   Most of the later writings in which he developed his political ideas were inspired by his hostility to the doctrines of Locke and his followers.   But whether he was theorizing in early life as an anti-Jacobite or afterwards as an anti-democrat, his political thought is free from serious inconsistency.

The origin of government Tucker ascribed not to the will of man but to the will of God as manifested in human nature.   Like Aristotle, he believed that man is by nature political, and he dissented vehemently, as was his wont, from Locke's doctrine that the state originated in a delib-erate and explicit com act between individuals who were not impelled to political association by natural inclination, but were actuated solely by a desire for a securer enjoyment of their natural rights than had been possible under an assumed preëxisting "state of nature."   Civil society and government were as natural to men, he contended, as community life to bees, ants and beavers.   Distinguishing between government and forms of government, he held that government was of divine origin, though its forms were of human contrivance and subject to change in cases of necessity. Locke's idea of an original state of nature, to which men reverted in times of revolution, he rejected as a figment of the imagination, and he showed that it received no support from what had actually happened in the course of revolutions.[145]

Government, being of divine origin, must serve a divine purpose, and this, according to Tucker, is the good of the people. Whatever its form, government is always, in essence, a public trust, "to be executed for the good of the whole, and not for the private advantage of the governors and directors,"[146] but it does not follow that the trust has been explicitly reposed in the governors by the governed, as Locke maintained, or that there is any direct contract between them. There is always, however, an implied contract, or "quasi-contract," by which Tucker meant that the relationship between them always implies mutual obligations. "In all human *trusts* whatever . . . where there is a duty to be performed, which is not actually expressed, specified, or contracted for,—but nevertheless is strongly implied in the nature of the trust;—the obligation to perform that implied duty is of the nature of a quasi-contract; a contract as binding in the reason of things, and in the court of conscience, as the most solemn covenant that was ever made."[147] Under this trust, or quasi-contract, the government owes protection, and the citizen owes obedience.[148]

Any established government, no matter how it has originated, says Tucker, is entitled to the allegiance of the people so long as it serves the purpose for which government exists. With regard to the question of obedience, a subject which is vital in any political theory, he took issue both with the Jacobites, who held that obedience was due only to kings who ruled by hereditary right, and with his democratic contemporaries, who argued that it was due only to governments based upon the consent of the governed. The latter, as he pointed out, had much in common with the Jacobites, both being equally intolerant of governments of whose original title they did not approve.[149] What mattered, for him, was not

---

[145] *A Treatise concerning Civil Government*, Pt. I, chaps. ii and iii. *Two Dissertations on Certain Passages of Holy Scripture*, 43. *A Sequel to Sir William Jones' Pamphlet*, 11 ff.

[146] Below, 412.   [147] Below, 480.

[148] Below, 482. *A Calm Address*, in *Reflections on the Expediency of a Law for the Naturalization of Foreign Protestants*, Pt. II, 58. *A Sequel to Sir William Jones' Pamphlet*, 10.

[149] Below, 450 ff. According to Tucker, many of those who had been Jacobites in 1745 were "republicans" in 1776; see *A Series of Answers*, 95, footnote.

how a particular form of government had come into existence, but how it was functioning.   As a zealous upholder of the Glorious Revolution he could not deny the right of resistance in all cases, but he did deny that it was ever justifiable to resist a government on the ground that its original title was defective.   In the *Calm Address* he cites the well-known statute of Henry VII to show that as a general rule of English law *de facto* kings are possessed of the same powers and entitled to the same allegiance as *de jure* kings.[150]

Though Scriptural texts no longer spoke as conclusively in politics as they had done in the seventeenth century, Tucker thought it well worth while to draft St. Paul in the service of George II against the Pretender.   The apostle, in his oft-cited injunction to the Christians of Rome, commanded them to obey "the powers that be," since these are ordained of God, threatening with damnation those who should resist. This text had been much used by the Jacobites in condemnation of the Revolution of 1688, but Tucker gave it a different interpretation.   The true meaning of the Pauline injunction, he said, was that an existing government (the powers that be) ought never to be resisted because of any defect in its original title, but that, on the contrary, "every *settled* government . . . exercising that office for the good of the people, is *so far* ordained of God, as to have a *sufficient*, and therefore in that sense a *divine right*, to the loyalty of the subject."[151]   Even a government founded on usurpation "may nevertheless be deemed the *Ordinance* of God to the people for good, after it is *peaceably* settled and established."[152] But St. Paul, when condemning resistance to government, was not thinking of governments that abused their powers to the injury of the people, for these could not be the Ordinance of God, and he did not mean to command obedience to such.   There could be no divine right "to govern wrong."   Tucker leaves us to infer that the apostle would have been a revolutionist in 1688, a strong Hanoverian in 1745—and a good Whig on both occasions.   He would also, presumably, have consigned to perdition those champions of democracy who, in Tucker's later years, were proclaiming that no government was entitled to obedience unless it was based on consent.

---

[150] This statute, says Hallam (*Constitutional History of England*, chap. i), "remains an unquestionable authority for the constitutional maxim that possession of the throne gives a sufficient title to the subject's allegiance and justifies resistance of those who may pretend to a better right."

[151] *Reflections on the Expediency of a Law for the Naturalization of Foreign Protestants*, Pt. II, 59.

[152] *Two Dissertations*, 47.

Since the people, under any system of government, were always entitled to be governed well, Tucker recognized an ultimate right of revolution. If a government was intolerably and incorrigibly bad, manifestly not the Ordinance of God, resistance was justifiable, and the governed, in last resort, were warranted in changing their governors. The time for the application of this desperate remedy was when, "according to the most impartial calculation," the ill consequences of submission clearly outweighed those of resistance.[153] Who the impartial calculators should be, Tucker did not specify, but from his approval of the Glorious Revolution it may be inferred that he would have left the decision to the rich and the well-born. One of his many objections to the "Lockian" system was that (so he said) it gave the right to depose rulers, in effect, to "the first mob that can be got together, provided they are strong enough to undertake and execute the work."[154] He was emphatically opposed to talking about the right of revolution, and especially to any attempt to specify the precise conditions under which resistance would be warranted. The English constitution contained no such specifications, "for fear crafty and designing men should mislead the giddy populace to deem that to be legal liberty, which in truth and reality is no better than a rampant licentiousness and lawless anarchy."[155] One of the great evils of Locke's teaching, in his opinion, was its tendency to inculcate distrust and dislike of government in general and to encourage talk of revolution.[156]

Though obedience, in Tucker's theory, was due to any established government that was not palpably abusing power to the injury of the governed, some forms of government were preferable, that is, better adapted to the purpose for which government existed, than others. In his *Treatise* he undertook to determine which of the principle types of government—monarchic, aristocratic, democratic and mixed—afforded the best security against "misapplication of the trust reposed in the governors for the sake of the governed."[157] His opinions concerning monarchy, by which he meant absolute monarchy, and hereditary aristocracy, though not favorable, are expressed calmly and without emotion, but his passionate hostility to democracy is obvious. Here the real object

---

[153] Below, 412. *Two Dissertations*, 47. *The Respective Pleas and Arguments* (2d ed., 1776), 23.

[154] Below, 451.   [155] *Treatise*, 421–22.

[156] *Four Letters on Important National Subjects*, 16. *A Sequel to Sir William Jones' Pamphlet*, 28.

[157] *Treatise*, Pt. II, chaps. iii and iv.

of his attack was not any existing system of government, but the ideal of
the ultra-democratic disciples of Locke, a "wild and visionary plan . . .
absolutely impracticable in any district of larger extent than a common
country parish."   By democracy he meant a form of government under
which all the adult males (and also, logically, all the adult females) were
supposed to meet together "whenever they will, in order to deliberate
and vote on all public affairs, to change and alter, to pull down and build
up, without control, and as often as they please."   Such a "reptile, democratical institution" would be utterly lacking in capacity for self-
defense and could not exist for any length of time except in some remote
wilderness.   Having proved to his own satisfaction that there were serious
defects in each of the three simple forms of government, he reached the
conclusion, not original with him, that the best was that which combined
monarchic, aristocratic and democratic elements in a system of checks
and balances, and this, needless to say, was the British form.   It would
be a mistake, however, to attribute Tucker's praise of his own government to any sentiment of patriotic pride; he was saying only what distinguished foreign publicists had said.   Moreover, he found considerable room for improvement even in the British system.   The balance
between the three parts of the constitution seemed to him to be far from
perfect.   Unlike those reformers who were calling for a diminution of the
influence of the crown, he saw no serious menace to good government in
the monarchic element, and he thought that the aristocracy had scarcely
enough weight.   The licentiousness of the masses, on the other hand,
he took to be a very real and imminent peril, and he presented a series of
proposals for holding the democratic part of the constitution in check.[158]

He was strenuously opposed to what the political radicals of his day had
chiefly at heart, a reform of the parliamentary system.   In his *Instructions for Travellers*, written before the rise of the democratic movement, he
had proposed an alteration and simplification of the qualifications for
the exercise of the parliamentary franchise which would exclude for the
most part "the idle, extravagant and debauched" and include "the sober,
virtuous and ingenious."   He had then advocated the restriction of the
county franchise, which was still based on the old forty-shilling freeholder act of 1430, to those in possession of freeholds of an annual value
of ten pounds or above, while for the boroughs he suggested a uniform
occupation franchise similar to that which was finally adopted in 1832.[159]
The principal items in the radical program of parliamentary reform were

---

[158] Below, 542 ff.   [159] Below, 267.

the extension of the suffrage to all adult male citizens, representation according to population, involving a redistribution of seats and the enfranchisement of the new industrial towns, and more frequent elections. To each of these Tucker objected vehemently.[160] He maintained that the suffrage qualifications ought to be such that a sober frugal man could become a voter within a reasonable length of time, while an idle spendthrift would be in danger of losing his electoral privilege. In accordance with the principle of virtual representation, in which he fully believed, he thought that the qualifications should be so prescribed that the electors could not combine against the non-electors without combining against themselves and their friends and relations.[161] But it was his firm conviction that it would be disastrous to give a vote to every man, and he took an almost gleeful pleasure in pointing out that the radicals were inconsistent in advocating universal male suffrage and at the same time favoring the continued exclusion of women from the suffrage.[162] His chief objection to the principle of representation by population was that it would have the effect of increasing greatly the influence and power of the populace in the large towns, which he regarded as "the seats of faction and sedition, and the nurseries of anarchy and confusion."[163] The radicals were agitating to have the maximum duration of Parliaments, which had been fixed at seven years by the Septennial Act of 1716, reduced to three years, and many of them even favored annual elections. Tucker denied that more frequent elections would do away with bribery, as the reformers hopefully anticipated, and believed that they would have several positive bad political and economic results.[164]

The subject of Anglo-Irish relations was one in which Tucker took great interest, and he expressed his mind freely upon it. Though Ireland, in the eighteenth century, had a Parliament of its own, the British Parliament, prior to 1782, legislated for that country whenever it desired to do so and passed some laws injurious to Irish industry and commerce, to the indignation of Irish patriots who claimed that no other Parliament than their own had any lawful authority over them. In his *Essay on Trade* Tucker proposed, as a means of increasing British commerce and credit, the incorporation of Ireland with Great Britain in a single kingdom, with a common Parliament and a common fiscal and commercial system. The political division of the British Isles into two

---

[160] See, e.g., Appendix to *Four Letters on Important National Subjects.*
[161] Below, 542–3.   [162] Below, 515.   [163] Below, 536–7.   [164] Below, 538 ff.

kingdoms was, he thought, impolitic and indefensible, and he believed that an organic, parliamentary union would be mutually beneficial, anticipating from it results comparable to those that ensued from the union of England and Scotland in 1707, which he lauded as an accomplishment of the highest statesmanship.[165]   One of the subjects which he intended to discuss in his projected treatise on economics was "a polity for a perfect incorporation with Ireland."[166]   In 1775 he wrote: "No good reason uɒon earth can be given for such a separation: And it has long been the ardent wish of every true patriot in both nations to see them united."[167] When Ireland secured a constitutional status of legislative equality with Great Britain in 1782, with an independent Parliament of its own, Tucker was convinced that this was contrary to the true interests of both kingdoms and prophesied that in time the Irish would themselves ask for a legislative union.[168]

William Pitt the Younger was in favor of free trade between Great Britain and Ireland, and early in his administration resolutions looking to this end were approved by the Irish Parliament, but British industrial and commercial interests took fright, and the resolutions were altered to the detriment of Ireland.   They were passed, as altered, by the British Parliament, but in this form they were unsatisfactory to Ireland, and the project was abandoned.   While it was under public discussion some of Tucker's friends were anxious to know what he thought of it, and his *Reflections on the Present Matters in Dispute between Great Britain and Ireland*, published in 1785, was written for their use.   In this he took the view that the proposed commercial arrangements were premature and should be deferred in the interest of both countries.   A political, legislative union was evidently not practicable at the time, but he was confident that it would eventually take place, "when many of those obstacles, which now appear so formidable, shall be smoothed by the lenient hand of time."[169]

One of those with whom Tucker discussed the commercial proposals of 1785 and the question of a political union with Ireland was the Reverend Dr. Clarke, chaplain to the Prince of Wales.   The two men conversed and corresponded on the subject, and Tucker undertook to answer

---

[165] *Essay on Trade* (3d ed.), 58–62, 142.
[166] Below, 215.
[167] *An Humble Address and Earnest Appeal*, 42.
[168] *Four Letters on Important National Subjects*, 11–15.
[169] Page 34.

certain popular objections to union submitted to him by Clarke.   In 1799,
when union was the paramount issue of domestic British politics, Clarke,
thinking that the dean's opinions upon so momentous a subject, though
expressed nearly fifteen years before, should be made public, included
them in a pamphlet which he published, entitled *Union or Separation*.
It is clear that Tucker did not regard the existing constitutional arrangements between Great Britain and Ireland as permanent.   To his mind the
only eventual alternatives were total separation or organic union.   If the
former should be resolved upon by the Irish in an outburst of patriotism,
"according to the unalienable doctrines of Locke and Molineux, Price
and Priestly, and according to the pattern set by the Americans," he
thought that no attempt ought to be made to coerce them.   Self-interest
would presently teach them that separation did not pay.   He had lived
too long and observed too much to suppose that deep-rooted prejudices
could be overcome by reason alone, and he did not rely upon reasoned
argument to bring about union.   *"But there is a tide in human affairs to
which prejudice itself must yield, because it cannot resist it."*[170]   In 1800,
the year after Tucker's death, the Act of Union was passed.

---

[170] Clarke, *Union or Separation*, 29.

THE ELEMENTS OF COMMERCE
AND THEORY OF TAXES

EDITORIAL NOTE

This work is published here for the first time. It was privately printed in 1755 for the purpose indicated in the Advertisement. Only three copies are known to be extant, one in the New York Public Library, one in the Library of the British Museum, and one in the private library of Professor H. S. Foxwell, which has been acquired by the University of London. One of those whose criticism Tucker solicited was Thomas Secker, who had been bishop of Bristol and soon afterwards became archbishop of Canterbury. The copy in the New York Public Library, from which this reprint has been made, is the one which was sent to Secker, who wrote many comments and suggestions on the margins; it contains, also, some annotations, interlineations and corrections by the author. These have not been reproduced. The title (see below, page 61) is struck out, and for it is substituted, in Tucker's handwriting, "The Moral and Political Theory of Trade, and Taxes".

ADVERTISEMENT.

THE present Impression of this Treatise is not designed for public Use: The Press being no otherwise employed on this Occasion, than as an expeditious Amanuensis. The Author therefore humbly hopes, That those Gentlemen who favour him with perusing these Sheets, will please to consider the Work as still in Manuscript, and oblige him with their Corrections and Improvements as soon as possible. The Margins are made particularly large for that Purpose. And it is proposed, that after a general Revisal, the Treatise shall be correctly and neatly printed, and published with Expedition.

IT is moreover to be observed, That the Principles laid down in the ensuing Treatise, are, for the most part, General and Universal; viz. such as would suit (with very little Alteration) any Kingdom, State, or Climate whatever; and are therefore called THE ELEMENTS OF COMMERCE: — A Title designed by the Author, as his Friends know very well, several Years before a French Writer appeared with the same. But if a more particular Application of these general Principles to certain Branches of foreign or domestic Commerce should be judged necessary, the Author humbly conceives, that this would best be effected by a separate Treatise, wherein justice might be done to each particular Subject. For as such Dissertations would be too long to be inserted in the Body of the present Work, and would cause too great an Interruption in the Thread of the Discourse, it seems most expedient, at least for the present, to omit them. The Author is the more confirmed in this Opinion, by observing to what an unexpected Length some of the ensuing Chapters are spun out; a Length, for which he is desirous of making the following Apology to the Reader, viz. That as his manner of treating this Subject is entirely new, he is obliged to be the more explicit in setting it forth. For in a new System every thing must be proved, and scarce any thing taken for granted. But if this System should have the good Fortune to be established in the Judgment of the Public, some future Writer, when old Prejudices are removed, may reduce all that has been said into a very little Compass.

A PRELIMINARY
DISCOURSE,
SETTING FORTH
The natural Disposition, or instinctive Inclination of Mankind towards COMMERCE.

THE Powers with which it hath pleased the munificent Creator to form Mankind, are suited to such important Ends, that a wrong Application of them cannot but be productive of great Infelicity; as a right Use of such Endowments is the Source of all the Enjoyments for which human Nature was created. Now these Powers are various, according to the different Ends proposed to be obtained by them; all which Ends center in a joint Happiness. If, for Example, you consider a human Creature as *a mere Animal*, you will find, that he has most of those Instincts which other Animals feel, in order to answer the Demands of Animal Life. But when you take a View of him in an higher Character, as a Member of *Civil Society*, and a Subject of *Moral Government*, you will observe, That he is not only furnished with a Set of *social* Tempers, but also that he enjoys the Prerogative of *Reason* and *Reflection*, to guide each Instinct and Disposition to its proper End. And therefore the general and constituent Principles of human Nature may be thus summed up: Man hath the Appetites of an *Animal*,—the Temper and Affections of a *social* Being,—and the Understanding of a *rational Agent*.

LET us take a View of human Nature under each of these Capacities.

I. As *mere Animals*, Mankind are powerfully incited by various Instincts to provide for their *animal* Wants; which, in general, are much the same with those of other Animals; Only I think it deserves to be taken Notice of, That Mankind are more deficient by *Nature* than any other Tribe of Beings. For it is obvious, that they are left by Nature destitute of a *proper Covering*, or *Clothing*: And as to *Food* and *Dwelling*, if we consider Men in their mere Animal State, without the Improvements of *Society*, and the Assistance of each other, they will be found less able to make Provision for themselves than any other

55

Creature. Now these are very remarkable Variations in the Ways of
Providence, and yet not to be consider'd as real Imperfections or Omis-
sions in regard to Man; but as a most admirable and gracious Contrivance of the Author of Nature to answer great and good Ends; —
which, it is hoped, will be more fully shewn in the Sequel. Indeed
other Beings, who are only designed for the Uses of *Animal* Life, are
not endued with any Qualification but what is necessary for this Purpose:
And therefore all their Sagacity and Knowledge shine forth at once.
For Instance, the first Nest that is built by any of the feathered Tribe
is as curious in its Contrivance, and as exquisite in its Workmanship,
as the last: And the Lion and the Vulture do not much *improve* in the
Use of their respective Weapons. In short, the same *original* Plan
continues throughout: — Nor do Beasts, Birds, or Fishes discover any
Disposition to divide the Labour of the Community into different
Branches, or assign distinct Parts to the respective Individuals.

THIS, I think, is the Case in general with respect to the Brute Creation.
But if there are any Traces of superior Abilities, they are so few and
inconsiderable, as not to deserve a particular Inquiry.   Nay, wheresoever
any Tribe of Animals distribute the Labour of the *Community* into
different Parts (as is reported to be the Case among the Bevers, Ants, and
Bees) it hath been always observed, that there they make some Advances
superior to the Condition of mere Animal Life, having a Species of
Commerce, and a Form of Government.

BUT if Man had no other Powers but what he receives in common
with the *Brutes*, he would not only be *one* of them, but perhaps the
lowest and most miserable of all.   For, as was observed before, he hath
many *Defects* considered as a mere Animal, which they have not: Nay,
the least bad Circumstance which must attend such a State, would be the
Levelling and *Degrading* human Nature to such a degree, that the *social*
Relations of High and Low, Rich and Poor, Benefactor and Receiver,
Governor and Governed, Learned and Illiterate, would be absolutely
unknown.

II. LET us therefore in the next Place consider Mankind as actuated
by a Set of *social* and *benevolent* Affections,   These social Instincts are,
for the most part, the Prerogative of Man: For though other Animals
herd together, (which may be called *conversing*) yet we cannot observe
that they are *naturally* inclined to do *good Offices* to each other.   They
shew no Disposition to part with any share of their *Food* or *Dwelling*
to relieve the Miseries of the Hungry and Afflicted, or to shelter their
Fellow-Creature from the Pursuits of the merciless Hunter.   And when a

Stranger is introduced among them, they are so far from shewing any Signs of *Hospitality*, that, till Time has familiarized them, they treat him as a common Enemy.

I WILL allow indeed, that all Animals discover, for a Season, the strongest Affection for their Offspring: The Males and Females likewise give many Proofs of a *temporary* domestic Kindness for each other. But these Regards are distinct from what is properly called *social Benevolence*. The Male and Female have a mutual Passion implanted in them for the Propagation of their Species; and they are *naturally* disposed to love their Young, the Females especially, during their *helpless* State, with a most ardent Affection; which Affection vanishes away in Proportion as their Young grow up, and become capable of providing for themselves. Now it is evident, that all this is different from *social* Friendship, different from the Love of *virtuous* Characters, and the Delight that is felt in the *Communication* of good Offices to the rest of the Species, when they either *deserve*, or stand in *need* of them.

MANKIND therefore being thus under the Influence of *social* and *benevolent* Affections, as naturally seek Society in order to gratify these *social Instincts*, as they require Food for appeasing the Appetite of Hunger. And when human Creatures are once brought together, they find a vast number of Advantages in each other by *mutual* Assistances, to which they must have been Strangers in their separate and independent State. Consequently then it is, that the common Labour of the Society is branched out into separate and distinct Parts: Then it is that each Individual chooses a *particular* Course of Life, according as his Circumstances, or *Genius* shall determine his Pursuits. — I mention GENIUS the more emphatically, because some Men are formed by *Nature* to peculiar Imployments, being born with *Talents* (which are a kind of *instinctive* Knowledge) for one Pursuit preferably to another: A Circumstance not discoverable in any of the Brute Creation. Therefore among the Human Species some are imployed in the several Articles of *Clothing*, others in raising of *Provisions*, and a third Set in preparing Materials and building *Habitations*. Thus are the *first* Wants of Mankind, viz. *Food*, *Raiment* and *Dwelling*, much better supplied by dividing the general Labour into different Branches, than if each Individual depended on himself alone for the Supply of them. And these different Parts of the common Labour are nothing else, in other Words, but distinct *Trades* and *Manufactures*; and may therefore be considered as the *first Draught*, or *Rudiments* of Commerce.

BUT if Society is the best Means of procuring a Supply for our *animal* or *natural* Wants, it creates a multitude of *artificial* Needs, which may be called *social*, because both their first Rise, and subsequent Increase, must be ascribed to Society. Now these *artificial* Needs are more or less extensive, according to the several Ranks and Stations in Society, the different Improvements, Customs, Education, and other Qualities of Mankind. And as our present *secular* Happiness appears to arise from the Enjoyment of superior Wealth, Power, Honour, Pleasure, or Preferment, SELF-LOVE, the great Mover of created Beings, determines each Individual to aspire after these *social Goods*, and to use the most probable Means of obtaining them.

THUS therefore the Passion of Self-Love operates with much greater Force, when excited by such a long Train of Objects, than it possibly could do, were Men strangers to the artificial Wants, the Refinements and Decorations of social Life. And yet were this Passion to proceed without Direction or Controll, it would in a great measure defeat its own Ends. For Self-Love is narrow and confined in its Views, and admits of no *Sharers* or *Competitors*, where-ever it *can exclude* them. Therefore when you see a Set of Individuals forming *Combinations* and *exlusive Societies*, you may observe, that the Members of this exclusive Company are still *Rivals* and *Competitors* among themselves; and after having excluded the rest of their Fellow-Subjects, would, in the next Place, exclude each other, *if they could*. And though, in Fact, all such *mutual* Exlusions must end in *mutual* Poverty, so that even *Self-Interest* is a *Loser* in the End by these pernicious Schemes, yet the Mass of Mankind ever did, and ever will proceed in this Way, *as far as they have Power:* They will always regard the present Moment, and be blind in respect to distant Consequences. Hence it is, that *Monopolies* are formed and *Charters* granted, under the ridiculous and absurd Pretence of the Public Good, when, in Fact, private Advantage is the only Point aimed at. Hence it is, that unjust Combinations are sanctified by positive Laws, and those very Exclusions are stiled RIGHTS and LIBERTIES, by which other Men have their *Rights* taken from them, and are *denied* the Liberty of being useful to themselves, and serviceable to their Country.

INDEED I grant, that the social Instinct of *Benevolence* is some Check upon this selfish *monopolizing* Principle; but it is so very feeble, that it would be quite ineffectual to prevent the Mischiefs arising from inordinate Self-Love, were there no stronger Curb to rein it in: For the Love of Self is implanted in Mankind much more strongly than the Love of Benevolence; according to the English Proverb, *Self knows no Fellow.*

III. THEREFORE REASON and REFLECTION must be called in to the Aid of the *social* and *benevolent* Principle. But what is the *Office* of Reason? — Not surely to *extinguish* Self-Love; that is impossible: And it might be questioned whether it would be right to attempt even to *diminish* it: For all Arts and Sciences, and the very Being of Government and Commerce, depend upon the *right Exertion* of this vigorous and active Principle. And were it once restrained, or greatly weakened, human Nature would make but feeble Efforts towards any thing great or good. Nay, in such a Case, the social Temper itself would want a Spur; and all the benevolent Affections being destitute of their proper Incitement, would be very faint and languid in their Operations. Consequently, the main Point to be aimed at, is neither to extinguish nor enfeeble Self-Love, but to give it such a Direction, that it may promote the public Interest by pursuing its own: And then the very Spirit of Monopoly will operate for the Good of the Whole.

AND if this is the proper Business of *Reason*, consider'd in the Abstract; the Reason or *public Wisdom* of a *State*, or *Community* is particularly called upon to pursue such a Plan. Indeed it can execute no other consistently with its own Interests, and the Good of those who are under its Protection. Divert therefore the Pursuits of Self-Love from vicious or improper Objects, to those that are commendable and virtuous; Grant no Privileges to Indolence and Ignorance; Give no Assistance to the ingrossing Schemes of Monopolists; but raise a general Emulation among all Ranks and Professions in Things relating to the public Good; And let superior Industry and Skill, Integrity and Virtue, receive all your Incouragement, because they alone deserve it: — Then such a Government must have good Subjects, because it has removed the Temptation to be bad ones; The Country will be blessed with Plenty, and abound in Commerce, by means of the Industry of its Inhabitants in their respective Callings; And the Subjects of such a State must feel the good Effects of its Influence, and be happy in each other, because their several Pursuits, Interests and Happiness do all coincide.

Now this politic Direction of the Pursuits of various Individuals to one common End, the Study of Philosophers, and the Aim of every wise Legislature, will be found to be nothing more than a strict and scrupulous Observance of Christian Morality. For this *truly* social System furnishes us with the strongest Motives towards restraining inordinate Self-Love, having so linked our Duty and Interest with that of the Community, and prescribed such Regulations for our Conduct and Behaviour, that a Man cannot act the Part of a *good Christian*, without being good and useful, and a public Blessing in every other Relation of Life.

Thus far as to the Uses of Reason in framing or directing any Systems of *National* Commerce: And the Reflection I would draw from the Whole is this, — That when the *auxiliary* Motives of *Reason* are called in to the Aid of *social* Love, or diffusive Benevolence, this latter becomes, in a good degree, a *Counter-Agent* to inordinate Self-Love. So that the *Circulation* of *Commerce* may be conceived to proceed from the *Impulse* of two distinct Principles of Action in Society, analogous to the *centrifugal* and *centripetal* Powers in the Planetary System. But unerring Wisdom being the Guide and Director of these Powers in the heavenly Bodies, causes that *Constancy* and *Regularity* in their Motions, which is never observable in the Affairs of Commerce. And why is that? — It is because the Circulation of Commerce being only directed by the Reason or Wisdom of Man, is therefore subject to all those Impediments, Obstructions and Irregularities, which result from the Vices and Extravagancies, the partial Interests, the false Conceptions, and mistaken Policy of Mankind.

However, from this general View of the Subject, the Evil doth not appear wholly without a Remedy; at least, if it will not admit of an *absolute* Cure, it may be so greatly *palliated*, as to render the present Scene of Things very desirable; which is as much as can be expected during an imperfect State. Let us therefore enter upon the ensuing Work with the following Maxim strongly upon our Minds, *viz.* That universal Commerce, good Government, and true Religion, are nearly, are inseparably connected. For the Directions and Regulations of each of these, are no other, than to make private coincide with public, present with future Happiness. And whoever is conversant with the Affairs of the World, cannot fail to observe, That whenever the Parts of this *extensive System* have been separated by the Arts or Folly of Men, Religion has sunk into Superstition or Enthusiasm, Government has been turned into Tyranny and *Machiavelian* Policy, and Commerce has degenerated into Knavery and Monopoly.

THE
Elements of COMMERCE, AND
Theory of TAXES.

INTRODUCTION.

AS the natural Disposition of Mankind to *Commerce* hath been
set forth at large in the *Preliminary Discourse*, and as *Self-Love*
is known to be the great Mover in human Nature, it may not be
improper to begin with the following Observation; *viz.* That every Legislature should consider these two Principles as the Foundation of their
future Proceedings, or as Materials in the Stores of Nature for them to
work upon. They cannot *create* new Powers or Faculties in human
Nature; but they can cultivate and improve those that are already
subsisting: They can, by a proper Application of their Influence and
Authority, prune away Luxuriancies, and check the Progress of *unbearing*
Branches, at the same Time that they promote and encourage the Growth
of every Thing good and useful in Society. Now when the legislative
Powers act upon this Plan, they will consider, That a lasting and extensive *National Commerce* is no otherwise to be obtained, than by a prudent
Direction of the Passion of Self-Love to its *proper Objects*, — by *confining*
it to those Objects, — and there giving it all possible *Assistance* and
Incouragement. The Passion of Self-Love therefore must be taken hold
of by some Method or other; and so *trained* or *guided* in its Operations,
that its Activity may never be mischievous but always productive of the
public Welfare. When Things are brought to that pass, the Consequence
will be, that every Individual (whether he intends it or not) will be promoting the Good of his Country, and of Mankind in general, while he is
pursuing his own private Interest.

BUT Self-Love is no otherwise to be taken hold of in the Case before us
than either by having recourse to PENAL LAWS, or by establishing a
JUDICIOUS POLITY. The Business of Penal Laws is to *terrify* or *punish*;
but the Use of a judicious Policy is to *incline* and *incourage:* The one is
to *deter* the Multitude from offending, the other to lead them by their
own *free Choice* to virtuous Industry. This being the Case, it is easy

to see which Method deserves the Preference, — especially in a *free* Country. Indeed the Multiplication even of *Penal Laws* would be of no Service, unless you armed the Magistrate with a proportionable Power to put them in Execution: And this in other Words, would be giving him something too like a *Carte Blanche* to act as he pleases. Such a degree of absolute Power is too great a Trust to be reposed in *Man:* And perhaps is safe and beneficial only in the Hands of that Great Being, whose *Wisdom and Goodness are over all his Works.*

WHEREFORE the only Thing desirable in our Situation, is a *judicious Polity:* — Which may be farther described as a *preventive Regimen* of State, whereby the Temptations to Vice are removed, and such In- couragements given to Virtue, as would induce a Man to execute the proposed Regulations of his own free Choice, without the Appearance of Restraint or Compulsion. Thus a Traveller may be said to *choose that Road*, which the *Public* hath *laid out* for him, when he finds that the *By-Roads* are deep, intricate, and disagreeable, and the other straight, easy, safe, and good: — He prefers the public Road, not because he is *compelled* by any penal Statute, but because he finds his own Advantage in his Compliance, and cannot find it any other way.

THIS may serve to explain in some measure the great Difference between *Polity* and *Law:* But if any thing is yet wanting to complete the Description, it may be farther suggested, That the one is like a beauti- ful Machine, which regulates and adjusts its own Motions; and the other a clumsy imperfect Work, which is always out of Order, unless the Maker stands by to correct and amend it. Now from these Hints and Illustrations it plainly appears; that the Influence of the one must be much more extensive and universal than that of the other. And indeed thus it comes to pass, that the *distinguishing* Characteristics of a People chiefly depend on their *National Polity*; whereas the general *System of Laws* makes no such Difference. Antient and modern *Rome*, for Ex- ample, do not differ much from each other in the main Tenor of their Laws, relating to the common Principles of Justice and Equity: But as to the whole Body of their Polity, it is in a manner diametrically opposite. And what is the Consequence?—Plainly this; That the very Temper and Genius of the People are changed, and that there is not a greater Contrast in Nature, than between the antient *Romans*, and modern *Italians*.

THE Subject has hitherto been considered only in a *general* View; *viz.* That Self-Love should be so directed as to promote its own, and the public Interest at the same Time; and that *Polity* is a properer

Method than *Penal Laws* for giving it this Direction. — But the immediate Inquiry comes yet to be resolved; *viz.* In what Particulars doth the Public Good consist? And how shall the Passion of Self-Love be directed so as to produce the happy Effects intended?—In answer to the former Part of the Inquiry, it may be proper to observe, That the Good of any State doth plainly arise from the *Increase, Imployment,* and *Morals* of its Subjects; because a *numerous, industrious,* and *virtuous* People, cannot fail of Plenty and Content at Home, of Respect and Influence Abroad. And in regard to the Method or System of Polity, How these great and good Ends are to be obtained, this is to be the Subject of the ensuing Discourse.

PART I.

Containing certain Polities for increasing the Number of People.

THE Necessity of attempting some Polity of this Nature, will abundantly appear from the following Considerations.

I. WHERE a Country is thinly peopled, it is impossible to promote a brisk and general Circulation of Industry and Labour, by reason of the Distance and Dispersion of the People from each other, and the Consequence of that, their Want of Rivalship and Emulation: — So that the greater Part of those few Inhabitants must lead a sauntering, lazy, and savage Life, thereby making near Approaches to the State of *mere Animals,* the most wretched of all others for an human Creature to be in. This Observation is confirmed by Experience; For in every Country, extremely thin of Inhabitants, the People are proportionably poor and miserable, and lead such Lives as are but a few Removes from the brute Savages of the Woods and Mountains. Suppose only Ten Thousand Inhabitants left in *Great Britain,* and what would be the Consequence? — These few Inhabitants would soon degenerate into *British* Savages, correspondent to the Clans of the Highlands of *Scotland,* or the *Indians* of *America.* Suppose the Country better peopled, and then the Evil would lessen in Proportion. It is moreover observable, That in Country Places, where there is a Scarcity of Inhabitants, one Trade will not be sufficient for a Man's Subsistence, but several distinct Occupations must be joined together in order to obtain a bare and wretched Support: — By which means it comes to pass, that there cannot be that *Quantity* of Work performed, as where every one exercises and improves himself in one particular Calling: And as to the *Quality,* or Workmanship itself, that must necessarily be clumsy, rude, and imperfect.

II. WHERE a Country is thinly peopled, the very Activity, or in other Words, the *exciting Cause* of that Activity, *viz.* the Self-Love of the Inhabitants, will take a wrong Turn. For in such a Situation, the Figure that *Commerce* can make, must be very mean and contemptible: So that Country Gentlemen, who at the best do not entertain a very kind Opinion of the Advantages of Commerce, are confirmed in their Prejudices against it, and choose rather to vie with each other in the Dangers of the Chace, or the Pretensions of Birth and Family, and the Length of their Pedigrees, than in giving Incouragement to the Increase of low-born Tradesmen and Mechanics.

III. WHERE a Country is thinly peopled, the Property of Lands will be the more easily ingrossed, and intailed in a few Families; by which means the Land-holders become more absolute and despotic over their Vassals. In this Case, Numbers are kept in Poverty and Wretchedness to raise the *comparative* Grandeur of one Family, and flatter the Pride of their petty Tyrant: — I say, the *Pride* only; for as to the *Comforts* of Life, he will not be on a Level with a common Tradesman in a populous and industrious Country; because he cannot have the Convenience of Markets, the Supplies of Foreign Trade, the Variety of useful Manufactures, or even the Pleasures of Society: And all that he has to put in the Scale against these *real* Disadvantages, is the imaginary and ungenerous Satisfaction derived from the greater Misery of his wretched Dependents. Whereas Commerce, as it is calculated to extend Industry, Happiness, and Plenty, equalizes Mankind more than any other Way of Life; and at the same time that it connects them together in Bonds of *mutual Interest*, it renders them FREE. Trade and Vassalage, Commerce and Slavery are, in their Natures, repugnant to each other.

IV. A COUNTRY thinly peopled, has neither the *Strength*, nor *Riches* it would have, were it better inhabited; so that it cannot make that Figure in Peace, or War, it ought to do. For Numbers of People are the Strength, as Industry is the Riches of a Country. Nay, this very Depopulation, unless preventive Remedies are used, and a proper Polity introduced, must occasion a farther Diminution of Inhabitants; because several Persons will be obliged to seek for Work in other Countries, as not having sufficient Imployment, or a proper Consumption of the Produce of the Lands, or the Labour of the Manufacturer among themselves. The Lands must lie waste, where there are no Markets; and the Artificers cannot be employed without Customers.

Now when a Country, blessed with the Advantages of Liberty and Peace, commodiously situated, and happy likewise in a mild and healthy

Climate, with a Soil productive of great Quantities of good Materials both for foreign and domestic Commerce; — When such a Country increases very slowly in the Number of its Inhabitants, which might have increased very fast, we must conclude, that some Canker in Polity, or lurking Disorder, is preying upon the Vitals of that Commonwealth; which, if not timely prevented, may bring on the most fatal Consequences.

Now though *Great Britain* enjoys many signal Advantages, yet she will be found to labour under sore Difficulties at present, through a bad System of Polity, and the mistaken Notions of public Welfare, and National Commerce, in the following Respects;

I. BECAUSE the Marriage State is loaded with many Taxes and Expences, from which a Single Life is free. For this Burden has the same Effect in its Operations, as if the Legislature had actually passed a Law to discourage Marriage, and incourage Celibacy. For the Father of a numerous Family, in paying the several Duties and Excises laid on those Commodities which his Family consumes, is *fined* as it were in those respective Sums, from which a Batchelor is exempt: And yet the Batchelor is not put under any Discouragements of another Nature, whereby the Scale might be brought even, or rather inclined to favour the Matrimonial Side. Nay, as Places of Diversion are continually multiplying, a Single Person with 200 *l.* a Year, can make a more *modish* Appearance, and partake of a greater Variety of Pleasures, and consequently appear in a Condition *more desirable* to the Generality of Mankind, than a married Man with twice that Sum.

II. SUCH an Inducement to Celibacy must be greatly prejudicial to good Morals; because an Increase of Temptation will always cause an Increase of Vice. And again, a general Corruption of Morals is fatal to the Populousness of a Country in various Ways. Thus the Evil operates back upon itself, spreading and increasing as it goes on. Nay, as the Sexes will naturally associate together in the single State, and form Parties of Pleasure, the very least bad Consequence that can happen, is a giddy, thoughtless Turn of Mind, and an utter Indisposition for the Discharge of those domestic Duties, on which the Good and Happiness of Society greatly depend.

III. THE Country grows thinner of Inhabitants in those Parts of the Kingdom where the Practice of destroying Cottages prevails, and joining several small Farms together to make one *great Farm:* For every Cottage or Farm-House thus destroyed, occasions the Loss of so many laborious, working Families to the Country. The same bad Effects are also produced by the unlimited Power of ingrossing Landed

Estates; by the Power of intailing them upon the Male Heir; the Power of settling them all upon the Eldest Son at the Marriage-Contract; and lastly, by the Common Law of the Land, which gives all the Landed Estates of *intestate* Persons to the First-born Son, without shewing the least Regard to the rest of the Children. These Monopolies of Land must occasion, according as they prevail, a great Diminution of People. — Besides, it is always observable, that in Proportion as the Property of Lands are more equally divided, in the same Proportion the Ground is better manured, cultivated and improved: And a great number of Farms, and middling Landed Estates, thick set together, not only occasion a very great Number of Inhabitants, but also render it necessary that many of the Children of such Inhabitants should be brought up to Trades and Manufactures. And I will venture to add, that Manufacturers of this Class are the most useful, and the least subject to Corruption of Morals. — But more of this hereafter.

IV. THE Nobility and Gentry of *England* are deterred from entering into the married State during the *Prime* of Life, because they can have little or no Command over their Children, when they advance towards Years of Maturity. And a Father is by no Means desirous of being treated disrespectfully by his Son, merely because he is not likely to make a Vacancy as soon as the young Heir could wish him. Yet this Consequence, bad as it is, too frequently happens to a middle-aged Man, as his Son draws towards the Years of twenty one. For at that Period of Life (such is our wrong Polity) the Parental Authority is almost at an End, and the Son can shew an undutiful Behaviour with Impunity.

THEREFORE to avoid this disagreeable Circumstance, the Father sends his hopeful Heir to travel into Foreign Parts, at the Age of Sixteen or Eighteen, a Season of all others, in which it is most improbable he should make any real Improvement; an Age in which he is too old for a School-boy, and too young to be able to make any useful Observations on Men or Things, being destitute of a proper Stock of Knowledge to form Comparisons between his own and foreign Countries, and without knowing the Difference between the Religion or Laws, the Polity or Government, the Commerce or Taxes of one Country from another. In short, he is strictly and literally a *Traveller*, that is, a *Passenger* through various Countries, and the greatest *Stranger* to his own. However, as he stays Abroad for several Years, this is some Comfort and Relief to his Father.

BUT in general, as I said before, Men of Fashion do not marry in the Prime of Life. And it is observable, that they stay later in *England*, than in any other Country in *Europe*, — as if it were on purpose to be ready to move off the Stage, when their Successors come on. But alas! if they continue single during the Prime of their Years, in what manner do they spend their Time? — Generally in all the Excesses of Riot and Debauchery: so that those of higher Rank, who ought to set the Example, seldom think of raising a Family, till they are fitter for an Hospital than the Bridal Bed. What an Offspring! what Members of Society, or Defenders of their Country, are we to expect from such Parents!

V. THE very Liberty which the *English* enjoy above other Nations, becomes in the Event, as Matters are *now* circumstanced, a means of dispeopling the Country. For it corrupts their Morals, hurries them into Vice and evil Courses, shortens their Days, and destroys the natural Fertility of the Sexes. In one Word, If the regular Course of Providence hath taken off its *Thousands* by natural Death, the Gallows and Electioneering, Spirituous Liquors and Debauchery have destroyed their MILLIONS.

VI. OUR numerous Colonies, extensive and distant Navigation, perilous and unwholesome Trades, are great and continual Drains upon us. — Add to all this, That *Holland, France,* and *Spain* keep great Numbers of *British* Troops in their Pay. Moreover, almost all the States in *Europe* draw off as many as they can of the Artificers, Sailors and Manufacturers of these Kingdoms, into their own; whilst we are so far from retaliating the like upon them, that we are for discouraging those few Foreigners who would voluntarily come over.

THE way to supply these Losses, and to put a Stop to many of the Evils here complained of, is to establish such a Polity as shall give Incouragement for increasing the Numbers of People both by Matrimony, and by the Introduction of industrious Foreigners.

CHAP. I.

A Polity for the Incouragement of the Married State.

MARRIAGE is not only the express Appointment of Divine Providence, but will be found upon Examination to be the only *effectual* Means (whatever licentious Talkers may pretend) for the Continuance and Preservation of the Human Species. This will appear, if we consider, that Nature has implanted in other Animals only a *temporary* Instinct towards each other; and in the Gratification of it hath given neither *Choice*, nor *Preference*, nor fixed any Ideas of *Beauty*;

or *Merit* in the Male or Female Objects, as far as we can discover.   Therefore Nature herself seems to have forbid any proper *Marriage*, or *lasting*
Cohabitation among other Tribes of Animals.   And this universal Law
of Nature is universally observed throughout the Brute Creation.   But
in regard to the Human Species, the great Author of our Being hath taken
a quite contrary Course, having implanted Appetites, which are *not*
periodical, and given Ideas of *Merit* and *Beauty*, of *mental* as well as
corporeal Excellence.   Judge therefore how absurd it must be to reason
from the Nature of Brutes to the Nature of Men, when these very
Natures are in *direct Opposition* to each other.   In short, the very
Circumstances in which Men and Women find themselves, suggest to them
this plain Lesson, That they were designed by Providence not only for
brutal, but *social* Converse.   To which End they have Capacities and
Inclinations given them to choose and prefer, to esteem and improve
one another.

THE same Argument might appear in another Light by considering
the Property of the Marriage Bed, as the Foundation of Civil Society,
and consequently of all the Advantages resulting from it.   For, if a
Man has no reasonable Security that the Children imputed to him are
his own, what Motive has he to extend his Care and Concern beyond
the Period of his own Life?   And yet it is a most certain Fact, that the
Progeny of the Human Species are in a more helpless State than those of
any other Animals yet known in the World: For they not only require to
be nursed and reared a much longer Time, than is necessary for the
Young of any other Creature, but must be also clothed, housed, educated,
and enabled to get a Livelihood in some Trade, Business, or Profession;
otherwise they will not be fit to fulfil the Part incumbent on them as
Members of human Society.

Now the Way to render Marriage a Matter of universal Choice, and the
Aim of both Sexes, is,

I. To cause a Law to be enacted, That no Persons shall either elect,
or be elected to any Post of Honour or Profit throughout the Kingdom,
but those who either are, or have been married: And with regard to
conferring Titles of Honour, and to the Disposal of such Civil Imployments as are lucrative or honourable, but not elective, they may likewise
be subject to the same Regulations.   As to any Objections that may be
made against such a Law, the like may be raised against every Proposal
calculated for the public Good; every legal Disqualification whatever
having been observed to bear hard upon particular Persons: And were
such kind of Objections to be admitted, they would tend to prevent all

new Laws from ever being made, and repeal all the old ones now in being.

II. It is proposed, That all Persons shall be adjudged to be *Minors*, till they arrive at the Age of *Twenty Five* Years,—unless they *marry* before that time, *with* the *Consent* of their Parents or Guardians, and so be admitted to be of Age at the present Period of *Twenty One*. And in case they should marry *against* the Consent of Parents or Guardians, between the Years of twenty one and twenty five, the Marriage itself shall be deemed *firm* and *valid*, but the young Person shall still be a *Minor* in Law, till the full Age of twenty five; that being the general Date from which a *Majority should commence*. And indeed in most other Countries, the usual Time of *Majority*, as the celebrated Marquiss of *Halifax* well observes in his Miscellaneous Tracts*, is *twenty five*. And it would be difficult to alledge any Reason why it should be earlier among us: For surely, as the Marquiss says,—*It is not that we are earlier Plants than our Neighbours*. One thing is certain, That there are more Fortunes spent, more Constitutions ruined, and bad Principles infused into the Minds of young Men of Fashion between the Years of twenty and twenty five here in *Britain*, than in all the other Parts of Life. That *commercial* People the *Dutch* think it full soon for their Youths to be of Age at *twenty three:* And yet they do not lay the same Temptations in the Way of the *eldest* Son to be *riotous* and a *Spendthrift* that we do; because they divide their Substance much more equally among their Children, than is done in *England*.

III. It is proposed, That the Statute made in the fifth Year of Queen *Elizabeth* against Persons exercising any Mystery, Craft, or *mechanic* Trade, who have not served an Apprenticeship for seven Years, be repealed as to *married* Men, but remain in force against *Batchelors*. The Statute itself is one of those which has the Public Good for its Pretence, but was really meant to serve the base Ends of private Interest and Monopoly;—in which even the Self-Interested themselves were grossly deceived: For this Statute, by being universal in its *Restraint*, and confining almost all Trades alike, excludes *Customers* as well as *Rivals*, so that in fact every Person is hurt, and no body benefited.—As to a Zeal for the Public Good, this Principle could never lead any Man, in his Senses, to exclude the *Industrious* and *Ingenious* from the *Common Rights* of Society: And yet the Framers of this Statute had plainly nothing else in View. For they knew full well, *from Fact and universal*

---

* Cautions and Considerations for choosing Members of Parliament, *Article* IX.

Experience, That Nature herself has formed certain Persons for certain Trades, and given them such Knowledge by *Instinct*, as no human Artist could communicate by Instruction: And it is very remarkable, That not only all new Inventions, but almost all the Improvements in Arts and Sciences were the Discoveries of those, who had not served a *regular Apprenticeship* to the Business.   Why then should such Men be debarred from following their *natural* Genius, and making a *proper* Use of their *Talents* for their own, and their Country's Welfare?   Besides, what is it to the Wearer of a Pair of Shoes, for instance, whether the Maker served seven Years or not?—By *wearing* them he himself becomes the *best Judge* of the *Goodness of the Work:* And if they are good, he will buy again of the *same* Maker; but if they are not, it is no Consolation to him, That he has bought *bad Shoes* of a *regular bred* Shoemaker, who is *free* of the Company, has walked in a Procession, and wore a fur Gown.   However, since the Statute is made, and has been long in force, and since the Prejudices of Mankind are obstinate things, and not to be overcome at once,—the most advisable Method seems to be, To graft a good National Polity upon this bad Law, rather than absolutely repeal it, and by making it subservient to the Promotion of Matrimony, *to draw Good out of Evil.*

   IV. It is proposed, That *married* Men shall be *free*, not only to work as Journeymen, but also to set up all Sorts of *mechanic* Trades in every City and corporate Place whatever, without *Fee*, or Acknowledgment in any Shape or Form.   And to make this Proposal go down the better with those Persons, who pique themselves upon the *imaginary* and *fallacious Distinction* (*Right* I cannot call it) of being *Freemen*, it may be enacted, That the Privilege of hanging out *Signs, Shewboards,* or *Names,* and of keeping *open* Shops (that is to say, A Shop with a Bulk to it, and without Glass Windows) be confined to Citizens and Burgesses; and that all others be content with displaying their Names and Goods within-side of the Glass.

   V. It is proposed, That *married* Men shall be free to reside where-ever they please, with their Wives and Children, without regard to Parish Settlements or Certificates;—provided some substantial Person (an Inhabitant in the Parish to which they come) shall give Five Pounds Security to the Overseers of the Poor, or the proper Officer, That such *new Comers* shall not be chargeable to the Parish for three Calendar Months after their Arrival.   Such a Security may possibly be expedient on many Accounts: And as it would serve to blunt the Edge of Opposition, it might be considered as the Basis of a new Regulation concerning Parish Settlements, wherein Cavilling and Contention could have no Place. For the very Date of the Bond would be *one* authentic Proof, whether the Person or Family in question had resided upwards of three Calendar Months or not; and consequently whether intitled to a Parish Maintenance, in Case of Sickness, Disability, &c.—But if any Parish admitted a Person or Family to reside among them for a longer Space than *six Weeks*, without this *Caution*,—be that at their own Peril; and they must take the Consequence upon themselves, in Case the Stranger should become a Burden. Thus would every Parish know what they had to trust to, and the Poor would never be without a Settlement.— As to the present Set of Laws concerning Paupers and Parish Settlements, they are equally absurd and unjust; nor is there any *one* good Consequence resulting from them.

In the first Place, the Parishes themselves, for whose Benefit these Laws were intended, are so far from receiving any Advantage, that they are greatly hurt by them. For by their means every Parish is put into a State of War with the rest of the Kingdom; and if a Man hath an Estate in two Parishes, he is frequently obliged to join in this unnatural War against his own self concerning Parish Settlements. Besides, suppose even that a Parish, now and then, prevents the Incumbrance of a Pauper and his Family, by means of these Laws;—do not other Parishes the same? that is, If *Bristol* prevents the Incumbrance of a Pauper coming from *York*, will not *York* make the like Retaliation upon *Bristol?* Where then is the Advantage to either?—Not to mention that these Parish Refusals and passing of Paupers are necessarily attended with great Expence, and perhaps with Law-Suits which cost ten times the Sum in question. To these Absurdities there is another, if possible, yet greater; *viz.* That one Parish is frequently obliged to be at the whole Expence of maintaining a poor Person, and another shall receive the Benefit of all his Labour. In his Infancy he is a Burden and Expence; when he grows to Maturity he leaves his Native Place, and works as a *Journeyman* or a *Labourer* for Years together, without gaining a *legal* Settlement; but when he is taken Sick, or is past his Labour, he is sent home again to his original Parish, who are obliged to receive him, and to maintain him as long as he lives. What can be the Charm in old Customs which infatuates the Minds of Men to such a Degree, that they cannot see the most palpable Absurdities, whereby their immediate Interest is so greatly injured?

In the next Place, if the Parishes themselves are such Losers, the Public must be so in all Capacities.—Not to mention, That in a Commercial State it ought to be the constant Aim of the Legislature to continue

Matters in such a Manner, that every Hand should be employed, and none kept idle that are either willing or able to work. But how can this be effected, unless there is either sufficient Work provided for the Poor at home, at *all Times and Seasons*, (a Supposition too extravagant to be admitted) or the Poor be suffered to seek for Imployment where-ever they can find it? Besides, there are many Trades which are only *temporary*, and in their own Nature *periodical:*—others have a *Glut* of Business at one time, and none at all at another; either therefore the labouring Poor ought to have *double* or *treble* Wages for the Time they can have Work, in order to lay up against the *long Vacation*, or they should be permitted to seek for some Imployment or other, at every Place and in every Season.

LASTLY, If the Parishes and the Public are Losers, what must the Poor be, who are the Persons immediately affected? And indeed the Inhumanity frequently practised on these Occasions is quite shocking to relate. An industrious Man shall be forced from his Business and his Bread, where he his enriching his Country by his Labour, and be sent to starve with a large Family upon *Parish Pay*, merely because he is not a *legal Parishioner* in the Place where his Business lies, and may *possibly* be chargeable. If he demands a Certificate from the Parish to which he *legally* belongs, they will certainly deny him, in hopes he may gain a *legal* Settlement elsewhere. And if any Parish finds that a Labourer or a Journeyman has by chance obtained a Certificate of his Settlement, they will not let him contract, as a Covenant-Servant, for longer time than eight, ten, or at farthest *eleven* Months, in order to have it in their Power to send him to his original Parish whenever they please. Thus are the Poor treated in regard to their Labour;—and even as to *Marriage*, the Overseers and the Justices frequently exercise a Power, for as to Right, in reality they have none, of forbidding the Banns of poor Persons, lest they should bring a Charge upon the Parish. Now all these, and indeed many more Impositions of the like Kind, arose originally from the despotic and tyrannical Notions of *Baron* and *Vassal*, which answered in former Times to the modern Ideas of *Planter* and *Slave;*—Ideas very unfavourable to the Increase of Inhabitants, and to the Circulation of Industry in every View. The Baron, the Planter, and the Parish-Officer act all upon the same Principle, when they would restrain their Vassals, Negroes, or labouring Poor from stirring beyond the respective Bounds prescribed. However, as I said concerning a former Article, since the Laws are enacted and daily executed, and since the Nation are *habituated* to this absurd and cruel

Practice, it would be more adviseable to graft a good Polity on these bad Laws, than absolutely to repeal them. And the Security above-mentioned of Five Pounds, will effectually prevent the Idle and the Vagabond from being troublesome, at the same time, that it will allure the Ingenious, Industrious, and Ambitious to push their Fortune, where-ever they can find it will answer best.

VI. IT is proposed, That Men shall not be allowed to work at, to set up, or carry on certain Trades, which properly belong to Women,—unless they *marry*, and so may be considered as *Assistants* to their Wives. These Trades will be more fully set forth, when we come to treat of the Polity proper for securing and promoting good Morals. And *Note*, All the four last Articles, *viz.* That relating to serving an Apprentice-ship,—That relating to Corporate Places,—That relating to Parish Settlements,—and the present concerning the Trades proper for Women, must come frequently under Consideration in the Progress of this Work; because the Polities here attempted to be grafted upon them, are not only means to increase the Numbers of People, but also the most effectual Methods of promoting Commerce, Industry, and good Morals.

VII. IT is proposed, That all Men for the first twelve Calendar Months after Marriage, shall be exempted from serving any Offices they shall please to decline; also be freed from paying all *personal* Duties and Taxes whatsoever.—In regard to this seventh Proposal, be it remembered, That it is a Transcript of a Part of that admirable Polity which *Moses* introduced by Divine Command into the *Hebrew* Constitution; whereby the little Territory of *Palestine* (not much larger than the Principality of *Wales*) became the most populous and the best cultivated Country on the Face of the Globe. Nor let any one object, That such Exemptions throw the Burden upon others; for surely the most effectual Way to *lighten* the Weight of any Burden is, To lay a Scheme for increasing the Numbers of those who are *speedily* to contribute towards the Support of it Thus, therefore, might the married State be rendered desirable, and become the Object of the Wishes of both Sexes. For it is humbly presumed, that all the Regulations here proposed, are such as would want very little Inforcement from Courts of Judicature; because they would execute themselves, and consequently must be effectual. As to the first Regulation, which excludes Batchelors from Titles of Honour, and Offices of Honour, Power, or Profit;—and the second which fixes the Time of *Majority* to twenty five Years, both these may be softened by a *saving Clause*, as far as regards the present Generation: That is, the *present* Admirers of a single Life may be *excepted* from the Disqualifications here proposed, if they shall have attained to the Age of twenty one Years *before* the passing of such a Law. And as this Exception may be necessary in order to disarm the Fury of their Opposition, and will likewise be only a *temporary* Thing, the Inconveniencies attending it will *diminish* every Day.

But after all, it ought not to be concealed, that there is one Difficulty still remaining, and such a one as, will sometimes defeat, if it cannot be removed, the Intent of the best of these Regulations in favour of Marriage. It is the Difficulty of obtaining a Divorce in Cases of Adultery. For as the Law now stands, the Innocent are punished, while the Guilty triumph. A Man, for Example, though convicted of the most notorious Adultery, shall still enjoy his whole Fortune; and the injured Wife obtain no other Satisfaction, than to be separated from *Bed* and *Board*; which can be no Punishment at all to the Adulterer. Again, If the Husband is the innocent Person, and the Wife the Adulteress, he shall not be allowed a second Marriage, even though he should declare in open Court, that he hath Reasons both of *Prudence* and *Religion* against continuing in a single State. Thus is he punished, as if he was the guilty Person;—unless he hath Friends and Money to obtain a Divorce by Act of Parliament.

Now if such Divorces *à Vinculo Matrimonii*, as they are called, are *unjust* in themselves, no Power on Earth hath a Right to grant them; nor can a thousand Acts of Parliament dissolve that Marriage which is not cancelled by the Laws of God. But if the Parliament is justified for disannulling a Marriage upon plain Proofs of Adultery, why should not the inferior Courts of Justice have the same Power, when the same Proof is laid before them?—Nay, such a Proof, on which the Act of Parliament itself is built? For it is observable, That no Act of Parliament can be obtained, till the Adultery hath *first* been proved in another Court. Moreover, if Husbands are intitled to the Privilege of being *totally* divorced, upon full Evidence of the Infidelity of their Wives, why should not the same Liberty be granted to the other Sex? Sure I am, that the Marriage Vow of Faithfulness and Affection, is the same in both Cases; the Men likewise are as capable by Nature of adhering to their Ingagement: and though a Breach on the Part of the Women may sometimes be attended with greater *temporal* Inconveniencies, yet if the Contract itself is not to be disannulled by the Crime of Adultery, the mere Plea of greater Inconvenience will appear a very weak one. Besides, it is such a Plea, as in certain Cases, may be made with greater justice on the Woman's Side, than on the Man's; therefore it would follow, that when *such* Circumstances occur, the Woman ought to have the full Power of a *total* Divorce, and not the Man.

THIS being the present State and Imperfection of our Laws, let us now see what Lights may be drawn from the holy Scriptures towards correcting and amending them.

FIRST therefore it appears, That when *Moses* constituted the Body of the Jewish Law, the Practice of divorcing Wives *at Pleasure* was very frequent in that Age, and in those Countries. For even in the Books of *Leviticus* and *Numbers* we find the Affair of Divorces spoken of as a *settled* Usage, and a Custom *universally* prevailing: So that *Moses* was so far from introducing this Practice, that he *moderated* the Exercise of it by confining it to *narrower* Bounds. And this agrees with the Words of our Lord, who said, "That *Moses SUFFERED* them to put away their Wives, because of the *Hardness* of their Hearts;"—a strong Intimation, That if these *arbitrary* Divorces could have been *intirely* prevented at *that Juncture*, it would have still been better. However, what *Moses* did, was a considerable Check upon *hasty, passionate*, and *capricious* Separations, though it was very far from being a thorough Prevention of the Evil.

SECONDLY, We must farther observe, That all Divorces under the Mosaical Dispensation were *total* and *final:* That is, They were Separations not only from *Bed* and *Board*, as the Canonists speak, but total Dissolutions of the Marriage Covenant: So that the Phrase, *To put away one's Wife*, carried the same Signification to them, as a *Parliamentary Divorce* doth to us; and each of the Parties might marry again whom and when they pleased. Such was the Language and Meaning of the Words in our Saviour's Time: And therefore when the Pharisees asked him, "Whether it was lawful for a Man to put away his Wife," they included the *Power* of marrying another, as a necessary Part of the Idea. Indeed these two Expressions were generally considered as equivalent Terms. For when our Lord preached his Divine Sermon on the Mount to a mixed and popular Audience, he used the very same Expressions as equivalent one to the other, *viz.* "It hath been said, Whosoever shall *put away his Wife*, let him give her a Writing of Divorcement; but I say unto you, that whosoever shall *put away his Wife, saving* for the Cause of *Fornication, causeth* her to commit Adultery. And whosoever shall *marry* her that is divorced, committeth Adultery," *Matt.* v. 31, 39. Where we may observe, That he takes it for *granted*, that the *Jewish* Wife, according to the Custom of her Country (where Matrimony was strictly required, and universally countenanced) would *not* remain in a *single* State, but would soon *marry* again: which Marriage he pronounces to be an Act of Adultery. —But why so? why is this Marriage to be reckoned adulterous more than others? The Reason is assigned by our Lord himself, *viz.* "Because the former Marriage Contract holds good, unless it is *vacated* by the Crime of *Infidelity:* For this is the *only Crime* which dissolves the Nuptial Tie, and allows a Man *to put away his Wife;* that is, *marry again.*"

THIRDLY, It is also to be observed, That Divorces were still more *frequent* and *arbitrary* among the *Greeks* and *Romans,* than among the *Jews.* For both Men and Women had a Power of *divorcing each other,* without assigning any Cause, Motive, or Reason whatever; and might afterwards marry whom they pleased. This being the Case, let us consider ourselves as stript of all *modern* Ideas relating to these things, and let us fix the same Meaning to the Words, which the *Jews* did in our Saviour's time, and the *Greeks* and *Romans* in the time of St *Paul.*

Now the Pharisees, in their Application to our Lord, put the Question in this Form, "Is it lawful for a Man to put away his Wife for EVERY CAUSE?" That is, in other Words, Is it lawful for a Man to be divorced *at Pleasure?* —For such they were *willing* to hope, was the Indulgence granted them by *Moses.* To which Inquiry he replied in two Places, viz. *Mark* x. 2—12. and *Luke* xvi. 18. That such *arbitrary* Divorces were *not justifiable;* — giving a general Answer to a general Question. But in two other Places, viz. *Matt.* v. 31, 32. and Chap. xix. 3—9. He not only gives the *general* Answer, but also adds the *particular* Exception, by shewing, That a Divorce is lawful in the Case of Adultery, and *in that only.*

MOREOVER, when St *Paul* wrote to the *Corinthians* in Answer to a Question of theirs concerning Marriages and Divorces, it is evident from the Context, That he meant nothing more than to express his Disapprobation of those *arbitrary* and *capricious* Divorces, which were then in use among the Gentiles. For these People, knowing their Power of dissolving the Marriage Contract, whenever they pleased, were *tempted* to carry every little domestic Quarrel and trifling Dispute to this fatal Extremity. Indeed, *healing* Counsels and *mutual* Forgiveness were scarce known, and seldom practised in any of those Countries, where both the Parties could wreak their Revenge upon each other by insisting upon the Privilege of a Divorce. And therefore this unlimited Privilege, as some are pleased to call it, would be so far from being advantageous to Society, or even to *domestic* Happiness, could it be attainable in our Days, that it would always *exasperate* and *inflame,* instead of *cooling* and *calming* the Passions of Mankind. Excellent therefore was the Advice of the Apostle, "If the Woman *will* depart, let her remain *unmarried*, or be *reconciled* to her Husband: And let not the Husband put away his Wife." He had before been exhorting them to live in Union and Harmony: But if Differences should arise, and these be carried to so great a Height as to cause a Separation between them, then he directs, That they must not think of entering into *new* Marriage Contracts with other Persons, but remain unmarried in order to come together again, and *be reconciled*. This State of the Case is farther illustrated by what follows, "If any Brother hath a Wife that believeth not, and she be pleased to dwell with him, let him not put her away. And the Woman which hath an Husband that believeth not, if he be pleased to dwell with her, let her not leave him." Where we may observe, That the Apostle was guarding against *Family Disputes* on Account of the Differences of Religion: —and not at all entering into the Reasonableness or Unreasonableness of Divorces on Account of Adultery: Indeed our Lord himself had determined that Question long before.

UPON the Whole therefore, thus much must now be surely taken for granted, That our Lord and St *Paul* introduced no *new Distinctions* into the Nature of a Divorce, but only confined the Practice of it to much narrower Bounds than either *Jews* or *Gentiles* had been accustomed to. If therefore a Man is allowed by the Gospel of Christ to *put away* his Wife for the Cause of Adultery, he is likewise allowed to *marry another*; these two Phrases signifying the same Thing in the Language of the Gospel. As to the Popish Distinctions of a Divorce *à Mensa & Thoro*,—and a Divorce *à Vinculo Matrimonii*, they were not known in that Age, nor in many hundred Years afterwards; but were the Invention of the Canonists and the Court of *Rome*, in order to create a Market for their own Dispensations, Pardons, Indulgencies, Absolutions, &c. &c. And the Misfortune was, that at the Time of the Reformation, People were in too great an Agitation of Spirits, to be able to examine with Deliberation how far the Corruptions of Popery had interwoven themselves into the more distant Parts of the Constitution: nor indeed was it an easy Matter, at such a Juncture, to prescribe a Remedy for the more latent and less obvious Disorders, when the best Heads and the warmest Hearts had enough to do to recover the *vital* Parts of the Constitution from the principal and more malignant Evils it laboured under. And thus it comes to pass, That at this Day we retain a monstrous Share of Popery (that is, the *Effects* of Popery) in many Branches of our Religious, Civil, and Commercial Polity, after it hath been banished out of our Articles of Faith, and Systems of Belief.

BUT having now cleared up the Difficulty which embarassed this Affair, I have only to remark, That the *Cautions* to be observed in giving Sentence in Cases of Divorce are obvious and plain enough: For if every Divorce was attended with six, or twelve Months Imprisonment of the *Guilty*, together with a *very large* Fine to be levied out of the *proper* Estate or Fortune of such offending Persons for the Use of the *Innocent*, there could be no such Thing as a *collusive* or *fraudulent* Divorce: And if both Parties accused, and proved each other guilty of Adultery, then both ought to suffer Imprisonment, and their respective Forfeitures be given to the Poor.

FROM hence therefore, let us take a View of the happy Consequences which must result from the whole of such a System operating *uniformly* together.

I. THEN, If the proposed Regulations took Place, every general Election, instead of being so extremely pernicious to the Morals and Manufactures of the Kingdom, as Elections are now observed to be, would eventually promote the Happiness of Society in all Respects:— Also as no Man would attempt to offer himself a Candidate for Places of Honour, Profit, or Preferment in the *State*, nor could enjoy any Titles of Honour, unless he were married;—and as the exlusive Privileges of Cities, Boroughs, and Corporate Societies,—and the restraining Laws relating to Trades and Parish Settlements would operate *only* against *Batchelors*, the CONSEQUENCE would be, that the whole Kingdom, without Force or Compulsion, would prefer the married State to any other Condition; so that it would become even the *Fashion* of the Times to be a married Man; and a Batchelor would be looked upon with Ignominy and Contempt.

II. As Matrimony became more desireable, or, if you please, more *fashionable*; the Taste for public Pleasures and Diversions would subside of Course; and both Sexes would begin to cultivate such Tempers and Dispositions of Mind, as would be the fittest Qualifications for the Married State, and become the most useful in domestic Life.

III. THE Consequence of this would be, that the Persons actually engaged in the married State and the Cares of a Family, would be much happier in themselves than can now be expected from them.—Because at present they see with Regret those Pleasures, which they cannot partake of so frequently and completely as single Persons do: And upon the Strength of this Circumstance, they make themselves miserable in forming Comparisons to their own Disadvantage.—Such a Source of domestic Uneasiness is not to be removed, till the first Cause and Origin of it is taken away. For Mankind in general will always be found to be better or worse, in proportion to the Increase or Decrease of the Temptations that surround them.

IV. Men of the greatest Property and Fortune would then marry in the Prime of Life, both as they could not make any Figure in their Country without this Qualification, and as the great Temptations to Debauchery would then be removed: nor would their Sons be sent abroad so young, raw, and unexperienced as they now are.

V. After Persons are married and have Families, the very Principle of *Self-Love* inclines them much more strongly than when in a single State, to a sober and industrious Course of Life; because Sobriety and Industry are the *natural Means* of supporting themselves with Credit and Reputation, and of making a Provision for their Family.

VI. The same Principle of Self-Love would induce them to give their Children a Religious Education, and train them up in some virtuous and honest Calling: For it never can be the *general* Interest of Parents (not to mention Motives of a higher Nature) to bring up their Children to *Idleness* and *Irreligion*.

VII. Were that Regulation to obtain, which fixes the Age of *Twenty Five* for the Time of *Majority*, the Parental Power would be sufficiently enlarged, which at present is undoubtedly too low in *England*; and Parents would have a reasonable Influence over their Children in the Disposal of them in Marriage, without Tyranny or Compulsion. Indeed, Cases of this Nature are attended with perplexing Difficulties on all Sides; but there are fewer Difficulties on this side, than on the other; and the Advantages both to Society, and to the Individuals themselves would be, upon the whole, much greater.

VIII. When the Morals of the People are in general amended, fewer will perish by drinking *Spirituous* Liquors, and other Habits of Intemperance, the present fruitful Sources of Disease and Villainy; also the Numbers of Convicts will be lessened, and very few will be obliged to leave their Country through *Shame* or *Want*.

IX. When Matrimony is duly encouraged, the unnatural Lusts themselves will then grow less frequent than they are now reported to be. For these horrid Vices, generally speaking, are derived from one or other of the following *bad Sources*, viz. Either from a *Prohibition* of the natural Use of the Sexes, or the *Satiety* of abandoned Lewdness and shameless Prostitution. Now as the latter Vice prevails at present in this Country, it is no wonder that the Crimes against Nature should be the Consequence: For this was ever the Case both in antient and modern Times, as all Histories do testify.

X. As nothing in this Life can be absolutely perfect,—we will suppose the Marriage State, notwithstanding these good Regulations, to prove sometimes greatly unhappy through the Infidelity of one of the Parties:— Yet even then the Remedy of a Divorce would be at hand to relieve the *Innocent*. And this itself might be a Means to engage many Persons to venture upon that State, which, at the worst, would not then be, as it is now, without a Remedy: Indeed such a Check would be a Motive to all in general to observe a regular and unblameable Behaviour, knowing the *Penalty*, as well as *Infamy* attending the *guilty* Person in Case of a Divorce.

BUT, as we have observed before, the Crime of Infidelity, as well as all other Crimes, would be much less frequent in both Sexes, in proportion as the Temptations and Tempters were removed or decreased.

CHAP. II.

A Polity for the Admission of Wealthy and Industrious Foreigners.

THE Reasons for instituting such a Polity, and the Advantages arising from the free Admission of wealthy and industrious Foreigners, will appear at large by the following Considerations.

I. MANY of the *best* and most *useful* Subjects in foreign Countries and arbitrary Governments, are often harrassed and oppressed by the *Minions* in Power. For any Pretext will serve, where Merit is dangerous, and Wealth a treasonable Crime, to prevent the Increase of such Subjects, or reduce them to a Level with others. Therefore such Persons as are the most deserving and the most industrious, are the best intitled to our Protection, and the fittest to be incorporated into a free State.

II. THE *Romish* Religion never ceases to persecute the Protestants in every Country, where it can; and these Protestants, generally speaking, are Merchants and Mechanics, Persons the most useful in a State, and the most wanted in our own,—and more especially deserving the Regard of that Kingdom on a *religious* Account, which is at the Head of the *Protestant* Religion.

III. IN some Countries Merchants and Tradesmen are treated with great *Contempt* merely on Account of their *Profession,* and dare not make that *display* of their Riches which their Fortunes could easily support, lest they should give umbrage to the Government to oppress them with Taxes, or for fear of exciting the Envy and Jealousy of the *Noblesse* by the superior Figure they could make in Society. Now such

Persons as these ought to be particularly invited to settle in a Country, which prefers the Glory of Commerce to that of Conquest.

IV. It is the Interest of this Nation to *invite* those Foreigners who have Money in the Public Funds to reside in *Great Britain*, because the Savings of the Remittances of so much *Yearly Interest* (now constantly sent abroad) would be a very great Addition to the National Stock. But the present Expences of a private Bill for Naturalization are so great, that many Foreigners (having Money in our Funds, and who are willing to make a Purchase of an House, or a Piece of Land, or to engage in some Branch of Merchandise) are deterred from settling in *England*, seeing they cannot enjoy the Emoluments of their own Fortune, without paying so dearly for it. Suppose therefore the Mind of a Foreigner to be *balancing*, whether he shall settle here, or continue in his own Country;—in such a Situation a very little would turn the Scale:—And whatever a prejudiced *Englishman* may suppose of the Charms of *Old England*, an indifferent Foreigner, who doth not see with the same Eyes, will not esteem it a very signal Favour to be allowed to spend his Money among us, and to enrich this Country at his own Expence.

V. As the Introduction of Foreigners brings in Riches, so doth it open also larger Correspondencies; — it presents us likewise with the Inventions and Sagacity of other Nations, creates more Imployment for the Natives, helps and improves all our old Manufactures, and sets up new ones;—thus impoverishing our Rivals, at the same Time that it enriches ourselves.

VI. When a Country is *open* for the Reception of Foreigners, it is proper to inquire, What sort of foreign Adventurers are likeliest to come in, and to try their Fortunes.—Foreign Beggars, for Example (concerning whom so great a Dread hath been pretended) are ignorant of the Language of any Country but their own. Judge therefore, to what Purpose should they come over to exercise the Trade of Begging, without being able to tell their doleful Tale, in which consists the very Art and Mystery of their Trade? Besides, as Idleness and Laziness are their grand Characteristic, they will not engage in any Enterprize, that is to cost them long Journies and much Fatigue: Add to this, that their very Poverty is a Bar against the Expence of a Voyage into *England;* an Expence still heightened to Strangers, as they are unacquainted with the Ways of Living of the Country, and know not *how* or *where* to be accommodated on the cheapest Terms. Now this reasoning ought to be attended to, because it is confirmed by Fact and Experience: For though *Great Britain* is *open* to all the Beggars of the Universe (who cannot be *legally* driven away after they are *once arrived here*) yet perhaps there is not a single Instance of any Person coming into this Country with a View to exercise the Trade of Begging.—And what has been observed concerning Beggars, holds equally true concerning the *Lazy* and *Undeserving* of any other Profession.   For such Creatures have neither the Talents nor Ambition for pushing their Fortunes in a strange Country: And indeed it is scarce possible, that any Foreigners should succeed, but those who are conscious to themselves of superior Talents, Industry, or Frugality in some respect or other.—Now such Adventurers as these are a Blessing to every State where they settle: And would to God, they were properly encouraged to settle here!

VII. As the Rent of Lands depends on the Numbers of People, (for Land is quite useless without a Market for its Produce) so the Introduction of Foreigners is a sure Means of creating a Demand for all the Produce of a Landed Estate;—and consequently of raising the Value and Price of Land.   Whereas at present, for want of a sufficient Consumption at home, we are obliged to send great Quantities of Corn abroad, and to levy a Tax upon ourselves to promote the Exportation of it to our Rivals. Thus they are fed cheaper than our own Manufacturers; and the greater the Years of Plenty, the higher is the Tax which we pay to foreign Countries.—Now if the People, who consume this Corn abroad, were transplanted into *England,* we should not only save this Expence, but likewise imploy a prodigious Number of Hands in manufacturing the said Corn into Bread, at the same Time that we should reap the Benefit of additional Labour and Industry, Strength and Riches, in every other Instance.

VIII. THE same Benefits must accrue to the Nation from the Admission of Foreigners, as would follow by the Increase of our own People in the Way of Marriage:—with this advantageous Circumstance, that Foreigners *immediately inrich* a State by their Industry, Commerce and Manufactures, which our natural-born Infants cannot do, but must remain a dead Weight upon the Community, till they are grown up, and actually imployed in some useful Calling.   Now this Consideration alone hath determined the Polity of *France,* not only to put the Foreigners on the *same Footing* with the natural-born Subjects, but also to grant them (particularly the *Swiss*) superior Privileges, in order to allure the greater Numbers into the Kingdom.

IX. THE Genius of the *English* Nation particularly requires, that it should be *piqued* by the Example of industrious, skilful, and deserving

Foreigners. Tell an *Englishman*, That it is a Shame for him to be excelled by a *Frenchman*,—that he ought to keep up the Glory of his Country, and not suffer himself to be out-done by a Foreigner; and this will have as great, perhaps a greater Effect to quicken his Industry, and mend his Morals, as any Consideration whatever.

X. As the Country is *already* open, not only to *Beggars*, were they disposed to come, but also to *Singers, Fidlers, Strollers, Dancers, Tumblers*, &c. &c. of every Climate and Religion, for the bringing over of whom *large Subscriptions are yearly made*,—one would think, there could be no great harm in going *one Step* farther, *viz.* To give a *Parliamentary* Invitation to the industrious and wealthy *Merchant*, to the ingenious and frugal *Mechanic*, and the oppressed and persecuted *Protestant:* For if Numbers of these were introduced among us, their Examples and Behaviour might, in some degree, counter-act the Corruption, Idleness, and Debauchery occasioned by the others.

XI. WHEN *English Protestants* express any kind of *backwardness* to receive persecuted and distressed *Protestants* of *other* Countries, they act in direct Opposition to the Spirit and Intention of their own Religion, and commence *Papists* in that particular Part of *Popery*, which is most injurious to the Christian Religion, dishonourable to human Nature, and detrimental to Society.

BUT as it is our *Duty*, so it is our Interest to *naturalize* the Virtuous and Industrious of every Nation, and to make them one People with ourselves. For Numbers of Inhabitants are the Strength, Riches, and Security, nay the *Beauty* of a Country:—Whereas the Depopulation of a Territory is not only its Ruin, but its *Deformity*.

THUS far I have proceeded in the *argumentative* Way, proving from the clearest Principles of Religion, Reason, and National Welfare, the great Expediency of a Bill for a general Naturalization. But alas! this harmless Word has by Art and Industry been made such a *Bugbear*, that the very Sound of it carries Dread and Terror, and, like a dark Night to a timorous Person, is full of

Gorgons, fierce Hydras, and Chimeras dire!

THEREFORE all that can be done at present, is to substitute such a Polity, as may answer the chief Ends of a general Naturalization, without naming that odious Word.—And this may be done two Ways; *first* by apprizing Foreigners of the true Nature and Genius of the *English* Constitution, as far as relates to this Affair; and *secondly*, by enacting such Laws as shall remove all the Difficulties which Foreigners now labour under, without naturalizing them.

I. THEREFORE, The principal Thing to be done, is to apprize the Inhabitants of Foreign Countries of the Genius of the *English* Constitution. For the governing Powers abroad take great Pains to conceal from their Subjects the true State of this Affair: And they so well understand the vast Advantages of having their Territories well peopled, that *Art* and *Power* are both made use of to prevent their Subjects from leaving their Native Country.—Yet such is our Infatuation, that we cannot see, that what is a *Loss* to our Rivals, is a *double Gain* to us! However, hence it is, that the Bulk of the People in *France* and other Countries, are made to believe every Time the Naturalization Bill is rejected, That the *British* Parliament have *refused* to admit Foreigners into their Kingdom. And indeed it is natural for other Nations to conclude, That this Bill, concerning which such a *mighty Clamour* hath been raised, must convey some *extraordinary* Privilege, without which the Residence of Strangers in *England* would be either *uncomfortable*, or *dangerous:* Whereas, in fact, this is a grand Mistake; and the Privileges conveyed by Naturalization are so *trifling*, that not one Foreigner in a thousand would be benefited by them. This may appear strange to many Persons; But it is not more strange than true: For when a Foreigner arrives in *England*, he is as much *naturalized* by his personal Residence, and enjoys as *full Privileges*, as an Act of Parliament itself could give him,—excepting in the four followings Particulars.

1. HE cannot possess Estates in *Fee*, unless the King grants Leave.

2. HE cannot merchandise without paying Alien Duty.

3. HE cannot obtain the Freedom of the *Turky*, and one or two more exclusive Companies.

4. HE cannot be imployed when he goes abroad, as Factor for the *English* in *Russia*, or in our Plantations, and a few other Places.

As to the *first* of these, very few Foreigners would chuse to buy Lands at all, because their principal Stock is imployed to better Advantage in Trade; and if they have Children born in *Great Britain*, or *any* of its Dominions, such Issue are in *every respect*, upon an equal Footing with the original Natives. But suppose a Foreigner should be inclined to make a Landed Purchase; Suppose he wants, for Example, an House to *dwell* in, being willing to continue his Riches in the Country where he got them, or perhaps to bring over his paternal Fortunes in order to enjoy them in this Kingdom of Liberty, (which Circumstance, by the by, ought not to be the *Motive* for us to *quarrel* with him) I say, such a Purchase is *valid in Law against all the Subjects of the Kingdom:*—Indeed the King himself could take it from him; but there is not any Probability that he ever would; nay, those very Persons who have exclaimed the most vehemently against the Naturalization Bill, would be the loudest in their Exclamations against such an Exertion of the Royal Prerogative. But what is much more to the present Purpose is, That the Foreigner himself can prevent this oppressive Use of the Prerogative several Ways; as (1.) By obtaining a private Bill of Naturalization. (2.) By Letters of Denization from the Crown. (3.) By making the intended Purchase in the Name of a Native, with a Declaration of Trust;—a frequent Practice with the *Roman* Catholics, in order to avoid the Payment of double Taxes. (4.) By contracting for such Estates as are deemed *Chattels* by the Common Law, and not *Freeholds*, of which kind of Tenures there are many thousands in the Kingdom, and more might be made at pleasure.

BUT as this latter Article seems to require some farther Explication, I shall therefore observe, That by the antient Common Law of the Realm, all *Lay* Estates or *Lay* Fees were supposed to be held of the Crown (either directly or indirectly) by some kind of *Military* Service. Therefore if a Foreigner should buy a landed Estate, he must become the King's *liege Man*, that is, do *Military* Service for that Estate. But in former Times, when the Kingdom was in perpetual Wars, and Estates in Land the only *considerable* Property;—also when the Possessors of such Estates were the *Military* Tenants, or STANDING ARMIES, of their Prince, it lay at the *Option* of the King, whether he would admit a Foreigner to be his Military Tenant, or not: So that the Reason or Grounds of the Distinction made between a Native and a Foreigner, arose from the Idea of the *Unfitness* of the latter to be the *King's Soldier*:—that Circumstance being the only Thing attended to in those gothic and barbarous Times. This farther appears by reflecting, That in all Cases where no Military Service was demanded, the Distinction between Foreigner and Native ceased of Course: of which take the following Instances for Proofs;—Before the Introduction of Commerce, Goods and Chattels were such inconsiderable Things, that no Military Service was ever demanded for them; and consequently a Foreigner could possess them equally with a Native. The same Observation holds in regard to Landed Estates of *Base Tenure*; for these are deemed *Chattels* in the Eye of the Law, because the *Fee* of them is supposed to reside in some other Person, who, by being the Lord of the Manor, is legally the King's Soldier, or his Military Tenant. Wherefore the Vassals, Villains, or Under-Tenants, being exempt from this gothic Military Service, may be of any Country or Climate whatever.

THE *Second* Thing to be considered, is the Burden of *Alien* Duty. This indeed is laid upon the Foreign Merchant with all the Art and Skill that Monopolizers could devise; a Race of Men who are ever setting up their own private Interest against that of the Public, and always raising a canting Cry (when any Attempts are made to free the Nation from these Oppressions) That Trade is in danger;—meaning thereby, that their own destructive Trade, their Monopoly is in danger; for they have a Regard for nothing else.   But nevertheless Time has shewn, That the Monopolists have been defeated at their own Weapons; for though the City of *London* got the Laws to be passed for laying an Alien Duty upon the Goods of Foreigners, yet the Citizens themselves were the first in shewing the Way to elude it by covering such Goods under their own Names; so that at present this Inconvenience is very little felt.   For when a Citizen once begun such a Practice, all the rest were obliged to do the same, lest he should ingross the Custom of Foreigners to himself: And at this Day the Usage is become so universal, that if one Citizen should refuse, hundreds would gladly do it.—Thus far therefore a Naturalization Bill is not absolutely necessary, though it may be expedient:—And indeed it is particularly expedient in a moral and religious View, in order to prevent numberless Lies and Perjuries.— Those who would know more on this Subject, must consult the Tenor of the Oaths taken by Citizens and Burgesses throughout the Kingdom.

As to the *third* Article, *viz.*   The Freedom of the *Turky*, the *Russia* and the *Hudson's-Bay* Company, the Want of the Power of obtaining these Freedoms is certainly a great Disadvantage to Foreign Merchants, and consequently to the Commerce of the Nation; inasmuch as their very Situation in Life, their large Correspondencies, and enterprising Genius, particularly qualify them for ingaging in these Branches of Trade: by which means vast Quantities of our own Manufactures might be exported, and raw Materials imported.

THE *fourth* Restraint upon Foreigners relates to the Affair of Factorage in *Turky*, in our own Plantations, and a few other Places.—But as to our own Plantations, it is one of those Laws which is too absurd to be executed: For the People of *America* will naturally imploy those Factors (notwithstanding our Acts of Parliament) who use them best, whether they are *English* or Foreigners.   Besides, a Foreigner is naturalized of Course, if he resides seven Years in any of our Plantations.   So that upon the whole, the Disadvantage in this Respect is very inconsiderable, and can affect but very few Foreigners; nor is it to be set in Counterbalance to the inestimable Privileges which Foreigners may enjoy in all other Instances, Religious, Civil, and Commercial.

AND thus having given a general State of the Case, we see at one View, That a Naturalization Bill is not so much wanted as the World may imagine, for the Admission of Foreigners; because such a Bill is rather to be considered in the Light of a National Advertisement to be published in foreign Countries, than as conveying any important or substantial Privileges. In a Word, were Foreigners properly acquainted with the Nature of our *English* Constitution, there would be little need of a general Naturalization Bill.

WHEREFORE the Proposal to be made on this Head is briefly this, —That the Lords of Trade, or any others in the Administration, should cause a few Paragraphs to be drawn up explanatory of this Affair, and get them inserted regularly three or four Times in the Year in all those Foreign Gazettes which are circulated among the Commercial and Manufacturing People of the Northern and Southern Parts of *Europe*.— Thus far as to the apprising Foreigners of the Nature and Genius of the *English* Constitution.

II. THE second Thing to be done is, To enact such Laws as shall remove all the Difficulties which Foreigners now labour under, without naming the *scare-crow* Word *Naturalization*.

THUS, for Example, a Law might be made, or a Clause inserted in the Body of any other Act, to abridge the Crown of the gothic Prerogative of taking away a Foreigner's Landed Estate, and to cause such Estate to descend regularly among his Children, according to the Nature of other Descents. Such a Law would easily pass for Reasons that are very obvious:—Nor would it be in the Power of any pretended Patriots to raise a Clamor against it. A Statute, intitled, *An Act to abridge or limit the Prerogative of the Crown in certain Cases*, carries the Air of Popularity, and would be received with Greediness. Nay, such is the Force of a proper Title, that if the late *Jew* Bill itself had been called, *A Bill to prevent the Jews from profaning the Christian Sacraments*, (which was the real Tendency of the Bill) instead of,—*A Bill to enable the Parliament to naturalize Foreign Jews*, all would have been well; and the Zeal for *Old England!* and Christianity for ever! would have still been asleep.

ANOTHER Law might be passed, whose Title should be, *An Act for incouraging the Exportation of English Manufactures, and the Importation of raw Materials*. And one single Clause in this Law might be sufficient to repeal all kinds of Alien Duty.

A *third* might be added with a popular Title, *For the Incouragement of Shipping and Navigation:* And therein it might be specified, That

all Persons residing in *Great Britain* or any Part of its Dominions, shall
be permitted to make themselves free of any of our exclusive Companies.

A *fourth* might be stiled, *An Act for impowering all British Merchants
to imploy such Agents or Factors as they shall judge most conducive for
carrying on their Affairs in Foreign Parts.*

Now these four Clauses (whether in separate Statutes or in one
general Law, it matters not) comprehend every Power or Privilege which
a Naturalization Bill itself can give. And yet not one of such Laws,
if they have proper Titles, is capable of being made an Engine for raising
popular Clamours, or serving the Ends of *Electioneering* Patriots. It is
therefore humbly apprehended, That these four Clauses, joined to the
Proposal before mentioned for issuing public Advertisements from the
Board of Trade, would induce as many sober, religious, and industrious
Foreigners to fly from the Tyranny of their respective Governments,
and to strengthen and inrich this Country, as the most extensive Naturalization Bill whatever. Indeed it cannot be expected, that Foreigners
would come over in Swarms to devour the Land, like the *Egyptian*
Locusts; to whom they have been so often compared:—Neither would
they have done so, whatever the Ignorant may fear, or the Designing
pretend, though the Parliament was to give them a thousand Invitations.
For all Mankind are fond of their native Soil, and have strong Attachments to the Manners and Customs, the Air and Situation of the Places
of their Birth and Education. This we see visibly enough here at home
in the little Contests between the Inhabitants of one Parish, Hundred, or
County, and those of another; each pretending, that the Spot of their
Nativity vastly excels the other, tho' both are under the same Government, partaking of the same Laws, Religion, and Climate, and no otherwise separated than by an Hedge, a River, a Moor, or a Mountain.
Nor ought it to be omitted, That though an *Englishman* may fancy his
own Country the finest under the Sun, the Glory and Garden of the
Universe, an unprejudiced Spectator will not see it with the same Eyes:
And therefore a Foreigner is not so strongly tempted, as we may imagine,
to break through the dear Connections of Family and Relation, and to
sacrifice his Interests, Friendships, and Pleasures, merely to come and
reside in a Country, which, though a good one, is destitute of many
real Beauties and Advantages which other Countries plentifully enjoy.

However, though there is no manner of Reason for apprehending,
That Foreigners will overwhelm us like a Torrent that hath broke its
Banks; yet there are good Hopes, that many of the Religious and In-
dustrious, the Frugal or the Wealthy, the Lovers of just Liberty, and

of Course the best Friends to the *English* Constitution, will flow in upon us from various Climes, like a constant, though gentle Stream, always useful, always agreeable, inriching the Country with a continual Verdure, and causing no Waste or Desolation.

CHAP. III.

Other Polities for increasing the Number of People.

THOUGH the Polities for promoting Marriage, and inviting Foreigners are the more immediate Ways of increasing the Number of People, yet all other Polities which tend to imploy Mankind in useful Labour, and to preserve and improve their Morals, are greatly subservient to the same good End.

A SET of Polities, for Example, which promote Industry and discourage Vice, hath the same (nay indeed a much better) Effect in its Operations, as a Sum of Money given by way of Portion to incourage Marriage. For it puts Mankind into a Capacity of increasing their Species, without bringing Misery on themselves, or intailing it on their Posterity; and by opening new Sources of Wealth and Prosperity, it incourages them to ingage in the Marriage State with a good Prospect of supporting their Families with Credit and Comfort. When Idleness is removed, Poverty is removed likewise; and when Industry is properly and generally excited, Numbers of Hands will of Course be *wanted*; so that a Stock of Children may be so far from being a Burden in certain Circumstances, that they may very literally and truly become the Wealth and Riches of the Parents. Now the Polities which seem best calculated to answer these good Ends will be set forth at large in PART II. wherein the Methods of employing Mankind, and for preserving a lasting and extensive Commerce, will be particularly treated of.

AGAIN, All those Polities which tend to promote good Morals, have an immediate Influence on the Increase and Preservation of the human Species: For good Morals are not only an Antidote against the spreading of Diseases, and the Destruction of Lives through Intemperance and Excess; they not only prevent the *barren* and *unfruitful* Vices of Lewdness and Debauchery, but also teach Mankind, That the natural Desires of the Sexes towards each other may, and ought to be gratified by lawful Marriage.—And the married State, as hath been proved already, is the only efficacious Method of increasing the Numbers of Mankind, and rendering a Country truly populous:—But the Influence of good Morals will appear still in a stronger Light, when we come to PART III. wherein the Polities for the Preservation and Improvement of them are to be distinctly considered and recommended.

THESE Hints therefore may suffice at present as to those Polities which are yet for to come:—On the other Hand it may be just proper to take Notice, That the Polities already inlarged upon in the two foregoing Chapters concerning Marriage and Naturalization, will be found equally subservient to the good Purposes of Industry and Moral Virtue. For the several Parts of the great Commercial System do indeed mutually support and strengthen each other; inasmuch as populousness hath a natural Tendency to promote Industry and good Morals,— and these in their Turn as naturally create Populousness.

PART II.

Containing certain Polities for the Extension and Improvement of Commerce.

NATIONAL and extensive Commerce is only another Name for the right and useful Imployment of the Individuals: And this Imployment is derived either from the *natural*, or the *artificial* Wants of Mankind. The *natural* Wants, as hath been observed before, are such as belong to Man in common with other Animals: But the *artificial* are peculiar to him as a rational Agent, and a Member of Civil Society:—Though indeed in another Sense these very artificial Wants may be stiled natural, because they arise from the *peculiar Nature* of Man as distinguished from other Creatures. But this being a less intelligible Way of speaking, it would be better to keep to the former Division of Wants, into *natural*, and *artificial*. If therefore a Man is *poor*, he is scarce able to purchase or supply himself with any thing beyond the *bare* Necessaries of Life; so that his Condition will approach the nearer to the *Brutal* State, which admits of no Commerce at all: But if he is *rich*, he need not deny himself the Injoyment of many things both useful and convenient. By which means it comes to pass, That several other Persons, besides himself, may be imployed in making or procuring them. Now if this is the Case, it plainly follows, That the Support and Extension of Commerce must result from the Multiplication of the *artificial* Needs of Mankind.

BUT as this System of *Commercial Industry* is equally the Plan of Providence with the System of *Morals*, we may rest assured, That both are consistent with each other: And therefore, for the present, let us take

it for granted, that they are so;—deferring the Proof till we come to
PART III. which is to treat particularly on this Subject: And then it
will be fully shewn, That these artificial Needs must be under the Direction of *good Morals*, before they can produce that *beneficial, perpetual*,
and *extensive* Commerce, which Providence intended by them.

LEAVING therefore this Subject till a future Occasion, let us now
observe, That all Commercial Imployment may be divided into two
kinds, *Husbandry*, and *Manufacture*; the immediate Object of the one
being to provide *Food*, and that of the other to procure *Raiment*, and
Dwelling: And from the CONCURRENCE *of these three* every other Trade,
Calling, or Profession derives its Origin and Support. If therefore this
is the Case, how wrong must have been that System of Politics, which
endeavoured to set Husbandry, and Manufactures at perpetual Variance?
How base and disingenuous to stir up Jealousies between them, and to
represent the one an Enemy to the other? For in Fact the *Landed*, and
the *Trading* Interests are only the different Markets for each other's
Produce, the one being the respective *Maker*, and the other the *Consumer*.
And consequently, the real Exaltation, or Depression of either, must
really exalt, or depress them both.

INDEED, if by the *Landed* Interest is to be understood the Interest
of the Gothic Barons (as it formerly subsisted here in *England*) or the
Interest of the Lairds of Clans in *Scotland*,—between *that* Interest and
the Commercial there ever was, and ever will be a strong Opposition.
For the Power and Importance of these *petty Tyrants* over their Slaves
or Vassals, can be no otherwise preserved, than by chaining down the
Mass of the People in Slavery and Want. It is therefore their Interest
to depress Commerce; because every Increase of Property in the lower
and middling Class of People tends to render them more free and independent;—and perhaps at last more considerable than their former
Superiors. In short, the poorer the Inhabitants of a Country, the
greater by *Comparison* is the Baron, the Laird of the Clan, or the Landed
Squire. Granting therefore that the Estates of such *Old English Gentry*,
who value themselves on the Antiquity of their Houses, would be
bettered by the Introduction of Trade and Manufactures, and that they
themselves would enjoy more of the Conveniencies, Elegancies, and
Ornaments of Life, than they otherwise could do;—yet as their *Inferiors*
by Birth might sometimes equal, and perhaps surpass them in these
Injoyments, the *Country Gentlemen* are strongly tempted to regret this
Diminution of their former Importance, and the Eclipsing of their antient
Grandeur by the Wealth of these *Upstarts*.

BUT then, if the Systems of Baronage and Commerce do thus necessarily clash, it is likewise as true, That Baronage is as great an Impediment to Improvements in Agriculture and good Husbandry.   For a Baron, or any other landed Gentleman, acting upon the old Baron Principles, cuts himself off from making any considerable Improvements on his Estates, both on Account of his Enmity to Manufactures, and his Tryanny over his Vassal Tenants.   As he is an Enemy to Manufactures and that *independent* Spirit which Trade necessarily introduces, he prevents, as much as in him lies, the having a Market for the Produce of his Estate.   And as he esteems it inconsistent with his own Greatness and the Dignity of his House to give his Vassals a Taste for Liberty, consequently he takes away every Spur to Industry, and chains them down in Sloth, Ignorance, and Poverty.   In a Word, a Gothic Baron in the Landed Interest is just the same kind of Monster as an *Exclusive* Company in the Commercial: They are both *Monopolists* in their several Ways; and their chief Wealth consists rather in preventing others from acquiring Wealth, than in being rich themselves: They are indeed *comparatively* great, because they render their Neighbours and Dependents *extremely* poor and miserable.

BUT to return;—If the true Interests of Agriculture and Manufactures are inseparably united, nay are indeed the same, we may therefore now consider them under the same View: Agriculture, for instance, is nothing else but a distinct Species of Manufacture, in relation to which the Ground or Soil is properly the *raw Material*, and the Land-Owner or Farmer is the *head* Manufacturer.   This being the Case, it must necessarily follow, That every *general* Principle of Commerce, which tends to establish and promote other Manufactures, must likewise be productive of good Effects in Husbandry.   And therefore our next concern is to make a suitable Application.

CHAP. I.

Certain Polities for incouraging and improving Husbandry.

IT IS not the Design of this Chapter to set forth the Rules of Agriculture, or to give Directions for the inclosing, planting, tilling, watering, draining, or manuring of Lands: No; all these are to be learned from other Books;—But the proper Design of this Chapter is to shew, That the *universal* Mover in human Nature, SELF-LOVE, may receive such a Direction in this Case (as in all others) as to promote the Public Interest by those Efforts it shall make towards pursuing its own.

And when this comes to be the State of Affairs, we may venture to foretel, from the necessary Connection between Causes and Effects, That the Science of Agriculture and Husbandry will be studied with more Care and Attention, and a swifter Progress will be made in the Arts of improving Estates, than have ever yet been known in these Parts of the World.

SECTION I.

A Polity for dividing large Estates.

WHEN this Kingdom was subject to the Gothic Baronage, it became a necessary Part of that Constitution, to transfer the whole Landed Estate, after the Death of the Father, to the eldest Son, without taking any Notice of the rest of the Children. For all Lay Estates being then *military Fees*, the Lords or Possessors thereof were bound by the Conditions of their Tenure, to arm their Vassals and Dependents, and to bring them into the Field when the King required. In such a Situation it is easy to see, That the Landlords of those Days were vested with a much greater Sway over their Tenants, in order to have them always at Command, than Landlords have at present. And such Powers must be annexed only to great Estates, otherwise they would become an useless and ridiculous Farce. For a Landlord would make but a burlesque Figure in the Day of Battle, acting as a Colonel, or heading a Battalion of half a dozen, or a dozen Tenants. The eldest Son therefore being naturally regarded as the Representative of the Family, and the next in Command over his Father's Tenants, succeeded of Course to the whole Landed Patrimony, in order to keep the Command intire.

THE Custom being thus originally founded in the Necessity or Convenience of the Times, was presently seconded by human Pride. For the Views of Ambition were gratified by this Display of Military Prowess: And as each Gentleman became more formidable and dangerous to his Neighbours in proportion to the Numbers he could raise of these ragged Dependents, it became a necessary Part of Self-Defence to invest the Lands of the Realm in such Hands as might be able to protect both themselves and others from Assaults. Add to this, that the Motives of vain Glory in keeping up the Name of the Family, and supporting the Grandeur of the antient House, strong Motives at all times! were particularly prevalent at that Juncture.

BUT after the Abolition of the Gothic Baronage, and the Introduction of Industry and Manufactures, one might have expected, That our Laws and Customs would have received some Alteration in Conformity to this

great Change.   Yet so it is, That though the Gothic Vassalage is ended,
the Baron-Scheme in many Instances still remains.   For Estates are
still permitted to be *intailed* on Heirs Male, to the Exclusion of all the
nearer Relations that are Females: And if a Person dies *intestate*, the
Common Law at this Day gives the whole Landed Estate to the eldest
Son, without making any Provision for the rest.   Now this Absurdity
becomes the more glaring, inasmuch as this same Common Law divides
all the Personals, be they ever so great, equally among the Children.—
But in Truth, we must repeat an Observation made several Times before,
viz.   That the Amount of Personals, before the Introduction of Commerce, was so very insignificant, as to cause little Difference how they
were divided.   Whereas in our Times, the Amount of these Things in
Trade, Cash, Mortgages, the Funds, Plate, Household Goods, &c. &c. is
prodigious and immense.   Either therefore the former Practice, which
gives all to the Eldest, or this latter which makes no Distinction between
the First-born and the Younger, must be intirely unjustifiable upon the
present Footing of Things, and repugnant to Common Sense and Equity.

BUT indeed, the most useful Measure of any for the Public, and perhaps the most equitable regarding Individuals, would be to steer a middle Course between these two Extremes.

SUPPOSE therefore, That the Law relating to *Personals* should remain
as it is, but the other regarding *Landed Estates* should be made more
conformable to Commercial Ideas by the following Regulation; *viz.*
That the Landed Estates of *Intestates* should be divided, one half
to the oldest Son, or (in Case of no Issue) to the Heir at Law, and the
other half to the rest of the Children, or to the Relations of equally
near Kin with the Heir at Law;—in which Number the Eldest, or
the Heir at Law should be always reckoned as *one* and come in for a
Share accordingly.

Now in Consequence of this Regulation the Eldest would always
enjoy a Sufficiency to distinguish him from others, and yet the rest of
the Children not be left destitute.   For his Proportion, by means of
having one half clear to himself, and a Child's Share in the Remainder,
would always keep Pace with the Number of Children; so that the
comparative Dignity of the Family would be decently preserved, and
the Mansion House might still remain in the Possession of the eldest
Branch.   As to the Cadets, or younger Children of great Families, they
would be rendered much more happy in themselves, and useful to
the Community, by receiving a Share in the Paternal Estate, than they
could possibly be, when they lay at the Mercy of their elder Brother,

and were too high born to take to mechanic Labour, too poor to ingage in a creditable Branch of Trade, and had no Estates of their own to exercise their Genius upon. Such a Situation hath rendered many Persons, of valuable natural Qualifications, both miserable in themselves, and the Pests of Society, or at best but an useless Race of Mortals, humourously and yet movingly described in *The Spectator* under the Character of *Will Wimbles*.

BUT the peculiar Advantage of such a Polity appears from hence, That most of the great *unwieldy* Estates throughout the Kingdom would undergo such Dismembrings, in a Course of Years, as would serve to raise up a respectable Number of new, independent Families, possessing from one hundred, to one thousand Pounds a Year:—That is, though the Lands were not worth, or not rented for near so much, when only Branches of the great Estate, yet they would be soon raised to a superior Value, when parted from it. For it is a most undoubted Fact, that if you should sever nine thousand Acres from an Estate of twenty thousand (that is, portion out nine Children, Male or Female, with one thousand Acres each, and reserve eleven thousand Acres for the eldest Son or the Heir at Law) each of these Freeholds of a thousand Acres, *generally* speaking, would soon be made to produce above double the Quantity of Grass, Hay, Corn, Flax, Hemp, Timber, and other Materials, and to rear and feed a much greater Stock of Sheep, Horses, and Cattle, than it ever did, when only a Part of one great Monopoly, and let out on a Lease, or Rack Rent. Moreover, the Effects of such a Regulation would induce the eldest Sons, or the Representatives of great Families, to study Frugality and Oeconomy more than they do at present, and to strive to improve their Shares of the Paternal Estate, so as to raise them to be equal in Value to what the former was before the Division. And indeed a proper Attention to the Principles of National Commerce and good Husbandry, would hardly fail of Success: For it is with Landed Estates as with Kingdoms, where a little Territory rendered rich by Industry, and populous by Numbers, is infinitely more valuable and powerful than immense Regions, where Poverty and Desolation universally prevail. And in Fact, what other Reason can you assign, but the Neighbourhood of the Market of *London*, why the Lands of *Hertfordshire*, naturally very poor in themselves, should be at least an hundred Times more valuable than the rich and fertile Plains of *Hungary?* And what is true in a greater Instance, holds likewise true in a smaller. If therefore the eldest Branch of an antient Family can raise a Market for the Produce of his Lands, as Mr *Charwell* is represented to do in the ninth *Guardian*, he will soon make Amends for any Dismembrings of the Estate, and raise the Value of one Acre to be worth four times as much as it was in his Grandfather's Time.

As to the Case of small Landed Estates, which will not bear a minute Division, these will naturally devolve to the eldest Son; because it will be both his Interest, and that of the rest of the Family, to preserve the Estate intire: For the Land will not be so valuable, when subdivided into *trifling* Parcels, as when kept together: And therefore his only Course will be either to marry a Woman with a suitable Fortune in ready Money, or to borrow a Sum sufficient for paying off the Demands of the younger Children: And either of these Consequences would have no bad Effect upon the Commerce of the Public, or the Morals of the Individuals.

THUS far as to the Effects of the Polity here proposed;—A Polity, it must be owned, not very extensive, if considered simply in itself, but greatly so, when viewed in all its Consequences. For though this Regulation pretends to no more than to dispose of the Estates of Persons who die *intestate*, yet the Influence of such a Law would operate in Multitudes of Cases by way of *Pattern* and *Example:* And though Mankind would be left at perfect Liberty to make what Marriage Settlements, Deeds of Gift, or Wills they pleased; yet they would naturally consider, That they could not do better, than to follow that equitable Rule, which the Wisdom of their Country hath recommended to them.—Nay indeed it is very probable, That many Persons would *choose* to die intestate, because they could not propose to make a wiser Disposal of their Effects, than the Legislature hath done ready to their Hands.

SECTION II.
A Polity for inclosing Commons and Common Fields.

THE Notion of having Lands in common, is to be derived from the Barbarian or Scythian Way of Life, when Men were Strangers to any higher Occupation than that of Shepherds or Hunters. Nay, in those Countries where the People still remain Savages, their Lands lie all in common to this Day. But if the Origin of this Custom is to be traced so far back, it is natural to ask, Why did not the Custom cease, when the Inhabitants of this Island became more civilized, and were better instructed in the Principles of Industry and Property?— To which I answer, That old Customs will frequently remain (as we find by sad Experience) long after the original Cause of them hath been taken away. And this Prejudice for old Customs sticks the closer, if the *Self-Love* of any of the Individuals in a Society is made to believe, That their own private Interest is concerned to support such a Custom.

Now, it is to be observed, That when the Barons parcelled out their vast Manors among their Dependents and Followers, these latter, together with their Under-tenants, Slaves, or Villains, were not many Removes from a Savage State: That is, tho' the Knights and Squires were Men of some Property in Lands, and considerable by Birth, yet they lived a lazy, sauntering Life when in Peace, destitute of every Ornament and Convenience, and when at War had little to lose besides the bare Walls of their Castles, and their Military Glory. Indeed it is hardly conceivable, That the Life of a Soldier should be spent in the Cultivation of Lands, and good Husbandry: And in those Times every Man was either a Soldier by Profession, or a Slave in Condition. Now Slavery, as hath been remarked before, is of all Conditions the most opposite to Industry and Improvement. Therefore it is very evident, That though the Bulk of the Nation were not absolute Savages, yet they made nearer Approaches to that State of Life, than many Persons who seem to boast of the Glory of *Old England* are willing to acknowledge. In short, when there was no Industry, no Commerce, and no Markets, Lands were worth little: And therefore it was no Loss to the Baron, and seemed to be some kind of Favour granted to the Vassals and Tenants, to set out a District of ten, fifteen, or twenty Miles square, for Hunting Grounds, and common Herbage. Nay, if the Lands had been divided into equal Shares of five hundred Acres apiece throughout the Kingdom, it is much to be questioned, whether there were Families enough, free or villain, to have settled in half of them: Consequently the other Moiety must have still remained in the Hands of the Baron, or great Landlord, *untenanted* and *unoccupied*, which therefore at such a Juncture, would soon have been regarded as *open* or *common* Grounds. And what was thus true in regard to the Manors of the Barons, was equally true in respect to those immense Domains which formerly belonged to the Crown:—Not to mention, That our former Race of Kings kept prodigious Tracts of Ground in almost every County in the Kingdom waste and desolate, under the Name of *Chaces* and *Forests*, for the Diversion of Hunting and Hawking.

THE Tenants therefore and Vassals having thus a Liberty of Common, transmitted the same to their Successors, and so downwards to the present Times. And therefore we call things by the same Names at this Day, though the whole Nature of the Constitution is perfectly changed:—Nay we pretend to find out Reasons, why these Commons should still continue in their original State of Desolation, (so ingenious is deluded Self-Love) though there is not one Reason now remaining for their Continuance.

I. THEREFORE it is objected, "That if we break up our Commons, our Sheep-Walks will be destroyed."—Now this Objection takes for granted, That if our Commons were inclosed, they would become Arable Land;—or at least would not be applied to the Purposes of rearing and feeding Sheep. But surely this is supposing a great deal too much, without proving any thing: For though it is probable, That two or three Corps of Corn would be sown in the fresh Grounds, upon their first Inclosure, yet it is as probable, That each Field in its turn, would afterwards be laid down in Grass, Clover, Cinque-Foin, or other Seeds; and it is certain, That a Crop of Turnips, together with a little Hay, (natural or artificial it matters not) would support more Sheep during the hard Time of the Winter, or Spring, than ten thousand Acres of Common, where they can have neither Grass, nor Shelter. Besides, it is a known Fact, That since the Inclosing of Downs, Commons, and common Lands, the Number of Sheep hath been vastly increased in those Countries where the Inclosures have been made:—And what is more, The Quantity of Wool growing upon the same Sheep's Back hath been increased likewise. Moreover, if this is the Case with respect even to dry Heaths and upland Commons,—what shall we say of such Commons, which are mere Moors and Marshes? For who is to drain, to trench, to manure, and cultivate them, while they remain open and common? And without this Husbandry what are they worth for three Parts in four of the whole Year? In short, this Affair is too absurd to bear a long Debate. And the Whole may be summed up in a few Words, *viz.* That Commons, whether Downs or Marshes, afford a tolerable Feed during a few Months in the Summer, when Food is plenty, and Shelter unnecessary, but they afford none at all in the Winter, and the Beginning of the Spring, when both Food and Shelter are mostly wanted.

II. IT is objected, "That Inclosures tend to spoil the Fineness of our Wool; because it is found by Experience, That after open Grounds have been inclosed, the Wool of the Sheep grows of a longer and a coarser Staple, than it did before."

Now in regard to Fineness, this is not the essential Quality of *English* Wool; nor are the Cloths and Stuffs sent to foreign Markets, made out of our finest Wools, but out of our coarse, middling, and long Wools; so that our Fabrics can receive no Discredit, nor our Trade any Disadvantage upon that Account. Nay it is certain, That our finest Wool is chiefly used for home Consumption, partly to make Cloth by itself, and partly to mix with *Spanish:* And the true superfine Cloths are all *Spanish* Wool.

BUT we have yet had no Proof, That the bare Inclosing of Grounds renders the Wool coarser:—Indeed it must be allowed, That a short, poor, close Feed, such as Downs and Commons generally afford, will render the Fibres more feeble, and consequently the Wool *weaker*, and in that Sense *finer:* Whereas a strong, hearty Feed, causes the Fibres of the Animal to be stronger, and the Perspiration more vigorous; and perhaps by that means the Wool is rendered somewhat coarser and longer. But this Wool is the fittest of all others for Combing, and making Stuffs and Worsteds; which in Fact is thought to be the chief Excellence for which the *English* Wool is preferable to that of other Nations. However, if a short Feed is so necessary for preserving the Fineness of the Wool, and if the Fineness itself is so necessary to preserve the Credit of our Manufactures, I humbly conceive, That Inclosures may be fed down as close as open Commons, and that therefore this can be no real Objection. But to come nearer to the Point, what shall we say of the Wools of *Urchenfield* in *Herefordshire*, which are indisputably the finest in *England*; and yet this Part of the County is as much inclosed as any Part in the Kingdom, if not more; and the Lands in general are of a very rich, deep, and fertile Soil? The Facts on both Sides are unquestionable; and therefore the Inference seems to be, That we have not yet discovered the true Cause of the Fineness, or Coarseness of Wool;—I mean, any farther than what may be accounted for by the Strength or Weakness of the Animal.—Certain it is, That on the Hills of *Mendippe* in *Somersetshire*, a Range of Common of near twenty Miles in Length, there is an apparent Difference in the Wool of almost every Parish. And yet what Hypothesis can account for this Difference? But as to the Fineness of the Wool of *Urchenfield*, the most probable Way of accounting for it upon general Principles, seems to be this; That if an equal Degree of Perspiration causes the best Growth of Wool, which seems to be generally allowed, then the Farmers in *Urchenfield*, who house or cot their Sheep by Nights, keep their Sheep in an equal Temperature, and so prevent those Extremes of Heat and Cold, which would damage their Wool.—This being their Practice, it is a Pity the like Practice was not tried in other Counties, in order to ascertain the Effects of it; for the Experiment is easy, safe, and not expensive; and the *Urchenfield* Wool is near *Cent. per Cent.* more valuable than the Wools of *Leominster*, and other Places.

III. IT is objected, "That by inclosing so much Common and Common

Fields, we shall lessen the Quantity of Arable Lands; inasmuch as it will be more advantageous to lay down inclosed Fields for Grass, than to sow Corn in them."

Now this Objection is just the Reverse of the first; For that supposed, That all the Lands would be plowed up, so as to leave no Grounds for Pasture; and this is built upon a contrary Supposition, *viz.* That every Inclosure would be converted to Pasture only. But both these Objections are alike founded on a Mistake, and seem to arise from a partial View of the Subject. For the true State of the Case seems to be this. *viz.* As the Produce of Arable and Pasture Grounds are very different in themselves, and are both (we will suppose) to be brought to the same Market;—The Question therefore is, Which of these Grounds *must* lie nearest, and which *may* be farthest off from the Place where the Produce is to be vended? Now the Produce of Pasture Grounds, considered in a general View, is Milk, Butter, Cheese, and Flesh: And each of these Articles, (large Cheeses excepted) are to be brought to the Market fresh and fresh; consequently the Grounds to be set apart for Pasture ought to be contiguous to the Town or City where the Market is held; or at most the Distance ought not to be very great, nor the Roads bad, because the Carriage of these things must be repeated often, perhaps every Week or every Day, Winter and Summer. Whereas Corn may be brought from far, and so may Flour, either by Land or Water, and brought in such vast Quantities at a time, as not to need frequent Repetitions. Hence therefore it comes to pass, not to mention other Reasons, That in Proportion as a Town or City increases, the Grounds around it are converted into Pasturage; and therefore from this partial View of the Case, some People have hastily concluded, That the Quantity of Arable Lands is decreasing, because they have happened to observe several Arable Lands laid down in Grass. Whereas in fact the Increase of Towns or Cities is a Proof of just the contrary;—only with this Difference, That the Corn brought to Market comes from a greater Distance, than the Milk, Cheese, and Butter. But it is plain, That if the Markets for Corn increase, the Quantity of Arable Lands will not be diminished.— As to the Breed of Sheep, there is no fear that this will lessen, while the Inhabitants are increasing in Numbers, and are desirous of being fed with Lamb and Mutton, and continue well-disposed to wear worsted Stuffs and woolen Cloaths.

IV. ANOTHER Objection sometimes brought is, "That Inclosures deprive many poor People, who had a Right to Common, of their just Privileges, and thereby render them poorer than they were before."—

To which a very short Answer may be given, *viz.* That as to the Poor, their Circumstances are rendered much more eligible by the Discommoning of open Grounds, and Increase of Husbandry, than ever they were before. For the poorest Person now living, if he is industrious, may eat, sleep, and wear better, and have better Household Goods, and consequently be a Man of more *Property*, than Persons even of middling Fortunes in former times; so much is the comparative Wealth of this Nation increased. And indeed it is quite repugnant to Reason and Common Sense to suppose, That the Poor should be hurt by that very Method, which creates them constant Labour and Imployment, and enables the Farmer to pay them good Wages. But in regard to their Right or Privilege of Common, that ought not to be taken from them without a full and ample Compensation: Nor on the other Hand ought either Poor or Rich to be indulged in a Petulancy of Humour to obstruct the Public Good, merely because they are resolved to adhere obstinately to the absurd and foolish Prejudices of their Forefathers.

V. LASTLY, It is pretended, "That Commons are good for rearing young Cattle: Therefore by destroying them, you destroy the Nursery." Now if it had been said, That Commons are good for starving and stunting young Cattle, there would have been much greater Truth in the Assertion. For the Fact is, That when the People of a certain District have an *unlimited* Right of Common, the Ground is so overstocked with Numbers, that no large sized, or generous Animal, whether Sheep, Horse, or Beast, can be bred upon it. And even where the Right is *limited*, Frauds are so very easily and frequently committed, that it amounts in the Event to near the same, as if there had been no Limitation at all. And indeed where no one Person is particularly called upon to watch and detect the Fraud, and where every one may hope to be winked at in his turn, it is absurd to suppose, that a very strict Inquiry will be made. Nay, who will take upon him the odious Character of an *Informer* against his Neighbours? And why should this Man be over-busy, more than another? This is the Language, and these are the Sentiments, however unjustly it matters not, that will always prevail on such Occasions. As to the Article of rearing Lambs, Colts, or Calves, it is humbly apprehended, That clean Grounds and spacious Inclosures, properly watered and sheltered, can rear them as well, and afford Grass as good and plentiful, as wild barren Commons, overrun with Heath, Furze, Fern, or Brush-Wood:—Nor doth it appear, that there is any Virtue in stinking Marshes full of Pits and Holes, and covered with Sedges and Rushes, and particularly baneful to Sheep, more than in dry, rich, healthy Ground, with better Feed and less Danger.—If it should be said, That inclosed Ground, cannot be put to such Uses, because the Ground is too dear;—the Answer is, That we know the Fact to be otherwise already; and the more Ground there is inclosed, the less Weight there will be in this Objection.

WHEREFORE the Polities here proposed are as follow:

I. THAT in Case each Claimant's Right of Common is *limited*, it shall be a necessary Condition for applying to Parliament, That the Petitioners for dividing the Commons, or Common Fields, shall be the Proprietors of at least two thirds of this limited Right: *viz.* If the Number of Sheep are limited to six hundred, Horses to one hundred and fifty, and Cattle to one hundred and fifty, then if the Petitioners can make it appear, That they are possessed of the *Right* of sending two thirds into the Common, *viz.* four hundred Sheep, one hundred Horses, and one hundred Cattle, they shall have the Benefit to be hereafter mentioned.

II. THAT in Case the Right of each Claimant is *unlimited*, then it shall be necessary, That the Petitioners shall be two thirds more in *Number*, than the Non-Petitioners or Opponents. And Guardians may have the Liberty, both in this and the former Case, to give Consent for Minors.

III. THAT upon the fulfilling of these two Conditions, all Acts of Parliament for dividing Commons, and Common Fields, shall be considered as a truly *National Concern*; and consequently, That the *Parliamentary* Fees shall be defrayed by the Public, and charged to the current Service, according to the Custom in such Cases.

IV. THAT in Case all the Claimants can agree, they may divide the Common among themselves, without farther trouble; and cause the Instrument of Division to be recorded among the Records of the County, either at the general, or the quarter Assizes.

Now by means of these Polities, all Persons will be incouraged to apply, who are now deterred by Reason of the great Expence. And yet as two thirds either in *Number* or *Property*, must become Petitioners in the one Case, before they can be intitled to obtain the Act *gratis*; and all must become unanimous in the other, before they can register it in the County Records, a reasonable Security is provided against Injustice or Oppression.—Indeed if such Polities could be obtained, they would be considered by all the Kingdom, as an *Invitation* to apply: And therefore many would apply who now remain silent: Particularly we would hope, that the Parishes and Districts within a Circle of forty Miles round about the Metropolis would not let such immense Tracts lie waste, and in a Manner useless, for want of Application to Parliament, or for want of agreeing among themselves to inclose them, as they now do—Nay, in Fact, in the present State of these Commons, they are not only useless, but a Nusance to Society. For so many Heaths and Commons round *London*, can answer no other End, but to be a Rendezvous for Highwaymen, and a commodious Scene for them to exercise their Profession. Whereas, had they been all cultivated and inclosed, an Hue and Cry might easily be raised; and it would be very dangerous, if not impossible, for Highwaymen to attempt to Rob in an inclosed Country thick set with Farm-Houses and Villages. Not to mention, that every Common near a Town or City is an irresistible Temptation to Horse-Racing, Idleness, Gaming, and all Sorts of Debauchery, which, if inclosed, might go in Aid of the Poor-Tax. Therefore it is certain that the Quantity both of Arable and Pasture, and Garden Grounds, and consequently the Increase of Riches, Industry, and Labour, would be much greater than indolent or self-interested People are willing to suppose. For it is a very moderate Calculation to allow, That at least two Millions of Acres within a Circle of forty Miles radius from the Suburbs of *London*, might be so improved, as to be worth five Shillings *per* Acre, one with another, more than they are at present. Now this is an Acquisition of *Landed* Property of Five hundred thousand Pounds a Year; which if Sold at twenty five Years Purchase, would yield Twelve million five hundred thousand Pounds Sterling! Is such a Sum as this to be lost to the Nation,—to a Trading, Commercial Nation, and a Nation vastly in Debt, only for the Want of asking! And are Party or Faction, or Electioneering Interests, or the bewitching Temptations of an Horse-Race, to prevent such a Benefit as this!

LASTLY, Were the abovementioned Polities to be obtained, the rich Marshes, or Moors of *Somersetshire*, and of several other Counties in *England*, now lying in Common, and consequently of little Use the far greater Part of the Year, might all be *drained*, and rendered as fertile Districts as any in *Europe*. And our Sedge-Moors, Mark-Moors, Weston-Moors, Nailsy-Moors, Glastonbury-Moors, &c &c. of *Somersetshire*, might then vie with, if not excel the* *Beemsters*, the *Purme-*

---

* "When a Stranger is at *Amsterdam*, it is worth his while to cross over to *North Holland*, alias *West Friesland*, and make a Tour of that small, but beautiful spot. Formerly it was a perfect Marsh, composed of many great Lakes, separated from each other only by high Roads or Dikes; but now nothing remains of them, except their Names and Dimensions in Maps. They are entirely drained, and metamorphosed into one of the most delightful Countries in the World. It is full of Towns and Villages, in the midst of pleasant Gardens and rich Pastures. With the Milk of their numerous

rendes, the *Schermers*, the *Wormers*, and the *Waerts* of *North Holland*. Particularly let me be permitted to observe, That as the Lands of *Somersetshire* have a certain Quality of producing the best and toughest Flax in the known World, a Polity of this Sort might be attended with such Consequences, as might imploy many Thousands of Families in this single Article of Manufacture:—Besides the good Effects which such a Circulation of Industry and Labour would necessarily occasion in every other Part of Commerce. And would not such an Acquisition be more valuable, than a thousand Victories either by Land, or Sea? Nay, what need is there, that any State or Kingdom should ingage in OFFENSIVE Wars to inlarge their Dominions, while so great a Part of what they already possess, remains uncultivated and unimproved?—In short, The mistaken Part of Mankind may call that Man an Hero, who makes a Country desolate: But certainly he is the true Hero who peoples a Country, and renders future Generations easy and happy, maugre all the foolish Opposition of his Cotemporaries, and their absurd Prejudices.

SECTION III.

A Polity for changing Tithes into Glebe.

WHEN *Moses* instituted the Polity of the *Hebrew* Commonwealth, he balanced the Landed Property so equally between the twelve Tribes, that it was morally impossible for any one Tribe to make a Conquest of the rest. For he ordered the Land to be divided to each Tribe by Lot; and each District was again subdivided among the particular Families of the Tribe. Now these Families were not suffered to intermarry with any others, but those of their own Tribe: And lest some more potent Families should arise and swallow up the rest, either by failure of Issue, intailing of Estates on Heirs Male, Purchases, or Mortgages; it was ordained, that in Case of failure of Issue, the next of Kin should marry the Widow, and raise up a new Family; in Case of failure of Sons, the Daughters should be joint Heiresses; and in Case of Purchases, the Purchase should be valid only for forty nine Years at *the*

Herds of Cows they make vast Quantities of excellent Cheese and Butter, which inrich the Country. Sir *William Temple* did not let this Corner escape his Observation. He says, the *Beemster* (formerly a *rotten* Marsh) is so well planted with Gardens, Orchards, Rows of Trees, and fertile Inclosures, [and *note*, he might have mentioned the vast Flocks of Sheep grazing upon it] that it makes the pleasantest Landskip he ever saw.—This Lake was drained in 1612, after four Years Labour. It contains 7090 Acres, besides the Highways and Dikes." See *Description of* Holland, Page 380, 381.

farthest, and then at the fiftieth Year, or Year of Jubilee, the Estate was to return to the Heirs at Law; lastly, in regard to Mortgages and Fore-closures, these were absolutely prevented by the Prohibition against lending Money on Interest or Usury. This being the State of Things, it is easy to see, That there could be no undue Monopoly of Land in such a Government. All were to have a Sufficiency, and none to have too much.

BUT as the Tribe of *Levi* was set apart for the Service of Religion, the Question is, How were they to be provided for? And this Question is the properer to be asked, because it was almost impossible to accommodate them with a Settlement or District after the Manner of the other Tribes. And therefore we find it expressly injoined, That *Levi should have no Part, nor Inheritance with his Brethren*, Deut. x. 9. For indeed the very Nature of such an Inheritance would have confined them to one Spot; whereas it was intended, That they should be scattered among all the Tribes and Families of *Israel*, in order to be the Ministers and Teachers of Religion in every Place. On the other Hand, if they had been suffered to inherit, or ingross Lands at Pleasure throughout all the Tribes, this Privilege, together with the Influence of their sacred Character, might have created them such an undue Share of Power, as would have indangered the whole Constitution. Lastly, if they had been supported only by a certain invariable Tax, this would have degenerated into the Nature of a *Modus*, and have never kept Pace with the compara-tive Riches, or Poverty of the rest of the People:—Not to mention, that a Modus, or *fixt* Salary, would have been a very weak Incitement to the Passion of Self-Love to co-operate with the Genius of the Constitution, and the Design of the Legislature; it having been the grand Plan of this divine Legislator to constitute such a Polity in all Respects, as would ingage the Individual to pursue the Interest of the Public, because he would pursue his own.

HENCE therefore some other Settlement or Appointment must have taken Place, in order to do Justice to the Tribe of *Levi* for the Loss they sustained in being deprived of their Share of their Inheritance among their Brethren, and to support them properly as Ministers of Religion. And that Appointment was TITHES; a Method of Support the best calculated for the Genius of that Government, and the Circumstances of the *Hebrew* People. Nay, it deserves to be taken Notice of, That *Moses* interwove the Appointment of Tithes with the Discharge of Religious Offices in such a Manner, That in Proportion as the Priests and Levites were remiss in the one, they lost their Quota of the other:

So that it became their *immediate Interest*, as well as *Duty*, to inculcate the Ordinances of the Law, on which depended their present Support, and to prevent the People from deviating into Idolatry, or falling off from the Terms of the Covenant. Now this admirable Polity, so deeply laid and surprizingly judicious, was relative only to that *Theocratic* Constitution, which *Moses* established;—A Constitution now no more, and which it would be both impious, and absurd to attempt to revive at this Day. Consequently those antient Fathers, *Origen*, St *Ambrose*, St *Austin*, &c. &c. who maintained, That Tithes were of divine Right under the Gospel, because they were so under the Law, must have had very imperfect Notions both of Law and Gospel, and had made little Progress in distinguishing the *Peculiarities* of the one, from the *Universality* of the other.

INDEED it is certain, That every Order of Men, Clergy or Laity, who are useful to Society, have a just and equitable, and therefore a *divine* Right to be supported in their Profession, suitably to their Station: And consequently in this Sense the Christian Clergy have most indubitably a divine Right to a decent and sufficient Subsistence,—such a Subsistence as will put them above the Contempt of the Poor, and below the Envy of the Great. And this doth well agree with St *Paul's* Declaration, who delivers it not as from himself, but immediately from God: viz. *Even so hath the Lord ordained, that they which preach the Gospel, should live of the Gospel.* But neither our Lord, nor St *Paul*, nor any other inspired Writer of the New Testament, suggest a Syllable concerning the *Necessity* of continuing that Part of the Jewish Law which relates to Tithes: Nay, if the Practice of St *Paul*, and his Advice to the *Corinthians* and *Galatians* were to be considered as a *Rule* in this Case, the quite contrary might be gathered from them. It is therefore exceeding strange, That so many Christians, antient and modern, who thought they could never express too great an Abhorrence of Jewish Rites and Doctrines, should yet adopt some of the *most glaring* Parts of Judaism (for this is not the only one) and so far commence JEWS themselves.

THE Reason therefore for the original Appointment of Tithes having ceased with the Levitical Priesthood, it is natural to conclude, even without farther Proof, That the Introduction of this Law into the Christian Dispensation must have been improper, or at least unnecessary. Let us now therefore inquire, what Effects have followed from it.

AND *first*, This Appointment, in a Commercial and Political View, must be considered as a *Tax* upon the Subject for the Support of an useful and necessary Order of Men.—But alas! it is such a Tax, as plainly tends to stop Industry, to discourage Improvements and good Husbandry, to favour Idleness, and introduce Poverty. For the more diligent and industrious a Man is, the more he is subject to the Impositions of this Tax: Whereas the bad Husbandman and the Sluggard, who are really the Drones of Society, escape in a manner Scot-free. Now this Proceeding is the very Reverse of what a good Tax ought to be: And though I am far from thinking, that the Clergy in *England* have too much, or even a sufficient Provision in Proportion to the present *increased* Wealth of the Laity, yet I do maintain, that this Tax is more heavy and oppressive in its Consequences, than many others, though they produce three times the Sum. For the Nature of Taxations ought never to be judged of from the Amount of the Sum collected, but from the Effect of the Tax upon the Dispositions and Resolutions of Mankind. And Fact it is, That when a Farmer finds he cannot exert his Industry, without paying so dearly for a *License*, he will often content himself with sitting still. Instances of this kind are daily occurring, especially in regard to the Introduction of new Improvements. Nor is it to any Effect to say, That the Landholder by so doing is chiefly his own Enemy: For a Fact is no less certain, because the Motives to it may not be solid: And such is the Disposition of Mankind, that it is with Difficulty you can persuade them to be industrious, unless you can prove likewise, that their Gettings shall become their own. And it is this very Principle in regard to the Land-Tax, which hath so effectually induced the Landholders in *England* to cultivate and improve their Estates: For they know, That the Land-Tax will not be raised the higher in a well-cultivated County, Hundred, or Parish, than if the County, Hundred, or Parish, had remained unimproved: Therefore all the additional Improvements become their own. Whereas were the Land-Tax to rise in Proportion to the *increased* Value of the Lands (which is the Case in *France*, where both the *Taille*, and the *Dizieme* vary every Year) this Island, which hath been so surprizingly improved within these last sixty Years, would have remained in *Statu quo*, like the rest of its Neighbours; and the Spirit of Industry and good Husbandry would have been nipped in the Bud.

SECONDLY, In a religious View the Appointment of Tithes is to be considered as the Support of the Ministers of Religion:—But it is such a Support, as naturally, I had almost said necessarily, tends to set the Incumbent and his Parishioners at Variance with each other. For when the Maintenance of the Clergyman is to depend on Tithes, it is obvious, That every Parishioner can cheat him if he pleases: And therefore, without intending any Reflection, we may justly conclude, that where the Temptation is so strong and universal, a great many will yield to it, and cheat in some degree or other. Hence it comes to pass, that tho' the Incumbent should be of the sweetest Temper, and mildest Disposition in the World, this is enough to sour him and make him fretful: And if he should happen to be naturally choleric or contentious, he will never want Provocations, while he has to do with Tithes. Perhaps the Charge of Fraud, which he can *legally* support in a Court of Judicature against any particular Person, may be but a Trifle;—such a Trifle as would cause a Man to be greatly exclaimed against, if he went to Law for the Recovery of it: And yet the Amount of these Trifles all over the Parish may make one third, or one half of his whole Income: So that the poor Man is reduced to this unhappy Dilemma, either to sit down quietly, and see himself defrauded of half his Income, while himself and his Family are wanting it,—or to bear the Character of an angry, litigious Person, who, though the Minister of Peace, is always at war with his Parishioners, and insisting upon such mean, trifling Article, as a Layman would scorn to contend for. In short, when the Case is thus circumstanced, what can be expected, but the very Things which the Apostle saith ought to be put away among Christians, *viz.* Bitterness and Wrath, Anger, Clamor, and Evil-speaking? And why should the Polity of our Constitution concerning the Maintenance of the Clergy *counter-act* those very Principles of Christian Love and Benevolence, which the Clergy are particularly called upon to recommend to others, and to practise themselves?—Surely it would be judged the wrongest and most absurd Proceeding in the World, in the Affairs of Government and Civil Life, to require one Thing by Principle, and yet to institute a Polity for inflaming the Passions, the Passion of Self-Love especially, strongly in behalf of another.—But nevertheless as the Evil is inveterate, and of a very long standing, we must not be precipitate or violent in the Means of a Cure, but apply those Methods only which are gentle and gradual.

WHEREFORE the Polity here proposed is such, as will scarce admit of any Difficulty in the Execution, when once established: *viz.* To pass a Law for impowering the Parties concerned to exchange Tithes for Lands, whenever they shall find it their mutual Interest so to do.—But in order to guard against those Collusions and Impositions, which may attend such a Power of exchanging, it may be necessary to make both the Patron of the Living, and the Bishop of the Diocese, Parties in this Case, together with the Incumbent. And then, when the Incumbent, the Patron, and the Bishop, are all satisfied, that the proposed Exchange will be for the Advantage of the Church in question, they may sign an Instrument of Exchange to the Landholder, in the same Manner as he is to deliver over a Counter-deed to them. Moreover, as such Exchanges will naturally create a great many petty Glebes in different Parts of the Parish, and perhaps in different Parishes, it will be necessary to continue a like Power of exchanging these scattered Parcels of Glebe for other Lands, that may happen to lie more convenient and contiguous.—In the mean Time, till these second Exchanges can be effected, the Incumbent will certainly be benefited, not only because the first or original Exchange was to his Advantage, but also because the worst Circumstance of scattered Glebes are more desireable than those of scattered Tithes,— especially such which are *Vicarial*. And when he can have drawn his Glebes together by subsequent Interchanges, he may make the Rectory or Vicarage both a very valuable, and compact Endowment. But be that as it may; certain it is, That the Farmer or Landholder will behold this Endowment of Glebe with very different Eyes, to what he doth that of Tithes; nor will he grudge his Parish-Minister the full Enjoyment of his legal Rights, be they more or less. On the other Hand, all Causes of Complaint and Dispute on the Part of the Incumbent, will then be taken away; so that both may live in mutual Harmony, as they ought to do, and be assisting to each other in mutual good Offices. Add to this, That when the Landholder can have all his Lands Tithe-free, the very Addition of Straw and Hay, and consequently of Manure, hence occasioned, will enable him both to support a larger Stock of Sheep, Horses, and Cattle, and also to dress and manure his Grounds more effectually, for raising greater Quantities of Corn.—Nor will he then be discouraged from putting in Execution any Scheme for Improvement, when he knows, That all his Labour and Industry will be his own.

Thus therefore might the whole Tithes of the Kingdom be changed in a Course of Years into Glebe, without Ferment, Opposition, or Contention. For as all Transactions would be voluntary, no Man could have a Right to complain: And yet every Man concerned would be desirous of making the Exchange here proposed, because his own Interest would suggest it to him. And such a Method of supporting the Clergy, though it may be subject to some Inconveniences, (as every thing is) would certainly be preferable, in our Situation, to any other. For in regard to the Appointment of Tithes, the very great Inconveniences attending this System, have been set forth already: And in relation to a fixt Tax, a Pound Rate, or Modus, this would not only be wrong, because it makes no

Distinction between the *comparative* Wealth, or Poverty of the rest of the Nation at different Periods of Time, but because no kind of *annual* Tax, be it more or less, will ever be paid by the Parishioners to their Clergy, with an hearty good Will, and sincere Approbation.

LASTLY, As the Case of the Levitical Priesthood, which was hereditary in one Tribe, hath no Analogy with that of the Clergy of the Church of *England*, whose Wealth, if they have any, sinks again into the common Stock of the Laity, and who can have no separate Interests from the rest of the Nation; so likewise it will be proper to observe, That the Science of Agriculture may probably receive considerable Improvements, when Men of Letters are ingaged in its Pursuit. For the Ignorance of the common Herd of Mankind, and their Prejudices and Attachments to old Customs, are really astonishing. And though much might be expected from Farmers and Occupiers of Land, because they are daily conversant in these Affairs, yet in Fact it will be found, that they too often proceed on by Rote, keeping to the Practice of their Forefathers, without inquiring whether it was right, or wrong. If *Virgil* of old, or the very worthy Dr *Hales* of modern times, had proceeded upon the same Plan, the one had never wrote that very judicious, as well as beautiful Poem, called the *Georgics*, nor the other his *Vegetable Statics*.

SECTION IV.

A Polity for increasing Buildings in low, fenny or marshy Grounds, and rendering them healthy.

IF suitable Polities can be established for the Draining, and Cultivation of Fens, Moors, and Marshes (which was the Thing attempted to be proved in the second Section of this Chapter) it follows of Course, That Houses ought to be built in them, and these Houses rendered as desireable, and healthy as the Situation will admit. And it is humbly conceived, That Art and good Management can go a great Way in this Matter. But before we enter directly upon the Subject, it will be necessary to premise a few Observations.

IT appears therefore to be a general Rule, That Lands are best cultivated and taken Care of, *cæteris paribus*, when the Farm-house is pretty near the Center, and equidistant from all Parts of the Estate; because all the Estate can be better looked after. And the same Reason should weigh with Gentlemen to part their Estates into moderate Farms, rather than join moderate Farms together to make large ones; or in Case they are very large already, it would be certainly right to divide them into two, or three Shares. For when the Farm is of such a vast Extent, the

Estate will not be duly cultivated; nor will the Farmer mind his Business as a *Farmer*; but will commence a kind of Gentleman, doing no Work himself, and only riding about to inspect others. And this Principle will extend itself to the rest of his Family; so that the Work of an whole Family will be intirely lost to the Community. In short, it is in Agriculture, as in Manufactures; *viz.* The more Rivals, where all may live decently, but none superfluously, the more industrious they will all be; and they will do their Work in greater Perfection. Now a Farm of four or five, not to mention seven or eight hundred Pounds a Year is certainly a *Monopoly* in its kind; because it would have afforded a comfortable Subsistence to three, or four Families, if divided into so many distinct Farms. And indeed it is attended with all the bad Effects which other Monopolies are, such as dispeopling a Country, and preventing the Increase of Inhabitants, raising one sort of Persons too high, and depressing others too low: All which must be greatly injurious to national Industry, good Husbandry, and extensive Commerce. Moreover it is impossible to suppose, that a Man who hath ten or twenty Servants to inspect, can look after them as well, as he that hath only two or three, and is working himself together with them.

Now if these Arguments are conclusive even in respect to dry, champaign Countries, they will be found to conclude much stronger in regard to Fens or Marshes. For in the first Place, rich, fat, and fertile Grounds, such as those generally are, do not require a large Extent of Country to make up a competent Farm. For a Quantity of two hundred, perhaps one hundred Acres of such Grounds may be a more valuable Estate, than two thousand Acres upon barren and bleak Hills. In the next Place the very Cottagers can derive a better Maintenance from two Acres of Ground in such Low-lands, than from forty in many Sorts of High-lands. For out of this little Plot they may spare an half, or a third every Year, for sowing of Flax, which Vegetable never can flourish well but in a moist, deep, and rich Soil; and requires to be watered after it is pulled; otherwise it will never be fit for use. Now in marshy Grounds, where the whole Country is intersected by Canals (as shall be described hereafter) there can be no want of Water: And even if we could suppose, That a Man was denied the Use of the public Canals for that purpose, he might dig a Pit in his own Garden at Pleasure; so that the Flax sown on this Acre of Ground, from the sowing it, throughout all the Stages, till the manufacturing it into Yarn or Thread, and perhaps into Cloth, may be performed by a Cottager within his own Family, and reward his Industry with at least twenty, perhaps thirty, or even forty Pounds a

Year. Judge now what an Advantage this would be both to the *local* Interests of a County, and to the general Interests of a Kingdom;— especially when it is considered, that most of this Labour is performed at spare Hours, when the Family would have had little else to do, if they had not done this. Therefore what an astonishing Loss must this Nation sustain in leaving such immense Quantities of its richest Grounds to lie waste and uninhabited! Surely, surely it is high time to rouse out of this Lethargy! But there is yet one Reason more to be given for rendering a Fenny or Swampy Country as populous as possible, which certainly deserves a very particular Regard; and that is, That the more populous you render a marshy Country, the more healthy it becomes. For every Fire, and every Drain is of Service to purify the Air, and to prevent or correct those Fogs and Damps which are so noxious to animal Life.

But still it must be owned, That according to the present Method of Building in such low Places, there is no Incouragement to build more. For the Agues and Seasonings, the Scurvies and putrid Fevers bred in marshy Grounds, make such Havock among the Inhabitants, that very few would care to live there, who can live any where else. Now the Unwholsomness of these Places must certainly be owing to those Effluvia and Exhalations which arise from rotten Grounds and stagnating Waters, whereby the Air is filled with noxious Particles and various Animalcula, and consequently rendered unfit for Animal, at least for *Human* Use. This being the Case, the very Nature of the Disease suggests the Cure: For if the corrupted State of the Atmosphere is the Original of these Disorders, two Things are necessary to be done: viz. *First,* To purify the Air as much as possible by Fires and Drains, according to what hath been observed above. And *secondly*, To build the Houses in such a manner, as shall cause the Inhabitants to live out of the reach of the noxious Part of this Atmosphere.

Now the latter is the peculiar Aim and Design of this Polity: And then, if the Habitations can be made healthy, there is no need to fear, but that the Country would soon be rendered populous; and by Consequence, the additional Number of Drains and Fires will still correct the natural Dampness of the Situation. Suppose therefore, That an Act was passed for granting certain Privileges or Exemptions (herein after mentioned) to such Dwelling-Houses situated in Fens and Marshes, as shall be built according to the following Direction; *viz.* That the Ground or First Floors shall be raised two Feet at least above the common Surface, and be arched over, but have no Chimnies in them; That all the Floors above them, being built upon these Arches, shall be at least fourteen Feet in the clear, higher than the Ground Floors, and be accommodated with Fire-places;—And then the rest of the Building (where higher Stories are required) may be left to the Pleasure and Discretion of the Proprietors. Now by Virtue of this Regulation, the Rooms which the Family shall inhabit, (for they cannot inhabit the Ground-Rooms below Stairs without a Fire-place) these Rooms, I say, built upon Arches, will necessarily be dry and warm; And as they are likewise raised sixteen Feet at least above the Level of the Country, they will be placed in a different Climate, so that the Inhabitants will breath a much purer Air, than they otherwise could do. For it is observable, that the more noxious Damps and Vapours seldom rise higher than eight, or ten Feet; And the most malignant Steams of all do not rise so high; As appears by the Experiment of the famous *Grotto del Cano* in Italy. —But even though we should allow, that sometimes Fumes and Exhalations will rise to the Height of sixteen Feet, and upwards; yet they will necessarily become harmless and inoffensive in Proportion as they spread through a greater Space, like the expanding Rays of a Circle; and therefore the Quantity of noxious Matter will always be diminished according as the Squares of the Distances from the Surface are increased: So that tho' you should allow, That a Dose of eighty Grains of any poisonous Vapour, will prove fatal to human Life at the Distance of four Feet from the Surface, it by no Means follows, That a Dose of only ten Grains at the Distance of sixteen Feet, shall be attended with any ill Effect whatever. Add to this, That the higher the People live above this gross and corrupt Atmosphere, the greater Advantage they will receive, generally speaking, from a Current of Wind dissipating and dispelling the unwholesome Effluvia, and bringing a Stream of fresh and sweet Air from a drier Country.

THESE Reasonings perhaps may appear to some Persons too finely spun, and inconclusive:—I must therefore add, That they are not merely Speculations, but fully warranted by Fact and Experience: For the famous City of *Venice*, besides other Places, affords such a Proof of the Truth of these Assertions, as should remove all Doubt, and silence Objections; this City being built not only in a Marsh, but, what is much worse, on a watry Ooze, where there is little, if any Tide; and where there is no strong Current to preserve the Waters from Putrefaction:— Yet this City is not remarkably unhealthy, nor do the Inhabitants find so much Inconvenience from their damp Situation, as the Inhabitants of the Hundreds of *Essex*, the Fens of *Ely*, or the Marshes of *Somersetshire*. But the Advantage which this City injoys is, That it is built in the manner above described, the first or ground Floors being used only for Magazines or Storehouses, and the Floors above them being the constant Residence of the Family: Moreover the like Practice obtains at *Marseilles, Bourdeaux*, and other Places. And why it should not obtain universally here in *England*, where Cautions of this sort are very necessary, is hard to say:—For undoubtedly an House so constructed, would cost very little, if any thing more (especially in Fens and Marshes, where Bricks can be made upon the Spot) I say, it would hardly cost any thing more, than one built after the present Form: Add to this, That the Arches of such an House would last much longer than Timber can be supposed to do; and the Danger from Fires would be much less; nor would these lower Rooms be at all useless or improper in any Family.

But Custom hath determined it otherwise in *England*; and Custom is a Tyrant not easily overcome. Let us see therefore, how far we might prevail with Self-Love and Self-Interest to withstand this Tyrant. For old Prejudices are never to be *nationally* subdued, till the Individuals, of which the Nation consists, are brought to make it a common Cause. This being the Case, let us not aim at too many Things at first, but confine the Polity to such Buildings only as shall be erected in fenny and marshy Grounds, and those Grounds which were before Common, because their Situation doth most require it, and because there can no Objections be raised against granting Privileges and Exemptions to Common Grounds, which never paid any Tax before.

First then, If an House, built as above described, should be exempt from paying the Window-Tax the first ten Years after its Erection, this would be some Encouragement to build.

Secondly, If the Occupier or Inhabitant should likewise be free from serving any Offices he should please to decline for the first ten Years, this would be some farther Inducement.

Thirdly, If the Inhabitant and the Lands were to be exempted from all County, Hundred, or Parish Taxes, for the like Space of ten Years, this would operate still more strongly.

Lastly, If the House, together with all the Grounds belonging to it, not exceeding two hundred Acres, were to be freed from the Payment of the Land-Tax for the first ten Years, this, together with the other three, would undoubtedly be effectual Incouragement to build. And thus might the fenny Wastes, and desolate Marshes of *England*, which at present pay no Taxes of any kind, and contribute very little, if any thing to the public Utility, thus might they, I say, be covered with good, comfortable, and wholesome Dwellings, and contribute as much towards inriching the Community, and defraying the necessary Expences of the State, in the Course of a few Years, as any other Part of the Kingdom. And surely it is much more delightful even by way of Prospect from an Eminence, to see a rich Vale, where the industrious Inhabitants are at Work, like the Bees, each at his proper Imployment, and to view their decent Houses, numerous Flocks and Herds, fine Plantations and well cultivated Grounds, than it is to behold a large standing Lake in Winter, or a dead, flat Plain in Summer, with nothing to diversify the Scene but Black Cattle for a few Months.

AND now, as the Subject falls naturally in our Way, it may not be amiss to set down an easy Method for draining large Fens or Marshes, where it is not practicable to open a Passage for carrying off the Waters. Suppose a Fen or Meer of a quadrangular Figure, containing about ten thousand Acres, which Fen is two Feet under Water during the greater Part of the Year. Now the first Thing to be done in such a Case is, to choose a very dry Summer for digging a large Trench of at least twelve Feet deep, and sixty broad, at the very Edge of the Meer, to go quite round it; and with the Earth taken out of this Trench you should make firm, broad, and high Banks, especially that Bank which is on the outer-side.—Then, the next Year, when the Ground hath been somewhat drained by this Trench, you are to dig, at the Distance of an hundred Yards, an *inner* Trench of about ten Feet deep, and forty wide, which is likewise to be carried quite round the Meer; and with the Earth of this second Trench make good the inner Bank of the first Year's Trench: Let both these Banks be raised to the Height of ten or twelve Feet above the Level, but made exceeding strong and firm; for all will depend upon their Strength and Goodness. Then the third Year you are to cut Trenches across, and along, so as to divide the whole Ground into Shares of about two hundred Acres each, and these Trenches may be made only six Feet deep;—but all should communicate, either directly or indirectly, with the Trench of the second Year, *viz.* that which is ten Feet deep: And the Earth taken out of these Trenches should not be raised into Banks, but spread abroad upon the Surface, in order to raise the Ground somewhat above its natural Level.

Now it is obvious, That as all the Trenches of six Feet deep communicate with that of ten, which we will term the *Canal*, the Water will have a sufficient Descent to run into that Canal; wherefore the only remaining Difficulty is, to get the Water out of this Canal into the great Canal of all, *viz.* that which was first made, and is incompassed with Banks twelve Feet high;—and for the Sake of Distinction, may be

called the *Grand Reservoir*. Now this is easily performed by the help
of a Windmill or two, placed at proper Distances, and so contrived as to
work a Set of Pumps for raising the Water out of the Canal into the
Reservoir. But when there happens to be no Occasion for making these
Evacuations, the Mills may be imployed in grinding Corn, sawing
Timber, making Paper, expressing Oil, and the like, according to the
Custom in *Holland*. Lastly, In regard to the Waters of the grand
Reservoir, if any Danger should be apprehended from their rising too
high, Pipes may be laid in the outermost high Bank for carrying off the
surplus Water into some neighbouring Brook or River, or to the Sea.
And surely this may be done without much Charge or Difficulty. For
though the Thing was impracticable, while the Water lay upon a Level
with the rest of the Country, yet when it is raised eight or ten Feet above
the Surface by means of these high Banks, there can be no great Art,
Expence, or Difficulty in laying Pipes for carrying it away.

AND thus might the whole Fen, or Meer, be turned into dry Lands,
as the Meers in *Holland* have frequently been, at the Expence of thirty,
or at most forty thousand Pounds Capital; and create a Landed Interest
of about seven thousand Pounds a Year. For after the most ample
Allowance is made for the Ground taken up in Banks, Reservoirs, Canals,
Trenches, Public Roads, &c. there will remain about six thousand six
hundred Acres of extremely rich and fertile Lands. And if these are
divided into thirty three Shares, they will make so many distinct Estates
of two hundred Acres each. Now if one of these Shares, *viz.* That
which is nearest the Center, was set apart for a Church, a Glebe, and
a little Town, (which might easily be done by allotting one hundred
and fifty Acres for the Glebe, one for the Church and Church-yard,
and forty nine for the Town) this District would be converted into a
very comfortable and happy Neighbourhood of middling Gentry, substantial Shopkeepers, industrious Tradesmen, and useful Mechanics.—
A District, I say, which was a wide Waste and Desolation before.

MOREOVER, each Gentleman's Estate might be adorned with Plantations of Planes and Poplars, Withies and other Trees, which delight in a
moist Situation;—and these might be so placed round the Trenches on the
Confines of their Estates, that no Ground would be really lost, but all
contribute both to Use and Beauty. Indeed the Trenches would
require to be new dug every three or four Years, but the Expence would
not be very great, and the rich Mould taken out, would both serve to
manure the Surface, and to raise it. As to the great Canal, and the great
Reservoir, these two would answer all the Purposes of an inland Naviga-

tion; and the grand Reservoir, in which there would be no Necessity of steeping Flax, might be well stocked with various kinds of Pond Fish.

SECTION V.

A Polity for creating a Plenty of Timber.

THE Necessity of establishing such a Polity in every Commercial and Maritime State must certainly be very great, and the Reasons for it are strong and cogent.—But yet these Reasons, in my humble Opinion, are somewhat different from what are generally imagined.

FOR first, though it is the received Opinion, That the Quantity of Timber in this Island hath greatly decreased of late Years, and that the present Scarcity and Dearness are to be ascribed to that Cause; yet, with due Deference to the public Judgment, I apprehend, That it is not quite so clear, that the *Quantity* is diminished, as that the *Demand* is increased; and therefore, that the Scarcity and Dearness of the Commodity are properly to be ascribed to the prodigious Increase of the Demand. But as this is very far from being the generally received Notion, let us endeavour to examine the Matter with the more Accuracy. Be it therefore remembered, That, in antient Times, the different Parts of this Kingdom, like every other uncultivated Country, were quite upon the Extremes in regard to Wood. For where the Timber grew naturally, without Care or Culture, there the Country was covered with a thick impenetrable Forest of many Miles extent: But on the other Hand, where the Soil was not naturally disposed for Timber (tho' Trees might have been raised by means of skilful Husbandry, proper Shelter and Inclosures) in those Parts, I say, the Scene was quite the reverse. This being the Case, it must certainly follow, That almost all sorts of heathy Grounds, chalky, gravelly, and flinty Commons, high Uplands, wild Downs, Fens and Swamps, besides all Places exposed to the Air of the Sea, were very naked and bare of Trees. Whereas, in modern Times, these Things are brought more to a Medium: For excellent Grass and Corn are raised in many Places where nothing but Wood grew formerly: And on the other Hand, since so many Fens and Marshes have been drained, since heathy Grounds, Commons, Uplands, and Downs have been inclosed and cultivated, the Numbers of Vistas, Clumps, Plantations, Parks, Groves, Gardens, Walks, Hedge Rows, Orchards, &c. have greatly increased the Quantity of Trees:—So that perhaps, when one thing is weighed with the other, it will not be found, that the real Quantity of Timber hath so much decreased as People do hastily imagine.   And this will farther appear by considering the Subject in another Light, *viz.*   That the present Scarcity of Wood is really owing to the prodigious Multiplication of its Uses of late Years: For if the Mass of the People were to use no more Timber in their Shipping, Houses, Furniture, Utensils, Manufactures, Mines, Iron Works, &c. &c. than their Forefathers did about seven hundred Years ago, the present Quantity of Timber would be so far from being insufficient to the Demand, that it would be really a Drug.   But the Truth is, that though perhaps the Number of People is not six Times greater than in the Reign of *Henry* II. the Uses and Application of Timber are certainly six hundred Times more.—In short, if you were to suppose, that all the common and middling People of *England* consumed no more Timber at present than the Highlanders of *Scotland*, and the old Natives of *Ireland* now do in building and furnishing their Huts and Cabbins, and that they had no more Shipping, Trade and Manufactures, you would soon find, that there would be Timber enough in this Island, and to spare.

SECONDLY, Though it is a Notion almost universally received, that *English* Oak is the best in the World for building Ships of War, and though it is the vulgar Opinion, that the *British* Fleet acquires a Superiority over all others by means of the superior Qualities of *British* Oak; yet these Opinions having no Foundation in Reason and Nature, ought to be rejected by Men of Sense as VULGAR ERRORS.   For it is impossible that *English* Oak can be fit for building large Ships of War, inasmuch as *English* Timber never can arrive at a Size large enough for that Purpose till it is past its Prime, and is decaying and perishing with Age.   Indeed the *English* Oak may serve for *Ribs* and *cross Timbers* as well as any other: But as to the *outward Planks*, or Sides of the Ship, that *English* Oak cannot serve for these Purposes, will appear both from the Reasonings, and Authority of the following Paper, taken from the Memoirs of Mr *Pepys*, Secretary to the Admiralty.

"RESOLUTIONS taken at a Conference held at the Office of the Navy, *April* 17, 1686, between His Majesty's Commissioners there, and us the underwritten Shipwrights, upon Inquiries then proposed by the Secretary of the Admiralty on the Behalf of His Majesty, touching the present Condition of this Kingdom in reference to Plank for Ship-building.

"INQUIRY I.   How far may it be depended on, that *England* may at this Day supply itself with a Sufficiency of that Commodity, for answering the Occasions both of the Merchants and His Majesty's Service (in the State the Royal Navy now is) without foreign Helps?

"RESOLUTION. That it is in no wise to be relied on: Forasmuch as from the Want of Plank of our own Growth, and consequently the Highness of the Price of what we have, the Shipwrights of this Kingdom (even in our Out-Ports, as well as in the River of *Thames*) have been for many Years past driven to resort to Supplies from Abroad; and are so at this Day, to the occasioning their spending of one hundred Loads of foreign, for every twenty of *English*. Besides, were our own Stock more, the Exclusion of foreign Goods would soon render the Charge of Building insupportable, by raising the Price of the Commodity to double what it is, and more, at the Pleasure of the Seller.

"INQUIRY II. From whence is the best foreign Plank understood to be brought?

"RESOLUTION. Either out of the East Sea, from *Dantzick*, *Quinborough* or *Riga*; of the Growth of *Poland* or *Prussia*; or from *Hamburgh*, namely, that Sort thereof which is shipped from thence, of the Growth of *Bohemia*, distinguished by its Colour, as being much more black than the other, and rendered so (as is said) by its long sobbing in the Water during its Passage thither.

"INQUIRY III. What Proportion this foreign Plank may be reckoned to bear to the *English*?

"RESOLUTION. For so much as concerns smaller Vessels, of fourscore Tons downwards, whose Works call for not more than two-inch Plank, of twenty Foot long at the highest, meeting at thirteen or fourteen Inches in breadth, our *English* Plank will, from the Nature of the Wood, *last longer* than any foreign of the same Dimensions. But [*Note*,] for Ships of *three hundred Tons upwards*, which require the Service of three or four-inch Plank, from twenty six to forty Foot long, meeting at fourteen or fifteen Inches breadth at the Top-End, *universal Practice* shews, that the White Crown Plank of *Prussia*, and the forementioned black of *Bohemia*, do in their *durableness* equal, or rather *exceed* that of our *English* Productions of the like Dimensions: Which we conceive to arise from this plain Reason, *viz*. That the foreign Oak being of much quicker growth than ours, their Trees arrive at a Stature capable of yielding Plank of these Measures, while they are yet in their sound and vigorous State of growing; whereas that of *England*, advancing in its Growth more slowly, arrives not at these Dimensions, till it becomes to, or rather is past the full of its Strength; fifty Years sufficing for raising the foreign, to what the *English* will not be brought in an hundred and fifty. But whether we are right or not in this Reasoning, it is, upon *daily Experience*, most evident, that our *East India* and other Ships of *greatest*

Burden, built with this large foreign Plank well chosen, *prove in their Durableness without Exception:*—Variety of Instances lying before us of Ships built wholly of *English* Stuff, as well in His Majesty's Yards, as Merchants, which *have perished in half the Time*, others of the like Burden, composed wholly of foreign have been observed to do.

ALSO it is, that *English* Plank of *short length*, cut out of *young*, growing Timber, is manifestly better than East Country, and therefore is preferred thereto in laying of a Gun-Deck, as far as the three Streaks next the Ship's Sides, where short Stuff will serve (the Quality of its Wood bearing better with being kept wet and dry, as it generally is in that Place) yet where, upon the same Gun-Deck, long Plank is necessary, that of foreign Growth, for *Strength* and *Duration*, is always preferred, from the Reason, as we conceive, before given; *viz.* That of its being cut while in its Vigour, which the *English* will not admit so as to bear those Scantlings. And to this is to be farther added the general Waniness, want of Breadth at the Top-End, and ill Method of Conversion of our *English* Plank; daily Practice shewing, that twenty Loads of foreign, shall, in working go further upon a Ship's Side, or Deck, than an hundred Loads of the like Lengths of *English*, after its Wanes, and other Defects shall be cut away.

"MOREOVER, it is yet to be noted, That in planking of a Ship with foreign Plank, the Builder shall not be driven to put in above three or four Pieces; whereas in a like Ship, done with *English*, he shall be obliged to use an hundred, to the *no less Impairment of the Strength of the Work*, than Increase of its Charge both in Stuff and Labour. So that upon the Whole, our UNANIMOUS OPINION is, That large Plank well chosen, of the foreign Growths before mentioned is, in its Service, *at least as durable*, in its Cost *less chargeable*, and the Use of it, through the Scarcity of *English*, become at this Day *indispensable.*

> *Jonas Shish, Hen. Johnson, Pet. Narberry, Abr. Greaves, Jos. Lawrence, John Shish, Jam. Yeames, Wm Collins, Rob. Castel.*

"WE do fully concur in the Resolutions above written.

A. DEAN,   J. NARBOROUGH,

J. BERRY,   PH. PET,

WILL. HEWER,   B. S. MITCHEL.

Now from this, and the former State of the Case, it appears very clearly, That the present Scarcity of Timber arises, *principally* at least, from the increased Demand; and that this increased Demand is chiefly owing to the superior Numbers of People, and to the rapid Progress which the Inhabitants of this Island have lately made in almost all Arts and

Sciences, Trades and Manufactures. Consequently it must follow, That in proportion as the Country shall still grow more populous, and make farther Advances in the Arts and Ornaments of Living, the Demand for Timber will still increase, and our present Necessities will yet be greater. Moreover as to Shipping and Navigation, though it hath been fully proved, that the *English* Plank is not fit for building large Ships of War, and consequently that our wooden Walls, so much our Glory, are not altogether *English*; yet the same Judges have declared, that *English* Oak is particularly excellent for Ships of a small Burden:—Nay they give plain Hints, that the Plank will serve very well for any Ships not exceeding two hundred and fifty, or three hundred Tons. Now the far greater Part of the Shipping imployed in the Merchants Service, and all the Coasting Vessels, are within the Dimensions here prescribed. And as to the Royal Navy itself, though the Planks must be Foreign, the Ribs and Knees, and crooked Timbers, might all be *English*;— and such *English* as need not exceed their prime State of growing, when cut down. So that upon the whole, after vulgar Errors are set aside, there are still Reasons sufficiently strong and cogent (and surely they ought not to be the less convincing, because they are *true*) for incouraging the Growth of all Sorts of Timber as much as possible, and Oak particularly. In a word, Timber is a *raw Material*, whose Demand is increasing, and whose Uses are multiplying every Day.

HENCE therefore it is natural to ask, How comes it to pass, that Self-Love, the grand Mover of *created* Beings, should want an Incitement in this Case more than in any others? For when the Demand increases, the Price increases likewise: And if the Price is inhanced, is not this itself a sufficient Spur for planting Timber, without any other political Inforcement? To this I answer, That if planting of Timber was of the same Nature with raising of Corn or Cattle, or ingaging in Merchandise or Manufactures, the Reasoning would hold true. For certainly there is no need of any Inducement but Self-Interest, where Self-Interest can properly take place. But in the Case before us, the Misfortune is, that he who plants, unless he begins very young, cannot expect to reap much Benefit in his own Person: For Trees are of a slower Growth than Corn; and a Plantation of Forest Timber will recompense the Grandson, instead of the Planter. This being the Case, it is very obvious, that *present* Self-Love is as much the ruling Passion in this Delay or Omission of planting Timber, as it is in any other: And therefore we may venture to foretell, That till a different Direction can be given to this ruling Passion, no Scheme or Proposal, no Law or Regulation will ever prove

effectual.   In short, we must take human Nature as we find it; and make
the best Uses of it we can.   And therefore, if we really expect a Growth
of Timber equal to the Demands of a Maritime and Commercial People,
we must come to the Point; That is, we must render it the *present* and
immediate Self-Interest of every considerable Land-Owner in the Kingdom to make Plantations.

Now these Plantations ought never to be less, but as much more as
the Owner shall please, than twenty Acres well fenced and inclosed:
Because a less Plantation, if near the Sea, or on a bleak, high Ground, is
in danger of being destroyed by high Winds, and the Extremity of
Weather: Whereas in a large Plantation one Tree shelters another, and
all are preserved.   And this Observation holds *particularly* true on the
Sea-Coasts; where if you plant one, or ten, or perhaps an hundred Trees,
they will come to nothing; such is the blighting Nature of the Sea Air:
But if you plant a thousand, the outermost Ranks may perhaps be shriv-
elled, but in proportion as you advance inwards, the Trees will appear
healthy and flourishing: An ocular Demonstration of which may be had
at the Hill above *Margum* House in *Glamorganshire*, and at Mount
Edgecombe in *Cornwall*.—Though indeed the safest Way in all Cases,
where either the Soil, or Situation is not kindly disposed for Timber
(after having prepared the Ground, and laid out proper Spaces for Walks
and Avenues) is, to sow Acorns, and all Sorts of Timber Seeds together,
in order that Nature, in such a Variety, may take her Choice.   And then,
when these young Plants come up, they will be a mutual Screen and
Defence to each other; and as they advance in Growth, may be transplanted, or thinned out at Pleasure.—So much as to the Reasons for
allotting twenty Acres at least to every Plantation near the Sea, and
upon bleak Exposures: And indeed in every Situation a Grove of twenty
Acres is not too large: But will be found to be much more commodious,
when proper Allowances are made for Walks and void Spaces, in order
that Carriages may pass and repass, and that the Underwood may be
cleaned out, and made into Charcoal;—I say, such a Plantation will be
found much more commodious to the Owner, and advantageous to the
Growth of Trees, than one of a less Size.

BUT the Polity itself for inforcing these Regulations, by taking strong
hold on the Passion of Self-Love, and giving it the *useful Direction*,
hath not yet been mentioned.   Suppose therefore, That every Land-
Owner for each Quantity of four hundred Acres that he possesses within
one Parish, Tithing, or Hundred, should be obliged by Law to allot twenty
Acres for making a Plantation of Timber under the following Penalties, *viz.*

1. THAT he should pay double Land-Tax for all his Estate situated in that Parish, Tithing, or Hundred, till he hath made as many Timber Plantations, as he had four hundred Acres.

2. THAT he should pay likewise double Window-Tax for all his Houses upon that Estate, without receiving any Allowance for those Cottages, or small Tenements, which have not *nine* Windows.

3. THAT he should pay double to the Poor-Tax, and to every other Parochial, Hundred, or County Tax, assessed on Lands or Houses, till he complies with the Terms here required.

4. THAT all reasonable Expences in making and preserving these Plantations should be allowed by Minors to their Guardians in passing their Accounts; moreover that every Husband holding an Estate during the Life of his Wife, should be permitted to charge the Estate with *two thirds* of the Expence hence occasioned, in case he survives her; but if a Person is Tenant only for his own Life, then he may be allowed to charge no more than *one third* of this Expence as a Debt on the Estate, payable to his Representative, or Heir at Law.

Now, when all these Clauses are operating jointly together, it is humbly conceived, that they must be effectual: For every Man would feel himself strongly disposed to concur with the public-spirited Designs of the Legislature, rather than bring so many Inconveniencies immediately upon himself by his Refusal: Present Self-Interest therefore would teach him this Lesson without Art or Logic. And thus might almost every Parish be adorned with Groves, and be inriched, as well as beautified; and the whole Kingdom, equally throughout, receive as full a supply of Timber, as could reasonably be expected. For it may be computed, that after Allowances are made for all Estates under four hundred Acres, and for such likewise as are above four hundred, but short of eight hundred, and so on,—I say, after these Allowances, it may fairly be computed, that for every thousand Acres of Land thro'-out the Kingdom, twenty Acres will be stocked with Timber; which Proportion amounts to just a fiftieth Part of the whole; and would certainly be sufficient for the Demand. And to ascertain the Nature of these Plantations, so as to prevent litigious Disputes, it might be enacted, That a certain Period, suppose *twelve Years*, shall be allowed, from the Date of the Act, for making these Plantations, and for the Growing of the Trees; and that, *at all Times*, after that Period, every good Inclosure of twenty Acres or upwards, wherein are growing at least four hundred Saplings or young Timber, shall be adjudged to be a sufficient Plantation, within the Intentions of this Act. Now this being the Case, every

Man will have a plain Rule to walk by; and therefore, if he will not comply with it, he has none to blame but himself.   And as this would be the Rule of judging, What was a legal or Parliamentary Plantation, and what was not, the same might serve, in case a Person was disposed to change one Plantation for another: For every new Plantation with four hundred Saplings would be a sufficient Security against the Penalties of the Law.   And when once the Plantation is set out, it would be the Proprietor's own Interest to make it both as *profitable* and as *ornamental* as he could: For in such a Case, he would need no farther Incitement.

Now though this Polity appears under somewhat of a different Aspect from any of the former, by carrying the Air of *Force* and *Compulsion*, yet in Fact it can hurt none, but the most obstinate of Men.   For the Expence of making such a Plantation would be inconsiderable in itself; and as it would fall on Persons of respectable Landed Property, it could scarcely be felt: Nay, though a Man might not live to be himself a Gainer, his Heirs or Representatives infallibly must; and if even *he* was obliged to sell the Estate, it would sell the better.   The Rich therefore, who are the Persons immediately concerned, cannot be said to be hurt by such a Law; because it only would spur them on to do those Things, which they ought to have done without Compulsion. And if Benevolence to the Public, the Love of their own Families, and the Desire of doing Good to Posterity, had been so prevalent with the Bulk of Mankind, as *Self*-Attachments and *present* Gratifications, there would have been no more need to have made a Law of this Nature, than there is to oblige Men to eat, or sleep.—But, waving this, if the Rich would not be hurt, nay, in Fact, would be greatly benefited in the Course of Things, by such a Law; the Poor, the middling Sort, the Mechanic, the Manufacturer, the Merchant, and in short, all Orders and Degrees of Men whatever, would likewise reap the Advantage; Iron-Works might then be erected in almost every Parish or Hundred, if there were Occasion; Ships might be built in every Port, and Flotes of Timber might be brought down all our Rivers.

SECTION VI.

A Polity for Registring the Title Deeds of Houses and Landed Estates.

THIS is a Subject, on which very little need be said: For the Case is so plain, That every Man who buys an Estate, or lends Money upon it, ought to have a good Title, that it would be the Height of Folly to pretend to illustrate the Matter, or make it plainer.   All therefore that is to be done, is to point out the true Reason, why some

Persons are so averse to a Register, and then to shew, how their Opposition may be disarmed, and yet the Thing effected.

As to the Cause of their Aversion, it is plainly this, Either their Estates are incumbered with Mortgages, Settlements, Jointures, Annuities, &c. &c. and then perhaps they may want to borrow more on them by means of double Deeds;—or else their Titles are not so clear as they could wish, and therefore they are desirous of concealing this Flaw from the World. Now both these Circumstances are the strongest Reasons imaginable for the Necessity of a Register, and plainly shew the Use and Advantage of it. But the more cogent these Reasons are, the more violent will be the Opposition from all those who have cause to fear a Discovery. And therefore it seems morally impossible to get such a Law to be past, were it to oblige all Persons to come in, and register their Title Deeds directly.

BUT what cannot be done at once, may be done gradually; and though a strong Opposition would certainly be made in the one Case, perhaps there would be very little, or none at all in the other. Suppose therefore a Law was enacted, to make Marriage Settlements, Sales, Mortgages, &c. not be deemed valid *for the future*, unless they were registered among the County Records. Now such a Provision, respecting only Futurity, would not be much opposed by the present Generation; and yet in a short Space of Time it would operate as effectually, as if all Deeds were registered at once. For every Year and every Month would add some Estate or other to the Number of the registred ones; and when such Estates became the greater Number, the rest of the County, finding the Advantages of a Register, and the Disadvantages of borrowing Money, buying or selling an Estate without one, would voluntarily inroll their Title Deeds, and do that by Choice, which they would not do by Compulsion.

CHAP. II.

Certain Polities for the Increase and Improvement of Manufactures.

IT hath been observed before, Page 91, "That all Commercial Imployment may be divided into two Kinds, *Husbandry* and *Mechanic Arts;* the immediate Object of the one being to provide *Food*, and that of the other to procure *Raiment* and *Dwelling:* And from the *Concurrence* and *Modifications* of these three, *viz.* Food, Raiment, and Dwelling, every other Trade, Calling, and Profession, derives its Origin and Support." For even the liberal Arts themselves, and all the literary Professions could never have existed, had it not been, that the Labour of the Husbandman, and the Skill and Industry of the Mechanic Artificer had first supplied the Scholar, the Philosopher, and Man of Contemplation, with the Necessaries and Conveniencies of Living. It hath been likewise farther observed, "That the *Landed* and the *Trading* Interests, or in other Words, that the Husbandman and the Artificer, are the *mutual Customers* to each other, the one being the respective Maker, and the other the Consumer." Hence therefore it should follow, That in proportion as any Nation improves in either of these, it improves likewise in the other; and if so, then we must conclude, that the Polities in the foregoing Chapter for the Increase and Improvement of Husbandry, become in the Event so many Polities for the Extension of Commerce and increasing the Number of Artificers and Tradesmen. And indeed these Consequences will necessarily follow, if all Obstacles are removed out of the way; but if Things are diverted from their natural Course by the Mistakes or sinister Arts of Mankind, the good Consequences will always be lessened in Proportion to the Number, and Nature of such Obstructions.

THIS being the Case, it is obvious to remark, That the Business and Aim of the insuing Sections, must be to remove those Obstructions which impede the *industrious* and *useful* Operations of Self-Love, and to set Mankind and Nature FREE:—Free, I mean, in that Sense in which consists our true Liberty. For if Self-Love is *restrained* from doing Good to Society, it will do Mischief; and if prevented from doing Mischief, it will do Good. Hence therefore the Physician to the Body Politic may learn to imitate the Conduct of the Physician to the Body Natural, in removing those Disorders which a bad Habit, or a wrong Treatment hath brought upon the Constitution; and then to leave the rest to Nature, who best can do her own Work. For after the Constitution is restored to the Use and Exercise of its proper Faculties and natural Powers, it would be as wrong to multiply Laws relating to Commerce, as it would be to be for ever prescribing Physic.

ONE Thing more I have to add, by way of Preface or Introduction, *viz.* That the Terms *Mechanic Trades* and *Manufactures*, here made use of, are to be understood in their largest and most extensive Signification: And therefore every Branch of Commercial Industry, even Shipping and Navigation, must be supposed to be comprehended under these Articles. But if any Person should object to this Method, and choose rather to say, That Shipping and Navigation ought to be con-

sidered as the *primary* Objects of our Attention, because we are a maritime People; To such an one I must beg leave to make this short Apology,
viz. That in a systematical Treatise it would seem very preposterous to
begin with that Article first, which is the last in the Order of Succession:
And therefore as Shipping and Navigation are only Sea-Carriage, they
must *pre-suppose*, in the very Nature of the Thing, that there are Goods
first to be carried.

SECTION I.

*A Polity for opening such exclusive Companies, as relate principally to our
Home-Trade, or Domestic Commerce.*

WHEN a Set of Families, be they many or few in Number, are
under the same Legislature, and constitute one People or political Society, the Commerce carried on between the Members of
this State among themselves, is called *internal* or *domestic:* But when they
trafic with the Subjects of different States or Legislatures, such Intercourse with other Nations, and exchange of Commodities, is termed
Foreign Commerce. Hence therefore it is very apparent, that the Ideas
of Foreign and Domestic Commerce do not arise from the *Distance* or
Nearness of Situation of one Place to another, but from the *different
Legislatures* which these Places may be respectively under. For when
Goods are sent from *Dover* across the narrow Streight to *Calais*, such
Goods are said to be *exported*, i. e. carried to a foreign Country; but
if shipped off from *London* to *Newcastle*, they are only reputed as carried
Coast-wise, though more than fifty times as far. This Observation is
yet strengthened by considering, that before the Union of *North* with
South Britain, the Trade to *Scotland*, though at no greater Distance than
crossing a River, was a Branch of Foreign Commerce, and so reputed by
the Laws of both Kingdoms.—Nay, the Trade to *Ireland* is still considered in that disadvantageous Light, and consequently discouraged by
hundreds of prohibitory Laws still in being, merely forsooth because
these neighbouring Islands happen to be under Legislatures in some
Respects different, though the general Government is the same, and the
Interests both of Church and State, are the same likewise. However,
since Things are in this Situation, our first Concern should be to set that
Trade *free*, which circulates, or might circulate at Home, and then to
extend our Attention to those Fabrics and Commodities which are, or
might be exported Abroad.

Now any Trade may be said to be FREE, in which every Person may
ingage if he pleases: And consequently those Trades are really *confined*,

where the Liberty of exercising them is denied to some, tho' granted to others; or where the Expence and Difficulties of obtaining this Liberty, are a great Burden and Discouragement. And therefore two Questions naturally arise on this Subject, *viz. First*, What Trades ought to be free and unrestrained? And *secondly*, What *Means* are the most desireable, and the least obnoxious to popular Prejudices towards obtaining this Freedom? As to the first, can it once be made a Doubt, whether such Trades ought to be free, as tend to create *mutual Imployment* for Mankind, and to promote useful industry and commendable Labour?— Surely it is impossible to conceive (*Self-Interest apart*) that any Trades deserve to be discouraged by a wise Government, but those only which administer Temptations to Vice and Idleness: For all others are an absolute Benefit to Society; and the more free and unconfined they are, the greater and more universal is this Benefit. If therefore those Trades ought to be free, whose Extension and Increase are a public Advantage, we are now to consider in the second Place, what Means would be the most eligible for obtaining this End.

ALL Liberty may be considered in two Views, Civil, or Religious: Religious Liberty, otherwise called Liberty of Conscience, is that whereby a Person is permitted to exercise his *own Judgment* in the Choice of his *own Religion*, and consequently to worship God in that manner which he believes to be most acceptable to the divine Being. This is certainly a Privilege which every Man hath a Right to enjoy, provided his religious Tenets cause no Disturbance to Civil Society, and are not repugnant to good Morals. And this Right we of *Great Britain* do now possess in as reasonable and ample a Manner, as can be desired. Nothing therefore is to be suggested in relation to this Article, as a Matter of Complaint, but of Commendation. For the Contemplation of it should inspire us with Praise and Gratitude, first to God, and then to his subordinate Agents.—And indeed, as the Ways and Systems of Providence are all uniform, and co-operating with each other, this Liberty of Conscience, so justifiable upon a religious Account, is not only compatible with, but greatly conduces to the Extension of Trade and Commerce. Whereas, on the contrary, it hath been the Observation of many Ages, that Bigotry and Industry, Manufactures and Persecution, cannot possibly subsist together, or cohabit in the same Country.—So far as to that Liberty, which is termed Religious.

AND as to *Civil* Liberty, we joyfully acknowledge with all Thankfulness, that in regard to the Crown and Government, never were a People more free than the *English* at this Juncture. But alas! though we are emancipated from the former Yoke of oppressive Power in one Sense, we are still Slaves to it in another: And, what is very astonishing, we now tamely submit to that *Usurpation* of our natural Rights from our Fellow-Subjects, which we would not bear from a crowned Head. The Nation, for instance, would rise as one Man, should the Crown attempt at this Day to exercise the *Prerogative* (as it did formerly) over the *natural* Rights and Liberties of the Subjects, by prescribing what particular Persons should exercise such and such Trades, and who should not,—by searching their Houses and taking away their Goods, under a Pretence that they were not made after a Workman-like Manner,—by stopping them from pursuing their honest Callings any longer,—by levying Fines and inflicting Penalties,—and doing other like Acts of despotic Violence and Oppression:—Such a Proceeding, I say, would raise a general Horror and Indignation: And yet, Reader, these very Powers derived originally from the Crown, and varnished over with the delusive Appearance of CHARTERS and CORPORATIONS, are exercised every Day, not only with Impunity, but with Applause. You will please to observe, that they are the same Powers still: For, in Fact, the whole Difference consists in the Persons, that are to execute them. Thus it is, that if the Crown should commission any Persons to see them put in Execution, *as from itself*, this would be esteemed, and justly too, a very high Infringement on Men's natural Rights and Liberties: For surely nothing can be plainer, than that every Man hath a Right *by Nature* to subsist himself, by his own Labour and Industry, in *any way that is compatible with the Good of the Whole*; for this is the *only Limitation* that should take Place: And the Common Law of the Land not only agrees with, but greatly inforces this Doctrine. But lo! these very Powers, shocking and oppressive as they are, intirely change both their Names and Natures, when deputed to a Set of our Fellow-Subjects, and exercised by them, under the foolish and fallacious Pretence of *supporting* their PRIVILEGES. Such is the Force of Custom! Such the Delusion of Words and Sounds! The *persecuted* Person, who was inriching both his Country and himself by his Genius and Industry, is by a Jury found *Guilty*; the oppressive, incorporated Drones, and injurious Monopolists are stiled the *Injured* and the *Innocent*.—In short, the plain Rules of common Justice, common Honesty, common Sense, good Government, and national Commerce,— are one thing in *Westminster* and *Southwark*, and quite the Reverse within the Liberties of the City of *London*.

Now when Nonsense and Absurdity, when bad Polity and Injustice have gained an Establishment, and are covered over with the sacred

Dust of Time, many Persons will always be found, whose supposed Interest, or real Inclination it is to defend them. And thus it hath happened in the Case before us: For a Multitude of Arguments have been coined to gloss over those Practices, which, if they had not been introduced in the Ages of Ignorance, Tyranny, and Barbarity, and settled by long Custom, would now have been detested by all the World. —However, as they have at present a kind of prescriptive Right, let us hear what can be offered in their Defence.

I. THEREFORE, It is pretended, that these Incorporated Societies were right at the Time of their original Institution, in order to keep up the Goods to a Standard, and to support the Credit of the Manufacture.

1st Answer, WHOEVER will be at the Pains to inquire into the Origin of these Grants, and to trace the Motives both of Granters, and Grantees, will find, That the Improvement of Commerce, and the Perfection of Mechanic Arts, were no Part of their Intention. For the Persons, to whom these Exclusions were granted, acted upon as base and disingenuous Motives, as ever disgraced human Nature: Their Designs were to exclude all Competitors, to monopolize the Trade into a few Hands, and to oblige the Buyer to take what they would please to sell him, however *dear*, or *bad*. And as to the Princes who granted these Privileges, they frequently sold them, as Goods in a Market, to the highest Bidder. For the Royal Prerogative was then so high and uncontrolable in Things of this Nature, that all Law and Parliament bowed before it: And therefore, if at any Time the Parliament did not readily grant Money in the ordinary Way, this Method always occurred to supply a present Pinch. Moreover, the Favourites and Courtiers of the Times had by means of these *Jobbs*, a Power of inriching themselves, without draining any thing out of the Royal Coffers.—But if any one should yet doubt of the real Intentions of these Monopolists, in regard to Commerce and Manufactures, he need only read the Form of those horrid Oaths, which they obliged their Fellow-Subjects to take before they would admit them to be free of their Incorporated Societies. This is enough;—but if he hath a Mind to search farther into these Iniquities, he may consult *Rymer's Fœdera*, Sir *Simon Dewes's* Journal of the House of Commons during the Reign of Queen *Elizabeth*, *Townshend's* Historical Collection of her four last Parliaments, the Preambles of several of the Statutes at Large, and other Tracts of the like Nature.

2d Answer, THE very Notion of keeping Manufactures up to a Standard is absurd and ridiculous; for different Nations, Countries, and Climates, different Ages, Sexes, and Stations, different Times and Seasons of the

Year, different Customs and Caprices, and consequently *different Prices* require different Sorts of Goods. And every Manufacturer must, and will endeavour to suit his Fabrics to the Taste, or Pocket of his Customers, let the Standard be what it will. In short, who can pretend to fix that Standard, which must alter with every Fashion, and vary as often as the Whims and Humours, the Abilities and Inclinations of Mankind differ from themselves, and from each other.—Therefore if the Goods have no hidden Flaw and Imperfection, and if they are intrinsically as valuable as they appear to be, they have all the Qualities which the Nature of the Thing will admit of. But suppose they should have some concealed Fault or Blemish, then, I ask, are the Wardens and Masters of Companies the proper Persons for detecting these Frauds? Will these Men, who have their own Wares to sell, will they impeach themselves for making bad ones?—or indeed will they impeach a Brother of the *Craft*, who may soon be in Office, and will surely retaliate the Favour to them?—No; the Thing is incredible and absurd: And Fact it is, that there have been more bad Goods manufactured and vended, *especially for foreign Markets*, by such as have born Offices in exclusive Companies, than by any other Set of Men whatever.

3d Answer, ALLOWING, for Argument sake, that it is necessary to establish, or continue these Incorporated Societies for the Purposes above mentioned, then it follows, *à fortiori*, as the Schoolmen speak, that the like Incorporations should be established and continued for the due manufacturing of all other Commodities, which can be brought to a Standard, and are least liable to the Changes and Alterations of Times and Fashions. Butter and Cheese, for Instance, are valuable Commodities, and require much greater Skill and Ingenuity in the making them, than is necessary for practising several Mechanic Trades, which yet are dignified with exclusive Charters: Likewise the Taste or Judgment for good Butter and Cheese is more general, fixed, and certain, than the Judgment for most other Manufactures. Suppose therefore, that a Company were erected for the proper making of Butter and Cheese; and that the Rulers of this *worshipful Company* had a Power of searching for, and confiscating all bad Butter and Cheese within twenty Miles of *London*;—How would the Masters and Wardens of our present exclusive Companies like this? For this is their own Argument in the strongest Sense: And yet there is not a Man that breathes, that would expect to find these two Articles of Living either cheaper, or better by such an Institution.

4th Answer, BUT even granting (what is utterly false) that Mechanic

Arts and Manufactures are to be improved by exclusive Charters·—still
what is that to other Trades, which do not make, but only sell and retail
these Manufactures?   For though a Manufacturer must be incorporated,
it doth not follow, that his *Broker* must: And, in Fact, all Shopkeepers
and Retailers are nothing more than *Brokers* between the Manufacturer
and the Buyer.   Surely, by Parity of Reason, the Carrier, and the
Carrier's Horse, may as well put in their Claim for Charters and Exclusions; and upon the same wise Principle, a Law ought to be enacted,
That for the due and proper Exercise of the Art or Mystery of carrying
Goods, and drawing a Load in a *Carrier-like* Manner, all the Horses
imployed therein, shall be Duns, Blacks, or Bays!

II. The *second* Pretence is, That exclusive Companies were necessary
at first, in order to give proper Incouragement to ingenious Artists to
settle among us.

1st Answer, This Plea is more ridiculous, if possible, and more extravagant than any of the former.   For the very Intention of an exclusive Company is to shut out Rivals, and to prevent, as far as may
be, the very Possibility of Competitions.   Where then can be the Motive
to excel, when Emulation is stifled, and the idlest Blockhead, if free of a
Corporation, is preferred to the most ingenious and industrious Artist
that is not free?—In short, where Privileges and Charters are to determine the Merit of a Man's Performance, his chief Regards will be paid
to *them*; and even if he should happen to be endowed with brighter
Parts, and a superior Genius, his Ambition will not be called upon to
exert them in such a Situation.

2d Answer, As to the Incouraging of new Trades, it ought to be
considered, that every Trade at its first Commencement, is properly in
its infant State; which therefore during that Period must be *nursed*;
and all nursing is attended with Expence.   Now, if a new Trade is to
be introduced at home, or a new Branch of Commerce is to be carried
on abroad, there are two Ways of nursing it, till it is able to shift for
itself; *viz.*   First by granting a Charter to the first Artists at home, or
to the first Adventurers abroad, and to their Successors after them,
with an Exclusion to all others; and secondly, To issue forth a general
Invitation to all, and to advance such Premiums or Bounties, as shall
induce many Individuals, from Prospects of Self-Interest, to ingage in it.
This being the Case, let us now consider which Method of Nursing is the
cheapest, and best?   Which, for Example, will make the Child thrive
fastest, or bring the Trade the speediest to Perfection, so that it may no
longer require the Support of Leading-strings?   Now in regard to the

first Method,—Indeed, I own, that the exclusive Grant will always appear the cheapest to those who do *not attend to the Nature of it*; but is in Fact the dearest. For those Taxes, which are raised by Monopolists and exclusive Companies, both in the Sale of their Goods, and in purchasing from others, are the most grievous and detrimental of any that ever existed; inasmuch as they nip Industry in the very Bud, and prevent that Circulation of *mutual* Labour and Imployment, in which consist the Riches and Prosperity of a Kingdom. And as to the nursing Part, to carry on the former Allusion, it is neither their Interest, nor their Inclination, that the Child committed to their Care should subsist without its Nurse: For when the Exclusion is discontinued, and the Trade thrown open, their monopolizing Gains are gone. Therefore it is their Business to stint the Growth of this Trade, within such Bounds as shall make the exclusive Charter *appear* still necessary for carrying it on. On the contrary, when a new Trade is supported by Premiums and Bounties, the very additional Expence in one respect is more than *repaid* by the additional Increase of Labour and Industry, and consequently of Riches in another. Moreover, as the Invitation is general, the Emulation will be so likewise; which is itself the best Guard against Combinations. Therefore as the Improvements come on, and the Trade extends, the Bounty or Premium may be proportionably diminished; so that in a few Years this kind of nursing may totally cease. Nay, in a Course of Time, perhaps this Trade itself may bear a Tax in order to support, and rear up other infant Trades, if such a Proceeding is judged requisite.—But indeed no Manufactures or Branches of Commerce ought to be burdened with Taxes, according to the Rules of sound Polity, but those only which administer to Idleness, Pleasures, and Diversions. However, from the above State of the Case, we see plainly, that exclusive Companies, whether for a Foreign or Domestic Trade, are the worst Nurses in the World, as well as the most expensive. And if from Theory we descend to Facts, the Proofs will appear in a very striking Light. For in regard to Foreign Commerce, tho' there was a *Greenland* Company subsisting for a great many Years, scarce any thing was done, and the little Quantity of Oil and Whalebone taken by them, was sold at most exorbitant Prices. But when this Trade was thrown open, and a Bounty given, the Increase and Improvement, within a very short Space, were astonishingly great and rapid; no less than eighty Sail of large, stout Ships (such Ships as would have been judged fit to form a Line of Battle in the Reign of Queen *Elizabeth*) having been fitted out in one Year, and that but a few Years distance from the Commencement of the Trade. And in respect to home Concerns, The City of *Worcester* hath by its Situation on the *Severn*, and by every other natural Cause, greatly the Advantage over *Birmingham:* But *Worcester* hath no Trade, and *Birmingham* a great deal; And why so?—*Worcester* hath exclusive Charters, and *Birmingham* none at all.

III. THE *third* Pretence is, That if it were not for exclusive Companies, there would be too many of a Trade:—The Trade would be over-done.

I. *Answer*, IF ever the Tricks of *Legerdemain* imposed upon the Eyes of Mankind, these Delusions of exclusive Companies impose as much upon their Understandings. For, in Fact, when all the several Trades are under their respective Exclusions or Monopolies, (which is the very Case in regard to our *home* Trades) what Advantage hath one Set of Trades-men over another? And if all Trades are *mutually impeded* by these Restraints, what is the Consequence, but mutual Poverty? Suppose, for Instance, any given Number of exclusive Companies living together within the Liberties of the City of *London*, viz. A Company of Bakers — Brewers — Taylors — Shoemakers — Carpenters — Masons — Smiths — Grocers — Mercers, &c. &c. and that each of these should resolve to support their *Privileges*, as they are pleased to call them, and to expel those Tradesmen who are not free: — The Bakers therefore begin with expelling the Non-freemen, or interloping Bakers; and the Brewers expel the interloping Brewers, and so on: — Now I ask, in the Name of Common Sense, after this Exploit, what have the Bakers, or Brewers, or Taylors, or any others gained by these Expulsions? — For the Matter, you see, is not one Jot mended; and the Complaint, *That the Trade is overstocked*, remains as strong as ever; there being as many of the Trade remaining, *in Proportion to the Number of their Customers*, as there were before. Either therefore let all continue, — or seek for some other Reason, and give up the foolish Pretence of lessening the Number of your *Rivals* by such Methods, whereby the Companies of other Trades are lessening the Number of your *Customers*.

II. *Answer*, GRANTING, that a Trade may be accidentally overstocked with Numbers; — when that is the Case, the best and safest Way is to let the Evil alone, and then it will infallibly cure itself. For in process of Time, some of these Persons will go off to other Trades; and, as the Trade is out of repute, there will not so many young Recruits be bred up to it. Thus the Occupation that was once overstocked, will soon be reduced to a Medium, and may in its turn want Hands again; the Con-sequence of which may probably be, that it will be again overstocked: For such is the Rotation of human Affairs, Dearness begets Cheapness, and Cheapness Dearness. But if you should take any other Course than what is here mentioned, which is in Fact the *Course of Nature, and of Providence,* like Summer and Winter in the natural World, your Attempts will not only be frustrate, but by endeavouring to remove one *seeming* Evil, and *temporary* Inconvenience, you will certainly introduce a thousand real ones, which will grow more dangerous, and inveterate by Length of Time.

IV. THE last Pretence is, That these Liberties and Privileges are *bought* by the great Sums given with Apprentices, and by the Money expended in taking up the Freedoms of Cities, Companies, &c. — Therefore if they are to be given up, some Recompence should be made to the present Proprietors.

1st Answer, IF any Money was really given for these Privileges, more is the Pity: For positively they are WORTH NOTHING: Nay, they are so vile a Drug, that if you were to carry them to *Manchester, Birmingham,* or any other free Town, they would not accept of your intended Present. But indeed, how is it possible, that these Privileges can be of any Valuation, inasmuch as it hath been made evidently to appear, that they do not increase the Trade of any one particular Person, and greatly prevent the general Trade of the Nation?

2d Answer, THE Position is not just, That the great Sums of Money given with Apprentices, are in Consideration of obtaining these imaginary Privileges. For, as great, nay much greater Sums are given in open Towns, where they neither have, nor desire such Privileges. And I will venture to assert, that many Tradesmen in *Westminster* and *Southwark,* have much larger Sums with their Apprentices than those of like Occupation in the City of *London:* And as to Merchants, it is now grown into a kind of Custom, even within the Liberties of the City, for Merchants to refuse taking up their Freedom, lest they should be burdened with the usual Inconveniencies attending it: And yet these Merchants have very large Sums with their Apprentices, or Clerks: — So little Regard is paid to these trifling Gewgaws by the best Judges, and most experienced Practitioners in the Commercial World.

UPON the whole, After having examined and refuted every Pretence, we must now recur to the Observation we set out with, *viz.* That an *Englishman,* notwithstanding his boasted Liberty, is, in regard to Commerce, still NOT FREE: — For he is still in Bondage, not to the Crown indeed, as formerly, but to his Fellow-Subjects; and we still want the GLORIOUS REVOLUTION in the Commercial System, which we have happily obtained in the Political. Then indeed, and not till then, may we be said to have abolished all the *Remains* of antient, despotic Power, and Gothic Barbarity. For as long as these Charters and Exclusions continue, so long we bear about us the Marks of our former Slavery.

HOWEVER, seeing these Chains are now looked upon by a considerable Part of the Nation as a Matter of Ornament, instead of a Badge of antient Slavery, we must pay that Deference to the Foibles and Pre-judices of Mankind, as may best promote the great End we aim at, *National Prosperity*. And therefore, far from endeavouring to take these pretended Privileges away at once, let us rather undermine them by degress, and by that Means render the People themselves weary of their Chains.

THEREFORE, the Set of Polities here proposed, are those which have been mentioned already under another Article, Page 18 and 19, viz. *Polities for incouraging the Married State*. And indeed, if all *married* People were allowed, as there set forth, the intire Liberty of working at what *mechanic* Arts they pleased, and of keeping Shops within Glass Windows, these two Articles would go a considerable Way towards redressing the Evil complained of. And as an Act for this Purpose might, and ought to bear the most popular Title, *viz. An Act for the more effectual Incouragement of Marriage among industrious People*, an Opposition to it would not be able to sound a general Alarm through-out the Nation. Nay, the far greater Part being pleased with the Title, would not trouble their Heads about the Contents: For Names and Sounds are the chief Things, in Cases of this Nature, either of doing Good, or doing Mischief. Besides, the very Contents of the Act not being levelled against any *particular* Set of Men, and consequently not raising any particular Enemies, there would be no *Demetriuses* to stir up the People, That their *Craft* was in Danger. Moreover as the Effects of such a Law could not appear instantaneously, but would creep on by slow Degrees, there would be no Danger to be apprehended at its first Commencement; Because there would be no immediate Object of *public Hatred*, like as in the Case of the *Jew* Bill, for the popular Fury to vent itself upon. So that in every View, the Electioneering Patriot must invent some other Cry, and here be silent: And if the Law was past the second, third, or fourth Session of Parliament (which would be the only *proper Seasons* for passing it) perhaps he himself would, for once, do Good undesignedly, and be among the first to promote it: — Indeed he could have no particular Interest to serve by opposing it. But be that as it may, certain it is, that after a Course of Years these pretended Privileges would grow into great Disesteem, and become at last as much the Subject of Derision and Contempt as the Coronation Challenges of *Dimmock* the Champion (another Remnant of Gothic Barbarity) are at present.

AND now, notwithstanding so much hath been said on this Subject, something seems necessary yet to be added by way of guarding against, as far as that is possible, the disingenuous Arts of Cavil and Chicane. For it is easy to foresee, that many Difficulties will be started, and Objections raised by narrow-minded Persons at the Beginning of this, as of every other Reformation. And though they cannot defend the absurd and iniquitous Practices intended to be reformed, yet they think themselves very happy (from what Motive it is many times hard to say) if they can succeed in perplexing the Argument, or misrepresenting the Intention of the Reformers.

I. THEREFORE it will be pretended, That if such a Course is taken in dissolving, or undermining Charters, all Order and Regularity will be overturned, and the usual Channels of Justice, and Civil Government will be stopped up.

Now it may be greatly questioned, whether the Persons themselves, who would urge this Plea, can possibly believe the Reality of it. And yet, as the Words made use of, are plausible and sonorous, it will be necessary to obviate the ill Impressions that such Words may occasion: Be it therefore remembered, That Charters for the *Administration of Justice,* are one Thing, and Charters for the *Limitation of Commerce* are another; and therefore, if any Man will confound these two together, he must be very weak, or, what is much worse, very wicked. Now the Force of the Arguments here advanced, as well as the Intent of the Polities proposed, tend only to the opening of exclusive Charters relating to Commerce, but have no Reference whatever to Charters for the Administration of Justice. These latter therefore are to remain in full Possession of all their Powers of administring Justice to the Subject; and as to the former, it is not even proposed to repeal these Charters but only to take away their noxious and malignant Qualities. For the Charters may still remain as far as relates to all Points of Honour, Pleasure or Profit: The Rents of the vast Estates belonging to these Companies are still to be at their Disposal; and their Furs and Scarlet Gowns, their Colours and Streamers, their Offices and Dignities, and what is the most essential of all, their frequent Feastings and Carousings, are still to be held sacred and inviolable: And nothing more is to be taken from them, but the Power of stopping Industry, and doing Mischief. Judge therefore with what Appearance of Truth it can be said (and yet

I am persuaded, it will be said) that this Scheme tends to dissolve all Charters whatsoever, and to annihilate the best Part of the Rights, Liberties, and Privileges of a *free-born Englishman*.

II. IT will be said, That according to the Principles on which this Scheme is built, every *other* Trade, Calling, or Profession, ought to be as free and independent, without Restraint or Examination.

Now, in order to give this Objection its full Answer, four Observations ought to be made;

(1.) THERE are a Set of Trades and Callings, whose very Business it is to draw others into Idleness and Expence; — Thus, for Example, the greater the Number of Alehouse-Keepers, and the more industrious they are, so much the less Industry there will be among other People. For they cannot succeed in their Imployments, without impeding the Success of others. This being the Case, it therefore follows, that the very same Principle, which would take off Restraints from other Trades, would lay Restraints upon these, and prevent their Increase. — But of what Nature these Restraints are, will particularly appear in PARTS III. and IV. when we come to treat of Polities for promoting good Morals and to set forth the Theory of judicious Taxes.

(2.) THERE are certain Occupations (*Mechanic*, or *Manufacturing* Trades I think there are none) whose Professors ought to be subject to a *Licence*, or *Examination* before they Practice, because the Injury done by unskilful Practitioners may be irreparable and fatal. And this Observation holds particularly strong in the Case of Physic and Surgery: For a bold plausible Pretender may do that Mischief at once, which is never afterwards to be remedied. And then it is of no avail to turn off the Quack, and have no farther Dealings with him, after he has killed, or ruined his Patient. In short, the Cases of Physic, and Manufactures are not at all parallel; and therefore no Argument relating to the one, ought to conclude for the other.

(3.) IN relation to the Professions of Law and Divinity, the very Nature of these Sciences renders it necessary, that the Professors of them should undergo some Examination, or give some Proof of their Abilities and Proficiency, before they commence Teachers and Practitioners. For in regard to Divinity, it is absurd to suppose, that the Persons to be *taught*, are the proper Judges of the Abilities and Learning of the *Teachers*. Nay indeed, Tares of bad Principles may be made to resemble Wheat so much in the outward Look and Appearance, that the best disposed *unlettered* Person may be deceived, if he is not likewise endowed with a most uncommonly solid and sagacious Judgment. Moreover in regard to Law, the *implicit Faith* which the Mass of Mankind must repose in the Practitioners of it, makes it necessary, that as many Securities should be taken by the Public, both of their Integrity, and Abilities in their Profession, as the Nature of the Case will bear. For their Clients can be no Judges of their Abilities; and after they have lost their Fortunes by trusting them in dishonest, or unskilful Hands, it will then be too late to turn off their Counsellors, or Attorneys, and chuse others.

BUT, (4.) there is one general Reason for restraining the Numbers of the Professors of Law, Physic, and Divinity, which concludes quite the contrary, if applied to Husbandry, or Manufactures: And that is, that as these Scholars and *literary* Gentlemen live by the Labour of others, the Increase of their Numbers would be so far from adding to the Public Stock of Wealth, that it would greatly diminish it in every View:—A dead Weight themselves, and depriving the Public of so much Labour. A few indeed are necessary in every State, but many are a Nusance both to themselves, and to the Public: And in short, an Increase of their Numbers should never be attempted till all other Orders and Professions have *led the Way, and greatly increased theirs:* For the Number of Parishioners, Clients, and Patients, should first be multiplied, before that of Clergymen, Lawyers, or Physicians.

WE have now, I think, viewed the Subject in all Lights, and in every Position:—And the Result of the whole is this, That no Discouragement ought to be put upon Industry and Labour; that every Trade, productive of National Commerce, Wealth, and Prosperity, ought to be free and unrestrained; that Monopolies and Exclusions, *in the Case before us*, are both a *foolish*, and a *knavish* Scheme; because they are a Detriment to all, without being a private Advantage to any: And to sum up every thing, it hence appears, That Excellency of Work, Cheapness of Labour, right Application of Genius, good Morals in private Life, Plenty and Prosperity in regard to the Public, are the sure Consequences of universal Freedom, and universal Emulation: For such is the Order of Things, and the Course of Providence. Put therefore your Commercial Affairs into that Method, which is planned out by Providence itself; and then all will go well. As to our present *numerous*, and *contradictory* Laws concerning the Quality and Price of Goods, Hours of Working, Hire of Journeymen and Labourers, high Wages, oppressive Combinations, &c. &c. they are only the poor Efforts of *After-Thought* to prevent the ill Effects of *original* Blunders. And as they frequently do more harm than good, if *attempted to be executed*, our old Legislators may be very justly compared to an unskilful Physician, first stopping up one Sore, and then another, instead of correcting the ORIGINAL MALADY, from whence all proceeded.

SECTION II.

A Polity for opening those exclusive Companies, which relate to Foreign Trade.

FOREIGN Trade, as was observed before, is only another Name for carrying on a Commercial Intercourse between such Countries as are not under the same Government, or Legislature with ourselves. For the Trade between *South*, and *North Britain*, when these Kingdoms were under different Governments, was esteemed *foreign;* nay, it was so reputed, when only the Legislatures were different, though the Crowns were united: But when there was an Union both of Crowns, and Legislatures, then the Idea of Foreign Commerce immediately vanished. Moreover, if all *Europe* were *united* under *one great Monarch*, and *one Legislature*, the Trade carried on between the different Parts of this extended Monarchy, would not be considered under the Idea of Foreign Commerce. And this Reasoning is fully confirmed by Facts; for in regard to *Turky* (that immense Collection of numberless States, Kingdoms, and Republics, as they formerly subsisted, but now swallowed up in one great Gulph of *uniform* despotic Power) I say, in regard to this vast Empire, no one looks upon that Trade as foreign which is carried on between *Smyrna* and *Constantinople*, tho' the Distance of the one from the other is very great, and they formerly belonged to different Kingdoms, and are now situated in different Quarters of the World. In short, *Constantinople* is the Metropolis, and *Smyrna* is one of the Out-Ports; and the Trade between them answers to the same Idea in this vast Empire, as the Trade between *London* and *Bristol* doth in *Great Britain*. —But this Observation will have its farther Use in settling right Notions of National Industry and Riches, and in confuting popular Errors concerning the Ballance of Trade, and the Nature of Money, as we proceed in this Work.

THE Ideas of Foreign, and Domestic Commerce being thus adjusted, we must now observe, That all kinds of Exclusions sprung from the same Origin, *viz.* Despotic Power in the Prince, and dishonest Selfishness in the Subject: For these were the Parents of this monstrous Brood: The despotic Power of the Prince, I know not for what Reason, was called Prerogative; and this Prerogative was purchased by the monopolizing Subject either of the Prince himself, or of some favourite Courtier, in order to prey upon, and oppress his Fellow-Subjects with Impunity.—

Now, though we have at present but few exclusive Companies relating to Foreign Trade, yet we had formerly almost as many Companies for Trading abroad, as Trading at home.—And then indeed, the Exclusions being mutual, all were hurt, and none benefited; so that the Knavery of these Men was amply rewarded with their Folly; but at present, as other Exclusions are taken off, and the Trade thrown open, the Monopolies that still remain, are certainly Gainers; and consequently the Imputation of Folly doth not fall to their Share. But in order to avoid Repetitions as much as possible, let us now omit those Pretences which have been already confuted in the former Section, and pass on to such Apologies, as seem more particularly calculated for the Defence of exclusive Companies in a Foreign Trade.

I. "THEREFORE it is pretended, That exclusive Companies are necessary in order to maintain Forts, Governors, and Soldiers along the Coast;—otherwise these Establishments must be supported at the public Expence."

1st Answer, IT is not so clear a Point, that any Forts are necessary, if *National* Commerce is the only thing aimed at. For let me ask, To what *Commercial* Uses are these Forts to be applied? If they are in order to plant a Colony;—then the having a few Forts, without making farther Settlements, is only being at a continual Expence to answer no End. If they are to awe and bridle the Natives, It would be difficult to shew, what Advantage can accrue to Trade by insulting and disobliging the People you trade with: And sure I am, that that Shopkeeper would be deemed a strange kind of Creature, who would go and *bully* all his Customers, in order to bring Custom to his Shop.— But perhaps it may be said, That Forts are necessary, in order to prevent other European Nations from trading with these Countries: If so, then I ask, Do these Forts prevent any Nations whatever from trading, if they have a mind to trade? Do the *English* Forts, for Example, prevent the *French*, or the *French* the *English* from trading to *India?* Not at all. Nay, those European Nations which have not one Fort, find the Way to trade as well as others; witness the *Ostend* Company formerly; and the *Embden* and *Gottenburg* Companies at present. Moreover the *English* themselves have no Forts in *China*;—tho' the Country itself is at a much greater Distance, and our Trade thither of more Extent and Importance; and though the same Pretence might serve against the *Mandrins* of *China*, as against the *Nabobs* of *India*. Suppose therefore, that the *Flemish*, the *Spaniards*, the *Genoese*, the *Tuscans*, *Neapolitans*, *Venetians*, or any of our European Neighbours, were to lay aside their present unhappy Systems, and to act upon *true Commercial Principles*, what is their to hinder them from opening a Trade to *India?* And can any one pretend to say, that they could not possibly succeed, when he knows that the *Dutch* did succeed, without Forts themselves, and against all the Forts of the united Crowns of *Spain* and *Portugal*, the greatest Powers then in *Europe*, and the only European Powers in *India?* This is a notorious Fact, which cannot be controverted; nay, the *Dutch East India* Company was not then *incorporated:* And had they always acted according to their *original* Plan of being *Traders*, instead of *Conquerors*, they would have imployed a much greater Number of Shipping than they now do, they would have exported and imported larger Quantities of the Merchandises of the respective Countries, and they would have spread that Wealth among all the Individuals of the State, which, by being ingrossed and monopolized in a few Hands, hath done more real Mischief to the Vitals of their Constitution, than all their other Enemies put together. But indeed, the very Notion of having Forts for the Purposes of Commerce (where no Colonies are intended) is extravagant and foolish: For either these Forts must be so numerous and strong, as to oblige the Natives to submit to the Will and Pleasure of their Commanders; or else it is absurd to suppose, that on a Coast of perhaps a thousand Miles extent, half a Dozen little Forts, scattered up and down, can prevent the Natives from trading with those Customers, which will use them best. In short, the only Use of Forts is *Perquisites, Jobbs*, and *Salaries*; viz. *Perquisites* to the Clerks, Factors, and Supercargoes; *Jobbs* to the Directors; and *Salaries*, with all their Appendages, to the Governors, Sub-Governors, and so forth. Indeed Sir *Josiah Child* (with whom the Writer of these Sheets had the Honour to agree in *every other Commercial Point*, before ever he read his Book) seems to intimate, that Forts are absolutely necessary in the *East Indies.*—But if the Reader will please to recollect, that Sir *Josiah Child* was the Chairman and Director of the Company at home, and that his Brother, Sir *John Child*, was their Governor abroad;—And if he will also consult *Harris's Collection of Voyages and Travels*, Edit. 1744, Vol. I. Page 899 to 905, he will be at no Loss in guessing at the true Reason for this Partiality in Sir *Josiah Child* towards Forts and Military Establishments in the *East Indies.*

2d Answer, GRANTING even that Forts are necessary,—How doth this prove that exclusive Companies are necessary? and what immediate Reference have the one to the other? If it is said, That exclusive Companies defray the Expences of maintaining these Forts,—This certainly is a palpable Falshood; for the Companies no otherwise defray the Expences, than as our *Tax-Gatherers* here at home may be said to defray the Expences of the Kingdom. Other Persons pay, and they collect:—So it is in relation to exclusive Companies; they TAX the European Goods which they sell in *Asia*, and the *Asiatic* Goods which they sell in *Europe*, with an *higher Price* than the private Trader would do; and then apply a Part, and a very small Part, of this Tax to the Purposes of their Military Establishments, and put the rest in their Pockets. But of all Taxes, this is the worst and most pernicious in its Consequences; for a Tax upon the *Exporation of our own Manufactures*, is a Tax upon our own Industry and Labour; and a Tax upon the *Importation of raw Materials*, is no other than a Method of tying Mens Hands behind them, lest they should do themselves and their Country Service.— The only Tax of this Nature which is justifiable, is that which our *East India* Company lays upon Tea, and such other Articles and foreign Manufactures, as do not promote general Industry *at home*, so far the Tax is right: But then it ought to be considered, That in Proportion as these Articles are taxed by the Company, in the same Proportion is the public Revenue defrauded of its just Due. For certain it is, That were the Trade to *India* and *China* as free and unrestrained, as the Trade is to *Spain* and *Portugal*, the Consequence would be, that Tea and all other Articles would be sold to the Consumer much cheaper than they now are, even though the present Customs were doubled upon them. And thus would the Revenue itself be prodigiously increased; nay, the Temptations of smuggling Teas, and other *Asiatic* Commodities from *Denmark*, the Isle of *Man*, *France*, and *Holland*, would be proportionably decreased; and this likewise would prove another Source of great Gainings and Savings to the Nation. Now, after it hath been thus demonstrably proved, that the Nation, and not the Company, support these Forts even in Times of Peace, one might reasonably expect, that the Advocates for such Exclusions would have the Modesty to give up this Plea, and be silent for the future; but alas! the less they have of Reason and Argument on their side, the more liberal they are in confident Assertions, and specious Chicane, in order to dazzle and perplex an honest Mind. However, supposing even that exclusive Companies maintain their own Quarrels in Times of Peace, (*i. e.* in such Times, when there are no Quarrels, and consequently when no Forts are necessary, but by way of *Prevention*) the Question still returns, *viz.* Who maintains them in Time of War? And to whom is Recourse had in real Danger? — For surely a Monopolist himself would hardly say, That the Nation have been put to no Expence on this Account:—Unless he thinks, that we have so soon forgot, that, during the last War, numerous and expensive Squadrons, were continually sent to defend the Company's Forts and Settlements in the *East Indies*. Therefore, to put an End to this Article, let it be considered, that the present Argument stands thus; — In Times of Peace, our exclusive Companies impose the very worst, and most detrimental Taxes on *their Fellow-Subjects*, that any Nation can suffer; and in Times of War they are so far from assisting us, that they do not defend themselves, and expect that we should do it for them:—So just therefore, as well as severe, was that Sarcasm of the *Indian Nabob*, viz. "That if he had intrusted a Town of his to be defended by his dancing Girls, he would have expected them to have given a better Account of it, than the *English* gave of Fort *St George.*"

3d Answer, GRANTING still, that these Forts are necessary:—An unlucky Question here occurs, *viz.* To whom are they necessary? If it is said, That they are necessary to the exclusive Company, then let this Company injoy the sole Benefit of them. But if it is farther pretended, That private Adventurers cannot carry on their Trade without the Protection of such Forts and Castles, then the Dispute is ended, and the Difficulty solved at once, *viz.* Let the private Adventurers trade wherever they can, but *not dare* to come into that Town, Port, or Place, where the Company have any *Military* Establishment: Nay, let the Excluders be considered, what they really are, the perpetual and avowed Enemies of the rest of their Countrymen; and therefore let them act like the most cruel Enemies in *open War*, whenever they can catch the private Traders *within their Territories:*—Then it follows, That, *according to this Hypothesis*, the private Traders must necessarily give over their Pursuits; inasmuch as they *cannot* trade without Forts, and *dare not* make use of those of the Company. Therefore what need is there of any further Exclusion, since this Circumstance itself will effectually exclude them? And why so much Pains taken to deny the poor Adventurer the Liberty of a *free Trade*, when, after all, he could not use this Liberty, were it granted to him? Now if the Advocates for the *East India*, and the *Hudson*'s Bay Companies do really think, that the above Argument is a good one, let them rest their Cause upon it; and we will be contented: But if they only bring it by way of Flourish and Illusion, they must be told, That those Persons who are excluded from a free Trade, by virtue of the partial, malevolent Charters of Men, are not excluded by the impartial divine Benevolence from the common Benefit of Sense and Reason.

II. THE second Pretence is, "That exclusive Companies are necessary, in order to keep up the Price of our own Goods in foreign Markets, and the Price of foreign Goods at home; or, in other Words, to *sell dear*, and *buy cheap*."

1*st Answer*, WE freely allow all the Premises, for most undoubtedly all exclusive Companies were set up with this View, and *this View only*; But what Conclusions can be drawn from hence regarding national Commerce?   Is it in the first Place, for the Interest of this Nation, that we should sell *our Manufactures* dear to Foreigners?   And doth it follow in the second Place, that the Monopolists, who buy *raw Materials* cheap abroad, will sell them cheap at home?—*Sic Notus Ulysses?*

2*d Answer*, IF this Principle of selling dear, and buying cheap, by means of Monopolies, is a good Principle for national Commerce, then it follows, that all foreign Trade whatever ought to be put under Monopolies and Exclusions, as soon as possible.   For where there are *no Rivals* either in buying or selling, the Monopolist will certainly have it more in his Power to fix his own Price: The Question therefore is, What will the Nation gain by this Monopoly?   Will greater Quantities of our own Manufactures, that is, our own Labour be exported?   Will greater Quantities of Raw Materials, that is, Provisions for future Labour be imported?—If neither of these will be the Case, what are the Gains of the Monopolist, but the *Nation's Loss?*   And if we were to suppose, That the Trade to *Holland, Flanders, Spain, Portugal, Italy, Germany*, the *Baltic*, &c. &c. were to be put under a Set of exclusive Companies, would the Ports of *London, Bristol, Liverpool*, &c. be as crowded with Shipping as they are at present?   Would the interior Parts of the Kingdom, and the great manufacturing Places of *Birmingham, Manchester, Leeds, Halifax, Sheffield, Norwich, Bradford, Stroud*, &c. &c. I say, would these, and many such Places, be as rich, populous, and flourishing, as they now are?—A plain and honest Answer to these Questions, ends all the Controversy at once.

III. A third Pretence is, "That exclusive Companies are necessary, because they are a Means of preventing the Exportation of Coin and Bullion.   For, say their Advocates, if exclusive Companies buy Goods in a foreign Market at a less Price, and in less Quantities, than free Traders would do; the Consequence is that the Ballance of Trade is the more likely to turn in their Favour:—And therefore if the Ballance of the *East India* Trade is vastly in our Disfavour, even when under the Management of a Company; what would it be, were this Trade let loose to all Adventurers, who, by vying with, and rivalling one another, would certainly enhance the Price abroad, and bring the greatest Quantities home?"

1st Answer, IF this Bullion, or Coin, is carried out to purchase *Raw Materials*, for the Imployment of our People, the Trade is good and beneficial to the State, because it creates Industry, and promotes Labour. For Industry and Labour are the only real Riches; Money being merely the Ticket or Sign belonging to them; and the Use of Money is TO CERTIFY, that the Person possessing that Piece of Coin, hath likewise been in Possession of a *certain Quantity of Labour*, which he hath transferred into other Hands, and now retains the *Sign* of it.—Money therefore being nothing more than a Certificate of Labour, it necessarily follows, that national Industry will always command as many of these Certificates, *i. e.* as much Gold and Silver, as are wanted for these Purposes. For if *Great Britain* hath Industry, and another Country Money, the Industry of the one will soon extract the Money of the other, in Spite of every Law, Penalty, and Prohibition that can be framed. Nay, to go a Step farther, Suppose a Country *separated from all the World*, and yet abounding in the Metals of Gold and Silver; it is very possible, that this Country may be in a *starving* Condition; and the Inhabitants of it much poorer than the poorest Beggar in our Streets. But if you will suppose, that the Inhabitants are likewise *nationally* Industrious, being skilful Husbandmen, and ingenious Artificers; and then I ask, What can they want? For surely they may live in that Country as happily as human Nature was designed to do.—This being the Case, let us now proceed to suppose, that all the Gold and Silver in that Country was lost and annihilated in one Night; and what would be the Consequence, but plainly this, that the Inhabitants would then devise some other Ticket, or Counter, for the Exchange of mutual Industry, and the Circulation of Labour among one another?—Industry therefore being the only Riches of a State, what have we to fear from the Exportation of Gold and Silver, if it is to *promote Industry?*

2d Answer, IF the Coin, or Bullion, is carried out, in order to bring back such Things as tend to Idleness, and are preventive of national Industry, then the only proper Method of *checking* such a Trade is, to lay very high Duties upon the Commodities imported:—which will be itself a Means of increasing the Revenue, and of saving the Imposition of other Taxes. And thus may any Trade, not deserving national Incouragement, be checked and restrained to what Degree you please; and the Public avail itself in the mean time both by the Increase of Taxes, and the Discouragement of Idleness, Luxury, and expensive

Pleasures;—So far therefore, it is to be hoped, there is no need of having recourse to exclusive Companies.

3d Answer, IT is not true, that exclusive Companies are a Means of preventing the Extraction of Gold and Silver out of the Kingdom: —Nay, the Truth is, that they themselves are the *principal Cause* of it, as far as this Extraction is to be considered as a bad Thing.—For let us now inquire, what can be the Reason, that the Trade to the *East Indies* is a perpetual Drain of Gold, and more especially of Silver, from every Country in *Europe*, that trades thither? Indeed the great Monsieur *Montesquieu* is of Opinion, that Nature itself produces this Effect. "For, says he, the *Indians* have their Arts adapted to their manner of Living. Our Luxury cannot be theirs, nor their Wants ours. They go, in a great Measure, naked; such Cloaths as they have, the Country itself furnishes. And their Religion, which is deeply rooted, gives them an Aversion for those Things which serve for our Nourishment. They want therefore nothing but our Bullion, to serve as the Medium of Value; and for which they give us in return Merchandises, which the Frugality of the People, and the Nature of the Country, furnish them in great Abundance." *Spirit of Laws*, Book XXI. Chap. 1. Now, with all due Respect to the Opinion of so great a Man, I humbly conceive, that his supposed Solution of this Phenomenon is, by no means, satisfactory. For he supposes, that these People are devoid of Ambition or Avarice (call it which you please) in one Respect; and yet greatly influenced by it in another. They have no Desire or Ambition after European Goods of any sort, or kind; and yet they are continually at Work, and take prodigious Pains to acquire European Money.—This Account of human Nature is, in my poor Judgment, not a probable one. For why should the *Indians* be supposed to be devoid of all other Passions, but that of heaping up Money? And are there indeed no *European* Commodities, that might suit an *Eastern* Climate? What think you, for Example, of several Sorts of thin Stuffs, Linens, painted Linens and Cottons, Lawns, Cambrics, Thread Laces, Gold and Silver Laces, *Dresden* Works, Mignonettes, Ribbans, variety of Silks, and other Matters relating to Dress and Apparel? Surely the mere Heat of the Country can be no Bar against the Introduction of any of these Things, and a thousand Articles of the like Nature. Nor will it be any sufficient Answer to say, that these People will not wear any European Commodities, because they manufacture such Things in their own Country, as serve the same Ends. For this is contrary to every *tried* Principle in human Nature, and indeed is contrary to the known Practice of this very People. For they do ac-

tually consume many Pieces of warm *English* Broad Cloth, against the
Use of which much stronger Objections might be formed, were Men
to reason after this manner. I ask therefore again, Why are we to
suppose, that an *Indian* of Distinction would not be as proud of being
seen in a Robe of *English* Silks, Brocades, or Embroideries, painted
Linens or Cottons, and of being adorned with Lawns, Cambrics, Thread
Laces, Gold and Silver Laces, *Dresden* Works, Mignonettes, Ribbans,
&c. &c. as an European is to be seen in a right *India* Silk, and to be fond
of Callicoes, and Chintzes?—To this might be added, an infinite Variety
of Toys and Trinkets, and all the curious Manufactures of Gold and
Silver Vessels, Chase Works, and Jewelries; also the higher Manufactures of Brass, Iron, Steel, Glass, Paper, and Paper Hangings,
Tapestries, Watches and Clock Works, Cabinet Wares, and Inlaid
Works, Ingravings, Paintings, Globes, Maps, Mathematical Instruments,
&c. &c.—Granting therefore, that an *Indian* Climate forbids the Use of
Kerseys and Great Coats, and that their Religion will not allow of Wine
or Spirituous Liquors, yet both their Climate and Religion will admit of
such an infinite Variety of other Articles as might bring the Ballance of
Trade perfectly even, if not turn it in our Favour. And though we are to
suppose, that these Things are not made at present according to the
Indian Taste and Fashion, yet this Difficulty might soon be got over; for,
by the Help of a Pattern or two, our skilful Artificers might surely as
easily accommodate their Work to the Genius and Gout of the *Indians*,
as the Artificers of *China* do, in painting *English* Coats of Arms on *China*
Services. There is therefore nothing in the Reason and Nature of the
Thing, why it should come so universally to pass, that the Trade to the
East Indies should be a continual Drain of Coin and Bullion.—But as
the Fact is undoubtedly so, we must now endeavour to account for it
upon other Principles. Let us therefore lay this down as a Maxim to
build upon, *That Cheapness is a Temptation to buy, and Dearness a
Discouragement.* And hence it will follow, that in Proportion as European Goods are rendered *cheap* in *India*, in that Proportion the Inhabitants will come more and more to use, and wear them. Now, when
exclusive Companies are set up in *Europe* with a quite *opposite* Intent,
viz. To raise the Price of European Goods as high, and make them as
DEAR as possible, what must be the Consequence, but deterring and
discouraging the *Indians* from buying them?—And by being deterred in
general, they become perfect Strangers to many particular Sorts; so
that the whole Trade is confined to those few Articles, which the Monopolists know and experience, will find a Vent. Add to this, that every

Man, Monopolist or other, counts his Gains principally on what he *sells*, not on what he *buys:* But the Difference between them is this, that the free Trader, surrounded with *Rivals* and *Competitors*, sells as *cheap*, and as *much* as he can; reckoning his Gains by the *Quantity* sold, according to the old Proverb, *Many Littles make a Mickle:* Whereas the unrivalled Monopolist sells as *dear* as possible; and therefore cannot sell *much*. This being the Case, the judicious Reader will plainly see, that the Contest between *Great Britain* and *India* for the Ballance of Trade, is not carried on upon equal Terms: Because the *Indian*, who is surrounded with Rivals, sells to the exclusive Company as cheap as he can possibly afford, in order to secure the Custom to himself; but the exclusive Company acts upon a quite different Plan in regard to the *Indian*. Thus the Monopolist, and the free Trader, though both their Aims are Gain, yet pursue quite contrary Measures to obtain it. And the Consequence will ever be, *cæteris paribus*, that the free Trader shall carry the Ballance from the Monopolists. Put the Case therefore, that the Trade to *Portugal*, where we have at present so great a Ballance in our Favour, was erected into a Monopoly like that of the *India* Company;—But that all the *Portuguese* were *at full Liberty*, unrestrained by Civil Tyranny, or Ecclesiastical Bigotry, and all *Rivals* in trading with the *English*; and then I ask any reasonable honest Man, whether he doth not think, that the Ballance in our Favour would immediately lessen? Nay, whether he would not have Cause to fear, that in a few Years it would turn against us?—Now, were every Nation in *Europe* to trade with *Portugal* through the disadvantageous Medium of exclusive Companies, *Portugal* would then become, what *India* is now. Indeed this Matter is so reducible to the Affairs of common Life, that it may be illustrated by a very familiar Instance: Let the Town of *Birmingham* therefore, and the City of *London* contend for the Ballance of Trade, respecting each other: But let the City give up all its Right of free Trade to one Man, or Set of Men, called a Company. Now this exclusive Company neither will, nor can sell their Goods so cheap, as private Adventurers would gladly do: They *will not*, because they know, that they have the whole Market to themselves, no other Citizen daring to rival, or *undersell* them: They *cannot*, because of the vast Expence they are at, in Fees, Jobbs, and Salaries, and in all the Pickings and Squeezings from the Governor in Chief down to the lowest Porter, and Sweeper of the Storehouse: Nay, they must have **peculiar Sorts* of Waggons for the Carriage

---

* This refers to the *peculiarly expensive* methods of fitting up Ships for the *East India* Service, and the exorbitant Charges of the Voyage.

of their Goods; and their very Carriers and Drivers will stand them in double the Expence, they would do to other People. Therefore upon all these Accounts, the *few* Articles which they *can* sell, must be at an exorbitant Price;—perhaps *Cent. per Cent.* to what they otherwise would have been. This being the Case, the *London* Monopolists carry down Goods to the Value only of two thousand Pounds, were the Trade open; but as it is shut up, and confined, we must call the Value four thousand Pounds: The Goods are therefore sold at that Price; and the Money vested in the Manufactures of *Birmingham*, in order to make a back Freight, and profitable Return. But the *London* Monopolists finding these Manufactures so extremely cheap, and knowing, that they can dispose of them to prodigious Advantage, when brought home, are tempted to lay out four thousand Pounds more; that is, to carry out Coin, or Bullion, to that Amount. And thus it comes to pass, that the Ballance will ever be against the confined Trade, in favour of the free. Whereas, had the Trade on both sides been equally unrestrained, both would have strove to have sold the most as to Quantity, and the cheapest as to Price; and by that Means, would have created a mutual Imployment for each other. In a word, Where the greater Numbers are imployed, there lies the Ballance;—Such a Ballance, I mean, as only deserves the Public Regard, THE BALLANCE OF INDUSTRY; for Money without Industry, is an Hurt, not a Blessing.

IV. A fourth Pretence is, "That exclusive Companies are necessary in order to impress Awe and Respect on the Inhabitants of distant Countries: For, say their Advocates, were the Trade to be carried on by private Adventurers, or voluntary Associations, the Chiefs and petty Princes, more especially the *Rajahs* and *Nabobs* of *India*, would despise, insult, and maletreat single, unconnected Merchants, and oblige them to be for ever sending them Presents. But exclusive Companies, by supporting Governors, Sub-Governors, &c. make a great Display of Royal State, and Dignity; and the Appearance of these Things strike a Terror and Reverence in the Natives, and prevent these, and such like Impositions."

1st Answer, THIS Pretence of the Advantage of Governors, Sub-Governors, &c. is nothing else, but the former Apology for Forts and Military Establishments, put into a new Dress. And the Plea having been once confuted already, now makes its Appearance in another Form. But we will trust the judicious Reader with what has been said on that Part of the Subject, under the first Article.

2d Answer, THOSE Gentlemen, who insist so peremptorily on the

Necessity of keeping up the Appearance of great State and Dignity, in the Persons and Retinue of their Governors in *India*, have forgot to tell us, how comes it to pass, that these Things are more necessary in later, than in former Ages? For the Merchants of *Egypt*, of the *Roman* Empire, of *Palmira*, of the *Greek* Empire, and after them the *Saracens* and *Egyptians*, acted as *mere Merchants*, without any one Governor, Fort, or Military Establishment whatever. And yet we do not find, throughout all History, that the *Indian* Kings or Princes used them the worse for being thus without State or Pomp; nor did they maletreat these *unconnected* Merchants, but gave them all possible Incouragement to come, and trade among them. In short, Governors, and Sub-Governors, Forts and Military Establishments, were never thought of till the *Portuguese* introduced them. And what was their Motive for so doing?—Not to shelter Merchants, not to protect Trade, not to export a larger Quantity of their own Manufactures, and import Raw Materials, not to redress Wrongs, and to do themselves Justice; not all, or any of these: For none of these Things are so much as pretended by their own Advocates:—But their real View was, (as set forth by their own Historians) to make Conquests both in a *temporal* and a *spiritual* Sense; Conquests for the King, and for the Pope; having received a Commission from both for so doing. This now is the righteous, the blessed, the *Commercial* Origin of *East India* Governments, Forts and Castles! And yet bad as this is, the Portuguese had no exclusive Companies *at that Juncture*; their Trade was *free, and open to all their Subjects*; nor did the Notion of a Joint-stock Company and exclusive Privileges, obtain in *Europe* till many Years afterwards, when the Avarice of the *English* and *Dutch East India* Adventurers suggested this Conspiracy against the natural Rights and Liberties of the rest of their Countrymen; as shall be speedily shewn under proper Articles.

3d Answer, IF the Appearance of external Splendor and Royal Dignity is so necessary to the Well-being of Trade,—may we be permited to ask, How comes it to pass, that other Nations, who cannot make this Display, yet trade as freely, and beneficially without it, as the *English* themselves with all their Pomp and Pageantry. The *Ostend* Company, for Example, did trade, (maugre all the Endeavours of the *Dutch, French*, and *English* to the contrary, both in *India*, and in *Europe*) to as much Advantage as any others; and they would have remained flourishing Traders to this Day, had there been no other Difficulties to obstruct them. The *Embden* and *Gottenburg* Companies likewise are not in Possession of one Government in all *India*;—unless Factories, and Merchants Compting-

Houses are to be honoured with that sounding Name. For they have
no Towns to govern, or Castles to command throughout the Country.
Nay, the *English* themselves have no Governors in *China*; and are
obliged to appear with as little Display of Royal State, as any *unconnected* Merchants whatever.   Moreover what shall we say of the *East
India* Company itself, even in *India?*   Did they make this grand Appearance at first setting out, a Time of all others the most necessary so to do?
Or is their subsequent Greatness to be ascribed to that Awe and Reverence, with which the Natives were seized at their first Appearance?—
So far from it, that scarce any thing could have had a more mean and
paultry Aspect, than this mighty Company, when first they came to
trade in *India*.   For their whole Fleet consisted only of* one Ship of six
hundred Tons, another of three hundred, two others of two hundred, and
another of one hundred and thirty, making one thousand four hundred
and thirty Tons in all; a Force so little, that many private Merchants
have at present, upon their own single Account, double the Tonnage of
Shipping.   And as to the Cargo, the total Value of the Out-set of the
Voyage rose no higher than to twenty six thousand Pounds Sterling;—
which Sum might perhaps go as far, in those Days, in buying a Cargo
fit for *India*, as twelve or fourteen thousand Pounds would do at present:—I say *perhaps* it would go as far; for certain it is, that it could not
go much farther, the Prices of Goods proper for the *East Indies* being,
in many Instances, about *Cent. per Cent.* and in some Cases *three hundred
per Cent.* CHEAPER now than in the Days of Queen *Elizabeth*.   In short,
there are many fishing Towns now in *England*, that might, by a voluntary
Association, fit out as great a Fleet, and as richly laden, as this which
first sailed to the *East Indies*.

   4th Answer, BUT after all, if Forts and Castles, and their Excellencies
the Governors, with their pompous Train and Retinue are so very necessary, then it follows, that the Want of them is a Loss, which can fall only
upon the free Trader, and not upon the Company.   Why therefore are
the Company so anxious in a Point, in which their own Interest is not
at all concerned?   And doth it not look a little suspicious, that they
should debar the free Trader from making a Trial, one Experiment at
least, when they know he cannot succeed?—Perhaps they may tell us,
(as some indeed have told) that this is the Effect of their pure Benevolence and Good-will; for they, generous Souls! are unwilling to see their

---

   * This *exclusive* Charter was given by Queen *Elizabeth* the 31st of *December*, 1600,
two Years before the *Dutch exclusive* Charter.—The Motives for granting both which
will soon appear.

dear Fellow-Subjects aiming at such Projects as must prove their Ruin. Indeed, indeed this is too much!—And, to let them see that all this *disinterested* Benevolence, and pure Good-will are thrown away upon an ungrateful, disbelieving People, we will, in our turn, set forth our own Sense of the Matter: In the *first* Place, We are firmly persuaded, that if there never had been a Fort in *India*, the Trade had been infinitely more extensive than it is: And in the *second*, We are so far from dreading the Oppression or Violence of the Princes and great Men of the Country, that we should think our Traders much safer under their Protection, than under that of any Monopolizing Company whatever. And in support of this Assertion, let an Appeal be made to the Histories of every European Government in *India*; particularly to that of our own, as it was published in the last Edition of *The great Collection of Voyages*, Vol. I. Page 873, *Lond.* 1744: For there the Reader will find a Relation of such horrid Scenes of Lust, Avarice, and Cruelty, as will soon give him a Disgust for such kind of political Institutions. And as to the Use of Military Establishments, in order to preserve Peace and good Neighbourhood between the Natives and Europeans,—they are so far from contributing to this good End, that the contrary is evident beyond Contradiction; and indeed is acknowledged by all our own Historians. Nay, it must be confessed, if we will speak impartially, that for one Instance, in which the Natives have been the Aggressors, the European Governors have given the Provocation fifty times. And therefore when one considers what a Complication of Treachery, Insolence, and Oppression, these Strangers have been guilty of, for the Space of one hundred and fifty Years and upwards, towards the innocent and peaceable Proprietors of the Country, it might really be expected, that all the *Indian* Nations would unite, and rise as one Man (which they certainly would have done, had their separate Interests been more reconcileable) in order to expel these bloody Tyrants and Usurpers. In short, the real Fear of the exclusive Company is this,—Not that the private Traders would be ruined, but that the *Indians* would prefer dealing with them, rather than with the Agents of the Company: For they know very well, that the *Indians*, in such a Case, would both buy their Goods upon better Terms, and be better treated. And then their Governors might reign over the naked Walls of their empty Forts and Castles, without Trade, and without Inhabitants.

V. THE last Pretence is, "That exclusive Companies must certainly be right, because all Nations have made use of them, preferably to any other Method. And what is thus universal, seems to have some Foundation in Reason, and Nature."

1st Answer, IF this Reasoning were to hold good, the Consequence is, that no new Improvement could ever be made. For every new Improvement, Alteration of Measures, or Reformation of Conduct, suppose, in their own Nature, that the old Practice was very different.

2d Answer, THE Presumption, that exclusive Charters *must be right*, because they have so universally prevailed in *Europe*, is effectually overthrown by tracing the original Motives for their Institution. And to elucidate this Matter, we will pitch upon the greatest, and most successful Company that ever existed, *viz.* The *Dutch* Company trading to the *East Indies*. Now in all these Institutions, the *Grantors* may have one Motive, and the *Grantees* another: And therefore the fairest Way will be to present the Reader with a View of both; in order that he may make his own Reflections.

THEREFORE in regard to the Views of the *Grantors*, viz. The States General,—that truly great and honest Patriot* *John De Wit*, explains their Motives in a few Words; *viz.* "The erecting of the *East* and *West India* Companies was [at the Time of their Institution] a NECESSARY EVIL; because our People *would be* trading in, and about such Countries, where *our Enemies were too strong for particular Adventurers:* So that this seemed to be necessary in all Respects, to lay the Foundation of that Trade by a *powerful, armed Society*. And seeing this Country, ingaged in a War against the King of *Spain, had need of using all its Strength*, it was *very prudently* done to erect those two Societies." Here, you see, in the first Place, he joins the *East* and *West India* Trade together; and supposes, that exclusive Companies were equally necessary, *at that Juncture*, for the carrying on of both: For his own strong, and emphatical Words, are, "That Companies, at the Beginning, were *necessary Evils*." In the next Place, he explains the Reason, why he thought them necessary at that particular Juncture, *viz.* "That their Enemies the *Spaniards* (being then likewise in Possession of *Portugal*, and the *Portuguese* Settlements) were too strong for private Adventurers; and that the States General, being ingaged in a War with the King of *Spain, had need of using all their Strength*."—The plain Meaning of which is this, That nothing but the greatest Exigency of State could have justified these *necessary Evils*; and that their High Mightinesses took this indirect Method of taxing their Subjects for carrying on a War in all Places at once, against the common Enemy, rather than of levying more Taxes in

* *De Wit's* true Interest and political Maxims of *Holland*, Lond. 1702. Chap. XIX. *viz.* Compulsion of Traffic.

the ordinary Way; which they must have done, had they fitted out additional Fleets to support and protect the private Adventurers in the *East* and *West Indies*.   Now as the Subjects of *Holland* were, at that Juncture, loaden with Taxes beyond what is well conceivable; and the Emissaries of *Spain*, in the Heart of the Republic, taking all Advantages, and endeavouring to make the Revolters weary of their new Government;—perhaps it was expedient at that *critical* Time to practise a little Deception upon the Understandings of their People: I say, *a Deception*; for such, in Fact, is every exclusive Company, because it is a Tax, and a very grievous one, nay the most pernicious of all others: But as it proceeds *indirectly*, and *obliquely*, it escapes the Notice of the Vulgar, and is not felt, but in its remote and general Consequences.   However, the above Account of the Matter shews plainly, that according to the Judgment of this great and honest Statesman, the Trade both to the *East* and *West Indies* ought to have been intirely free and unconfined, had not the aforementioned unhappy Circumstances made a *temporary* Exclusion necessary.   Now, as we all know, that a Trade to the *West Indies* can be carried on without an Exclusion, it follows of Course, that upon removing *the one only Impediment* that to the *East Indies* can be carried on, and ought to be as free and open as the other.   Nay this great Man is very express, and I may say, *prophetical* in his Observations: For his Words are, "But that Trade [to the *East* and *West Indies*] being now *so well settled*, we may justly make it a Doubt whether the said Companies ought any longer to continue on the same Foot.—For it is certain, that the *first moving Reason* of those Grants to them, which was the War with the King of *Spain*, NOW CEASETH; and that in Case of any new War with that People, they would no longer be formidable to us, but we to them.   And secondly, as it is well known, that it was necessary at first to make some Conquests upon the *Spice Islands of the said Enemy*, because the more Lands they [the Company] conquered, the more Right and Ability they would acquire to the Trade which might happen in those Parts: So it cannot be denied, that when these good and necessary Conquests are made, the Grounds and Maxims of the Prosperity of the said Companies begin to *jostle* and *oppugn* the general Good of this Country; which is manifestly known to consist in a *continual Increase of our Manufactures*, Traffic, and Freight-Ships: Whereas nevertheless the true Interest of such Companies consists in seeking the Benefit of all the Members, even with foreign, as well as our own Manufactures, and (to the great Prejudice of all other our Inhabitants) by importing Manufactures, and other Mechanic Works into this Country, and vend-

ing them throughout *Europe*; and, in short, ☞ By making the greatest
Profit with the least Traffic and Navigation. As it is acknowledged,
that if the *East India* Company can gain more by importing *Japan*
Garments, *Indian* Quilts and Carpets, *&c.* than *raw Silk;*—or if the
Company, by causing a Scarcity of Nutmegs, Mace, Cloves, Cinnamon,
&c. could so raise the Price of them, that they might gain as much by
one hundred Lasts, as by a *thousand**; we ought not then to expect that
those raw Silks, and unnecessary and great Disbursements which they
are at, should cause a greater Trade and Navigation than those hundred
Lasts would just require, but that they would rather, to shun greater
Traffic and Navigation, *destroy* all the Superfluity they have in the
Indies. And it can be as little denied of such Companies, that the more
Lands they conquer, the more of their Stock they must necessarily spend
for the Preservation and Defence of such Lands †; and the more Domin-
ion they have, the less they are able to mind and augment their Traffic.
Whereas, on the contrary, our particular Inhabitants by those manifold
conquered strong Holds and Lands, would have so much the more
Conveniency and Security to trade in the *Indies.* We have now, to say
no more, quite lost our *open* Trade of *Guiney*, and that of Salt in the
West Indies, which were heretofore so considerable, *by the erecting of the*
West India *Company:* And the Mischief which was done to the King of
Spain in the *West Indies*, is recoiled back, and fallen upon ourselves:
So that we cannot cry up that Company, who have bound the Hands of

---

* The Translation here is strangely perplexed and obscure; but the Author's Meaning is plain enough; *viz.* That if the Company could get more by importing Manufactures, than Raw Materials, they would certainly import Manufactures; and would
likewise sell their Raw Materials as dear as possible. Moreover in regard to Spices,
his Remark is, That the Company would rather *destroy nine Parts in ten*, than be at the
Expence of carrying the nine Parts home, and then selling them for no more, than they
now sell the Tenth. Thus do the Company, in this single Article, imploy no more than
a *tenth Part* of the Shipping, Sailors, Storehouses, Porters, *&c. &c.* which an *open, free*
Trade would do.

† Here again is another strange Perplexity of Stile: But the Sense is very strong and
nervous: *viz.* That Trade and Conquest are two different Things, the latter being
quite incompatible with the former. If therefore Conquests are to be made, such Conquests ought to be undertaken by the Public; and then secured, and improved by planting Colonies; in short, *suum cuique*, the State to conquer, and the Subject to trade;
and a Conquest without a View of planting a Colony, is an Absurdity both in Trade,
and Politics. Hence therefore it follows, that in settling Colonies, the State should give
an intire Liberty to all the Inhabitants of the Mother Country to trade with the Colonies; for this is the only Way of strengthening, and supporting both.—Such is the Argument of this judicious and unprejudiced Writer: And I will venture to say, it is *unanswerable*.

particular Men, and made War instead of Traffic, unless at least they in the mean Time suffer all our Inhabitants freely to trade in all their Conquests. On the contrary, that Company hath *impoverished many of our good Inhabitants.* Whereas by an open Trade, and *consequently well settled Colonies*, we should not only, with small Charge, have easily defended those vast Lands of *Brazil, Guiney, Angola, St Thomas*, &c. against all foreign Power, but (which is more considerable) have been able to carry on a very great Trade with our own Nation, without Fear that any foreign Potentate should seize our Ships, Goods, or Debts, to which those *Hollanders* that trade only in *Europe* are continually exposed. And how profitable and secure that Trade would have been, may easily be apprehended, if it be well considered, that the said Lands yield the best Sort of Commodities that are in request over all *Europe*, and are not to be had so good elsewhere, *viz.* Sugar, Brazil-Wood, Elephants Teeth, Gold, &c. and that which those Inhabitants have need of in return, *Holland* could, for the most Part, have supplied them with, as Victuals, Drink, and Apparel; yea even with most Materials for building Houses, Ships, &c. whereas now we are deprived of all these Advantages. ☞ This is the ordinary Fruit and Punishment of *Monopolies*, and *Conquests*, which, *for want of Colonies*, they must keep up at a continual great Charge. May our *East India* Company consider this effectually, ere it be too late!"

THUS far this great Man: But alas! his patriotic Wish will never be regarded by an exclusive Company; for their Views are, to sacrifice the Good of their Country to their own Interest, and to bring every other Set of Members of the Commonwealth *so low*, as not to be able to oppose their Designs. However, we see from hence the original Motive of the States General in granting these Exclusions, and the subsequent Uses which the Monopolists made of them. Perhaps therefore it would have been better, that the States General had submitted to the *temporary* Inconveniences arising from the *Spanish* War, rather than to have sought to have redressed them by establishing exclusive Companies. For that *supposed* Remedy is only the changing of a *present* Evil, of no great Extent, for one that is *future*, and every Day extending, and increasing. Let this therefore be a Lesson to all States hereafter how they grant Monopolies, if they really regard the Good of their People. For the Establishment of an exclusive Company, *be the Motive what it will*, may be compared to the Hedge-Hog in the Fable; who at first was a most humble Petitioner to have one Night's hospitable Lodging in another's Apartment; but when he had once got Possession, he set up his Bristles, and was too strong to be removed.

BUT it is now high time, that we should take a View of the Motives of the Petitioners, or *Grantees*, in this Affair. It appears from the *Dutch* Histories, that at the Beginning of the Republic, several Persons entered into voluntary Associations, to carry on a Trade with *India*; and they not only made successful Voyages, (which by the By is a plain Proof, that a Trade can be carried on without an exclusive Company) but also beat their Enemies, the *Spaniards* and *Portuguese* in several Rencounters. "But * while their Navigation continued to be thus successful, and the Trade of the *Indies* flourished more and more, there happened an Accident that discontinued their former good Fortune, and threatned Ruin to the whole; I mean the Plurality of Companies [voluntary Associations] that were formed, and the sorry Understanding that was between them. Oftentimes many of them fitted out Ships for the same Port which lowered the Price of their Goods, and discouraged the Sailors. The States General being acquainted with these Inconveniences, called a Meeting at the *Hague* of the Directors of the Companies both of *Holland* and *Zealand*, and obliged them to unite in one Body for the future, to which their High Mightinesses joined their Consent and Authority. The Treaty that was then agreed upon, was confirmed by a Patent from the Sovereign Power, for twenty one Years, commencing from the Date, viz. *March* 20, 1602. The Patent being given out, the Company became a very considerable Body, and made a joint Stock of 6,600,000 Livres," which, I suppose, is about 300,000 *l.* Sterling.

HERE, Reader, the Truth is come out at last:—There were too many *Rivals* in the Trade! —The Price of European Goods was lowered in *India!* —And, dreadful to relate! by the coming of different Ships to the same Port, the Natives had the Liberty of trading with those that used them best! After this plain Demonstration, dare any Man mutter a Word against Monopolies and Exclusions? —For who is so blind, but must see the Necessity of them?—Alas, for want of these necessary Establishments, our Merchants trading to *Spain* and *Portugal* are often in the same Plight with the above mentioned honest *Dutchmen:* That is, for want of a *good Understanding among themselves*, they often send Ships to the same Port, and lower the Prices to that Degree, that the *Spaniards* and *Portuguese* are tempted to purchase ten times the Quantities of Woolen Cloths, and other *English* Manufactures, than they would have done, had the *Trade been properly managed:* Nay, the Evil is still greater; for they bring home such large Quantities of *Spanish* Wool, Oils, Iron, Steel, Dye Stuff, and other raw Materials, *that the Market is overstocked:*

---

* The great Collection of Voyages, Book I. Chap. ii. Sect. 6. Page 927.

And (Reader you *must* believe me, for I speak the true mercantile Dialect) *Trade is not worth carrying on, there is so little to be got by it.*—However, it is by means of this *bad Trade*, this Trade that is *not worth carrying on*, that the Nation subsists in its present Plenty, and is increasing in Wealth, and Manufactures every Day. And were you to make the Trade *worth carrying on*, in their Sense of the Word, you would soon have the Comfort of sinking the Value of Lands to twelve or fourteen Years purchase (as they were formerly) and of raising the Interest of Money to eight or ten *per Cent.* For these are the Blessings that always attend Monopolies and Exclusions, and Trades that are *worth carrying on.* Indeed the *Turky* Company in the Year 1718, made a noble Effort towards bringing these Blessings upon us, as speedily as possible. For they came to a very pious Resolution, in a general Court, held for that Purpose, the 20th of *March*, which was, *To prevent the Exportation of all English Manufactures, and the Importation of raw Materials for two whole Years and a Quarter:* And, like true Patriots, they honestly and bravely declared, *That this was done with an Intent of raising the Price of English Cloth in Turky, and of Turky raw Silk in England.*—Therefore with this Sample of *exclusive, monopolizing Patriotism*, let us (being sufficiently tired) conclude the Scene, and leave the indignant Reader to make his own Reflections, which, I make no doubt, he will not spare.

* * * * * * * * * * * * * * * * * *

AND now, after all this Pro-ing and Con-ning, and wading through the Shoals of Absurdity and Nonsense, and sounding the various Depths of Chicane and Dishonesty, I hope to be somewhat the shorter as to what is to follow.

I. THEREFORE, in regard to the *Turky* Company, the late Attempts towards opening this Exclusion were greatly defeated by the obstinate Opposition of its few Friends and Advocates. For indeed a very few, by dint of teazing, objecting, perplexing, and other the like honest Arts, have it in their Power, in such a Constitution as ours, to tire out the Patience of the many, and to gain those Advantages by assiduous Attendance and perpetual Opposition, to which they have no other Merit, or Pretence. But this Matter will appear the more fully by entering into Particulars.

FIRST, It was the Design and Aim of the Friends of Liberty, and an open Trade, to have demolished all Pretences of Fines of Admission. But alas! they could only obtain a Mitigation; the Fine being still 20 *l.* which, together with other Items, amount to 22 *l.* 12 *s.* 6 *d.* Now a Fine, in the Nature of the Thing, supposes a Punishment for having done something wrong; I ask therefore, What Crime is there in exporting the Labour and Industry of our own People, and importing raw Materials to keep them still imployed?—A Crime, I grant it is against the Monopolist and Excluder, and a very unpardonable one; but, with Submission, I do not apprehend it is any against the State.   However, the Answer is, That this Fine is necessary in order to pay the Expences the Company must be at; and at the same Time is so very small, as to prevent no Person of Substance from ingaging in the Trade, if he is inclined.—As to the Article of Expences, that shall be taken into Consideration in another Place; but in regard to the Smallness of the Fine, as being no Discouragement to Trade, I deny it absolutely.   For every Burden is a Discouragement, especially in a new Trade, where the Mind is ballancing, whether it shall ingage in it or not.   Put the Matter therefore home; and suppose, that every Man was obliged to pay a Fine of 20 *l.* before he *commenced* an Exporter of *English* Manufactures to *Spain*, or *Portugal*, or the *American* Plantations;—and then I ask, Can you think, that the Number of Exporters, or the Quantities exported, would be as great as they are at present?—If they would not in that Case, why should you expect them in this?   Besides, there is a wide Distinction to be made between opening a new Trade, and ingaging in an old one, well known and established.   And, in Fact, the *Turky* Trade is so little extended, that it may still be considered, in a great Measure, as unknown: And though the Probability of Success is very great, yet in Cases of Risques and Hazards, tell me, where is the Merchant that will give 20 *l.* for *a Licence*, merely for the Sake of making Discoveries and Experiments?—In short, a new Trade is necessarily *precarious* in one degree or other; and the old Stagers will throw all the Difficulties they possibly can, in the Way of a new Adventurer.   Therefore he ought rather to be assisted, than discouraged, by the Legislature.   For a new Trade is like a Nursery of young Trees: And as the sturdy Oak was once a tender Plant, I ask, Which, in your Opinion, is the best Policy,—To cherish and fence it round, while it is *young*; or to nip it in the Bud, and destroy it, before it can gather Strength?

SECONDLY, The Tax laid upon Exports, and payable in *Turky*, is a most unreasonable and absurd Duty.   For it is a Tax upon Industry and Manufactures; and is the unhappy Remains of those antient Blunders, under which the whole Nation formerly groaned.—I am well aware, that the present Pretence is, that this Tax must be levied in order to defray the Charges of keeping an Ambassador at the Port, and Consuls in other Cities: And therefore, if the Company did not take this Method of taxing themselves, the Burden would be laid upon the Public, which hath Burdens enough already. Here now lies the Delusion! As if a Tax upon Industry and Manufactures was no Burden to the Public! And as if the Nation itself did not pay the Tax, because the Tax-Gatherers are not called Excisemen, or Customhouse Officers! Strange Infatuation! For if this Tax had been levied, and paid in our own Customhouses at the Time of Exportation, every Man in the Kingdom would have acknowledged, in that Case, that it was a Tax upon the Public;—and (what is much worse) a Tax upon the *Manufacturing* Part of the Public, laid upon them at the very time in which they ought to be tax-free, viz. *while they are at work:* (Indeed a Tax upon them, *while they are idle,* would have been a good Thing; and the more of such Taxes, the more industrious Men would be, and consequently the *Richer*) Therefore this being the Case, surely the Nature of the Tax remains the same, whether the Sum is collected in *Turky*, or in *England*; and, say what you will, a Tax upon the Exports of Manufactures, is the heaviest, most oppressive, and most impoverishing Tax you can possibly lay. But

THIRDLY, This Power granted to the Company of taxing the Manufactures of the Kingdom, brings on another great Inconvenience along with it; *viz.* The Power of paying the Ambassadors and Consuls. For the Governors, or Directors of the Company are, of Course, in the sole Possession of this Power. And a very moderate Insight into human Nature, will suffice to teach us, that such a Prerogative carries a vast Influence along with it; An Influence the more dangerous, as there is no guarding against it by private Regulations, or detecting it in a legal Way; there being thousands of Instances, wherein the Ambassadors, and Consuls can favour one Set of Men, and prejudice the others, without doing any thing that a Court of Judicature can punish, or take hold of. This being the Case, whom, do you think, will they be so likely to favour, as the Men who can *accelerate*, or *retard* the Payment of their Salaries, and can always find out plausible Reasons for making them *additional Gratuities*, by way of Recompense for their *extraordinary* Services, and signal Merits? or, on whom will they turn the dark Side of their Horizon, but on those, who are not in the Interest of, perhaps in Opposition to the Governors and Directors? In short, this single Article, were there no others, hath a necessary Tendency towards throwing the whole Trade into the Hands of the Merchants belonging to the Metropolis, and excluding all the Out-Ports. Judge therefore, whether you can call such a Trade a *free one*. But as in other Cases one Evil begets another, so it is in this; for

FOURTHLY, The same Pretence of levying the Tax upon the Members of the Company, hath brought on a very remarkable Regulation, or By-Law, for shutting up the Trade, even since the last Act of Parliament was past for opening it. For it is such a Law, as in its obvious Consequences, defeats the whole Intention of the Act.—The By-Law referred to, as I am credibly informed, is to this Effect, *viz.* That all Members shall give in a List of the several Particulars they send abroad, in order that the Duties may be collected on them, when they arrive in *Turky*. Now the latent Mischief which will necessarily result from this Order, is the following, That the governing Part of the Company will always discover what kind of Trade is carried on by every other Member; whereas the other Members, especially those of the Out-Ports, will not have the same Advantage over them. And I appeal to every sensible, mercantile Person, whether he would chuse to inform his *Rival* of every Branch of Trade he is carrying on, and of every *new* Attempt he intends to make, at the same time that his Rival conceals all from him?—And whether he doth not think, that this single Disadvantage is not of prodigious Consequence in the Course of Trade, and hath an immediate Tendency towards a Monopoly, and Exclusion?

FIFTHLY, Another Difficulty still remaining is, The Prohibition against imploying any Agents or Factors, but *English-born* Subjects. For why should this Prohibition still continue? and what Interest can it serve but that of a Monopoly? If *English-born* Factors will vend the greatest Quantity of *English* Labour in *Turky*, they ought to have, and certainly will have the Preference, because they are best known at home; and it will be the Interest of the Exporter to imploy them. But if *English* Agents aim at great Profits upon small Exports, they are the worst Commercial Enemies the *English* Nation can have; and therefore deserve no kind of Preference, or Incouragement. Besides, every exclusive Privilege is a Temptation to do amiss; and when *English* Factors abroad know that their Constituents at home are restrained from imploying any but themselves, they are tempted to do such Things, and to make such had Uses of their Power, as never would have entered into their Heads, bad the Trade been free.

SIXTHLY, The Oath of Secrecy is another strange Absurdity still remaining. For what is a Member of the Company to keep secret? nay, why is he put at all under such an Obligation? Is he to keep secret, That he will sell as cheap as he can afford; and give as good a Price to the Natives for their Goods, as any other of his Rivals? If this is the Secret, it were better it were published on the House Top.—But undoubtedly the Reader expects to hear of Secrets of another kind; and he shall not be disappointed: For the Secrets referred to in this Oath are the *Secrets of Trade*, and the *Secrets of an exclusive Company*; of which the following Rule, or Order, may probably serve as a goodly Specimen; which you will find in their Books under the Article of BATTULATIONS; *viz.* "It was resolved and ordered, that as it is very expedient to avoid as much as possible the having Recourse to the Tribunals of the Country, in all Matters of Commerce in *Turky*, and as it hath been found by long Experience, that the Battulation of (or Interdiction of all farther Commerce with) such Subjects of the Country, as shall act fraudulently, and refuse to give just Satisfaction, or persevere in unwarrantable and irregular Practices, or, *in Case of Dispute in any Matter of Business*, refuse to submit to the National [*English*] Magistrate, or to an equal Arbitration,—has been of great Use towards this, and other good Ends for the Benefit of the Trade of His Majesty's Subjects into the *Levant:* If any Factor, or Factors, shall have *any manner* of Dealings with, or by any Person *battulated* by the Lord Ambassador, or by the Consul of any of the Scales in *Turky*, with the *Advice of the respective Factories*; such Factor, or Factors, shall pay a Fine for every Offence, to the Amount of three Consulages upon the Value of the Transaction by, or with such *battulated* Person. And the Lord Ambassador at *Constantinople*, and the Consuls at *Smyrna* and *Aleppo*, for the Time being, shall, upon full and legal Proof of such Offence, IMMEDIATELY levy the said Fine upon the Offender by DISTRAINT, or OTHERWISE, without admitting ANY APPEAL to the Company, to be paid to the Company's Treasurer for their sole Use and Benefit, and not chargeable to the Account of the Factor's Principal."

Now it must be owned, that such Resolutions as these ought to be kept *secret*: For no Government upon Earth would willingly submit to such an Indignity as is here offered to the *Ottoman* Port by the *Turky* Company; an Indignity the more outrageous, as it is committed within its own Territories, and by those Persons who reside there only upon Sufferance. Put the Case therefore, that the *Turks* traded to *England*, instead of the *English* to *Turky*; and that these INFIDELS and FOREIGNERS should take upon them to erect a Tribunal of their own, in Opposition to the Tribunals of the *English* Nation; and by Virtue of this extra-judicial Court should *battulate*, that is, excommunicate, or out-law, not only one another, but the Natives themselves;—I ask therefore, Is there a Man in *Great Britain*, that would not resent such an Affront, and think the Persons who committed it very unworthy of the Favour

and Protection of the *British* Nation? Besides, supposing that an
English Factor had a Difference with a Native *Turk*, or *Grecian*, why
must the other Factors quarrel with him upon this Account? For if
the Native of the Country has the Character of being a fraudulent,
dishonest Man, and really deserves it, the other Factors need not be
told, much less *compelled*, to break off their Connections and Correspondence with him; because it will be, at least, as much their Interest in
Turky to shun, or avoid a Rogue or a Knave, as it is their Interest in
England. But if the chief Crime of this *battulated*, or *outlawed* Person is,
that he hath not bowed the Knee to *Baal*, and has dared to disoblige the
lordly Consul, or some *leading* Factor at the Scale, what is that to the
British Nation? And why must every other Consideration be sacrificed
to the implacable Resentment of a *Bashaw* Consul, or a *Bashaw* Factor?
In short, this Rule, or Order of the Company, is worded so very loosely,
that it may be made to signify any Thing, or every Thing whatever:
And if a Native of *Turky* may be battulated *for persevering in unwarrantable, or irregular Practices, and for not submitting to the national*
English *Magistrates in any Case of Dispute about Business*, I should be
glad to know, what particular Rule the Company have (if this is not
likewise as great a *Secret* as the rest) to determine and limit the Meaning
of these general Words?—Sure I am, that if the Writer of these Sheets
was in the Power of the Company, he would be BATTULATED to a Purpose,
for his thus *persevering* in his *unwarrantable*, and *irregular Practices*,
in writing against Monopolies.—But though the Affair is so extravagantly absurd, as to tempt a Man to treat it ludicrously; yet it is too
tragical a Subject for Ridicule. And when the Reader has been informed, that even *Englishmen* themselves have been put under this imperial Ban of Battulation, nothing more need be added towards raising
in him a just Spirit of Indignation against these Tyrannies, and Oppressions. Thus much therefore may suffice by way of Specimen, concerning the *Secrets* and *Mysteries* of Monopolies and Exclusions.—And
I can assure the Reader, that the *Turky* Company (tho' several other
Samples might be given) are not worse, perhaps not so bad in these
Respects, as some others that might be named.

SEVENTHLY and lastly, The Continuance of the Prohibition against
exporting Coin, or Bullion, is another Absurdity, and tyrannical Imposition: It is an *Absurdity*, because the chief Call for Money in *Turky*,
according to the Company's own Account, is to purchase Raw Silk, and
Mohair Yarn: Judge therefore, which deserves the Preference among a
manufacturing Nation, a Lump of Gold or Silver, or a Bale of Raw

Materials? and consider, which imploys the most Hands, or circulates the most Labour?—It is likewise a *tyrannical Imposition*, because the governing Part of the Company never can, in the Nature of the Thing, be subject to this Restriction. For, *Quis Custodes custodiet ipsos?* Who will be able to restrain the leading Men, and chief Factors from exporting that kind of Goods, by which they are to get most? Therefore, if they can make use of such a Pretence in order to keep down the Market of Raw Silk in *Turky*, and so prevent their *Rivals*, especially those of the *Out-Ports*, from buying with ready Money, is it to be supposed, that they will not take the Advantage, and make the better Bargain for themselves?—Those who can believe the contrary, know very little of human Nature, and nothing at all of exclusive Companies.—But as the Affair of the Exportation of Coin, or Bullion, is to come more professedly upon the Carpet in the insuing Chapter, we will not anticipate it at present.

SUCH therefore being the present State of the *Turky* Company, I appeal to all the World, whether this Trade can be said to be truly FREE? Nay, whether it doth not still bear about it the evident Marks of Monopoly, and Exclusion? In short, there is not the least Shadow of a Pretence for keeping up an *incorporated* Company to trade to *Turky*, but what might equally serve for erecting a new one to trade to *Spain*, and *Portugal*, or almost any other Kingdom. And if the antient Company trading to *Spain* had not been yet demolished (for there was a Time, when even this Trade was under an Exclusion) the same sort of Pretences would now have been urged at this Day for the Continuance of the one, which are brought at present in Support of the other. Nay, if we consider the Nature and Temper of the *Spaniards*, their excessive Jealousy with regard to their Wives and Daughters, their extreme Bigotry, their frequent Processions and public Adorations of the Host, together with the Rigour and Strictness of the Inquisition; especially their searching after heretical, or prohibited Books;—and if we contrast these Things with the licentious Dispositions and Behaviour of an *English* Sailor, and the Thirst of a *British* Merchant after Gain, we must confess, that the Objections against opening a Trade to *Spain* would make a much more formidable Appearance than any that can be alledged in behalf of other Exclusions.—But if you once establish a Company, they will never want Pretences for the Continuance of it. And therefore there is but one way to make the Trade truly free and useful; and that is, to demolish the Company intirely, and thereby effectually cut off all Artifices, and Pretexts of making By-Laws and Regulations *for the good*

Government of Trade. For as long as these remain, do what you will, Monopoly and Exclusion will creep in, and cover themselves under a thousand different Disguises. In short, this Commercial Hydra must be *pierced to the Heart*, if you hope to destroy it: For the Lopping off an Head, or two, will signify little, when twenty others are ready to sprout up. Nay, the very *Russia* Company, which, one would think, hath the least Power of doing Mischief of any in the World, yet find Ways and Means to exclude those Persons, particularly *Russians* and Foreigners, from the Freedom of Trade, whose Interest interferes with that of the leading Men of the Company, or the chief Factors abroad; several Instances of this Nature having been clearly proved at the Bar of the honourable House of Commons a few Sessions ago. Let therefore the *Turky* Trade be put upon the same Footing as that to *Spain* and *Portugal*; and let the Expences of Ambassadors and Consuls be born by the Public, and carried to the Account of the *current Service of the Year:* And this Polity alone will be sufficient. [Indeed the Public bears all at present, and that in the most disadvantageous Way that could possibly be contrived. For the Method of taxing Manufactures exported, and Raw Materials imported, is the same Absurdity in Trade, as it would be in Mechanics to use the *disadvantageous Lever* in order to assist your natural Strength. And every Butcher can tell us, that a Quarter of a Pound at the long End of the Steelyard, can weigh down an hundred Weight placed at the short End: Just so it is in regard to Taxes; For a Tax upon Manufactures exported, or Raw Materials imported, is an heavier Tax than four hundred times the Sum, when properly laid on. Therefore, it is high time that all these absurd Practices should be abolished; and Things put upon their proper Footing.] And then, and *not till then*, the Trade will BE FREE.

II. In regard to another great Monopoly, *viz.* The *Hudson's* Bay Company, the Case stands thus; When King *Charles* II. was restored, he not only revived all the former Monopolies relating to foreign Trade, but created as many new ones, foreign and domestic, as the Times would then admit; I say, *then* admit: For the arbitrary Proceedings of *Charles* I. in relation to these Things, were too odious, and too recent for the Son to proceed immediately to the same exorbitant Lengths. And as these Stretches of the Prerogative in the preceding Reign brought on the first Complaints, according to Lord *Clarendon*'s own Account, so it is observable, That when the Parliamentary Party got to be uppermost, they abolished, or at least superseded all exclusive Charters relating to foreign Trade. And this Fact is the more remarkable, inasmuch as the *Turky*

Company (of whom so much hath been said in the preceding Article) were pleased to call it a *Grievance*, and to make it the Basis of their Petition to King *Charles* II. soon after his Restoration, in order to obtain a new Charter, and such other new Powers as were still more excluding and oppressive; *viz.* "And whereas by the humble Petition of the said Governor and Company of Merchants of *England* trading into the *Levant* Seas, We are given to understand, That in these *late Times of Libertinism*, many of the *known* Privileges of the said Company have been *violated*,— KNOW YE, &c." Now that the Reader may likewise know a little concerning these *libertine Violations*, it may not be amiss to recite one of them by way of Sample; *viz.* "And for that divers Persons our Subjects of refractory and perverse Minds, seeking as much as in them lieth to disturb the said Trade, by wilful refusing to Account with their Principals, and to pay the Company's Duties;—And otherwise by attempting, or practising to violate, break, and make void the Privileges of the said Company, or any of them; ☞ And being of scandalous Life do appeal oftentimes from the Justice of the *English* Ambassador, or Consuls, or Vice-Consuls, to *Turkish* Judicatories and Justice, to the great Prejudice of the said Company and Trade, and the Dishonour of the *English* Nation, and Scandal of their Religion. WE willing to prevent, &c."

SEE here now, a selfish, grasping, exclusive Company, transformed all of a sudden into a godly, benevolent Society for the Reformation of Manners! And, what is stranger still, the *Profanely-Popish* King *Charles* II. converted into an holy Zealot for the Honour of the Christian Religion, and the Protestant Faith! Surely we have great Reason to expect rare Doings in consequence of such good Beginnings! And therefore, after having re-established the **Turky* Company, the *East India* Company, and some others, the King proceeded to erect this new one of the *Hudson*'s Bay, putting them in Possession, as far as Parchment and Wax could do it, of a Country without Bounds or Limits, (but which we know for Certainty is about as big as half *Europe*, and how much more we cannot tell) and constituting twenty or thirty private Men the absolute Sovereigns of this immense, and hideous Waste. If you should ask, With what View this was done? I can answer, That the

---

* The Charter for the *Turky* Company is dated the 2d of *April*, 1661, that for the *East India* Company was granted the very next Day:—And I believe several others, *viz.* The *Guiney* Company, the *Morea* Company (a Sprout of the *Turky* Company) the *Muscovia* Company, and the *Greenland* Company (which was a Branch of it) the *Hamborough* Company, the *East Land* Company, &c. were re-established either this Year, or the ensuing.—In such Haste were the *Stuart* Family to return to their old Courses of Ruling by Prerogative.

View of the Company was, to export as little as possible of the *British* Manufactures, and to import as little as possible of raw Materials, in order to get the more exorbitant Price both for the one, and the other: And they have greatly succeeded in both these destructive Schemes. For the *British* Manufactures fell at *Hudson's* Bay, one with another, after the Rate of four hundred *per Cent.* more than they would have done, had the Trade been free: That is, * If you suppose the Quantity of Manufactures now exported, to cost here at home four thousand Pounds,

---

* This State of the Exports, and Imports of the *Hudson's* Bay Company, is much more favourable on their Side, than it need have been, had we gone to the Rigour of the Matter: But I was willing to let the Reader see the mischievous Effects of these De-vourers of Mankind, *Monopolies*, when viewed even in the most favourable Light.   For the Account given in the Pamphlet, entitled, *A short State of the Countries and Trade of* North America *claimed by the* Hudson's *Bay Company*, London, *Printed for* J. Robinson, 1749, Page 5, is as follows; "The Company, to engross this beneficial Trade to them-selves, and to prevent its being known, or inquired into by the Merchants of *Britain*, confine their Trade in this extensive Continent, to the Exporting of Goods and Man-ufactures to the Value of three thousand six hundred Pounds annually, at a Medium; *in which is included Provisions and Necessaries for their Servants at their Factories:* And for that Export, import annually Furrs, Peltry, &c. to the Value of about thirty or forty thousand Pounds: When, if these Countries were settled, and the Trade ex-tended and improved, by civilizing and incorporating with the Natives, ☜ allowing them a more equitable Trade, and carrying up our Manufactures into their Countries by these large navigable Rivers in Summer, and by Sledges in Winter, and by that means imploying more of the Natives in Hunting, and inabling them to become in-dustrious;—our *British* Exports might reasonably increase to two hundred thousand Pounds, and our Imports from thence to above four hundred thousand Pounds in a very short Time, as by presumptive Proofs may be easily made appear."   Now the Views of the Company are just the Reverse of every Thing here recommended.—And yet bad as this is, they have found a Man hardy enough to undertake their Defence in a *public Manner*; and even to justify the Smallness of their Exports, confidently asserting, That it is more for the Nation's Advantage to export four thousand Pounds worth of Labour, than sixteen thousand Pounds worth; that is, That it is better for the Kingdom, that one Fleece of Wool should be used, one Spinner, Weaver, Scribler, Dyer, Clothier, Carrier, Factor, Porter, Packer, Sailor, &c. &c. be imployed; than that four Fleeces should be used, or four Spinners, Weavers, and four times as many of all the rest of the long List of Trades-people should be imployed: And in short, that Industry and Rival-ship ought to be checked and discouraged, as being contrary to the Interests of a Na-tion, because they are repugnant to the Views of Monopolists.   Is this Man now a Judge of National Commerce, and of the means of promoting it?—Or if he is, can you look upon this as a Specimen of it?   Surely, either his *Head*, or his *Heart* must be greatly here in Fault.   If out of four Spinners, Weavers, &c. in a Parish, three of them should want Work by means of this Monopoly, and become chargeable to the Parish, will this Gentleman, or will the Company pay for their Maintenance, and take upon themselves that Burden, of which they have been the real Authors?

then, instead of sending out four thousand Pounds worth of Labour to purchase Furrs and Peltry, we should have sent out four times as much, *viz.* Sixteen thousand Pounds worth to purchase the *same Quantity* of Furrs and Peltry: Moreover, when this Quantity is brought home to *England*, it is sold at present *Cent. per Cent.* dearer than it would have been, had the Trade to *Hudson*'s Bay been as open to all Adventurers as that to *Newfoundland, Greenland, Nova Scotia,* &c. &c. that is, the same given Quantity of Furrs and Peltry which now sell for forty thousand Pounds, would gladly have been sold for twenty thousand Pounds: — which indeed would have been sufficient Profit, *viz.* twenty five *per Cent.* upon the Voyage. Therefore in regard to *Exports*, this Company defrauds the Nation of *three-fourths* of the Quantity of Labour or Industry, which it hath a Right to have, according to the Nature of Commerce; and in regard to *Imports*, it lays a Tax on *Raw Materials of Cent. per Cent.* as a Discouragement to future Industry; and by that Means actually stifles numberless Branches of Commerce in the very Birth. But this is not all: For if the rival Traders would have exported sixteen thousand Pounds worth of *British* Manufactures, where the *Monopolists* export only four thousand Pounds, in order to obtain the very same Quantity of *Indian* Goods; they would, for the like Reason, have augmented their Exportations, in order to augment their Imports: That is, they would send out still greater Quantities of Manufactures, in order to tempt the *Indians* by Cheapness, and good Usage, to bring down still greater Quantities of Furrs and Skins: And it is well known, that the *Indians* might, and would bring down ten times the Quantities, provided they had proper Incouragement so to do. Hence therefore it is plain, that even this single Article of Trade, as now carried on, might be extended, in relation to *Exports* from four thousand to sixteen thousand Pounds, and from sixteen thousand Pounds to one hundred and sixty thousand Pounds worth of Labour. And in relation to *Imports*, the Quantity of Raw Materials would have been just ten times as much, and at Half-Price. — So far as to the present staple Trade;—But we have, by no means, as yet seen thro' all the ill Consequences attending Charters of Monopolies. For these Exclusions not only prevent the natural Expansion of that Trade, in which they are at present concerned; but also are a Bar against opening any new Sources, or making any farther Discoveries. And indeed, why should a Monopolist, who can cooly, and quietly, and without Risque, get an *Exceeding* of four hundred *per Cent.* upon his Exports, and *Cent. per Cent.* upon his Imports,—Why, I say, should such an one think of opening new Channels, or of making farther

Discoveries in the Way of Trade?   For all new Attempts and Experiments must be attended at first with certain Expence, and with a considerable Degree of Uncertainty, as to the final Event, or future Success.
Therefore these Attempts are seldom, or ever made but in a *free Trade*,
where *rival* Adventurers, pushing against each other, *over-stock the Trade*,
as the Phrase is; and then some of them find it necessary to leave the old
frequented Road, wherein are too many Travellers, and to beat out new
Paths for themselves: A Circumstance this, though disagreeable to a
Monopolist, yet the most advantageous to National Commerce of any
in the World; because almost all new Trades, Improvements, and
Inventions, take their Rise from this Cause. — So far therefore may
suffice to set forth the Views of the Company in petitioning for the
Exclusion.   As to the Views of the Court in granting it, these Things
will come more fully under our Consideration in the insuing APPENDIX,
to which therefore we refer them.

BUT having traced the Matter thus far; the grand Question returns at
present, *viz.* What is to be done with this Company now it is established?
For you must know, that the Rights and Privileges of chartered Companies are sacred Things, and must not be violated; though the Monopolists themselves are violating the NATURAL RIGHTS of Mankind every
Day, and were incorporated for that very Intent. — Therefore two
Proposals will here occur; *viz.* Either the intire Resumption of the Charter,
upon a valuable Consideration given by the Public: Or a Permission
granted to all others to trade in such Places, which the Company have
left unoccupied, and where they have made no Establishments.   As to
this latter Proposal, it would certainly answer all the Ends of National
Commerce as well as the former, if the Country were already peopled,
as the *East Indies* are; and if no Colonies were intended to be planted.
But seeing the Country lies now in a desolate State, in a manner without
Inhabitants; and those few being *Savages* for this plain Reason, *because
they are so few*; — and seeing likewise, that this Country is extremely
proper for settling a Colony, as shall be presently made to appear; therefore the former Proposal is the only eligible one in the present Case;
viz. To resume the Charter, giving the Company a valuable Consideration.   Now were this Consideration to be given them only in Proportion
to their public Merit, or their private Expences in settling the Trade, the
Account would be soon made up.   For as to their public Merit, I am
persuaded every Reader (himself not interested in, or *connected with*
the Company) hath adjusted in his Mind already, what ought to be paid
them on that Score: And in regard to their Expences in settling the

Trade, one might really conclude, that a Trade which hath for these thirty or forty Years last past brought in a Profit of at least three hundred *per Cent.* clear of all Deductions whatsoever, hath by this Time pretty well paid for the *original* Expences; so that a Bill of this Nature could not be a *very* large one. But, here the Reader will be told by the Champion for Monopolies, that the Author of these Sheets is a PRATING SCANDALOUS LIAR; and perhaps too he may be told it (as was lately the Case) in such a Place, where the poor Author can make no Reply; — he therefore humbly hopes, that he may without Offence anticipate this Matter, by confessing his Guilt, and shewing, wherein he is a *Liar:* In the first Place then, as the whole annual Exports of the Company do not rise higher than four thousand Pounds, *communibus Annis*; nay, not near so high, when proper Deductions are made for the Provisions and Necessaries which are carried out on the Account, and for the Use of the Company's Servants; — and as their Returns and yearly Sales amount, at a Medium, to thirty five thousand Pounds a Year; the Author humbly conceives, that he cannot be reckoned a *very scandalous Liar* in affirming, that the *Clearings* of the Company are at least three hundred *per Cent.* In the next Place, as to the Dividend upon the Joint-Stock; — *here he confesses his Guilt:* For the Dividend is indeed so far from being three hundred Pounds, that it is nearer three *per Cent.* nay, if this Affair should ever be brought before the Parliament, perhaps it would then be MADE TO APPEAR, that the Dividend was hardly two *per Cent.* — Now this is one of those *Secrets* of Trade, which none but the Adepts should be initiated into. However, since they have fallen into such unhallowed Hands as mine, I will boldly divulge them, and take the Consequences. Know then, that the *original* Joint-Stock of this Company was ten thousand five hundred Pounds Sterling: And when they found, that the Profits of the Trade were immense on such a trifling Capital, they were pleased to *call* that ten, twenty; — and by the same *golden* Rule in Arithmetic they proceeded to *call* that twenty, forty; — and forty, eighty; — and from eighty, according to the last Accounts, it is swelled up now to an hundred and twenty: And how far this Joint-Stock Tumour, or monopolizing Tympany, is yet to extend itself, in order to prove me a *prating scandalous Liar* before the most August Assembly in the World, I cannot pretend to say. But, be that as it may: — If the *nominal* Joint-Stock were one hundred and twenty thousand Pounds, or even double that Sum, it would be the Interest of the *British* Nation to buy it out, and take Possession of the Country: And no Time should be lost; inasmuch as this Country is particularly adapted by Nature for the Reception of a *British* Colony: For

IN the first Place, If a *North-West* Passage is ever to be discovered, the settling of a Colony on the Continent of *Hudson*'s Bay is the only Way to do it, and the only Method of appropriating the Use and Benefit of such a Passage to ourselves. Nay, supposing even that there is no Passage (which is not a likely Supposition) yet the Distance between Sea and Sea cannot be great, because the Degrees of Longitude in *Hudson*'s Bay in *America*, and the Degrees of Longitude on the *Northern* Coasts of *Asia* have been found by the *English* on one side, and the *Russians* on the other, to approach very near to each other: And perhaps some future Navigators may bring the Discoveries on both Sides much nearer. But even grant the worst, grant, I say, that the Land from Sea to Sea, or from *East* to *West*, is twenty or thirty Degrees of Longitude; now this, in so *high a Latitude* as the upper End of *Hudson*'s Bay, cannot be more than four hundred, or at most six hundred Miles: And whoever considers the peculiar Conveniencies of carrying Goods in Northern Climates by means of Sledges in Winter, and navigable Rivers in Summer, will find, that this Distance is of no more Consequence in regard to Trade, than an hundred Miles with us. — Nay, the *Russians* bring all their Hemp from the *Ukraine*, and their Iron from *Siberia* to *Petersburg* at a much less Expence, than Goods are carried from *Bristol* to *London*; though the Distance is ten times as far. Thus therefore, even at the worst, might an easy Communication be opened between the two Seas; and a quick Passage found out for all the *English* Manufactures, particularly for the two chief (I mean the Woollen and Iron Manufactures) into all those immense Countries of *America* and *Asia* hitherto discovered, or undiscovered; and the Returns and Raw Materials of those Countries imported into *Great Britain*. Now if such a Consideration as this is still to be sacrificed to the Schemes and Cabals of an injurious Monopoly, usurping over the *natural Rights* of Mankind, who can we blame but ourselves? And what Pretence can we have to complain for the future of the Want of Trade, and the Burden of the Poor, if we neglect those Things which at any time we have the Power to command in regard to the Company, and the Ability to execute in respect to ourselves? — I say, the *Ability* in respect to ourselves: For

IN the second Place, The Highlanders of *Scotland* have every Qualification you could wish to have in the first Settlers of such a Country. Their Highland Dress, their Diet, their Dwellings, Genius, Imployments, and Diversions, — all bespeak them the fittest People in the World for such an Undertaking. And therefore, though the disloyal Clans of the *Camerons, Mac Donalds, Mac Phersons, Mac Cleans, Mac Intoshes,*

&c. &c. are very bad Neighbours in the Highlands of *Scotland*, yet they would make very useful Subjects, and be a sufficient Guard of the Frontiers against the Incroachments of the *French*, if four or five independent Companies were raised, and sent into the Southern Parts of *Hudson*'s Bay. Nay, in a very little Time these People, as they can already bear equal Hardships and Fatigue, would acquire the same Dexterity in Hunting, and catching Beaver, as the Natives themselves: And moreover, as the respective natural Dispositions, Ways of Living, Countries and Climates, are so similar one to the other, such new Comers would the more easily intermix, and incorporate with the original Inhabitants. A Circumstance always to be desired in establishing Colonies. — In short, for my Part, I can see but one possible Objection to this Proposal; and that is such an one, as none but the Advocates for an exclusive Company would attempt to make; *viz.* That this Proposal savours of Disaffection and Disloyalty, inasmuch as it would be paving the Way to make the Chevalier King of *Hudson*'s Bay. — However, while this Country is in the Hands of the Company, it is to be hoped, we have nothing to fear: For doubtless, they will give strict Orders to their *grand* Army of one hundred and twenty Men to make a *brave* Defence; such an one as they made in Queen *Ann*'s Wars, when a *French* Privateer of about fifty Men, summoned the best Fort in their vast Territories to surrender at Discretion:—Which the *prudent* Governor immediately did without striking a Stroke.

THIRDLY, Were the magic Spell of an exclusive Company dissolved, a Colony settled, and the Trade laid open, — the *British* Nation is, of all others, the most capable of trading with such a Colony to *mutual* Advantage, and consequently of promoting a mutual Interest, and beneficial Intercourse. — For in regard to the Colony, there is no Nation in *Europe* that can take off so great a Quantity of Furrs, and Peltry, both for their own Consumption, as well as for Exportation, as the Inhabitants of *Great Britain*. Moreover, should any new Sources of Trade be attempted to be opened, should Fisheries be established, Mines of Lead, Tin, Copper, *&c.* or Quarries of Marble, or indeed should any other Sort of Raw Materials be discovered, where is the Kingdom that could receive such Quantities, and find a Vent for them, as our own can do? Or where is the Nation that hath so great a Number of mercantile Persons, with large Capitals, willing and ready to ingage in such Undertakings? And on the other Hand, with regard to the Manufactures of *Great Britain*, the very Climate and Situation of *Hudson*'s Bay would oblige the Inhabitants to purchase the warm, and coarse Woollens, and all kinds of Iron Manufactures, and Houshold Goods, and almost all the Implements of Husbandry, and Fishing, from the Mother Country. Nay, even *British* Spirituous Liquors, or *West India* Rum, would be less noxious in such a Climate than in any other; and though the Importers of them into *Africa*, and the more Southerly Countries of *America*, are the *certain Murderers* of the Inhabitants, to the no less Detriment of Trade, than Breach of Morals, and Dishonour of Religion; yet they might import them for the Use of Fishermen at *Hudson*'s Bay without doing any Injury at all. In short, the Circumstances both of the Mother Country, and of the Colony proposed would be such, that their respective Interests must always co-incide, and never could clash with each other.— And what could you desire more?

FOURTHLY, The *British* Nation are in great want of such a Country as *Hudson*'s Bay, for the Purposes of disposing of their numerous Convicts and Malefactors in a proper Manner. For this Country is so situated by having the *French* Colonies to the *South*, and the Polar Circle to the *North*, with the Sea and *Terra de Labrador* to the *East*, and undiscovered Regions to the *West*, that it would effectually answer the same Ends to us, which *Siberia* doth to the *Russians*. Besides, the very Idea of Transportation as a Punishment for Crimes points out this Country, preferably to any other. For Convicts ought not to be sent into a *populous* Country, where their bad Example might corrupt the innocent Natives; nor into a rich, and fertile Country, where they have the same Opportunities, and consequently the same Temptations of returning to their evil Courses, which they had before; neither ought they to be placed in such a Situation, where they may return, almost at Pleasure, to the Mother Country. — Therefore the Method of sending Convicts to those Plantations on the Continent of *America*, that are populous already, rich and flourishing, where they may escape from one Colony to another, or return to *England* at Pleasure, is very wrong, absurd, and impolitic. And indeed most of the Provinces in *North America* are now so sensible of the Evils arising from this Cause, that they have prohibited the Importing of Convicts under very severe Penalties. Nor did they pass these Laws without great Occasion for them; it being a known Fact, that the *Men* Convicts actually carry on at this present Time a kind of regular Exchange of stolen Goods, particularly Horses, by the following Method; *viz.* The Thieves of the Southern and Northern Provinces meet each other half way, and there barter their ill gotten Merchandize, and then return home to dispose of them with Confidence and Impunity. And as to the *Women* Convicts, there is no need to be very descriptive in setting forth the numberless bad Consequences that must result from such experienced Tutrices, and diseased Tempters. — Now *Hudson's* Bay being a *cold, barren, uninhabited* Country, of an *immense Extent*, and yet *shut up* on all Sides, hath every Qualification that is requisite for making Transportation a real Punishment: And moreover, as all Temptations towards their former Crimes are effectually removed; and as there can be no living or subsisting without Industry and Labour, the Persons sent thither would have the best Chance in the World of reforming, and becoming Good,—the true End of Punishment; and, I will add, the true Interest of every State to promote. I ask therefore, would it not be the most useful Step that could be taken in our Circumstances, to destroy this Monopoly immediately, and erect a Colony? Nay more, would it not be expedient to enact a Law, changing the Punishment of Whipping and hard Labour into Transportation? For it is evident to all the World, that our Jails and Bridewells are no Schools of Reformation: Nay, it is certain, that for one Person, *Male* or *Female*, whose Morals are bettered by such a Punishment, thousands are hardened and corrupted. In short, were Death to be inflicted only in Cases of *Murder*, or *High-Treason*, and all other Crimes to be punished with Transportation to this *English Siberia* for a longer, or a shorter Time, according to the Nature of the Offence, we should approach nearer to the Rules of Equity, we should temper Mercy and Justice properly together, we should clear our Streets of bad Subjects, nay, of the Pests of Mankind, while they remained here at home; and yet by means of this single Polity, make them good, useful, and virtuous, by sending them abroad. — And *Hudson*'s Bay is of that prodigious Extent, that if ten thousand were transported every Year for an hundred Years to come, the Country could in no Degree be deemed *populous:* So that the former Objection against sending them to our other Plantations, can with no Colour of Truth, or Reason, be retorted here.

But if this Objection cannot be made, I am very sensible, that the Advocates for the present Monopoly will strive hard to muster up others: And therefore the great Pretence will be, *The Expence!* The Expence! — To which a very sufficient Answer might be returned, by asking a plain Question, *viz.* Who pays the Expence now? Who paid for building the Forts, if they may be called Forts? And who pays for the exorbitant Profits arising from the Shares, or Dividends, to the Proprietors, and the Jobbs to the Managers, and the Salaries to the respective Governors, Officers, and Men? — Who indeed, but the Public: The Public, I say, literally and truly pays all at present; with this cruel Circumstance, that the Tax is a thousand Times more heavy and oppressive, than if it had been judiciously laid on, and regularly collected by the Officers of the Revenue. And, Reader, as a Proof of what I am now saying, give me Leave just to lay before you a Specimen, or Sample of this Tax, taken from the Company's own Accounts,—*viz.* Their Standard of Trade at *Hudson*'s Bay. Now as Gold and Silver are never used in that Country, they all proceed by Barter, *fixed by Order of the Company:* And therefore you have nothing more to do, than to examine how much this Barter is set *higher*, than it would have been in a *free* and *open* Trade, in order to find out the *Company's Tax;* For ☞ all the *Exceedings*, are in Fact, a Tax laid, and levied on the Manufactures of their Fellow-Subjects exported, and on Raw Materials imported, by their own supreme Authority. Now as Beaver is the principal Article in the Trade, this is made the Standard whereby to value every Thing else; and moreover, as the Company sell this Beaver, at a Medium, after the Rate of Nine Shillings each; therefore by turning the Quantity of Beaver into the Valuation of *English* Money, we shall see with a single Cast of the Eye, the whole Mystery of this dark Affair.

Prices of the Linen and Woollen Manufactures, as fixed by the Company at *Hudson*'s Bay.

		£.	s.	d.
Duffles, 1 Yard.....as	2 Beavers	0	18	0
Flannel, 1 Yard.....as 1½	Beavers	0	13	6
Gartering, 1½ Yard..as	1 Beaver	0	9	0
Thread, 1 Pound....as	1 Beaver	0	9	0
Shirts, 1............as	2 Beavers	0	18	0
Stockings, 1 Pair....as	2 Beavers	0	18	0
Twine, 1 Scain......as	1 Beaver	0	9	0
Lace, broad orris 1½				
Yd..............as	1 Beaver	0	9	0
Worsted Binding, 1½				
Yd..............as	1 Beaver	0	9	0
Gloves, Yarn 1 Pair..as	1 Beaver	0	9	0
Blankets, 1 Yard....as	7 Beavers	3	3	0

Prices of the Iron and Metal, and other Manufactures, as fixed by the Company at *Hudson*'s Bay.

		£.	s.	d.
Brass Coat Buttons,				
4 Doz..........as	1 Beaver	0	9	0
Ditto Waistcoat, 6				
Doz.............as	1 Beaver	0	9	0
Awl Blades, 8......as	1 Beaver	0	9	0
Bayonets, 1........as	1 Beaver	0	9	0
Fish-Hooks, 14.....as	1 Beaver	0	9	0
Guns, 1............as	14 Beavers	6	6	0
Pistols, 1..........as	7 Beavers	3	3	0
Needles 12........as	1 Beaver	0	9	0
English Brandy, 1				
Gall.............as	4 Beavers	1	16	0
Feathers, Red, 2....as	1 Beaver	0	9	0
Tobacco Boxes, 1...as	1 Beaver	0	9	0
Flints, 16........as	1 Beaver	0	9	0
Vermillion, 1 Pound as	16 Beavers	7	14	0

AND now, my good Reader, what think you of such a Tax as this! Coarse Blanketing at Three Guineas *per* Yard! Woollen Gloves at Nine Shillings *per* Pair! Common Guns at Six Guineas each! Sixteen Flints for Nine Shillings! *English* Spirits at One Pound Sixteen Shillings *per* Gallon! And a Pound of Vermillion sold at Seven Pounds Fourteen

Shillings! Astonishing, and Prodigious! — But yet this melancholy Affair (for surely such it is) may afford us one useful Lesson of Instruction: And that is, that the Variety and Inequality of the Prices of these Things, is a Proof that the Company fixed their Valuations according to the Demand, which either the *Necessity*, *Luxury*, or *Vanity* of the *Indians*, made upon them. For Example, A Yard of warm Blanketing, or a Pair of Woollen Gloves, a Gun, Pistol, or Flint to strike Fire, were in some respects, Articles of Necessity; and therefore the respective Prices are set high: — A Gallon of Spirituous Liquors is a Matter of Luxury, and therefore the Price of that was high also: But it seems, that the Vanity of Dress is the ruling Passion of these poor People, for their Eagerness after a red Feather, and red Paint, scarce knew any Bounds; and therefore the *honest* Company took the Advantage of their Foible, and made them pay accordingly. And I am much afraid, that what is thus discovered to be the Case in relation to the Savages of *Hudson*'s Bay, will be found to be very similar to the Practice of the good Christians, and polite Inhabitants of *Great Britain*. However, by this single Circumstance, the Company have intirely confuted their own Arguments concerning the Laziness, the Indifference, and Inactivity of this People; nay, they themselves have shewn that they do not want a Spirit of Ambition, or Emulation. And therefore, if we could touch their Self-Love in a proper Manner, we should soon make them as industrious as other People; that is, they would become as willing to labour as ourselves (for the *Britains* were once such Savages) and to exchange the Produce of that Labour for the Produce, or Manufactures of other Countries:— And surely this is Commerce; or there is no such Thing in the World.— As to the Article of Expence, I humbly hope, that from what hath been set forth, no farther Difficulty can be alledged on that Head. However, if any Doubt should still remain, let it be considered, that if the Public shall get an additional Revenue of at least forty thousand Pounds a Year, by the Rise of the Customs on the greater Quantities of Goods imported, and by the Rise of the Excise, and all Inland Duties on Account of the greater Number of Manufacturers, and all Sorts of Persons being imployed (not to mention the Nursery for so many thousands of Seamen) I say, if this is the Case, as it infallibly will be, surely we may afford to pay eight or ten thousand Pounds a Year out of this Sum, without any Loss, or Burden. — Indeed, that Person must be a very sorry Calculator, who cannot discover, that the Increase of Manufactures, Trade, and Shipping, will necessarily be attended with a proportionable Increase in every Branch of the Revenue. — There is but one Thing more I have to add on this Subject, and I have done: And that is, that the Company, not content with the gainful Practice of *conscientious* Traders, who do as they would be done by, act likewise in the Capacity of *Quacks* and *Conjurers**, selling the People *Nostrums* to cure all Diseases, and *Charms* to make them successful in their Wars, or Hunting. And in honest Truth, if after what has been said, this Company shall still be suffered to trample upon our *natural* Rights and Liberties; and if the Subjects of this Kingdom will not make it a common Cause, to free themselves from this galling Chain, we must conclude, that the wise Inhabitants of *Great Britain* are as much the Dupes of the *Doctor*, and the *Cunning Man*, as the poor, illiterate Savages of *Hudson*'s Bay.

III. WE have yet to direct our Attack against another great Monopoly, and indeed the most unweildy Monster of them all: — The Reader need not be told, that this is the EAST INDIA COMPANY. But as for the Attack itself, the Work is already done to our Hands by an Act of the whole Legislature, past the third Year of his present Majesty; and we have nothing more now to do, than to pursue and execute the judicious Plan there laid down. The Purport of which Act of Parliament, as far as relates to the present Subject, is as follows; That after three Years Notice given by Parliament to the Company, and upon paying off the Principal and Interest of 3,200,000*l*. Sterling, which the Public have borrowed of the Company, "Then, and from thenceforth, the Right, Title, and Interest of the said Company to the whole, sole, and exclusive Trade to the *East Indies*, &c. shall cease and determine. But after the Determination of that Company's Right to the sole, and exclusive Trade to and from the *East Indies*, the Corporation [for the Company is still to remain a corporate Body, if they please] with all, or any of their Joint-Stock, Goods, Estates, &c. may trade in common with other Subjects of His Majesty trading to, and from those Parts." See *The great Collection of Voyages*, Vol. I. Page 915.

Now, if we really intend to put in Execution this excellent Law, what have we more to do, than to give the Public Notice, and pay off the Debt? The Debt may be discharged when Peace is established, in much less Time than three Years, by means of the Sinking Fund. And surely this Debt, of all others, ought to be discharged the first: Nay, were even the destroying of the Monopoly, and the Advancement of national

---

* See a Pamphlet, intitled, *A short State of the Countries and Trade of North America claimed by the* Hudson's *Bay Company*, Printed for *J. Robinson*, Page 16. The whole Pamphlet highly deserves the Regard and Attention of the Friends of Liberty and Mankind.

Commerce out of the Question, the very Behaviour of the Company in a late trying Affair, when the Reduction of Interest was upon the Carpet, is sufficient to determine this Point. For if ever there was an Instance of the blackest Ingratitude, and the most dangerous Combination against a just, and unblemished Government, this was one: Vices the more unpardonable in the present Case, as the Government had just been protecting their Forts and Settlements in *India* at a most immense Expence; and as the Company themselves had set the Example by reducing the Interest of their own Bonds to three *per Cent.* and yet they refused three and a half, and had the Conscience to demand four of the Government. No Thanks therefore to the *East India* Company, that this laudable Scheme for the Reduction of Interest hath so happily succeeded; for they opposed it with all their Might, and endeavoured to raise a senseless, popular Cry against it. But the Thanks are due, and ought to be paid to the Memory of that *honest Minister* lately deceased, and to his Fellow-Helpers still living; who so bravely and firmly broke the Neck of these Combinations, and gave a noble Specimen of the great Good that may be done by Men of *good Hearts* in a *good Cause.*

IV. LASTLY, As to the *South Sea* Company, this Monopoly is such an undefinable, unshapen, nameless Thing, that little can be said about it. For it hath not the least Sign of a Trading Company belonging to it, and yet hath a Grant to prevent all others from trading. It fits out no Ships, deals in no sort of Merchandize, neither buys nor sells any thing but Stocks, neither exports nor imports: — But nevertheless, if you were to send a Ship any where within the Reach of its extensive Patent, you would presently find, that it so far possesses the true Spirit of an exclusive Company, as to act like the Dog in the Manger, and hinder others from reaping any Benefit from that Trade, which it doth not injoy itself. However, as no present Design is formed for carrying on any Commerce with the * *Spicy* Countries within its Grant, *viz. New Guinea, New Holland,* &c. and as it will be necessary whenever this is attempted, that the State should either settle a Colony, or nurse up the Trade at first by means of Bounties to rival Adventurers (which are the only *national* Ways of opening new Sources of Commerce) we may defer this Subject at present, and resume it again when we come to the third Section, to treat more expressly of the Nature of Commercial

---

* See *The great Collection of Voyages,* Vol. I. Chap. I. Sect. IX. and X. Pages 62, 63, 64, and 65. See also Sect. XXII. Pages 330, 331, 332, 333, 334, and 335.

Colonies, the Reasons of their Institution, the Rules for settling them, and the Regulations they should be under in relation to the Mother Country.

AND now, to put an End to this tedious, and toilsome Affair, let us conclude all with this general Remark, *viz.* That every Rank and Condition of Men throughout the Kingdom, the Monopolists excepted, would find their Advantage by concurring and uniting together to break loose from these Chains of *Egyptian* Bondage.

THE Government and Administration, which, God be praised, no longer proceeds upon the old Maxims of Tyranny and Prerogative, but considers itself as the *equal* Protector *of*, and *equally* related *to* all its Subjects, would soon find the Effects of its Paternal Care in the growing Industry of the People. The Wheels of Government would go smoothly on; because the great Subject of repining would be taken away: And it would be neither the Interest, nor Inclination of the great Body of the People to complain of an open Trade, or to wish for any Change in their Commercial System. Therefore, as by this single Polity, Wealth would flow in from every Quarter, the People would be imployed in more useful Matters than to criticize on the Conduct or Management of their Superiors. Moreover, the Amount of Taxes would be every Day increasing, because the Numbers of the People would increase, and their Abilities to consume taxable Commodities would increase likewise: Consequently the Produce of the Sinking Fund would rise; the National Debt would lessen, and Money, when wanted, might be borrowed at almost any Interest. Moreover, as to external Affairs, the more powerful we are, the more we should be respected: And the less we aimed at Conquests, the more desirous would every People be to traffic with us. — Indeed all Nations would covet our Manufactures, because we could sell them the best, and on the cheapest Lay; and they would send us either the valuable Returns of raw Materials, or such other Commodities as would swell the Amount of our yearly Revenue by the Customs, Duties, and Taxes put upon them. In short, every Port would then have its Share of Commerce, and be industrious to rival, and exceed its Neighbour; and therefore every Port would augment the Riches, Strength, and Glory of the Kingdom, by its additional Contribution towards the Revenue, and its additional number of Ships, and Sailors. Thus therefore would the Interest of the Government be promoted by every Method which advances the Interest of the Individuals.

AND as to the *Patriot*, he surely would have Reason to rejoice at this Restoration of our *natural* Rights and Liberties. For when our Trade is once set free, we shall be intirely and completely free; having no other Thraldom to complain of: For all the Remains of our former Vassalage and Slavery in other Instances are already abolished. Indeed this Affair of Monopolies and Exclusions, is the *last Prerogative Tax* now remaining; and when that is demolished, the Patriot will find, by happy Experience, that these Prerogative Taxes, though the least attended to, were the heaviest and most oppressive of any.

MOREOVER, in regard to the *Country Gentleman*, as it is his immediate Interest to raise the Value of his Lands, to get good Tenants for his Farm, a ready Market for the Consumption, and to be eased from the Burden of a numerous Poor, he must regard these Monopolies, as so many Combinations particularly levelled against the *Landed Interest:* And therefore he should be the more active and indefatigable in abolishing them.

As to the whole Body of Merchants, Manufacturers, and other Classes of People, what can be more obvious, than that these Monopolies were intended to impoverish all besides, and to eat like a Canker into their Gains and Industry? For they were established with the very Intent of being detrimental to the *many*, in order to be exorbitantly profitable to the *few*. The Question therefore is no more than this, Whether the *few* or the *many* shall get the better in this Struggle; a Struggle in which the one Side are contending for their natural Rights and Liberties, and the other for the Continuance of an unjust and odious Usurpation. And as to the well-timing of an Application to Parliament, any Sessions may serve for that Purpose; Perhaps the sixth or seventh as well as any other; — indeed rather better. For the Case of foreign Monopolies is not the same with that of domestic ones; — I mean as to the *Popularity* of them. And the Reason is, because the Numbers ingaged in them, comparatively speaking, can be but few: And therefore it becomes a popular Topic to declaim against them. — For, in Fact, every Man is desirous, that all Monopolies should be abolished but his own: — Than which, I think, there cannot be a stronger Proof, *That they are all bad.*

An APPENDIX *to the First and Second Sections of the* Chapter *on* Manufactures.

HAVING laid down a Position, or Maxim, at the Beginning of the First Section, That all Trades and Branches of Commerce ought to be FREE, those only excepted, which administer Temptations to Vice, or are preventive of National Industry;—and having asserted both in the First and Second Sections, That the inslaving

of Commerce by exclusive Patents, and monopolizing Corporations, is a
Remnant of that antient despotic Power, and Gothic Barbarity, under
which this Kingdom long groaned; I think it very proper, in a Matter of
such vast Importance, to make good my Assertions by the most undoubted Authorities; by which Means the Reader will be able to form
the truer Judgment on the Merits of this Cause.   And if he shall be able
to discover the real Motives of those Princes, who granted these Patents
from time to time; — and the precise Views of the Grantees in so earnestly petitioning for, and eagerly defending them, he will be at no
Loss in determining, whether these Things were ever established with a
good Intent, and particularly whether they ought to have continued so
long as to the present Times.   And tho' many Authorities might be
brought, yet I shall content myself with two only, as being altogether
unexceptionable, full, and decisive.

THE first Instance which I shall here produce, is that which occurred
during the Reign of Queen *Elizabeth;* when the Dawnings of Commerce
began to break forth, and People's Eyes were opened a little, to see the
Advantages that would have resulted from a free, and uninterrupted
Trade *at home.*

THE second wholly concerns such Charters and Exclusions as relate
to *Foreign* Trade. — And by comparing both together the Reader will
find, that though our Forefathers were forced to kiss the Rod, they
thought it neither an Honour, nor Advantage, so to do; and would have
been glad to have injoyed a greater Degree of Liberty, but did not dare to
appear openly in its Defence.

I. IN the Reign of Queen *Elizabeth*, there were several Struggles to
shake off some of the most galling Links of that slavish Chain, in which
the People were held in regard to Commerce: Particularly the Struggles
in the forty third Year of her Reign deserve an especial Regard: Because
the Debates in Parliament then ran the highest about Monopolies and
Exclusions; as may be seen in *Townshend's Historical Collections*, himself a
Member *of*, and a Speaker *in* that very Parliament: *Note,* The same
Collections are likewise transcribed, with some Abridgments, into Sir
Simon D'ewes's Journal of the House of Commons, see Page 644—660.
But tho' the Members widely differed, whether they should proceed
against these Monopolies by Way of Bill, or Petition to the Queen;
yet they all agreed, that in regard to Commercial Matters, an Act of
Parliament itself was no Fence against the Prerogative.   Such was the
miserable and slavish Condition of *Old England!*   Such the *golden Days
of good Queen Bess*, so much envied and preferred to modern Times!   Mr

Francis [afterward Sir *Francis*] *Bacon* said, (Page 231) "The Queen, as she is our Sovereign, hath both an inlarging and restraining Liberty of her Prerogative: That is, she hath Power, by her Patents, to set at Liberty Things restrained by Statute Law, or otherwise; [*i. e.* Common Law] and by her Prerogative she may restrain Things that are at Liberty. — If Her Majesty makes a Patent, or Monopoly to any of her *Servants*, That we must go, and cry out against: ☞ But if she grants it to a Number of Burgesses, or Corporation, that must stand; and, forsooth, is no Monopoly."

MR *Francis Moor* [Member for *Reading*] said, Page 233, "Mr Speaker, I know the Queen's Prerogative is a Thing curious to be dealt withal; yet all Grievances are not comparable. I cannot utter with my Tongue, or conceive with my Heart, the great Grievances that the Town and Country for which I serve, suffer by some of these Monopolies: It bringeth the general Profit into a private Hand; and the End of all is Beggary and Bondage to the Subject. — But to what Purpose is it, to do any thing by Act of Parliament, when the Queen will undo the same by her Prerogative? Out of the Spirit of *Humility*, Mr Speaker, I do speak it: There is no Act of hers that hath been, or is more derogatory to her own Majesty, or more odious to the Subject, or more dangerous to the Commonwealth, than the Granting of these Monopolies."

MR *Martin* [Member for *Barnstaple*] said, Page 234, "I speak for a Town that grieves and pines, and for a Country that groaneth under the Burden of monstrous and unconscionable *Substitutes* to the Monopolitans of Starch, Tynn, Fish, Cloth, Oil, Vinegar, Salt, and I know not what; nay, what not. The principal Commodities of my Town and Country are ingrossed into the Hands of these Blood-Suckers of the Commonwealth. — The [foreign] Traffic is taken away by Wars; the inward and private Commodities dare not be used without Licence of these Monopolitans. If these Blood-Suckers be still let alone, to suck up the best and principalest Commodities, which the Earth hath given us, what shall become of us? — The Fruits of our own Soil, and the Commodities of our own Labour, which with the Sweat of our Brows (even up to the Knees in Mire and Dirt) we have laboured for, shall be taken from us by Warrant of supreme Authority, which the poor Subject dares not gainsay!"

SIR *George Moor* [Member for *Surry*] spoke next, and said, "We know the Power of her Majesty cannot be restrained by any Act. Why therefore should we thus talk? Admit that we should make the Statute with a *Non-obstante;* yet the Queen may grant a Patent with a *Non-*

obstante, to cross this *Non-obstante*. I think therefore, that it agreeth more with the Wisdom and Gravity of this House, to proceed with all *Humbleness*, rather by Petition, than Bill."

MR *Wingfield* [Member for *Stanford*] replied to this, as follows, "I would but put the House in mind of the Proceedings we had in this Matter the last Parliament: [which Parliament was held four Years before: For *note*, The Custom of holding *annual* Parliaments did not take Place till the happy Revolution] "In the End whereof our Speaker moved her Majesty by way of *Petition*, that the Griefs touching these Monopolies might be respected, and the Grievance redressed. Her Majesty answered by the Lord Keeper: That she would take Care of these Monopolies; and our Griefs should be redressed: If not, she would give us free Liberty to proceed in making a Law the next Parliament. The Wound, Mr Speaker, is still bleeding; and we grieve under the Sore, and are without Remedy."

MR *Fleming*, the Sollicitor General [Member for *Southampton*] said, Page 238, "That her Majesty in her provident Care had given Charge to Mr Attorney General and his self, that speedy and special Course may be taken with these Patents. This was the Beginning of Hillary Term last. — Since that nothing could be done therein for want of Leisure."

SIR *Robert Wroth* [Member for *Middlesex*] replied, "I would but note, Mr Sollicitor, that you were charged to take Care in Hillary Term last. Why not before? There was Time enough ever since the last Parliament [four Years ago] I speak it, and I speak it boldly, these Patentees are worse than ever they were. And I have heard a Gentleman affirm in this House, *That there is a Clause of Reversion in the Patents.* If so, what needed this stir by *Quo Warranto*, and I know not what? when it is but to send for the Patents, and cause a Re-delivery. There have been divers Patents granted *since the last Parliament*; these are now in being, *viz.* The Patents for Currants, Iron, Powder, Cards, Horns, Ox Shinbones, Train Oil, Lists of Cloth, Ashes, Bottles, Glasses, Bags, Shreds of Gloves, Aniseed, Vinegar, Sea-Coals, Steel, Aqua-Vitæ, Brushes, Pots, Salt, Salt-Petre, Lead, Accedence, Transportation of Leather, Calamint Stone, Train Oil of Blubber, Fumathoes, or dried Piltchers, and many others."

UPON reading of the Patents aforesaid, Mr *Hackwell* of *Lincolns-Inn* [Member for *Bossenny*] stood up, and asked this, "Is not Bread there? Bread! quoth one; Bread! quoth another: This Voice seems strange, quoth a third: No, quoth Mr *Hackwell*, but if Order be not taken for these, Bread will be there before the next Parliament."

But notwithstanding these Grievances were so numerous, and almost too great a Burden even for a *Turkish* Vassal to submit to, Mr *Spicer* [Member for *Warwick*] said upon the second Reading, Page 241, "I think it were good this Bill were committed. I am no Apostate, but stick to my former Faith; and upon that asserted, that by way of *Petition* will be our safest Course. For it is to no Purpose, to offer to tie her Majesty's Hands by way of Act of Parliament, *when she may loose herself at Pleasure.*"

Mr *Davies* [Member for *Corf-Castle, Dorsetshire*] spoke next, and said, "God hath given Power to ABSOLUTE Princes, which he attributeth to himself; *Dixi quod Dii estis:* And, as Attributes unto them, he hath given them *Majesty, Justice,* and *Mercy. Majesty,* in respect of the Honour that the Subject sheweth unto his Prince; *Justice,* in respect he can do no wrong; and *Mercy,* in respect he giveth Leave to his Subjects, to right themselves by Law: And therefore, in the forty fourth Assize an Indictment was brought against Bakers, and Brewers: For that by Colour of Licence they had broken the Assize: Wherefore, according to that Precedent, I think it most fit to proceed by Bill, and not by Petition."

The Reply made to this Speech was so very extraordinary, that I am persuaded, the Reader will not pass it over without taking some Notice of it: And the Comparison, that will result from thence, between *Old England,* and *Modern England,* may have its Uses in many Respects. The Reply was made by no less a Person than Sir *Robert Cecil,* Principal Secretary of State, and in these Words, — "I am a Servant to the Queen: And before I would speak, or give my Consent to a Case that should debase her Prerogative, or abridge it, I would with my Tongue cut out of my Head. — One Gentleman went about to possess us with the Execution of the Law, in an antient Record of the fiftieth of *Edwardi* III. Likely enough to be true at that time, when the King was afraid of the Subject. —If you stand upon Law, and dispute of the Prerogative, hark what *Bracton* saith, *Prærogativam nostram nemo audeat disputare.* For my own Part, I like not these Courses should be taken. ☞ And you, Mr Speaker, should perform the Charge her Majesty gave unto you at the Beginning of this Parliament, not to receive Bills of this Nature."—

This Speech seems to have thunder-struck the House: — However, after having a little recovered from the Fright, Mr *Mountague* [Member either for *Brackley* in *Northamptonshire,* or *Malmsbury* in *Wiltshire,* for there were two Members of the Name] had the Courage to say, "Mr Speaker, I am loth to speak what I know, lest perhaps I should displease. The Prerogative Royal is that which is now in Question, and which the Laws of the Land have ever allowed and maintained. My Motion then shall be but this, That we may be Suitors unto her Majesty, that the Patentees shall have no other Remedy, than by the Laws of the Realm they may have; and that our Act be drawn accordingly." This Motion was seconded by Mr *Martin*, and greatly approved of by the House; so that the Affair was settled according to this Plan.

Mr *Townshend*, at Page 243, then proceeds to give a List or Catalogue of the several Monopolies then in being; which, as they are much the same with what have been mentioned before, excepting some additional ones, I shall not now repeat. Only, I think, it may be proper to take Notice, that most of them were granted to *Members of Parliament*, or their *near Relations*, with Clauses of Revocation at Pleasure: And that the Patents themselves were of five Kinds, 1*st*, Such as were granted in order to countenance, and support an open Violation of the known Laws of the Land; of which number we are to reckon that granted to Mr *Cornwallis* to hold *unlawful* Games; likewise the Patent to Sir *Edward Dier*, to pardon, dispense, and release all Forfeitures, and Abuses committed by Tanners contrary to the Statute; and several others of the same Stamp. For when the Parliament enacted a *penal* Law, it was frequently the Practice of the Crown to grant a Patent of Dispensation, like the Popes of *Rome*, in order to raise Money upon the Subject by selling *Pardons*, and *Indulgences.* — 2*dly*, Another sort of Patents, and Exclusions, were those which were calculated to check the internal Trade, and Industry of the Kingdom; such were the Patents for Printing School-Books, &c. and making Salt, Steel, Brushes, Paper, Glass, Pottery Wares, Starch, &c. also the Patent for Salt-Petre, and the Licence for sowing Woade. As to that relating to Salt-Petre, it was of a Nature so extraordinary, that something farther ought to be said about it. For it not only gave an exclusive Grant to the Patentees to make Gunpowder, but also impowered them to enter forceably into any Man's House, and dig up his Floors, and Cellars, and do what Mischief they pleased, in search of Salt-Petre. Therefore these unwelcome Guests were sure to pay every Man a Visit, who did not buy his Peace and Safety by means of pecuniary Contributions. And it was upon this Account, that Sir *George Moore*, part of whose Speech hath been quoted before, Page 138, made a Sort of Pun upon the Word; *viz.* "Many Grievances have been laid open touching the Monopoly of *Salt*; but if you had added thereunto *Peter*, then you had hit the Grief aright with which my Country is perplexed." And Secretary *Cecil* says himself, Page 251, That the Patent for Salt-

Petre "digs in every Man's House, removes the Inhabitant, and generally troubleth the Subject." And *note*, This is the very Monopoly that was afterwards revived with so much Rigour and Cruelty in the Reign of *Charles* I. and caused such universal Murmurings. As to the Sowing of *Woade*, the Pretence for restraining the natural Liberty of the Subject in this particular, was really curious, *viz.* "That the Queen in her Progresses was offended with the Smell of it." See Secretary *Cecil's* Speech, Page 250. I suppose, when she granted two Licences, one to *William Aber*, and another to *Valentine Harris*, to Sow six hundred Acres each, that Woade had a better Smell. *3dly*, Another Set of Monopolies, were those which clogged and discouraged the Exportation of our own Manufactures: As, for Example, the exclusive Patent for exporting Iron Ordnance, Iron, and Tin; also the Patent for brewing Beer for Transportation, another to transport Lists, and Shreds, and another for exporting six thousand Calf Skins. *4thly*, There were Monopolies also to confine the Importation of Raw Materials, lest the Subject should have too much Imployment; *viz.* A Monopoly for importing *Spanish* Wool, another for importing Steel, a third for Oil of Blubber, and a fourth for *Irish* Yarn, &c. &c. *5thly*, Besides these Exclusions granted to single Persons, there were several others granted to Numbers, whereby they were incorporated: — And indeed you will find, upon Inquiry, that a great many of the Companies of Trades now subsisting, were of her creating; — But waving all domestic Matters, let us now confine ourselves to Foreign Trade; For in the first Place, we find in this very Catalogue of Monopolies, *A Patent for certain Merchants to traffic.* As to the Country to, and from which this Trade was to be carried on, this is not specified; but it seems to be either some Renewal of the Grant made to the *Muscovia* Company: — Or the Confirmation of the exclusive Charter of Merchant Adventurers, — or some new Monopoly for carrying on a Trade to *Barbary*. For all these Exclusions were granted much about the same Time, *viz.* in the Years 1584, 1585, or 1586. Now if it was a Renewal, or some Extension of Privileges of the *Muscovia* Company, her Conduct was still the more extraordinary, in regard to this Affair, because the Emperor *Theodore Joannides* had particularly expostulated with her on that Head*, "desiring her to grant Liberty to all the *English* to trade into *Russia*. For to permit some, says he, and to deny others, is Injustice: And Princes must carry an indifferent Hand betwixt their Subjects, and not convert Trade (*which by the Law of Nations ought to be common to all*)

---

* *Memoirs of Wool*, Vol. I. Chap. XXIV. Page 114.

into a Monopoly, to the private Gain of a few." These were the Sentiments of a Prince, whom the *English* then supposed a Barbarian, and almost a Savage. — But if the Grant here in Question was a Confirmation of the Charters of Merchants Adventurers, the Discussion of that Affair will come before the Reader in the second Part of this APPENDIX; where he will find, that the same hackney Apologies, and thread-bare Cant were used in support of Monopolies one hundred and fifty Years ago, as are used at present.—Moreover, if this Patent *to Merchants to traffic* was the *Barbary* Patent above mentioned, it may not be amiss to recite the curious Reasons for granting it, as given by the Reverend Mr *Smith* in his *Memoirs of Wool*, Vol. I. Page 115, from Mr *Camden*, viz. "*Anno Dom.* 1585. For the more advantageous and GAINFUL VENDING of *English* Cloths, Licence was granted to *Ambrose* Earl of *Warwick*, and his Brother the Earl of *Leicester*, *Thomas Starky*, *Gerard Gore*, and divers others, Merchants of *London*, for the Term of two Years, to trade with the Moors in the Eastern Parts of *Barbary*, to make good the Losses they had sustained in *Africa:* And all other Merchants were prohibited to Trade upon those Coasts." — In order that these Monopolists might have the MORE GAINFUL Vending of *English* Cloths; that is, in plain *English*, That they might enrich themselves at the Expence of their Country: An infallible Method of making Trade to flourish!

BUT alas! these Blood-suckers were not the only ones authorised by this Princess; for in the Year 1600, the very Year before this Parliament met, she fortified by her Letters Patents, two other destructive and devouring Monopolies, *viz.* That trading to the *East Indies*, and the other to the *Levant* Seas, the Seignory of *Venice*, and the Republic of *Ragusa;* and for this latter she stipulated to have an yearly Consideration paid her of four thousand Pounds. *Note,* This Grant to the *Turky* Company, was only the Renewal of a former one made about nine Years before. For her Custom was, to insert Clauses of Revocation in the domestic Patents, and to grant the foreign ones but for a short Space of Time; or at least to find out Pretences for *revising* them, in order to keep the Monopolitans, and their Agents, in a *continual Dependence* upon herself. However, it seems, this politic and crafty Princess now began to think, that she had stretched the String too far; and therefore concluded that the more prudent Step at such a Juncture, when *the Subsidies were likewise depending*, was to make a decent Retreat, with a good Grace: Which surely she did to Wonder, and Admiration! For, after having endeavoured to prevent the Affair from ever coming upon the Tapis, as appears by her Orders to the Speaker of the House of Commons: And after having opposed it with all her Might by her Privy-Counsellors, Place-men, and *Pensioned* Monopolists; she still found that the Storm was rising, and the Clamours growing louder. For indeed the Yoke was now grown quite intolerable, so that even the most passive Minds were worked up into a Sensibility of these continued, repeated, and increasing Evils. Nay, it is observable from all History, that there is a Point, beyond which even the most despotic Power cannot proceed. Therefore she artfully changed her Note, and appeared as ready to revoke these Monopolies, as her Subjects could be to remonstrate against them. For at Page 248, we find, "That the Speaker, after a Silence (and every one marvelling why the Speaker stood up) spake to this Effect:

"IT pleased her Majesty to command me to attend upon her Yesterday in the Afternoon: From whom I am to deliver unto you all, her Majesty's most gracious Message sent by my unworthy self. She yieldeth you all hearty Thanks for your Care, and special Regard of those Things which concern her State, and Kingdom, and consequently ourselves; whose Good she hath always tendred as her own: For our speedy Resolution in making so *hasty, and free a Subsidy;* which commonly succeeded, and never went before our Counsels. — For our Loyalty I will assure you, with such, and so great Zeal of Affection she uttered, and shewed the same, that to express it with our Tongues we are not able, neither our Hearts to conceive it. It pleased her Majesty to say unto me, That if she had an hundred Tongues, she could not express our hearty good Wills: And farther she said, That as she had ever held our Good most dear, so the last Day of ours, or her Life should witness it. And that if the least of her Subjects were grieved, and herself not touched, she appealed to the Throne of Almighty God, how careful she had been, and will be to defend her People from all Oppression. ☞ She said, That partly by Intimation of her Council, and partly by divers Petitions that had been delivered unto her both going to Chapel, and also walking abroad, she understood, That divers Patents, that she had granted were grievous unto her Subjects, and that the Substitutes of of the Patentees had used great Oppression. But, she said, she never assented to grant any Thing that was *Malum in se.* And if in the Abuse of her Grant there be any Thing that is Evil, which she took Knowledge there was, she herself would take present Order for Reformation thereof. I cannot express unto you the apparent Indignation of her Majesty towards these Abuses."

HERE the good Mr Speaker used a very proper Word in describing this Affair, without intending it; *viz. apparent Indignation:* For surely her

Indignation was only *apparent;* and her *real* Displeasure was not against the Monopolitans, but against the Advocates for a free Trade; as they would have found to their Cost, under some Pretence or other, had she lived any Length of Time after this Affair.   And as to her saying, That she never made any Grants that were *mala in se*; It is hard to define, What Salvo could be intended by this Excuse.   For certain it is, That she granted Patents for holding *unlawful* Games, and for dispensing *with*, or rather compounding *for*, the Breach of a great Number of Penal Statutes.   And one would think, That if such Patents were not absolutely *evil in themselves*, they approached so near to Evil, that the Distance was not very great or material.   However, let the Grants be what they will in themselves, we have the Authority of her own Secretary *Cecil* for asserting, that they were all evil in their Application.   For, as it was now no Time to dissemble, or deny, the Abuse of these Things, he seems to make a Merit of inveighing against them, and frankly acknowledges, Page 249, "That there was no Patent, which in the Execution thereof, hath not been injurious.   Would they had never been granted.   I hope there shall never be more.   (All the House said *Amen*.) In particular, most of these Patents have been supported with Letters of Assistance from her Majesty's Privy Council: But whosoever looks upon them, they shall find they carry no other Stile than with relation to the Patent.   I dare assure you, that from henceforth there shall no more be granted; and how many soever have been already granted, they shall all be revoked.   But to whom do they repair with these Letters? — To some Out-house, to some desolate Widow, to some simple Cottage, or poor ignorant People, who rather than they would be troubled, and *undo themselves by coming up hither*, they will give anything in reason for these *Caterpillars* Satisfaction."

A FINE Apology truly!   And a noble Justification of himself, his Fellow-Counsellors, and his Prince, for arming these devouring Caterpillars with *Writs of Assistance*, issued from the Privy Council; some of which had been executed in this manner for near thirty Years past. But, — as if he had made too great a Concession in confessing these enormous Abuses, he could not conclude his Speech without some kind of Reprimand.   For, towards the Close, he says, Page 251, "Why, Parliament Matters are ordinarily talked of in the Streets.   I have heard myself, being in my Coach, these Words spoken aloud: *God prosper those that further the Overthrow of these Monopolies!   God send the Prerogative touch not our Liberty!*"

HOWEVER, as these Declarations both of the Speaker, and the Secretary were very express, *That the Patents should be cancelled*; the Members, who before were trembling like Children under the Apprehension of the iron Rod of Prerogative, now burst out into vehement Transports of wild and extravagant Joy. And as their Acclamations upon the Occasion may give us the truest Picture, and the liveliest Idea of those Times, (which some would persuade us to prefer to the present) I shall select a few of them by way of Sample. Mr *Wingfield* said, Page 252, "My Heart is not able to conceive the Joy that I feel: And, I assure you, my Tongue cannot utter the same. If a Sentence of everlasting Happiness had been pronounced unto me, it could not have made me shew more outward Joy, than I now do; which I cannot refrain here to express (and here I think he wept.) There could nothing have been more acceptable to the Subject, than this Message. And I verily think, that if ever any of her Majesty's Words were meritorious before God, I do think these are." — This, you will say, is soaring pretty high: But what is to follow is much above it: For when Mr *Downold* moved the House, Page, 257, "*That the gracious Message sent from her Majesty, might be written in the Books of this House,*" [with a distant *Innuendo*, that if some such Course was not taken, perhaps they might be put off again with fair Speeches, as they were before, when they petitioned the Queen in a Body the last Parliament, four Years ago] Mr Secretary *Cecil* said, "I do not speak because I do dislike the Motion of that Gentleman that spoke last, but to defend the Diligence and Grace of the Queen. — And I do protest, there is not any Soul living, deserves Thanks in this Cause but our Sovereign." — Whereupon Mr *Davies* said, Mr Speaker, "That which was delivered unto you from her sacred self, I think to be *Gospel*, that is, *glad Tidings*. And as the Gospel is written and registered, so would I have that also: For *glad Tidings* come to the Hearts of the Subject. — This is all." And surely the Reader will say, *it is enough*. But if he likes to hear any more, Mr Speaker's Speech is still in a more exalted and pious Strain, *viz*. "My Heart is not able to conceive, nor my Tongue to utter the Joy I conceive for her Majesty's gracious, and especial Care for our Good and Welfare. Wherefore, as God said, *Gloriam meam alteri non daleo*; so may her Majesty say in that, that herself will be the only and speedy Agent, for the Performance of our most humble and wished Desires."

AND upon an Intimation given by the Secretary, that the Queen was willing to receive their Thanks upon the Occasion; and that, if the Speaker should come at the Head of forty, fifty, or an hundred Members, they should be all welcome; the general Cry of the House, instead of naming the particular Committee for that Purpose, was *All, All, All*; so no Committee was named.   Therefore [see Page 262] "The Commons attended the Queen at *Whitehall*, about three of the Clock, to the Number of one hundred and forty. — At length the Queen came into the Council-Chamber; where sitting under the Cloth of State, at the upper End, the Speaker, with all the Commons came in; and after three low Reverences he spake to this Effect:

"MOST sacred, and more than most gracious Sovereign,

WE your faithful, loyal, and most obedient Subjects, and Commons here present, vouchsafed of your special Goodness (to our unspeakable Comforts) Access to your Royal Presence; do, in all Duty and Humbleness, come to present that which no Words can express, our most humble, and thankful Acknowledgment of your most gracious Message, and most bounden, and humble Thanks for your Majesty's most abundant Goodness, extended and performed to us.

"WE cannot say (most gracious Sovereign) *we have called, and been heard; we have complained, and have been helped:* Though in all Duty and Thankfulness we acknowledge, *your sacred Ears are ever open, and ever bowed down to hear us, and your blessed Hands ever stretched out to relieve us.* We acknowledge (sacred Sovereign) we acknowledge, that before we call, ☞ Your preventing Grace, and all-deserving Goodness do watch over us for our Good; more ready to give, than we can desire, much less deserve.

"THE Attribute which is most proper unto God, *To perform all he promiseth* (most gracious Sovereign, Queen of all Truth, of all Constancy, of all Goodness, never wearied of doing Good unto us, which the Deeds themselves do speak) *that* we must render unto you, as being most zealous, most careful to provide all good Things for us, most gracious, most tender to remove all Grievances from us, which all your Princely Actions have ever shewed.   And even now, your most gracious published *Proclamation*, of your *own only mere Motion*, and special Grace, for the Good of all your People, doth witness unto us.

"WE come not (sacred Sovereign) one of ten, to render Thanks, and the rest to go away unthankful: But all, of all, in all Duty and Thankfulness, do throw down ourselves at the Feet of your Majesty.   Neither do We present our Thanks in Words, or any outward Thing, which can be nothing, which can be no sufficient Retribution for so great Goodness. But in all Duty and Thankfulness, *prostrate at your Feet*, we present our most loyal, and thankful Hearts, even the last Drop of Blood in our Hearts, and the last Spirit of Breath in our Nostrils, to be poured out, to be breathed up for your Safety.

☞ "After three low Reverences made, he with the rest kneeled down."

BEHOLD here a glorious Sight for the Admirers of *Old England*, and the golden Days of good Queen *Bess!* — See the whole Commons of the Realm in Parliament assembled, prostrate on the Ground, as to an *Eastern Tyrant*, using not only the most fulsome Compliments, and the most notoriously false, and abject Flattery, but even idolizing and adoring a Fellow-Mortal; and addressing their Prince in the same Language, which both Scripture, and our established Church have appropriated to the supreme Being! — And all this for what? Why truly, That this most sacred, *and more than most gracious Sovereign*, would condescend to pay some regard to her *Coronation-Oath*, and govern her People *according to Law:* — I say, *according to Law:* For every Grant of a Monopoly is a Violation of the Common Law of the Realm: and yet these are the Times that are eternally cried up; these are proposed as Patterns for us to copy after; nay, every false, and unjustifiable Artifice is made use of to render the People uneasy in their present IMPROVING Situation, and to wish for the Restoration of their former Miseries, and Oppressions. — In short, Sir *Robert Cecil*, and Sir *Robert Walpole*, are now both dead, and are gone to answer for what they have done amiss: Nor is there any Doubt to be made but that both had their *Faults*, as well as *Failings:* Yet, let the honest, and impartial World be the Judge between them, whether the one deserved so high a Degree of Applause, or the other so much Reproach, and Censure from the *English* Nation. Particularly, let their Conduct be examined in regard to the Liberty of the Subject, and a free Commerce. The former assisted in laying the most oppressive, and ruinous Taxes upon the People that any Nation can suffer; nay, he defended them in Parliament, when Attempts were made to repeal them; and what is still more, he *bullied* the Speaker, and the whole House, for admitting a Debate against them: The latter, of his own accord, brought a Bill into the House, and had it carried into a Law, for repealing at one time near two hundred of the most *impoverishing* Taxes: And the Speech made from the Throne on that Occasion, is justly recommended by Don *Geronymo de Uztariz* * as a Model for all

---

* See *The Theory and Practice of Commerce*, written by Order of his Catholic Majesty, Vol. I. Chap. XXVIII. The Speech here referred to, was delivered from the Throne, *October* 29, 1721. And in consequence thereof, about one hundred and fifty six Articles of *British* Manufactures were allowed to be exported *Duty free*, which before paid a Duty; and thirty eight Articles of Raw Materials were imported *Duty free*, by Virtue of the same Regulation. See *Crouch's Book of Rates*, Customs inwards, and Customs outwards, where a distinct Account is given of the Taxes repealed by the

Princes to proceed upon in regard to National Commerce.   Yet from that
Moment, of so much Advantage to *Great Britain*, this able and judicious
Minister was attacked with all the Rage and Bitterness, the Calumny
and Invectives, that private Malice and Disappointments, and public
Faction, joined to Disaffection, could possibly muster up.   Such an
ungrateful Treatment threw him into those Measures of *Self-Defence*,
which, though not to be *justified*, were certainly more excusable in his
Situation than in that of any other.   And therefore, without entering
into a Defence of all Parts of his Conduct, I am persuaded, that impartial
Posterity will do him the Justice to acknowledge, that if ever a Statesman
deserved well of the *British* Nation, Sir *Robert Walpole* was that Man. —
Indeed the only true Way of discovering, whether we are advancing, or
retreating in our Political, and Commercial Capacity, is to compare the
Past with the Present, and to examine whether we have the same Quantity of pernicious Taxes, and monopolizing Patents now subsisting, as we
had formerly: If we have not, it is our Business to be thankful for the

---

eighth of *George* I. Chap. XV.   Moreover, in the same Sessions, though not in the
same Act of Parliament, several other excellent Provisions were made for granting
Bounties and Premiums to the Importers of Pitch, and Tar, Hemp, and Naval Stores,
from our Colonies in *North America*.   And the Advancements which the *British*
Nation have made in Shipping, Commerce, and Manufactures, and in all kinds of
Industry, since the passing of this Law, have been prodigious.   This was at the Begin-
ning of his Ministry: And in the third Year of his present Majesty, that excellent Law
was enacted, which we mentioned before, Page 132, relating to the *East India* Com-
pany.   But, to omit Matters of lesser Note, the greatest Effort towards benefiting a
Nation, was that for which he received the greatest Insults and Abuses, THE EXCISE
SCHEME, by means of which the whole Island would have been made one general
FREE PORT, and a *Magazine*, and *common Storehouse* for all Nations.—Indeed the
Excise Scheme was not a perfect Scheme at its first Appearance: But the Foundation
was good; and a very few Alterations would have rendered it a most useful Institution
for the Purposes of *National* Commerce.   But the Business of those Times was not to
alter, mend, or improve, but to set up a Cry, and raise a Ferment.   However, this
Scheme, in its most imperfect State, would have defeated the Views of Monopolists,
and have proved of great national Advantage.   Nay, if the Bill had been so worded
as to be only *permissive*, not *compulsory*, every Man in the Kingdom would, by this
time, have made the Excise Scheme his own voluntary Choice: That is, he would
have preferred the Method of putting his Goods in a Warehouse, and paying the
Duties as he wanted them, rather than paying the Duties all at once at the Custom-
house.—As a Proof of this, let it be observed, that the very Men who made the loudest
Clamours about the Excise Scheme, in a few Years afterwards petitioned for a much
worse, I mean the present Law relating to Tobacco; which is allowed on all Hands to be
an Excise Scheme in Effect, and to have several Inconveniences, which that had not.—
But to give some Salvo to the Matter, the Word *Permit*, is changed into that of
Certificate.

Deliverance we have received, and to unite our Endeavours to be freed from the Remainder: And this is *real* Patriotism, and public Spirit. — Whereas the Persons who are pleased to assume to themselves the glorious Name of *Patriots*, act upon a very different Plan, and therefore deserve a very different Appellation. — But as the more immediate Design of this APPENDIX is to set before the Reader, the true Origin of Monopolies and Exclusions, this should lead us to set forth the true Reasons, why so shrewd and politic a Sovereign as Queen *Elizabeth* should chuse this Method of taxing, and impoverishing her Subjects by means of her Prerogative, rather than apply to Parliament for Fifteenths, Tenths, and Subsidies: For the doing this will prove to a Demonstration, that exclusive Grants were so far from ever having been an useful Institution in regard to the Public, that they were, from the Beginning, intended to be the Instruments of arbitrary Power, and Oppression. — To unravel which Affair three Propositions must be laid down.

I. THAT a Prince who intends to govern arbitrarily, ought not to ask such Favours of his People, as may lay a Foundation for them to make reciprocal Demands; — but he should fetch his chief Supplies out of the Stores of his own Prerogative.

II. THAT it is incompatible with the Views of such a Prince to permit his Subjects in *general* to grow Wealthy by means of Liberty, and a free Trade.

III. THAT if it is his Aim to be the Source of Power, he must contrive Matters in such a Manner, as to be likewise the Source of Property.

I. As to the first of these Propositions, surely it is self-evident. For what can be plainer than that a continual Dependence of the Crown upon the People for support, must exalt the Power of the one, and depress that of the other? Queen *Elizabeth* was so sensible of this Matter, that she resolved to make use of her Prerogative almost upon all Occasions, rather than apply to Parliament. And the great Secret of her artful Management consisted in this very thing. For her excessive Parsimony was owing to this Cause, and this only: And I think, it used to be a Saying either of hers, or some of her Ministers, That the Prince who applies often to Parliament, is like a Master borrowing Money of his Servants, who is consequently obliged to submit to their Humours. Therefore she had rather get one Shilling by means of her Prerogative, in which she was beholden to nobody, than a thousand Pounds by a Parliamentary Tax. And indeed, as she was very unwilling to apply to Parliament, even in the greatest Exigencies, so when she did it, she did not fail to urge the extreme Necessity, as a popular Topic of Justification.

Nay, we find, that once, she either refused, or returned the Subsidies (I forget which) when there was no immediate Occasion for them, and by that means gained infinite Applause: But we never find, that she consented to a Law to abridge any Part of her vast Prerogative; tho' certainly the public Good was much nearer concerned in that Case, than in returning a temporary Subsidy. As to the Extent of the Liberty of the Subject on one side, and the Royal Prerogative on the other, the little that remained to the Subject (tho' that little was often encroached upon by *forced* Loans, and Benevolences) seemed to consist in this single Particular, *viz.* That no Tax could be raised upon the Lands, Persons, or Properties, of the Subject, without consent of Parliament, provided the Chattels, or Produce of those Lands, were consumed within the Kingdom. For, as to things either going out of the Kingdom, or coming in, the Sovereign alone held the * *Claves Regni*, and could lock, or unlock all the Ports at Pleasure. And accordingly we find, that Queen *Elizabeth*, King *James* I. King *Charles* I. and many other of our Princes, laid on what Imposts, and Duties they pleased, merely by sending Warrants to the Collectors of the respective Ports. But, in regard to Matters of *Home Manufacture*, and *Home Consumption*, they seemed to take a more round-about Way. For instead of laying on a *direct* Tax, and so permitting all Persons to exercise the Trade, provided they would pay the Tax (which would have been a much juster, as well as a more advantageous Way of raising Money) they limited the Numbers to be imployed, and bargained for the Monopolies and Exclusions. And thus they set one Part of the Nation to prey upon the other; and, under the Notion of granting private Advantages to some, they riveted the public Chains on all: For every Man that was either concerned in any Exclusion, or hoped to be concerned, was of course a Wellwisher to this Part of the Prerogative, because he would support, what he thought, though *very erroneously*, his own Interest. — Thus much as to the Matter of Fact; but an inquisitive Reader will still be apt to ask, What Views could a Prince have in thus studying as it were to impoverish his Subjects? and what Benefit can redound to himself in laying a Scheme to prevent an Increase of that Wealth, which would increase his own? — Now the Answer to this Question will come under my

II. SECOND Proposition, *viz.* That it is incompatible with the Views of a Prince, who intends to govern arbitrarily, to permit his Subjects,

---

* This is my Lord *Bacon's* own Expression, who was as great an Instrument of Oppression in the Affair of Monopolies, and of other arbitrary Proceedings, as ever existed.

in general, to grow rich by Trade. For indeed, how can this be done without granting them a general Liberty? And if they are to have this general Liberty, he is no longer the absolute Prince he intended to be. In Fact, if you expect Mankind to be industrious, you must make it appear, that they themselves, and not others, are to injoy the Fruits of their Labours. And you cannot do this, till you grant them such *Securities*, as will put it out of your Power to recall these Concessions, if you were disposed. Besides, Trade and Industry naturally create an independent Turn of Thinking, which Circumstance necessarily inspires an Horror, and Detestation of arbitrary Power. Moreover, Freedom of Trade brings likewise with it Freedom of *Debate*, as well as Freedom of Thinking. Add to all this, that though the Revenue increases by means of a *free Trade*, the Greatness of the Prince is *comparatively* diminished; and ten Millions may be in that respect a less Sum than one Million. — To illustrate this *seeming* Paradox let us borrow an Idea from private Life, and then apply: A Country Gentleman, for Instance, is Lord of a Manor, which clears him five hundred Pounds a Year; being a certain Tax, or Rent (call it which you please) received from an hundred poor Tenants, each of which miserable Wretches hath no more than five Pounds a Year, after having paid his Lord's Rent, to subsist upon. Now this is so small a Pittance, that it can hardly keep Life and Soul together; and therefore the Lord of the Manor may beat, and abuse those poor Creatures as long as he pleases; for in short, their extreme Poverty prevents almost a Possibility of seeking a legal Redress. — This being the Case, we will now suppose, that by means of a free Trade, the Income both of the Landlord, and of the Tenants is raised to ten times the Value: I ask therefore, Is the Landlord now as great a Man, *comparatively* speaking, as he was before? Can he insult, and abuse his Tenants with the same Impunity, as he was used to do? Or, in plain *English*, can he be as much a Tyrant over his new, commercial, well-cloathed, and well-fed Subjects, as over his former, ragged, half-starved Slaves, and Vassals? — No; he cannot: For he will find, that fifty Pounds a Year hath created a vast Difference in their Way of Thinking, to what five Pounds did; and though the Tenants of five Pounds *per Annum* could spare nothing out of their wretched Income to make Head against Oppression, the Tenants of fifty Pounds will both *associate* themselves, and contribute largely towards procuring Assistance from others; they will harangue, *print*, and *publish*, and raise a general Ferment in order to defend their Rights, and Privileges, Properties, and Possessions, and secure them against all Attacks for the future. Therefore to apply this, — It is morally impossible, that an arbitrary Prince should wish the *Generality* of his Subjects to be rich: For he cannot promote their Riches, without diminishing at the same Time his own comparative Greatness: And this is not the Thing which we naturally expect from an absolute Monarch. Hence therefore it evidently appears, that though some arbitrary Governments may give *temporary* Incouragements to Trade, yet they never will do it but by Halves; they never can promote it but by partial Grants, and monopolizing Patents. For there is such a *Vice in the Constitution* of an arbitrary Government, as a late Author hath well expressed it in regard to *France*, as must obstruct all Attempts towards a generous, open, and universal Liberty. Hence therefore we now come to the

III. THIRD Point, which is, That if it is the Aim of the Prince to be the Source of *Power*, he must likewise endeavour to be the Source of *Property:* For the one cannot be supported without the other. And this follows so clearly from what hath been said, that very little need be added by way of Illustration. As to the Methods of compassing such an End, the old Gothic Constitution gave to the Crown such an immense Power in regard to the *Landed Property*, by means of the military Tenures, Wards, Liveries, Forfeitures, &c. &c. that surely there was no need of any more: And with respect to the *Commercial Property*, the foregoing Instances of Patents, Monopolies, and Exclusions, Writs of Assistance, Star-Chamber Prosecutions, &c. &c. have sufficiently proved, that no Man dared to be industrious, unless he acknowledged it both by Word and Deed, as an especial Favour, and Act of Grace obtained from the Prince. — Upon the whole, Thus much, I think, may now be insisted on, because it hath been fairly proved, *viz.* That Monopolies, and Exclusions, are the Remains of antient Tyranny and Oppression; — That they *never* were calculated for the public Good, and never can be productive of it: — Nay, that at the Time of their Institution, they actually were designed to create innumerable Dependents on the Court; such Dependents as, in modern Phrase, would be stiled *Placemen*, and *Pensioners;* and therefore we conclude that those Persons, who stand up in their Vindication, either *do not* know, or *will not* know, the manifold bad Consequences attending these Things.

II.

THE SECOND INSTANCE promised to be produced, relates wholly to Foreign Trade: And the principal View of producing it at present, is to shew, that the Pretences urged with such Confidence of late Years against opening the *Hudson*'s Bay, and *Turky* Companies, are no other, than the stale, hacknied Apologies, used in Defence of other Monopolies, above one hundred and fifty Years ago; and may serve with equal Force of Reason, to defend any Absurdity whatever. It will from hence likewise appear, that the Vindications of Monopolies, antient and modern, always come from the *same Quarter:* And consequently, that the less Regard ought to be paid to the Sentiments, and Opinions of such Vindicators, in whose Minds Partiality and Prejudice, *self,* and *local* Interests have so visibly the Ascendant. The Paper itself was drawn up by Sir *Edward Sandys,* the Ancestor, as I am informed, of the present Lord *Sandys:* — And I can add with Pleasure, that his Lordship seems to be as much the Inheritor of the Patriot Sentiments of his Ancestor, as of his Name, and Fortunes; having greatly distinguished himself by the Services done to his Country in the Affair of Monopolies. Indeed at the Time when Sir *Edward* drew up this Paper, *viz.* the third of *James* I. (see *The Journal of the House of Commons,* Vol. I. Page 218) it cannot be supposed, that the Principles of Commerce were so well understood, as they are at present. And therefore some few Errors are to be expected. But the Reader will easily believe, and this Paper will be a convincing Proof, that a good Head, joined to a good Heart, will at all Times do great Things. — This is all I have to add by way of Introduction; and as to what is the Author's own, that shall be marked by way of Quotation; and what is mine, shall be included in Hooks.

* "INSTRUCTIONS touching the Bill for a FREE TRADE.

"THE Committees from the House of Commons, sat five whole Afternoons upon the Bill. There was a great Concourse of Clothiers, and Merchants of all Parts of this Realm, and especially of *London,* who were so divided; as that all the Clothiers, and in Effect, all the Merchants of *England* complained grievously of the Ingrossing, and Restraint of Trade *by the rich Merchants of London,* as being the Undoing, or great Hindrance of all the rest. And of *London* Merchants three Parts named in the same Complaint against a fourth Part; and of that fourth Part some standing stiffly *for their Company,* yet *repining at other Companies;* divers Writings, and Informations, were exhibited on both

---

* This Struggle for the Liberties of the People was two Years after the former; and seems to have taken its Rise from the Speeches, and Remonstrances that were made on that Occasion. Mankind are naturally Friends to Truth; and if you once put them in the right Way, and stop up the By-Paths of Self-Love, and Self-Interest, they themselves will take a Pleasure in finding it out: And one Discovery will open the Way for many others.

Parts.   Learned Council was heard *for* the Bill, ☞ And divers of the principal of the Aldermen of *London against* it.   All Reasons exactly weighed, and examined, the Bill, together with the Reasons on both Sides, was returned, and reported by the Committees to the House; where at the Reading it was three several Times debated, and in the End past with great Consent, and Applause of the House (as being for the exceeding Benefit of all the Land) scarce forty Voices dissenting from them.

"THE most principal Reasons for the Inlargement of Trade were these:

"I. Natural Right, the first Reason for a free Trade.

"ALL free Subjects are born inheritable as to Heir-Land, so also to the free Exercise of their Industry in those Trades whereto they apply themselves, and whereby they are to live.   Merchandizing being the chief, and richest of all other, and of greater Extent and Importance, than all the rest; it is against the NATURAL RIGHT, and LIBERTIES of the Subjects of *England*, to restrain it into the Hands of some few, as it now is.   For although there may be now some five or six thousand Persons (counting Children and Prentices) free of the several Companies of Merchants in the whole, yet apparent it is, that the Governors of these Companies, by their monopolizing Orders, have so handled the Matter, as that the Mass of the whole Trade of all the Realm is in the Hands of some two hundred Persons, at the most!   The rest serving for a Shew only, and reaping small Benefit.

"II. Judgment of Parliament, the second Reason for a free Trade.

"THE Law stands for it.   And a Statute made the twelfth of *Henry* VII. never repealed by Parliament, ☞ Only restrained by Charters since procured (by which means all the Monopolies have had their Original.)   And the first of these Charters, since the making of that Statute, was *purchased* in the End of the Reign of *Henry* VII. at which Time *Empson*, and *Dudley*, were Instruments of wronging, and oppressing the People: Yet doth in no wise restrain the Liberty of free Trade, but expressly allows it, with Reference unto that very Act in the twelfth of his Reign, and so it continued until the Reign of *Elizabeth*." [*Empson*, and *Dudley*, were not the first who *sold* Monopolies; for it was a common Practice with almost every Prince, and Minister, from the Conquest down to the Revolution, to do the like: This being the usual Way of raising Money at a Pinch, without applying to Parliament; And the common Method of gratifying Court Favourites, and creating what we would call *Places* and *Pensions*. As to the Law of the Land, it is most undeniable, that both the Common and Statute Law were ever in favour of a free Trade, foreign and domestic. But alas! the Civil Power soon learned from the Popes of *Rome*, the pernicious Doctrine of *Non-obstantes;* and then all our Laws and Constitutions were of no avail. For it was but to insert in the Body of the Grant, or Patent, the all-conquering Word, *Non-obstante*, any Law, Custom, Statute, &c. (in Imitation of the Popes dispensing Power in Ecclesiastical Matters) and then neither the natural, nor civil Rights of the Subject were at all to be regarded; but every thing was to submit to this usurping *Non-obstante*. Thus it is, as I said before, and shall have too many Occasions to say again, that the Corruptions of Popery spread much wider, than is commonly imagined, and are lurking at this Day in several Parts of our Civil Constitution, after the Principles, on which they were built, were banished out of the Ecclesiastical. — But though *Empson*, and *Dudley*, were not the first who begun the Practice, they were the first who begun it after so express a Law was made to prevent it: And it is worthy of the Reader's Notice, that they did not pretend to contradict this Law in Words, but seemed to allow it, at the same Time that they were destroying its Force, and Intention. Their Pretence therefore was, to incorporate a Company for the Benefit of a free, and open Trade, *with a Power of making By-Laws for the good Government thereof.* And indeed whoever doth this, need do no more: For these *By-Law* Legislators will take effectual Care to do all the rest themselves: And if one Pretence, or one Disguise will not serve, another shall. Moreover, in regard to the particularizing *Empson*, and *Dudley*, as these Ministers were become very odious, the Author, Sir *Edward Sandys*, did right to mention *them*, and not others: Though he might with equal Justice, had it been prudent, have mentioned all the Ministry of Queen *Elizabeth*, and the Favourites of the Prince then reigning. For in regard to Sir *Robert Cecil*, and others, they were still living, and in high Credit at Court; and with respect to Sir *Francis Bacon*, the Extracts of his Speeches under the former Head, are a sufficient Proof of his manner of thinking, and acting upon such Occasions.— Indeed I was promised an original Letter of his, wrote in Confidence to a Friend, wherein he boasts that he got five thousand Pounds a Year by the Sale of Monopolies. — But as I have not yet procured it, the Reader must judge for himself, whether the Thing is probable or not. Certain it is, that in those Times, the Court would grant a Monopoly for almost any thing that was asked, and paid for. And I have seen myself in *Rymer's Fœdera*, a Grant from King *James* I. to six or eight Persons to teach the *noble Science of Defence*; together with a Power of examining, and licensing all other Masters of this noble Art; and what is truly shocking, a Power of administring Oaths!]

"III. Example of Nations, the third Reason for a free Trade.

"THE Example of all other Nations generally in the World, who avoid in themselves, and *hate* in us the monopolizing Way of Traffic. For it cannot be otherwise accounted than a Monopoly, when so large a Commodity is restrained into the Hands of so few in Proportion, to the Prejudice of all others, who by LAW, and NATURAL RIGHT might have Interest therein. And whereas some alledge, that there are like Companies in other Countries, as of the *East Indies* in *Lisbon*, the House of Contraction there, the *Frontega* at *Venice*, the *Treinsana* at *Noremberg*; these Allegations are either untrue, or improper. There are Places of Assembly for Merchants, and to consult for good Orders, in all other Countries, but without the Restraint of Trading from any Man. And how Merchandize by this Freedom doth flourish in other Nations, and principally in the Low Countries more than in ours [the *Dutch East India* Company being hardly then set up] "it is apparent to all the World.

"IV. Increase of Wealth, a fourth Reason for a free Trade.

"THE Increase of Wealth generally of all the Land, by the ready Vent of all our Commodities to the Merchant at higher Rate. For where many Buyers are, Wares grow dearer; and they that buy dear at home, must sell dear abroad. This will also make our People more industrious." [A latent Error runs through the Reasoning of every Part of this Paragraph, excepting the last Sentence:—The Error is, That *Money is Wealth*; whereas in Fact, *Industry is Wealth*; and Money is only the ready and expeditious Method of circulating the Produce or Manufactures of this Industry from hand to hand. It is therefore not true, that an open Trade would enhance the Price of our Manufactures, if either bought at home of the Maker, or sold abroad to the Consumer: Nay, the necessary Effect is just the contrary. For a free Trade is the necessary Cause of Rivalship, and Emulation, both in regard to the Manufacturer, and Exporter: And therefore in such a Situation, all Goods whatever will be made in as high Perfection, and sold at as low a Price, as can be afforded with a living Profit.—Indeed the Sums of Money actually circulating throughout the Kingdom, by this means would, in time, become almost immense; but this Increase of Money doth not arise from the *Dearness*, but from the *extraordinary Quantity* of the

Things that are vended. And to make this Matter yet plainer, I shall endeavour to illustrate it by a recent Example, which perhaps will make the strongest Impression on the Minds of *Gentlemen*, because they are more conversant with the Fact laid before them. It is the Case of Post-Horses, and Post-Chaises:—Now had there been a Company incorporated with the pompous Preamble, "For the better supplying of Post-Horses, and Post-Chaises, for His Majesty's loving Subjects; and for preventing of Impositions on Travellers, and extortionate Demands, on account of the Necessity they are under to proceed in their Journey, be the Price never so unreasonable. WE THEREFORE, taking these Premises into mature Consideration, do ordain, constitute, and appoint, *&c. &c.*" I say, had there been such a Company, and such a Preamble, what would have been the Consequence? Why truly this; The Price of Post-Horses, and Post-Chaises, would have been at least *Cent. per Cent.* as dear as they are at present; and the Parliament would have had enough to do every Sessions in making new Laws, and Regulations against the Combinations, and excessive Demands of this *incorporated* Company; the Mayors of Towns, and Justices of the Peace, would have been armed with new Powers to settle the Prices, the Judges of the Assize would be frequently appealed to for determining the Disputes relating to these Affairs: And, in short, this one original Blunder of the Legislature, would have created a thousand others. Whereas at present, by letting all Things alone, that is, by leaving Things free and open, as Naure and Providence designed them, the Prices have settled of themselves, and are become as moderate, and reasonable, as can be wished; no Combinations, no Quarrels, Appeals, or Litigations about the Price are formed: And yet Horses, and Chaises are to be had in Plenty all over the Kingdom, and *better*, and *cheaper* than in any Part of *Europe*. So that upon the whole, though the Price of riding Post is greatly reduced, the Use of Post-Horses, and Chaises, is proportionably multiplied: And the Consequence of both is, that the Sums of Money actually paid on these Accounts may perhaps be ten times greater than they would have been, had this Trade (for so it may be called) been put under the Management of Governors, and Directors, Courts of Assistants, Committees, Freemen of the Company, *&c. &c.*—Hence therefore, the Reader will be pleased to make one general Remark, *viz.* That if all Restraints were taken off, and every other Trade was as free as this, one half at least, of those cumbersome Volumes called the *Statutes at Large*, which are now so great a national Grievance, might be laid aside at once, or rather made a Bonefire of, by way of rejoicing for such an happy Deliverance.]

"V. Equal Distribution, a fifth Reason for a free Trade.

"THE more equal Distribution of the Wealth generally of all the Land, which is a great Stability and Strength to the Realm, even as the equal distributing of Nourishment in a Man's Body. The contrary whereof is inconvenient in all Estates, and oftentimes breaks out into Mischief, when too much Fulness puffs up some with Presumption, and too much Emptiness leaves the rest in perpetual Discontent, the Mother of Desire of Innovations, and Troubles. And this is the proper Fruit of Monopolies: Example hereof may be *London*, and the rest of the Realm. The Customs and Imports of *London* come to 110,000 *l.* a Year; and of the rest of the whole Realm but to 17,000 *l.*"

"VI. Increase of Shipping, and Mariners, a sixth Reason for a free Trade.

"THE Increase of Shipping, and especially of Mariners in all Parts of *England*, and how greatly the Mariners of the Realm have decayed in all Places of late time, and with how great Danger of the State in these late Wars, is known to them that have been imployed in that kind of Service, who do also attribute the Cause thereof to this Restraint of Trade; free Traffic being the Breeder, and Maintainer both of Ships, and Mariners; as by memorable Example in the Low Countries may be seen." [*Note*, The Number of Mariners thro'-out the Kingdom were then said to be but ten thousand. See *Hume's History of* James I. Chap. VI.]

"VII. Profit of the Crown, a seventh Reason for a free Trade.

"THE Increase of the Customs, and Subsidies to the King, which doth necessarily follow the Increase of foreign Traffic and Wealth, is to be considered: And they which say otherwise, will dare to say any thing. These Reasons are in great Part set down in the Act of the twelfth of *Henry* VII.—Other particular Reasons there are, which this present time doth yield.

"VIII. Present Opportunity abroad, an eighth Reason for a free Trade.

"UNDER our gracious *Solomon*, a Prince of Wisdom, and Peace, we are like to be in League, or Amity with all Nations; whereby as there will be greater Freedom abroad to trade to all Places, so it is fit to have greater at home for all Persons to trade. This Alteration of Times may make that fit now, which in Times of Hostility might have seemed unfit.

"IX. Necessity at home, a ninth Reason for a free Trade.

"As there will be greater Opportunity abroad, so also much more Necessity at home: For what else shall become of Gentlemens Sons, who cannot live by Arms, when there are no Wars? And Learning-Preferments are common to all, and mean: So that nothing remains fit for them, save only Merchandize; (and such is the Use of other politic Nations) unless they turn Serving-men, which is a poor Inheritance.

REASONS for continuing the Restraint on Trade stated, and answered.

"I. Imputation on the State.

"IT is a Taint to the King, and State, that these restrained Companies should be called, or counted *Monopolies*. And by this Act we justify, and strengthen the Complaint of the Hanse Towns, and other Nations against the State, for suffering such Companies.
Answer. "THE same Reason doth justify all the Monopolies that ever were: It is no Taint to the State, if Abuses creep in; but if Reformations desired by Parliament be denied. But surely this Taint can no way attaint his Majesty, who hath declared himself a just Enemy to all these unjust Monopolies." [The very Apology here brought by the Monopolists is a Proof, that other Nations would not be displeased to see these Exclusions set aside. For indeed every exclusive Grant is a reciprocal Disadvantage, and a Stop to mutual Industry; — though the Detriment is much greater to that Nation, which authorises the Exclusion, than to the other which doth not. However, as both are Losers, we have no need to fear, that our Correspondents abroad (though that hath been sometimes suggested) would resent our setting a Trade free: Nay, they would rejoice at it, because *their* Interest would be promoted as well as ours. As to the Compliment paid King *James*, That he was an Enemy to Monopolies, it was artful in Sir *Edward* so to do: But the Sequel will shew, that he was just such an Enemy to them, as his Predecessor Queen *Elizabeth* was before him; and as all other Monarchs are, who intend to rule arbitrarily, and to check a Spirit of Independency, and Liberty in the Minds of their People.]

"II. Not Monopolies.

"THESE Companies are not Monopolies: For a Monopoly is when Liberty of Selling, due to all Men by Right, is restrained to *one*, with Prejudice to all others.

Answer. "THE Name of Monopoly, though taken originally from personal Unity, yet is fitly extended to an improportionable Number of the Sellers in regard of the Ware that is [or might be] sold.   If ten Men had the only Sale of all the Horses in *England*, this were a Monopoly; much more the Company of Merchant Adventurers; which in effect are not above two hundred Persons: — And the Clothiers having no utterance of Cloth but to the Merchant Adventurers, they, by a Combination among themselves, will buy at what Time, what Quantity, and what Prices themselves list; whereby the Clothiers are fain often to lay their Cloths to pawn, to slack their Market, to the utter Undoing of their poor Workmen, their Wives, and Children."   [The Advocates for the *Turky* Company used the very same Plea to the Parliament with this here mentioned, *viz.*   That their Company is no Monopoly: And the precious Reason assigned for it was, that all *mere* Merchants (by which is meant, all Persons who buy in *gross*, and sell in *gross*, without ever dividing their Merchandize into *smaller Parcels*, than they receive them: And, by the By, if we go to the Strictness of the Letter, there are scarce *ten* such Merchants in the whole Kingdom) and likewise that all Lords, and Lords Sons, upon paying a Fine of fifty Pounds, had a Right to the Freedom of their Company.   It was thus that they proved themselves to be no Monopolists.   But one general Answer will suffice for all this Chicane: *viz.*   That in a *Commercial Sense*, every Exclusion from the common Benefit of Trade, due to all Men by *natural Right*, is a MONOPOLY.   And the Degrees of this Monopoly are either greater, or less, in proportion to the Restraints and Abridgments of such natural Right.]

"III. Keeping up our Commodities.

"THESE Companies keep up the Price of our Commodities abroad, by avoiding an Over-glut of our Commodities in Places whereunto they trade.   And this Experience doth witness: For our Cloth is sold of late Years much dearer than in former Times: Whereas contrariwise, when Trade is free, many Sellers will make more cheap, and of less esteem.

Answer.   "IT is true, that all Companies keep up their Commodities for their own private Lucre; but they do it unjustly, and to the Discontent of all other Men: Which have been the Cause of so many Edicts of the Empire against the Company of Merchant Adventurers (which hath driven them so often to shift their Mart) and it is the Cause, that our Merchants are *universally hated*; no other Christian State either using, or induring such restrained Companies in Matters of Merchandise."

[So far the Author was certainly in the right: For though all other Nations have at present as many Monopolies as the *English*, if not more, they had them not when this Author wrote. As to what follows, — he endeavours, in the Remainder of this Answer, to prove, that a free and open Trade would not sink the Price of *English* Commodities at a foreign Market; than which nothing could be more absurd, and incredible. But yet, I think, I can trace the Steps by which he, and many others, have fallen into this egregious Error. — In the first Place, the capital Mistake, that *Money is Riches*, is the Basis of all: And then, being unwilling to allow, that a free Trade would cause our Goods to be sold for *less Money* at a foreign Market, they are obliged to infer, that the *National Ballance* of Trade, and the *Mercantile Ballance* of Trade are one, and the same Thing: Whereas these Ideas are perfectly distinct, and may be (as they often are) intirely repugnant to each other. For the Business of the Merchant is to get as large a Profit as he can upon small Exports: And his perpetual Thirst after a Monopoly is for this very End: But the Interest of the Nation is to promote general Industry, and Labour at home; which consists in exporting the greatest Quantities at the smallest Profits; in order to tempt Foreigners by Dint of Cheapness to buy our Manufactures. Therefore what is Gains to the one, may be Loss to the other. Add to this, that the Views of the Merchant are *merely* and *solely* to get Money; and if he can get this by imploying the fewest Hands, he thinks it so much the better: Whereas the Views of a Nation should be *wholly* and *solely* to promote Industry; and then National Industry will always command as much Cash, and Credit as are wanted for the Purposes of Circulation. Nay, what is still more; if it were possible to increase the Quantity of Money in a Nation by diminishing the Quantity of Labour (which is the utmost that a Monopolist could propose, even upon his own Hypothesis) this would be so far from being a national Advantage, that it would become one of the most fatal Disasters, and impoverishing Systems that could befall any People. And yet the whole Defence of the *Hudson*'s Bay Company, when that Affair was last before the Parliament, turned upon this very Thing. — And whenever it shall come on again, we shall be told over and over the same idle Story, about the Ballance of Trade, Savings to the Nation, &c. &c. — Indeed their Advocates have fully proved, that this exclusive Company keep up the Price of *English* Commodities at *Hudson*'s Bay with a Vengeance; And if this is any Merit, if this is a Saving to the Nation, they certainly have it in the highest Degree, they certainly save nine Parts in ten of the Labour that might be exported. But every honest, impartial Man will readily confess, that it had been much more for the Interest of the Public, that Woollen Gloves had been sold to the *Indians* for *Sixpence*, than for NINE SHILLINGS the Pair, and other Things in Proportion.]

"IV. Vending all now.

"THE Companies that are now, do vend all the Commodities of the Land; and yet are they hardly able to live one by another.

Answer. "IT is not all vended which the Land might spare; and that by Reason of the Courses held by these Companies, to their own excessive Gain, and certain Loss of all other Men. Besides, when Traffic shall flourish with us, as it doth in other Countries where Trade is free, and namely in the Low Countries, who thereby have supported the huge Charge of their long Wars; Things merchantile will increase daily by this Incouragement to the Subject's Industry, even as they do there. For natural Commodities are more than trebled by the Access of Art and Industry: And howsoever, yet the Division of Wealth will be more equal: For now, by plotting of the Governors of these Companies, some few overgrown Men devour the Wealth, and make Merry, whilst the rest, even of their own Company, want and weep." [The Plea here made use of, That the Merchant Adventurers sell all the Commodities of the Land, is the same in effect with that of the late Advocates for the *Hudson*'s Bay Company, *viz.* That they buy all the Commodities produced; *i.e.* they buy all the Beaver and Fur, which the *Indians* bring down to the Forts; and if they brought more down, the Company would buy more. Now these Monopolists take that for granted in this Argument, which they know to be false by their own Practice; *viz.* That the Prospect of superior Gains is no Incentive to future Endeavours: They know, that they themselves would not endeavour to preserve this Monopoly, if they were sure of being Losers, instead of Gainers by it. And therefore as the Clothiers in the one Case, and the *Indians* in the other, have no Incouragement to Labour and Industry, what can we expect, but that they should take no more Pains, than what is barely necessary and unavoidable? The real Wonder would be to see any People desirous of being industrious, without Incouragement. For Self-Love, and Self-Interest, will as naturally prompt a Man to Idleness, and Laziness, if he foresees no Reward for his Industry, as it will teach him to be diligent, and indefatigable with the Prospect of Gain. Put the Case therefore, that the Monopolists, and the *Indians* had changed Stations; and then I ask, what Stomach would these active Monopolists have to bear the Fatigues of hunting Beaver, and suffer all the Inclemencies of Weather;

if they were sure, that after they had been at all this Pains, the *Indians* would give them in exchange but sixteen Flints for a Beaver Skin, or one Pound of Vermillion for sixteen Beavers?]

THE fifth, sixth, seventh, eighth, ninth, tenth, eleventh, and twelfth Pretences are so frivolous, and so little to our present Purpose, that I shall intirely omit them. As to the thirteenth, though it is in itself perhaps one of the weakest of all, yet as it hath been at all times the most prevalent with a certain Set of Men, and the most repugnant to the National Prosperity, I shall be obliged to mention, and to descant a little upon it. The Plea is this; "That the destroying of Monopolies would hurt the Interests of the City of *London*, which ought to be upheld, because it is the head City of the Kingdom." To which the Author returned the following Answer, "That the intended Bill was *for* the Interests of the City of *London*, unless we confine *London* into some two hundred Men's Purses. The rest of the City of *London*, with the whole Realm, sue greatly for this Bill, and cry they are undone, if it should be crossed." [Now though this Answer is good in the Main, yet it is not sufficiently explicit; and therefore may be considered more as an *Argumentum ad Hominem*, than a thorough Confutation of the Objection. And indeed as long as this Objection is supposed to have any weight, so long we may assure ourselves, that the Representatives of the City of *London* will be *instructed* by their Constituents to oppose all Endeavours towards putting Trade upon a broad, and national Basis. Nay, as these Gentlemen, on Account of their Situation, and Commercial Connections, have been generally supposed to be the best Judges in Commercial Matters, a kind of *implicit Faith* hath been reposed on their Opinions; and their Decisions have been too frequently regarded, as carrying a sort of *Papal Infallibility* in the Commercial World. It is therefore become absolutely necessary to examine into the Grounds of the foregoing Assertion, That an open and national Commerce would be prejudicial to the Interests of the City of *London*. — For the Reader will please to observe, that I do not once expostulate the Point with the Citizens on the Footing of Justice, natural Right, or common Equity; though surely one might say a little on that head, and venture to hint at least; That if the Interests of the Nation, and of the City of *London*, are in any respect incompatible, the latter ought to give way to the former. — But, waving all that, my present Business is to prove, that a free Trade in the Out-Ports can never be detrimental to the real Interests of the City of *London*. And in order to do this, I would beg leave to ask one Question, *viz.* Under what Idea would the City of *London* chuse to consider itself in this Affair?   If under that of a Shop, or Magazine to serve Customers, (which is certainly the most natural Idea for the Metropolis of the Kingdom) then, I say, it can never be the Interest of this Shopkeeper, that all his Customers should be poor, and ready to starve: For the poorer they are, the less able to become good Customers at his Shop. If the Citizens would chuse to consider themselves under the generous Notion of *Monopolists*, and *Excluders*, and the rest of the Nation as *excluded* from their natural Right to a free Trade; this State of the Case, so flattering to partial Self-Love, and Self-Interest, is both false in itself, and if it were true, would be of no Service, but a real Detriment to the Citizens of *London:* It is false, because the Citizens in general are the *Excluded*, and not the *Excluders* in regard to foreign Trade; inasmuch as the whole Number of the Freemen of *London* belonging to the *East India*, the *Turky*, and the *Hudson's* Bay Companies are hardly an hundredth Part of the Inhabitants of the City.   Nay farther, allowing that the Trade was free, and open to all the Inhabitants of *London*, without Fine, without By-Laws, or any other cramping Regulation, but shut up from the rest of the Subjects of the Kingdom; — yet this itself would create a Monopoly against the far greater Part of the Inhabitants of the Metropolis; because none could reap the Benefit of such an exclusive, detrimental Trade, but the Exporters, and Importers of Goods, who in the Nature of the Thing, can be but a very few in Comparison to the Numbers of other Tradesmen necessary in a large City.   And therefore the other Tradesmen must become the Slaves, and Dupes of these Monopolists, contributing to rivet the Chains on the Necks of others, nay on themselves too, without receiving any Profit or Compensation. — The monopolizing Merchant *taxes* his Fellow-Citizens both in his Exports and Imports; and yet expects, that they should blindly, and stupidly vindicate his Cause, and make it their own! — This being the Case, let the Citizens themselves be the Judges, whether in standing up for a Monopoly of some few of their Fellow-Citizens to their own Prejudice, they do not in reality leave the Substance, and catch at the Shadow.   Let them likewise consider, which are indeed their *real* Friends, — those who would promote a general, and universal Commerce all over the Kingdom, which must of Course center in the Capital; — or those others, who would check Labour, and tax Industry, who would squeeze all the Wealth of the Kingdom into the City of *London*, and the Wealth of the City of *London* into the Purses of a Score or two overgrown Monopolists, and tyrannical Ingrossers.]

As to the fourteenth, the fifteenth, and the rest of the Pretences, as they are both trifling in themselves, and contain nothing in particular relating to the present Times, I believe the Reader will readily excuse my not mentioning them. — It will be more to the Purpose to set forth the extraordinary Consequences of this honest, and in the Main, very judicious Representation. But alas! what shall I say on this Occasion? Shall I say, what every Lover of his Country would wish to hear, that this worthy Patriot received the Thanks of his King and Country for his modest, sensible, and nervous Vindication of the natural Rights of Mankind? No: Nothing of this was to be expected from the Prerogative, and arbitrary Government of *good Old England*. In short, this *deserving* Member of the *English* Parliament met with a Prison for his Reward, even during the Sitting of the House; such was the Regard paid to Civil Liberties, and *Parliamentary* Privileges in those Times! And the King, notwithstanding he was complimented with the Name of *Solomon* in this very Memorial, shewed no Disposition of pursuing *Solomon's* Maxim, viz. *Of establishing his Throne by Righteousness.* Indeed, a little before the Meeting of the Parliament, or at least before this Representation against Monopolies, the King had, of his own accord, recalled several of those Patents which were complained of in Queen *Elizabeth's* Time: But whether this was done out of a Regard to the Memory of his Predecessor, and to fulfil her Royal Promise, which she did not live to execute herself; — or whether with a View of gaining Popularity at his first Accession to the Throne, and in order to obtain the larger Subsidies from the *English* Parliament, is impossible now to determine. But certain it is, that, whatever his Motives were, he had no Views to the Benefit, and Extension of National Commerce, by these Revocations; because he not only refused to give his Assent to this Bill for abolishing the Company of Merchant Adventurers, but imprisoned those Members that were active in promoting it. Nay, immediately upon the rising of this very Parliament, he erected an exclusive Company for trading with *Spain*, and *Portugal*; and would have proceeded farther, so as to have included the Trade to *France* in the same Monopoly, had not the insuing Parliament interposed, and annulled both the one, and the other. See the Preamble of the third of *James* I. Chap. VI. — In short, his weak and childish Extravagancies obliged him to make frequent Applications to Parliament: This Measure, so cautiously avoided by his Predecessor, threw him into fresh Difficulties: For the Consequence was, That either he must give up some Points of his darling Prerogative, or obtain no Supplies. — Supplies were to be obtained at any rate, in order to feed his devouring Favourites. But wherever he could, he stuck to his Prerogative: And as a Proof of it, let it be observed, that he made a new Grant of most of those Patents, which he had formerly recalled; besides bestowing several others, foreign and domestic, on his Friends, and Favourites; and to complete the Scene, by Virtue of his own Warrant, without Vote of the House, or Act of Parliament, he frequently laid Impositions upon the Manufactures of the Kingdom, when exported, and on raw Materials, if imported, to the Value of five, and sometimes as high as twenty five *per Cent*.

JUDGE therefore by these Circumstances, whether the Taxes were most oppressive, and most impoverishing then, or now; and whether we ought to wish for the RESTORATION of those Times, and prefer them to the present: Judge likewise, whether Monopolies, and Exclusions were ever necessary, or ever vindicable; And above all, please to reflect, that every Plea, Pretence, or Apology urged at this Day in defence of these Things, is nothing else but a nauseous Repetition of the same idle, canting Story, which hath been confuted a thousand Times over. As to the *Spanish*, and *Portugal* Company, the Trade to those Countries is now free, and unlimited; therefore Experience hath fully shewn us, that it can be safely carried on, without the Management of an exclusive Company. But if the Exclusion had still continued, I must insist upon what I have proved before, and now repeat, That the Arguments which might be drawn from the Proceedings of the Popish Inquisition, the Bigotry of an ignorant, haughty, and furious People, and the natural Jealousy of the whole *Spanish* Nation, would have created a much more plausible, and specious Pretence for keeping up that Monopoly, than for any other now existing. With what Face then can any Man be an Advocate for others? —

AND now after this long and tedious Detail, I must beg the Reader to consider the Importance of the Subject, and in consequence thereof to judge the more favourably of the Length of this SECTION, and AP-PENDIX. Nothing of the like Nature will occur hereafter. But it seemed necessary in the present Case, to obviate every Plea, to refute every Cavil, to strip off all Disguises, and to lay naked before the Reader the base, but true Original of these odious, and inslaving Usurpations. In one word, As we are now blessed with Liberty of Conscience, and a free Government, we want nothing to complete our Happiness under a Race of excellent Princes, but that Liberty of Commerce, to which every Man is intitled both by the Right of Nature, and the general Tenor of the Laws of his Country: — And towards the attaining of which our gracious Sovereigns of the House of *Hanover* have ever manifested the readiest Concurrence. This I say, and insist upon, without fear of the Imputation of Flattery; because it is neither more, nor less than the *simple Truth:* For, since the coming of this *patriot* Family to the Throne, many Monopolies have been destroyed, and the Trade thrown intirely open; and many more greatly weakened, and rendered less oppressive; and yet not one new Exclusion hath been erected, not one monopolizing Patent hath been granted, excepting to the Inventors of new Discoveries as a reasonable *Recompense*, for fourteen Years. — Now this Circumstance of destroying, opening, and weakening so many Monopolies in so short a Time, is what no Nation in *Europe* can boast of but ourselves; neither could we do it in any Age but the present. — May we still go on, and complete what is wanting!

The End of the Appendix.

H AVING brought the Treatise thus far, the Author is desirous of laying it before his Commercial Friends, and other proper Judges, during this Recess from public Business; hoping to receive the Benefit of their Correction, and Improvement, while he is proceeding on with the rest. And indeed his general Plan being now sufficiently laid open, an intelligent Reader cannot fail of judging of the Nature, and Importance of what is to follow: And consequently, if he approves of the Author's Design, and Manner of conducting it, he may suggest such useful Hints, and Observations, as would probably have escaped the Author's Notice, but which he shall most thankfully receive, and incorporate into his Work.

THE Author is the more particularly earnest in making this humble Request to the judicious Lovers of their Country; inasmuch as without some kind Assistance of this Sort, it will be extremely difficult for him to go through all the Parts of this extensive Subject, especially that relating to Taxes, and to execute his Undertaking in the Manner he could wish. For indeed the Reasons on the *moral* Tendency, and *commercial* Use of *proper* Taxes, have never yet been exhibited to the Public; — or if they have, the Author hath not been so happy as to meet with them: And therefore, since he must still consider them as a *new System*, he would be the more desirous of producing it finished, and complete to public View, and in some Degree not unworthy of public Attention.

As to the Author's own Theory, it is certainly no complex Thing, but is sufficiently clear, and plain: *viz.* If you have a Mind to have your

People in *general* honestly, and usefully imployed, lay your chief Taxes upon Idleness, and Pleasures: For such Taxes will make all People frugal, and industrious: And Frugality, and Industry necessarily create Wealth: The INFALLIBLE CONSEQUENCE of Wealth is *Injoyment*; and Injoyment is the properest Subject for Taxation. Thus therefore the Circle goes round, the more Taxes (*of this sort*) the more Riches, — the more Riches the more Pleasures, — the more Pleasures the more Taxes, — the more Taxes the more Riches, &c. &c. — Or, if you prefer to consider the Subject in another View, then I would say, Abolish every Tax, and remove all Impediments whatever, which might prevent Self-Love, the *Grand Mover*, from operating for the Public Good: But bar up with high Taxes, Duties, and Impositions, all the Avenues, and By-Paths, which might make an Opening for irregular, or corrupt Self-Love to decline from the great Road of private Virtue, and public Happiness. And when you have set this Plan once in Motion, you have all the Certainty, which is to be expected in human Affairs, that it will not miscarry: For the daily, and hourly Collection of the Revenue, is a constant and never-ceasing Agent in the Execution of your System: Whereas all other Applications to Law, or Justice, can proceed, even at the best, only by Fits, and Starts. Thus therefore, Rewards and Punishments are the grand Hinges, on which, not only Government, and Religion, but national Commerce, and national Industry, ought to turn: And indeed, the nearer you bring your Commercial Ideas to the Standard of good Government, and sound Religion, the more lasting, the more extensive, and the more perfect is your Plan.

BUT though the general Nature of the Subject is so very plain, and intelligible; and though the Application of it would be extremely easy to a State *now in forming*; yet it requires the nicest and coolest Judgment to adapt the several Parts of it to a State *already formed*. And nothing should be offered to the Regard of the Public, but what is really practicable, and may be introduced, without throwing the Body Politic into unnatural, and dangerous Convulsions. As to the Remainder of this Work, the Skeleton thereof is as follows:

CHAP. II. of PART II. continued, *viz.*

SECTION III.

A Polity for improving our Colonies, and extending the Trade between them and the Mother-Country to their mutual Advantage.

SECTION IV.

A Polity for making all Ports free, and easing Trade of several Burdens.

SECTION V.

A Polity for suppressing Smuggling.

SECTION VI.

A Polity for a sure, and expeditious Manning of the Fleet without Pressing.

SECTION VII.

A Polity for making good Roads, navigable Rivers, and Canals.

SECTION VIII.

A Polity for establishing an Uniformity of Weights, and Measures throughout the Kingdom.

SECTION IX.

A Polity for a perfect Incorporation with Ireland.

CHAP. III.

On Coin, and Credit as the Mediums of Commerce.

SECTION I.

On the Nature, and Circulation of human Industry.

SECTION II.

On the Rise, and Origin, the Use, and Necessity of some Medium, Deposit, or Certificate, whereby the Exchange of the Produce of one Man's Labour may be facilitated for that of another. — And that this Medium, Deposit, or Certificate, is what we call Money.

SECTION III.

On the true Meaning of the relative Terms, Market Price, *and* Value *of Commodities,* Cheapness, Dearness, Scarcity, Plenty, &c. &c.

SECTION IV.

The Reasons assigned why Gold and Silver are found preferable to other Metals for the Purposes of making them into Money; *and how far a* Paper Certificate *may as truly become* Money, *as Pieces of the Metals of Gold, and Silver.*

SECTION V.

What is intrinsic *in these Metals, and what is more properly relative: —
viz. The Intrinsics in Gold, and Silver are Size, Weight, and Fineness:
The Relatives are the several Proportions of the Weight, and Fineness of
the Coins of one Country compared with those of another: And from these
Comparisons results that imaginary Coin, or Medium between the two,
called the* Par of Exchange. *— After this Comparison with foreign Coins,
whether Gold or Silver, there is a secondary or domestic Comparison, which
hath an universal Influence, tho' little attended to, viz.   The domestic
Proportion between Gold, and Silver, whether set higher or lower, than it
is in other Countries.*

SECTION VI.

*On the Doctrine of Exchanges, and the Nature of Banking, illustrated by
familiar Ideas taken from Common Life, and then applied.*

SECTION VII.

*Reasons for increasing the Quantity of Metal Money, and the Polities
for so doing.*

SECTION VIII.

Reasons for changing a considerable Part of the dead *national Debt into
circulating Certificates or Paper Money; and a Scheme proposed, whereby
every Man in the Kingdom may receive Interest every Moment for his
Money, and become his own Banker; so that the national Debt shall become
the most advantageous Institution to Commerce, Manufactures, Agriculture, and general Industry, that ever existed.*

PART III.

A System of Polities for the Preservation, and Improvement of Good Morals.

DISSERTATION I.

*On the Connection, and intire Harmony between National Commerce,
Good Morals, and Good Government: That they all promote each other;
nay, that they are but Parts of one general Scheme, in the Designs of
Providence, though considered by us as separate, and distinct, and
sometimes as unconnected.*

DISSERTATION II.

That as Commerce must be under the Guidance of Good Morals, the Rules of Good Morals are therefore to be applied to regulate these artificial Wants of Mankind, which are the Basis of Commerce: And these Reasonings illustrated by plain Facts, and Examples. Polities proposed.

SECTION I.

Proved, that all the former Polities relating to the Increase of Mankind, Part I, are useful to Good Morals.

SECTION II.

Proved, that all the former Polities relating to national Industry, and the right Imployment of Time, Part II, are productive of the same good Effects.

SECTION III.

A Polity for superintending all public Places of Expence, Pleasure, and Diversion.

SECTION IV.

A Polity for securing those Trades to the Female Sex, which are fittest for their Condition.

SECTION V.

A Polity for preventing the present bad Effects of Electioneering.

SECTION VI.

A Polity for preventing national Perjury.

SECTION VII.

A Polity for clearing the Streets of Street-walkers, for the well-regulating of Jails, and Bridewells, and for making Executions less frequent, but more decent, and solemn.

SECTION VIII.

An annual Survey, and Register of the Inhabitants.

PART IV.

A System of Taxes preventive of Idleness, Extravagance, &c.—promotive of good Morals,—and productive of national Industry, Wealth, and Plenty.

PART V.

Miscellaneous Reflections, and Observations.

SECTION III.

Rules for setting up any new Branch of Trade, Merchandize, or Manufacture.

SECTION IV.

General Directions for Travellers, whether through our own, or in foreign Countries; viz. What Questions to ask relating to Civil, Religious, or Commercial Liberty; the Tenure of Lands, different Holdings, and Jurisdictions, Nature of Government, Courts of Justice, Tendency of Taxes, and the like: And what Inferences to make from the respective Answers: — How to judge of the Genius of a People from their political Constitution, and vice versa: How to account for the Decay, or Improvement of Trade, Manufactures, Agriculture, Husbandry, &c. and of the Increase or Diminution of the Numbers of People: Also a true Method of finding out the comparative Riches or Poverty of the State, or Country through which you travel.

SECTION V.

The whole Science, and System of Commerce reduced into a Series of short Maxims, or Aphorisms. The Conclusion.

POSTSCRIPT.

IT is humbly requested of those Gentlemen, and honourable Persons, into whose Hands these Sheets shall be committed, that they would please to return them in two, or three Month's Time, (with their Corrections, and Amendments in the Margin) sealed up, and delivered either to

The Reverend Dr BIRCH, Secretary to the Royal Society, in *Norfolk-street*, in the *Strand*;

Mr SHIPLEY, Secretary to the new Society for Arts and Sciences, in *Craigs-Court, Westminster*;

The Reverend Dr HALES, at *Teddington*, in *Middlesex*; or to

Their most Obliged,

and most Obedient,

Humble Servant,

Josiah Tucker,
Rector of St *Stephen*'s in *Bristol*.

Bristol,
July 10, 1755.

INSTRUCTIONS FOR TRAVELLERS

EDITORIAL NOTE

This tract was privately printed in 1757 and was published in Dublin in 1758. In it the author develops one of the topics included in the skeleton of his projected treatise appended to *The Elements of Commerce.* See above, page 219.

INSTRUCTIONS

FOR

TRAVELLERS.

By *JOSIAH TUCKER*, M.A.

Rector of St. *Stephen*'s in *Bristol*, and Chaplain to the
Right Reverend the Lord Bishop of *Bristol*.

Author of

*A Brief Essay on the Advantages and Disadvantages
which respectively attend France and Great Britain,
with regard to* TRADE.

DUBLIN:

Printed for WILLIAM WATSON, at the

Poets Heads in *Capel-street.*

MDCCLVIII.

INSTRUCTIONS, &c.

A PLAN *for improving in the moral and
political Theory of Trade and Taxes, by
means of Travelling.*

PERSONS who propose to themselves a Scheme for Travelling,
generally do it with a View to obtain one, or more of the following
Ends, *viz. First,* To make curious Collections, as Natural
Philosophers, Virtuosos, or Antiquarians. *Secondly,* To improve in
Painting, Statuary, Architecture, and Music. *Thirdly,* to obtain the
Reputation of being Men of Vertù, and of an elegant Taste. *Fourthly,*
To acquire foreign Airs, and adorn their dear Persons with fine Cloaths
and new Fashions, and their Conversation with new Phrases. Or,
Fifthly, To rub off local Prejudices (which is indeed the most commend-

able Motive, though not the most prevailing) and to acquire that enlarged and impartial View of Men and Things, which no one single Country can afford. — These, I say, are the principal Inducements for modern Travelling: Though it must be owned, that there is one particular Class of Travellers yet to mention, whose Motives are very singular, and their Number very small; those, I mean, who resolve to visit the Countries of *Italy* and *Greece*, out of a kind of enthusiastic Reverence for Classic Ground, like the Pilgrims of old for the Holy Land, and paying a Sort of Literary Adoration to the very Rubbish of an antient City, or to any Spot of Earth that has been famous in antient Story.

[As to that Species of Beings found only here in *England* (a Country of universal Freedom and Opulence) who go Abroad with no other Views but because they are tired of staying at Home, and can afford to make themselves as ridiculous every where as they please: It would be a Loss of Time to take any other Notice of them, than just to observe, That they are sure of returning Home as Wise as they went out, but much more Impertinent, less Wealthy, and less Innocent.]

Now, though the Scheme to be proposed in the following Pages, is not immediately calculated for the Use of either of the Classes of Travellers abovementioned, yet the Author is humbly of Opinion, that all might peruse it without Disadvantage, if not with some Degree of Improvement. But still the Person, for whom this Plan is particularly intended, must be a Man whose Views in Travelling are of a different Nature from either of the former: That is, he must make those Things in which their Business and Employment chiefly consisted, to be only his Amusement and occasional Recreations; and must dedicate his principal Studies towards tracing such secret, though powerful Effects and Consequences, as are produced by the various Systems of Religion, Government, and Commerce in the World: He must observe, how these Systems operate on different People, or on the same People in different Periods, *viz.* Whether they enlarge, or contract the active Powers in human Nature, and whether they make those Powers become useful, or pernicious to Society. For in Fact the human Mind is in some Sense but as Clay in the Hands of the Potter, which receives its Figure and Impression, if I may so speak, according as it is moulded or formed by these different Systems: So that the Political, the Religious, and Commercial Characters of any People, will be found, for the most Part, to be the Result of this threefold Combination of Religion, Government, and Commerce on their Minds. Now Travelling into foreign Countries for the Sake of Improvement, necessarily pre-supposes, that you are no Stranger to the Religion,

Constitution, and Nature of your own. For if you go abroad, before you have laid in a competent Stock of this Sort of Knowledge, how can you make useful Comparisons between your own and other Countries? How can you judge concerning the Preference which ought to be given either to the one, or the other? Or select those Things from Abroad, which may with Advantage be naturalized at Home? Therefore let a young Gentleman begin with the Tour of his own Country, under the Guidance of a skilful Instructor: Let him examine the general Properties of the Soil, the Climate, and the like: And attend to the Characteristics of the Inhabitants, and the Nature of the several Establishments, Religious, Civil, Military, and Commercial; and then, and not till then, is he completely qualified to make Observations on foreign Countries.

BUT in order to proceed even thus far, a young Gentleman should not only have passed through the common Forms of a liberal Education, but also should have attentively perused such particular Treatises, as might best serve to instruct him in the Business he is to set about, and to answer the Purposes here proposed: For an ignorant Traveller is of all Beings the most contemptible; and the best that you can say of him is, that he sees strange Sights in strange Countries, with the same stupid, wondering Face of Praise, which the common People do Feats of Juggling and Legerdemain at Home. Besides, if a young Person is not sufficiently grounded in right Principles before he sets out, it will be seldom in his Power, and seldomer still in his Inclination, to acquire them afterwards; especially during his Travels. For Travelling is by no Means the proper Season for acquiring the Rudiments of Knowledge, but for making a judicious Application of former Acquirements.

THEREFORE the Author humbly hopes, that the candid and judicious Reader will forgive him, in his well meant Endeavours, in recommending a few Books to the Perusal and Study of the young Pupil before setting out; and in adding short Observations upon them.

Religion.	*Seed*'s Sermons, two first vol. *Sherlock*'s Sermons, three vol. Bishop of *Sodor and Man*'s Instructions for *Indians*.
Ethics, Civil Law, and Government in general.	*Burlamachi*'s Natural and Political Law; *Burnet*'s Essay on Government; *Montesquieu*'s L'Esprit de Loix.

Peculiar System of the *English* Constitution.
} *Rapin*'s Dissertation on the Government of the *Anglo-Saxons*, and his Dissertation on Whig and Tory; *Montesquieu*'s Chapters on the *English* Constitution, *viz.* Book XI. Chap. 6. and Book XIX. Chap. 27. The Analysis of the Laws of *England*; also the present State of *England*.

Establishment of the Church of *England*, and a Toleration.
} *Warburton*'s Alliance between Church and State.

Foreign Politics, and Balance of Power.
} *Campbell*'s Present State of *Europe*.

Commerce, and Taxes.
} Sir *Josiah Child* on Trade; Remarks on the Advantages, and Disadvantages of *France*, and *Great Britain*; *Crouche*'s Book of Rates.

OBSERVATIONS.

I. WE must first begin with Religion, not only because it is the most Important in its Nature, but because if a Traveller is not well grounded in the Principles of it before he sets out, he will run the Risk either of having none at all during his whole Life, or of being made a Convert to a very bad one, I mean the Popish. For if his Turn of Mind is naturally Contemplative and Philosophic, the great Variety of Religions he will meet with in his Travels will so stagger his Resolution as to make him indifferent to all alike; at the same Time, that the impudent Tricks and Forgeries of the Church of *Rome*, will tempt him to pronounce the Whole a Cheat. But if he should have any strong Tincture of Enthusiasm, or Superstition in his Composition; or if he should be pre-disposed either to an Excess of Gaiety, or of Gloom, or be captivated with outside Forms, at the same Time that he went on in a Round of thoughtless Pleasure; in all these Respects the Religion of the Church of *Rome* is particularly calculated for making Proselytes of young Minds, by applying her Snares, either to this Foible, or to that, according to the predominant Disposition. Therefore in every View, and upon every Account, it ought to be laid down as an indisputable Maxim, that a young Gentleman ought not to begin his Travels, while he is a Novice in the important Concerns of Religion.

Now the first Book recommended is *Seed*'s Sermons, which having the Advantage of a great Luxuriancy and Brilliancy of Stile, are fitter to make their Way into the Hearts of young People, than Authors more exact in their Composition, and of a less flowery Imagination. But there is besides this, a very peculiar Reason for recommending these Discourses, and that is, that as their Reasoning is, for the most Part, grounded on Bishop *Butler*'s *Analogy*, they exhibit in the gayest and most inviting Colours, the Strength, and Chain of Thought of that deep, sagacious Author, without his metaphysical Stile, or abstract Speculations. As to Bishop *Butler* himself, he certainly pursues a Method the fittest in the World to put to silence the superficial, licentious Extravagancies of modern Times, were his manner of Writing a little more pleasing and alluring. For by demonstrating, that there is a System actually carrying on by the Author of the Universe, both in the natural and moral World, he confutes the Sceptics on one Extreme; and by proving how imperfectly this System is yet comprehended by us, he checks that Arrogance, and Self-sufficiency on the other, which are too natural to young Minds, just tinctured with a Smattering of Knowledge. As to Bishop *Sherlock*'s Sermons, whether you consider the Author as the distinguished Defender of the sublime Truths of Religion, or as throwing new and unexpected Lights on old and common Subjects, or as a sagacious Textuarist, a sound practical Writer, a judicious Casuist, or an eminent Model of clear, nervous, and manly Eloquence: — In all these Respects he is great without a Rival. And no Man, whatever his future Profession in Life is intended to be, would misemploy his Time in giving him a careful and attentive Perusal. In regard to the Bishop of *Sodor and Man*'s *Instructions for the* Indians, it is enough to say, that it is the best Compendium of practical Divinity yet extant. And as a Gentleman ought to carry some little Tract or other with him Abroad both for Reading and Devotion (for I dare not suppose that the Life of a Traveller will be the Life of an Atheist) he cannot carry a fitter Author into foreign Countries than this here recommended; an Author, who by happily selecting the more essential and fundamental Truths of Religion, from others of less Importance, hath kept clear of all Controversy, and wrote in such a manner as to be acceptable to the Members of every Christian Communion whatever.

Note, This Author is translated into *French*.

II. NEXT to Religion, and indeed as a Part thereof, though too frequently considered in a different View, are Ethics, Civil Law, and the Rudiments of Government in general. In which Case *Burlamachie*'s two Treatises contain all the Instructions necessary for a young Gentleman just setting out upon his Travels: It being the great Happiness of this Author to express himself in very clear and intelligible Terms upon the abstrusest Subjects, and to reconcile the seemingly contradictory Opinions and Systems of those who wrote before him, by unravelling the Meaning of each, and shewing, that the chief Difference between them was a Difference of Expression. By these Means he hath fixed the Science of Legislation, if I may so speak, by clear and determinate Rules; and hath laid a firm Foundation for future Legislators to build upon; I say, *future* Legislators; because in a Constitution such as ours, it is not at all improbable, but the young Gentleman Traveller will, one Day, come to have a Share in making Laws for the Good of his Country: And therefore he ought certainly to know something of the Nature of them. In regard to Dr. *Burnet's Essay on Government*, as it is written with peculiar Clearness and Precision, and proceeds in a mathematic or scientific Way; it has undoubtedly great Merit; and being so very short and compendious, it will take up but little Time in Reading. *The Spirit of Laws* of Monsieur *de Montesquieu* is superior to all Elogiums whatever.

III. AFTER an Acquisition of the Rudiments of Ethics and Civil Law, and some Insight into the general Nature of Government, it will be highly requisite to enter into the peculiar Spirit of the *British* Constitution: To which End, *Rapin's Dissertation on the Government of the* Anglo-Saxons, and his *Dissertation on Whigs and Tories*, will be highly useful, both as they give a general Idea of the antient Gothic Plan, which is the Basis of the present, and as they point out those great and important Revolutions which have since ensued: So that by comparing both together, a judicious Reader may be the more able to form an exact Idea of the Benefits or Dangers proceeding either from the former, or the latter Constitution. But as to the modern Spirit of our Government, its Guards, Limits, and Correctives, perhaps no Author can equal the Baron *de Montesquieu* in his Chapters on the *English* Constitution, Book XI. Chap. 6. Book XIX. Chap. 27. Note also, that before a young Gentleman actually sets out to visit foreign Countries, he ought to have received a few Lectures on the Nature of our landed Tenures, Freeholds, Copyholds, &c. also on the Nature of our Courts of Law, and Equity, and the different Manner of proceeding in these respective Courts upon different Causes, Civil, Criminal, and Ecclesiastical. By these Means he would be able to compare the Land-holdings, and legal Processes in *England* with those Abroad, and form a truer Judgment upon his Return than most other Travellers have yet done, whether our own were better, or worse: And if worse, what might be mended, and how to do it. He would likewise then see, whether many of the Evils now complained of, are really such as could be mended without introducing greater; or whether they are of the Number of those that must be submitted to in the present imperfect State of Things. And the little Treatise lately published, called the *Analysis of the Laws of* England, seems to afford the best Assistance in this Case. If the Author shall complete the Lectures therein promised, and of which this is the Syllabus, with equal Judgment and Perspicuity (as there is great Reason to believe he will) such a Man will justly deserve the best Thanks of his Country. As to *The Present State of* England, it may be consulted occasionally in the Nature of a Dictionary, in order to see the Number of Offices, and the different Kinds of Jurisdictions exercised throughout the Kingdom.

IV. THE next Article is the legal Establishment of the Church of *England*, and a Toleration to Dissenters. A young Gentleman of a liberal Education, especially one who is to Travel into foreign Countries, ought to know upon what Grounds a Church or Ecclesiastical Society is formed, upon what Conditions it may receive the Sanctions of the Civil Legislature, and for what Reasons and within what Bounds, a Toleration ought to be allowed to those whose Consciences do not approve of the national Establishment. And for this Purpose Dr. *Warburton's Alliance between Church and State* seems to be the fittest, and to give the fullest Satisfaction of any thing yet extant. For though his System hath been greatly controverted by many, yet it hath never been properly answered or confuted. And as to making Exceptions to detached Parts of a Plan, or picking little Holes in it here and there, suffice it to say, that it is much easier to find Fault than to mend; and that almost every Man can object, and is too naturally disposed to cavil at the Performance of another, at the same Time, that that very few indeed are capable of producing an unexceptionable Plan of their own.

V. As to foreign Politics, and the Balance of Power, Dr. *Campbell's Present State of* Europe, has reduced all that Affair, which used to be the vague and unmeaning Talk of Coffee-house Politicians, into so regular a Science, and has fixed it upon such sure Principles, that his Treatise alone is very sufficient by way of Preparative.

VI. THE last Thing is Commerce and Taxes: And as this whole Treatise pretends to enter deeply into that Matter, the less may be said in this Place. However, as it may not be amiss to take the Judgment of one or two Authors more on the same Subject, I would beg Leave to recommend Sir *J. Child* as a Commercial Writer of the first Note: And then at a respectful Distance after him, the *Remarks on the Advantages and Disadvantages of* France *and* Great Britain *in regard to Trade* may be no improper Book; *viz.* because it exhibits a comparative View of the Commerce of both Kingdoms, and enters deeper into the Inconveniencies or Obstructions attending the *French* Government, regarding Trade, than any Author whatever.   This Tract is in a great Measure a Translation of my *Essay on Trade*, and other Commercial Pieces.   But as the Author is a Native of *France, viz.*   The Marquiss *D'Angeul* (though appearing under the borrowed Name of an *Englishman*, Sir *John Nicholls*) he was capable of making great Improvements on my Plan; and being likewise employed in the Finances, he could speak to the Difficulties and Discouragements attending Trade in that Kingdom, with more Experience and Certainty than a Stranger was capable of doing.   The last Author recommended is *Crouch's Book of Rates*, which is properer for a Scholar than any other (though perhaps not for the Use of the Merchant) because it sets forth the Improvements that have been made since the happy Revolution in the System of our Taxes: And because it may suggest the Improvements that are still to be made, by exposing the Absurdities which our former Princes and Parliaments committed in this Affair.   Moreover when the young Traveller takes this Book with him into foreign Countries, and there compares it with their Tarifs and Systems of Taxation, he can determine at one Glance, whether their Taxes are better or worse, more impoverishing or enriching than ours: And consequently, whether the Country so taxed, can make a Figure in Commerce, and the Arts of Peace and Industry, or not.   For it is an indisputable Fact, that a Progress in Commerce, and the Improvement of a Country, greatly depend upon the Nature of the national Taxes, *viz.* Whether they cramp Industry, or promote it; and whether they make the Passion of Self-Love (that ruling Principle of human Nature) subservient to the Public Good, or detrimental.   In short, That State or Kingdom which by means of proper Taxes converts Drones into Bees, will be Rich: But every Community which turns Bees into Drones, must be Poor.

WE will now suppose the young Traveller to enter upon the immediate Business of his intended Tour with these Accomplishments: And during his Travels he should constantly bear in mind the grand Maxim, That the Face of every Country through which he passes, the Looks, Numbers, and Behaviour of the People, their general Cloathing, Food, and Dwelling, their Attainments in Agriculture, Manufactures, Arts and Sciences, are the Effects and Consequences of some certain Causes; which Causes he was particularly sent out to investigate and discover.   Therefore let him consider, whether, and how far, the said Effects may be ascribed to the natural Soil and Situation of the Country. — To the peculiar Genius and singular Inventions of the Inhabitants. — To the Public Spirit and Tenor of their Constitution, — or to the Religious Principles established, or tolerated among them. For certain it is, that every considerable Effect must be ascribed, and may be traced up to, one or more of these Causes; which for the Sake of greater Distinction I will term Natural, — Artificial, — Political, — and Religious. Moreover, as it is extremely proper to assist a Beginner by raising some Queries for him under each Head, it will also, it is humbly presumed, not be amiss to return such Answers to them, as a Person may be supposed to give, who hath lately made the Tour both of his own, and foreign Countries; and is now striking out a general Comparison between them. For this will serve both to illustrate the Nature of the Plan, and at the same Time give a Sample or Specimen of the intended Manner of Proceeding. And note, Though the Scene is laid in *England*, yet the same Questions, *mutatis mutandis*, may serve for any Country or Climate whatever.

NATURAL CAUSES.

Q. Is the Soil of *England* naturally good and fertile, or barren and steril? Is it a shallow, or a deep Mould? inclinable to Sand, or Clay? And what seems to be the most natural Produce of the Country?

A. The Soil is generally good, and the Mould deeper than is usual in other Countries. Some Parts, such as *Surry, Hampshire, Norfolk*, &c. are inclinable to Sand. And others, (though of much less extent) are bound up with Clay. But for the most Part *England* hath a greater Variety of Sand, Clay, Loom, fat Earth, Marl, Chalk, Flint, Stone-Brush, &c. &c. within the same Space of Ground, perhaps the Compass of a County, or Hundred, nay even of a Parish, than most other Kingdoms in *Europe*; and seems to be a Compendium within itself of the Soils, Strata, Mountains, Valleys, Plains, Fens and Marshes of other Countries. The most natural Produce of the Ground is Grass, owing to the great Moisture of the Atmosphere. For as to the Plenty of Corn, with which *England* generally abounds, it is merely the Force of superior Art and Industry. In regard to Minerals, the Chief are Coal, Lead, Tin, and Copper.

Q. Is the Air dry or moist? The Climate healthy, or sickly? and how is it as to the Degrees of Heat, and Cold? What are the general Distempers of the Country? and at what particular Times of the Year do they usually come?

A. The Air is moist, the Sky subject to be cloudy, and the Climate remarkably mild, as to the Extremes of Heat, and Cold: But the Country cannot be pronounced so very healthy as some others Abroad.   The prevalent Distempers are such as proceed from Obstructed Perspirations, *viz*. Scurvies, Colds, Coughs: And in Consequence thereof, and of the Smoak of Sea Coal, Asthmas and Consumptions: Colds and Coughs usually come on, when the Chills of Autumn lock up the perspirable Matter, which used to pass in the Summer.

Q. ARE the married Women observed to be more, or less fruitful here than in other Countries?   And do many Children die from the Birth to two Years Old?

A. IT doth not appear that the married Women in *England* are altogether so prolific as in other Countries; and in Cities and great Towns it is certain they are remarkably otherwise: Whether this is to be ascribed to the superior Vice and Luxury reigning at present in our *English* Cities, is another Question.   But it is undeniable, that more Children die in *England* from the Birth to two Years old, than in any known Country whatever.

Q. How is *England* situated in regard to the neighbouring States and Kingdoms?   Has it a free and easy Communication with them, by Land or Water?   Or are other Countries difficult and dangerous of access? What Advantages doth it derive from good Ports and Sea Carriage? and what from inland Navigation?

A. *Great Britain* being an Island is situated very commodiously between the South and North Parts of *Europe*, to hold a Communication with either: Likewise as it is an Island, the Sea, which is a considerable Defence against Invasions, is of use to promote its Commerce: And the Ports are in such Abundance, that there is hardly a Spot in the Kingdom above sixty Miles distant from some Port on one Side, or other of the Island: As to Rivers naturally navigable, it hath not many, the *Thames*, the *Severn*, and the *Humber*, are the Chief: Some few have been rendered navigable by Art; but as the Undertakings have been carried on by private Subscriptions, the high Tolls or Duties laid upon these Rivers, in order to re-imburse the Proprietors, are a great Check to the Navigation. — If low priced Goods are to pay excessive Lockages, they are as effectually stopped from passing, as if the Water was shallow, or a Bank of Sand in the Way.

Q. WHAT Improvements might be easily made in Matters of Water Carriage both on the Sea Coast, and within Land?

A. Many new Ports might be made, and others improved by building Piers, driving down Piles, &c. &c. at the public Expence, under the

Direction of the Board of Trade. [Here specify Particulars; and see *Lewis Morris*'s Charts for the Coast of *Wales*.] And the Sums so expended would not amount to the hundredth Part of the Money, now laid out for securing the useless Navigation of many Parts of *America!* The same Remark holds good in regard to making Rivers and Streams navigable, and cutting Canals: Not to mention, that as every Canal and navigable River are high Roads in Times of Peace, so also are they easily made Fortifications in Times of an Invasion, *viz.* By lining the Banks with a few Troops to stop the Progress of the Enemy. And the Situation of *England* is such, that it might be intersected at least in eight or ten Places, so as to open a Communication with almost every Town of Note throughout the Kingdom. The more obvious Communications are those, which might be made between the Avon of *Bristol*, the *Kennet*, and the *Thames*, — the Avon of *Bristol*, and the Avon of *Salisbury*, — the Avon of *Bristol* and the *Thames* by way of *Letchlade* and *Cricklade*, — also between the *Severn*, the *Stroud*, and [by the Help of a short Land Carriage] to *Cirencester*, and so on to the *Thames* at *Cricklade*,—the *Severn*, the *Steur*, the *Penk*, the *Trent*, and the *Humber*,—the *Severn*, the Avon [of *Stratford*] with a small Land Carriage to *Banbury* on the *Charwell*, and so to the *Isis* at *Oxford*.—These, and many such like Communications might be opened in the Course of a few Years, by employing some Regiments of Soldiers during the Summer Seasons, on each Work, and paying them six-pence or eight-pence a Day above their usual Allowance.

Q. WHAT other Improvements do the Situation of the Country, the Nature of its Forests, Heaths, Wastes, Commons, Fens and Marshes, readily and properly suggest?

A. THE Situation of the Country between the North and South of *Europe*, and between the Continent of *Europe* and *America*, (not to mention *Africa* and *Asia*) plainly shews the Feasibility of making this Island become the common Depositum, Magazine, or Storehouse, for each other: So that the medium Profit might be made to center here. As to the Royal Forests, these might produce great Quantities of Timber, were the Right of Herbage, now belonging to the adjacent Parishes and Villages, totally abolished. But whilst this destructive Privilege remains, the Persons interested in the Verdure will take effectual Care to prevent the Increase of Timber, by setting on Fire the Grass, Leaves, Fern, &c. in the dry Season, and consequently burning the Seeds and Acorns, and destroying all the natural Nurseries of young Plants. In regard to Heaths, Wastes, Commons, Fens and Marshes, all these would soon become a great Addition to the Wealth, Strength, and Beauty of the Kingdom, were they converted into private Property, and made to yield those Productions, which Nature and Providence fitted them for.   Moreover, were a great part of the Wastes on the South Coasts from *Kent* to *Cornwall* to be parcelled out into small Shares, suppose ten or twenty Acres, as Portions to virtuous young Women remarkable for their Diligence in Spinning certain Quantities of Wool, Flax, or Cotton, provided they married Labourers or Farmers; this Circumstance alone would render that Country, which now looks like a desolate Wilderness, as populous and industrious as a Bee-Hive.   Add to this, that were other Portions of these immense Wastes, converted into spacious Barracks, well fortified, and having large Districts round them, to serve both for military Lines, and military Exercise within the Lines, in the Manner of the *Roman* Castra, with good Roads and easy Communications laid out between Barrack and Barrack; then the Consequence would be, that all the Country round would find a ready Market for their Provisions, and carry back the Soil and Manure of the Barrack or Town to raise more;— but above all, the Soldiers in these Places would be kept in good order, and properly disciplined, consequently, would be no Burden to the Innkeepers, and not be obliged, as they are at present, to take up their Quarters in Gin-Shops and Bawdy-Houses: Thus therefore, being less tainted in their Morals, healthy, well disciplined, and ready upon the Spot to give the Enemy a warm Reception in Case of an Invasion, to annoy him in Front, Flank, and Rear, and to defend their Fortress if besieged; they would, in all human Probability, be as great a Security to us as the Nature of this imperfect State of Things can be supposed to promise.

ARTIFICIAL CAUSES.

By the Term Artificial is here intended the Exercise and Progress of the *peculiar Genius* and inventive Powers of the Individuals in a State, considered in their *private* Capacity; whereby such Causes are distinguished from Religious, or Political, which are more properly the united Councils of the whole Society.

AND as all Inquiries of this Sort are reduceable to two Heads, *viz.* those respecting Agriculture, and those respecting Manufactures, I shall beg Leave to suit the several Queries accordingly.

First, *Queries on the Subject of Husbandry and Agriculture.*

Q. WHAT happy Discoveries have been made of late Years in regard to Husbandry? What Improvements, in turning, preparing, and dressing of Land? What new Implements, and how contrived? What Advantages and Disadvantages resulting from them?

A. THE Principles and Powers of Vegetation are still but little known; though perhaps more in *England*, and better applied to promote Husbandry and Gardening, than in most other Countries. What is discovered for certain is this, That all Vegetables, whether Herbs, Plants, Trees, or Corn suck out of the Earth, by means of their Roots and Fibres, their natural Mouths, the Particles of Food peculiar for them, and fitted for their Digestion. They also imbibe the Air, Rains and Dews, by means of their Bark, Stalks and Leaves; and they carry on a Circulation, and throw off perspirable Matter through their Pores, much in the same Manner as Animals do. This being the Case, they must have a Sufficiency of Food, or come to nothing and die. Now this Food is either got naturally on the Spot, or procured artificially from other Places. The Food got naturally, is that which is procured from the Earth, Air, Rains, Frost, and Snow, within the Reach of the Roots or Fibres, that is, the Mouths of the respective Tree, Plant, or Herb. But even in this Case, the Earth, by being turned and properly stirred, imbibes more of the Qualities of Frost and Snow, Air and Rain, than it would otherwise do: That is, it becomes more fruitful by the Help of human Industry and Labour. Likewise this turning, digging, or plowing of the Ground at proper Seasons, besides other Uses, destroys the Weeds, which when thoroughly putrified, and reduced to Mould, become the Food of better and more useful Vegetables, sown or planted in their stead. But for* more particular Directions, and for Cuts or Draughts of

---

* IT is next to impossible that any Traveller could note down all that can be said on each of these Heads; and it would be a mere Waste of Time to attempt it. Nevertheless, when a judicious Traveller meets with any thing very *singular*, curious, or remarkable, he would do well to pay a more peculiar Attention to it, and enter down the whole Process of the Affair. If nothing singular or striking occurs, there is no harm done; but if something should appear worth his Notice and Regard, the present System of Queries will serve both to fix his Attention, to improve his Reasoning, and to arrange his Thoughts and Ideas in their proper Order. And what is thus true in regard to Agriculture, Husbandry and Vegetation, is equally true with respect to every other Subject he will meet with in his Travels, whether Manufactures, Taxes, Politics, or Religion. Moreover, a few of the best and choicest Authors in every Country, and on every Subject, ought to be brought Home, in order to be consulted occasionally, and at one's Leisure: Also the Cuts or Draughts of Machines or Engines, where such are to be got, together with Descriptions of their Uses, and Calculations of their Expence both in making, and maintaining them.—Gentlemen, who travel after this manner, will travel to great Advantage, doing an Honour to their Country when Abroad, and to themselves when they return Home.

Hoes, Harrows, Plows, and other Implements, their Uses, or Inconveniences, it would be proper to consult the principal Books on Husbandry and Gardening, such as *Tull, Lisle, The complete Body of Husbandry, Bradley, Miller,* &c. And for a more analytic Theory, a chemical, and philosophical Knowledge of the Process of Nature, see Dr *Hales's Vegetable Statics,* and Dr *Home's Principles of Agriculture and Vegetation.*

Q. WHAT kind of Manure is applied to different Soils? How is the Manure made? from whence brought, and at what Expence?

A. MANURES of all kinds are such Food, as is prepared and brought by human Art and Industry to the Spot, where the Vegetables are growing, or designed to grow, in order to lay in a Stock for their Support and Nourishment. But as the Books of Gardening and Husbandry abovementioned, are full of Rules and Directions, and will answer all Queries of this Sort, it will be properer to refer to them, than to transcribe their Words in this Place. Only let it be always remembered, that the more populous any Country is, the more Manure and Soil will be made by the Inhabitants: So that large Towns and populous Villages do not only furnish a Market for the Produce of the Country round about, and thereby pay for the Labour, and excite the Emulation of the Husbandman, but also supply him with Dung, Rags, Horn-Shavings, Ashes, Soot, &c. &c. to load his Carriages back, in order to fructify his Grounds for fresh Crops. So little Cause is there to fear, that a Country can be too populous! So empty and frivolous the Pretence of making Wars for the sake of a greater Extent of Dominion! And such are the admirable Ways of Providence in providing for the Wants of Mankind, by the Arts of Peace and Industry, were we but to pay the Attention and Regard which are due to them!

Q. WHAT Methods are taken to water dry Grounds, or gutter wet ones? What is the Form of the Gutter, and the Expence and Manner of making it? What also are the Provisions, Machines, &c. for draining Fens and Marshes?

A. THESE Articles being Branches of Mechanics and Hydraulics, are best treated of by the Writers on the Mechanic Powers; who, together with the practical Writers on Husbandry, ought to be consulted on these Occasions. But for particular Facts, see the Account of stopping *Dagenham* Breach, draining the Fens in *Lincolnshire,* and the like.

Q. ARE the several Sorts of Grain, Seeds, Fruits, Trees, and Grasses, judiciously adapted to the Soils proper for them? Are sufficient Changes made from one Sort of Grain, Seeds, &c. to another, and from fibrous rooted Vegetables to bulbous rooted, and *vice versa,* so that the Soil may not be too fast clung together by the former, nor rendered too open and porous by the latter? Moreover, is the Grain well and properly got in, and by what Instruments; how secured from bad Weather, Mice, and Vermin? And how threshed out, cleansed and winnowed?

A. ALL these Inquiries are best answered from Books of Husbandry; inasmuch as it can be no Entertainment, nor much Improvement to an *Englishman* (whatever it might be to a Foreigner) to write down those Particulars, which he daily sees practised almost in every Farm throughout the Kingdom.

Q. WHAT Methods are taken for rearing Sheep, Horses, Cattle, and for curing or preventing their Disorders; also for providing a Sufficiency of Food for them, especially at such Seasons of the Year, when the natural Grass is gone?

A. SEE the Authors as before.

Q. ARE Things so contrived, as that the Raising or Fattening of Cattle, and the Raising of Corn shall assist each other? And if there is any Scheme of this Nature, what is it?

A. THIS is such an Important Article, as to deserve a peculiar Consideration.—In the South and West Part of *Ireland*, where Nature has been the most liberal of her Gifts; Arts and bad Policy have brought on a General Desolation, by the sole Fact of raising and fattening Cattle without regard to raising either Corn, or Flax, or Hemp, or any such Produce as might feed, or employ Numbers of People: So that nothing is to be seen for many Thousands of Acres, but Sheep and Cattle, except here and there a wretched *Irish* Cabbin, and two or three of its miserable, half-starved, naked Inhabitants, to add to the Dismalness of the Prospect. Whereas, in *Norfolk*, a Country naturally much more barren, the People are numerous, well-cloathed, well-housed, and well-fed; and all owing to the good Management of making the Raising of Corn, and the Rearing, or at least the Fattening of Cattle, be mutually assistant to each other. In this Country it is generally so contrived, that the Field intended to be manured for a Crop of Corn, is not very far distant from from a Field of Turneps: And when the Sheep have fed upon the green Leaves, or when the Frost hath nipped them off, then the Field to be manured is divided into smaller Plots by Hurdles; and twenty or thirty lean Cattle are put into a Plot: A Man is employed to draw up the Turneps, and to load a one-horse Cart, in order to bring them to the Cattle. There he scatters them about, cutting a few of them at first into Slices, in order that they may be induced to taste them. When they have tasted, they grow so excessively fond of them, as to be frequently in danger of Choaking; and therefore he is provided with a Piece of Rope of a proper Size to push the Turnep that sticks, down their Throats. He strews also a little Hay or Straw about the Plot for the Cattle to feed on occasionally, and to prevent their Teeth from being set on Edge by feeding altogether upon Turneps. When this Plot is sufficiently saturated with the Dung and Urine of the Animals, he moves them to another Plot, and so on to a third, till the whole Field is sufficiently manured, and fit to be plowed up. And thus, by the Time that the Cattle are grown fat and fit for a Market, the Ground likewise is properly enriched for a Crop of Corn: And both Articles are carried on without any Inconvenience, Loss of Time, or Expence to either; nay, perhaps in a better manner, than either of them could be done separately. As to the Turnep Field itself, the Feeding of the Sheep at first upon the Greens or Tops, and the Feeding of them again upon such of the Turneps or Roots, as will be occasionally left, though the Majority of them are carried away; I say, these two Circumstances will sufficiently enrich the Ground for sowing any common Grain, though perhaps the safer Experiment would be to sow Barley rather than Wheat.

Q. WHAT new Markets are opened for vending the Produce of the Ground? And what Encouragements are given, or might be given, for opening more?

A. THE Bounty upon the Exportation of Corn hath opened a Market to every foreign Country, where there is any thing of Demand. But it may be made a great Query, Whether that Bounty, which in the Infancy of Agriculture was so essentially necessary, ought not to receive at present very considerable Amendments and Reductions. And if the Legislature shall enact, which they seem at present to intend, that all Grain shall be sold by Weight, this Circumstance will go a great Way towards redressing the present Evils. As to new Markets at Home, every Road well mended produces that Effect in one Degree or other: And were more Rivers made navigable, and Canals cut, the Effects would still be greater and more beneficial.

Q. WHAT further Improvements in Gardening, Agriculture, and Husbandry, might be suggested?

A. MANKIND in general are very slow in leaving off old Prejudices, and have a strong Aversion even against thinking, much more against publicly acknowledging, that they have ever been in the Wrong. Even at this Day there are many Parts of the Kingdom, where the Arts of Guttering of wet Lands, the proper Sowing and Hoeing of Turneps, the Sowing of artificial Grasses, raising of Flax and Hemp, the Use of the

Wheel Plow, winnowing with the Toss of the Shovel, and the skilful Methods of Hedging and Ditching, with many the like Improvements, have scarce made their Appearance.—But for a more exact Knowledge in Gardening, Agriculture and Husbandry, as Branches of natural Philosophy (in order that such Knowledge might hereafter descend to the Farmer and the Labourer) the Scheme of a Society, or Committee to be expressly appointed for making, receiving, and communicating Experiments, seems the plainest and the best.—This is a Proposal of the Ingenious Dr. *Home*, in his *Principles of Agriculture and Vegetation*, Page 173.—And this is not the only one, by a great many, for which that worthy Gentleman deserves the Thanks of his Countrymen, and of Mankind in general.

Secondly, *Queries on the Subject of Trade and Manufactures.*

Q. WHAT principal Manufactures are carried on in this Country? and what is the Price of Labour?

A. THE principal Manufactures are the Woollen, the Metal, (*viz.* Iron, and Steel, Copper, Brass, Tin and Lead) the Silk, the Linen, and the Cotton.   But the Price of Labour in each Manufacture is so various, that it is impossible to give an Idea of it by any common Example.— Only it may be affirmed in general, that the Wages of Men (or what Men generally earn *per* Day) is for the most Part, from 1*s.* to 2*s.* 6*d. per* Day; and the Wages of Women from 4*d.* to 1*s.* throughout the Kingdom.

Q. Do Journey-men and Journey-women work by the Day, or by the Great?   And what Checks are invented to guard against Impositions of bad Work, or embezzling the Materials, or idling away Time?

A. ALMOST all Master Manufacturers now find it their Interest to pay their Work-people by the Piece, or the Great, wherever they can, rather than by the Day: Which Circumstance alone is a striking Proof, that no sufficient Check hath yet been invented against the loitering away of Time, when the Master was to pay for it:—Not to mention, that the Person who works by the Day hath scarce any Motives to exert an Industry, Dexterity, or Skill superior to others; whereas the Working by the Piece, or by the Great, calls them all forth; because he himself, and none others, are to reap the Benefit and Reputation of them. [And *N. B.* this single Remark, were there no others, is sufficient to prove, that Slaves, who very literally work by the Day, and can have no Motive whatever to exert any other Industry, Dexterity, or Skill, than what is just sufficient to escape the Whip of the Driver; nay, whose Self-Interest will naturally teach them to conceal any superior Talents from the

Knowledge of their Masters, lest their Masters should expect a greater Task from *them* than others, and punish them for not doing it;—I say this single Remark is a full Proof, that Slaves never did, nor ever will perform their Work either so cheap, or so well, as those Freemen who work by the Piece or the Great, and are spurred on every Moment by the Examples of others, by Self-Interest, and by the Glory of excelling.] As to Checks against bad Work, the Judgment of the Master or Overseer is the best, and perhaps the only Remedy that can be applied in such a Case. But in respect to embezzling of Materials, and various are the Methods contrived, and almost every Manufacture hath a different one; sometimes the Goods are weighed in and out, due Allowance being made for necessary Waste: At other Times Check-Engines are used to ascertain the Length or Measure, and in general Sleaing, or Weaving-Tables, are a tolerable Security against Impositions in the Weaving of Woollens, Stuffs, Linens, Silks, Cottons, &c.

Q. WHAT Machines are used to abridge the Process of a Manufacture, so that one Person can do the Work of many? And what is the Consequence of this Abridgment both regarding the Price, and the Numbers of Persons employed?

A. FEW Countries are equal, perhaps none excel the *English* in the Numbers and Contrivance of their Machines to abridge Labour. Indeed the *Dutch* are superior to them in the Use and Application of Wind-Mills for sawing Timber, expressing Oil, making Paper, and the like. But in regard to Mines and Metals of all Sorts, the *English* are uncommonly dexterous in their Contrivance of the mechanic Powers; some being calculated for landing the Ores out of Pits, such as Cranes and Horse-Engines:—Others again for draining off superfluous Water, such as* Water Wheels and Steam Engines: Others again for easing the Expence of Carriage, such as Machines to run on inclined Planes, or Roads down Hill with wooden Frames, in order to carry many Tons of Materials at a Time. And to these must be added the various Sorts of Levers used in different Processes: Also the Brass Battery Works, the Slitting Mills, Plate, and Flatting Mills, and those for making Wire of different Fineness. Yet all these, curious as they may seem, are little more than Preparations or Introductions for further Operations. Therefore when we still consider, that at *Bermingham, Wolverhampton, Sheffield*, and other Manu-

---

* THE celebrated Machine of *Marli*, so much boasted of by the *French*, is but a bungling Performance in the Eyes of an *Englishman*. The same Quantity of Water might have been raised, and is raised under *London* Bridge at a fortieth Part of the Expence.

facturing Places, almost every Master Manufacturer hath a new Invention of his own, and is daily improving on those of others; we may aver with some Confidence, that those Parts of *England* in which these Things are to be seen, exhibit a Specimen of practical Mechanics scarce to be paralleled in any Part of the World. As to Machines in the Woollen, and Stuff Way, nothing very considerable hath been of late attempted; owing in a great Measure to the mistaken Notions of the infatuated Populace, who, not being able to see farther than the first Link of the Chain, consider all such Inventions, as taking the Bread out of their Mouths; and therefore never fail to break out into Riots, and Insurrections, whenever such Things are proposed. In regard to the Silk Manufacture, the Throwsting Mills, especially the grand one at *Derby*, are eminent Proofs of the Abridgment of that Species of Labour: And some Attempts have been lately made towards helping forward the Cotton and Linen Manufactures by means of certain Engines.

IN regard to the other Part of the Query, *viz.* What is the Consequence of this Abridgment of Labour, both regarding the Price of the Goods, and the Number of Persons employed? The Answer is very short and full, *viz.* That the Price of Goods is thereby prodigiously lowered from what otherwise it must have been; and that a much greater Number of Hands are employed. The first of these is a Position universally assented to; but the other, though nothing more than a Corollary of the former, is looked upon by the Majority of Mankind, and even by some Persons of great Name and Character, as a monstrous Paradox. We must therefore endeavour to clear away these Prejudices Step by Step. And the first Step is, that Cheapness, *cæteris paribus*, is an Inducement to buy,—and that many Buyers cause a great Demand,—and that a great Demand brings on a great Consumption;—which great Consumption must necessarily employ a vast Variety of Hands, whether the original Material is considered, or the Number and Repair of Machines, or the Materials out of which those Machines are made, or the Persons necessarily employed in tending upon and conducting them: Not to mention those Branches of the Manufacture, Package, Porterage, Stationary Articles, and Book-keeping, *&c. &c.* which must inevitably be performed by human Labour. But to come to some determinate and striking Instance, let us take the Plow, the Harrow, the Cart, the Instruments for Threshing and Winnowing, and the Mills for Grinding and Boulting, as so many Machines for abridging Labour in the Process of making Bread: I ask, do these Machines prevent, or create Employment for the People? And would there have been as many Persons occupied in raising of Corn, and making of Bread, if no such Engines had been discovered?—The obvious Reply to this Query is, That probably the wheaten Loaf had been confined to one, or two Families in a State, who, on Account of this superior Rank, and vast Revenues, could have afforded to give an extravagant Price for their delicious Morsel: But it is impossible, that under such Circumstances, it ever could have become the common Food of the Kingdom. The same Remark would hold good, were it to be applied to the Art of Printing, and to the Numbers of People, from first to last, therein employed: For Printing is nothing more than a Machine to abridge the Labour, and reduce the Price of Writing.—But Examples are endless; and surely enough has been said, to convince any reasonable Man, though even the great Author of *L'Esprit des Loix* should once be of a different Mind, that that System of Machines, which so greatly reduces the Price of Labour, as to enable the Generality of a People to become Purchasers of the Goods, will in the End, though not immediately, employ more Hands in the Manufacture, than could possibly have found Employment, had no such Machines been invented. And every manufacturing Place, when duly considered, is an Evidence in this Point.

Q. Is that Labour, which is still to be performed by the human Kind, so judiciously divided, that Men, Women, and Children have their respective Shares in Proportion to their Strength, Sex, and Abilities? And is every Branch so contrived, that there is no Waste of Time, or unnecessary Expence of Strength or Labour? Moreover, what good Consequences attend these Circumstances in such Parts of the Kingdom, where they are observed, and what bad ones in other Parts, where they are not?

A. IN many Provinces of the Kingdom, particularly, *Staffordshire, Warwickshire,* and certain Districts of *Yorkshire,* with the Town of *Manchester, Norwich,* and some others, the Labour, for the most Part, is very properly proportioned, and great Judgment appears in the Methods and Contrivances for bringing the several Parts of the Manufacture so within the Reach of each other, that no Time should be wasted in passing the Goods to be manufactured from Hand to Hand, and that no unnecessary Strength should be employed. For an Instance of both Kinds, take one among a Thousand at *Birmingham, viz.* When a Man stamps a metal Button by means of an Engine, a Child stands by him to place the Button in readiness to receive the Stamp, and to remove it when received, and then to place another. By these means the Operator can stamp at least double the Number, which he could otherwise have done, had he been obliged to have stopped each Time to have shifted the Buttons: And as his Gettings may be from 14*d*. to 18*d*. and the Child's from a Penny to 2*d. per* Day for doing the same Quantity of Work, which must have required double the Sum, had the Man alone been employed; this single Circumstance saves above 80, or near 100 *per Cent.* at the same Time that it trains up Children to an Habit of Industry, almost as soon as they can speak. And hence it is, that the *Bijoux d' Angleterre*, or the *Birmingham* Toys, are rendered so exceedingly cheap as to astonish all *Europe*; and that the Roman Catholic Countries are supplied with such vast Quantities of Crucifixes, Agnus Dei's, &c. from *England*. A Dozen of these Crucifixes, as I am informed, being to be sold, in the wholesale Way, for 7½*d*.—But the good Effects of this proportioning of Labour to different Strengths and Sexes, is still more extensive than it at first appears. For in *Birmingham* the Numbers of poor Women on the Pay-Bill, compared to those of poor Men, are hardly as three to two; whereas in *Bristol*, where no such good Polities obtain, the Numbers are upwards of four to one; and in many Parts of *London*, it is still much worse: So great is the Difference, and such the Expensiveness and heavy Burdens of a wrong Conduct even in this Respect: not to mention, that Prostitution and Debauchery seem to be an unavoidable Consequence in the female Sex of Poverty and Idleness, when they are young; and when they grow old, what Refuge can they have, if they do not soon rot with their Diseases, but the Parish Pay?

Q. IN those Towns and Places, where great Manufactures are carried on, are there many independent Masters, and few Journeymen to each Master? or few independent Masters, and many Journeymen? And what is the Difference, in regard to Morals, Cheapness and Goodness of Work, Extent of Trade, Rioting, Mobbing and the like?

A. THIS Matter is better illustrated by comparing the same Manufacture, and the Consequences attending it, under the different Circumstances here referred to. In many Parts of *Yorkshire*, the Woollen Manufacture is carried on by small Farmers and Freeholders: These People buy some Wool, and grow some; their Wives, Daughters, and Servants spin it in the long Winter Nights, and at such Times when not employed in their Farms and Dairies; the Master of the Family either sells this Produce in the Yarn Market, or hath it wove up himself. It is then milled, cleansed, and brought to Market, generally to the Town of *Leeds*; but when sold there, he can be paid for no greater Number of Yards than the Cloth will measure, after having been well soaked in Water: By which means all Frauds in Stretching, Tentering, &c. are

effectually prevented.   The Persons who buy this Cloth, generally act
upon Commission at a very low Rate; and afterwards cause the Cloth to
be dyed (if it was not dyed in the Wool) and to be properly dressed and
finished.   Thus, the whole passes through various Hands independently
of each other.   And though in Fact the Spinner, Weaver, Millman,
Dyer, Dresser, &c. &c. are all of them the Journeymen of the Agent or
Commissioner, who stands in the Stead of him who is the Clothier in
other Places; yet by acting thus upon a distinct Footing, they conceive
themselves as far independent of him, and of each other, as any Buyer or
Seller whatever: And being thus independent, they are all Rivals, all
animated with the same Desire of bringing their Goods to Market upon
the cheapest Terms, and of excelling one another.   Their Journeymen
likewise, if they have any, being so little removed from the Degree and
Condition of their Masters, and likely to set up for themselves by the
Industry and Frugality of a few Years, have no Conception that they are
embarked in an Interest opposite to that of their Masters, or that they
are called upon to enter into Clubs and Combinations against them.
Thus it is, that the working People are generally Moral, Sober, and
Industrious; that the Goods are well made, and exceedingly Cheap; and
that a Riot or a Mob is a Thing hardly known among them.   Whereas
in *Gloucestershire*, *Wiltshire*, and *Somersetshire*, the Manufacture is
carried on by a quite different Process, and the Effects are accordingly;
viz. One Person, with a great Stock and large Credit, buys the Wool,
pays for the Spinning, Weaving, Milling, Dying, Shearing, Dressing, &c.
&c.   That is, he is Master of the whole Manufacture from first to last,
and perhaps employs a thousand Persons under him.   This is the
Clothier, whom all the Rest are to look upon as their Paymaster.   But
will they not also sometimes look upon him as their Tyrant?   And as
great Numbers of them work together in the same Shop, will they not
have it the more in their Power to vitiate and corrupt each other, to
cabal and associate against their Masters, and to break out into Mobs and
Riots upon every little Occasion?   The Event hath fully shewed, and is
now shewing, that these Conjectures are too frequently supported by
Facts.   Besides, as the Master is placed so high above the Condition of
the Journeyman, both their Conditions approach much nearer to that of a
Planter and Slave in our *American* Colonies, than might be expected in
such a Country as *England*; and the Vices and Tempers belonging to
each Condition are of the same Kind, only in an inferior Degree.   The
Master, for Example, however well-disposed in himself, is naturally
tempted by his Situation to be proud and over-bearing, to consider his

People as the Scum of the Earth, whom he has a Right to squeeze whenever he can; because they ought to be kept low, and not to rise up in Competition with their Superiors. The Journeymen on the contrary, are equally tempted by their Situation, to envy the high Station, and superior Fortunes of their Masters; and to envy them the more, in Proportion as they find themselves deprived of the Hopes of advancing themselves to the same Degree by any Stretch of Industry, or superior Skill. Hence their Self-Love takes a wrong Turn, destructive to themselves, and others. They think it no Crime to get as much Wages, and to do as little for it as they possibly can, to lie and cheat, and do any other bad Thing; provided it is only against their Master, whom they look upon as their common Enemy, with whom no Faith is to be kept. The Motives to Industry, Frugality, and Sobriety are all subverted by this one Consideration, *viz.* That they shall always be chained to the same Oar, and never be but Journeymen. Therefore their only Happiness is to get Drunk, and to make Life pass away with as little Thought as possible. This being the Case, is it to be wondered at, that the Trade in *Yorkshire* should flourish, or the Trade in *Somersetshire*, *Wiltshire*, and *Glocestershire* be found declining every Day? The real Surprize would be to discover, that such Causes did not produce such Effects: And if ever the Manufactures in the North should adopt the bad Policy of the West, and *vice versa*, Things will come round again.

Q. ARE the Manufactures of *England*, those especially in the Toy, Jewelry, Cabinet, Furniture, and Silk Way, chiefly adapted for high or middling Life? and what Species of People make up the Bulk of the Customers?

A. England being a free Country, where Riches got by Trade are no Disgrace, and where Property is also safe against the Prerogative either of Prince or Nobles, and where every Person may make what Display he pleases of his Wealth, without incurring a higher *Taille*, Poll, or Capitation the next Year for so doing;—the Manufactures of the Kingdom accommodate themselves, if I may so speak, to the Constitution of it: That is, they are more adapted for the Demands of Peasants and Mechanics, in order to appear in warm Circumstances;—for Farmers, Freeholders, Tradesmen, and Manufacturers in middling Life;—and for wholesale Dealers, Merchants, and all Persons of Landed Estates, to appear in genteel Life; than for the Magnificence of Palaces, or the Cabinets of Princes. Thus it is, according to the very Spirit of our Constitution, that the *English* of these several Denominations have better Conveniencies in their Houses, and affect to have more in Quantity of clean, neat Furniture, and a greater Variety (such as Carpets, Screens, Window Curtains, Chamber Bells, polished Brass Locks, Fenders, &c. &c. (Things hardly known Abroad among Persons of such a Rank) than are to be found in any other Country in *Europe, Holland* excepted. Moreover, as the Demand is great and continual, the Numbers of Workmen and their greater Experience excite the higher Emulation, and cause them to excel the Mechanics of other Countries in these Sorts of Manufactures. In a Word, it is a true Observation, that almost the whole Body of the People of *Great Britain* may be considered either as the Customers *to*, or the Manufacturers *for* each other: A very happy Circumstance this, on which the Wealth and Prosperity of a Nation greatly depends.— Were an Inventory to be taken of the Houshold Goods and Furniture of a Peasant, or Mechanic in *France*, and of a Peasant, or Mechanic in *England*, the latter would be found, upon an Average, to exceed the former in Value at least as three to one.

Q. IN what particular Manufactures, Arts, or Sciences, are the *English* Nation chiefly deficient?

A. THEY are said to be out-done by Foreigners in most of the higher or politer Arts, such as Painting, Engraving, Statuary, and Music. And one Reason seems to be, that neither the Religion, nor Political Constitution of the Country give that Encouragement to these Studies, which is to be met with Abroad; our Churches, for Example, admitting of little more than elegant Neatness; and our Situation, as an Island, besides other Circumstances, preventing our Artists from taking Models, or trying their Ingenuity in the Palaces of foreign Princes.

Q. ARE there any peculiar Institutions, or voluntary Societies erected with a View to give Encouragement, and distribute Premiums to those who shall excel in the mechanic Arts, and Manufactures?

A. Ireland seems to have been the first Place in the *British* Empire, which had the Honour of giving Birth to Institutions of this Nature. But now there is a numerous Society of Noblemen, and Gentlemen, formed in *London* for promoting Arts, Manufactures, and Commerce. The *Antigallican* Societies are likewise much upon the same Plan; except that they take in likewise the discouraging the Consumption of *French* Wine, and Use of their Manufactures. The Society of *Edinburgh* comprehends not only Arts and Manufactures, but also Agriculture, and the Study of Vegetation. And that at *Glasgow*, as I am informed, is intended to promote the finer Arts in Conjunction with the others. Moreover, the Gentlemen of *Brecknockshire* in the Principality of *Wales*, came to a very laudable Resolution, about two Years ago, of converting a monthly Hunting Club into "A Society for encouraging Improvements in Agriculture and Manufactures, and promoting the general Good of the Country." And the Success, which hath already attended this Institution, affords great Hopes, that many other Clubs and Societies throughout the Kingdom, will follow their Example, and convert themselves into public spirited Institutions of real Use, and extensive Benefit.

POLITICAL CAUSES.

THESE being as extensive as they are important, ought to be subdivided into separate Heads; *viz.* Such as constitute the Rights, Privileges, and Liberties of the Subject; — such as establish the national Taxes; — and such others, which being compounded of all Parts of the Constitution operating together, may be termed the Spirit or Essence of it.

Queries relating to the Rights, Liberties and Privileges of the Subject.

Q. WHAT are those Rights and Privileges of an *Englishman*, which seem peculiar to him, and whereby he may be distinguished from the Subject of another State?

A. Englishmen, as such, have several Privileges of a very valuable and extensive Nature; as *First*, Every Man hath the same equal Security, one as well as another, against arbitrary Imprisonments: That is, no Person, though the highest in the Kingdom, can imprison or detain the meanest, without alledging some legal Cause, and bringing that Cause to a judicial Hearing: And the same Observation may be applied to Security of Possessions against any Invader, as well as Security of Person. *Secondly*, When a Subject is accused of any Crime, of what Nature soever, the Accusers or Witnesses must appear Face to Face in open Court, to be interrogated by himself concerning the same; and he himself, after he hath finished his Defence, is then to be judged by Twelve of his Peers (*i. e.* by Persons of the same Condition, or nearly the same with himself) whether guilty, or not. *Thirdly*, He can have no Taxes levied upon him, but such as he is supposed to agree or consent to by his Proxy or Representative in the House of Commons, *i. e.* by the Member, or Members, of Parliament for the County, City, or Borough to which he belongs.

Q. WHAT are the Forms or Processes of Law, or general Methods of proceeding in Civil, Criminal, or Ecclesiastical Causes? And what Institutions might be borrowed from other Countries to render our Law Proceedings more certain, and expeditious, more adequate to natural Justice, and attended with less Chicane, and less Expence?

A. As to the former Part of the Query, a great deal depends at present upon that Knowledge which is to be gained by personal Experience, and Attendance in the Courts; there being no Treatise yet extant, as far as I can learn, to explain these Matters in a full and distinct Manner. But for a general or compendious Knowledge of them, see *The Analysis of the Laws of England*, Books III. and IV. *viz* "Of private Wrongs and civil Injuries; and of public Wrongs and Misdemeanors." In regard to the latter Part of the Query, the Author freely confesses, that he is not able to answer it: His Stay abroad having been too short, and too much taken up with other Avocations, to have acquired a sufficient Insight into these Matters: But the Query nevertheless may have its Use in a Treatise of this Nature, as it is to stand to be answered by those, who shall have more Time and Leisure, shall visit more Countries, and can return their Thoughts particularly to this Subject.

Q. ARE Tradesmen and Plebeians in *England* equally at Liberty to purchase landed Estates with Gentlemen or Noblemen? And are there any territorial Jurisdictions annexed to them? What likewise is the Power of Landlords over their Tenants?

A. ALL natural born Subjects of the Realm are upon an equal Footing as to the Liberty of purchasing, if they have the Ability. But as to territorial or hereditary Jurisdictions, there is scarce such a Thing now remaining in any Part of the Kingdom; those in *Scotland* being lately purchased, and annexed to the Crown. Indeed, the Courts Leet and Courts Baron, together with the Payments of Herriots and Services, still required in some Places, may be said to keep up the Shadow of the antient *Gothic* Constitution of Baron and Vassal; but the Substance of that Tyranny and Slavery is pretty well destroyed; and these customary Duties, Services, &c. are expiring every Day: So that, in short, the Tenant who pays his Rent, has as little to fear from his Landlord, as from any other Person.

Q. WHAT Encouragements, Exemptions, Privileges, or Honours are granted to the married State? And what Discouragements, Burdens, or Dishonours laid on the contrary?

A. NONE, or next to none, either Way, to the very great Detriment and dispeopling of the Country, Corruption of Morals, and Reproach of the Legislature. This Omission is the more to be lamented, as the very Nature of our Government, and Form of our Constitution, point out such easy and effectual Remedies; *viz.* to annex the Privileges of Voting, and the Posts of Honour and Profit to the married State; and to compel Bachelors of a certain Age, suppose Thirty, to pay double Taxes in all

Respects whatever, *viz.* Land, Window, Coach, Plate, Church and Poor, Tithes, and all County Taxes, Excise, and Customs, and to be obliged to serve all Offices of Burden and Expence.

Q. As Lands are best cultivated, when divided into moderate Shares, and that Country is the richest and most populous, and consequently the strongest, which hath the greatest Number of Freeholders and middling Gentry residing in it; What Polities are established by the Constitution to prevent the monopolizing of landed Property into a few Hands? What Care is also taken to make reasonable and judicious Wills for those who die Intestate? or, in other Words, to divide the Estates of such Persons agreeably to the Laws of right Reason and Equity among their Children, or nearest of Kin?

A. THE Constitution hath established no Polity whatever to prevent Monopolies of this Sort; but on the contrary, hath encouraged and encreased the natural Vanity of Mankind towards raising one Person to be the Head of the Family and Impoverishing, and sometimes Beggaring of all the rest. — To trace this Affair to its true Source, we shall find that in *England*, before the *Norman* Conquest, such landed Estates, *as had no civil or martial Jurisdiction belonging to them*, were to descend equally among all the Children, like as Goods and Chattels do now. This was, it must be owned, running too far into the *Agrarian* Scheme of Levelling and Equality; and had certainly some Inconvenience attending it: For, it cannot be at all proper, that such a System should take Place, in any Monarchy of considerable Extent. But on the other Hand, when the *Normans* took Possession of the *English* Estates, they introduced their own Customs, which gave *all* to the Eldest, and none to the rest of the Children: So that the Constitution was totally changed from one Extreme to the other. But though something might be urged at that Juncture in behalf of the *Normans*, who, by erecting almost all Estates into Knights Fees, could the easier keep the *English* in Subjection; inasmuch as every Knight was bound, when summoned, to appear with his military Tenants, to defend the Possessions of his immediate Lord; I say though this might be a good Plea for the *Normans* under such Circumstances, What Plea can it be for us at this Distance of Time, and in so different a Situation? Or is it really intended, by the late Clamours for a national Militia, to recur to the old Methods of making the same Person the hereditary Colonel of his Tenants, as well as their Landlord? If this is the Case, it may be a good Reason upon such Grounds, why the eldest Son ought to have all the Estate, and the rest none:—But at the same time it affords a very strong Argument against so great an Incroachment on our present Rights and Liberties, as such a national Militia must certainly be.   In short, the present *English* Practice of giving all to the Eldest, appears the more absurd, if we farther consider, that even in *France* itself, where Notions of high Birth and the Pride of Family certainly run sufficiently high, the Customs of *Normandy* are not the Customs of the rest of the Kingdom.   For in some Provinces, the eldest Son hath two thirds; in others he hath only one half, and then comes in for a Child's Share in the Division of the Remainder.   And this Practice, which I think obtains in all *Guienne*, a Country full of Noblesse, is attended with no Inconvenience whatsoever.   Why therefore should it not be introduced into *England*, a Country more particularly subsisting by Commerce and Navigation?   And why, in the Name of Common Sense, should the *Norman* Custom, so repugnant to the Rest of our Constitution, be continued any longer among us.   [See *The Elements of Commerce*, Pages 44, 47.]—To illustrate this Reasoning yet farther, we may observe, That the Custom of *Paris* is pure Gavelkind, or equal Division; a Custom not improper for Commercial Cities, or little Republics; and indeed highly requisite in small Islands, in order to prevent overgrown Landed Estates, and to keep all the Inhabitants in a State of Industry; a Custom also the most effectual of any towards peopling new Colonies:—Now this is the very Custom which the *French* Government hath judiciously introduced into all their Sugar Colonies: by Virtue of which, these Islands are well-peopled, well-defended, well-cultivated, and very assistant to their Mother Country: Their Sugars also, Indigo and Coffee, are better in Quality, and infinitely more in Quantity, and are almost *Cent. per Cent.* cheaper, Sugars especially, than any that come from our Plantations: Though, *N. B.* they buy their Negroes, their Lumber and Provisions at a much dearer Rate than our Planters do. *Jamaica*, on the contrary, is as thinly peopled as ever; and the Inhabitants, instead of affording any military Assistance to the Mother Country, are under perpetual Alarms of being destroyed by their own Negroes. Add to this, that the Expences which *Great Britain* hath been at in Fleets and Forces to protect *Jamaica*, and the Rest of the Sugar Islands, from foreign Invasions for these twenty Years last past, are almost incredible. Moreover, as to the Rest of the *English* Sugar Islands, Land is monopolizing, and the white Inhabitants are growing thinner every Day. This is the Fact; and a Fact too quite the Reverse of the *French*.   Judge therefore from these Circumstances, as we have paid so dearly for our Knowledge, and are still paying, whether we ought not to grow wiser, than to suffer the *Norman* Customs to prevail any longer in our Sugar Islands.—For surely, *Fas est & ab hoste doceri.*

Q. WHAT good Laws regarding Commerce and Manufactures are now in Force? And what Bounties and Premiums are given to support Manufactures in their Infant State?

A. As to the first Part of this Query, it must be observed, that there are very few, if any, Laws subsisting for that Purpose: Nor indeed is there that Necessity for them (I mean Laws of the *positive* Kind) which the generality of Men are apt to imagine. For let the Legislature but take Care not to make *bad Laws*, and then as to *good ones*, they will make themselves: That is, the Self-Love and Self-Interest of each Individual will prompt him to seek such Ways of Gain, Trades and Occupations of Life, as by serving himself, will promote the public Welfare at the same Time. The only Thing necessary to be done by positive Institutions is, to enforce the Observance of voluntary Contracts by legal Penalties speedily levied. Thus, for Example, If a Man contracts a Debt, he ought to be obliged to pay it in a Manner the least burdensome to the Creditor: And Debts contracted for Goods or Merchandise ought to have the Preference of all others. Moreover, if he sells Goods by Samples, the Goods sold ought not to be worse than the Samples; and the same Remark will extend to the Selling of Goods by the Piece, or in the wholesale Way: Because the outward Appearance of such Goods ought to be considered as a Sample of the inward Reality of them. And therefore, if they should prove to be worse than they *appeared*, having Flaws or Blemishes concealed within, or if they should be short of Measure, Weight, &c. the Seller ought to make ample Reparation to the Buyer, and be subject likewise to some Fine, or Mark of Infamy. But in Fact, such Laws as these are Laws of *Justice*, rather than of Commerce; and therefore cannot be said to promote its Interest, or the Interest of Manufactures, in any other Way, than as all Things necessarily do, which oblige us to do to others, as we would be done by. Indeed, it must be acknowledged with Gratitude and Pleasure, that the Legislature of late Years hath enacted many excellent Laws which have promoted Commerce, increased Industry, and extended Manufactures. This, I say, ought ever to be acknowledged; but then the Laws in Question are such, whose true Excellence consists rather in the Repeal of absurd and bad Laws formerly made, than in any particular Positions or Maxims of Commerce: And as to the pernicious Statutes formerly enacted, many such, as will soon appear, there are still remaining, which ought to be repealed.

IN regard to the other Part of the Query, *viz.* "What Bounties or Premiums are given to support Trades and Manufactures in their

Infant States?" The Answer is, That the Institutions of Bounties, Premiums, and Drawbacks, are in a Manner peculiar to *Great Britain* and *Ireland*; there being more of them introduced into our Commercial System within these sixty Years, than are to be met with in all *Europe* besides. And these Encouragements are of two Sorts, *viz.* First, such as are granted upon Manufactures, or super-abundant Produce to promote the *Exportation* of them; and secondly, such as are given upon raw Materials growing in our own Colonies, to promote the *Importation* of them. In regard to the former, we ought to distinguish between Bounties, and Drawbacks; the one being a Sum actually given or paid by the People in general to particular Exporters; the other being no more than a Return of that Tax or Duty upon Exportation, which was, or would have been levied upon the Goods, if used for home Consumption. Now the Commodities entitled to Bounties are at present Corn, and Spirits distilled from Corn, Fish, and Flesh, Gunpowder, coarse Linens, Sail-Cloth, and some Sorts of Silk Manufactures: To which may be added, as peculiar Cases, the Bounty on the Tonnage of Ships employed in the Royal *British*, and the *Greenland* Fisheries.—The Commodities entitled to Drawbacks are, refined Sugars, Soap, Candles, Starch, Leather, and Leather Manufactures, Paper, Ale, Mum, Cyder, Perry, also Spiritous Liquors, wrought Plate, Gold and Silver Lace, and Glass Also [foreign] Silks, Callicoes, Linens, and Stuffs, if printed, painted, stained, or dyed in *Great Britain*. The Commodities or raw Materials coming from our Colonies, entitled to a Bounty, are Pitch, Tar, and Turpentine, naval Stores and Indigo.—Now upon a Review of these several Articles, it is easy to see, that all our Manufactures ought to be exported *Duty free*; and therefore, the Institution of Drawbacks, or Return of Duties, should always make a Part in the commercial System of every wise Government: It is also easy to see, that such infant Manufactures, or raw Materials, as promise to become hereafter of general Use and Importance, ought to be reared and nursed during the Weakness and Difficulties of their infant State, by public Encouragements and national Premiums. But it doth by no means so clearly appear, that this nursing and supporting should be *continued for ever*. On the contrary, it seems more natural to conclude, that after a reasonable Course of Years, Attempts ought to be made to wean this commercial Child by gentle Degrees, and not to suffer it to contract a lazy Habit of leaning continually on the leading Strings. In short all Bounties to particular Persons are just so many Taxes upon the Community; and that particular Trade is not worth the having, which never can be brought to support itself. Were all Manufactures to receive a Bounty (and all have equal right to expect it) this Reasoning would appear unanswerable.

Q. WHAT bad Laws relating to Trade and Manufactures are now subsisting?

A. A PRODIGIOUS Number, as will appear by the following Detail.

1. ALL Laws and exclusive Privileges whatever; all Constitutions of Companies of Trade, Corporations, &c. &c. relating to the internal Commerce of the Kingdom: under which Head must likewise be comprehended that absurd Statute of the fifth of Queen *Elizabeth*, which restrains Persons from exercising those very Trades they may have the happiest Genius for, and in which they may have made great Improvements, and excelled all that went before them.—Yet, strong and unanswerable as these Reasons are, they are totally over-ruled by this single Law; and the unfortunate, ingenious Person, must be debarred from exercising that Trade, which Nature herself designed him for, and perhaps in which only he could be of use to his Country; because, forsooth, he had not served a regular Apprenticeship! But the pernicious Tendency of these several Restraints have been made more amply to appear in *The Elements of Commerce*, Pages 79—92.

2. ALL Statutes and exclusive Charters made for the Shackling and Confinement of foreign Trade, must undoubtedly come under the Denomitation of bad, nay, the worst of Laws. In relation to which see *The Elements of Commerce*, Pages 93—135.

3. THE Statutes relating to Pauper Settlements, are another great Confinement and Disadvantage to Trade: without being of real Benefit to any Set of Men whatever, the Lawyers excepted. See *The Elements of Commerce*, Pages 20—21.

4. THE Statutes for the due ordering and making particular Sorts of Goods, keeping them up to a Standard, regulating their Lengths and Breadths, appointing of what Materials, or at what Seasons of the Year they shall be made, &c. &c. are also a useless Farce and Burden; and only serve now and then as an Handle for one litigious, or lazy Rival, to vex his industrious, or ingenious Neighbour. For as to general Use, they are absolutely impracticable; and ever will so remain, as long as Buyers and Sellers vary in their Prices, Fancies, Tastes, &c. In one Word, if the Buyer is not *deceived* in buying them (that is, if they shall prove throughout such as they *appear* to be, and are in reality the same he bought them for) it is of no sort of Consequence when, or how, or where, or with what Materials they were made, or whether the Goods are longer or shorter,

broader or narrower, coarser or finer, better or worse, than those usually made before them.   See *The Elements of Commerce*, Page 88.

5. LASTLY, The Statutes for regulating Wages and the Price of Labour, are another absurdity, and a very great Hurt to Trade.—Absurd and preposterous it must surely appear, for a third Person to attempt to fix the Price between Buyer and Seller, without their own Consents: For if either the Journeyman will not sell his Labour at the fixed or statutable Price, or the Master will not give it, of what Use are a thousand regulating Laws?   Nay, how indeed can any stated Regulations be so contrived, as to make due and reasonable Allowance for Plenty or Scarcity of Work, Cheapness or Dearness of Provisions, Difference of living in Town or Country, Firing, House-Rent, &c. &c. also for the Goodness or Badness of the Workmanship, the different Degrees of Skill or Dispatch of the Workman, the unequal Goodness of Materials to work upon, State of the Manufacture, and the Demand, or Stagnation at home or abroad?   I say, How is it possible to make due Allowance for all these various and contingent Circumstances?   And yet, were even this possible, a great Difficulty still recurs, *viz.* Who shall, or how can you force the Journeyman to work, or the Master to give him Work, unless they themselves shall mutually agree about it? — And if they agree, why should you, or I, or any one else interfere?   And what need of any Regulations at all?   In short, such Laws as these can do no good, because they never can be carried into a regular, useful Practice: But on the contrary, they may cause a great deal of Mischief, Riots, and Disturbances; and will infallibly, sooner or later, drive the Trade from that Country, where Men are absurd enough to attempt to put them in Execution.

Now this being the Case, and these the Numbers of bad and pernicious Laws, it is very evident, that were they all repealed, one farther good Consequence would result, besides those already mentioned, *viz.* our *Statutes at Large*, as they are justly called, would not appear of so enormous a Bulk as they now do.   For perhaps a fourth, if not a third Part of their Number would be found upon Examination to be no other than Statutes relating either to Companies of Trades, and the Freedoms of Corporations at home,—or to exclusive Companies for trading abroad, —or to Pauper and Parish Settlements—or to the keeping of Manufactures to some supposed particular Standard,—or to regulate Wages and the Price of Labour.   Therefore the sooner all these were repealed and abolished, the better for the Public in every Respect.—As they stand at present, they are the Reproach and Nusance of a Free People, and the Plague of a Commercial Nation.

Queries relating to the Nature and Tendency of the National Taxes.

Q. As Taxes must be levied in all Countries for the Defence and Support of the State,—What constitutes a good Tax and what a bad one?

A. A good Tax is that which tends to prevent Idleness, check Extravagance, and promote Industry: A bad Tax, on the contrary, falls the heaviest of all upon the industrious Man, excusing, or at least not punishing the Idle, the Spend-thrift or the Vain. Taxes therefore when properly laid on, must enrich a Country; but when improperly, will as certainly impoverish it; and the Sum produced into the Exchequer ought not to be so much the principal Consideration, as the Nature and Tendency of the Tax.—Only it may be observed as a Corollary of what hath been here said, that an improper Tax can never amount to any considerable Sum; because it impoverishes the Country, and by that Means disables the People from paying it. Whereas a proper Tax, by causing Industry to flourish, by preventing Idleness, and checking Extravagance, is itself the Cause of that Riches which flow so abundantly into the Exchequer,—A Manufacturer, for Instance, if prevented by a judicious Tax from getting frequently drunk even with the cheapest Ale, or Gin, till he arrives at thirty five, or forty Years of Age; and if he is careful and industrious in the mean while,—may afterwards very probably be able to afford a Bottle of good Wine every Day at his Table, with House, and Furniture, and all Things suitable thereto: And yet neither do himself, nor his Family any real Disservice. Such is the Difference both to a Man's Self, and to the Public, between spending properly, and improperly: And so true it is, that Sobriety and Industry, at the long run, will contribute infinitely more in Taxes to the Support of the State, than Idleness, Drunkenness, or Extravagance.

Q. ARE all Persons, from the highest to the lowest, impartially taxed? Or are some Individuals, some Ranks and Orders of Men, or certain Towns and Districts, exempted from paying one, or more of the National Taxes?

A. *England* is much happier than most other Countries in regard to the universal Distribution and Impartiality of the Taxes; there being hardly any Exemptions or Privileges to one Person, to one Class or Degree of Men, to one Town or District, more than another.—Indeed, the Nobility and higher Gentry have some little, small Indulgence shewn them in the Affair of the Coach and Plate Tax: But these are Things so very inconsiderable, if compared with the large Exemptions that take Place in every Country abroad (*Holland* perhaps excepted) that they are not worth naming.   Be it rather observed, as a thing of much greater Consequence, that such partial Exemptions, in Proportion as they obtain, are ever found to impoverish a Country, and to cause all the useful, manufacturing, and mercantile People to grow weary of their Trades, and to run mad after Nobility.   And of the Truth of this *France* itself affords too many Instances; *Germany* still more; *Hungary* more than *Germany*; and *Poland* the most of all.   And what is the Consequence?— Why truly, *Hungary* and *Poland*, naturally two of the best, finest, and most fruitful Countries in *Europe*, are rendered by this wretched Art and bad Policy the poorest and most miserable of all.

Q. ARE any Taxes laid upon the Passage or Transport of Merchandise from one Place, one Country, or Province of the Kingdom to another? Or may they pass free of any Tolls, Town Duties, or other Burdens;— those only excepted which are appropriated to repair the Roads, and facilitate the Carriage?

A. HERE again *England* hath a great Advantage over most other Countries; inasmuch as all the old, narrow Methods of Tolls, and Town Duties, and other Contrivances for stopping the Circulation of mutual Industry and Labour, are deservedly exploded; so that hardly any Footsteps remain of this antient, *Gothic*, barbarous Custom.   Whereas in every Kingdom abroad, not excepting *France* itself, the Tolls, Town Duties, Customs, and other Impositions, have a most baleful Influence in stopping the Carriage of a Manufacture from one neighbouring Town, or Province, to the other.—And if Manufactures are prevented from being carried in order to be exchanged with each other, or in other Words, to be bought and sold, they are prevented from being made; and so much Labour is lost to the Community.

Q. UNDER what Heads might the National Taxes be the most properly ranged?

A. To omit lesser Divisions, they may be ranged with sufficient Accuracy for the present Purpose, under the Land Tax—the several Branches collected by the Officers of Excise (under which the Salt may be likewise comprehended)—and the Stamp Duties.

Q. WHICH of these several Duties do come under the Definition of good Taxes as above laid down; and ought therefore to be continued; —Which also are bad Taxes, and ought to be repealed?

A. THE Land Tax is become of late Years, a most excellent Tax for the exciting of Industry, and all kinds of Improvements; inasmuch as the Increase of Produce and Advancements of Value pay no higher a Tax, than the Grounds would have paid, had there been no Improvement at all. Therefore this Impost doth now operate in the very Manner which every Tax ought, and every good one necessarily will do: That is, it punishes the Idle and the Sluggards for not improving their Estates, but exempts the Diligent and Industrious. Whereas in all other Countries throughout *Europe*, the Taxes upon Land annually rise or fall in Proportion to the Value or Produce: by which means the Proprietor is intimidated from improving his Estate, lest it should be burdened with an higher Tax the succeeding Years.

MOREOVER, in regard to the Excise, many Branches thereof are very proper Taxes, and fit to be continued; those especially which are laid on intoxicating Liquors, or on Articles of Parade, Expence, and Pleasure. For, the further any Article is removed from the unavoidable Wants, and absolute Necessities of Life, the fitter it is to contribute towards the Support of the State by paying a Tax. And as to intoxicating Liquors, they are the farthest removed of any whatever, and the most detrimental to the State in their Effects and Consequences; therefore in every View, they are the properest to have very high and discouraging Duties laid on them.

As to the various Customs or Duties on Goods imported, or exported, there is one certain Rule, whereby a Person of any moderate Capacity might judge with sufficient Exactness, whether such Customs are right, *i. e.* properly laid on, or not; *viz.* Let him suppose the State to be a living Personage, standing on the Kay of some great Sea Port, and examining the Goods as loading,—or unloading. In the former Case, if the Goods to be exported, are completely manufactured, having undergone the full Industry and Labour of his own People, he ought to lay no Embargo whatever upon them, but to shew the Exporters all the Favour he can, and to protect them in that good Work. Whereas if the Goods are only manufactured in Part, or, what is worse still, if they are absolutely raw Materials, he should lay such Taxes upon them to check and discourage their going out of the Kingdom in *that* Condition, as may be proportionate to their unmanufactured, or raw-material State: That is, if they are absolutely raw Materials, they ought to have the highest Tax laid upon them, and in some Cases even such as may amount to a Prohibition. But if they are partly manufactured, and partly otherwise, the Tax should be lessened in Proportion as they recede from the State of raw Materials, and approach to complete Manufactures.—In regard to Goods imported, his Conduct ought to be just the very reverse of the former; that is, he ought to lay the highest and most discouraging Taxes upon foreign *complete* Manufactures, in order to prevent their being worn or used in this Kingdom,—a less discouraging upon others that are incomplete,—and still less upon those that are but little removed from the raw-material State. As to raw Materials themselves, they ought to be admitted into every Port of the Kingdom, *Duty free*; unless there are some very peculiar Circumstances to create an Exception to this general Rule. Now the Grounds or Foundation of all this Reasoning, is —national Industry and Labour: Because these are the only Riches of a Kingdom. And therefore, if foreign Manufactures are to be discouraged by Taxes, lest they should prevent the Labour of our own People; foreign intoxicating Liquors ought to be discouraged still more:—Because they are not only to be considered under the Notion of complete Manufactures in their Kind, but such Manufactures likewise as take up the Time, and destroy the Industry of our own People in the using them. A Man may wear a Coat of *French* Cloth, and yet not lose an Hour in his proper Trade or Business; but he cannot lay out so much Money in *French* Wines or Brandies, without losing a great many.

THE last Article of Taxes is the Stamp Duties; and as some of them are very proper, and none of them amiss, we shall here conclude this Head of the Query with one short Reflection, *viz.* as that Tax which promotes Labour, and checks Idleness, is a very good one; so no others ought to be esteemed absolutely *bad*, but such only which produce the contrary Effect.

WHEREFORE, from this Observation, let us now pass on to consider, what Taxes ought to be repealed, according to the Principles here laid down.

IN the first Place, the Salt Tax can have no shadow of an Argument to plead in its behalf. For if Salt is a good Manure for Lands, the taxing of Salt is the taxing of Manure. And surely all Manures are raw Materials of the most important, most extensive Nature. Judge therefore, how impolitic it must be to stop so many Improvements, and the Circulation of so much Labour, by one single Tax; which, according to the Nature of all bad Taxes, produces but very little into the Exchequer. But further, Salt is an absolute Necessary of Life, administering to no Pride, Vanity, or Excess whatever, and consequently the most improper to be taxed.—To illustrate this by its Contraries: A Man who keeps a Coach, may expect to be respected, and therefore deserves to be rated for it; because a Coach is to be considered as a Display of his Rank and Riches: But the Man who keeps a Salt-Box, only shews the Necessity he is under of preserving his Meat sweet and wholesome: And he is not esteemed by his Neighbours to be the greater, or richer Man upon that

Account. Once more, a Man may idle away a great deal of his Time in Taverns, drinking to the Prejudice of his Health, the Spending of his Substance, ruining his Family, subversion of good Morals, and setting a bad Example. Therefore, since intoxicating Liquors may, and often do produce these bad Effects, they are fit Subjects for Taxation. But the Use of Salt is liable to none of these Evils; nor will the Man who wastes away Hours and Days together at his Bottle, keep his Saltseller a Moment longer by him than he really wants it. Why therefore should this useful raw Material, this Necessary of Life, this harmless, inoffensive Thing, incapable of Abuse, Vanity, Extravagance, or Excess; — Why, in the Name of Common Sense, should it be taxed?

2dly, THE Duty on Coals is a very pernicious Duty; and subject to all the Objections of the former; only some of them in a lesser Degree.

3dly, THE Duty on Soap and Candles is not a good Tax; and yet not wholly bad. — That Part which affects the Poor, or even the middling People, must certainly be bad. But the Soap and Candles used by the Great, in which the chief Consumption and Extravagance consist, ought to pay a Duty; and it would be really a Pity, that Beaux and Belles should not contribute something to the Support of Government, in Proportion as they frequented Balls, Assemblies, Operas, Plays, Masquerades, Routs, Drums, &c. &c. But in regard to the Poor, perhaps were the Duty on Candles so constituted, that only great Candles should pay, and the small ones, *viz.* those of twelve and upwards to the Pound be exempted; this would be a very useful Emendation. — As to the Duty on Soap, it is exceeding difficult to suggest any Amendments of this Nature, though it much wants it. Yet, seeing that Drawbacks are allowed for all Soap and Candles used in Manufactures, we must in Justice acknowledge, that the Effects of this Tax are not so prejudicial as many People are apt to imagine.

4thly, The Duty on Leather is subject to some Objections, as it affects the Poor almost equally with the Rich. But yet of bad Taxes, it is far from being the worst.

5thly, The extravagant Duty upon the Importation of coarse Olive Oil, a raw Material incapable either of Excess, Vanity, or Waste of Time, and a most necessary Article for our Woollen Manufactures, and in making *Castile* Soap, is one that calls the loudest for Redress. And surely, after what hath been said, it is needless to expatiate any more on the Impropriety or Absurdity of such a Tax. But there are two peculiar Circumstances attending this Affair, which to many Persons are but little known, and yet deserve an especial Consideration. The one is, That our

Sugar Islands, and Southern Colonies, where the Heat is so intense as to render *Tallow* Soap in a great Measure useless or offensive, are under a Necessity of having *Oil* Soap from the *French*, and other Foreigners; because the high Duties upon the Materials are a Discouragement to the making of such Soap in *England;* and also because the Drawback upon Exportation bears no Proportion to the Duty paid for the raw Materials on Importation.   And if a Country is under a Necessity of taking *one* Manufacture, that one will introduce many more. — The other is, That when *Castile*, or Oil Soap is made in *England*, and used by the Clothier, he receives no greater a Drawback for it than if he had used Tallow Soap; whereas the Drawback upon foreign-made Soap is equal, or very nearly equal to the original Duty: So that, in Fact, according as Matters now stand, our own Manufacture is discouraged in both Respects, and that of Foreigners preferred.

AND having thus finished the present Examination, it may not be improper to add, for the Credit of our Country, and Praise of the Legislature, that upon the most impartial Survey, there seem to be only these five Taxes of any Consequence, which can strictly be denominated *Bad;* and among these, the Duties on Salt, Coal, and coarse Olive Oil are by much the worst, and therefore ought to be the first repealed.—At least the Duty on Oil, if not totally repealed [which perhaps would be objected to; because, if Duty free, it might come in so cheap as to supersede the Use of Train, or Fish Oil] should nevertheless be considerably lessened, and reduced from 6 *l.* 3 *s.* 2 *d. per* Ton, the present Rate, to 30 *s.* or 40 *s. per* Ton.

BUT after having specified the bad Taxes, will it be amiss, or can it be judged unseasonable, to suggest *one* great Improvement easily to be made in some of the good ones? *viz.* In regard to the Customs, To permit (though not oblige) the Merchants to land their Goods without prompt Payment of Duties at the Custom-house? — Were this Permission granted, those who accepted of it should be obliged to give Bond for the Payment, and to put their Goods under the Lock and Key of the Officer, by way of additional Security.   And then they should be allowed to dispose of their Effects, and to pay the Duties gradually; according as they could find Purchasers, or as they wanted to remove such or such particular Parcels, Hogsheads, Butts, Pipes, *&c.* out of the public, to their own private Warehouses.   By these Means, every Merchant could extend his Trade and Credit to an infinitely greater Degree than he can do at present; because he would need to make no Reserves of Cash or Credit for prompt Payments at the Custom-house; every Merchant also could buy when and where, and as much as he pleased on Speculation;

and sustain no Loss of Interest of that Money, which must be *now* advanced to pay the Duties; and which Interest, even in the Case of Drawbacks, upon the present Footing, never is, and never can be returned. — Because, though the Duty is returned, the Interest of the Money paid for it still remains unreturned, a great Loss to the Merchant, yet no Gains to the Government. — In short, this single Regulation would go a great Way towards making *Great Britain* a Magazine and Store-house for other Countries, and render all her Ports FREE.

Q. WHAT new Taxes ought to be laid on, according to the present Doctrine of preventing Idleness, promoting Industry, and checking Extravagance?

A. TAXES ought to be laid on Dogs, on Saddle-Horses, when exceeding two in Number; on Livery Servants, on all Places of public Resort and Diversion, such as public Rooms, Music-Gardens, Play-Houses, &c. also on Booths and Stands for Country Wakes, Cricket Matches, and Horse Racing, Stages for Mountebanks, Cudgel Playing, &c. moreover on Fives Places, and Ball Courts, Billiard Tables, Shuffle Boards, Skittle Alleys, Bowling Greens, and Cock Pits: — Also Capitation Taxes should be levied on itinerant Players, Lottery-men, Shew-men, Jugglers, Ballad Singers, and indeed on all others of whatever Class or Denomination, whose very Trades and Professions have a natural Tendency, and whose personal Interest it is to make other People profuse, extravagant, and idle. Lastly, The Stamp Duty might very properly be extended to take in printed Songs, Novels, Romances, Music, Plays, and such like Articles of mere Amusement, to be stampt in the same Manner as Almanacks are. — Now it is obvious, that such Taxes as these are so far from impoverishing, that they must necessarily enrich every State where they take Place. And therefore, let it be laid down as an infallible Rule, that in Proportion as this System of Taxation, or its Contrary, doth prevail in any State throughout the World, in the same Proportion doth Industry or Idleness, Plenty or Want, Riches or Beggary prevail likewise. For in short, the Course of Nature is fixed, and cannot be altered. What have we then to do but to endeavour to accommodate ourselves to the invariable Rules of Divine Providence; and not foolishly expect, that wrong should be made right, or the crooked be pronounced straight to please us?

Queries relating to the Spirit and Essence of the Constitution.

Q. WHAT is the general Result of the *present English* Constitution, considered as operating upon the Minds of the People, and producing certain, distinguishing Effects in their Conduct and Behaviour?

A. THE general Result is — An Independence of the lower and middling People in regard to the Great, — but a Dependence of the Great upon them. And from the Clashing or Mixture of these two opposite Principles, arises that medley, or Contradiction of Characters so remarkable in the *English* Nation. The People are independent, because they have nothing to fear, and very little to hope from the Power of the Great; but the Great are rendered dependent upon them; because, without the Assistance or Approbation of the People, they cannot be considerable either in the Senate, or out of it; they cannot either be Ministers themselves, or raise an effectual Opposition to the Ministry of others. Hence it is, that the Bulk of the People are always appealed to in every Dispute; and being thus erected into sovereign Arbitrators, they act without Disguise, and indeed without Reserve; so that both the good and bad Qualities in human Nature, appear bolder and more prominent in the Inhabitants of *England*, than in those of any other Country. For if the People are good, they are remarkably so; but if they are bad, they will take no Pains to conceal their Vices. Their unbounded Generosity, Frankness of Disposition, great Sincerity, and above all, their glowing Spirit of Patriotism, are Proofs of the former; and the Surliness, Brutality, and daring, declared Venality and Prostitution of many among them, are too sad Instances of the latter. In other Countries, the Mass of the People know nothing of State Affairs; being Things indeed dangerous to be meddled with: And therefore they are simple and credulous, believing what is told them, and inquiring no farther. — But in *England*, every Creature is a Politician; and has formed in his own Mind the best System both for Peace and War. He dislikes the Ministry, because he is no Minister himself; and therefore reckons up all their Failings, and a great many more than ever belonged to them: and if Things go on unsuccessfully, he is sure to impute it to the Fault, rather than the Misfortune of the Administration; because it is natural to a free People to be suspicious of their Governors; but he never distrusts his own Opinion, or imagines another may see farther, or know better than himself. Thus it is, that the *English* Populace are too deeply versed in Politics, — and yet too little; too deeply to obey with Readiness and Chearfulness; and too little, to make a wise and prudent Choice for themselves. On the other Hand, the Great, finding no other Way to the Honours and Emoluments of the State, and the Gratification of their Ambition, but through the Labyrinths of Popularity, take the shortest and the surest Road they can find, to arrive at them; that is, they apply to the Passions and Foibles of the People, rather than inform their

Reason, or enlighten their Judgments. For the Mass of Mankind are much sooner cajoled, than instructed. Flattery is pleasing, Instruction disagreeable and forbidding. Therefore a Candidate at an Election, is servile and fawning to an astonishing Degree: He consults the Humours, Tempers, Caprices, Follies, nay, the Vices of the voting Mob, their Friends and Acquaintance; and suits his own Behaviour accordingly. Nothing is too abject for him to stoop to, no Lye so absurd, no party Distinction so ridiculous, that he will not by himself, or his Agents, make use of on that Occasion. And while the mental Part of these unhappy People is thus continually inflamed with Noise and Nonsense; their brutal and animal Part is gorged and intoxicated with Gluttony and Drunkenness. — But if the Candidate is out-done by his Antagonist in these *disguised* Methods of Bribery and Corruption; if he is inferior to the other in the Arts of political Lying, popular Declamation, Carousing, and Huzzaing: then he has Recourse, as the last Shift, to the tempting Influence of pecuniary Bribes; and so corrupts the Heart, where he cannot corrupt the Understanding. Thus it is, that many of the Nobility and Gentry in *England*, are too frequently found to have certain Meanesses and Basenesses in their Conduct, which are seldom to be met with in other Countries among Persons of the same elevated Rank and Station. And yet, as a great deal must still depend upon the Reputation of a good Character, and as it is impossible, that popular Deception should last long, or serve in all Cases; the very same Motives of Popularity, which lead them to do much Evil in some Instances, operate as powerfully towards doing great Good in others. Hence that diffusive Charity, great Liberality, and Condescension, so conspicuous in Persons of Fortune in this Country; hence those noble Instances of public Beneficence for the Relief of the Poor, in Times of Scarcity and general Distress; hence also that Rivalship and Emulation in some of the Members of the Legislature, to patronize a public-spirited Scheme, and to take the Lead in doing the most signal Service to their Country. In short, this Independency, and this Dependency create such a Mixture of good and bad Effects, both in the inferior, and superior Stations, that it is difficult to say which of them at present doth preponderate, and whether the Balance at the Foot of the Account can be placed to the doing more Benefit, or more Harm to Society. — But it is to be hoped and earnestly wished, that some Method or other may be happily hit upon to produce the same, or more Good, and yet avoid the Evil.

Q. IF the Constitution hath this universal, and almost irresistible Influence on all Ranks and Conditions of Life, What is the Consequence in regard to certain Professions, Trades and Stations? And hath it rendered some of them more, or less honourable and eligible than others?

A. As the Spirit and Bent of the Constitution so strongly point towards Liberty and Independency, the Consequence is, that every Profession or Occupation is deemed honourable or eligible, in Proportion as it can attain this great End. And hence it is, that the military Service, so much coveted in other Countries, as the most honourable, is not entitled to a very great Respect in this; *viz.* because it creates a Dependency, instead of promoting an Independency; hence also the true Reason, why Trades, even mechanic Trades, are no Disgrace, provided they produce Riches; because Riches in every free Country necessarily make the Possessors independent. In *England*, an Haberdasher in his Coach, is certainly as much considered as a Captain in his Scarlet; and if he should happen to be a Member of Parliament, which is no impossible Case, the military Man would be much more likely to sue to him for Favour with the Ministry, than he to the other. Thus therefore, as Wealth creates Independency, so it is, for the most Part, that Trades and Professions are rated and valued in Proportion as they produce Wealth. Why else is the Brewer preferable to the Baker, or the Pinmaker to the Butcher? There may indeed be some Exceptions to this general Rule: but there are so few, as not to deserve a distinct Consideration. And certain it is, that though the low bred Mechanic may not always meet with Respect equal to his large and acquired Fortune; yet, if he gives his Son a liberal and accomplished Education, — the Birth and Calling of the Father are sunk in the Son; and the Son is reputed, if his Carriage is suitable, a Gentleman in all Companies, though without serving in the Army, without Patent, Pedigree, or Creation. In one Word, Trade begets Wealth, and Wealth Independence: But the Assistance of Learning and Education must be called in, in order to set off, and embellish them both. Thus therefore it cometh to pass, that a competent Share of Wealth, Learning, and improved Sense, is more generally diffused throughout all Orders and Degrees of Men in this Country, than perhaps in any other: And the different Stations of Life so run into, and mix with each other, that it is hard to say, where the one ends, and the other begins. — In other Countries it is not so.

Q. ARE the *English* Nobility and Gentry more disposed to Town Residences than Country ones, or *vice versa?* And what Effects doth the Spirit of the Constitution seem to produce in regard to either, or both these Things?

A. WERE the present Constitution removed, or altered, perhaps a Town Residence would be the chief Delight: But as Matters now stand, the Constitution strongly, though silently, disposes them to chuse both in their respective Seasons. To explain this, let it be observed that a Country Residence is necessary in order to create a Country Interest: For, was the great Man never to see, to converse with, or reside among his Country Neighbours (I mean the Neighbours to his Country Estate) he would soon find, that another of much less Property would eclipse him in Influence and Power; and that the independent *Britons* would give their Votes to that Candidate who studied most to please them. Hence therefore a kind of constitutional Necessity is formed of residing at least some Time in the Country; and since a Residence for some Part of the Year or other must be chosen, a Summer Residence is certainly the most agreeable. [Not to mention, that in the Winter, the very same Constitution calls them up to Parliament.] And when Persons are once habituated to a Thing, they take a liking to it, and seem to prefer it to another. Therefore a Country Seat becomes a Matter of Choice; and as such, is ornamented and improved, till at length it doth an Honour to the Owner, and raises the Emulation of others. Then the Example spreads and catches; and Building and Planting become a Fashion. Thus it is, that the Country Seats of the *English*, their Parks and Woods, their Gardens, Plantations, Fish-Ponds, and Canals are infinitely more numerous, more beautiful, and formed upon a better Plan, and kept in neater Order (having more Care, as well as Expence bestowed upon them) than is usual in other Countries. But, were it ever to come to pass, that the Parliament should chuse their own Members, by filling up Vacancies as they happened; — this one Circumstance would cause a total Revolution; and the whole Taste for Country Improvements, rural Decorations, and Summer Residences, would be soon at an End; *viz.* Because the great Families would then reside wholly at the Capital, as they do in other Countries; or else they would resort to Places of public Diversions, Baths, mineral Waters, &c. instead of cultivating an Acquaintance with their Country Neighbours. This therefore is a striking Instance of the Power and Influence of the present Constitution. — An Influence, which operates much stronger than any positive Law whatever. For were this Constitution, obliging to Country Residences, altered or destroyed, you might make a thousand penal Laws for the keeping up of the Country Seats, embellishing of Parks, Gardens, Canals, &c. and yet without Effect; because they would soon be forgot and disregarded. But when a Polity of this Nature is once formed, and set a going, it proceeds on of itself, requiring neither Judge nor Jury, Plaintiff nor Informer, to enforce its Execution.

RELIGIOUS CAUSES.

Q. WHAT are the moral and social Effects, which the Religion publicly professed in *England*, hath a natural Tendency to produce?

A. IN regard to Society, as this is the only View in which the Religion publicly professed, is to be here considered, it may not be amiss to give an *authorized*, and therefore an unexceptionable Account of its Nature and Tendency; *viz.* "It teaches us to love our Neighbours as ourselves,— and to do to all as we would they should do to us, — to love, honour, and succour our Parents,—to honour and obey the King, and all that are put in Authority under him, — to submit ourselves to all our Governors, Teachers, Spiritual Pastors, and Masters, to order ourselves lowly and reverently to our Betters, — to hurt no Body by Word or Deed, — to be true and just in all our Dealings, — to bear no Malice or Hatred in our Hearts, — to keep our Hands from Picking and Stealing, — our Tongues from Evil-speaking, Lying and Slandering, — to keep our Bodies in Temperance, Soberness, and Chastity, — not to covet or desire other Mens Goods — but to learn and labour truly to get our own Living, — and to do our Duty in that State of Life unto which it shall please God to call us."

Now from the above Account, it is easy to deduce one plain Inference, *viz.* That the Rules of Religion, and the Rules of social Industry do perfectly harmonize; and that all Things hurtful to the latter, are indeed a Violation of the former. In short, the same good Being who formed the religious System, formed also the commercial; and the End of both, as designed by Providence, is no other than this, That private Interest should coincide with public, self with social, and the present with future Happiness. Those Men therefore, who would represent the Principles of Religion, and the Principles of Commerce as at Variance with each other, are in reality Friends to neither, and quite ignorant of both.

Q. HATH the civil Constitution unhappily established any Circumstances in the State, which *eventually* counteract the natural good Tendency of Religion? And if it hath, how might they be removed or altered?

A. THERE are several Circumstances established, which almost necessarily introduce bad Morals; but the two Principal, and such as are chargeable altogether upon the Constitution, are Electioneering, and the

Frequency of Oaths. With regard to the former, so much hath been said already, that it is become a very needless, as well as a disagreeable Task to repeat it. Let us therefore, having seen too much of this loathsome Disease, endeavour to find out a Cure. — Or if not a total Cure, at least a considerable Remedy: And such, I think, is not difficult to discover. *Viz.* Let the Qualifications for Voting be put upon such a Footing as would exclude, for the most Part, the idle, extravagant, and debauched, but include and encourage the sober, virtuous, and ingenious: That is, let Voting excite an Emulation in Virtue, Industry, and Sobriety, not in Vice, Intemperance, and Debauchery. Now this would be greatly effected by fixing the Qualification both of a Freeholder and a Burgess, upon one simple, equal Plan, throughout the Kingdom; *viz.* Let that Estate which is rated for ten Pounds a Year or upwards to the Land-Tax, be the Qualification of Voting for a Freeholder: — And that Dwelling-house, if occupied wholly by a Man's self, and not let out to Lodgers, or In-Tenants, — that Dwelling-house, I say, in a Borough or City, which likewise pays to the Land-Tax after the Rate of ten Pounds a Year or upwards, be the Qualification of Voting as a Citizen or Burgess; and then, when these are fixed and settled, let all other Qualifications, Freedoms, Liberties, and exclusive Privileges be for ever abolished and destroyed.

Now were this the Case, waving all Commercial Views, the moral good Consequences would be exceeding great and extensive; and public Elections would in some Sense be Incitements to Virtue, instead of being, what they notoriously are at present, the Seminaries and Nurseries of Vice. Moreover, the Liberties of the People would be as well secured as ever; nay, much better, because they would be founded on superior Wisdom and Knowledge, and on undoubted Substance, and real Property; instead of that which is too much at present the Basis of popular Power; *viz.* Rags and Vermin, Noise and Nonsense. In short, nothing would suffer by this proposed Alteration; nothing would be demolished or diminished but Idleness, Drunkenness, and Extravagance; Lying, Swearing, and Forswearing; the Meanness of Superiors, and Insolence of Inferiors; Confusion, and every evil Work. And truly these are the Things which might be parted with without Regret.

As to the Frequency of Oaths, were the Arch-Fiend himself, the grand Enemy of Mankind, to have studied all means possible towards annihilating the good Impressions of Religion, he could not have devised a more effectual Method than this, which is here ready contrived for him; there being scarce a considerable Branch of Duty either towards God or

Man, but what is directly counteracted by these Institutions. In regard to God, the Idea of Him as an omnipresent Judge and almighty Avenger, is obliterated and lost by the frequent Appeals made to Him, in such Cases, where the Subject-Matter is either amazingly low and trifling, or excessively improper. — Trifling surely would many Things appear, were one to give a formal Detail of all the absurd, or insignificant Passages, which might be collected out of the Statutes of Colleges and Universities, — out of the Customs, Charters, and By-Laws of Cities, Boroughs, corporate Companies, and legal Societies; — or even out of the public Statutes of the Realm. And yet, young Gentlemen at their Admission into the University, Election upon Foundations, or taking of Degrees; — also all Citizens or Burgesses either upon receiving their Freedoms, Admittance unto the Exercise of certain Trades, or serving of Offices in exclusive Companies, — and in short, civil Magistrates of every Denomination, are respectively sworn to observe and enforce these Articles, according to their Rank and Station. It is not therefore,— indeed it is not for want of Instances, that I here forbear to produce the particular Passages referred to; but because the Subject itself is too serious to be laughed at; being fitter to excite Horror, than Ridicule.

As to *improper Occasions*, what shall we think of such Oaths, which either, in a Manner, require *Impossibilities?* or *unnecessarily* lay the Mind and Conscience under the most distressful Difficulties? And yet thousands, and hundreds of thousands of such Oaths are constitutionally imposed every Year. This is a Fact, which alas! there is no necessity of proving; because those, who are obliged to serve the Offices of Church-wardens, Constables, &c. &c. and those who must transact Business in the several Branches of the Revenue, especially the Excise, the Salt and the Customs, know it already but too well: And as to others, whose Scenes of Life lead them not into this fatal Knowledge, there is no need of drawing them out of their happy State of Ignorance.

BUT if the Duty towards God is thus intrenched upon, by such a Multiplication of useless, or improper Oaths; the Duty towards Man is not less affected by the malignant Tendency of many of them. And by this I do not mean to say, that the Obligations to social Virtue, Justice, Honesty and Integrity are necessarily relaxed in Proportion as the first Principle of Religion, *viz.* the Idea of an omnipresent Judge, and almighty Avenger, is become less awful and affecting (though surely this itself is a most alarming Consideration.) But what is here intended is, that the express Tenor, and almost the very Words of many of these Oaths are altogether repugnant to the Duties of universal Benevolence and Goodwill; and that a Man cannot possibly observe *them*, and at the same Time observe the Christian Maxim of—Doing as he would be done by. For Example, if the Concealments of Fraud and Iniquity, under the specious Title of the MYSTERIES OF TRADE; and if the grossest Disingenuity, and such selfish, sordid Views as are diametrically opposite to the public Good, are to be enforced by the Sanction of an Oath, as most undoubtedly they daily are;—What considerable Assistance can we expect from Religion, when it is thus employed to destroy itself? And if the Light that is in Us, is thus turned into Darkness, How great must that Darkness be? In short, were all the several Instances to be enumerated, wherein the natural Efficacy of Religion is unhappily counteracted by some positive civil Institution; it would perhaps appear a greater Wonder, that Religion, under such Circumstances, should produce any good Effects at all, than that it should produce so few.

BUT yet, these Evils, great and crying as they are, may most easily be removed, if heartily and sincerely set about. And what is better still, there is hardly a Possibility that any bad Consequences should attend the Alteration; for in such a Case, no Mobs, no Insurrections, nor even popular Clamours could be raised to oppose the Reformation; no Struggles for Power, or Convulsions in the State could be excited; nor any Prospect of a Change in the System of Religion, or Government could, in Consequence thereof, be wished for by some, or feared by others. And now, should you ask, What is the Remedy proposed, that can be so safely administred, and yet be adequate to so great an Evil? The Answer is plainly this; let all common or private Subjects, who are not called to *especial Engagements* of Trust or Fidelity in the Discharge of some particular Offices, or in Accounting with the Revenue, be suffered to live quietly under the Laws of the respective Societies to which they belong, without previously requiring any express Covenant whatever:—But let every other Person, who is more immediately called to some particular Engagement, be expressly obliged under large Bonds and Penalties, besides the usual legal Punishments, to discharge it faithfully. And thus, by these two simple, easy Reformations, at least a Million of Perjuries would be prevented every Year. For by the first, all Students in the Universities, Citizens, Burgesses, Freemen of Trading Companies, Voters at Elections, &c. &c. would be left free from the horrid Abuse and Entanglement of Oaths; and yet be as much under the Command, *Jurisdiction* and *Punishment* of their respective Laws, as they are at present: And in regard to the second, all Civil Magistrates, from the highest to the lowest Order; all Officers in the Revenue, Merchants,

Captains of Ships, Tanners, Tea-Sellers, &c. &c. would thereby be discharged from such Oaths, which, as Matters now stand, are in many Respects impossible to be kept, and in others are but little, very little observed, when found to interfere with immediate Interest and present Profit:— Yet, though these several Classes of People would be discharged from Oaths, they would still remain under the Obligation of Bonds, Penalties, and legal Punishments; nay, be liable to higher Bonds and Penalties, than at present they are subject to. This being the Case, What further Securities are to be given, or can you require?—Indeed, let me ask, What are the present Securities (such I mean, on which any Stress or Confidence is put) were you to suppose all Bonds, Penalties, and legal Punishments to be totally set aside? As to the Multiplicity of Oaths, so frequently taken; that these are not looked upon as any real Security, is evident from hence; viz. every Merchant, or Master of a Vessel who swears to his Import at the Custom-house, hath his Goods as much watched and guarded by the Officers, as if they did not believe one Word which he had sworn. Why therefore is he compelled to swear at all, since his Swearing produces no Sort of Confidence, and gives no Satisfaction whatever to the Imposer of the Oath? In one Word, let daily Experience determine this Affair.—We have, for Example, a prodigious Multitude of Employments now in the Kingdom; all which may be termed *Offices* or *Places*, in a general Sense, with no great Impropriety: That is, they may be stiled Posts of Honour, or Profit, or perhaps both; Posts of Trust, or Gain, or probably of both united. This being the Case, I shall, for the Sake of greater Distinction, beg Leave to divide them into two Classes; viz. Those of the *new*,—and those of the *old* Creation. The Offices of the new Creation, are such as have partly arisen, and partly been instituted since the Reformation; and will be found to consist chiefly of Governorships, Guardianships, Treasurerships, and Trusteeships in the Management of Schools, Hospitals, Almshouses, Infirmaries, and many other Foundations of late Erection: To these may be likewise added the Masterships, and Usherships of Schools; the Places of Physicians, Surgeons, Apothecaries, Matrons, and Nurses in Hospitals and Infirmaries; also all Employments arising from mercantile Commissions, Agencies, Factorages, Partnerships, Purserships, and the like; not to mention those belonging to Compting-houses, Storehouses, Magazines, Bankers-shops, and many others. Be it therefore sufficient to observe, that all these Employments (call them Offices, or otherwise, it matters not;) yet all are attended with a considerable Share either of Honour, or Profit according to their respective Natures; and that some of them are among the most important, and others the most lucrative Stations in the whole Kingdom; requiring the greatest Degree of Diligence, and Integrity in their Discharge and Execution. Yet, great, important, and lucrative as many of them are, you can hardly say, that a single Oath of Admission is required in any one of them. This is a striking Circumstance, and highly deserves the public Attention.—On the contrary, The Offices of the Old Creation, are all the Parts of Government, of Civil Magistracy, and of the Revenue from the highest to the lowest; also the several Masterships, Wardenships, Treasureships, &c. of Corporations, and Companies of Trades; and indeed of almost every other Charter, and Foundation, Civil, Commercial, or Religious, if granted, or established prior to the Reformation. Now in regard to the Admission into each of these, the Reader is desired to take especial Notice, that the Solemnity of an Oath is required over and over, even though the Subject-Matter to which it relates, should be of no more Importance than the Office of a Scavenger. This being the Case, and these the Distinctions between the Offices of the old, and of the new Creation, permit me to ask this one Question, viz. In what Respects are the Swearers observed to discharge their respective Duties, better than the Non-Swearers? or did you ever discover, that the Administering so many Oaths was attended with any solid Advantage in the one Case; or the Non-Administering with any real Disadvantage in the other? Nay, to go farther; were your own Clerk, Steward, Bailiff, Butler, Groom, House-keeper, and all the menial Servants in your House now to take ever so many Oaths, that they would behave with Honesty, Diligence, Fidelity, and Sobriety in your Service:—Would you repose one Jot the more Confidence in them upon that Account? No; I am certain, you would not. Why therefore should such Oaths be continued any longer in similar Cases; seeing it hath been made out as clear as the Sun, that they serve to no other Purpose in the World, but to involve Thousands and Millions in the Guilt of Perjury?

But the Origin of these Oaths is a farther Reason why they should be now abolished: Of which take the following brief Relation, viz. When the Tyranny and Wickedness of Popery prevailed, the Priests invented and recommended the Use of Oaths upon almost every Occasion. This they did under a Pretence of mixing the Duties of Religion with the Affairs of Civil Life; but with a real View of extending their Empire of auricular Confession, and thereby of bringing the Laity under the Necessity of applying to them for Pardon, and purchasing Absolution. And the Design thus deeply laid, succeeded to their Wishes for many

Ages. But as the Reformation came on, the Doctrine of auricular Confession, and judicial Absolution sunk and died away: Yet in the Hurry and Confusion of the Times, some of those very Corruptions, which made auricular Confession appear necessary, or at least plausible, were over-looked and forgot: So that the shameful Frequency, and improper Use of Oaths not only continued, in the Instances above related, but even gained Ground in after Times, to the particular Disgrace of this Protestant State and Nation. And thus is too fully verified that Remark, frequently repeated in *The Elements of Commerce, viz.* That we still remain in the Dregs of Popery, in regard to certain Points of Practice, tho' we have fully abjured those Principles, on which such corrupt Practices were originally built. Indeed the pious and well-meaning Father *Quesnel* honestly endeavoured to reform these Abuses, even in the Church of *Rome*, setting forth the Unreasonableness and Wickedness of continuing such Oaths, and the Dangers thence arising to the Souls of Men. But alas! this very Position, which certainly hath not a Spark of Heresy, or Enthusiasm belonging to it (whatever some other Parts of his Works might have) was condemned by the Pope in the hundred and first Proposition of the famous Bull *Unigenitus*, as heretical, ill-sounding, and offensive to catholic Tradition.—Thus far as to the historical Account of the Rise and Progress of the Evil here complained of—And now let me be permitted to close the Whole with this one Reflection; *viz.* That tho' the Pope may condemn any Attempts towards the Discontinuance of unnecessary or improper Oaths, through Motives best known to himself; yet the Sense of Reason and Revelation is evidently this, *viz.* That Swearing, or a solemn Appeal to the Court of Heaven should be the last Resource of all; and only to be used on the most important Occasions, and where other Methods cannot succeed. Therefore in Proportion as you deviate from this Rule, you prostitute one of the most sacred Ordinances of Religion; you counteract its Design, and make Religion become a Parricide to itself; you loosen the Bands of human Society; and in every Respect you take *the Name of God in vain.*

Q. DOTH the Religion by Law established allow a Toleration to those Persons, whose Consciences will not permit them to join in its Worship and Communion?

A. THE Principles of the Protestant Religion being founded in the Right of private Judgment (for our first Reformers had no other Right to justify their Separation from the Church of *Rome*) it evidently follows, that all Protestants, if they will act consistently, must allow that Right to others, which they claim themselves. And yet, clear as this Proposition now appears, its Evidence was not seen, at least not acknowledged by Prostestants of *any* Denomination whatever, till a great many Years after the Reformation. So difficult a Thing it is for the Light of Truth to make its Way, where the Minds of Men have been long wrapped up in Darkness:—And herein we must ingenuously confess,

Illiacos intra muros peccatur, & extra.

THE *Dutch* were the first People, who caused the Doctrine of a Toleration to be incorporated into their civil Constitution: And yet, it is much to be queried, whether their true Motives had not more of the commercial, than religious Merit belonging to them. But be that as it may, this Doctrine was certainly adopted here in *England* upon Motives of Conscience, at the Time of the happy Revolution; and seems now so firmly rooted in the Judgments of the whole Kingdom; that scarce a Person can be found to oppose it openly. Nay, were any Author to assert, at this Time of Day, that three or four hundred Thousand Persons ought to be imprisoned, or expelled the Realm, or otherwise persecuted; rather than be permitted to live in a Non-conformity to the Established Church; he would meet with that universal Contempt and Indignation, he had so justly deserved. And as to the Church of *England* itself, What is the Consequence of this Lenity and Indulgence? Why truly, the Effects are so far from being prejudicial to her, that they strengthen her Interests every Day: And in Proportion as the former Heats and Animosities subside, in the same Proportion do Men seem better disposed to join in her Worship and Communion. Indeed some few prejudiced Persons, perhaps naturally of a malevolent Temper, may still remain on both Sides, who would be for reviving the former Contentions: But they are in all Respects so very inconsiderable, as to merit no Share of the public Regard. If any Competition is now subsisting, it is of a much nobler Kind, *viz.* Which Side, the Church, or the Dissenting, shall have the Honour of producing the most eminent Persons in all Branches of useful Learning, particularly the Knowledge of the Scriptures. And Competitions of this Sort, will never do any Mischief to either Church, or State.

Q. DOTH the Religion of the Country create a great Number of idle Holidays, and pompous Processions? And what are the Consequences regarding both the Industry, and Morals of the People?

A. AN *Englishman*, who is to travel into foreign Countries, must see the Propriety of inserting these Questions in a Treatise of this Nature: Though as far as regards his own Country and Religion, thanks to the happy Reformation, they are become unnecessary and superfluous.

Q. DOTH the Religion of the Country enjoin a long and severe Lent, requiring its People to conform strictly to a Fish-Diet, as a meritorious Act of Piety towards God? if so,—What Excesses of Gluttony and Gormandizing are observable, either at the Approach, or after the Conclusion of this extraordinary Season?   And what Diseases or Distempers are discoverable, as proceeding from such a sudden and unnatural Change both of the Quality, and Quantity of the usual Food.

A. THE present Reply to this Question must be the same as the former.

Q. DOTH the Religion of the Country inculcate Celibacy, and recommend a Solitary, or monastic Life as the most meritorious; instead of giving the Preference to the active, industrious, and the social?   Moreover, are there any Orders of religious Beggars to be found? and are such Institutions to be imputed to the avowed Principles of the Religion of the Country?

A. A LIKE Answer to be returned, as before.

Q. WHAT public Provisions are made either by the Religious, or Civil Institutions of the Country towards the proper Training up of Youth in the Principles of Religion and Virtue?   And are there any parochial Lists annually required to be given in, of such young Persons, as having been instructed during the preceding Year, are capable of giving a sufficient Account of those Duties, which constitute the good Christian,— and the good Citizen?

A. THE ecclesiastical Establishment hath done tolerably well; but the civil having done nothing at all in this Respect, the Consequence is, That every Effort of the religious Part of the Constitution becomes fruitless and vain.   The Methods of public Instruction proposed by the Church, are Catechising on Sundays in the Afternoon; which Methods are undoubtedly good in themselves, and would certainly soon produce a visible Reformation, were they properly attended.   But the Misfortune is, That as Catechising is an Application to the Judgment, and not to the Passions of Mankind; it is destitute of those Charms which draw Numbers together, whether of young or old.   For as it hath nothing belonging to it, to captivate either the Eyes of the Spectators, or the Ears of the Audience; and as it is neither of the Comedy, nor Tragedy kind, its Influence on an independent [not to say, a *licentious*] People, is just as much as they please themselves; — which is almost just nothing at all. This is a Fact, which the Author of these Sheets is sorry to say, he can too well attest upon the Experience of many Years.   Add to this, that the Rich will not scruple to declare, That they do not chuse to send their

Children to mix with the Poor, lest they should be injured in their Morals by contracting Acquaintance with them, (not to mention other Reasons, which perhaps have their Foundation in Pride and Vanity): And as to the Poor, those few among them, who are disposed to send their Offspring to be instructed, think it very sufficient to oblige them to attend at such a Period of Childhood, when they are fitter for the alphabetical Rudiments of the School-mistress, than the rational Instructions of the Pastor. In short, the properest Seasons for Catechising are those, when the Understanding is opened, and the Passions are on the Wing in pursuit of Objects. For if you begin sooner, you instruct the Parrot, and not the Man: But alas, if you defer it to the proper Time, and expect that Youth should the more constantly attend, in Proportion as they advance towards Maturity, you will find, that those of the better Sort esteem themselves above it, and those of the inferior judge themselves past it: — And in both these unhappy Prejudices, they are too much abetted by their respective Parents. This being the Case, the Religious Part of our Constitution cannot be blamed, if so little Good is effected; because it is impossible to go to the Root of the Evil, unless the temporal Power will lend some Assistance. Were indeed some Civil Polity established in order to enforce the Business of Catechising both on the Catechist, and Catechumen; (and such might easily be devised, without making any Intrusions on Liberty of Conscience) a considerable Good might be effected. Or rather were the parochial Pastors universally obliged to deliver to their Diocesans annual Lists of such young Persons belonging to their Charge, as either are, or might be instructed in the Duties of Religion, (specifying the several Impediments or Preventions); this single Circumstance would do more than perhaps at present can be well imagined. Certain it is, That it would give Countenance and Protection to those worthy Clergymen, who are inclined and desirous to do their Duty; and it would shame and expose others, if they did not make the like Returns: Not to mention, that it would dispose the Laity to acquiesce *in*, and to approve *of* such a Regulation, when made a standing Part of their Pastor's Duty; which otherwise, they would censure, and object to, and undoubtedly oppose, as a peculiar Officiousness, and meddling Temper in *him*. In short, when any Affair is made a regular Part of a Man's Duty, he is never blamed, but rather commended for discharging it faithfully: whereas were he to attempt to do the same Thing, through any Zeal, or voluntary Act of his own, he would soon find, that they would put a very different Construction upon the Matter, and oppose him with all their might — The Pastors in *North Britain*, as I am informed, are bound by public Authority to go through these, or such like annual Examinations, and to make regular Reports to their respective Synods.   In this they find no Difficulty, but are the more commended and respected for it, in Proportion as they use the greater Care.   And the Morals of the People committed to their Charge, are a sufficient Proof of the Excellence of the Institution.   Why therefore must *South Britain* alone be distinguished from all the World, wherein, the Institutions of Religion, and those of Civil Government concord so little with each other?

One general Query more especially adapted for discovering the comparative
   Riches, or Poverty of a Country in passing through it.

Q. ARE there any general Rules to be laid down for the Use of Travellers to enable them to judge of the comparative Poverty, or Riches of a City, Town, or Country, in passing through it?

A. YES there are several; and such as mutually prove, and corroborate each other:

1. LET the Traveller enquire the relative Price both of Land, and Money; these being the certain Criteria of the Riches, or Poverty of a Country; Criteria, like the alternate Buckets of a Well, where the Ascent of the one necessarily supposes the Descent of the other.   Thus, for Example, where the Interest of Money is high, the Price of Lands must be low; because the Height of the Interest is a Proof, that there are many to borrow, yet few to lend.   And if so, then it follows, that wherever there are but few Lenders of Money, there cannot be many Purchasers of Land. On the contrary, were the Interest to be exceeding low, the Price of Lands must rise in Proportion; because the Lowness of Interest is an infallible Proof, that there are many Persons in that State capable of making Purchases; and yet but few, who want to sell, or mortgage their Estates.   But the Effects of high, or low Interest are yet to be extended a great deal farther; inasmuch as the Employment, or Non-employment of a People, and consequently their Riches, or Poverty, will be found to depend, in a considerable Degree, on one or other of these Things.   To illustrate this, let us suppose the Interest of Money to be low in *England*, as it really is, but high in *France*.   Therefore an *English* landed Gentleman can afford, and often doth borrow Money on his Estate, in order to advance the Value of it, to build, and plant, and make other Improvements: All which give Employment to the common People, at the same Time that they bring clear Gains to himself.   And the Employment of a People is their Riches.   On the other Hand, a *French* landed Gentleman

cannot afford to do the like; that is, to employ the People; because the high Interest of Money would be greater than his Returns of Profit, or Advantage.   Therefore the Estates in *France* are in no Degree improved, and advanced in Value like the Estates in *England*.   And what is here observed in regard to the landed Interest, is equally applicable to the mercantile, and manufacturing: It being a certain Fact, That a Tradesman in *France* would rather chuse to put out his Money to Interest (which by the By, creates no Employment) than be content with those small Profits, which an *English* Tradesman is glad to accept of, because he cannot turn his Stock, or Credit to a better Account. — Not to mention, That when a *French* Merchant, or Manufacturer rises to a Capital of twelve, or fifteen thousand Pounds, he begins to be sick, and ashamed of his Occupation; and will use all his Power, and not a little of his Money, to get himself and Family ennobled, in order to wipe off the Disgrace of his original Condition.   This being the Case, it evidently follows, that the *English* in general must have larger Capitals in Trade than the *French*; and consequently can, and do employ a greater Number of People in Proportion.   Nay, it follows likewise, that an *English* Tradesman with a Stock of ten thousand Pounds, will actually undersell his *French* Rival of five thousand Pounds; even though he should pay dearer for every Article of Work, and Labour.   This may seem a Paradox to many Persons, who are unacquainted with Calculations of this Nature: But it can be none to those, who will consider, that if the *Englishman* is content with Five *per Cent*. Profits; while the *Frenchman* expects Eight or Ten *per Cent*. the former may afford to undersell the latter (especially as he hath a double Capital) and yet pay higher Wages to all his Journeymen, and common Tradesmen.

2. LET the Traveller observe the Condition of the public Inns on the great Roads: For they likewise are a kind of Pulse, by which you may discover the Riches, or Poverty of a Country.   If therefore you find them in a flourishing State, you may depend upon it, that many Passengers frequent that Road: And the Frequency of Passing and Re-passing is a sure Proof, that Business of some kind or other is going forwards.   The public Inns on the great Roads in *France* are generally bad; — bad, I mean, if compared with the Inns in *England:* Those in *Languedoc* are some of the best: and if you ask, What is that owing to?   It is, because the Trade of *Languedoc* is more considerable than the Trade of most other Provinces in the Kingdom.

3. LET the Traveller make the like Observations and Enquiries concerning the Number of Waggons, which pass and re-pass the Road.— Waggons never travel for the Sake of Pleasure, but for Use: Because

their Inducement must be the Carriage, and consequently the Sale of Goods: And wherever these Goods are made, there the People have found Employment in Proportion.

4. LET him be particularly attentive to the Quantity and Quality of the Wares to be found in the Shops of the Country Towns, and Villages through which he passes.   For in Fact, such Shops are no other than the Magazines of the Place; and by that means become the surest Indications of the Wealth, or Poverty of the adjacent Neighbourhood.   In a Word, rich Customers create rich Shops; but no Shopkeeper will be so imprudent, as to provide great Stores of valuable Goods, where he can have no reasonable Expectation of vending them.   Therefore, let the Traveller, who goes abroad for the Sake of knowing the State of other Countries, always call at such Places, whenever he can have Time: For, a little Money judiciously laid out in purchasing any Trifle which the Shop affords (though perhaps not worth the carrying to the next Stage) will enable him to make more useful Discoveries, and authorise him to ask more searching Questions concerning the Trade, Manufactures, Improvement, or Non-Improvement of the Country, than he could otherwise have done, had he resided whole Months, or even Years among them. And as this is a Fact which the Author may be permitted to speak to from his own Experience; therefore he hath a better Right to recommend it to others.

5. LET the Traveller also enquire into the State of Living in Cities and Towns, viz. whether the Inhabitants in general occupy separate Dwelling houses; or whether many Families are crouded into one.   If the latter is the Case, depend upon it, that the People are poor in Reality, whatever Appearance they put on.   For scarce any Family would submit to the Inconvenience of Lodgers, or In-tenants, if their Circumstances were such, as would enable them to be exempt from it. — Not to mention, that if a Family is to be pent up in a Room or two, the Quantity of Houshold Goods cannot be great: And yet, were a national Inventory to be taken in every Country, the greatest Riches of a State will always be found to consist in Houshold Goods.

6. LET him further observe both in Town and Country, whether the Generality of the Inhabitants decorate, or keep neat the Outside of their Houses; and bestow some Kind of Ornament on their Grounds and Gardens.   For if they do, they certainly are not in distressful Circumstances; the exterior in this Respect being a sure Proof of the interior. And the very doing of these Things creates a considerable Quantity of Labour.   But, wherever the Houses look decayed or miserable, and the adjacent Gardens and Grounds appear neglected, and Nature lies unim-

proved; — there you may assure yourself, that the Inhabitants either never felt the Blessing of Prosperity, or have lost it.

7. LASTLY, let him particularly enquire, whether Tenants in the Country usually pay their Rents in Money, or in Produce. For this is a capital Article in discovering the relative Riches, or Poverty of a Country. If the Rent is paid chiefly, or altogether in Corn, or Cattle; or any the like Productions of the Farm, it is a sure Sign, that Money is exceeding scarce, and that there are no convenient Markets at Hand for the Tenant to sell his Produce, and convert it into Cash. For if there were, neither Landlord, nor Tenant would approve of this Method of Payment, could another be obtained. Not the Landlord, because it would not always suit him to take it in Kind; and because he cannot so conveniently exchange it for other Necessaries or Conveniences: Not the Tenant, because he would certainly prefer a free and open Market for the Sale of his Goods; and would be very unwilling to see the best of his Produce be carried to his Landlord for the Payment of Rent; — nay, in such a Case, he will not think of raising *so good* a Produce, as he otherwise would have done.

AND thus have I ventured, with due Deference to those, whose more immediate Province it may be, to conduct my young Traveller, and to lead him, as it were by the Hand, not only through various Climes, but even through the different Systems of Commerce, Government, and Religion of different Countries. The Manner of doing this, it must be acknowledged, is entirely new; but if the general Method, or Plan proposed is not an improper one; and if some Treatise, or other of this Nature was really wanted; it is humbly hoped, that the Errors and Mistakes of the Author, occasioned by his making his Way over vast, untrodden Grounds, where he had no Guide or Direction, will be looked upon as the more excusable. Indeed, the Apology which will best suit him, and which he is desirous of using on this Occasion, is no other, than what would suit every honest Writer, who hath the public Good really at Heart, and hopes, that his Labours may at some Time or other, though ever so distant, or in some Degree, though ever so small, be of Use and Advantage to Mankind. That is, he humbly desires, that these Sheets may be considered only as a rude Essay, or the first Attempt of a well-meaning Person on a very important Subject. And if they should prove to be the Means of exciting the superior Abilities of others; or if any Hints here thrown out, shall hereafter be corrected and improved upon; the Design of the Author will be fully answered; and the *Horatian* Motto of *Fungar vice cotis*, will then be his own.

As to the Queries themselves, they are such as may be easily altered, and adapted to the Genius of any Country, People, or Government whatever.   And though the young Traveller may at first Sight, be discouraged at their Nature, or Number, as if they would impose a greater Task upon him than he is able, or willing to perform; yet he may assure himself, that the farther he proceeds, the more Delight he will take in these Studies.   Moreover, as he is not called upon to hasten, or make any fatiguing Dispatch, but to take Time, and advance gradually, he will find that the Difficulties will lessen every Day; and that these Researches, which at the Beginning perhaps appeared to be a *Labour*, will turn to an *Amusement*.   Nay more, seeing that the Questions are already stated (and by that means the great, and perhaps the only real Difficulty taken off his Hands) he will find likewise, that every Person he shall converse with, from the highest to the lowest, will be capable of answering some, or other of these Questions, to his full Content and Satisfaction.

In regard to what the Author hath said particularly about his native Country, the candid and judicious Reader will easily perceive, that his Design was neither to commend, nor blame indiscriminately; but to speak as impartially as he could, and then, having set forth, what appeared to him to be the *Truth*, to leave it to operate and take its Course.   Many great Improvements have been undoubtedly made of late Years in this Kingdom; yet many more there are still to make.   And as it would be very disingenuous to deny a Blessing, it would be equally wrong to conceal a Fault: — Especially, if together with the mention of the Fault, a Method is proposed for redressing it.   As to the Times and Seasons, *when* these, or such like Methods are the properest to be carried into Execution, that is not the Author's Concern; his Province being only to state Facts, and to submit Proposals to public Consideration.   Perhaps indeed the Time is approaching, and not afar off, when the peculiar Circumstances, and Crisis of Affairs, will require the Adoption of some of these Plans much sooner than could otherwise have been expected. But, be that as it may, when an important Truth is once laid down, it will be perceived to be always growing, though very slow in Growth. *Crescit occulto velut arbor ævo*, is the Characteristic of it; and in this, it is just the Reverse of Error.   Such therefore being the Case, may we not hope, that sooner, or later, Truth will certainly prevail?   But whether the Author himself shall have the Pleasure of seeing these Polities established during his own Life-time, is much less material, than whether they shall be established at all.

FINIS.

THE CASE OF GOING TO WAR

EDITORIAL NOTE

This tract was published in 1763 as "A Fragment of a greater Work". It was republished as Tract II of *Four Tracts together with Two Sermons* (Gloucester, 1774).

TRACT II.

The CASE *of* going to War;

BEING

The FRAGMENT of a greater Work.

CHAP. III. *Prevention of Wars.*

DID the Difficulty in this Argument consist in the Dubiousness of the Fact, 'Whether Wars were destructive to Mankind or not,' that Difficulty would not long subsist; for, if ocular Demonstration can be allowed to be Proof, it is but too manifest, That both the conquering, and conquered Countries, are prodigious Losers by them. But, alas! in this Case the Difficulty lies not in the Obscurity of the Proof, but in the Feebleness of the Attempt to dissuade Men from a Practice they have been long accustomed to consider in a very different Light from that in which it will be here set forth: And such is the Inveteracy of bad Habits, such the bewitching, tho' empty Sounds of Conquest and Glory, that there remains only the *bare Possibility* of Hopes of Success in these Endeavours; for as to all the Degrees of *Probability*, they are certainly on the contrary Side.

HOWEVER, as the Nature of my Argument leads me to set forth the several Means of rendering a Country populous, certainly the Prevention of Wars, as one of the most capital Means, cannot be omitted: And therefore I must consider myself in this Case as People do when they commence Adventurers in a Lottery; where, though there are perhaps almost an infinite Number of Chances against any single Adventurer, yet every Individual cherishes the flattering Expectation, that he shall be the happy Man to whose Share the great Prize will fall. Now, if a Conduct, grounded on so much Improbability, can escape the Censure of general Ridicule, it is to be hoped, that my Folly, for such I acknowledge it, may escape likewise; at least, as it is of so innocent and harmless a Nature, let me be allowed to petition, that mine may be esteemed less irrational than that military and political Folly which consists in seeking for Empire by Means of Desolation, and for national Riches by introducing universal Poverty and Want.

IN ancient Times, Men went to War without much Ceremony or Pretence: It was thought Reason good enough to justify the Deed, if one Man liked what another Man had; and War and Robbery were the honourable Professions: Nothing was adjudged dishonourable but the Arts of Peace and Industry.   This is *Herodotus*'s Account of the Manner of living of the Barbarians of *Thrace*; and this, with very small Alterations, might serve to characterise all other Barbarians, either of antient or modern Times.

BUT at present, we, who chuse to call ourselves civilized Nations, generally affect a more ceremonious Parade, and many Pretences.   Complaints are first made of some Injury received, some Right violated, some Incroachment, Detention, or Usurpation, and none will acknowledge themselves the Aggressors; nay, a solemn Appeal is made to Heaven for the Truth of each Assertion, and the final Avenger of the Oppressed, and Searcher of all Hearts, is called upon to maintain the righteous Cause, and to punish the Wrong-doer.   Thus it is with both Parties; and while neither of them will own the true Motives, perhaps it is apparent to all the World, that, on one Side, if not on both, a Thirst of Glory, a Lust of Dominion, the Cabals of Statesmen, or the ravenous Appetites of Individuals for Power or Punder, for Wealth without Industry, and Greatness without Merit, were the only real and genuine Springs of Action.

Now the Aims of Princes in these Wars are partly the same with, and partly different from, those of their Subjects: As far as Renown is concerned, their Views are alike, for Heroism is the Wish and Envy of all Mankind; and to be a Nation of Heroes, under the Conduct of an heroic Leader, is regarded, both by Prince and People, as the Summit of all earthly Happiness.   It is really astonishing to think with what Applause and Eclat the Memoirs of such inhuman Monsters are transmitted down, in all the Pomp of Prose and Verse, to distant Generations: Nay, let a Prince but feed his Subjects with the empty Diet of military Fame, it matters not what he does besides, in regard to themselves as well as others; for the Lives and Liberties, and every Thing that can render Society a Blessing, are willingly offered up as a Sacrifice to this Idol, GLORY.   And were the Fact to be examined into, you would find, perhaps without a single Exception, that the greatest Conquerors abroad, have proved the heaviest Tyrants at Home.   However, as Victory, like Charity, covereth a Multitude of Sins, thus it comes to pass, that reasonable Beings will be content to be Slaves themselves, provided they may enslave others; and while the People can look up to the glorious Hero on the Throne, they will be dazzled with the Splendor that surrounds him, and forget the Deeds of the Oppressor.

Now, from this View of Things, one would be tempted to imagine, that a Practice so universally prevailing, was founded in the Course and Constitution of Nature. One would be tempted to suppose, that Mankind were created on Purpose to be engaged in destructive Wars, and to worry and devour one another. "Perhaps the Earth would be overstocked with Numbers was it not for such Evacuations, salutary upon the whole, and necessary for the Good of the Remainder. Perhaps, likewise, there may be some Truth in what is vulgarly given out, that one Nation cannot thrive but by the Downfall, and one People grow rich but by the impoverishing, of its Neighbours."

AND yet, when we examine into this Affair, neither Reason, nor Experience will give the least Countenance to this Supposition. The Reason of the Thing we will consider now, and reserve the Fact 'till by and by. Here then, if Principles of Reason are to be our Guide, one would think, that a Being overflowing with Benevolence, and not limitted in Power, might have made a much better Provision for his Creatures, than what is here suggested: Certainly he might have rendered their several Interests less repugnant to each other; or rather, he might have caused them all to spring from one common Center, or to unite in one common Basis. And we are confirmed in this Train of Reasoning, when we reflect, that even the Benevolence and Power of human Governments, narrow and imperfect as they are, do actually provide for the Safety and Welfare of their respective Subjects by this very Method of an Union and Coalition of separate Interests. Thus, for Example, the Inhabitants of one County, or of one City, have not so much as an Idea, that they are, and must be, according to the unalterable Course of Things, the constitutional Foes of those of another County or City under the same Government: Nor do we at all conceive, that this or that particular Town, or District, can grow rich, or prosper, 'till the Districts, or Towns around it are reduced to Poverty, or made a dreary Waste. On the contrary, we naturally conclude, and justly too, that their Interests are inseparable from our own: And were their Numbers to be diminished, or their Circumstances altered from Affluence to Want, we ourselves, in the Rotation of Things, should soon feel the bad Effects of such a Change. If, therefore, this is the Case, with respect to human Governments; and if they, notwithstanding all their Faults and Failings, can regulate Matters so much for the better; how then comes it to pass, that we should ascribe so much Imperfection, such Want of Benevolence, such Partiality, nay such premeditated Mischief to that great and equal Government, which presideth over all? Is it, do you think, that Al-

mighty God cannot govern two large Districts, *France* and *England* for
Example, as well, and as wisely as you can govern two small ones?   Or
is it, that he hath so egregiously blundered in his first framing the
Constitution of Things as to render those Exploits, called Wars, necessary
for the Good of the Whole under his Administration, which you would
justly consider to be a Disgrace to yours, and severely punish as an Outrage?   Surely no: And we cannot, without Blasphemy, ascribe that
Conduct to the best of Beings, which is almost too bad to be supposed
of the worst: Surely it is much more consonant to the Dictates of
unbiassed Reason to believe, that our common Parent and universal
Lord regards all his Children and Subjects with an Eye of equal Tenderness and Good-will; and to be firmly persuaded, that in his Plan of
Government the political Interests of Nations cannot be repugnant to
those moral Duties of Humanity and Love which he has so universally
prescribed.

So much as to the Reason of the Thing: Let us now consider the Fact,
and be determined by Experience.   Princes expect to get by successful
Wars, and a Series of Conquests, either more Territory, or more Subjects,
or a more ample Revenue; or perhaps, which is generally the Case, they
expect to obtain all three.   Now, in regard to Territory, if mere Super-
ficies were the Thing to be aimed at, it must be allowed, that a Country
of a Million of square Miles is more in Quantity than one of half that
Extent.   But if Countries are not to be valued by Acres, but by the
Cultivation and the Produce of those Acres, then it follows, that ten
Acres may be better than a thousand, or perhaps ten thousand; and
Bishop *Berkley*'s Query may come in here very apropos, — "May not a
Man be the Proprietor of twenty Miles square in *North-America*, and yet
be in Want of a Dinner?"

As to Numbers of Subjects, surely War and Conquest are not the most
likely Means for attaining this End; and a Scheme, which consists in the
Destruction of the Human Species, is a very strange one indeed to be
proposed for their Increase and Multiplication: Nay, granting that
Numbers of Subjects might be acquired, together with the Accession of
Territory, still these new Subjects would add no real Strength to the
State; because new Acquisitions would require more numerous Defences,
and because a People scattered over an immense Tract of Country are, in
fact, much weaker than half their Numbers acting in Concert together,
and able by their Vicinity to succour one another.

MOREOVER, as to the Affair of the Revenue, and the Produce of Taxes,
the same Arguments conclude equally strong in this Case as in the

former: And the indisputable fact is, that an ill-peopled Country, though large and extensive, neither produces so great a Revenue as a small one well cultivated and populous; nor if it did, would the neat Produce of such a Revenue be equal to that of the other, because it is, in a Manner, swallowed up in Governments, Guards, and Garrisons, in Salaries and Pensions, and all the consuming Perquisites and Expences attendant on distant Provinces.

IN reference to the Views of the People: As far as such Views coincide with those of the Prince, so far they have been considered already: But seeing that the Thirst of inordinate Riches in private Subjects, which pushes them on to wish so vehemently for War, has something in it distinct from the Avarice of Princes; let us now examine, whether this Trade of War is a likely Method to make a People rich, and let us consider every Plea that can be offered.   "Surely, say these Men, to return Home laden with the Spoils of wealthy Nations is a compendious Way of getting Wealth; surely we cannot be deceived in so plain a Case: For we see that what has been gathering together and accumulating for Years, and perhaps for Ages, thus becomes our own at once; and more might be acquired by a happy Victory within the Compass of a Day, perhaps of an Hour, than we could otherwise promise to ourselves by the tedious Pursuits of Industry through the whole Course of a long laborious Life."

Now, in order to treat with this People in their own Way, I would not awake them out of their present golden Dream; I would therefore suppose, that they might succeed to their Heart's Desire, though there is a Chance at least of being disappointed, and of meeting with Captivity instead of Conquest: I will wave likewise all Considerations drawn from the intoxicating Nature of Riches, when so rapidly got, and improperly acquired: I will also grant, that great Stores of Gold and Silver, of Jewels, Diamonds, and precious Stones, may be brought Home; and that the Treasures of the Universe may, if you please, be made to circulate within the Limits of our own little Country: And if this were not enough, I would still grant more, did I really know what could be wished for or expected more.

THE Soldier of Fortune, being made thus rich, sits down to enjoy the Fruits of his Conquest, and to gratify his Wishes after so much Fatigue and Toil: But alas! he presently finds, that in Proportion as this heroical Spirit and Thirst for Glory have diffused themselves among his Countrymen, in the same Proportion the Spirit of Industry hath sunk and died away; every Necessary, and every Comfort and Elegance of Life are grown dearer than before, because there are fewer Hands, and less Inclination to produce them; at the same Time his own Desires, and artificial Wants, instead of being lessened, are greatly multiplied; for of what Use are Riches to him unless enjoyed?   Thus therefore it comes to pass, that his Heaps of Treasure are like the Snow in Summer, continually melting away; so that the Land of Heroes soon becomes the Country of Beggars.   His Riches, it is true, rushed in upon him like a Flood; but, as he had no Means of retaining them, every Article he wanted or wished for, drained away his Stores like the Holes in a Sieve, 'till the Bottom became quite dry: In short, in this Situation the Sums, which are daily and hourly issuing out, are not to be replaced but by a new War, and a new Series of Victories; and these new Wars and new Victories do all enhance the former Evils; so that the relative Poverty of the Inhabitants of this war-like Country becomes so much the greater, in Proportion to their Success in the very Means mistakenly proposed for enriching them.

A FEW indeed, incited by the strong Instinct of an avaricious Temper, may gather and scrape up what the many are squandering away; and so the Impoverishment of the Community may become the Enrichment of the Individual.   But it is utterly impossible, that the great Majority of any Country can grow wealthy by that Course of Life which renders them both very extravagant, and very idle.

To illustrate this Train of Reasoning, let us have recourse to Facts: But let the Facts be such as my Opponents in this Argument would wish of all others to have produced on this Occasion: And as the Example of the *Romans* is eternally quoted, from the Pamphleteer in the Garret, to the Patriot in the Senate, as extremely worthy of the Imitation of *Britons*, let their Example decide the Dispute.   "The brave *Romans*! That glorious!   That God like People!   The Conquerors of the World! Who made the most haughty Nations to submit!   Who put the Wealthiest under Tribute, and brought all the Riches of the Universe to centre in the Imperial City of *Rome!*"

Now this People, at the Beginning of their State, had a Territory not so large as one of our middling Counties, and neither healthy, nor fertile in its Nature; yet, by Means of Frugality and Industry, and under the Influence of *Agrarian* Laws (which allotted from two to six, or eight, or perhaps ten Acres of Land to each Family) they not only procured a comfortable Subsistence, but also were enabled to carry on their petty Wars without Burden to the State, or Pay to the Troops; each Husbandman or little Freeholder serving gratis, and providing his own Cloaths and Arms during the short Time that was necessary for him to be absent from his Cottage and Family on such Expeditions.

BUT when their Neighbours were all subdued, and the Seat of War removed to more distant Countries, it became impossible for them to draw their Subsistence from their own Farms; or in other Words, to serve gratis any longer; and therefore they were under a Necessity to accept of Pay. Moreover, as they could seldom visit their little Estates, these Farms were unavoidably neglected, and consequently were soon disposed of to engrossing Purchasers: And thus it came to pass, that the Lands about *Rome*, in spite of the *Agrarian* Laws, and of the several Revivals of those Laws, were monopolized into a few Hands by Dint of their very Conquests and Successes: And thus also the Spirit of Industry began to decline, in Proportion as the military Genius gained the Ascendant. A Proof of this we have in *Livy*, even so far back as the Time of their last King *Tarquinius Superbus:* For one of the Complaints brought against that Prince was couched in the following Terms, That having employed his Soldiers in making Drains and Common Sewers, "they thought it an high Disgrace to Warriors to be treated as Mechanics, and that the Conquerors of the neighbouring Nations should be degraded into Stone-cutters and Masons," though these Works were not the Monuments of unmeaning Folly, or the Works of Ostentation, but evidently calculated for the Health of the Citizens and the Convenience of the Public. Had he led forth these indignant Heroes to the Extirpation of some neighbouring State, they would not have considered that as a Dishonour to their Character.

BUT to proceed: The Genius of *Rome* being formed for War, the *Romans* pushed their Conquests over Nations still more remote: But alas! the *Quirites*, the Body of the People, were so far from reaping any Advantage from these new Triumphs, that they generally found themselves to be poorer at the End of their most glorious Wars than before they begun them. At the Close of each successful War it was customary to divide a Part of the Lands of the Vanquished among the veteran Soldiers, and to grant them a Dismission in order to cultivate their new Acquisitions. But such Estates being still more distant from the City, became in fact so much the less valuable; and the new Proprietor had less Inclination than ever to forsake the Capital, and to banish himself to these distant Provinces. [For here let it be noted, that *Rome* was become, by this Time, the Theatre of Pleasure, as well as the Seat of Empire, where all, who wished to act a Part on the Stage of Ambition, Popularity, or Politics; all who wanted to be engaged in Scenes of Debauchery, or Intrigues of State; all, in short, who had any Thing to spend, or any Thing to expect, made *Rome* their Rendezvous, and resorted

thither as to a common Mart]   This being the Case, it is not at all surprising, that these late Acquisitions were deserted and sold for a very
Trifle; nor is it any Wonder, that the Mass of the *Roman* People should
be so immersed in Debt, as we find by their own Historians they continually were, when we reflect, that their military Life indisposed them for
Agriculture or Manufactures, and that their Notions of Conquest and of
Glory rendered them extravagant, prodigal, and vain.

However, in this Manner they went on, continuing to extend their
Victories and their Triumphs; and, after the Triumph, subsisting for a
while by the Sale of the Lands above-mentioned, or by their Shares in
the Division of the Booty: But when these were spent, as they quickly
were, then they sunk into a more wretched State of Poverty than before,
eagerly wishing for a new War as the only Means of repairing their
desperate Fortunes, and clamouring against every Person that would
dare to appear as an Advocate for Peace: And thus they encreased their
Sufferings, instead of removing them.

At last they subdued the World, as far as it was known at that Time, or
thought worth subduing; and then both the Tribute, and the Plunder of
the Universe were imported into *Rome*; then, therefore, the Bulk of the
Inhabitants of that City must have been exceedingly wealthy, had
Wealth consisted in Heaps of Gold and Silver; and then likewise, if ever,
the Blessings of Victory must have been felt had it been capable of
producing any.   But alas! whatever Riches a few Grandees, the Leaders
of Armies, the Governors of Provinces, the Minions of the Populace, or
the Harpies of Oppression might have amassed together, the great Majority of the People were poor and miserable beyond Expression; and while
the vain Wretches were strutting with Pride, and elated with Insolence,
as the *Masters of the World*, they had no other Means of subsisting,
when Peace was made and their Prize-Money spent, than to receive a
Kind of Alms in Corn from the public Granaries, or to carry about their
Bread-Baskets, and beg from Door to Door.   Moreover, such among
them as had chanced to have a Piece of Land left unmortgaged, or
something valuable to pledge, found, to their Sorrow, that the Interest
of Money (being hardly ever less than twelve per Cent. and frequently
more) would soon eat up their little Substance, and reduce them to an
Equality with the rest of their illustrious Brother-Beggars.   Nay, so
extremely low was the Credit of these Masters of the World, that they
were trusted with the Payment of their Interest no longer than from
Month to Month;—than which there cannot be a more glaring Proof,
both of the abject Poverty, and of the cheating Dispositions of these
heroic Citizens of Imperial *Rome*.

Now this being the undoubted Fact, every humane and benevolent Man, far from considering these People as Objects worthy of Imitation, will look upon them with a just Abhorrence and Indignation; and every wise State, consulting the Good of the Whole, will take Warning by their fatal Example, and stifle, as much as possible, the very Beginnings of such a *Roman* Spirit in its Subjects.

THE Case of the antient *Romans* having thus been considered at large, less may be requisite as to what is to follow. And therefore suffice it to observe, that the Wars of *Europe* for these two hundred Years last past, by the Confession of all Parties, have really ended in the Advantage of none, but to the manifest Detriment of all: Suffice it farther to remark, that had each of the contending Powers employed their Subjects in cultivating and improving such Lands as were clear of all disputed Titles, instead of aiming at more extended Possessions, they had consulted both their own, and their People's Greatness much more efficaciously, than by all the Victories of a *Cæsar*, or an *Alexander*.

UPON the Whole, therefore, it is evident to a Demonstration, that nothing can result from such Systems as these, however specious and plausible in Appearance, but Disappointment, Want, and Beggary. For the great Laws of Providence, and the Course of Nature, are not to be reversed or counter-acted by the feeble Efforts of wayward Man; nor will the Rules of sound Politics ever bear a Separation from those of true and genuine Morality. Not to mention, that the Victors themselves will experience it to their Costs sooner or later, that in vanquishing others, they are only preparing a more magnificent Tomb for their own Interrment.

IN very deed, the good Providence of God hath, as it were, taken peculiar Pains to preclude Mankind from having any plausible Pretence for pursuing either this or any other Scheme of Depopulation. And the Traces of such preventing Endeavours, if I may so speak, are perfectly legible both in the natural, and in the moral Worlds.

IN the *natural* World, our bountiful Creator hath formed different Soils, and appointed different Climates; whereby the Inhabitants of different Countries may supply each other with their respective Fruits and Products; so that by exciting a reciprocal Industry, they may carry on an Intercourse mutually beneficial, and universally benevolent.

NAY more, even where there is no remarkable Difference of Soil, or of Climates, we find a great Difference of Talents; and, if I may be allowed the Expression, a wonderful Variety of Strata in the human Mind. Thus, for Example, the Alteration of Latitude between *Norwich* and

Manchester, and the Variation of Soil are not worth naming; moreover, the Materials made Use of in both Places, Wool, Flax, and Silk, are just the same; yet so different are the Productions of their respective Looms, that Countries, which are thousands of Miles apart, could hardly exhibit a greater Contrast.   Now, had *Norwich* and *Manchester* been the Capitals of two neighbouring Kingdoms, instead of Love and Union, we should have heard of nothing but Jealousies and Wars; each would have prognosticated, that the flourishing State of the one portended the Downfall of the other; each would have had their respective Complaints, uttered in the most doleful Accents, concerning their own Loss of Trade, and of the fomidable Progress of their Rivals; and, if the respective Governments were in any Degree popular, each would have had a Set of Patriots and Orators closing their inflammatory Harangues with a *delenda est Carthago*. "We must destroy our Rivals, our Competitors, and commercial Enemies, or be destroyed by them; for our Interests are opposite, and can never coincide." And yet, notwithstanding all these canting Phrases, it is as clear as the Meridian Sun, that in case these Cities had belonged to different Kingdoms (*France* and *England* for Example) there would then have been no more Need for either of them to have gone to War than there is at present.   In short, if Mankind would but open their Eyes, they might plainly see, that there is no one Argument for inducing different Nations to fight for the Sake of Trade, but which would equally oblige every County, Town, Village, nay, and every Shop among ourselves, to be engaged in civil and intestine Wars for the same End: Nor, on the contrary, is there any Motive of Interest or Advantage that can be urged for restraining the Parts of the same Government from these unnatural and foolish Contests, but which would conclude equally strong against separate and independant Nations making War with each other on the like Pretext.

Moreover, the Instinct* of Curiosity, and the Thirst of Novelty, which are so universally implanted in human Nature, whereby various Nations and different People so ardently wish to be Customers to each other, is another Proof, that the curious Manufactures of one Nation will never want a Vent among the richer Inhabitants of another, provided

---

* Indeed this Instinct, like all other Instincts and Passions, ought to be put under *proper Regulations*, otherwise it may do more Hurt than Good.   But this Necessity of due Regulation is no more an Objection against the good Tendency of the Instinct itself, than the Rules of Temperance and Sobriety are Objections against Eating and Drinking in a moderate and reasonable Degree.   The Instinct itself is certainly good; but it may be misapplied:—And what may not?   The *political Regulations* it should be under, will be mentioned elsewhere.

they are reasonably cheap and good; so that the richer one Nation is, the more it has to spare, and the more it will certainly lay out on the Produce and Manufactures of its ingenious Neighbour. Do you object to this? Do you envy the Wealth, or repine at the Prosperity of the Nations around you? — If you do, consider what is the Consequence, *viz.* that you wish to keep a Shop, but hope to have only Beggars for your Customers.

LASTLY, the good Providence of God has further ordained, that a Multiplication of Inhabitants in every Country should be the best Means of procuring Fertility to the Ground, and of Knowledge and Ability to the Tiller of it: Hence it follows, that an Increase of Numbers, far from being a Reason for going to War in order to thin them, or for sending them out to people remote Desarts, operates both as an exciting Cause to the Husbandman to increase his Quantity, in Proportion to the Demand at Market; and also enables him to raise more plentiful Crops, by the Variety and Plenty of those rich Manures, which the Concourse of People, their Horses, Cattle, &c. &c. produce: And it is remarkable, that very populous Countries are much less subject to Dearths or Famines than any other. — So much as to those Stores of Providence, which are laid up in the natural World, and graciously intended for the Use of Mankind.

As to the *moral* and *political* World, Providence has so ordained, that every Nation may increase in Frugality and Industry, and consequently in Riches*, if they please; because it has given a Power to every Nation

---

* The Wealth of this Nation—that amazing Wealth, which has been so profusely squandered away in the two last general and devouring Wars, is principally owing to the wise Regulations of that able Minister, Sir ROBERT WALPOLE. Justice to his Character, and Gratitude to his Memory, demand this Tribute of Acknowledgement to be paid him when dead, which was shamefully denied him while alive. *Sed opinionem commenta delet dies!* And the Time is now come when his very Adversaries frankly confess, That his Plan of Commerce was manly and rational; that his Endeavours to prevent an infatuated People from quarrelling with their best Customers, were truly patriotical; and that his very *Crimes* were more owing to the Extremities to which he was driven by his implacable Enemies, than to any Malignity of his own. When he came into Administration, he found the *English* Book of Rates almost as bad as any in *Europe*; but he left it the very best. And were you to compare what he did for promoting general Trade, (and much more he would have done, had it not been for the Madness of some, and the Wickedness of others) were you but to compare what he actually did, with what has been done either before or since, in this, or any other Country, not forgetting the SULLYS, the COLBERTS, and the FLEURYS of *France,* you would find that he shone as much above all other Ministers, as *England* hath exceeded the rest of the World in her late enormous Expences.

to make good Laws, and wise Regulations, for their internal Government: And none can justly blame them on this Account. Should, for Example, the *Poles*, or the *Tartars* grow weary of their present wretched Systems, and resolve upon a better Constitution; should they prefer Employment to Sloth, Liberty to Slavery, and Trade and Manufactures to Theft and Robbery; should they give all possible Freedom and Encouragement to industrious Artificers, and lay heavy Discouragements on Idleness and Vice, by Means of judicious Taxes; and lastly, should they root out all Notions of beggarly Pride, and of the Glory of making maroding Incursions; — what a mighty, what a happy Change would soon appear in the Face of those Countries! And what could then be said to be wanting in order to render such Nations truly rich and great?

PERHAPS some neighbouring State (entertaining a foolish Jealousy) would take the Alarm, *that their Trade was in Danger*. But if they attempted to invade such a Kingdom, they would find to their Cost, that an industrious State, abounding with People and with Riches, having its Magazines well stored, its frontier Towns* well fortified, the Garrisons

---

The Author is in no Pain for what he has advanced on this Head. Truth—unbought, unpensioned, and impartial Truth, is his only Motive: Indeed, what other Motive can any Man have for speaking well of a *dead* Minister? Nay, he will further add, That tho' the Minister was neither complimented by Corporations, nor huzza'd by Mobs; yet as long as the 8th of Geo. I. Cap. 15 (see the Statute Book) shall remain among the Laws of this Realm, so long will these *Commercial Regulations* be regarded by the thinking and considerate Part of Mankind, as doing more *true Honour*, than all the Gold Boxes, or honorary Freedoms that could have been bestowed.

* As a Confirmation of the above, it may be observed, that this very Country of *Great-Britain* is become much more capable of Defence against a foreign Invasion, than it used to be; and that the numberless Enclosures, new Canals, and artificial Navigations, which are now forming almost every Day, render it a Kind of Fortress from one End to the other. For while a few Regiments were posted in Villages, or behind Hedges, or to line the Banks of Rivers and Canals; and while a few Light Horse were employed in harassing both the Front and Rear of the Enemy, in falling on his Convoys, destroying his Magazines, and keeping him in a perpetual Alarm;—his Progress would be so retarded, and his Forces so weakened, at the same Time, that our own would be encreasing in *Strength* and *Numbers*, as would oblige him to retire without Danger to us, but with great Shame and Loss to himself. Had HAROLD used the same Precaution against the Duke of *Normandy*, instead of coming to a decisive Engagement with him on his landing; the latter must have returned ingloriously, perhaps with not a fourth Part of his Troops; — if indeed he could have returned at all, after he had penetrated a great Way into the Country, *far from* the Resources of his Shipping, Provisions, and Supplies. An Invasion of this Country is certainly *a possible Thing*, notwithstanding all our Fleets, and all the Vigilance of their Commanders. But the Invader would not have the least Chance of conquering the Country, unless the headstrong Impatience of the *English* to come to Blows, should give him an Opportunity of bringing the Affair to *one decisive Battle*.

duly paid, and the whole Country full of Villages and Enclosures; I say, they would feel to their Cost, that such a State is the strongest of all others, and the most difficult to be subdued: Not to mention that other Potentates would naturally rise up for its Defence and Preservation; because, indeed, it would be their Interest that such a State as this should not be swallowed up by another, and because they themselves might have many Things to hope from it, and nothing to fear.

BUT is this Spell, this Witchcraft of the Jealousy of Trade never to be dissolved? And are there no Hopes that Mankind will recover their Senses as to these Things? For of all Absurdities, that of going to War for the Sake of getting Trade is the most absurd; and nothing in Nature can be so extravagantly foolish. Perhaps you cannot digest this; you don't believe it: — Be it so: — Grant, therefore, that you subdue your Rival by Force of Arms: Will that Circumstance render your Goods cheaper at Market than they were before? And if it will not, nay if it tends to render them much dearer, what have you got by such a Victory? I ask further, What will be the Conduct of foreign Nations when your Goods are brought to their Markets? They will never enquire, whether you were victorious or not; but only, whether you will sell cheaper, or at least as cheap as others? Try and see, whether any Persons, or any Nations, ever yet proceeded upon any other Plan; and if they never did, and never can be supposed to do so, then it is evident to a Demonstration, that Trade will always follow Cheapness, and not Conquest. Nay, consider how it is with yourselves at Home: Do Heroes and Bruisers get more Customers to their Shops because they are Heroes and Bruisers? Or, would not you yourself rather deal with a feeble Person, who will use you well, than with a Brother-Hero, should he demand a higher Price?

Now all these Facts are so very notorious, that none can dispute the Truth of them. And throughout the Histories of all Countries, and of all Ages, there is not a single Example to the contrary. Judge, therefore, from what has been said, whether any one Advantage can be obtained to Society, even by the most successful Wars, that may not be incomparably greater, and more easily procured, by the Arts of Peace.

As to those who are always clamouring for War, and sounding the Alarm to Battle, let us consider who they are, and what are their Motives; and then it will be no difficult Matter to determine concerning the Deference that ought to be paid to their Opinions, and the Merit of their patriotic Zeal.

1. THE first on the List here in *Britain* (for different Countries have different Sorts of Firebrands) I say the first here in *Britain* is the *Mock-*

Patriot and furious *Anti-Courtier*, He, good Man, always begins with Schemes of Œconomy, and is a zealous Promoter of national Frugality.* He loudly declaims against even a small, annual, parliamentary Army, both on Account of its Expence, and its Danger; and pretends to be struck with a Panic at every Red-Coat that he sees.   By persevering in these laudable Endeavours, and by sowing the Seeds of Jealousy and Distrust among the Ignorant and Unwary, he prevents such a Number of Forces, by Sea and Land, from being kept up, as are prudently necessary for the common Safety of the Kingdom: This is one Step gained.   In the next Place, after having thrown out such a tempting Bait for Foreigners to catch at, on any trifling Affront he is all on Fire; his Breast beats high with the Love of his Country, and his Soul breathes Vengeance against the Foes of *Britain:* Every popular Topic, and every inflammatory Harangue is immediately put into Rehearsal; and, O LIBERTY! O MY COUNTRY! is the continual Theme.   The Fire then spreads; the Souls of the noble *Britons* are enkindled at it, and Vengeance and War are immediately resolved upon.   Then the Ministry are all in a Hurry and a flutter; new Levies are half-formed, and half-disciplined: Squadrons at Sea are half-manned, and the Officers mere Novices in their Business. In short, Ignorance, Unskilfulness, and Confusion, are unavoidable for a Time; the necessary Consequence of which is some Defeat received, some Stain or Dishonour cast upon the Arms of *Britain.*   Then the long-wished-for Opportunity comes at last; the Patriot roars, the Populace clamour and address, the Ministry tremble, and the Administration sinks.   The ministerial Throne now being vacant, he triumphantly ascends it, adopts those Measures he had formerly condemned, reaps the Benefit of the Preparations and Plans of his Predecessor, and, in the natural Course of Things, very probably gains some Advantages.   This restores the Credit of the Arms of *Britain:* Now the Lion is roused, and now is the Time for crushing our Enemies, that they may never be able to rise again.   This is Pretext enough; and thus the Nation is plunged into an Expence ten Times as great, and made to raise Forces twenty Times as numerous, as were complained of before.   "However, being now victorious, let us follow the Blow and manfully go on, and let

---

* All the Speeches and all the Pamphlets poured forth against Standing Armies during the Administration of Sir ROBERT WALPOLE, were levelled at a Number of Troops so small that their highest Complement did not exceed 20,000 Men.   Yet these were represented as very formidable to the Constitution by their Numbers; and more formidable still by that vast Accession of Power, which accrued to the Crown from the Disposal of such a Multitude of Places.—How are the Times altered since !

neither Expence of Blood nor of Treasure be at all regarded; for another Campaign will undoubtedly bring the Enemy to submit to our own Terms, and it is impossible that they should stand out any longer." Well, another Campaign is fought, — and another, — and another, — and another, and yet the enemy holds out; nor is the *Carte blanche* making any Progress in its Journey into *Britain*. A Peace at last is made; the Terms of it are unpopular. Schemes of excessive Œconomy are called for by a new Set of Patriots; and the same Arts are played off to dethrone the reigning Minister, which he had practised to dethrone his Predecessor. And thus the patriotic Farce goes round and round; but generally ends in a real and bloody Tragedy to our Country and to Mankind.

2. THE next in this List is the hungry Pamphleteer, who writes for Bread. The Ministry will not retain him on their Side, therefore he must write against them, and do as much Mischief as he can in order to be bought off. At the worst, a Pillory or a Prosecution is a never-failing Remedy against a political Author's starving; nay, perhaps it may get him a Pension or a Place at last: In the Interim, the Province of this Creature is to be a Kind of Jackall to the Patriot-Lion; for he beats the Forest, and first starts the Game; he explores the reigning Humour and Whim of the Populace, and by frequent Trials discovers the Part where the Ministry are most vulnerable. But above all, he never fails to put the Mob in mind, of what indeed they believed before, that Politics is a Subject which every one understands, — except the Ministry; and that nothing is so easy as to bring the King of *France* to sue for Peace on his Knees at the Bar of a *British* House of Commons, were such — and such — at the Helm, as honest and uncorrupt as they ought to be. "But alas! What shall we say! *French* Gold will find an Admission every where; and what can we expect, when the very Persons, who ought to have saved us, have sold their Country?" This is delightful; and this, with the old Stories of *Agincourt* and *Cressy*, regales, nay intoxicates, the Mob, and inspires them with an Enthusiasm bordering upon Madness. The same Ideas return; the former Battles are fought over again; and we have already taken Possession of the Gates of *Paris* in the Warmth of a frantic Imagination: Though it is certain, that even were this Circumstance ever to happen, we ourselves should be the greatest Losers; for the Conquest of *France* by *England*, in the Event of Things, would come to the same Point as the Conquest of *England* by *France*; because the Seat of Empire would be transferred to the greater Kingdom, and the lesser would be made a Province to it. — [The philosophic Dr. FRANKLIN adopts the same Ideas in regard to the present Contest between *North-*

America and *Great-Britain*. He supposes, agreeably to the *Newtonian* Philosophy, that there is a mutual Attraction and Gravitation between these two Countries; but nevertheless, that the Powers of Gravitation and Attraction being so much stronger in the vast Continent of *North-America*, than in the little Spot of *Great-Britain*, it therefore follows, that the former will swallow up, or absorb the latter, and not *vice versa*. The present astonishing Emigrations from *Great-Britain* and *Ireland* seem to confirm the Hypothesis of this eminent Philosopher but too well: And it were greatly to be wished, that the magical Spell, which is to chain this our Island to those immense Regions, were dissolved, 'e're it be too late.]

3. NEAR a-kin to this Man, is that other Monster of modern Times, who is perpetually declaiming against a Peace, *viz.* the Broker, and the Gambler of Change-alley. Letters from the *Hague*, wrote in a Garret at Home for Half a Guinea; — the first News of a Battle fought (it matters not how improbable) with a List of the Slain and Prisoners, their Cannon, Colours, &c. Great Firings heard at Sea between Squadrons not yet out of Port; — a Town taken before the Enemy was near it; — an intercepted Letter that never was wrote; — or, in short, any Thing else that will elate or depress the Minds of the undiscerning Multitude, serves the Purpose of the Bear or the Bull to sink or raise the Price of Stocks, according as he wishes either to buy or sell. And by these vile Means the Wretch, who perhaps the other Day came up to *London* in the Waggon to be an Under-Clerk or a Message Boy in a Warehouse, acquires such a Fortune as sets him on a Par with the greatest Nobles of the Land.

4. THE News-writers are a fourth Species of political Firebrand: A Species which abound in this Country more than in any other; for as Men are in this Kingdom allowed greater Liberty to say, or write what they please; so likewise is the Abuse of that Blessing carried to a higher Pitch. In fact these People may be truly said to *trade in Blood:* For a War is their Harvest; and a Gazette Extraordinary produces a Crop of an hundred Fold: How then can it be supposed, that they can ever become the Friends of Peace? And how can you expect that any Ministers can be their Favourites, but the Ministers of War? Yet these are the Men who may be truly said to govern the Minds of the good People of *England*, and to turn their Affections whithersoever they please; who can render any Scheme unpopular which they dislike, and whose Approbation, or Disapprobation, are regarded by Thousands, and almost by Millions, as the Standard of Right and Wrong, of Truth or Falshood: For it is a Fact, an indisputable Fact, that this Country is as much News-mad,

and News-ridden now, as ever it was Popery-mad, and Priest-ridden, in the Days of our Forefathers.

5. THE Jobbers and Contractors of all Kinds and of all Degrees for our Fleets and Armies; — the Clerks and Pay-Masters in the several Departments belonging to War; — and every other Agent, who has the fingering of the public Money, may be said to constitute a distinct Brood of Vultures, who prey upon their own Species, and fatten upon Human Gore. It would be endless to recount the various Arts and Stratagems by which this Tribe of Devourers have amassed to themselves astonishing Riches, from very slender Beginnings, through the Continuance and Extent of the War: Consequently, as long as any Prospect could remain of squeezing somewhat more out of the Pockets of an exhausted, but infatuated People; so long the *American* War hoop would be the Cry of these inhuman Savages; and so long would they start and invent Objections to every Proposition that could be made for the restoring Peace, — because Government Bills would yet bear some Price in the Alley, and *Omnium* and *Scrip.* would still sell at Market.

6. MANY of the Dealers in Exports and Imports, and several of the Traders in the Colonies, are too often found to be assistant in promoting the Cry for every new War; and, when War is undertaken, in preventing any Overtures towards a Peace. You do not fathom the Depth of this Policy; you are not capable to comprehend it. Alas! it is but too easily explained; and when explained, but too well proved from Experience. The general Interest of Trade, and the Interest of particular Traders, are very distinct Things; nay, are very often quite opposite to each other. The Interest of general Trade arises from general Industry; and, therefore can only be promoted by the Arts of Peace: But the Misfortune is, that during a Peace the Prices of Goods seldom fluctuate, and there are few or no Opportunities of getting suddenly rich. A War, on the contrary, unsettles all Things, and opens a wide Field for Speculation; therefore a lucky Hit, or the Engrossing a Commodity, when there is but little at Market, — a rich Capture, — or a Smuggling, I should rather say a traiterous, Intercourse with the Enemy, sometimes by Bribes to Governors and Officers, and sometimes through other Channels; — or perhaps the Hopes of coming in for a Share in a lucrative Job, or a public Contract: These, and many such like notable Expedients are cherished by the Warmth of War, like Plants in a Hot-bed; but they are chilled by the cold languid Circulation of peaceful Industry.

THIS being the Case, the warlike Zeal of these Men, and their Declamations against all reconciliatory Measures, are but too easily accounted for; and while the *dulcis odor lucri* is the governing Principle of Trade, what other Conduct are you to expect?

But what if the Men of landed Property, and the numerous Band of *English* Artificers and Manufacturers, who constitute, beyond all Doubt, the great Body of the Kingdom, and whose real Interests must be on the Side of Peace; what if they should not be as military in their Dispositions as these Gentlemen would wish they were? Why then all Arts must be used, and indefatigable Pains be taken to persuade them, that this *particular War* is calculated for their Benefit; and that the Conquest of such, or such a Place would infallibly redound both to the Advantage of the landed Interests, and the Improvement and Extension of Manufactures. "Should (for Example) the *English* once become the Masters of *Canada*, the Importation of Skins and Beavers, and the Manufacture of fine Hats, would extend prodigiously: Every Man might afford to wear a Beaver Hat if he pleased, and every Woman be decorated in the richest Furs; in return for which our coarse Woollens would find such a Vent throughout our immense Northern Regions as would make ample Satisfaction for all our Expences," Well, *Canada* is taken, and is now all our own: But what is the Consequence after a Trial of some Years' Possession? Let those declare who can, and as they were before so lavish in their Promises, let them at last prove their Assertions, by appealing to Fact and Experience. Alas! they cannot do it: Nay, so far from it, that Beaver, and Furs, and Hats are dearer than ever: And all the Woollens, which have been consumed in those Countries by the *Native Inhabitants*, do hardly amount to a greater Quantity than those very Soldiers and Sailors would have worn and consumed, who were lost in the taking, defending, and garrisoning of those Countries.

"However, if *Canada* did not answer our sanguine Expectations, sure we were, that the Sugar Countries would make amends for all: And, therefore, if the important Islands of *Guadaloupe* and *Martinico* were to be subdued, then Sugars and Coffee, and Chocolate, and Indigo, and Cotton, &c. &c. would become as cheap as we could wish; and both the Country Gentleman and the Manufacturer would find their Account in such Conquests as these." Well, *Guadaloupe* and *Martinico* are both taken, and many other Islands besides are added to our Empire, whose Produce is the very same with theirs. Yet, what Elegance of Life, or what Ingredient for Manufacture, is thereby become the cheaper? and which of all these Things can be purchased at a lower Rate, at present than before the War? — Not one can be named. On the contrary, the Man of landed Property can tell but too circumstantially, that Taxes are risen higher than ever, — that the Interest of Money is greater; — that every additional Load of National Debt is a new Mortgage on his exhausted, and impoverished Estate; — and that, if he happens to be a Member of Parliament, he runs the Risque of being bought out of his Family Borough, by some upstart Gambler, Jobber, or Contractor.

THE *English* Manufacturer, likewise, both sees and feels, that every foreign Material, of Use in his Trade, is grown much dearer, — that all Hands are become extremely scarce, — their Wages prodigiously raised, — the Goods, of course, badly and scandalously manufactured, — and yet cannot be afforded at the same Price as heretofore, — that, therefore, the Sale of *English* Manufactures has greatly decreased in foreign Countries since the Commencement of War; — and what is worse than all, that our own Colonies, for whose Sakes the War was said to be undertaken, do buy Goods in *Holland*, in *Italy*, at *Hamburgh*, or any other Market where they can buy them cheapest, without regarding the Interest of the Mother-Country, when found to be repugnant to their own. All these Things, I say, the *English* Manufacturer both sees and feels: And is not this enough? Or must he carry his Complaisance still farther, and never be a Friend to Peace 'till it becomes the Interest of the Merchant to befriend it likewise? Surely, surely, this is rather too much to be expected. In one Word, to return to the Point from which we set out, the Interest of the Merchant, and the Interest of the Kingdom, are two very distinct Things; because the one may, and often doth, get rich by the Course of Trade, which would bring Ruin and Desolation on the other.

7. THE Land and Sea Officers are, of course, the invariable Advocates for War. Indeed it is their Trade, their Bread, and the sure Way to get Promotion; therefore no other Language can be expected from them: And yet, to do them Justice, of all the Adversaries of Peace, they are the fairest and most open in their Proceedings; they use no Art of Colouring, and as you know their Motive, you must allow for it accordingly. Nay, whether from a Principle of Honour natural to their Profession, or from what other Cause I know not; but so it is, that they very frankly discover the base and disingenuous Artifices of other Men. And the Author of these Sheets owes much of his Intelligence to several Gentlemen of this Profession, who were Eye and Ear-witnesses of the Facts related.

BUT after all, What have I been doing? and how can I hope for Proselytes by this Kind of Writing? — It is true, in regard to the Points attempted to be proved, I have certainly proved them. "Neither Princes nor People can be Gainers by the most successful Wars: —

Trade in particular, will make its Way to the Country where Goods are manufactured the best and cheapest: — But conquering Nations neither manufacture well nor cheap: — And consequently must sink in Trade in Proportion as they extend in Conquest." These Things are now incontestibly clear, if any Thing ever was so. But, alas! Who will thank me for such Lessons as these? The seven Classes of Men just enumerated certainly will not; and as to the Mob, the blood-thirsty Mob, no Arguments, and no Demonstrations whatever, can persuade them to withdraw their Veneration from their grim Idol, the *God of Slaughter*. On the contrary, to knock a Man on the Head is to take from him his All at once. This is a compendious Way, and this they understand. But to excite that Man (whom perhaps they have long called their Enemy) to greater Industry and Sobriety, to consider him as a Customer to them, and themselves as Customers to him, so that the richer both are, the better it may be for each other; and, in short, to promote a mutual Trade to mutual Benefit: This is a Kind of Reasoning, as unintelligible to their Comprehensions, as the Antipodes themselves.

SOME few perhaps, a very few indeed, may be struck with the Force of these Truths, and yield their Minds to Conviction: — *Possibly* in a long Course of Time their Numbers may encrease; — and *possibly*, at last, the Tide may turn; so that our Posterity may regard the present Madness of going to War for the Sake of Trade, Riches, or Dominion, with the same Eye of Astonishment and Pity, that we do the Madness of our Forefathers in fighting under the Banner of the peaceful Cross to recover the Holy Land. This strange Phrensy raged throughout all Orders and Degrees of Men for several Centuries; and was cured at last more by the dearbought Experience of repeated Losses and continual Disappointments, than by any good Effects which cool Reason and Reflection could have upon the rational Faculties of Mankind. May the like dear-bought Experience prevail at last in the present Case!

A LETTER FROM A MERCHANT IN LONDON
TO HIS NEPHEW IN AMERICA

EDITORIAL NOTE

This tract was published in 1766, during the course of the controversy over the Stamp Act, and was republished as Tract III of *Four Tracts together with Two Sermons* (Gloucester, 1774). In the Preface to *Four Tracts* Tucker explains that the piece was written at the request of "an elderly Gentleman," who was well versed on the subject of colonial trade and gave him interesting information regarding colonial smuggling during the Seven Years' War. His informant admitted that the colonies had grown ungovernable and that they were a burden to the mother country, but "he startled as much at the idea of a *separation*, as if he had seen a spectre!" Accordingly, says Tucker, "I was obliged, as the reader will see towards the conclusion, to give the argument such a turn as expressed rather a casual threat to separate, than a settled project of doing it."

TRACT III.

A

Letter from a Merchant in *London*

TO HIS

NEPHEW in *AMERICA*.

DEAR COUSIN,

YOUR Letters gave me formerly no small Pleasure, because they seem to have proceeded from a good Heart, guided by an Understanding more enlightened than is usually found among young Men: And the honest Indignation you express against those Artifices and Frauds, those Robberies and Insults, which lost us the Hearts and Affections of the *Indians*, is particularly to be commended; for these were the Things, as you justly observed, which involved us in the most bloody and expensive War that ever was known; and these, by being repeated, will stimulate the poor injured Savages to redress their Wrongs, and retaliate the Injury as soon as they can, by some Means or other. You did therefore exceedingly right, in manifesting the utmost Abhorrence and Detestation of all such Practices.

BUT of late I cannot say, that I receive the same Satisfaction from your Correspondence: You, and your Countrymen, certainly are discontented to a great Degree; but whether your Discontent arises from a Desire of Change, and of making Innovations in your Form of Government, or from a mistaken Notion, that we are making Innovations in it, is hard to say.

GIVE me Leave therefore to expostulate with you, on this strange Alteration in your Conduct. You indeed talk loudly of Chains, and exclaim vehemently against Slavery: — But surely you do not suspect, that I can entertain the most distant wish of making any Man a slave, much less my own Brother's Son, and my next of Kin. — So far from it, that whether I can make you a Convert to my Way of thinking or not, I shall still act by you as my nearest Relation; being always desirous of allowing that Liberty to others, which I hope ever to enjoy myself, — of letting every Man see with his own Eyes, and act according to his own Judgment: — This, I say, I would willingly indulge every Man in, as far as ever is consistent with good Government, and the public Safety.

For indeed Governments there must be of some Kind or other; and Peace and Subordination are to be preserved; otherwise, there would be no such Thing as true Liberty subsisting in the World.

IN Pursuance therefore of this rational Plan of Liberty, give me Leave to ask you, young Man, What is it you mean by repeating to me so often in every Letter, *The Spirit of the Constitution?* I own, I do not much approve of this Phrase, because its meaning is so vague and indeterminate; and because it may be made to serve all Purposes alike, good or bad. And indeed it has been my constant Remark, That when Men were at a Loss for solid Arguments and Matters of Fact, in their political Disputes, they then had recourse to the *Spirit* of the Constitution as to their last Shift, and the only Thing they had to say. An *American*, for Example, now insists, That according to the Spirit of the *English* Constitution, he ought not to be taxed without his own Consent, given either by himself, or by a Representative in Parliament chosen by himself. Why ought he not? And doth the Constitution say in so many Words, that he ought not? Or doth it say, That every Man either hath, or ought to have, or was intended to have a Vote for a Member of Parliament? No, by no Means: The Constitution says no such Thing.— But the Spirit of it doth; and that is as good, perhaps better. — Very well: See then how the same Spirit will presently wheel about, and assert a Doctrine quite repugnant to the Claims and Positions of you *Americans*. *Magna Charta*, for Example, is the great Foundation of *English* Liberties, and the Basis of the *English* Constitution. But by the Spirit of *Magna Charta*, all Taxes laid on by Parliament are *constitutional*, *legal* Taxes; and Taxes raised by the Prerogative of the Crown, without the Consent of the Parliament, are *illegal*. Now remember, young Man, that the late Tax or Duties upon Stamps was laid on by Parliament; and therefore, according to your own Way of reasoning, must have been a regular, constitutional, legal Tax. Nay more, the principal End and Intention of *Magna Charta*, as far as Taxation is concerned, was to assert the Authority and Jurisdiction of the three Estates of the Kingdom, in Opposition to the sole Prerogative of the King: So that if you will now plead the Spirit of *Magna Charta* against the Jurisdiction of Parliament, you will plead *Magna Charta* against itself.

LEAVING therefore all these shifting, unstable Topics, which, like changeable Silks, exhibit different Colours, according as they are viewed in different Lights; let us from the *Spirit* of the Constitution, come to the Constitution *itself*. For this is a plain, obvious Matter of Fact; and Matters of Fact are said to be stubborn Things. Now the first Emigrants, who settled in *America*, were certainly *English* Subjects, — subject to the Laws and Jurisdiction of Parliament, and consequently to parliamentary Taxes, *before* their Emigration; and therefore subject *afterwards*, unless some legal, constitutional Exemption can be produced.

Now this is the Question, and the sole Question between you and me, reduced to a plain, single Matter of Fact. Is there therefore any such Exemption as here pretended? And if you have it, why do you not produce it? — "The King, you say, hath granted Charters of Exemption to the *American* Colonies." This is now coming to the Point; and this will bring the Dispute to a short Issue. Let us therefore first enquire, Whether he could legally and constitutionally grant you such a Charter? And secondly, Whether he did ever so much as attempt to do it? And whether any such Charters are upon Record?

Now, upon the first settling an *English* Colony, and before ever you, *Americans*, could have chosen any Representatives, and therefore before any Assembly of such Representatives could have possibly met, — to whose Laws, and to what legislative Power were you then subject? To the *English* most undoubtedly; for you could have been subject to no other. You were *Englishmen* yourselves; and you carried the *English* Government, and an *English* Charter over along with you. This being the Case, were you not then in the same Condition, as to Constitutional Rights and Liberties, with the rest of your Fellow-subjects, who remained in *England?* Certainly you were. I most cordially agree, that you ought not to have been placed in a worse; and surely you had no Right to expect a better. Suppose therefore, that the Crown had been so ill advised, as to have granted a Charter to any City or County here in *England*, pretending to exempt them from the Power and Jurisdiction of an *English* Parliament; — what would the Judges? what would the Lawyers? nay, what would you *Americans* have said to it? Apply this now to your own Case; for surely you cannot wish to have it put upon a fairer Footing; try therefore, and see, and then tell me; is it possible for you to believe, that the King has a Power vested in him by the Constitution of dividing his Kingdom into several independant States, and petty Kingdoms, like the Heptarchy in the Times of the *Saxons?* Or can you really imagine, that he could crumble the parliamentary Authority and Jurisdiction, were he so minded, into Bits and Fragments, by assigning one Parliament to one City or County, another to another, and so on? Is it possible, I say, for you to believe an Absurdity so gross and glaring? And yet gross and palpable as this Absurdity is, you must either believe it, or adopt a still greater, *viz.* that, though the King cannot do these strange Things in *England*, yet he can do them all in *America*; because the Royal Prerogative, like Wire coiled up in a Box, can be stretched and drawn out almost any Length, according to the Distance and Extent of his Dominions. Good Heavens! what a sudden Alteration is this! An *American* pleading for the Extension of the Prerogative of the Crown? Yes, if it could make for his Cause; and for extending it too beyond all the Bounds of Law, of Reason, and of Common Sense!

But though I have for Argument's Sake, and merely to confute you in your own Way, here supposed, that the Crown had been so ill-advised, as to grant Charters to the Colonies so unconstitutional and illegal, as these undoubtedly must have been; — yet the Fact itself is far otherwise*; for no such Charters were ever granted. Nay, many of your Colony Charters assert quite the contrary, by containing express Reservations of Parliamentary Rights, particularly that great one of levying Taxes. And those Charters which do not make such Provisoes in express Terms, must be supposed virtually to imply them; because the Law and Constitution will not allow, that the King can do more either at home or abroad, by the Prerogative Royal, than the Law and Constitution authorize him to do.

However, if you are still doubtful, and if you would wish to have a Confirmation of this Argument by some plain Fact, some striking Proof, and visible Example, I will give you one; and such an one too, as shall convince you, if any thing can, of the Folly and Absurdity of your Positions: The City of *London*, for Instance, — a Body Politic as respectable, without Offence, as the greatest of your Colonies with regard to *Property*, and superior to many of them with respect to *Numbers;* — this great City, I say, the Metropolis of the whole *British* Empire, hath long enjoyed, before the Colonies were ever thought of, the threefold Power of Jurisdiction, Legislation, and Taxation in certain Cases: But no Man in his Senses ever yet supposed, that the City of *London* either

---

* Our former Princes claimed a Right, and frequently exercised the Power of levying Taxes, without the Consent of Parliament. But upon settling the Colonies, this supposed Right, which cost Charles I. his Crown, and his Life, was not insisted on in any of the Charters, and was expressly given up in that which was granted to Lord *Baltimore* for *Maryland*. Now this Clause, which is nothing more than the Renunciation of *obsolete* Prerogative, is quoted in our Newspapers, as if it was a Renunciation of the Rights of Parliament to raise Taxes. Whereas the King in that Charter stipulated only *for himself, his Heirs, and Successors*, not to raise Taxes by Virtue of the Prerogative Royal; which certainly he might do, and which was very proper to be done for the Encouragement and Security of a new Colony. But he could not stipulate for the Parliament; and indeed he did not attempt to do it.

was, or could be exempted by these Charters from Parliamentary Jurisdiction, or Parliamentary Taxes; and if any Citizen should plead the
Charters in Bar to Parliamentary Authority, or refuse to pay his Quota
of the Land-Tax, because that Tax is not laid on by an Act of the Lord-
Mayor, Aldermen, and Common Council; — I do not say, indeed,
that the Judges would commit him to *Newgate*; — but I do verily believe,
that they would order him to another Place of Confinement, much
fitter for a Person in his unhappy Situation.

AND now, my good Friend, what can you say to these Things?—The
only Thing which you ought to say is, that you did not see the Affair
in its true Light before; and that you are sincerely sorry for having been
so positive in a wrong Cause. Confuted most undoubtedly you are
beyond the Possibility of a Reply, as far as the Law and Constitution of
the Realm are concerned in this Question. But indeed it seems to me by
certain Passages in your Letters, that, though you raise a terrible Outcry
against the supposed Violation of your Charters; you yourself would not
rest the Merits of your Cause upon the Proof of such a Violation; and
that you would rather drop that Point, than attempt to justify the
Charge, if called upon to do it.

WHAT then is it, which you have next to offer? Oh! "The Unreasonableness! the Injustice! and the Cruelty of taxing a free People,
without permitting them to have Representatives of their own to answer
for them, and to maintain their fundamental Rights and Privileges!"

STRANGE, that you did not discover these bad Things before! Strange,
that though the *British* Parliament has been, from the Beginning, thus
unreasonable, thus *unjust*, and *cruel* towards you, by levying Taxes on
many Commodities outwards and inwards,—nay, by laying an internal
Tax, the Post-Tax for Example, on the whole *British* Empire in *America*;
—and, what is still worse, by making Laws to affect your Property,—
your Paper Currency, and even to take away Life itself, if you offend
against them:—Strange and unaccountable, I say, that after you had
suffered this so long, you should not have been able to have discovered,
that you were without Representatives in the *British* Parliament, *of
your own electing*, 'till this enlightening Tax upon Paper opened your
Eyes! And what a Pity is it, that you have been Slaves for so many
Generations, and yet did not know that you were Slaves until now.

BUT let that pass, my dear Cousin; for I always choose to confute you
in your own Way. Now, if you mean any thing at all by the Words
unreasonable, unjust, and cruel, as used in this Dispute; you must mean,
that the Mother Country deals worse by you, than by the Inhabitants

of *Great-Britain*; and that she denies certain Constitutional Rights and Privileges to you abroad, which we enjoy here at home. Now pray what are these constitutional Rights and Liberties, which are refused to you? Name them, if you can. The Things which you pretend to alledge are, "The Rights of voting for Members of the *British* Parliament; and the Liberty of chusing your own Representatives." But surely you will not dare to say, that we refuse your Votes, when you come hither to offer them, and choose to poll: You cannot have the Face to assert, that on an Election Day any Difference is put between the Vote of a Man born in *America*, and of one born here in *England*. Yet this you must assert, and prove too, before you can do any thing to the present Purpose. Suppose therefore, that an *American* hath acquired a Vote (as he legally may, and many have done) in any of our Cities or Counties, Towns, or Boroughs; suppose, that he is become a Freeman, or a Freeholder here in *England*;—on that State of the Case, prove if you can, that his Vote was ever refused, because he was born in *America:*—Prove this, I say, and then I will allow, that your Complaints are very just; and that you are indeed the much injured, the cruelly treated People, you would make the World believe.

BUT, my good Friend, is this supposed Refusal the real Cause of your Complaint? Is this the Grievance that calls so loudly for Redress? Oh! no, you have no Complaint of this Sort to make: But the Cause of your Complaint is this; that you live at too great a Distance from the Mother Country to be present at our *English* Elections; and that in Consequence of this Distance, the Freedom of our Towns, or the Free-holds in our Counties, as far as voting is concerned, are not worth attending to. It may be so; but pray consider, if you yourselves do choose to make it inconvenient for you to come and vote, by retiring into distant Countries,—what is that to us? And why are we to be reproached for committing a 'Violation on the Birth-rights of *Englishmen*, which, if it be a Violation, is committed only by yourselves?' It seems, you find it to be your particular Interest to live in the Colonies; it seems, that you prefer the Emoluments of residing there to your Capacity, or Capability (take which Word you please) of residing and voting here. Now this is your own free Choice; and we leave you at full Liberty to act as you think proper: But then, are we obliged to alter our Political System merely to accord with your Convenience? Are we to change and new model our fixed and ancient Constitution, just as you shall see fit to command us? and according as it shall please you to remove from Place to Place? And is this the Complaisance, which you expect the

Mother Country should shew to her dutiful Children? Yes, it is; and you demand it too with a loud Voice, full of Anger, of Defiance, and Denunciation.

HOWEVER, the Lion is not always so fierce as he is painted; and 'till we are beaten into a Compliance, it is to be hoped, that we may be allowed to expostulate with you in a few harmless, unbloody Words. Granting therefore, that the Colonies are unrepresented in the *British* Parliament: Granting that two Millions of People in *America* have, in this respect, no Choice, nor Election of their own, through the Necessity of the Case, and their Distance from the Place of Election:—What would you infer from this Concession? And wherein can such Kind of Topics support your Cause? For know, young Man, that not only two Millions, which are the utmost, that your exaggerated Accounts can be swelled to;—I say, not only two Millions, but six Millions at least of the Inhabitants of *Great-Britain*, are still unrepresented in the *British* Parliament. And this Omission arises, not from the Necessity of the Case, not from consulting Interest and Convenience as with you, but from original Ideas of Gothic Vassalage,—from various Casualties and Accidents,—from Changes in the Nature of Property,—from the Alteration of Times and Circumstances,—and from a thousand other Causes. Thus, for Example, in the great Metropolis, and in many other Cities, landed Property itself hath no Representative in Parliament; Copyholds and Leaseholds of various Kinds have none likewise, though of ever so great a Value. This you yourself very well know; because when you were here last, you knew, that I was possessed of considerable landed Property in *London*, and of several Copyholds and beneficial Leaseholds in the Country, and yet that I never had a Vote. Moreover, in some Towns neither Freedom, nor Birth-right, nor the serving of an Apprenticeship, shall entitle a Man to give his Vote, though they may enable him to set up a Trade: In other Towns the most numerous, the most populous, and flourishing of any, there are no Freedoms or Votes of any Sort; but all is open; and none are represented. And besides all this, it is well known, that the great *East-India* Company, which have such vast Settlements, and which dispose of the Fate of Kings and Kingdoms abroad, have not so much as a single Member, or even a single Vote, *quatenus*, a Company, to watch over their Interests at home. What likewise shall we say in regard to the prodigious Number of Stock-holders in our public Funds? And may not their Property, perhaps little short of ONE HUNDRED MILLIONS Sterling, as much deserve to be represented in Parliament, as the scattered Townships, or straggling

Houses of some of your Provinces in *America?*   Yet we raise no Commotions; we neither ring the Alarm-Bell, nor sound the Trumpet; but submit to be taxed without being represented; and taxed too, let me tell you, for your Sakes.   Witness the additional Duties on our Lands, Windows, Houses; also on our Malt, Beer, Ale, Cyder, Perry, Wines, Brandy, Rum, Coffee, Chocolate, *&c. &c. &c.* for defraying the Expences of the late War, — not forgetting the grievous Stamp-Duty itself.   All this, I say, we submitted to, when you were, or at least, when you pretended to be, in great Distress; so that neither Men, almost to the last Drop of Blood we could spill, — nor Money, to the last Piece of Coin, were spared: But all was granted away, all was made a Sacrifice, when you cried out for Help.   And the Debt which we contracted on this Occasion, is so extraordinary, as not to be paralleled in History.   It is to be hoped, for the Credit of human Nature, that the Returns which you have made us for these Succours, and your present Behaviour towards us, which perhaps is still more extraordinary, may not be paralleled likewise.

But as you *Americans* do not chuse to remember any thing, which we have done for you;—though we, and our Children shall have Cause to remember it 'till latest Posterity;—let us come to the Topic, which you yourselves do wish to rest your Cause upon, and which you imagine to be the Sheet Anchor of your State Vessel.   "You are not represented; and you are Two Millions; therefore you ought not to be taxed."   We are not represented; and we are Six Millions; therefore we ought not to be taxed.   Which now, even in your own Sense of Things, have most Reason to complain?   And which Grievance, if it be a Grievance, deserves first to be redressed?   Be it therefore supposed, that an Augmentation ought to take place in our House of Commons, in order to represent in Parliament the prodigious Numbers of *British* Subjects hitherto unrepresented.   In this Case the first Thing to be done, is to settle the Proportion.   And therefore if Two Millions (the Number of Persons actually represented at present) require Five Hundred and Fifty-eight Representatives (which I think is the Number of our modern House of Commons) how many will Six Millions require?—The Answer is, that they will require One Thousand Six Hundred and Seventy-four Representatives.   Now this is the first Augmentation, which is to be made to our List of Parliament Men.   And after the Increase, we are to be furnished, by the same Rule of Proportion, with Five Hundred and Fifty-eight more from the Colonies.   So that the total Numbers will be Two Thousand Seven Hundred and Ninety Representatives in

PARLIAMENT! A goodly Number truly! and very proper for the Dispatch of Business! Oh, the Decency and Order of such an Assembly! The Wisdom and Gravity of Two Thousand Seven Hundred and Ninety Legislators all met together in one Room! What a Pity is it, that so hopeful a Project should not be carried into immediate Execution!

BUT, my noble Senator,—for certainly you yourself must figure a way in such an august Assembly,—permit an old Man to reveal one Secret to you, before you proceed any further in your representing Scheme:— That the Complaint itself of being *unrepresented*, is entirely false and groundless. For both the Six Millions at home, and the Two Millions in the Colonies, are all represented already. This perhaps may startle you; but nevertheless this is the Fact. And though I have hitherto used a different Language merely to accommodate myself to your Ideas, and to confute your Folly in your own Way, I must now tell you, that every Member of Parliament represents you and me, and our Interests in all essential Points, just as much as if we had voted for him. For though one Place, or one Set of Men may elect, and send him up to Parliament, yet, when once he becomes a Member, he is then the equal Guardian of all. And he ought not, by the Duty of his Office, to shew a Preference to his own Town, City, or County, but in such Cases only, where a Preference shall not interfere with the general Good. Nay, he ought in Conscience to give his Vote in Parliament against the Sense, and against the Instructions of his Electors, if he should think in his Conscience, that what they require, is wrong in itself, is illegal or injurious, and detrimental to the public Welfare. This then being the Case, it therefore follows, that our *Birminghams*, *Manchesters*, *Leeds*, *Halifaxes*, &c. and *your Bostons*, *New-Yorks*, and *Philadelphias*, are all as *really*, though not so nominally represented, as any Part whatsoever of the *British* Empire:—And that each of these Places have in fact, instead of one or two, not less than Five Hundred and Fifty-eight Guardians in the *British* Senate. A Number abundantly sufficient, as far as human Prudence can suggest, or the present imperfect State of Things will permit, for the Security of our Rights, and the Preservation of our Liberties.

BUT perhaps you will say, That though it may be a Senator's Duty to regard the Whole rather than a Part, and to be the equal Protector of all;—yet he will, in fact, regard that most, which can best promote his own Interest, and secure his Election another Time. It may be so: For who can guard against all Possibility of Danger? And what System can there be devised, but may be attended with Inconveniences and

Imperfections in some Respect or other?—Nevertheless, if your general Objection proves any thing, it proves a great deal too much: For it proves, that no Man ought to pay any Tax, but that only, to which the Member of his own Town, City, or County, hath particularly assented: Because all other Members being chose by other Persons, and not by him, and perhaps by Persons of an opposite Interest, are therefore not *his* Representatives, and consequently not the true Guardians of *his* Property. Being therefore *without a Representative* in such a Parliament, he is under no Obligation to obey its Laws, or pay any of its Taxes.

WHERE now, my Friend, will you turn? And what can you do, to extricate yourself from the Difficulties which arise on all Sides on this Occasion? You cannot turn about, and say, that the other Representatives, whom this Man never chose, and for whom he had no Vote to give, and against whom perhaps he had particular Exceptions, have nevertheless a Right of taxing him, because he makes a Part of the Body Politic *implied* in, and concluded by the rest;—you cannot say this, because the DOCTRINE of IMPLICATION is the very Thing to which you object, and against which you have raised so many Batteries of popular Noise and Clamour. Nay, as the Objection is entirely of your own making, it must go still further: For if your Argument is good for any thing, it is as good for *North-America* as it is for *Great-Britain*; and consequently you must maintain, that all those in your several Provinces who have no Votes (and many Thousands of such there are) and also all those Votes, whose Representatives did not expressly consent to the Act of your Assemblies for raising any of your own provincial Taxes,— ought not to be compelled to pay them. These now are the happy Consequences of your own Principles, fairly, clearly, and evidently deduced: Will you abide by them?

BUT however, not to push you into more Absurdities of this Kind, let us wave the present Point, and come to another. For, after all your doleful Complaints, what if it should appear, that these Five Hundred and Fifty-eight Parliamentary Guardians, who represent you only by *Implication*, have, in fact, been *kinder* and *more bountiful* to you *Americans*, than they have been to their own *British* Voters, whom they represent by *Nomination?* And, what if even this Argument, so full of Sorrow and Lamentation, should at last be retorted upon you, and made to conclude, like all the rest, the very Reverse of what you intended? This, I believe, is what you little expected: But nevertheless, this is the Case: For if there be any Partiality to be complained of in the Conduct of the *British* Parliament, it will appear to be a Partiality in Favour of the

Colonies, and against the Mother Country. Do you demand my
Authority for this Assertion? I will give it you:—The Statutes of the
Realm are my Authority; and surely you cannot demand a better.
By these then it will appear, that a Colonist, who is consequently subordinate to the Mother Country in the very Nature of Things, is nevertheless put upon a better Footing, *in many Respects*, than an Inhabitant
of *Great-Britain*. By these it will appear, that the Parliament, like an
over-indulgent Parent to his Favourite, froward Child, hath been
continually heaping Favours upon you, which we were not permitted to
taste. Thus, for Example, you have your Choice, whether you will
accept of my Price for your Tobacco,—or after bringing it here, whether
you will carry it away, and try your Fortune at another Market: But I
have no Alternative allowed, being obliged to buy yours at your own
Price; or else to pay such a Duty for the Tobacco of other Countries, as
must amount to a Prohibition. Nay, in order to favour your Plantations, I am not permitted to plant this Herb on my own Estate, though
the Soil should be ever so proper for it. Again, the same Choice, and the
same Alternative are allowed to you, and denied to me, in regard to Rice;
with this additional Advantage, that in many Respects you need not
bring it into *England* at all, unless you are so minded. And what will
you say in Relation to Hemp? The Parliament now gives you a Bounty
of 8l. per Ton for exporting your Hemp from *North-America*; but will
allow me nothing for growing it here in *England*; nay, will tax me very
severely for fetching it from any other Country; though it be an Article
most essentially necessary for all the Purposes of Shipping and Navigation. Moreover in respect to the Culture of Raw Silk, you have an
immense Parliamentary Premium for that Purpose; and you receive
further Encouragements from our Society for Arts and Sciences, which
is continually adding fresh Rewards:—But I can receive no Encouragement either from the one, or from the other, to bear my Expences at
first setting out; though most undeniably the white Mulberry-Trees
can thrive as well on my Grounds, as they can in *Switzerland*, *Brandenburgh*, *Denmark*, or *Sweden*, where vast Quantities are now raising.
Take another Instance:—Why shall not I be permitted to buy Pitch,
Tar, and Turpentine,—without which I cannot put my Ships to Sea;—
and Indigo, so useful in many Manufactures;—why shall not I be permitted to purchase these Articles wherever I can, the best in their Kind,
and on the best Terms?—No, I shall not; for though they are all raw
Materials, which therefore ought to have been imported Duty free, yet I
am restrained by an heavy Duty, almost equal to a Prohibition, from

purchasing them any where, but from you:—Whereas you on the
contrary, are paid a Bounty for selling these very Articles, at the only
Market, in which you could sell them to Advantage, *viz.* the *English**.

MUCH more might have been said on this Subject; and the like Observations might have been extended to the Sugar Colonies: But I
forbear.   For indeed enough has been said already (and as it exposes our
Partiality and Infatuation a little severely, perhaps too much)—in order
to prove to the World, that of all People upon Earth, you have the least
Reason to complain.

BUT complain you will; and no sooner is one Recital of imaginary
Grievances silenced and confuted; but, like the Hydra in the Fable,
up starts another.   Let us see therefore, what is your next Objection,
which I think, is the last, that with all your Zeal, and Good-will, you are
able to muster up.—"The Inexpediency and Excessiveness of such a
Tax! a Tax ill-timed in itself, and ill digested! unseasonably laid on! and
exceeding all Rules of Proportion in regard to the Abilities of those, who
are to pay it!"

Now, my Friend, had there been any Truth in these Assertions, which
I shall soon make to appear, that there is not;—but had there been,
the Plea itself comes rather of the latest, and out of Place from you;—
from you, I say, who peremptorily object to the very Power and Authority of the *British* Parliament of laying *any internal* Taxes upon the
Colonies, great or small, or any Time seasonable, or unseasonable.   And
therefore, had you been able to have proved the *Illegality* of such a Tax,
it would have been quite superfluous to have informed us afterwards,
that this Usurpation of your Rights and Liberties was either an excessive,
or an unseasonable Usurpation.   But as you have failed in this first
Point; nay, as all your own Arguments have proved the very reverse of
what you intended; and very probably, as you yourself was not originally
quite satisfied with the Justice of your Cause;—and must have seen
abundant Reason before this Time to have altered your former hasty,
and rash Opinion;—I will therefore wave the Advantage, and now
debate the Point with you, as though you had acknowledged the Parliamentary Right of Taxation, and only excepted to the Quantum, or
the Mode, the Time, or the Manner of it.

Now two Things are here to be discussed; first, the pretended *Excessiveness* of the Tax; and secondly, the *Unseasonableness* of it.   As to the
Excessiveness of the Stamp Duties, the Proof of this must depend upon

---

* Those who have not the Statutes at large, may see the Things here referred to,
and many others of the like Sort, in *Crouche*'s or *Saxby*'s Book of Rates.

the Proof of a previous Article,—the relative Poverty, and Inability of
those, who are to pay it.   But how do you propose to make out this
Point?   And after having given us for some Years past such Displays of
your growing Riches and encreasing Magnificence, as perhaps never any
People did in the same Space of Time; how can you now retract and call
yourselves a poor People?   Remember, my young Man, the several Ex-
postulations I had with your deceased Father on the prodigious Increase
of *American* Luxury.   And what was his Reply?   Why, that an Increase
of Luxury was an inseparable Attendant on an Increase of Riches; and
that, if I expected to continue my *North-American* Trade, I must suit
my Cargo on the Taste of my Customers; and not to my own old-
fashioned Notions of the Parsimony of former Days, when *America* was a
poor Country.   Remember therefore the Orders given by him, and
afterwards by you, to have your Assortment of Goods made richer, and
finer every Year.   And are your Gold and Silver Laces;—your rich
Brocades, Silks, and Velvets;—your Plate, and China, and Jewels;—
your Coaches and Equipages;—your sumptuous Furniture, Prints, and
Pictures.   Are all these Things now laid aside?   Have you no Concerts,
or Assemblies, no Play Houses, or Gaming Houses, now subsisting?
Have you put down your Horse Races and other such like Sports and
Diversions?   And is the Luxury of your Tables, and the Variety and
Profusion of your Wines and Liquors quite banished from among you?—
These are the Questions, which you ought to answer, before an Estimate
can be made of your relative Poverty, or before any Judgment can be
formed concerning the Excessiveness of the Tax.

BUT I have not yet done with you on this Head.   For even though you
were poor (which you know, you are not, compared with what you were
Thirty Years ago) it may nevertheless happen, that our relative Poverty
may be found to be greater than yours.   And if so, when a new Burden
is to be laid on, the proper Question is, which of these two Sorts of poor
People, is the best able, or, if you please, the least unable to bear it?—
especially if it be taken into the Account, that this additional Load is an
American Burthen, and not a *British* one.   Be it therefore granted,
according to what you say, that you are Two Millions of Souls; be it also
allowed, as it is commonly asserted, that the Public Debt of the several
Provinces amounts to about 800,000l. Sterling; and in the next Place,
be it supposed, for Argument's Sake, that were this general Debt equally
divided among the Two Millions, each Individual would owe about the
Value of Eight Shillings.   Thus stands the Account on one Side.   Now
we in *Britain* are reckoned to be about Eight Millions of Souls; and we

owe almost One Hundred and Forty-four Millions of Money; which
Debt, were it equally divided among us, would throw a Burthen upon
each Person of about 18l. Sterling.   This then being the State of the
Case on both Sides, would it be so capital an Offence? would it be High-
Treason in us to demand of you, who owe so little, to contribute equally
with ourselves, who owe so much, towards the public Expences;—and
such Expences too as you were the Cause of creating?   Would it be a
Crime of a Nature so very heinous and diabolical, as to call forth the
hottest of your Rage and Fury?   Surely no:—And yet, my gentle
Friend, we do not so much as ask you to contribute equally with our-
selves, we only demand, that you would contribute *something*.   And
what is this something?   Why truly it is, that when we raise about Eight
Millions of Money annually upon Eight Millions of Persons, we expect,
that you would contribute One Hundred Thousand Pounds (for the
Stamp Duty upon the Continent alone, without comprehending the
Islands, cannot possibly amount to more) I say, we expect, that you
should contribute One Hundred Thousand Pounds to be raised on Two
Millions; that is, when each of us pays, one with another, Twenty
Shillings per Head, we expect, that each of you should pay the Sum of
One Shilling!   Blush! blush for shame at your perverse and scandalous
Behaviour! — Words still more keen, and perhaps more just, are ready
to break forth, through an honest Indignation: — But I suppress them.

PERHAPS you will say, and I think it is the only Thing left for you to say
in Excuse for such Proceedings, that you have other Public Taxes to pay,
besides those which the *British* Parliament now requires.   Undoubtedly
you have, for your Provincial and other Taxes are likewise to be paid:
But here let me ask, is not this our Case also?   And have not we many
other Taxes to discharge besides those which belong to the Public, and
are to be accounted for at the Exchequer?   Surely we have: Witness our
County Taxes, Militia Taxes, Poor Taxes, Vagrant Taxes, Bridge Taxes,
High Road and Turnpike Taxes, Watch Taxes, Lamps and Scavenger
Taxes, *&c. &c. &c.* — all of them as numerous and as burthensome as
any that you can mention.   And yet with all this Burthen, yea, with an
additional Weight of a National Debt of 18l. Sterling per Head,—we
require of each of you to contribute only One Shilling to every Twenty
from each of us! — yes; and this Shilling too to be spent in your own
Country, for the support of your own Civil and Military Establishments;
together with many Shillings drawn from us for the same Purpose.
Alas! had you been in our Situation, and we in yours, would you have
been content with our paying so small, so inconsiderable a Share of the

Public Expences? And yet, small and inconsiderable as this Share is, you will not pay it. No, you will not! And be it at our Peril, if we demand it.

Now, my Friend, were Reason and Argument, were Justice Equity, or Candour to be allowed by you to have any Concern in this Affair; I would then say, that you *Americans* are the most unfortunate People in the World in your Management of the present Controversy. Unfortunate you are; because the very Attempts you make towards setting forth your Inability, prove, to a Demonstration, that you are abundantly able, were you but truly willing to pay this Tax. For how, and in what Manner do you prove your Allegations? Why truly, by breaking forth into Riots and Insurrections, and by committing every Kind of Violence, that can cause Trade to stagnate, and Industry to cease. And is this the Method, which you have chosen to pursue, in order to make the World believe, that you are a poor People? Is this the Proof you bring, that the Stamp Duty is a Burthen too heavy for you to bear? Surely, if you had really intended our Conviction, you would have chosen some other Medium: And were your Inability, or Poverty the single Point in Question, you would not have taken to such Courses, as must infallibly render you still the poorer. For in fact, if, after all your Complaints of Poverty, you can still afford to idle away your Time, and to waste Days, and Weeks, in Outrages and Uproars; what else do you prove, but that you are a prodigal, and extragavant People? For you must acknowledge, that if but Half of this Time were spent, as it ought to be, in honest Industry and useful Labour, it would have been more than sufficient to have paid double the Tax which is now required.

BUT you will still say, that though the Tax may be allowed (nay indeed it must be allowed) to be very moderate, every thing considered, and not at all excessive; "It may nevertheless be laid on, very unseasonably; it may be wrong-timed, and ill-digested."

Now, here I must own, that I am somewhat at a Loss how to answer you, because I am not quite certain that I understand your Meaning. If, for Example, by the Term *ill-digested*, you would insinuate, that the *American* Stamp Duty would grind the Faces of the Poor, and permit the Rich to escape; — that it would affect the Necessaries, and not the Superfluities of Life; — that it would prevent the Building of Houses, or the clearing of Lands, or the Cultivation of Estates already cleared; — or lastly, that it would diminish the Number of your Shipping, or stop the Pay of your Sailors: If these, or any of these are the Evils, which you would lay to the Charge of the Stamp Duty, nothing upon Earth could be a falser Charge; and you could not give a stronger Proof either of your Defect in Judgment, or Want of Integrity, than by uttering such Assertions as these; — Assertions, which both daily Experience and the Nature of Things evidently demonstrate to be void of Truth. We in *Britain* have been subject to a Stamp Duty for many, very many Years; a Duty much higher than that which is intended for *America;* and yet we know by long Experience, that it hath not been attended with any of the dreadful Consequences which are here supposed.

AGAIN, as to the *wrong-timing*, or the *Unseasonableness* of this Tax: — If by this you mean to say, that it was laid on, at a Time, when you were poorer, and less able to bear it, than you were before; — that is *false* also. For you never were richer, and you never were more able to contribute your Quota towards the general Expences, than at the Juncture of laying on this Tax. To prove this, let it be observed, that just before this Event, you had not only been draining the Mother Country by the immense Sums drawn from us to pay our Fleets and Armies, when acting in Defence of *America;*—and that your Jobbers and Contractors had not only been sucking our Blood and Vitals by their extortionate Demands;—but you had also been enriched by the Spoils, and by the Traffic of the numerous Colonies of *France* and *Spain*. For you were continually acting the double Part either of Trade, or War, of Smuggling, or Privateering, according to the Prospect of greater Gain. And while we at Home were exerting our utmost to put a speedy End to the War by an honourable Peace, — you on the contrary were endeavouring to prolong it as much as possible; and were supplying our Enemies with all Manner of Provisions, and all Sorts of warlike Stores for that Purpose. Nay, because a Part of these ill-gotten Riches was laid out in *English* Manufactures (there being at that Time hardly a Possibility of purchasing any but *English*, when our Fleets were absolute Masters of the Sea) your Advocates and Authors trumpeted aloud the prodigious Profits of this *North-American* Trade; — not considering, or rather not willing that we should consider, that while a few Individuals were getting Thousands, the Public was spending Millions.

ONCE more: — If by the Epithet *unseasonable*, you would be understood to mean, that there was *no need* of taxing you at all at that Juncture; *because the Mother Country was still as able to carry the additional Load, which you had brought upon her, as she had been to bear all the rest:* If this be your Meaning, I must tell you once for all, that you are egregiously mistaken. For we can bear no more; we cannot support ourselves under heavier Taxations, even were we ever so willing; we have strained every Nerve already, and have no Resources left for new Impositions. Therefore let what will come of the present Affairs, let the Stamp Duty be repealed, or not; still the Expences of *America* must be borne by the *Americans* in some Form, or under some Denomination or other.

BUT after all; perhaps you meant none of these Things; perhaps you meant to insinuate (though it was Prudence in you not to speak out) that the late Act was *ill-contrived* and *ill-timed*; because it was made at a Juncture, when neither the *French*, nor *Indians* were in your Rear to frighten, nor the *English* Fleets and Armies on your Front to force you to a Compliance. Perhaps this was your real Meaning; and if it was, it must be confessed, that in that Sense, the late Act was not well-timed; and that a much properer Season might have been chosen. For had the Law been made five or six Years before, when you were moving Heaven and Earth with your Cries and Lamentations; not a Tongue would then have uttered a Word against it; all your Orators would have displayed their Eloquence on other Topics; and even *American* Patriotism itself would at that Season have made no Difficulty in acknowledging, that the Mother Country had a Right to the Obedience of the Colonies in Return for her kind and generous Protection.

UPON the whole therefore, what is the Cause of such an amazing Outcry as you raise at present? — Not the Stamp Duty itself; all the World are agreed on that Head; and none can be so ignorant, or so stupid, as not to see, that this is a mere Sham and Pretence. What then are the real Grievances, seeing that the Things which you alledge are only the pretended ones? Why, some of you are exasperated against the Mother Country, on account of the Revival of certain Restrictions laid upon their Trade: — I say, a **Revival*; for the same Restrictions have been the

---

* Ever since the Discovery of *America*, it has been the System of every *European* Power, which had Colonies in that Part of the World, to confine (as far as Laws can confine) the Trade of the Colonies to the Mother Country, and to exclude all others, under the Penalty of Confiscation, &c. from partaking in it. Thus, the Trade of the *Spanish* Colonies is confined by Law to *Old Spain*,—the Trade of the *Brazils* to *Portugal*,—the Trade of *Martinico* and the other *French* Colonies to *Old France*, — and the Trade of *Curacoa* and *Surinam* to *Holland*. But in one Instance the *Hollanders* make an Exception (perhaps a wise one) *viz.* in the Case of *Eustatia*, which is open to all the World. Now, that the *English* thought themselves entitled to the same Right over their Colonies, which other Nations claim over theirs, and that they exercised the same Right by making what Regulations they pleased, may be seen by the following Acts of Parliament, *viz.* 12 of Car. II. Chap. 18. — 15 of Car. II. Ch. 7. — 22 and 23 of C. II. Ch. 26.—25 of C. II. Ch. 7.—7 and 8 of Will. III. Ch. 22.—10 and 11 of W. III. Ch. 21.—3 and 4 of Ann. Ch. 5 and 10.—8 of Ann. Ch. 13.—12 of Ann. Ch. 9.—1 of G. I. Ch. 26.—3 of G. I. Ch. 21.—8 of G. I. Ch. 15 and 18.—11 of

standing Rules of Government from the Beginning; though not enforced at all Times with equal Strictness.   During the late War, you *Americans* could not import the Manufactures of other Nations (which it is your constant Aim to do, and the Mother Country always to prevent) so conveniently as you can in Times of Peace; and therefore, there was no Need of watching you so narrowly, as far as that Branch of Trade was concerned.   But immediately upon the Peace, the various Manufactures of Europe, particularly those of *France*, which could not find Vent before, were spread, as it were, over all your Colonies, to the prodigious Detriment of your Mother Country; and therefore our late Set of Ministers acted certainly right, in putting in Force the Laws of their Country, in order to check this growing Evil.   If in so doing, they committed any Error; or, if the Persons to whom the Execution of these Laws were intrusted, exceeded their Instructions; there is no Doubt to be made, but that all this will be rectified by the present Administration.   And having done that, they will have done all that in Reason you can expect from them.   But alas! the Expectations of an *American* carry him much further: For he will ever complain and smuggle, and smuggle and complain, 'till all Restraints are removed, and 'till he can both buy and sell, whenever, and wheresoever he pleases.   Any thing short of this, is still a Grievance, a Badge of Slavery, an Usurpation on the natural Rights and Liberties of a free People, and I know not how many bad Things besides.

BUT, my good Friend, be assured, that these are Restraints, which neither the present, nor any future Ministry can exempt you from. They are the standing Laws of the Kingdom; and God forbid, that we should allow that dispensing Power to our Ministers, which we so justly deny to our Kings.   In short, while you are a Colony, you must be subordinate to the Mother Country.   These are the Terms and Conditions, on which you were permitted to make your first Settlements: They are the Terms and Conditions on which you alone can be entitled to the Assistance and Protection of *Great-Britain*; — they are also the fundamental Laws of the Realm; — and I will add further, that if *we* are obliged to pay many Bounties for the Importation of *your* Goods, and are excluded from purchasing such Goods, in other Countries (where

---

G. I. Ch. 29.—12 of G. I. Ch. 5.—2 of G. II. Ch. 28 and 35.—3 of G. II. Ch. 28.— 4 of G. II. Ch. 15.—5 of G. II. Ch. 7 and 9.—6 of G. II. Ch. 13.—8 of G. II. Ch. 18.—11 of G. II. Ch. 29.—12 of G. II. Ch. 30.—13 of G. II. Ch. 4 and 7.—15 and 16 of G. II. Ch. 23.—with many others of a later Date.   I might also mention the Laws made in the Reign of his present Majesty; but as these Laws are now the Point Controversy, I forbear.

we might purchase them on much cheaper Terms) in order to promote *your* Interest; — by Parity of Reason *you* ought to be subject to the like Exclusions, in order to promote *ours*. This then being the Case, do not expect, from the present Ministry, that which is impossible for any Set of Ministers to grant. All that they can do, is to connive a while at your unlawful Proceedings. But this can be but of short Duration: For as soon as ever fresh Remonstrances are made by the *British* Manufacturers, and *British* Merchants, the Ministry must renew the Orders of their Predecessors; they must enforce the Laws; they must require Searches, and Confiscations to be made; and then the present Ministers will draw upon themselves, for *doing their Duty*, just the same Execrations, which you now bestow upon the last.

So much as to your first Grievance; and as to your second, it is, beyond Doubt, of a Nature still worse. For many among you are sorely concerned, That they cannot pay their *British* Debts with an *American* Sponge. This is an intolerable Grievance; and they long for the Day when they shall be freed from this galling Chain. Our Merchants in *London, Bristol, Liverpool, Glasgow, &c. &c.* perfectly understand *your* many Hints and Inuendoes to us, on this Head. But indeed, lest we should be so dull as not to comprehend your Meaning, you have spoken out, and proposed an open Association against paying your just Debts. Had *our* Debtors in any other Part of the Globe, had the *French* or *Spaniards* proposed the like (and surely they have all at least an equal Right) what Name would you have given to such Proceedings? — But I forget: You are not the faithless *French* or *Spaniards:* You are ourselves: You are honest *Englishmen.*

Your third Grievance is the Sovereignty of *Great-Britain.* For you want to be independent: You wish to be an Empire by itself, and to be no longer the Province of another. This Spirit is uppermost; and this Principle is visible in all your Speeches, and all your Writings, even when you take some Pains to disguise it. — "What! an Island! A Spot such as this to command the great and mighty Continent of *North-America!* Preposterous! A Continent, whose Inhabitants double every five and twenty Years! Who therefore, within a Century and an Half will be upwards of an hundred and twenty Millions of Souls! — Forbid it Patriotism, forbid it Politics, that such a great and mighty Empire as this, should be held in Subjection by the paltry Kingdom of *Great-Britain!* Rather let the Seat of Empire be transferred; and let it be fixt, where it ought to be, *viz.* in *Great America!*"

Now, my good Friend, I will not stay to dispute with you the Calculations, on which your Orators, Philosophers, and Politicians have, for some Years past, grounded these extravagant Conceits (though I think the Calculations themselves both false, and absurd); but I will only say, that while we have the Power, we may command your Obedience, if we please: And that it will be Time enough for you to propose the making us a Province to *America*, when you shall find yourselves able to execute the Project.

IN the mean Time, the great Question is, What Course are *we* to take? And what are we to do with *you*, before you become this great and formidable People? — Plain and evident it is by the whole Tenor of your Conduct, that you endeavour, with all your Might, to drive us to Extremities. For no Kind of Outrage, or Insult, is omitted on your Part, that can irritate Individuals, or provoke a Government to chastise the Insolence, not to say the Rebellion of its Subjects; and you do not seem at all disposed to leave Room for an Accommodation. In Short, the Sword is the only Choice, which you will permit us to make; unless we will chuse to give you entirely up, and subscribe a Recantation. Upon those Terms indeed, you will deign to acknowledge the Power and Authority of a *British* Parliament; — that is, you will allow, that we have a Right and a Power to give you Bounties, and to pay your Expences; but no other. A strange Kind of Allegiance this! And the first that has ever yet appeared in the History of Mankind!

HOWEVER, this being the Case, shall we now compel you, by Force of Arms, to do your Duty? — Shall we procrastinate your Compulsion? — Or shall we entirely give you up, and have no other Connections with you, than if you had been so many Sovereign States, or Independent Kingdoms? One or other of these three will probably be resolved upon: And if it should be the first, I do not think that we have any Cause to fear the Event, or to doubt of Success.

FOR though your Populace may rob and plunder the Naked and Defenceless, this will not do the Business when a regular Force is brought against them. And a *British* Army, which performed so many brave Actions in *Germany*, will hardly fly before an *American* Mob; not to mention that our Officers and Soldiers, who passed several Campaigns with your Provincials in *America*, saw nothing either in their Conduct, or their Courage, which could inspire them with a Dread of seeing the Provincials a second Time. — Neither should we have the least Cause to suspect the *Fidelity* of our Troops, any more than their *Bravery*, — notwithstanding the base Insinuations of some of your Friends here (if indeed such Persons deserve to be called your Friends, who are in reality your greatest Foes, and whom you will find to be so at the last); not-withstanding, I say, their Insinuations of the Feasibility of corrupting his Majesty's Forces, when sent over, by Means of large Bribes, or double Pay.   This is a Surmise, as weak as it is wicked: For the Honour of the *British* Soldiery, let me tell you, is not so easily corrupted.   The *French* in *Europe* never found it so, with all their Gold, or all their Skill for Intrigue, and insinuating Address.   What then, in the Name of Wonder, have you to tempt them with in *America*, which is thus to overcome, at once, all their former Sense of Duty, all the Tyes of Conscience, Loyalty and Honour?—Besides, my Friend, if you really are so rich, as to be able to give *double* Pay, to our Troops, in a wrong Cause; do not grudge, let me beseech you, to give *one third* of *single* Pay (for we ask no more) in a right one:—And let it not be said, that you complain of Poverty, and plead an Inability to Pay your just Debts, at the very Instant that you boast of the scandalous Use which you intend to make of your Riches.

But notwithstanding all this, I am not for having Recourse to Military Operations.   For granting, that we shall be victorious, still it is proper to enquire, before we begin, How we are to be benefited by our Victories? And what Fruits are to result from making you a conquered People?— Not an Increase of Trade; that is impossible: For a Shop-keeper will never get the more Custom by beating his Customers: And what is true of a Shop-keeper, is true of a Shop-keeping Nation.   We may indeed vex and plague you, by stationing a great Number of Ships to cruize along your Coasts; and we may appoint an Army of Custom-house Officers to patrolle (after a Manner) two thousand Miles by Land.   But while we are doing these Things *against you*, what shall we be doing *for ourselves?*   Not much, I am afraid: For we shall only make you the more ingenious, the more intent, and the more inventive to deceive us.   We shall sharpen your Wits, which are pretty sharp already, to elude our Searches, and to bribe and corrupt our Officers.   And after that is done, we may perhaps oblige you to buy the Value of twenty, or thirty thousand Pounds of *British* Manufactures, more than you would otherwise have done,—at the Expence of two, or three hundred thousand Pounds Loss to *Great-Britain*, spent in Salaries, Wages, Ships, Forts, and other inci-dental Charges.   Is this now a gainful Trade, and fit to be encouraged in a commercial Nation, so many Millions in Debt already?   And yet this is the best, which we can expect by forcing you to trade with us, against your Wills, and against your Interests?

Therefore such a Measure as this being evidently detrimental to the Mother Country, I will now consider the second Proposal, *viz.* to procrastinate your Compulsion.—But what good can that do? And wherein will this Expedient mend the Matter? For if Recourse is to be had at last to the Military Power, we had better begin with it at first; it being evident to the whole World, that all Delays on our Side will only strengthen the Opposition on yours, and be interpreted by you as a Mark of Fear, and not as an Instance of Lenity. You swell with too much vain Importance, and Self-sufficiency already; and therefore, should we betray any Token of Submission; or should we yield to these your ill-humoured and petulant Desires; this would only serve to confirm you in your present Notions; *viz.* that you have nothing more to do, than to demand with the Tone of Authority, and to insist, with Threatenings and Defiance, in order to bring us upon our Knees, and to comply with every unreasonable Injunction, which you shall be pleased to lay upon us. So that at last, when the Time shall come of appealing to the Sword, and of deciding our Differences by Dint of Arms, the Consequence of this Procrastination will be, that the Struggle will become so much the more obstinate, and the Determination the more bloody. Nay, the Merchants themselves, whose Case is truly pitiable for having confided so much to your Honour, and for having trusted you with so many hundred thousand Pounds, or perhaps with some Millions of Property, and for whose Benefit alone such a Suspension of the Stamp Act could be proposed; they* will find to their Costs, that every Indulgence of this Nature will only furnish another Pretence to you for the suspending of the Payment of their *just* Demands. In short, you declare, that the Parliament hath no Right to tax you; and therefore you demand a Renunciation of the Right, by repealing the Act. This being the Case, nothing more than a Renunciation can be satisfactory; because nothing else can amount to a Confession, that the Parliament has acted illegally and usurpingly in this Affair. A bare Suspension, or even a mere Repeal, is no Acknowledgment of Guilt; nay, it supposes quite the contrary; and only postpones the Exercise of this usurped Power to a more convenient Season. Consequently if you think you could justify the Non-payment of your Debts, 'till a Repeal took Place, you certainly can justify the Suspension of the Payment 'till we have acknowledged our Guilt. So that after all, the Question must come to this at last, *viz.* Shall we renounce any Legislative Authority over you, and yet maintain you as we have hitherto done? Or shall we give you entirely up, unless you will submit to be governed by the same Laws as we are, and pay something towards maintaining yourselves?

---

* The Event has severely proved this Conjecture to be but too justly founded.

THE first it is certain we cannot do; and therefore the next Point to be considered is (which is also the third Proposal) Whether we are to give you entirely up?—*And after having obliged you to pay your Debts*, whether we are to have no further Connection with you, as a dependent State, or Colony.

Now, in order to judge properly of this Affair, we must give a Delineation of two Political Parties contending with each other, and struggling for Superiority:—And then we must consider, which of these two, must be first tired of the Contest, and obliged to submit.

BEHOLD therefore a Political Portrait of the Mother Country;—a mighty Nation under one Government of a King and Parliament,— firmly resolved not to repeal the Act, but to give it Time to execute itself,—steady and temperate in the Use of Power,—not having Recourse to sanguinary Methods,—but enforcing the Law by making the Disobedient feel the Want of it,—determined to protect and cherish those Colonies, which will return to their Allegiance within a limited Time (suppose twelve or eighteen Months)—and as determined to compel the obstinate Revolters to pay their Debts,—then to cast them off, and to exclude them *for ever* from the manifold Advantages and Profits of Trade, which they now enjoy by no other Title, but that of being a Part of the *British* Empire. Thus stands the Case; and this is the View of Things on one Side.

OBSERVE again a Prospect on the other; *viz.* a Variety of little Colonies under a Variety of petty Governments,—Rivals to, and jealous of each other,—never able to agree about any thing before,—and only now united by an Enthusiastic Fit of false Patriotism;—a Fit which necessarily cools in Time, and cools still the faster, in Proportion, as the Object which first excited it is removed, or changed. So much as to the general Outlines of your *American* Features;—but let us now take a nearer View of the Evils, which by your own mad Conduct you are bringing so speedily upon yourselves.

EXTERNALLY, by being severed from the *British* Empire, you will be excluded from cutting Logwood in the Bays of *Campeachy* and *Honduras*,—from fishing on the Banks of *Newfoundland*, on the Coasts of *Labrador*, or in the Bay of *St. Laurence*,—from trading (except by Stealth) with the Sugar Islands, or with the *British* Colonies in any Part of the Globe. You will also lose all the Bounties upon the Importation of your Goods into *Great-Britain*: You will not dare to seduce a single Manufacturer or Mechanic from us under Pain of Death; because you will then be considered in the Eye of the Law as mere Foreigners, against

whom these Laws were made.   You will lose the Remittance of 300,000l.
a Year to pay your Troops; and you will lose the Benefit of these Troops
to protect you against the Incursions of the much injured and exasperated
Savages; moreover, in Case of Difference with other Powers, you will
have none to complain to, none to assist you: For assure yourself, that
Holland, France, and *Spain,* will look upon you with an evil Eye; and
will be particularly on their Guard against you, lest such an Example
should infect their own Colonies; not to mention that the two latter will
not care to have such a Nest of professed Smugglers so very near them.
And after all, and in Spite of any thing you can do, we in *Britain* shall
still retain the greatest Part of your *European* Trade; because we shall
give a better Price for many of your Commodities than you can have any
where else; and we shall sell to you several of our Manufactures, especially
in the Woollen, Stuff, and Metal Way, on cheaper Terms.   In short, you
will do then, what you only do now; that is, you will trade with us, as
far as your Interest will lead you; and no farther.

TAKE now a Picture of your *internal* State.   When the great Power,
which combined the scattered Provinces together, and formed them
into one Empire, is once thrown off; and when there will be no common
Head to govern and protect, all your ill Humours will break forth like a
Torrent: Colony will enter into Bickerings and Disputes against Colony;
Faction will intrigue and cabal against Faction; and Anarchy and Confusion will every where prevail.   The Leaders of your Parties will then
be setting all their Engines to work, to make Fools become the Dupes of
Knaves, to bring to Maturity their half-formed Schemes and lurking
Designs, and to give a Scope to that towering Ambition which was
checked and restrained before.   In the mean Time, the Mass of your
People, who expected, and who were promised Mountains of Treasures
upon throwing off, what was called, the Yoke of the Mother Country,
will meet with nothing but sore Disappointments: Disappointments
indeed!   For instead of an imaginary Yoke, they will be obliged to bear a
real, a heavy, and a galling one: Instead of being freed from the Payment
of 100,000l. (which is the utmost that is now expected from them)
they will find themselves loaded with Taxes to the Amount of at least
400,000l.: Instead of an Increase of Trade, they will feel a palpable
Decrease; and instead of having Troops to defend them, and those Troops
paid by *Great-Britain,* they must defend themselves, and pay themselves.
Nay, the Number of the Troops to be paid, will be more than doubled;
for some must be stationed in the back Settlements to protect them
against the *Indians,* whom they have so often injured and exasperated,

and others also on each Frontier to prevent the Encroachments of each Sister Colony. Not to mention, that the Expences of your Civil Governments will be necessarily increased; and that a Fleet, more or less, must belong to each Province for guarding their Coasts, ensuring the Payment of Duties, and the like.

UNDER all these Pressures and Calamities, your deluded Countrymen will certainly open their Eyes at last. For Disappointments and Distresses will effectuate that Cure, which Reason and Argument, Lenity and Moderation, could not perform. In short, having been severely scourged and disciplined by their own Rod, they will curse their ambitious Leaders, and detest those Mock-Patriots, who involved them in so many Miseries. And having been surfeited with the bitter Fruits of American Republicism, they will heartily wish, and petition to be again united to the Mother Country. Then they will experience the Difference between a rational Plan of Constitutional Dependence, and the wild, romantic, and destructive Schemes of popular Independence.

AND you also, after you have played the Hero, and spoke all your fine Speeches; after you have been a *Gustavus Vasa*, and every other brave Deliverer of his Country; after you have formed a thousand Utopian Schemes, and been a thousand Times disappointed; perhaps even you may awake out of your present political Trance, and become a reasonable Man at last. And assure yourself, that whenever you can be cured of your present Delirium, and shall betray no Symptoms of a Relapse, you will be received with Affection by

> *Your old Uncle,*
> > *Your true Friend,*
> > > *And faithful Monitor,*

A. B.

THE TRUE INTEREST OF GREAT BRITAIN SET FORTH IN REGARD TO THE COLONIES

EDITORIAL NOTE

This tract was published in 1774 as a separate pamphlet and as Tract IV of *Four Tracts together with Two Sermons*. In it Tucker advances his plan for solving the imperial problem by separation.

TRACT IV.

THE

True Interest of *Great-Britain*

SET FORTH

In REGARD to the COLONIES;

And the Only MEANS of

Living in Peace and Harmony with them.

A VERY strange Notion is now industriously spreading, that 'till the late unhappy Stamp-Act, there were no Bickerings and Discontents, no Heart-burnings and Jealousies subsisting between the Colonies and the Mother Country. It seems, 'till that fatal Period, all was Harmony, Peace, and Love. Now it is scarcely possible even for the most superficial Observer, if his Knowledge extends beyond the Limits of a Newspaper, not to know, *That this is entirely false.* And if he is at all conversant in the History of the Colonies, and has attended to the Accounts of their original Plantation, their Rise, and Progress, he must know, that almost from the very Beginning, there were mutual Discontents, mutual Animosities and Reproaches. Indeed, while these Colonies were in a mere State of Infancy, dependent on their Mother-Country not only for daily Protection, but almost for daily Bread, it cannot be supposed that they would give themselves the same Airs of Self-Sufficiency and Independence, as they did afterwards, in Proportion as they grew up to a State of Maturity. But that they began very early to shew no other Marks of Attachment to their antient Parent, than what arose from Views of Self-Interest and Self-Love, many convincing Proofs might be drawn from the Complaints *of*, and the Instructions *to* the Governors of the respective Provinces; from the Memorials of our Boards of Trade, presented from Time to Time to his Majesty's Privy Council against the Behaviour of the Colonists; from the frequent Petitions and Remonstrances of our Merchants and Manufacturers to the same Effect; and even from the Votes and Resolutions of several of their Provincial Assemblies against the Interest, Laws, and Government of the Mother-Country; yet I will wave all these at present, and content myself with Proofs still more authentic and unexceptionable; I mean the public Statutes of the Realm: For from them it evidently appears, that long before there were any Thoughts of the Stamp-Act, the Mother-Country had the following Accusations to bring against the Colonies, *viz.* 1st, That they refused to submit to her Ordinance and Regulations in Regard to Trade.—2dly, That they attempted to frame Laws, and to erect Jurisdictions not only independently of her, but even in direct Opposition to her Authority.—And 3dly, That many of them took unlawful Methods to skreen themselves from paying the just Debts they owed to the Merchants and Manufacturers of *Great-Britain*.

THESE are the Objections of the Mother-Country to the Behaviour of the Colonies long before their last Outrages, and their present Conduct:—For even as early as the Year 1670, it doth appear, that MANY COMPLAINTS (the very Words of the Act) had been made against the *American* Proprietors of Ships and Vessels, for engaging in Schemes of Traffic, contrary to the Regulations contained in the Act of Navigation, and in other Statutes of the Realm made for confining the Trade of the Colonies to the Mother-Country. Nay, so sensible was the Parliament, above an hundred Years ago, that Prosecutions for the Breach of those Laws would be to little or no Effect, if carried on in *American* Courts, or before *American* Juries, that it is expressly ordained, "It shall, it may be lawful for any Person or Persons to prosecute such Ship or Vessel [offending as described in the preceding Section] in any Court of Admiralty in *England*; the one Moiety of the Forfeiture, in Case of Condemnation, to be to his Majesty, his Heirs, and Successors; and the other Moiety to such Prosecutor or Prosecutors thereof." [See 22 and 23 of *Ch*. II. Cap. 26, § 12 and 13.] And we find, that two Years afterwards, *viz.* 25 of *Ch*. II. Cap. 7, the same Complaints were again renewed; and in Consequence thereof higher Duties and additional Penalties were laid on, for the more effectually enforcing of the Observance of this and of the former Laws: But in Spite of all that was done, Things grew worse and worse every Day. For it is observable, that in the Year 1696, the very Authority of the *English* Legislature, for making such Laws and Regulations, seemed to have been called in Question; which Authority, therefore, the Parliament was obliged to assert in Terms very peremptory;— and I may likewise add, very prophetical. The Law made on this Occasion was the famous Statute of the 7th and 8th of *William* III. Cap. 7. wherein, after the Recital of "divers Acts made for the Encouragement of the Navigation of this Kingdom, and for the better securing and regulating the Plantation Trade, it is remarked, that notwithstanding such Laws, great Abuses are *daily* committed, to the Prejudice of the *English* Navigation, and the Loss of great Part of the Plantation Trade to this Kingdom, by the Artifice and Cunning of ill-disposed Persons." Then, having prescribed such Remedies as these great Evils seemed to require, the Act goes on at §. 7. to ordain, "That all the Penalties and Forfeitures before mentioned, not in this Act particularly disposed of, shall be one third Part to the Use of his Majesty, his Heirs, and Successors, and one third Part to the Governor of the Colony or Plantation where the Offence shall be committed, and the other third Part to such Person or Persons as shall sue for the same, to be recovered in any of his Majesty's Courts at *Westminster*, or in the Kingdom of *Ireland*, or in the Courts of Admiralty held in his Majesty's Plantations respectively, where such Offence shall be committed, *at the Pleasure of the Officer or Informer*, or in any other Plantation belonging to any Subject of *England*, wherein no Essoin, Protection, or Wager of Law shall be allowed; and that where any Question shall arise concerning the Importation or Exportation of any Goods into or out of the said Plantations, in such Case the Proof shall lie upon the Owner or Claimer; and the Claimer shall be reputed to be the Importer or Owner thereof."

Now here it is obvious to every Reader, that the Suspicions which the Parliament had formerly conceived of the Partiality of *American* Courts, and *American* Juries in Trials at Law with the Mother-Country, were so far from being abated by Length of Time, that they were grown higher than ever; because it appears by this very Act, that the Power of the Officer or Informer was greatly enlarged, having the Option now granted him of three different Countries for prosecuting the Offence; whereas in the former of *Charles* II. made 16 Years before, he had only two. Moreover it was this Time further ordained, that the *Onus probandi* should rest on the Defendant, and also that no *Essoin, Protection, or † Wager of Law should be allowed him.

BUT above all, and in order to prevent, if possible, every Sort of Chicane for the future, and to frustrate all Attempts of the Colonies, either to throw off or evade the Power and Jurisdiction of the Mother-Country,—It was at §9. "further enacted and declared by the Authority aforesaid, that all Laws, Bye-Laws, Usages, or Customs, at *this Time*,

---

* An Essoin signifies, in Law, a Pretence or Excuse.

† A Wager at Law, is a Power granted to the Defendant to *swear*, together with other *Compurgators*, that he owes nothing to the Plaintiff in the Manner set forth. — It is easy to see what Use would have been made of such a Power, had it been allowed.

or which *hereafter* shall be in Practice, or *endeavoured*, or *pretended* to be in Force or Practice, in any of the said Plantations, which are in *any wise* repugnant to the before-mentioned Laws, or any of them, so far as they do relate to the said Plantations, or any of them, or which are any ways repugnant to this present Act, OR TO ANY OTHER LAW HEREAFTER TO BE MADE IN THIS KINGDOM, so far as such Law shall relate to, and mention the said Plantations, are ILLEGAL, NULL, AND VOID TO ALL INTENTS AND PURPOSES WHATSOEVER."

WORDS could hardly be devised to express the Sentiments of the *English* Legislature, more fully and strongly, than these have done: And if ever a Body of uninspired Men were endowed with a Spirit of Divination, or of foreseeing, and also of providing against untoward future Events, as far as human Prudence could extend, the King, Lords, and Commons of the Æra 1696, were the very Men. For they evidently foresaw, that a Time was approaching, when the Provincial Assemblies would dispute the Right of *American* Sovereignty with the great and general Council of the *British* Empire: And therefore they took effectual Care that, whenever the Time came, no Law, no Precedent, nor Prescription, should be wanting, whereby the Mother-Country might assert her constitutional and inherent Right over the Colonies.

BUT notwithstanding these wise Precautions, some of the Colonies found Ways and Means to evade the Force and Meaning even of this express Law; at least for a Time, and 'till the Legislature could be sufficiently apprized of the Injury designed. The Colonists, who practised these disingenuous Arts with most Success, were those who were endowed with *chartered Governments*, and who, in Consequence of the extraordinary Favours thereby indulged them, could nominate or elect their own Council, and (if my Memory doth not fail me) their own Governors likewise;—at least, who could grant such Salaries to their Governors, and with such Limitations, as would render them too dependent on the Will and Pleasure of their Pay-Masters. Hence therefore it came to pass, that in the Colonies of *Rhode-Island* and *Providence* Plantations, *Connecticut*, the *Massachusett's Bay*, and *New Hampshire*; the Governors of these Provinces *suffered themselves to be persuaded* to give their Sanction to certain Votes and Resolutions of their Assemblies and Councils; whereby Laws were enacted first to issue out Bills of Credit to a certain Amount, and then to make a Tender of those Bills to be considered as an adequate discharge of Debts, and a legal Release from Payment. A most compendious Method this for getting out of Debt! And were the like Artifice to be authorized every where, I think it is very evident, that none but the most stupid Ideot would be incapable of discharging his Debts, Bonds, or Obligations; and that too without advancing any Money.

HOWEVER, as soon as the *British* Legislature came to be fully apprized of this Scheme of Iniquity, they passed a Law, "to regulate and restrain Paper Bills of Credit in his Majesty's Colonies or Plantations, of *Rhode-Island* and *Providence* Plantations, *Connecticut*, the *Massachusett's Bay*, and *New Hampshire*, in *America*; and to PREVENT THE SAME BEING LEGAL TENDERS IN PAYMENTS OF MONEY."—This is the very Title of the Statute; but for further Particulars, and for the different Regulations therein contained, consult the Act itself, 24th of *George* II. Cap. 53, *Anno* 1751.

Now will any Man after this dare to say, that the Stamp-Act was the first Cause of Dissention between the Mother-Country and her Colonies? Will any Man still persist in maintaining so gross a Paradox, that 'till that fatal Period, the Colonies shewed no Reluctance to submit to the Commercial Regulations, no Disposition to contest the Authority, and no Desire to question the Right of the Mother-Country? The Man who can maintain these Paradoxes, is incapable of Conviction, and therefore is not to be reasoned with any longer. "But the Stamp-Act made *bad* to become *worse:*—The Stamp-Act irritated and inflamed, and greatly encreased all those ill Humours, which were but too predominant before." Granted; and I will further add, that any other Act, or any other Measure, of the *British* Government, as well as the Stamp-Act, if it were to compel the Colonists to contribute a single Shilling towards the general Expence of the *British* Empire, would have had the same Effect. For, be it ever remembered, that the Colonists did not so much object to the *Mode* of this Taxation, as to the Right itself of levying Taxes. Nay, their Friends and Agents here in *England* were known to have frequently declared, That if any Tax were to be crammed down their Throats without their Consent, and by an Authority which they disallowed, they had rather pay this Stamp-Duty than another.

BUT indeed, and properly speaking, it was not the Stamp-Act which increased or heightened these ill Humours in the Colonists; rather, it was the Reduction of *Canada*, which called forth those Dispositions into Action which had long been generating before; and which were ready to burst forth at the first Opportunity that should offer. For an undoubted Fact it is, that from the Moment in which *Canada* came into the Possession of the *English*, an End was put to the Sovereignty of the Mother-Country over her Colonies. They had then nothing to fear from a foreign Enemy; and as to their own domestic Friends and Relations, they had for so many Years preceding been accustomed to trespass upon their Forbearance and Indulgence, even when they most wanted their Protection, that it was no Wonder they should openly renounce an Authority which they never thoroughly approved of, and which now they found to be no longer necessary for their own Defence.

BUT here some may be apt to ask, "Had the Colonies no Provocation on their Part? And was all the Fault on one Side, and none on the other?" Probably not:—Probably there were Faults on both Sides. But what doth this serve to prove? If to exculpate the Colonies in regard to their present refractory Behaviour, it is needless. For I am far from charging our Colonies in particular with being Sinners above others; because I believe (and if I am wrong, let the History of all Colonies, whether antient or modern, from the Days of *Thucydides* down to the present Time, confute me if it can; I say, 'till that is done I believe) that it is the Nature of them all to aspire after Independence, and to set up for themselves as soon as ever they find that they are able to subsist, without being beholden to the Mother-Country. And if our *Americans* have expressed themselves sooner on this Head than others have done, or in a more direct and daring Manner, this ought not to be imputed to any greater Malignity, or Ingratitude in them, than in others, but to that bold free Constitution, which is the Prerogative and Boast of us all. We ourselves derive our Origin from those very *Saxons*, who inhabited the lower Parts of *Germany*; and yet I think it is sufficiently evident, that we are not over complaisant to the Descendants of these lower *Saxons*, i.e. to the Offspring of our own Progenitors; nor can we, with any Colour of Reason, pretend to complain that even the *Bostonians* have treated us more indignantly than we have treated the *Hanoverians*. What then would have been the Case, if the little insignificant Electorate of *Hanover* had presumed to retain a Claim of Sovereignty over such a Country as *Great-Britain*, the Pride and Mistress of the Ocean? And yet, I believe, that in Point of Extent of Territory, the *present* Electoral Dominions, insignificant as they are sometimes represented, are more than a Moiety of *England*, exclusive of *Scotland* and *Wales:* Whereas the whole Island of *Great-Britain*, is scarcely a twentieth Part of those vast Regions which go under the Denomination of *North-America*.

BESIDES, if the *American* Colonies belonging to *France* or *Spain*, have not yet set up for Independence, or thrown off the Masque so much as the *English* Colonies have done,—what is this superior Reserve to be imputed to? Not to any greater filial Tenderness in them for their respective antient Parents than in others;—not to Motives of any national Gratitude, or of national Honour;—but because the Constitution of each of those Parent States is much more arbitrary and despotic than the Constitution of *Great-Britain*; and therefore their respective Offsprings are *awed by the Dread of Punishments from breaking forth into those Outrages which ours dare do with Impunity. Nay more, the very Colonies of *France* and *Spain*, though they have not yet thrown off their Allegiance, are nevertheless as forward as any in disobeying the Laws of their Mother-Countries, wherever they find an Interest in so doing. For the Truth of this Fact, I appeal to that prodigious clandestine Trade which they are continually carrying on with us, and with our Colonies, contrary to the express Prohibitions of *France* and *Spain:* And I appeal also to those very free Ports which the *British* Legislature itself hath lately opened for accommodating these *smuggling* Colonists to trade with the Subjects of *Great-Britain*, in Disobedience to the Injunction of their Mother-Countries.

ENOUGH surely has been said on this Subject; and the Upshot of the whole Matter is plainly this,—That even the arbitrary and despotic Governments of *France* and *Spain* (arbitrary I say, both in *Temporals* and in *Spirituals*) maintain their Authority over their *American* Colonies but very imperfectly; in as much as they cannot restrain them from breaking through those Rules and Regulations of exclusive Trade; for the Sake of which all Colonies seemed to have been originally founded. What then shall we say in Regard to such Colonies as are the Offspring of a free Constitution? And after what Manner, or according to what Rule, are our own in particular to be governed, without using any Force or Compulsion, or pursuing any Measure repugnant to their own Ideas of civil or religious Liberty? In short, and to sum up all, in one Word, How shall we be able to render these Colonies more subservient to the Interests, and more obedient to the Laws and Government of the Mother-Country, than they *voluntarily chuse to be?* After having pondered and revolved the Affair over and over, I confess, there seems to me to be but the five following Proposals, which can possibly be made, *viz.*

1st, To suffer Things to go on for a While, as they have lately done, in Hopes that some favourable Opportunity may offer for recovering the

---

* But notwithstanding this Awe, it is now pretty generally known, that the *French* Colonists of *Hispaniola* endeavoured lately to shake off the Government of *Old France*, and applied to the *British* Court for that Purpose.

Jurisdiction of the *British* Legislature over her Colonies, and for maintaining the Authority of the Mother-Country. — Or if these temporising Measures should be found to strengthen and confirm the Evil, instead of removing it; — then,

2dly, To attempt to persuade the Colonies to send over a certain Number of Deputies, or Representatives, to sit and vote in the *British* Parliament; in order to incorporate *America* and *Great-Britain* into one common Empire. — Or if this Proposal should be found impracticable, whether on Account of the Difficulties attending it on this Side of the *Atlantic*, or because that the *Americans* themselves would not concur in such a Measure; — then,

3dly, To declare open War against them as Rebels and Revolters; and after having made a perfect Conquest of the Country, then to govern it by military Force and despotic Sway.—Or if this Scheme should be judged (*as it ought to be*) the most destructive, and the least eligible of any; — then,

4thly, To propose to consent that *America* should become the general Seat of Empire; and that *Great-Britain* and *Ireland* should be governed by Vice-Roys sent over from the Court Residencies, either at *Philadelphia* or *New-York*, or at some other *American* imperial City. — Or if this Plan of Accommodation should be ill-digested by home-born *Englishmen*, who, I will venture to affirm, would never submit to such an Indignity; — then,

5thly, To propose to separate entirely from the Colonies, by declaring them to be a free and independent People, over whom we lay no Claim; and then by offering to guarantee this Freedom and Independence against all foreign Invaders whomsoever.

Now these being all the Plans which, in the Nature of Things, seem capable of being proposed, let us examine each of them in their Order.

FIRST SCHEME.

AND 1st, as to that which recommends the suffering all Things to go on as they have lately done, in Hopes that some favourable Opportunity may arise hereafter for recovering the Jurisdiction, and vindicating the Honour of the Mother-Country.

THIS first Proposal is very unhappy at first setting out; because it takes that for granted, which History and Experience prove to be false. It supposes, that Colonies may become the more obedient, in Proportion as they are suffered to grow the more headstrong, and to feel their own Strength and Independence; than which Supposition there cannot be a more palpable Absurdity.   For if a Father is not able to govern his Son at the Ages of 14 or 16 Years, how can it be supposed that he will be better able when the Youth is become a Man of full Age and Stature, in the Vigour of Health and Strength, and the Parent perhaps more feeble and decrepid than he was before?   Besides, it is a Fact, that the Colonies, from almost one End of *North-America* to the other, have already revolted from under the Jurisdiction of the *British* Legislature; — each House of Assembly hath *already* arrogated to themselves a new Name, by stiling themselves an HOUSE OF COMMONS; in Consequence of which Stile and Title, they have already declared, that the *British* House of Commons neither hath, nor ought to have, any Right to intermeddle in their Concerns.   Now, after they have advanced thus far already, what Rhetoric would you use for calling these Revolters back?   And is it at all probable, that the Provincial Assemblies would be induced by the Force of Oratory to renounce their own Importance, and to acknowledge that to be a *Crime*, which both they, and the People whom they represent, glory in as their Birth-right and unalienable Prerogative?   The Man who can suppose these Things, must have a most extraordinary Opinion of his own Eloquence.

BUT here perhaps some may be inclined to ask, Why would you meddle with the Colonies at all?   And why not suffer Things to remain in *statu quo?*   The obvious Answer to which Questions is this, — *That it is not the Mother-Country which meddles with the Colonies, but the Colonies which meddle with the Mother-Country: For they will not permit her to govern in the Manner she ought to do, and according to the *original Terms* of the Constitution; but are making Encroachments on her Authority every Day.   Moreover as they increase in Riches, Strength, and Numbers, their civil and military Establishments must necessarily increase likewise; and seeing that this Circumstance is unavoidable, who is to defray the growing Expences of these increasing and thriving Colonies? — "The Colonies themselves you will naturally say, because none are so fit, and none so able:" And perhaps some *American* Advocates will likewise add, "That the Colonies do not refuse

---

* See the preceding letter from a Merchant in *London* to his Nephew in *America*, wherein it is proved, to a Demonstration, that the Powers, which the Colonies will not allow the Mother-Country *now* to exercise over them, are no other than what always belonged to her from the very first Period of their Settlements, and according to the *original Terms* of their Constitution.   The Question therefore is, Which of the two, the Colonies, or the Mother-Country, usurps on the legal Rights and constitutional Privileges of the other?

to defray these Expences, provided they shall be the *sole Judges* of the Quantum to be raised, or the Mode of raising it, and of the Manner of its Application." But here lies the Difficulty, which remains yet to be solved: For if the Colonies are to be allowed to be the *sole Judges* in these Matters, the Sovereignty of the *British* Legislature is entirely at an End; and these Colonies become in Fact, as much independent of their Mother-Country, as we are independent of *Hanover*, or *Hanover* of us;— only indeed with this Difference (which an *American* always chuses to forget) That whereas we lay a *Duty* on all *raw Materials* coming from the Electoral Dominions, we give a Bounty on those which are imported from the Colonies. Besides, many will be apt to ask, Could not this Matter be compromised in some Degree? And will nothing less content the Colonies than a total Revolt from under the Jurisdiction of the Mother-Country?—Some well-meaning Persons have proposed, that each Colony, like each County here in *England*, should be allowed to raise Taxes for its own internal Uses, whilst the *British* Parliament, the sovereign Council of the *British* Empire, should preside over the whole; and therefore should enact such Laws for the levying of those general Taxes, which are to be applied for the common Protection, the Good, and Benefit of all. But the Misfortune is, that the Colonies will not consent to this Partition of Power and Jurisdiction; consequently any Scheme of this Nature is utterly impracticable. Indeed the late Stamp-Act itself was no other than a Part of this very Scheme: For the Money to be raised by that Tax, was to be applied to the *sole Use* of the Colonies, and to be *expended no where else* but in the Colonies. Nay it was not the Moiety, nor yet the third, nor the fourth Part of the Sum which *Great-Britain* was to have raised on the same Account, and to have expended in the same Provinces: — So anxious was the antient indulgent Parent not to lay too heavy a Burden on her favourite Children. But alas! Favourites of all Kinds seldom make those returns of Gratitude and Obedience, which might be expected. For even as to that boasted Loyalty, which the Colonies have hitherto professed to maintain towards his Majesty King *George*, — this stands, and must stand, according to their present political System, on as precarious a Footing as any of the rest of our Claims. For if the *British* Parliaments have no Right to make Laws to bind the Colonies, they certainly ought not to be allowed to prescribe to them *who shall be their King*; — much less ought they to pretend to a Right of enacting, That it shall be a most capital Offence, even HIGH TREASON itself, in a Colonist to dare to controvert the Title of any Prince, or any Family, to the *American* Throne, whom the *British* Parliament shall place thereon.

BESIDES, some of those lower Houses of Assemblies (which each Province now affects to call *its House of Commons*) have already proceeded to greater Lengths of Sovereignty and Independence than a *British* House of Commons ever presumed to do except in the Days of the grand Rebellion. For they have already arrogated to themselves a Power of *disposing*, as well as of *raising* the public Monies, without the Consent of the other Branches of the Legislature; which is, in fact, nothing less than the Erection of so many sovereign and independent *Democracies*. Nay more, there is a general Combination and Confederacy entered into among them all: For each House of Assembly hath lately appointed a standing Committee for corresponding with the standing Committees of other Provinces, in order the more effectually to oppose the Authority and Jurisdiction of the Mother-Country.

WHAT then is to be done in such a Case? Evident it is beyond a dispute, that timid and temporising Measures serve to no other Purpose but that of confirming the Colonies in their Opposition, and strengthening them in their present Revolt.

SCHEME II.

WHEREFORE the 2d Proposal is, To attempt to persuade the Colonies to send over a certain Number of Representatives to sit and vote in the *British* Parliaments, in order to incorporate *America* and *Great-Britain* into one common Empire.

* THIS is the Scheme of a very worthy Gentleman, eminently versed in the Laws and Constitution of *Great-Britain*, and what is still better, a real, not a pretended Patriot. Let us therefore examine it with as much Respect and Deference to his Opinion, as the Cause of Truth will permit; which I am well persuaded, is full as much as he would require.

HE begins with observing very justly, Page 4, "That the Subjects of the Crown of *Great-Britain*, must (i.e. ought to) continue to be so in *every* Respect, in all Parts of the World, while they live under the Protection of the *British* Government; and that their crossing the *Atlantic* Ocean with the King's Licence, and residing in *America* for the Purposes of Trade, cannot affect their legal Subjection to the governing Powers of the Community to which they belong.

"BUT yet he observes, that the total Want of Representatives in the

---

* See a Pamphlet, — "Considerations on the Expediency of admitting Representatives from the *American* Colonies into the *British* House of Commons." — *London*, printed for B. WHITE, 1770.

great Council of the Nation, to support their Interests, and give an
Assent on their Behalf to Laws and Taxes by which they are bound and
affected, is a *Mistune*, which every Friend to Liberty and equal Government must be sorry to see them labour under, and from which he must
wish them to be relieved in a regular and constitutional Manner, *if such
Relief can possibly be afforded them, without breaking the Unity of the
British Government.*"

HE therefore proceeds, at Page 10, to propose his Scheme for remedy-
ing this Misfortune; *viz.* "That about eighty Persons might be admitted
to sit in Parliament, as *Members* of the Commons House of Parliament for
all the King's Dominions in *America*, the *West-Indies*, as well as *North
America*; and that their Stile and Title should be THE COMMISSIONERS
OF THE COLONIES OF AMERICA." After this he goes on to fix the Numbers requisite to represent each Colony, their Qualification, and the
Mode of their Election; also the Time of their continuing in Office, and
the Manner of their being re-elected, or superseded by others, if that
should be judged necessary: In all which, tho' the Proposals are not
quite consistent with the *Unity* of the *British* Government, yet as he has
obviated the principal Difficulties, it would be both ill-natured and unjust
to spy out every small Fault, or to magnify Objections.

BUT when he comes to give us the Form, the Extent, and the Limitation of these Commissions; nay, when he proposes to circumscribe the
Authority and Jurisdiction of the *British* Parliament itself, even after it
hath been strengthened by the Accession of these Colony-Representa-
tives; there, I humbly apprehend, the Importance of the Subject should
preponderate over mere Deference and Complaisance. Nay I will go
still further, and add, that if the Measures proposed should be shewn to
have a Tendency to beget endless Jealousies, Quarrels, and Divisions,
between the Mother-Country and the Colonies, instead of proving a
Means of Reconciliation, and a Center of Union, the Gentleman himself,
I am fully persuaded, would be among the first in rejecting his own Plan.
Let us therefore now descend into Particulars.

AND 1st, it is proposed, Page 11, That they (the Commissioners)
should receive a Commission in Writing from their Electors (*viz.* the
* Assemblies in each Province) "IMPOWERING them to sit and vote in the

---

* *Quere*, Whether it is intended that the *lower* Houses in each Assembly should have
the sole Right of voting for these Commissioners? Or both Houses jointly? If the
former, then the Colony Governments would become still more *democratical* than they
now are, tho' already so, to such an excessive Degree, as to be almost incompatible with
any Idea of Monarchy: But if each House is to vote separately, what Jars and Factions, and reciprocal Reproaches, would this occasion! And how would they be able to
agree? In short, either Way, the Prospect is alarming!

British House of Commons, and consult with the King, and the Great Men of the Kingdom, and the Commons of the same in Parliament assembled, upon the great Affairs of the Nation, and to CONSENT on the Behalf of the Province, for which they were chosen, to such Things as shall be ordained in Parliament, &c."

Now this *Form* might pass very well among ourselves at Home, where the Majority are not continually on the Watch to spy out every Flaw, real or imaginary: But in regard to the Colonists, and especially an Assembly of Colonists, the Case is widely different: For it is well known that their Wits are perpetually at work to avail themselves even of the Shadow of an Argument to oppose the Right and Authority of the Mother-Country. Therefore they will immediately seize on the Words *impowering* and *Consent*, and reason after the following fallacious Manner: — "The Assemblies who elected the Commissioners, have a Right to instruct them; and these Instructions, when properly drawn up, are no other than so many Trusts or Powers granted to them from Time to Time, by the Assembly which elected them; which Assembly hath therefore a Right to contract or enlarge their Commission, as they shall find it to be the Interest of the Province so to do. Consequently, if these Commissioners should at any Time vote *contrary* to their Instructions, that is, to their Commission, it follows, that in these Respects they have exceeded the Bounds prescribed by their Electors. Therefore, being themselves prohibited from voting, and having no Authority to vote in such a Question, every Law wherein they gave their Suffrage, affecting the Interests of the Colonies in general, or any Province in particular, is *ipso facto null* and *void*."

AGAIN, — "The Colony Commissioners are to give their *Consent in Behalf of the Province* for *which they are chosen, to such Things as shall be ordained in Parliament*. This is the Foundation and Corner-Stone of all the Building: And therefore, if such or such Commissioners did *not give their Consent* in Behalf of the Provinces for which they were chosen, then it follows, of Course, that no Law, affecting the Interests of such respective Provinces, is obligatory, no Tax due or payable, nor any Regulations made by the pretended Authority of the *British* Parliament without the Consent of such Commissioners, are to be at all regarded by the *American* Electors." — These are a few of those blessed Conclusions, which the Politicians on the other Side of the *Atlantic* will certainly draw from the Terms and Expressions contained in such a Form. And what is still worse, both our own hair-brained Republicans, and our Mock-Patriots at Home will as certainly adopt the same Language, and echo back the same specious, tho' false Allegations, from one End of the Kingdom to the other. Indeed many there are, even among ourselves, who, with the most honest and upright Intentions, are at a Loss at present how to disintangle themselves from these fallacious Reasonings. For having unhappily learnt in Newspaper Dissertations, and from Coffee-house Harangues, that the Deputies sent to the great Council of the Nation, are the *mere Attornies* of those who elected them; — the Inference is but natural, that these Attornies ought to do *as they are bid*; and that in Case of Competition, they ought not to prefer their own private Opinions to the Judgments of their Constituents. — I say, this Inference is natural; nay it is necessary, just, and true, were the Premises but true from whence it is deduced.

WHEREFORE, having often had the Advantage of hearing no less a Person than the late excellent Judge FOSTER, that true Friend to all *reasonable* Liberty, Civil and Religious, — I say, having often heard him discoursing on the Rise and Origin of Parliaments, I will venture to lay his State of the Case before my Reader, hoping that it may remove all his Difficulties (if he has any) and work the same Fulness of Conviction in his Mind, which it did in mine.

"To reason accurately, said this upright and able Lawyer, on the Origin of Parliaments, we must trace the Matter up to its constituent Principles. Now the first Idea which strikes one on this Occasion is, that of a large Assembly of different Tribes of Warriors, either preparing for some military Expedition, or got together, after a Victory, to share the Booty, and divide the Lands among the Conquerors. When all are met together in one Place, they chuse a *Committee* for managing their Affairs; having found it impracticable to transact any Business of Consequence in any other Way. Now this Committee, chosen by the whole Nation, actually assembled, gives us the first rude Draught of a national Parliament, or a national Council. But in Process of Time, and when the Nation had made large Conquests, and was cantoned into distant Provinces, it was found to be extremely inconvenient to assemble the whole Nation together into one Place. Therefore the next, and indeed the only Expedient, was, that each Canton, or each District, which could assemble, should be authorized to elect a Deputy, or Deputies, *not for itself alone*, THAT IS THE GRAND MISTAKE, but for the Nation at large, which could not assemble; and the Powers to be granted to such Deputy, or Deputies, were just the same as the Nation would have granted to them, had it been actually assembled. Hence therefore it comes to pass, that each Deputy represents the whole Nation in general, as much as if he had been elected by the whole Nation; and consequently such a Deputy is the *Attorney* (if he must be called by that Name) not of any one particular Tribe, Society, or District, but of the *whole collectively:* So that it becomes the Duty of his Office to take Care of the Interests of all the People in general, *because he represents them all.* In short, he cannot, consistently with the Duty which he owes to the whole, pay any Deference to the Request, Instruction, Remonstrance, or Memorial, of his particular Electors, except in such Cases only wherein he is convinced in his Conscience, that the Measures, which they require him to pursue, are *not incompatible with the public Good.*"

THUS far this great Judge of the *British* Constitution. And tho' many important Inferences might be drawn from hence, which would effectually remove those Difficulties, with which the Subject has of late been artfully and studiously perplexed (and particularly in the Case of the Expulsion* of a Member of the House of Commons) yet I shall content myself with one general Remark at present; *viz.* That as each Class of Men, each Society or District, throughout the *British* Empire, are as much represented by those Deputies, whom they did not personally elect, as they are by those whom they did; it therefore follows, that there is no need, that the Deputies, particularly elected by them, should give their *personal Consent* to any Acts of the Legislature; because a Vote of the Majority is in fact a Vote of the Nation to all Intents and Purposes.

BUT it is now high Time to attend to another Part of this Gentleman's Plan for admitting Commissioners from the Colonies to sit and vote in the *British* House of Commons.

AND that is, 2dly, the *Extent* of their Commission, and indeed the boundary Line prescribed to the *British* Parliament itself, whenever it shall interfere in *American* Affairs. For it seems (see P. 14) "That this legislative Power of Parliament should be exercised but *seldom*, and *on Ocassions of great Necessity*. Whatever related to the internal Government of any particular Colony (such as raising the necessary Taxes for the support of its civil Government, and passing Laws for building Bridges, or Churches, or *Barracks*, or other public *Edifices*) should be left to the Governor and Assembly of that Colony to transact among themselves, unless in Cases where the domestic Dissentions of the Colony

---

* Surely the Nation might have expelled Mr. WILKES, or have struck his Name out of the List of Committee, had it been assembled, and had it thought proper so to do. What then should hinder the Deputies of the Nation from doing the same Thing? And which ought to prevail in this Case, the Nation in general, or the County of *Middlesex?*

put a Stop to public Business, and created a Kind of Necessity for the Interposition of the supreme Legislature. But when any general Tax was to be impcsed upon all the *American* Colonies for the *Support of a War*, or any other such general Purpose; or any new Law was to be made to regulate the Trade of all the Colonies; or to appoint the Methods by which Debts owing from the Inhabitants of one Colony to those of another, or of *Great-Britain*, should be recovered; or to direct the Manner of bringing Criminals to Justice who have fled from one Colony to another; or to settle the Manner of quartering the King's Troops in the several Colonies; or of levying Troops in them, and the Number each Colony should contribute; or to settle the proportionable Values of different Coins that should be made current in the several provinces; or to establish a general Paper-Currency throughout *America;* or for any other general Purpose that relates to several Colonies: — In these Cases the Authority of Parliament should be employed.''

HERE now is a Kind of Barrier set up between these two contending Powers, the *British* Parliament, and the Provincial Assemblies; — a Barrier, which must be held so sacred by both Parties, as to limit their respective Pretensions, and to extinguish all further Claims. Let us therefore see how well this Scheme is calculated to answer such good Purposes.

AND first it is said, that the Parliament ought to interfere but *seldom*; and then only on Occasions of *great Necessity*. Now here permit me to ask, Who are to be the *Judges* of what is *seldom*, or what is *frequent?* Moreover, who is to determine between the Parliament and the Provincial Assemblies, when there is a *great* Necessity for the Interference of the former, and when there is but a *little* one, or *none* at all? — Obvious it is, to all the World, that these jealous Rivals will never settle such Points among themselves; and if *they* will not settle them, indeed if they cannot, who is to be their common Umpire or Referee? Besides, granting even that this Difficulty could be got over in some Degree, another formidable one immediately starts up, like another Hydra; *viz.* What are these Colony-Agents to do in our House of Commons, when no Colony Business happens to be transacted? Are they to remain as so many MUTES, without speaking a Word, or giving a single Vote for Weeks, or Months, or perhaps for a whole Session together? — Or are they to sit and vote in all *British* Causes, great or small; notwithstanding that the *British* Senators are precluded from voting, excepting in extraordinary Cases, in respect to the Colonies? In either Case here seems to be something introduced into the *British* Constitution of a very heterogeneous Nature;

something very repugnant to *that Unity* of Government, which the Gentleman himself allows ought to be preferred to every other Consideration: And I will add further, that if the Colony-Commissioners are to sit and vote in all our Causes, tho' our *British* Representatives are restrained from voting in theirs, perhaps ninety-nine Times in an Hundred, this will be the setting up of one of the most partial, unequal, and unjust Systems of Pacifications, that ever yet appeared in the World.

WE therefore proceed to another weighty Objection against the present Plan. — The Terms of this new Compact are declared to be, That the Colony Assemblies shall be invested with the Right of *internal* and *provincial* Jurisdiction and Legislation; while the *British* Parliament, even after the Accession of these 80 Colony Commissioners, shall be content to retain only that which is *external* and *general*. — But here alas! the very same Difficulties return which pressed so hard before: For who is to judge between the *British* Parliament and the Provincial Assemblies in these Respects? Who will venture to ascertain in every Case what is external and general; and what is merely internal and provincial? Nay indeed, may not the very same Things justly pass under both Denominations, according as they are seen from different Points of View? — Surely they may; and to convince any Man of this, let him attend to the very Catalogue of Articles, with which this Gentleman hath himself presented us. For at Page 14, he observes, "That whatever related to the internal Government of any particular Colony, should be left to the Governor and Assembly of that Colony to transact among themselves;" among which Articles belonging to internal Government, he enumerates the building of *Barracks*, and of other PUBLIC Edifices; and yet both he and every Man must allow, that the building of Barracks, of Forts, and Fortresses, the making of King's Docks and Careening Places for the Navy, the laying out of military Roads, and the providing of Magazines for Provisions and military Stores, considered in another View, are of a general Nature; in the Erection and Preservation of which, the whole *British* Empire is deeply interested. And yet were the *British* Parliament to frame Laws, and to levy Taxes on the *Americans* for these Purposes, what Outcries would immediately be raised against the Mother-Country! Every Fortress, nay every Barrack, would be described as an odious Badge of Slavery; and every little Magazine would be termed a Monument of Tyranny and despotic Power, and a Prerogative for destroying the few Liberties that were left. Again, at the Bottom of the same Page, he declares, that the Authority of Parliament should be employed in *settling the Manner of quartering the King's Troops in the several Colonies.* I will not object to the Interposition of Parliament in such a Case: For well I know, that if the Parliament did not interfere, the Troops would very often have no Quarters at all; and yet this very Circumstance would afford an *American* Assembly the most inviting Opportunity for Exclamation and Opposition. "What! The *British* Parliament to take upon them the Manner of quartering Troops in our own Province, and on our own Inhabitants! Who so proper Judges as ourselves, when or where, or after what Manner, they should be quartered? And how came the Gentlemen, met at *Westminster*, to be acquainted with the Circumstances of our People, and the Situation of Places, better than we, who reside on the Spot? No! These Acts of the *British* Parliament are all barefaced Encroachments on our Liberties, and open Violations of our Rights and Properties: They are the Chains which our pretended Protectors, but in Reality our *Egyptian* Task-Masters, have been long forging for us. Let therefore all unite, and manfully resist them; let us postpone the paying of Debts, and enter into a general Association to refuse their Goods, to distress their Trade, and to harrass our cruel Enemies by every Method in our Power; and if we are thus united, they *must yield*, as *they did before*." In short it would be endless to recount all the Topics which such a Scheme as this Gentleman has proposed would certainly furnish to every popular Declaimer in every popular Assembly; and the more improbable, the more absurd and unjust his Harangues were in Point of sound Argument and just Reasoning; so much, generally speaking, the more greedily would they be received.

HOWEVER, there is one Point more which I cannot omit, because it will throw a further Light on this Matter, and disclose a new Scene of patriotic Manœuvres, and the Wiles of Politicians. At Page 13, this Author lays down a *general Rule* for the Conduct of Parliament with Respect to *America, viz.* "That it ought to be made a standing Order of both Houses of Parliament, never to pass any Law, whether for imposing a Tax, or for regulating Trade, or for any other Purpose whatsoever relating to any of the *American* Colonies, 'till one whole Year after the first reading of the Bill; unless it be to renew some expiring Laws of great Importance, and of immediate and urgent Necessity, such as the Act for *billeting* the King's Troops, and perhaps some few others that might be specially excepted in the Order."

THIS is the Restriction in Point of Time, which our Author proposes to lay on the Parliament of *Great-Britain*. "They never must pass any Law for imposing a Tax 'till one whole Year after the first Reading of the

Bill:" Why? — "In order to give the several Colonies an Opportunity of making *proper Representations* against it, and to prevent the Parliament from making injudicious Laws, not suited to the Condition of the Colonies." A fine Contrivance truly! and a most effectual Expedient to prevent the Parliament from ever making any Laws to oblige the *Americans* to discharge their Duty towards their Mother-Country: For this Gentleman might have known, indeed it is hardly possible, that the Fact could have escaped his Notice, had he recollected it, that this very Circumstance of *a Year's Procrastination* was the main Engine employed to batter down the late Stamp-Act. When the Duty on Stamps was first proposed, the *Americans* made as little Objection to it, as could be supposed to be made to any new Tax whatever. Nay, several of their popular Orators and Leaders used considerable Interest to be employed as Agents in the Distribution of these Stamps: And *one* among the rest, whom I need not name, was more than ordinary assiduous in his Application on this Head: So that had the Act passed within the usual Time, instead of being a flaming *American* Patriot, he would probably have acted the Part of a Tax-Gatherer and an *American* Publican. But when the *Outs* and the *Pouters* on this Side the Water, saw the Advantage which the Minister gave them by a whole Year's Delay, they eagerly seized the Opportunity; Emissaries and Agents were dispatched into all Quarters;—the Newspapers were filled with invectives against the new-intended Tax. It was injudicious!—it was ill-timed!—oppressive! tyrannical! and every Thing that was bad! Letters upon Letters were wrote to *America* to excite the People to associate, to remonstrate, and even to revolt. The most ample Promises were made from hence, of giving them all the Assistance which Faction, and Clamour, and Mock-patriotism, could muster up. And then it was that this very Man, this self-intended Publican, changed Sides, and commenced a zealous Patriot: Then he appeared at the Bar of the House of Commons to cry down that very Measure which he himself had espoused; and then, as the avenging Angel of *America,*

He rode in the Whirlwind to direct the Storm.

WELL, the Storm fell on the Minister for the Time being, and overset him. Our *Outs* at Home became the *Ins*; and the Storm having now done its Business, they had no further Occasion for it, were its most obedient humble Servants, and wished it to subside. But here they found themselves egregiously mistaken. For the *Americans* had, in their Turn, learnt the Art of making Tools of them, instead of being made Tools by them: So that having been taught by these Preceptors to feel their own Weight and Independance, they were not to be wheedled by soothing and cajoling Letters to give over their Enterprize, or to become a tractable, obedient People for the future.   In short, hence it came to pass, that even during the Continuance of this new and favourite Administration, the *American* Spirit was rising all the while, instead of sinking.   And as like Causes will always produce like Effects, especially since Things have been suffered to grow to such an Height, evident it is to common Sense, that any future Attempt of the *British* Parliament to levy a Tax on *America*, will meet with no better a Fate than the Stamp-Act has done. Moreover, a Year's Delay in laying it on will be just so much Time given the Colonies to prepare for Battle; and Woe to that Administration which shall propose it; for they will certainly be overturned by the same Arts and Managements which the former were, and with much greater Ease.

I should now have done with this Gentleman's Scheme, were it not that I find him, at Page 28, making a Kind of Apology to the *Americans* for the Conduct of our Parliament in paying the King's Debts of his Civil List.   And I own myself more hurt by this Paragraph, than by all the rest of his Pamphlet: For as I am thoroughly persuaded, he wrote from Conviction, and not from any sinister Views, one is sorry to find so able, so honest, and upright a Man, carried away by the Torrent of the Times to such a Degree, as to adopt Notions, which are almost too crude for a Club of Livery Politicians met in some blind Alley at a City Ale-house.   His Words are these: — "It is certain, that no such (exorbitant) Grants as are above mentioned have been made, unless in the single Instance of the Sum of 513,000l. granted to his present Majesty for the Discharge of the Debts of his Civil List.   And in this Case I can easily suppose, that a Motive of Compassion for a Number of innocent Persons, who would otherwise have been Sufferers from that Load upon his Majesty's Revenue, and an affectionate Desire of relieving their excellent Sovereign (who has in no Instance endeavoured to violate the Liberties of his Subjects) from the unworthy Streights and Inconveniences, ill becoming the Royal Dignity, *into which some of his Ministers had brought him by the injudicious Management of his Revenue*, may have induced many Members of the House of Commons to consent to this Grant, without any View to their own private Interest; though at the same Time I acknowledge it to be, *considering all its Circumstances*, a dangerous Compliance, and not worthy to be drawn into Example."

Now if the Compliance of the Parliament in discharging this Debt was dangerous, the Reason must be, because the Circumstance of contracting the Debt itself was really infamous; therefore ought not to be avowed, but had better be suppressed in Tenderness to the Royal Cause. But can this Author point out any such infamous Circumstances, if he were minded to make the Discovery? — I dare answer for him, that he cannot. And as I will not suppose that he has more Tales to tell than any other private Gentlemen, or much less that he himself was an Accomplice in, or privy to any such Scenes of Iniquity as are here insinuated, — I will now undertake to prove to him and the World, how as great a Debt as this, nay a much greater, might have been contracted in the Space of ten Years, without the least Impeachment of Waste, Profusion, Mismanagement, or any other *Misapplication* whatsoever.

EVERY Office, Dignity, Rank, or Station, has a certain Character to sustain, which necessarily requires a correspondent Train of Expences; so that whether you consider the Demands upon a King with a Salary of 800,000l. a Year, or the Demands on a private Gentleman with only a clear Rental of 800l. a Year, the Scale of Expences must be proportionate, the Demands and Expences being relative one to the other.

WE will therefore reason on what we are most conversant with (and with Respect to which we may be allowed to be competent Judges) *viz.* on the Case of a young Gentleman of a respectable antient Family, just come to take Possession of an Estate, which clears him 800l. a Year.

1st. THEREFORE, being appointed Sheriff of the County, he must and ought to go through that expensive Office in such a Manner as would reflect no Disgrace on himself, or the respectable Family from which he is descended (and the Office of Sheriff belonging to a private Gentleman is of much the same Import in Point of Expence, as the Circumstances of a *Coronation* in respect to Majesty.)

2dly. MANY *Deaths* and *Funerals* within the above-mentioned Period create another Article of Expence, which must be borne; with this peculiar Circumstance attending it, That tho' he must bury a Grandfather suitably to his Rank, also an Uncle, Aunts, a Brother and Sisters,— yet he himself acquires no Addition of Fortune by their Deceases.

3dly. SEVERAL *Marriages* in the Family, and his own* in particular,

---

* Some shrewd Politicians have been wise enough to ask, Why did not his Majesty's marry a *large Fortune*, in order to re-imburse some of these Expences? — What large Fortune would these Wiseacres have wished him to have married? A Duchy or Principality on the Continent, in order to engage us still more in *Continental* Measures? — Or was it to be a large landed Estate at Home, to be annexed to the Crown, like another Dutchy of *Lancaster?* — This would have had a fine Influence on Electioneering, and *English* Liberties. — But perhaps they meant, that he should have

bring on a third Charge, which surely in Reason and Conscience ought
not to be objected to.

4thly. SIX or seven Christenings and Lyings-in, expensive Articles in
all Families, necessarily happen from the Circumstance of the Case,
to be peculiarly expensive in this: And yet neither the young Gentleman
himself, nor any of his Friends and Well-wishers to the Family, ought
to be supposed even to have wished to have saved these extraordinary
Charges.

5thly. A Train of unexpected Visitants bring on another heavy Load;
and though they were not invited, yet, as they chose to come, they must
be received with an Hospitality suitable to his and their Dignity, and the
Relation of Friendship and Family-Ties subsisting between them.

ADD to all this, 6thly, The uncommon Dearness of all Sorts of Provisions, which for some Years past hath exceeded any Thing known in
former Times; and which alone hath actually swelled the Amount of
House-keeping in every Family to a very considerable Sum.

Now the young Gentleman having supported himself under these
several Pressures and growing Expences for ten Years together, at last is
obliged to request his nearest Friends and dearest Relations to grant
him some Assistance; because he is 513l. *or almost three Quarters of a
Year* in Debt. Heavens! What a Sum! And is this all against which
such loud Outcries have been raised? Yes, this is all! Indignant
Reader, whoever thou art, *Englishman* or *American*, lay thy Hand on
thy Heart, and ask thyself this plain Question, What wouldst thou have
thought of such a young Man, had he been thine own Son, thy Grandson,
or the Heir-apparent of thy Fortune? And what Sort of Treatment
would he have deserved at thy Hands? Therefore, *mutato nomine*. —
But I will add no more: Let Nature and Humanity, Justice and Equity,
plead their own Cause.

WE have now, I think, very sufficiently discussed every Part of this
Gentleman's Plan: Nay, we have amply and particularly shewn, that
his Apology to the Americans in Behalf of the *British* Parliament, for
paying the Arrears of his Majesty's Civil List, was quite a needless Thing.
For if no stronger Proofs can be brought of their Venality and Corruption
than this Instance, they still may be safely trusted with the Guardianship

---

gone into the City, and have paid his Addresses to Miss *Plumbe*, the rich Grocer's
Daughter, or to Miss *Rescounters* the Heiress of the great Broker in Change-Alley. And
to be sure, such a Match as this would have corresponded rarely well with the sublime
Ideas of City-Politics. Our antient Nobility would have been delighted in giving the
Precedency to such illustrious Princes of the Blood.

of those Liberties and Properties, which they have hitherto not only preserved, but also strengthened and encreased to a Degree unknown before in this, or any other Country. In one Word, the Scheme of an Union under our present Consideration, is of such a Nature, as would necessarily tend to exasperate both Parties, instead of mollifying or reconciling either. And as the *Americans* have already given us to understand, both in their Provincial Assemblies, and at their General Congresses, that they will not accept of an Union with us; and as *Great-Britain* ought not to petition for it; surely more need not be added for laying the Scheme aside. Indeed the Gentleman himself, towards the Close of his Pamphlet, expresses but little Hopes of its Success: For, after all, the best Use he can put it to, seems to be the Justification of the Mother-Country in declaring War against the Colonies, in order to oblige them to submit to her Authority, and to return to their Obedience. So that this Scheme of Pacification is to end in a War at last. Therefore we are now come to consider the

THIRD SCHEME.

THE Expediency of having Recourse to Arms, in order to compel the Colonies to submit to the Authority and Jurisdiction of the supreme Council of the *British* Empire, the Parliament of *Great-Britain*.

IN regard to which important Point, the Gentleman reasons after the following Manner: — "After such an Offer (of an Union, as above described) and the contemptuous Refusal of it by the Colonies, we may well suppose, that they (the Inhabitants of *Great-Britain*) will act as one Man, to support the just and lawful, and necessary Authority of the supreme Legislature of the *British* Nation over all the Dominions of the Crown. The Justice of their Cause will give Vigour to their Measures; and the Colonies that shall have the Folly and Presumption to resist them, will be quickly reduced to Obedience."

IT is possible, nay indeed it is very probable, that if a War was to be speedily undertaken, before *Great-Britain* and *Ireland* had been too much exhausted of their Inhabitants, emigrating to *North-America*,—the Forces of the Mother-Country might prevail, and *America*, however unwilling, be forced to submit. But alas! Victory alone is but a poor Compensation for all the Blood and Treasure which must be spilt on such an Occasion. Not to mention, that after a Conquest of their Country, the *Americans* would certainly be less disposed, even than they are at present, to become our good Customers, and to take our Manufactures in return for those Injuries and Oppressions which they had suffered from us:—I say, *Injuries and Oppressions*; because the Colonies would most undoubtedly give no softer an Appellation to this Conquest, tho' perhaps it would be no other in itself, than a just Chastisement for the manifold Offences they had committed.   Moreover, as the *Americans* are endeavouring even at present to set up all Sorts of mechanic Trades in order to rival us, or at least to supersede the Use of our Manufactures in their Country,—can any Man suppose, that their Ardor for setting up Manufactures would be abated, by their being *forced* to deal at the *one only European* Shop, which they most detested?

BUT what is still worse, if possible,—though the *British* Troops might over-run the great Continent of *North-America* at first, it doth by no Means follow, that they could be able to maintain a Superiority in it afterwards for any Length of Time; and my Reason is, because the governing of a Country after a Peace, is a much more arduous Task, in certain Circumstances, than the conquering it during a War.   Thus for Example, when a Peace ensues (and surely it is not intended that we shall be for ever in a State of War) then a civil Constitution of some Kind or other must necessarily be established; and in the Case before us, there seems to be no other Alternative, but either the permitting the Colonies to enjoy once more those Advantages of *English* Liberty, and of an *English* Constitution, which they had forfeited; or else a Resolution to govern them for the future by arbitrary Sway and despotic Power. If the latter should be the Plan adopted, I then humbly submit it to be duly weighed and considered, what a baleful Influence this *Government a la Prusse* would have on every other Part of the *British* Empire.   *England* free, and *America* in Chains!   And how soon would the enslaved Part of the Constitution, and perhaps the greater, contaminate the free and the lesser?   Nay, as *America* was found to encrease in Strength and Numbers, an Army of *English-born* Soldiers (for no others could be trusted) first of 50,000, and afterwards perhaps of 100,000, would scarcely be sufficient to keep these turbulent Spirits in Awe, and to prevent them, at such a prodigious Distance from the Center of Government, from breaking out into Insurrections and Rebellions at every favourable Opportunity.   But if the former were to prevail, and a Return of *English* Liberties was again to take Place, it must also follow, that the System of Trials by Juries must return with them: And then, when *America* shall grow stronger and stronger every Day, and *England* proportionably weaker, how is an Insurrection to be quelled in *America?*   And what *English* Officer, civil or military, would dare to do it?   Nay, I ask further. granting that he was so brave, or rather so fool-hardy, as to attempt to do his Duty, who is to protect him in the Execution of his Office? Or how is he to be preserved, *by due Forms of Law*, against the Determination of an *American* Jury? A Tumult is excited;—the Military is called forth;—the Soldiers are insulted;—many perhaps wounded, and some even killed. The Patience of the Officers worn out, and in their own Defence, they are obliged to give the Word of Command to *fire*. The Relations of those who *fell* by this Fire, bring on an Appeal of Blood. The *American* Jury find the Officers who commanded, and perhaps the whole Corps who fired, guilty of wilful Murder; and then all the Power of the Crown, *legally exerted*, is not able to save the Lives of these poor innocent Men. Pitiable sure is such a Case; and yet it is a Case which would and must frequently then happen in the natural Course of Things, according to our legal Constitution.

PERHAPS it might be said, that *American* Juries are as conscientious as other Juries in bringing in their Verdicts according to Law; and that it is very uncharitable even to suppose the contrary. — Be it so: But the Question here turns on, What will be the Suggestions of Conscience in the Breast of an *American* on such an Occasion?—What would be his Ideas of Law, Justice, or Equity, when *England* and *America* stood in Competition?—Certainly, if ever the Inhabitants of that Country should come (and they are almost come already) to be fully persuaded, that the *British* Parliament hath no Right to make Laws either to tax or to govern them [and the having once beaten them will not be taken as a convincing Proof that we always have either the Right or the Power to beat them] then every Attempt towards throwing off this odious Yoke, would appear in their Eye, as so many noble Struggles for the Cause of Liberty: And therefore the base *English* Hireling, who would dare to injure this sacred Cause, deserved to die a thousand Deaths. Such undoubtedly would be the Language, and such the Sentiments of the great Majority of *Americans*, whenever such a Case should happen. In a Word, an erroneous Conscience, and a false Zeal, would have just the same bad Effects in the new World respecting civil Government, as they have formerly had in the old, in regard to Religion: And therefore, either Way, whether we should treat these *Americans* as an enslaved People, or whether we should restore to them, after a Conquest, the same Constitution which we enjoy ourselves, the final Event would come to this,—That *England* would be the greatest Sufferer; and that *America* is not to be governed against its own Inclinations. Wherefore let us now come to the

FOURTH SCHEME,

Viz. To consent that *America* should become the general Seat of Empire, and that *Great-Britain* and *Ireland*, should be governed by Vice-Roys sent over from the Court Residencies either at *Philadelphia*, or *New-York*, or at some other *American* Imperial City.

Now, wild as such a Scheme may appear, there are certainly some *Americans* who seriously embrace it: And the late prodigious Swarms of Emigrants encourage them to suppose, that a Time is approaching, when the Seat of Empire must be changed. But whatever Events may be in the Womb of Time, or whatever Revolutions may happen in the Rise and Fall of Empires, there is not the least Probability, that this Country should ever become a Province to *North-America*. For granting even, that it would be so weakened and enfeebled by these Colony-Drains, as not to be able to defend itself from Invaders, yet *America* is at too great a Distance to invade it at first, much less to defend the Conquest of it afterwards, against the neighbouring Powers of *Europe*. And as to any Notion that we ourselves should prefer an *American* Yoke to any other,—this Supposition is chimerical indeed: Because it is much more probable, were Things to come to such a dreadful Crisis, that the *English* would rather submit to a *French* Yoke, than to an *American*; as being the lesser Indignity of the two. So that in short, if we must reason in Politics according to the *Newtonian* Principles in Philosophy,—the Idea of the lesser Country gravitating towards the greater, must lead us to conclude, that this Island would rather gravitate towards the Continent of *Europe*, than towards the Continent of *America*; unless indeed we should add one Extravagance to another, by supposing that these *American* Heroes are to conquer all the World. And in that Case I do allow, that *England* must become a Province to *America*. But

Solamen miseris socios habuisse doloris.

DISMISSING therefore this Idea, as an idle Dream, we come now lastly to consider the

FIFTH SCHEME, *Viz.*

To propose to separate entirely from the *North-American* Colonies, by declaring them to be a free and independent People, over whom we lay no Claim; and then by offering to guarrantee this Freedom and Independence against all foreign Invaders whatever.

AND, in fact, what is all this but the natural and even the necessary

Corollary to be deduced from each of the former Reasons and Observations? For if we neither can govern the *Americans*, nor be governed by them; if we can neither unite with them, nor ought to subdue them;— what remains, but to part with them on as friendly Terms as we can? And if any Man should think that he can reason better from the above Premises, let him try.

BUT as the Idea of Separation, and the giving up the Colonies for ever will shock many weak People, who think, that there is neither Happiness nor Security but in an over-grown unwieldy Empire, I will for their Sakes enter into a Discussion of the *supposed* Disadvantages attending such a Disjunction; and then shall set forth the manifold Advantages.

THE first and capital *supposed* Advantage is, *That, if we separate from the Colonies, we shall lose their Trade.* But why so? And how does this appear? The Colonies, we know by Experience, will trade with any People, even with their bitterest Enemies, during the hottest of a War, and a War undertaken at their own earnest Request, and for their own Sakes;—the Colonies, I say, will trade even with them, provided they shall find it their Interest so to do. Why then should any Man suppose, that the same Self-Interest will not induce them to trade with us? With us, I say, who are to commit no Hostilities against them, but on the contrary, are still to remain, if they please, their Guardians and Protectors?

GRANTING, therefore, that *North-America* was to become independent of us, and we of them, the Question now before us will turn on this single Point,—Can the Colonists, in a general Way, trade with any other *European* State to greater Advantage than they can with *Great-Britain?* If they can, they certainly will; but if they cannot, we shall still retain their Custom, notwithstanding we have parted with every Claim of Authority and Jurisdiction over them. Now, the native Commodities and Merchandize of *North-America*, which are the most saleable at an *European* Market, are chiefly Lumber, Ships, Iron, Train-Oil, Flax-Seed, Skins, Furs, Pitch, Tar, Turpentine, Pearl-Ashes, Indigo, Tobacco, and Rice. And I do aver, that, excepting Rice and Tobacco, there is hardly one of these Articles, for which an *American* could get so good a Price any where else, as he can in *Great-Britain* and *Ireland*. Nay, I ought to have excepted only Rice; for as to Tobacco, tho' great Quantities of it are re-exported into *France*, yet it is well known, that the *French* might raise it at Home, if they would, much cheaper than they can import it from our Colonies. The Fact is this,—The Farm of Tobacco is one of the great five Farms, which make up the chief Part of the Royal Revenue; and therefore the Farmers General, for Bye-Ends of their own, have hitherto had Interest enough with the Court to prohibit the Cultivation of it in *Old France, under the severest Penalties. But nevertheless the real *French* Patriots, and particularly the Marquis de *Mirabeau*, have fully demonstrated, that it is the Interest of the *French* Government to encourage the Cultivation of it; and have pointed out a sure and easy Method for collecting the Duties;—which was the sole Pretence of the Farmers General for soliciting a Prohibition. So that it is apprehended, that the *French* Government will at last open their Eyes in this Respect, and allow the Cultivation of it. Tobacco therefore being likely to be soon out of the Question, the only remaining Article is Rice: And this, it must be acknowledged, would bear a better Price at the *Hamburgh* or *Dutch* Markets than it generally doth in *England*. But as this is only one Article, out of many, it should be further considered, that even the Ships which import Rice into *England*, generally bring such other Produce as would not be saleable to Advantage in other Parts of *Europe:* So that there is no great Cause to fear, that we should *considerably* lose the Trade even of this Article, were the Colonies to be dismembered from us. Not to mention that all the Coasts of the *Mediterranean* and the South of *Europe* are already supplied with Rice from the Colonies, in the same Manner as if there had been an actual Separation;—no Rice-Ship bound to any Place South of *Cape-Finistere* being at all obliged to touch at any Port of *Great-Britain*. So much, therefore, as to the staple *Exports* of the Colonies.

LET us now consider their *Imports*. And here one Thing is very clear and certain, That whatever Goods, Merchandize, or Manufactures, the Merchants of *Great-Britain* can sell to the rest of *Europe*, they might sell the same to the Colonies, if wanted: Because it is evident, that the Colonies could not purchase such Goods at a cheaper Rate at any other *European* Market. Now, let any one cast his Eye over the Bills of Exports from *London, Bristol, Liverpool, Hull, Glasgow*, &c. &c. and then he will soon discover that excepting Gold and Silver Lace, Wines and Brandies, some Sorts of Silks and Linens, and perhaps a little Paper

---

* Great Quantities of Tobacco are permitted to be raised in *French-Flanders, Alsace*, and all the Païs conquises, i.e. the newly *conquered Provinces*; because the Inhabitants of these Countries are indulged in many Liberties, which are denied to the Provinces of *Old France*. But the Farmers General keep a strict Watch, that none of this Tobacco shall be permitted to be carried into *Old France*, except by themselves or their Agents. And the Penalty against Smuggling in this Case is very cruel and severe.

and Gun-powder; I say, excepting these few Articles, *Great-Britain* is become a Kind of a *general Mart for *most other* Commodities: And indeed were it not so, how is it conceivable, that so little a Spot as this Island could have made such a Figure either in Peace or War, as it hath lately done?   How is it possible, that after having contracted a Debt of nearly One Hundred and Forty Millions, we should nevertheless be able to make more rapid Progresses in all Sorts of Improvements, useful and ornamental, public and private, agricolic and commercial, than any other nation ever did? — Fact it is, that these Improvements have been made of late Years, and are daily making: And Facts are stubborn Things.

BUT, says the Objector, you allow, that Gold and Silver Lace,—that Wines and Brandies,—some Sorts of Silks,—some Sorts of Paper, Gunpowder, and perhaps other Articles, can be purchased at certain *European* Markets on cheaper Terms than they can in *England:* And therefore it follows, that we should certainly lose these Branches of Commerce by a Separation, even supposing that we could retain the rest. Indeed even this doth not follow; because we have lost them already, as far as it was the Interest of the Colonies, that we should lose them. And if any Man can doubt of this, let him but consider, that the Lumber, and Provision-Vessels, which are continually running down from *Boston*, *Rhode-Island*, *New-York*, *Philadelphia*, *Charles-Town*, &c. &c. to *Martinico*, and the other *French* Islands, bring Home in return not only Sugars and Molasses, but also *French* Wines, Silks, Gold and Silver Lace, and in short every other Article, in which they can find a profitable Account: Moreover those Ships, which sail to *Eustatia* and *Curacoa*, trade with the *Dutch*, and consequently with all the North of *Europe*, on the same Principle.   And as the Ships which steer South of *Cape-Finistere*, what do they do?—Doubtless, they purchase whatever Commodities they find it their Interest to purchase, and carry them Home to *North-America*.   Indeed what should hinder them from acting agreeably to their own Ideas of Advantage in these Respects?   The Custom-house Officers, perhaps, you may say, will hinder them.   But alas! the Custom-house Officers of *North-America*, if they were ten Times more numerous, and ten Times more uncorrupt than they are, could not possibly guard a tenth Part of the Coast.   In short these Things are so very notorious

---

* I am credibly informed, that it appears by Extracts from the Custom-house Books, that more *English* Goods are sent up the two Rivers of *Germany*, the *Weser* and the *Elbe*, than up any two Rivers in *North-America*. Yet the *North-Americans* and their Partisans are continually upbraiding us, as if we enjoyed no Trade, worth mentioning, except that with the Colonies.

that they cannot be disputed; and therefore, were the whole Trade of *North-America* to be divided into two Branches, *viz.* the *Voluntary*, resulting from a free Choice of the *Americans* themselves, pursuing their own Interest, and the *Involuntary*, in Consequence of *compulsory* Acts of the *British* Parliament;—this latter would appear so very small and inconsiderable, as hardly to deserve a Name in an Estimate of national Commerce.

THE 2d Objection against giving up the Colonies is, that such a Measure would greatly decrease our Shipping and Navigation, and consequently diminish the Breed of Sailors. But this Objection has been fully obviated already: For if we shall not lose our Trade, at least in any important Degree, even with the northern Colonies (and most probably we shall encrease it with other Countries) then it follows, that neither the Quantity of Shipping, nor the Breed of Sailors, can suffer any considerable Diminution: So that this Supposition is merely a Panic, and has no Foundation. Not to mention, that in Proportion as the *Americans* shall be obliged to exert themselves to defend their own Coasts, in Case of a War; in the same Proportion shall *Great-Britain* be exonerated from that Burden, and shall have more Ships and Men at command to protect her own Channel Trade, and for other Services.

THE 3d Objection is, That if we were to give up these Colonies, the *French* would take immediate Possession of them. Now this Objection is entirely built on the following very wild, very extravagant, and absurd Suppositions.

1st, IT supposes, that the Colonists themselves, who cannot brook our Government, would like a *French* one much better. *Great-Britain*, it seems, doth not grant them Liberty enough; and therefore they have Recourse to *France* to obtain more:—That is, in plain *English*, our mild and limited Government, where Prerogative is ascertained by Law, where every Man is at Liberty to seek for Redress, and where popular Clamours too often carry every Thing before them,—is nevertheless too severe, too oppressive, and too tyrannical for the Spirits and Genius of *Americans* to bear; and therefore they will apply to an arbitrary, despotic Government, where the People have no Share in the Legislature, where there is no Liberty of the Press, and where General Warrants and *Lettres des cachets* are *irresistible*,—in order to enjoy greater Freedoms than they have at present, and to be rescued from the intolerable Yoke, under which they now groan. What monstrous Absurdities are these! But even this is not all: For these *Americans* are represented by this Supposition, as not only preferring a *French* Government to a *British*, but even to a

Government of their *own modelling and chusing!* For after they are set free from any Submission to their Mother-Country; after they are told, that for the future they must endeavour to please themselves, seeing we cannot please them; then, instead of attempting to frame any popular Governments for redressing those Evils, of which they now so bitterly complain,—they are represented as throwing themselves at once into the Arms of *France*;—the Republican Spirit is to subside; the Doctrine of passive Obedience and Non-resistance is to succeed; and, instead of setting up for Freedom and Independence, they are to glory in having the Honour of being numbered among the Slaves of the Grand Monarch!

BUT 2dly, this Matter may be further considered in another Point of View: For if it should be said, that the *Americans* might still retain their Republican Spirit, tho' they submitted to a *French* Government, because the *French*, through Policy, would permit them so to do; then it remains to be considered, whether any arbitrary Government can dispense with such Liberties as a republican Spirit will require. An absolute Freedom of the Press! No controul on the Liberty either of Speaking or Writing on Matters of State! Newspapers and Pamphlets filled with the bitterest Invectives against the Measures of Government! Associations formed in every Quarter to cry down Ministerial Hirelings, and their Dependents! The Votes and Resolutions of the Provincial Assemblies to assert their own Authority and Independence! No landing of Troops from *Old France* to quell Insurrections! No raising of new Levies in *America!* No quartering of Troops! No building of Forts, or erecting of Garrisons! And, to sum up all, no *raising of Money* without the express Consent and Approbation of the Provincial *American* Parliaments first obtained for each of these Purposes! — Now I ask any reasonable Man whether these Things are compatible with any Idea of an arbitrary, despotic Government? — Nay more, whether the *French* King himself, or his Ministers, would wish to have such Notions as these instilled into the Subjects of *Old France?* Yet instilled they must be, while a Communication is kept open between the two Countries; while Correspondences are carried on; Letters, Pamphlets, and Newspapers, pass and re-pass; and in short, while the *Americans* are permitted to come into *France*, and *Frenchmen* into *America*. So much therefore as to this Class of Objections. Indeed I might have insisted further, that *Great-Britain* alone could at any Time prevent such an Acquisition to be made by *France*, as is here supposed, if she should think it necessary to interfere, and if such an Acquisition of Territory would really and truly be an Addition of Strength in the political Balance and Scale of Power*.   But surely I have said enough; and therefore let us now hasten briefly to point out

The manifold Advantages attendant on such a Scheme.

AND 1st, A Disjunction from the northern Colonies would effectually put a Stop to our present Emigrations.   By the Laws of the Land it is made a capital Offence to inveigle Artificers and Mechanics to leave the

---

* The Phænomenon of that prodigious Increase of Trade, which this Country has experienced since the happy Revolution, is what few People can explain; and therefore they cut the Matter short, by ascribing it all to the Growth of our Colonies: But the true Principles and real Causes of that amazing Increase, are the following:

1. The Suppression of various Monopolies and exclusive Companies existing before, for foreign Trade.

2. The opening of Corporations, or the undermining of exclusive Privileges and Companies of Trade at Home; or, what comes to the same Thing, the eluding of their bad Effects by Means of legal Decisions in our Courts of Law.   And N. B. The like Observation extends to the Case of evading the Penalties of the Act 5th of Queen *Elizabeth*, against exercising those Trades, to which Persons have not served regular Apprenticeships.

3. The Nursing up of new Trades and new Branches of Commerce by Means of Bounties, and national Premiums.

4. The giving of Drawbacks, or the Return of Duties on the Exportation of such Goods, as were to have paid a Duty, if used and consumed at Home.

5. The Repeal of Taxes formerly laid on raw Materials coming into the Kingdom. See 8 G. I. C. 15.

6. The Repeal of Taxes formerly laid on our own Manufactures, when exported. See ditto.

7. The Improvements in various Engines, with new Inventions and Discoveries for the Abridgment of Labour.

8. Better Communications established throughout the Kingdom by Means of Turnpike Roads and Canals, and the speedy Conveyance of Letters to every great Town and noted Place of Manufacture, by Means of Improvements in the Post-Office.

9. Happy Discoveries and Improvements in Agriculture and in the mechanic Arts.

10. Larger Capitals than usual employed both in Husbandry and Manufactures; also in the Importation and Exportation of Goods.

Now all these Things, co-operating together, would render any Country rich and flourishing, whether it had Colonies or not: And this Country in particular would have found the happy Effects of them to a much greater Degree than it now doth, were they not counter-acted by our Luxury, our Gambling, our frequent ruinous and expensive Wars, our Colony-Drains, and by that ill-gotten, and ill-spent Wealth, which was obtained by robbing, plundering, and starving the poor defenceless Natives of the *East-Indies*. — A Species of Villainy this, for which the *English* Language had not a Name, 'till it adopted the Word *Nabobing*.

Kingdom. But this Law is unhappily superseded at present as far as the Colonies are concerned. Therefore when they come to be dismembered from us, it will operate as strongly against them, and their *Kidnappers*, as against others. And here it may be worth while to observe, that the Emigrants, who lately sailed in such Multitudes from the North of *Scotland*, and more especially from the North of *Ireland*, were far from being the most indigent, or the least capable of subsisting in their own Country. No; it was not Poverty or Necessity which compelled, but Ambition which enticed them to forsake their native Soil. For after they began to taste the Sweets of Industry, and to partake of the Comforts of Life, then they became a valuable Prey for these Harpies. In short, such were the Persons to whom these Seducers principally applied; because they found that they had gotten some little Substance together worth devouring. They therefore told them many plausible Stories— that if they would emigrate to *North-America*, they might have Estates for nothing, and become Gentlemen for ever; whereas, if they remained at Home, they had nothing to expect beyond the Condition of a wretched Journeyman, or a small laborious Farmer. Nay, one of these false Guides was known to have put out public Advertisements, some few Years ago, in the North of *Ireland*, wherein he engaged to carry all, who would follow him, into such a glorious Country, where there was neither Tax, nor Tithe, nor Landlord's Rent to be paid. This was enough: It took with Thousands: And this he might safely engage to do. — But at the same Time, he ought to have told them (as Bishop *Berkley* in his Queries justly observes) That a Man may possess twenty Miles square in this glorious Country, and yet not be able to get a Dinner.

2dly. Another great Advantage to be derived from a Separation is, that we shall then save between 3 and 400,000l. a Year, by being discharged from the Payment of any civil or military Establishment belonging to the Colonies: — For which generous Benefaction we receive at present no other Return than Invectives and Reproaches.

3dly. The ceasing of the Payment of Bounties on certain Colony Productions will be another great Saving; perhaps not less than 200,000l. a Year: And it is very remarkable, that the Goods imported from the Colonies in Consequence of these Bounties, could not have been imported into any other Part of *Europe*, were there a Liberty to do it; because the Freight and first Cost would have amounted to more than they could be sold for: So that in Fact we give Premiums to the Colonies for selling Goods to us, which would not have been sold at all any where else. However, when the present Bounties shall cease, we may then consider, at our

Leisure, whether it would be right to give them again, or not; and we shall have it totally in our Power to favour that Country most, which will shew the greatest Favour to us, and to our Manufactures.

4thly. WHEN we are no longer connected with the Colonies by the imaginary Tie of an Identity of Government, then our Merchant-Exporters and Manufacturers will have a better Chance of having their Debts paid, than they have at present: For as Matters now stand, the Colonists chuse to carry their ready Cash to other Nations, while they are contracting Debts with their Mother-Country; with whom they think they can take greater Liberties: And provided they are trusted, they care not to what Amount this Debt shall rise:—For when the Time for Payment draws on, they are seized with a Fit of Patriotism; and then Confederacies and Associations are to discharge all Arrears; or, at least, are to postpone the Payment of them *sine die*.

5thly. AFTER a Separation from the Colonies, our Influence over them will be much greater than ever it was, since they began to feel their own Weight and Importance: For at present we are looked upon in no better a Light than that of Robbers and Usurpers; whereas, we shall then be considered as their Protectors, Mediators, Benefactors. The Moment a Separation takes Effect, intestine Quarrels will begin: For it is well known, that the Seeds of Discord and Dissention between Province and Province are now ready to shoot forth; and that they are only kept down by the present Combination of all the Colonies against us, whom they unhappily fancy to be their *common Enemy*. When therefore this Object of their Hatred shall be removed by a Declaration on our Parts, that, so far from usurping all Authority, we, from henceforward, will assume none at all against their own Consent; the weaker Provinces will intreat our Protection against the stronger; and the less cautious against the more crafty and designing: So that in short, in Proportion as their factious, republican Spirit shall intrigue and cabal, shall split into Parties, divide, and sub-divide,—in the same Proportion shall we be called in to become their general Umpires and Referees. Not to mention, that many of the late and present Emigrants, when they shall see these Storms arising all around them, and when their promised earthly Paradise turns out to be a dreary, unwholesome, inhospitable, and howling Wilderness,—many of them, I say, will probably return to us again, and take Refuge at last in *Old England*, with all its Faults and Imperfections.

LASTLY. Our *West-India* Islands themselves will receive signal Benefit by this Separation. Indeed their Size and Situation render them incapable of substracting all Obedience from us; and yet the bad Precedents of their Neighbours on the Continent hath sometimes prompted them to shew as refractory a Spirit as they well could. — But when they come to perceive, what are the bitter Effects of this untractable Disposition, exemplified in the Case of the *North-Americans*, it is probable, it is reasonable to conclude, that they will learn Wisdom by the Miscarriages and Sufferings of these unhappy People; and that from henceforward they will revere the Authority of a Government, which has the fewest Faults, and grants the greatest Liberty, of any yet known upon Earth.

But after all, there is one Thing more, to which I must make some Reply. — many, perhaps most of my Readers, will be apt to ask,— What is all this about? And what doth this Author really mean?— Can he seriously think, that because he hath taken such Pains to prove a Separation to be a right Measure, that therefore we shall separate in good Earnest? And is he still so much a Novice as not to know, that Measures are rarely adopted merely because they are right, but because they can serve a present Turn? — Therefore let it be asked, What present Convenience or Advantage doth he propose either to Administration, or to Anti-Administration, by the Execution of his Plan?—This is coming to the Point, and without it, all that he has said will pass for nothing.

I frankly acknowledge, I propose no *present* Convenience or Advantage to either; nay, I firmly believe, that no Minister, as Things are now circumstanced, will dare to do so much Good to his Country; and as to the Herd of Anti-Ministers, they, I am persuaded, would not wish to see it done; because it would deprive them of one of their most plentiful Sources for Clamour and Detraction: And yet I have observed, and have myself had some Experience, that Measures evidently right will prevail at last: Therefore I make not the least Doubt but that a Separation from the northern Colonies, and also another right Measure, *viz.* a *complete Union* and *Incorporation* with *Ireland* (however unpopular either of them may now appear) will both take Place within half a Century:— And perhaps that which happens to be first accomplished, will greatly accelerate the Accomplishment of the other. Indeed almost all People are apt to startle at first at bold Truths:----But is is observable, that in Proportion as they grow familiarized to them, and can see and consider them from different Points of View, their Fears subside, and they become reconciled by Degrees:—Nay, it is not an uncommon Thing for them to adopt those salutary Measures afterwards with as much Zeal and Ardor as they had rejected them before with Anger and Indignation.

NEED I add, That the Man, who will have Resolution enough to advance any bold unwelcome Truth (unwelcome I mean at its first Appearance) ought to be such an one, whose Competency of Fortune, joined to a natural Independency of Spirit, places him in that happy Situation, as to be equally indifferent to the Smiles, or Frowns either of the Great, or the Vulgar?

LASTLY, some Persons perhaps may wonder, that, being myself a Clergyman, I have said nothing about the Persecution which the Church of *England* daily suffers in *America*, by being denied those Rights which every other Sect of Christians so amply enjoys.   I own I have hitherto omitted to make Mention of that Circumstance, not thro' Inadvertence, but by Design; as being unwilling to embarrass my general Plan with what might be deemed by some Readers to be foreign to the Subject: And therefore I shall be very short in what I have to add at present.

THAT each Religious Persuasion ought to have a full Toleration from the State to worship Almighty God, according to the Dictates of their own Consciences, is to me so clear a Case, that I shall not attempt to make it clearer; and nothing but the maintaining some monstrous Opinion inconsistent with the Safety of Society,—and that not barely in Theory and Speculation, but by *open* Practice and *outward* Actions,— I say, nothing but the *avowedly* maintaining of such *dangerous* Principles can justify the Magistrate in abridging any Set of Men of these their natural Rights.   It is also equally evident, that the Church of *England* doth not, cannot fall under the Censure of holding Opinions inconsistent with the Safety of the State, and the Good of Mankind,—even her Enemies themselves being Judges: And yet the Church of *England* alone doth not enjoy a Toleration in that full Extent, which is granted to the Members of every other Denomination.   What then can be the Cause of putting so injurious a Distinction between the Church of *England*, and other Churches in this respect?   The Reason is plain.   The *Americans* have taken it into their Heads to believe, that an Episcopate would operate as some further Tie upon them, not to break loose from those Obligations which they owe to the Mother-Country; and that this is to be used as an Engine, under the Masque of Religion, to rivet those Chains, which they imagine we are forging for them.   Let therefore the Mother-Country herself resign up all Claim of Authority over them, as well Ecclesiastical as Civil; let her declare *North-America* to be independent of *Great-Britain* in every Respect whatever;—let her do this, I say, and then all their Fears will vanish away, and their Panics be at an End: And then, a Bishop, who has no more Connections with *England* either in Church or State, than he has with *Germany*, *Sweden* or any other Country, will be no longer looked upon in *America* as a Monster, but a Man. In short, when all Motives for Opposition will be at an End, it is observable, that the Opposition itself soon ceases and dies away. In a Word, an Episcopate may then take Place; and whether this new Ecclesiastical Officer be called from a Name derived from the *Greek*, the *Latin*, or the *German*,—that is, whether he be stiled Episcopus, Superintendent, Supervisor, Overseer, &. &c. it matters not,—provided he be invested with competent Authority to ordain and confirm such of the Members of his own Persuasion, as shall voluntarily offer themselves, and to inspect the Lives and Morals of his own Clergy.

A LETTER TO EDMUND BURKE

EDITORIAL NOTE

This tract was called forth by Burke's famous speech on conciliation with America. In it Tucker undertakes to show that the specific causes enumerated by Burke to explain the "fierce spirit of liberty" in the colonies were in reality reasons for separation, not for conciliation.

A

LETTER

TO

EDMUND BURKE, Esq;

MEMBER OF PARLIAMENT FOR THE CITY OF BRISTOL,

AND

AGENT FOR THE COLONY OF NEW YORK, &c.

IN ANSWER TO

HIS PRINTED SPEECH,

SAID TO BE SPOKEN IN THE HOUSE OF COMMONS
ON THE TWENTY-SECOND OF MARCH, 1775.

SECOND EDITION, Corrected.

BY JOSIAH TUCKER, D. D.

DEAN OF GLOCESTER.

GLOCESTER:
PRINTED BY R. RAIKES;
AND SOLD BY
T. CADELL, IN THE STRAND, LONDON.
M.DCC.LXXV.
[PRICE ONE SHILLING.]

ADVERTISEMENT.

THE present critical Juncture obliges the Author to postpone his Animadversions on Mr. LOCKE's Theory of Government for some Time longer. But the Public may be assured, that he has not dropped the Design; and that he only postpones it because the present Subject seems to require a more immediate Attention. In the mean while, the Learned and Judicious will easily perceive from several Parts of this Discourse, and particularly from what he has advanced, Page 11, that he is fixed in his Plan, and that he has selected these Positions out of Mr. LOCKE's Book for his future Animadversion, which are the most inconsistent with any Form of Government, Republican or Monarchical, and therefore the most dangerous to real Liberty.

EDMUND BURKE, Esq;

MEMBER OF PARLIAMENT FOR THE CITY OF BRISTOL,

AND

AGENT FOR THE COLONY OF NEW YORK, &c.

SIR,

AS YOU have been pleased to bestow much Abuse and Scurrility on me in your public Speech of the 19th of *April*, 1774; — and also many Commendations in private both before, and since that Publication; — I shall take no other Notice of either, than just to assure you, that I am neither elated by your Praises, nor chagrined at your Censures; and that I hold myself indifferent in respect to both. My Business with you is solely of a public Nature; and therefore, without farther Preface, I beg Leave to inform you, that I propose to examine your last Performance, entituled, *The Speech of* EDMUND BURKE, *Esq; March* 22, 1775, with as much Freedom, as you do the Writings and Opinions of other Men; but, I hope, with more Decency and good Manners.

IN this Speech you lay down certain Premises respecting the Disputes between the Parent-State and her Colonies: And from them you infer a most extraordinary Conclusion. My Province it shall be to enquire, whether this Conclusion is justly and regularly made;—and whether a quite different one ought not to have been drawn from such Premises.

MY only Difficulty is, to state your Meaning with Accuracy and Precision: — Not that you yourself are unable to express your own Thoughts with the utmost *Clearness*, as well as *Energy*; but you are *unwilling*. For you excel in the Art of ambiguous Expressions, that is, in giving one Sense to your Readers, and of reserving another to yourself, if called upon to defend what you have said; — you excel, I say, in this Art, perhaps the most of any Man living. Sometimes you express more than you mean; and at other Times less; but at all Times, you have one general End in View, viz. To amuse with Tropes and Figures, and *great swelling Words*, your Audience or your Readers, and not to let them see your Drift and Intention, 'till you have drawn your Net around them.

At Page 15 [1st Edit.] you observe, "That in the Character of the *Americans*, a Love of Freedom is the predominating Feature, which marks and distinguishes the whole: — And that the *Americans* become suspicious, *restive* and *untractable*, whenever they see the least Attempt to wrest from them by Force, or Shuffle from them by Chicane, what they think the only Advantage worth living for."

Sir, I perfectly agree with you in your Description: And I will add farther, what you chuse to conceal, that the same People were *restive* and *untractable* from the Beginning. For as far back, as the 7th and 8th of King *William* C. 22. §. 9. [1696] it appears, that they manifested the plainest Intention of disowning the Authority of the *English* Legislature in every Instance, which they thought incompatible with their own Interest. Nay, it is evident from the Words of the Act, that even at this early Period, they pretended to set up Laws, By-laws, Usage, and Customs in Opposition to *English* Acts of Parliament.

You add farther at Page 16 "That this fierce Spirit of Liberty is stronger in the *English* Colonies, probably than in any other People upon Earth." I think so too: And I will give a most striking Proof of it in the Liberty they took with, and in the Contempt they shewed to the Circular Letter even of their darling Advocate and Patron, Mr. Secretary Pitt, now Lord Chatham. For when he wrote to them to desist from the infamous and traiterous Practices of supplying the Enemy with Provisions and Military Stores during a War, undertaken at their Request, and for their immediate Protection; — what Effect had this official authoritative Letter on their Conduct and Behaviour? — None at all. For they not only continued, but increased the Practice of supplying the Enemy with every Means of protracting the War; — greatly to their own Profit, it must be owned;---but to the lasting Detriment of this Country, whose Lands and Revenues are mortgaged for Ages to come, towards defraying the Expence of this ruinous, consuming War. Nay, such was the *fierce Spirit of Liberty* prevailing in our *English* Colonies on this trying Occasion, that the Provincial Governors dared not so much as commence a Prosecution against any of the numerous Offenders. And their Friends and Agents here at Home [You know best, whether Mr. Burke was among the Number: Dr. Franklin certainly was] — I say, their Friends and Agents were so far from being ashamed of such infamous and traiterous Practices, that they openly vindicated them in our public News-Papers, pouring forth the bitterest Reproaches on Administration for attempting to restrain these Northern Merchants (such was the gentle Phrase) in the Pursuit of their undoubted and unalienable Rights and Liberties. After this, there is certainly no Need of any further Confirmation of your assertion, *That the fierce Spirit of Liberty is stronger in the* English *Colonies probably than in any other People upon Earth.*

Now, as such is the Fact, you give us at Page 21 a Summary of the several Causes, which have produced it. "From these six capital Sources, — Of Descent, of Form of Government, of Religion in the Northern Provinces, of Manners in the Southern, of Education, of the Remoteness of Situation from the first Mover of Government: — From all these Causes [co-operating together] a fierce Spirit of Liberty has grown up."

I. AND first as to Descent. "The People of the Colonies (P. 16.) are the descendents of *Englishmen. England*, Sir, [addressing yourself to the Speaker] is a Nation which still, I hope, respects, and formerly adored, her Freedom. The Colonists emigrated from you, when this Part of your Character was most predominant. And they took this Bias and Direction the Moment they parted from your Hands. They are therefore not only devoted to Liberty, but to Liberty according to *English* Ideas, and on *English* Principles:---It happened, you know, Sir, that the great Contests for Freedom in this Country were from the earliest Times, chiefly upon the Question of *Taxing.*---The Colonies drew from you, as with their Life-Blood, these Ideas and Principles. Their Love of Liberty, as with you, fixed and attached on this *specific Point of Taxing.*"

HERE, Sir, you tell some Truth; you disguise some; and you conceal more than you disguise.

OUR first Emigrants to *North-America* were mostly Enthusiasts of a particular Stamp. They were of that Set of *Republicans*, who believed, or pretended to believe, *that Dominion was founded in Grace.* Hence they conceived, that they had the best Right in the World both to *tax*, and to *persecute* the *Ungodly.* And they did both, as soon as they got Power into their Hands, in the most open and atrocious Manner. The Annals of the Quakers will tell you, that they *persecuted* Friends even to the Death. And in regard to *Taxation*, if you will be so hardy as to assert, that they taxed none, but such as were represented in their Provincial Assembly, I will undertake to prove the contrary:---I will undertake to prove, that they themselves paid no Regard, in a Variety of Instances, to that very Point, on which they insist so much at present in their disputes with us, the Right of Representation, and of not being taxed without their own Consent.

IN Process of Time, the Notion, that Dominion was founded in Grace, grew out of Fashion. But the Colonists continued to be Republicans still, only Republicans of another Complection. They are now Mr. LOCKE's Disciples; who has laid down such Maxims in his Treatise on Government, that if they were to be executed according to the Letter, and in the Manner the *Americans* pretend to understand them, they would necessarily unhinge, and destroy every Government upon Earth. I shall at present only mention the four following.

1. "THAT Men are by Nature all free, equal, and independent; *and no Man can be put out of this Estate, without his own Consent.*" Book 2, Chap. 8.

2. "THAT Governments have no Power over the Son, because of that which they have over the Father." Chap. 8.

3. "THAT submitting to the Laws of any Country, living quietly, and enjoying Privileges and Protection under them, makes not a Member of that Society;—because nothing can make any Man so, *but his actually entering into it by* POSITIVE ENGAGEMENT." Chap. 8.

4. "THAT the Supreme Power cannot take from any Man *any Part* of his Property [that is, cannot Tax him] WITHOUT HIS OWN CONSENT." Chap. 11.

Now, Sir, if these crude, undigested Notions are to be understood absolutely, and without Correction or Limitation;—and if such are the true, original Ideas of *English* constitutional Liberty,—I will frankly acknowledge, that *Great-Britain* hath not so much as the Shadow of a Right to tax the Colonies:—Nay, I will go farther, and scruple not to declare, that she has no Right to make any Regulation whatever respecting them, without their own express Consent and full Approbation first obtained. But, after having made this Concession, I hope you will be so candid on your Part, as to acknowledge, that no Government upon Earth did ever yet subsist on such a Plan of wild, Utopian Liberty. And I do presume, that I do not ask too much in making this Request; seeing that your celebrated *American* Fellow Labourer, Dr. PRIESTLY, has already gone a good deal farther. For he has already informed the World, in his Essay on Civil Government, that as all Governments whatever have been in some Measure compulsory, tyrannical, and oppressive in their Origin, THEREFORE they ought to be changed, and new-modelled as soon as ever the People [who, N. B. according to him and Mr. LOCKE, have always an unalienable and indefeasible Right to change and alter, *what*, and *whenever they please*] shall feel themselves strong enough to throw off this Usurpation, and can bring about a glorious Revolution. Nay, another great Man, and Disciple of Mr. LOCKE, no less than the patriotic JEAN JAQUES ROUSSEAU (I think in his Letters from the Mountains) suggests an happy Expedient for accomplishing this desirable Work of perpetual Alterations. He proposes, that once a Year, at least, the People should assemble together for the express Purpose of consulting and debating, whether they should permit the same Form of Government, or the same Officers to continue for *one Year longer*; or change them all, and begin another Form, or try another Set. The People, you know, according to this republican Doctrine, are, in all Instances, the supreme Head, and Lord Paramount: And Government, even the best of Governments, ought implicitly to submit to their Authority and Controul. Therefore, whether the same Form of Government, or the same Administrators of it, shall be, or not be,—*that's the Question!*

THE *Americans* of late have acted very agreeably to this shifting Scene of *new Lords and new Laws*; for not only their general Congresses, and their Provincial Congresses, but their Town-Meetings, their select Meetings, and their Liberty-Tree Meetings, have a natural Tendency to beget a popular, republican Spirit, and to subject every Degree of Magistracy and Government to the perpetual Controul and Caprice of the Mob. In short, it is already an established Maxim in that Country, *that the Voice of the People,*—is the VOICE OF GOD. And were any one to dare to gainsay it, Tarring and Feathering would be the mildest Punishment, which such a Rebel against this [Mob-cratic] Constitution could expect.

AND you, Sir, when you were enumerating them any signal Advantages we derive from our Connections with *America*, ought to have mentioned this among the rest:—You ought to have exulted, that the fierce *American* Spirit begins to operate so very rapidly here in *England*; and to have expressed your Hopes that it will spread more and more, the longer we are connected with that People.

BUT perhaps you had your Reasons against being thus explicit.—It is a tender Point; and you have a very difficult Part to act. Certain it is, that both the *American* and the *English* Republicans expect great Things from you: They expect, that you would assist them in reducing the Power of the Crown, and of the House of Peers to a mere Cypher;— or rather to abolish them totally, Root and Branch: And they expect likewise, that you would co-operate with them in subjecting the House of Commons itself to the Instructions of Town-Meetings, select Meetings, Liberty-Meetings, &c. &c. &c.: And in short, that every Thing should be subjugated both within Doors, and without, *arbitrio popularis auræ*. On the other Hand, it is equally certain, that you are endeavouring to make Use of these factious Republicans, as the Tools and Instruments of your own Advancement, without gratifying them in their darling Object. This is a curious Farce, in which each Party must act at present under borrowed Characters; (for even the Republicans must, as yet, express their Wishes more by *dumb Shew*, than by open Declarations) and in which one, or other must be duped at last. But more of this hereafter.

II. THE second Source you mention, from whence the fierce Spirit of the *Americans* is derived, is their Forms of Government strongly tending to become Republics. And here, as you had no Interest either to conceal, or to disguise the Fact, you have given us a just Representation of it. "Their [*the American*] Governments (Page 17) are popular in an high Degree. Some are merely popular; in all the popular Representative is the most weighty: And this Share of the People in their ordinary Government never fails to inspire them with lofty Sentiments, and with a strong Aversion from whatever tends to deprive them of their chief Importance."

BUT you insinuate, that you will not decide, whether this Indulgence to the Colonies at first, in granting them such popular [alias republican] Forms of Government, arose from *Lenity* or *Indolence*, from *Wisdom*, or *Mistake*. Alas! Sir, one can easily perceive by your very Insinuation and your Caution, that you had already decided this Point in your own Mind, tho' you did not chuse to speak out. And indeed it is now evident to all, that if the Parent-State really intended to retain an actual and effectual Supremacy over her Colonies, (which was certainly her Intention) such Forms of Government were of all others the most unfit for that Purpose; and the most likely to beget a Spirit of Independence and Revolt. In fact, what was so likely to have happened, has actually come to pass, and would have come to pass in the natural and necessary Course of Things, tho' the Stamp, or the Tea acts had never been thought of. And I agree with you, that it is now by much too late to think of correcting an Error, so strengthened by Time, and grown inveterate by Habit, that it may be said to be interwoven into the very Constitution of the present *Americans*. Here therefore, as we are agreed in the Fact, let every one draw his own Inference.

III. YOUR third grand Cause is Religion: On which Subject you deliver yourself in the following Strain, at Pages 17 and 18.

"IF any Thing were wanting to this necessary Operation of the Form of Government [to beget or infuse a fierce Spirit of Liberty] Religion would have given it a complete Effect. Religion, always a Principle of Energy, in this new People, is no Ways worn out or impaired. And their Mode of professing it, is also one main Cause of this free Spirit. The People are Protestants; and of that Kind, which is the most adverse to all implicit Submission of Mind and Opinion. This is a Persuasion not only favourable to Liberty, but built upon it.—The Dissenting Interests have sprung up in direct Opposition to all the ordinary Powers of the World; and could justify that Opposition only on a strong Claim to natural Liberty. Their very Existence depended on the powerful and unremitted Assertion of that Claim. All Protestantism, even the most cold and passive, is a Sort of Dissent. But the Religion most prevalent in the Northern Colonies is a Refinement on the Principle of Resistance; it is the Dissidence of Dissent: And the Protestantism of the Protestant Religion. This Religion, under a Variety of Denominations, *agreeing in nothing, but in the Communication of the Spirit of Liberty*, is predominant in most of the Northern Colonies. The Colonists left *England* when this Spirit was high, and in the Emigrants the highest of all."

SIR, this Account is not exact, and stands in Need of some Correction. When the Emigrants fled from *England*, they were universally Calvinists of the most inflexible Sort. But they were very far from being of that Species of Protestants, whom you describe; and of which spreading Sect, there are but too many Proselites both in *Great-Britain*, *Ireland*, and *America*; I mean, the modern *new-light* Men, who protest against every Thing, and who would dissent even from themselves, and from their own Opinions, if no other Means of Dissention could be found out. Such Protestants as these are very literally PROTESTERS; but it is hard to say, what they are besides. And Fact it is, that they have no Manner of Affinity with the Calvinists of old respecting Church Government. For tho' the Calvinistical Emigrants were professed Enemies to the Popery of the Church of *Rome*, and to the Arminianism of the Church of *England*, yet were they no Enemies to religious Establishments. Nay, their great Aim was, to establish the *solemn League and Covenant*, as the only System which ought to be admitted into a Christian State. Nor would they have suffered any other religious Persuasion to have existed, if they could have prevented it. Moreover, tho' they were for pulling down proud and lordly Prelacy; yet were they most indefatigable in erecting Classes, and Synods, and Elderships, in the genuine Spirit of High-Church, Presbyterian Hierarchy, and armed with the Terrors and Powers of an Inquisition. In short, their Aim was to establish a republican Form of Government built on republican Principles both in Church and State. But, like all other Republicans ancient and modern, they were extremely averse from granting any Portion of that Liberty to others, which they claimed to themselves as their unalienable Birth-Right.

THE present Dissenters in *North-America* retain very little of the peculiar Tenets of their Fore-fathers, excepting their Antipathy to our established Religion, and their Zeal to pull down all Orders in Church and State, if found to be superior to their own. And if it be this you mean, by saying, that the dissenting Interests [in *America*] have sprung up in direct *Opposition* to all the ordinary Powers of the World;—and that the Religion most prevalent in the Northern Colonies is a *Refinement* on the Principles of *Resistance*; the *Dissidence* of *Dissent*, and the *Protestantism* of the Protestant Religion:—In short, if you ascribe the fierce Spirit now *raging* in the Northern Colonies to these Causes, I make no Objection to your Account of the Matter; provided you will allow that the Religion of the Gospel is a very different Thing from theirs. But nevertheless I must beg the impartial World to judge between us, as to the *Conclusion* to be drawn from such Premises; and whether it be, or be not, a desireable Thing to continue a Connection with a People who are actuated by Principles so very repugnant to our own Constitution both in Church and State, and so diametrically opposite to the Spirit of the Gospel.

IV. To the before-mentioned Sources, from whence this ungovernable Spirit is derived, you add another, viz. The Domination of the Masters over their Slaves in the Southern Colonies. For it seems, he that is a Tyrant over his Inferiors is, of Course, a Patriot, and a Leveller in respect to his Superiors. And I am afraid, there is but too much Truth in this Observation. However, let us consider the Drift and Tendency of your own Expresions.— "In *Virginia*, and the *Carolinas*, they have vast Multitudes of Slaves. Where that is the Case, *in any Part of the World*, those who are free, are by far the most proud and jealous of their Freedom. Freedom is to them not only an Enjoyment, but a Kind of Rank and Privilege.—I do not mean to commend the superior Morality of this Sentiment, which has at least as much Pride, as Virtue in it: The Fact is so; and these People of the Southern Colonies, are much more strongly, and with an higher and more stubborn Spirit, attached to Liberty than those of the Northward. Such were all the antient Common-wealths; such were our Gothic Ancestors; such in our Days were the Poles; and such will be all Masters of Slaves, who are not Slaves themselves. In such a People the Haughtiness of Domination combines with the Spirit of Freedom, fortifies it, and renders it invincible." P. 18, and 19.

HERE, Sir, you trace out many important Matters for our due Regard and Attention. And first of all, you suggest, that the Southern Colonies, who have such Multitudes of Slaves, and who, in Consequence thereof, are by far the weakest, standing in Need of our daily Protection, are nevertheless the most obstinately bent against contributing any Thing towards their own Defence. Why? Because they are by far the most proud and jealous of their Liberty; for in them the Haughtiness of Domination combines with the Spirit of Freedom: And therefore as they will not condescend to contribute any Thing towards their own Defence, we, who are not so proud and jealous, must submit to be their Guards and Centinels. And then perhaps, they *may* make us some Acknowledgments, or they *may not*; — according as it shall please their High Mightinesses! Grand and noble on their Part, it must be owned! Humiliating and mean on ours! Surely, Sir, one would have thought, that a very different Inference might have been drawn from such Premises: — One might have supposed, that it would not have been altogether unreasonable, or unjust to say, that if Men of such Principles will not contribute their fair Quota towards their own Preservation; let them take the Consequence; and let us give ourselves no further Concern about them.

BUT it seems, the antient Republics, and our Gothic Ancestors, the modern Poles, and all Masters of Slaves, who are not Slaves themselves, were, and are, in every Part of the World, possessed with the Haughtiness of Domination respecting others, and with an invincible Spirit of Freedom regarding themselves. Probable enough: The fierce Spirit of the *Goths* and *Vandals* was a Spirit of Freedom for themselves to do whatever they listed, at the Expence of the Lives, Liberties, and Properties of the rest of Mankind: The modern Poles prosecuted just the same Plan over their Dependents; 'till a Tyrant arose of more extensive Power, and of greater Capacity, who has lately served some of them in the same Manner, in which they serve all their Vassals. As to the Institution of Slavery in any of our Colonies; let those be Advocates for it, who approve of it. For my Part, I am thoroughly convinced, that the Laws of Commerce, when rightly understood, do perfectly co-incide with the Laws of Morality; both originating from the same good Being, whose Mercies are over all his Works. Nay, I think it is demonstrable, that *domestic* or *predial* Slavery would be found, on a fair Calculation, to be the most onerous and expensive Mode of cultivating Land, and of raising Produce, that could be devised. And I defy you, with all your Learning and Acuteness, to produce a single Instance from History either

antient or modern, of a Country being well cultivated, and at the same
Time abounding in Manufactures, where this Species of Slavery (I mean
the *domestic* or *predial*) is preferred to the Method of hiring free Persons,
and paying them wages.   In the mean Time, I do most readily subscribe
to the Doctrine implied in your Description, viz.   That the Masters of
such Slaves, are, for the most Part, haughty, insolent, and imperious in
private Life; and also, that they are turbulent and factious in respect to
the Public, incessantly endeavouring to pull down and lay low, even with
the Dust, every Order and Degree of Men above themselves.   *Jura
negant sibi nata.*

WITH respect to the ancient Republics (and you might have added
the modern likewise) the same Remark holds good.   The Haughtiness
of Domination, generally speaking, renders these republican Governments
the most insolent and tyrannical upon Earth.   And it is observable,
that their Subjects retain less of Liberty, both in Form and Substance,
than most of the Subjects even of monarchical Governments.   Now,
that this is the Fact, I appeal to all Men of Reading, to all who have
travelled, and to all who can make a just Observation on Men and
Things.   Nay, to go no farther than our own Country, the Specimen we
had of the manifold Tyrannies, and grievous Oppressions (without even
the Colour of Law) of those UPSTARTS, who called themselves, *The Common-Wealth of England*, after the Murder of King CHARLES I.   I say,
this Specimen is such, that no Man, either wise, or good, would wish
to have the like Tragedies acted over again;—notwithstanding the high
Encomiums, which some celebrated republican Writers of late have
passed on those Times.

IN short, Sir, very unfortunate have you been hitherto in heaping
together such a Number of Arguments, and such Examples as these:
All of which militate so very strongly against your own Conclusion.   And
yet what is to follow, will be found to do so much more strongly.

V. For 5th.   You say (Page 19) "Permit me, Sir, to add another
Circumstance in our Colonies, which contributes no mean Part towards
the Growth and Effect of this UNTRACTABLE SPIRIT: I mean their
Education.   In no Country perhaps in the World is the Law so general
a Study.   The Profession itself is *numerous* and *powerful*; and in most
Provinces it takes the Lead.   The greater Number of the Deputies sent
to the Congress were Lawyers.   But all who read, and most do read,
endeavour to obtain some Smattering in that Science.   General GAGE
marks out this Disposition very particularly in a Letter on your Table.
He states, that all the People in his Government are Lawyers, or Smat-

terers in Law: And that in *Boston* they have been enabled by successful Chicane wholly to evade many Parts of your capital penal Constitutions. The Smartness of Debate will say, that this Knowledge ought to teach them more clearly the Rights of the Legislature, their Obligations to Obedience, and the Penalties of Rebellion.   All this is mighty well: But my honourable and learned Friend on the Floor [the Attorney General] who condescends to mark what I say for Animadversion, will disdain that Ground.   He has heard, as well as I, that *when great Honours, and great Emoluments do not win over this Knowledge to the Service of the State, it is a formidable Adversary to Government.*   If the Spirit be not tamed and broken by these happy Methods, it is STUBBORN and LITIGIOUS.   *Abeunt studia in mores.*   This Study renders Men acute, inquisitive, dextrous, prompt in Attack, ready in Defence, FULL OF RESOURCES."

SIR, you say, *In no Country perhaps in the World is the Law so general a Study.*   True: And you might have added, That in no Country perhaps in the World are there so many Law-Suits, or so much open and barefaced Chicane.   An *American* Gentleman of great Discernment and good Sense assured me about the Time of the Stamp-Act, that if that Act would make the Going to Law so dear, as to lessen the Number of Law-Suits (but of that he doubted) it would become in the Event, tho' not by Design, the greatest Blessing that ever could befall *America.*   He observed further, that in one small District of about 800 taxable Persons, the number of Law-Suits was so great in one Year, that I am afraid to repeat it after him; for nothing but the Character you give of the perverse Litigiousness and chicaning Disposition of this People, could make his Account appear credible.   But leaving their own petty-fogging Tricks and Quirks to themselves, we will now consider this wrangling unhappy Turn of Mind, as it affects the Trade and Commerce, the Peace and Prosperity of *Great-Britain.*

SIR, the Trade to *North-America* (which, after all your pompous Accounts, I take upon me to aver, and DISPROVE IT, IF YOU CAN,)* is

---

* The Amount of the Value of the Exports (extracted from the   *l.*   *s. d.*
Custom-House Books) from *England* to *Holland* and *Germany*, for
nine Years, *viz.* from *Christmas* 1763, to *Christmas* 1772, was   30,294,126 11 3
    The Amount of the Value of the Exports (taken from the same
Books) and for the same Length of Time, from *England* to the
present *revolted Provinces* of *America*, was only   ——   —— 20,061,023   3 8
    According to this Account it appears, that *Holland* and *Germany*
    were better Customers to *England* than the revolted Provinces
    of *North-America*, during these nine Years, by the Sum of   —— 10,233,103   7 7
Before a Comparison was drawn between the Trade to *North-America*, and the

much less than that to *Holland* and *Germany*; yet this Trade alone has made more Bankrupts, and ruined more Merchant Exporters, for these fifty Years last past, than almost every other Export-Trade besides. This is a Fact, which I am well persuaded, could have been no Secret to Mr. BURKE; yet, as he has studiously concealed it from his Hearers, or his Readers, I will, in Justice to them, endeavour to explain it in the best Manner I am able.

THE People of other Countries, *Holland*, *Germany*, *France*, or *Spain*, &c. &c. are, *generally speaking*, afraid of giving Orders for a greater Quantity of Goods, than they can see a Prospect of paying for.   Not so in *North America*.   For if you will give them *Credit*, they will give you *Orders* to what *Amount* you please.   [I speak this in *general*, for undoubt-

---

Trade to other Countries, *where we have no Colonies*, the general Cry of the Mal-contents was, Let us appeal to the Custom-House Books, and there you will find, that the Trade to our Colonies is worth all other Trades besides.   This was the Language which Dr. FRANKLIN held, in my Hearing, about twenty Years ago.   But, as I never believed him in any public matter, excepting in his Electrical Experiments, I was resolved to see with my own Eyes, whether what he advanced was true or not; having a strong suspicion that he fibbed disignedly, like Sir HENRY WOTTON's Embassador, *patriæ causa*.   The Extract which I then obtained, is now mislaid.   But I remember perfectly well, that the Balance was at that Time much greater in Favour of *Germany* and *Holland*, even than it is, at present, as given above.   Nay, I think that the Exports to *Holland* alone were then equal, or nearly equal, to the Value of all the Exports to *North-America*.   And it is reasonable to suppose, that at *that Juncture*, the Case was not far distant from this State of it; for then we had not altogether spent 70,000,000l. Sterling in Defence of that Country; which Circumstance, as it greatly enriched the *Americans*, enabled them proportionably to extend their Trade, and to purchase much greater Quantities of Goods than they had done before.   And we had not then drained ourselves of *Men* as well as Money, to fight their Battles, and to settle among them, to their Gain, but to our irreparable Loss: — Nor lastly, had the Emigrations from the different Parts of *Europe*, and especially from *Germany*, *Ireland*, and *Scotland*, then taken Place to the Degree they have since done; all which Circumstances conspire to swell the present Account in Favour of *America*, much beyond its due Size and real Value, and to lessen both the Consumption at Home, and our Exports to other Countries.   For it is evident to a Demonstration, that if our old Customers will remove from *Germany*, *Ireland*, *Scotland*, &c. or from among ourselves, to settle in *North-America*; — they cannot be *European*, and *American* Customers at the same Time: So that what we get in one Respect, we must lose in the other.   And yet, with all these Advantages, and taking the *American* Trade at its most flourishing Period, *viz.* from the Year 1763 to the Year 1772, as above stated; — what is it to make such a mighy boast of?   And why is our Commerce with other Countries so much vilified and degraded, if brought into Comparison with the Trade of *North-America?* — But I throw out these Reflections only as *Hints* at present, and reserve to myself a more full Consideration of the Matter in the Treatise that is to follow, *viz. An Address to the Landed Interest of* Great-Britain *and* Ireland.

edly there are *numerous* Exceptions.] And then, when the Time of Payment approaches, they are the very People you have described, *dextrous*, *prompt* in Attack, *ready in Defence*, and FULL OF RESOURCES: Some of which Resources, as practised between forty and fifty Years ago, I will lay before the Reader.

FIRST, after they had run so far in Debt, that they could be no longer trusted; — they required that the *English* Creditor should make his Appearance in their Courts of Law, or before some of their Magistrates, in order to prove his Debt. Now it is easy to see, that in many Cases, it would be better for the *English* Merchant to compound his Debt at any Rate, or even totally to relinquish it, than to prosecute the Recovery of it after this Manner. Then, secondly, they insisted, that their Lands, Houses, and Slaves were not liable to the Payment of Commercial or Book Debts, because they were not *Assets*; — though these Possessions were purchased, or procured by that very Credit, and those very Capitals, which they had obtained from *England*. The Merchants of *Great-Britain*, finding themselves thus shamefully cheated of their Property, petitioned the Parliament for a Redress of Grievances; and obtained an Act the 5th of G. II. C. 7. *Anno* 1732, entituled, "An Act for the more easy Recovery of Debts in his Majesty's Plantations and Colonies in *America*." In which Act there are special Clauses inserted for defeating both these Schemes of your *ingenious* Friends, the *Americans*. However, a People so *full of Resources*, as you have described them to be, soon recovered themselves from this Overthrow: For in a very few Years, they contrived another successful Mode of cheating their *English* Creditors: And the four *New England* Provinces, now in actual Rebellion, were particularly concerned in this Conspiracy. The Trick was, to issue out a Paper Currency, and to oblige the *English* Creditor to accept of it as a *legal Tender*, in full Discharge of all Demands. The *Englishman*, who, in *Great-Britain*, is not obliged *by Law* to accept even of a Bank-Note, as a Tender of Payment, was shocked and alarmed to the last Degree, at this repeated Attack upon his Property: And therefore applied again to the Legislature for Assistance and Protection. Nor did he apply in vain: For in the Year 1751, viz. 24th of G. II. C. 53, an Act was passed, entituled, "An Act to regulate and restrain Paper Bills of Credit in his Majesty's Colonies and Plantations of *Rhode-Island* and *Providence* Plantations, *Connecticut* and *Massachusets Bay*, and *New Hampshire* in *America*; and [N. B.] to prevent the same being legal Tenders in Payment of Money."

Now, Sir, you see even here, and without mentioning those numerous

Instances of a growing Disposition to rebel, which occasioned the famous declaratory Law of 7th and 8th of WILLIAM III. C. 22 about 80 Years ago; — and without referring to the Archives of the Board of Trade, whose Presses are loaded with *English* Complaints and Memorials against *American* Injustice and Chicane, against their Violation of our Trade-Laws, and other bad Practices; — I say, without referring to any of these, and confining ourselves simply and solely to the Acts of Parliament here mentioned, it appears evident to a Demonstration, that the present Disputes with the Colonies derive their Origin from Causes much more ancient and remote, than either the Stamp, or the Tea Act. And it is really astonishing, that you should have the Courage even to insinuate the contrary; — much less to assert it, so peremptorily, as you do at P. 34. and in the Face of such stubborn Facts. But alas! All Things are now inverted. For that very Boldness, which nothing but a Consciousness of Truth, the *Mens conscia recti*, ought to inspire, is become the Privilege of the most bare-faced Falshoods.

BUT to return, after both these Acts of Parliament (obtained, not during the present, but during the late Reign;) one would have thought, that an effectual Stop had been put to *American* Chicaning, and *American* Subterfuges. Alas, Sir, no such Thing. Your Friends and Fellow-Labourers are ever *dextrous, ever ready* in *Defence*, and *full of Resources*. The tricks last in Vogue as I am credibly informed (I mean, before ever the Stamp-Act was thought of) were to procrastinate a Law-Suit to an immoderate Length; which it seems, this People, *so addicted to the Study of the Law*, have discovered the Art of doing, at a very small Expence on their Part; and then, when they could ward off the Blow no longer, and when the Lands, Houses, and Effects must be sold, in Consequence of the afore-mentioned Act, — the *last Resource* was, to get a Friend to buy the Estate back again at the Public Vendue; in which Case these *good Men and true* were sure of favouring one another against the *common Enemy*. In short, it frequently came to pass, that the *English* Creditor, at the Foot of the Account, found himself so loaded with Expences and *Items* of various Kinds, that it was well for him, if the Sale of the Premises would defray the Charges, without taking into the Account his original Debt, his Loss of Interest, expected Profit on his Capital, Loss of Time, &c. &c. Nay, it has been sometimes known, that the Sheriff himself has absconded with the Purchase Money.

HENCE, Sir, and from a Variety of such Causes, it has actually come to pass, that so many Merchants of *London, Bristol, Liverpool*, &c. &c. have failed, and become Bankrupts, if they traded *chiefly* and *principally* to

North-America:—An that so very few have acquired any considerable Fortunes by this Trade, notwithstanding the great Riches which have been acquired by almost all others.

BUT here, to use your own Words, the *Smartness of Debate* will retort upon me:—Granting the Case to be as you have stated it, "What do you propose to do with these *Americans?* Your own Scheme of a total Separation from them, recommends nevertheless the trading with them, as with any other independent, neutral Powers. And then, if they should have Recourse to their former Tricks and Chicaneries, the same Complaints will be made by the *English* Merchants, and the same Difficulties, or perhaps greater, might again perplex the *British* Crown and Parliament." To which Objection I return the following Answer:—That if the *North-American* Provinces were erected into independent States, their Subjects would be afraid to insult us with such shocking Provocations as they have done with Impunity for many Years past. No neutral Power dares to attempt the like against *Great-Britain*. And in Case the *Americans* should ever betray a Disposition to return to their former Practices, a few Letters of Marque Ships sent upon their Coast, would soon teach these *Smatterers in the Law*, to be honest in Spite of their Teeth. Nay, the *Americans* themselves have not, as far as appears, practiced these infamous Cheats on any *European* Nation, excepting the *English*. For tho' they have, for at least these last fifty Years, carried on an increasing Trade with *Holland* and *Germany*, with *France, Spain, Portugal*, and *Italy*, either by Means of the *Dutch, French, Spanish*, or *Portuguese* Colonies, or by a more direct Communication; — yet they have, for the most Part, paid *ready Money* wherever the Balance was against them: And then they traded with the good-natured credulous *English* on *long Credit*; which induced them, when the Times of Payment drew on, to be guilty of the infamous Practices before described.

So much for their private Character respecting their commercial Intercourse with their Fellow-Subjects.—We will now consider the same People in another View,—in the Treatment they shew to that very Legislature, which they themselves do *in Words and in Tongue* acknowledge to be supreme.

GENERAL GAGE, you say, declares in one of his Letters, that [as all the People in his Government "are either Lawyers, or Smatterers in Law] they have in *Boston* been enabled by Successful Chicane, wholly to evade many Parts of one of our capital penal Constitutions." Most probably this penal Statute was one of our Laws for the Regulation of their Trade, and for confining it to the Mother Country; which System of Laws you well know (tho' you will not own it) has ever been their Aim either to undermine, or over-turn. And, Sir, if you will be pleased to attend to the very Terms made Use of, both by the Provincial, and General Congresses, in their respective Resolves, you will find, that these zealous Protestants, who are, in your Opinion, the very Quintessence of Protestantism, are nevertheless as great Adepts in the Science of Equivocation, and mental Reservation, as the most subtile Jesuit; you will find, that when they seemed to approach the nearest to a Compromise, they really intended to be as far distant from it as ever; and only used soothing and ambiguous Expressions in order to deceive the Unwary. — That this is the Fact, you may learn at once from that remarkable Expression in all their Congress Resolves, EVERY IDEA of Taxation. Now what is *every Idea?* What are its Limits and Boundaries? And who can fix the Meaning of so vague a Term? According to the Explanations which the *American* News-Papers, and their political Writers, have already given of this Phrase of doubtful Signification, it appears, that they intend to object under Cover of it, to every Restriction you can form for confining their Trade to the Mother-Country; seeing that the Sanctions or Penalties, by which such Regulations must be enforced, may be considered as coming under the Idea of Taxation. "For, say they, every *English* Law, which either diminishes our Property, or deprives us of the Means of acquiring it, is in Fact, a Tax laid on the Inhabitants of *America* for the Benefit of *England.*" And under this Head, they have already classed that Act of Parliament, which required the Billeting the Troops in their respective Provinces.

BUT lest, Sir, you should despise what I have here suggested, (what you often magisterially affect to do,) give me Leave to refer you to a Prophet of their own, who delivers his Oracles on this Head. "If, says he, the British Parliament has a legal Authority to order, that we shall furnish a single Article for the Troops here [in *America,*] and to compel Obedience to that Order; they have the same Right to order us to supply those Troops with Arms, Cloaths, and every Necessary, and to compel Obedience to that Order: In short, to lay any Burdens they please upon us: What is this but taxing us at a *certain Sum*, and leaving to us only *the Manner* of raising it? How is this more tolerable than the Stamp-Act? Would that Act have appeared more pleasing to *Americans*, if being ordered thereby to raise the Sum total of the Taxes, the mighty Privilege had been left to them of saying, how much should be paid for an Instrument in Writing on Paper, and how much for another on Parchment. AN ACT OF PARLIAMENT COMMANDING US TO DO A CERTAIN

Thing, if it has any Validity, is a Tax upon us for the Expence that accrues in complying with it." [Letter 1st of the Letters from a Farmer in *America*, printed at *Philadelphia*; *London* re-printed for Almon, P. 8.]

And now, Sir, if it be possible to suppose, that any Thing further can be wanting to prove the Expediency, and even Necessity of separating speedily from such a People, and so circumstanced; — you yourself have furnished us with one grand Argument still more cogent than all the rest, under your next and concluding Head. Strong indeed, and very emphatical are your Words on this Occasion!

VI. "The last Cause of this disobedient Spirit in the Colonies is hardly less powerful than the rest, as it is not merely *moral*, but laid deep in the *natural* Constitution of Things. *Three Thousand Miles of Ocean* lie between you and them. No contrivance can prevent the Effect of this Distance in Weakening Government. Seas roll, and Months pass, between the Order and the Execution: And the Want of a speedy Explanation of a single Point, is enough to defeat a whole System. You have indeed winged Ministers of Vengeance, who carry their Bolts in their Pounces to the remotest Verge of the Sea. But there a Power steps in, that limits the Arrogance of the raging Passions and furious Elements, and says, so far shalt thou go, and no farther. Who are you that should fret and rage, and bite the Chains of Nature?— *Nothing worse happens to you, than does to all Nations who have extensive Empires: And it happens in all the Forms to which Empire can be thrown.* In large Bodies, the Circulation of Power must be less vigorous at the Extremities. Nature has said it. The *Turk* cannot govern *Ægypt*, and *Arabia* and *Curdistan*, as he governs *Thrace*; nor has he the same Dominion in *Crimea* and *Algiers*, which he has at *Boursa* and *Smyrna*. Despotism itself is obliged to *truck* and *huckster*. The Sultan gets such Obedience as he can. He governs with a loose Rein, that he may govern at all; and the whole of the Force and Vigour of his Authority in his Centre, is derived from a prudent Relaxation in all its Borders. *Spain* in her [*American*] Provinces, is, perhaps, not so well obeyed as you are in yours. She complies too; *she submits, she watches Times*, This is the immutable Condition, the eternal Law, of extensive and detached Empire." — [Page 20.]

The immutable Condition! the eternal Law! Extensive and detached Empire! Pray, Sir, on which Side of the Question were you retained? And whose Cause are you now pleading? I have heard of Lawyers in great Practice, who, thro' Hurry and Inattention, mistook one Brief for another, and then, pleading on a contrary Side to that on which they were retained, did not perceive their Error, 'till their Clients had lost their Cause. Whether any Thing of the like Kind has happened to you, is more than I can say. But it is Matter of Astonishment to all, to your own Friends and Admirers, as well as to others, that you should bring such Arguments as these, to prove the Necessity of continuing an Union of Empire between *Great-Britain* and the detached continental Powers of *North-America*. You instance the Case of *Spain:* But to what End or Purpose have you brought it into the present Argument? For if it be, to display the Benefit and Advantage of distant and extensive Colonies, you surely are the most unfortunate of all Men living in the Nature of your Proofs: *Spain* being a striking Example, and a full Illustration of the direct contrary. *Spain*, Sir, as you well know, was, before it was seized with an epidemic Madness of settling Colonies in *America*, one of the richest, the best peopled, the best cultivated, and the most flourishing Country in *Europe*. It was said to have contained at least twenty Millions of Inhabitants: Its Cities were numerous and opulent, abounding with Manufactures of various Kinds, and particularly with those of Silk and Wool. But now alas! how fallen! what is *Spain!* where are its Manufactures! where its Inhabitants!

THE last Enumeration of its Inhabitants was, I think, in the Year 1766: And the Numbers then given in were between six and seven Millions of Persons of an Age sufficiently adult to receive the Sacrament at *Easter*. The Question therefore between you and me is reduced to a few single Points, simple in themselves, and easy to be understood, viz. 1st. Whether *Spain*, with its present Number of Inhabitants (or if you please, with *double its present Number*) and also with vast and extensive Colonies in *South-America*, is richer and stronger than it was, with its Twenty Millions formerly, and without any Colonies at all? And 2dly. What prudential Course ought *Spain* to take in its present Situation,---Whether to call off as many *American* Subjects as it can, and then entirely to abandon all those immense and distant Regions, *which it cannot govern*, turning its Cares wholly to the *re-peopling*, and improving of *Old Spain?* Or whether to go on still in its present Mode, *trucking* and *huckstering*, and *getting such an Obedience as it can* [which you say is the Case even with the Grand Turk] *watching Times*, governing and submitting by Turns, and *complying with this* American *Spirit as with a necessary Evil?* Now, Sir, as these are the Questions to be decided; let the impartial World judge between, and determine for us. And after that Decision, let an Application be made, *mutato nomine*, to *Great-Britain* and her Colonies.

Two words more about *Spain*, and I have done. The first is, that before the Discovery of *America*, there were upwards of 30,000 Hogsheads of Sugar raised in the Kingdom of *Granada*; and all raised by free People, without domestic, or predial Slavery. Whereas at present there are hardly any. Why? Because *Spain* has now Sugar Colonies in *America*; and the making of Sugar in *Granada* would interfere with their Interests. We have, I think, made no less than six Acts of Parliament here in *England*, on a similar Plan, to prevent the Cultivation of Tobacco, in order to favour the Colony of *Virginia*.

THE second is, that the only Province in all *Spain*, which seems to begin to lift up its Head, and to get a little forward in Population, Agriculture, and Manufactures, is the province of *Catalonia*. And the Reason is, because *Catalonia* is happily by its Situation the farthest removed from the baleful Influence of Colony-Connections, and suffers the least by Emigrations.

AND now, Sir, as if the six Causes, which you had already produced, were not enough to overthrow your whole System, you are so kind, in the Sequel, as to present me with two more, which prove very strong Arguments against yourself. The first is the *growing Population* of the Colonies, which you say [P. 24] is evidently *one Cause of their Resistance*. And therefore in whatever Ratio this Population is to be supposed to increase, in the same must their Resistance increase with it, and our Authority decrease. The other Cause of Resistance is, the prodigious Expansion of the Back-Settlements. "Many of the People in the Back-Settlements are already little attached to particular Situations. Already have they topped the *Apalachian* Mountains. From thence they behold before them an immense Plain, one vast, rich, level Meadow, a Square of Five Hundred Miles. Over this they *would* wander, *without a Possibility of Restraint*. [And surely, Sir, if it is *impossible* for us to restrain them, undoubtedly they *will* wander whenever they chuse so to do.] "They would soon change their Manners with the Habits of their Life; would soon forget a Government by which they were disowned: Would become Hords of *English* Tartars; and pouring down upon your unfortified Frontiers a fierce and irresistible Cavalry, become Masters of your Governors, and Counsellors, your Collectors and Comptrollers, and of all the Slaves that adhered to them." [Page 24.]

THANKS to you, Sir, for these kind, and prophetic Declarations! The Description alone is sufficient; without staying to put the Matter to an actual Trial. And if after this, we will persevere in retaining Governors and Counsellors, Collectors and Comptrollers in such a Coun-

try, on any Account, or under any Modification whatever, we deserve
to suffer all that you have predicted. For indeed, whether the Colony
was placed in *Asiatic*, or *American Tartary*, the Folly and Absurdity of
pretending to govern such a Colony, and to make it subservient to the
Purposes of Commerce, is just the same. Nature opposes it, as you
justly observe: And Nature will be obeyed.

BUT I forget: — You have a Scheme of your own to propose: A
Scheme, which will remove all Difficulties, be they ever so great; an
infallible Scheme, which can unite the most distant Situations, reconcile
the most jarring Interests, the most opposite Principles, and discordant
Tempers; — A Scheme in short, which, as you say on another Occasion,
will *annihilate both Space* and *Time*, and *make two Lovers happy.* — "The
Proposition is PEACE. [Page 5.] Not Peace thro' the Medium of War;
not Peace to be hunted thro' the Labyrinths of intricate and endless
Negociations; not Peace to arise out of universal Discord, fomented
from Principle, in all Parts of the Empire; not Peace to depend on the
juridical Determination of perplexing Questions: or the precise marking
the shadowy Boundaries of a complex Government. It is simple Peace,
sought in its natural Course, and its ordinary Haunts.---It is Peace sought
in the Spirit of Peace, and laid in Principles purely pacific."

WHAT a pompous Description is here!

——Mulier formosa supernè,
Desinit in piscem——

FOR after all, what is this Heaven-born pacific Scheme, of which we
have heard so laboured an Encomium? Why truly; *if we will grant*
the Colonies all that they shall require, and stipulate for nothing in Return;
then they will be at Peace with us. I believe it; and on these simple Principles of simple Peace-making I will engage to terminate every Difference
throughout the World: I say, throughout the World: For even your
own *Dissidents* of *American* Dissenters, whom you have described as
the most difficult of all Men living to be pleased, cannot, I should think,
ask for more, than to have their Demands always granted, whenever
they make them.

IT is, Sir, a Thing worthy of Observation in your Writings, that
whenever you are advancing some strange Paradox, which will not bear
a Discussion in open Day, there you attempt either to envelope yourself
in such a Cloud of Metaphors, as may prevent your Readers from seeing
what you are about;—or else to draw up your Paragraphs with such

Guards and Salvoes, that while you present one Sense to your Readers, you reserve another for yourself in Case of Attack. Of the former of these I have given some glaring Instances already; and shall now exhibit some Specimens of the latter.

At Page 52, you say, "I do not know, that the Colonies have, in *any general Way*, or in any *cool Hour*, gone *much beyond* the Demand of Immunity in relation to Taxes. It is not fair to judge of the Tempers and Dispositions of any Man, or of any Set of Men, when they are composed, and at rest, from their Conduct or their Expressions, in a State of Disturbance and Irritation."

Now a plain, honest Man, not aware of your mental Reservations, would think, that you had expressly told him, that before the Colonies were *provoked* by the Stamp-Act, they were all Love and Duty to the Mother-Country; and that 'till this fatal Period, they had never manifested any Disobedience to her Authority, or shewn the least Reluctance to comply with her Demands: But as you know the contrary, you were unwilling to risque the Merits of your Cause on this Issue: And have cautiously added, that the Colonies have not in *any general Way*, in their *cool Hours* gone *much beyond*, &c. &c. Therefore should I undertake to prove that the Colonies, as far back as the Year 1696, manifested a strong Disposition to set up Laws, Bye-laws, Usages and Customs in Opposition to the Navigation-Act, and other Acts of the like Tendency, (where Taxation was out of the Question) — your Reply is ready: "The Colonies might be then in a State of Disturbance and Irritation: And I had only affirmed, that they did not break out into Acts of Disobedience in their *cool Hours:*" Or if I could prove, (which I think I can) that in the Year 1696, there was no Appearance of Disturbance or Irritation in the Colonies, but that all was peaceable, — you then can have Recourse to your other Distinction, viz. "That their Reluctance to comply with *particular* Acts of Parliament, which they esteemed to be peculiarly oppressive, was very consistent with their Conduct as good Subjects in *general*." In short, by the Help of these Distinctions and mental Reservations every Instance of their Disaffection and Disobedience to, and Ill-treatment of, their Parent State may be accounted for, palliated and glossed over: And nothing will remain for us at Home, but to take Shame to ourselves for having brought such a frivolous Accusation. Their tempting General Bradock to set forward on a March, and then refusing to supply him with necessary Provisions at the Places appointed, unless he would advance the Price, which had been agreed upon, to a most enormous Height; — and after all deceiving him [would to GOD, that we had taken Warning by this Treachery, and left them, and the *Indians* to have fought their own Battles;] their aiding and abetting our declared Enemies, the *French* and *Spaniards*, during a War undertaken for their Sakes; — their refusing to pay their just Debts to their *English* Creditors, while they were trafficking with other Nations for ready Money; with numberless other Artifices and Chicaneries, which are daily practised by these *Smatterers in the Law*; all, all are to be veiled over by these disingenuous Sophistries, and pitiful Evasions. But what is still more extraordinary, their very Grants of Money, of which you make your Boast with peculiar Exultation; I mean their own Grants made in their own Assemblies, and for the particular Uses and Defences of their own Provinces during the last War, are a further Illustration of this Matter. Sir, by your Manner of expressing yourself on this Head, P. 16. you have endeavoured to make the good People of *England* believe, that the *Americans* have been the most liberal People upon Earth of their Grants of Money; provided there was a Requisition made to them in due Form and Manner, and that there was a just and sufficient Reason alledged for making such a Requisition. How surprized therefore will they be to hear so different an Account given of this Matter by the most unexceptionable of all Witnesses, even by themselves! The Authority I shall quote at present, as being the most recent, and likely to be contradicted, had it been false, is the Speech of Governor FRANKLIN made to the Assembly of *New Jersey, May* 16, 1775: "The Necessity of some supreme Judge [*whether*, and *when* each Province contributes its just Quota for the general Service] is evident from the very Nature of the Case; as otherwise some Colonies might not contribute their due Proportion. During the last War, I well remember, it was ardently wished by some of the Colonies, that others, who were thought to be delinquent, might be *compelled by Act of Parliament* to bear an equal Share of the public Burdens. It appears by the Minutes of Assembly, in *March* and *April* 1758, that some of the neighbouring Colonies, thought *New Jersey* had not at that Time contributed its due Share towards the Expences of the War; and that President READING (the then Commander in Chief of the Colony) was of the same Opinion. And since my Administration, when the Assembly in 1764 was called upon to make Provision for raising some Troops on Account of the *Indian* War, they declined doing it for some Time, but on Condition a Majority of the Eastern Colonies, as far as to include *Massachusets-Bay* should come into his Majesty's *Requisition* on the Occasion. But [N. B.] as none of the Assemblies of the *New-England* Governments thought themselves *nearly* concerned, *nothing was granted by them:* And the *whole Burden* of the Expedition then carried on, fell upon *Great Britain* and three or four of the middle Colonies, with which this Colony was dissatisfied, and the Assembly complained of it in one of their Addresses to me on the Occasion."

Now, Sir, in this Extract from Governor FRANKLIN's Speech, you see, that both Fact and Argument directly confute your fine-spun aerial Theory of a *voluntary Revenue,* for the general Support even of the *American* Part of the Empire;—without hinting a Word about the *European* Interests of *Great-Britain.* For, here, all their Governments were left to their own free Choice, without the Shadow of a Compulsion. Here the Parliament did not interfere at all: Nor did the King interfere in any other Mode, than by *Requisition*; and that too for their own Sakes, and for the Sake of their Sister-Colonies. Yet, what was the Consequence? —Why, all the Governments throughout the Continent, excepting three or four of the middle ones, granted,—"the voluntary Flow of heaped-up Plenty, [Page 59] bursting from the Weight of its own rich Luxuriance, ever running in a most copious Stream of Revenue;"—that is to say, they granted, JUST NOTHING AT ALL: And poor *England*, with what tiny Assistance it could draw from these three or four middle Colonies, was forced to *bear all* the Burden, as is usually her hard Fate. Nay more, the Reason given, why the *New-England* Governments refused to contribute *any Share* in Aid of their Sister-Colonies, is a Circumstance, which, I hope, no Inhabitant of *Great-Britain* or *Ireland* will pass over, without due Attention, and without making a Self-Application to his own Cause and Country, viz. These *New-England* Governments did not think themselves *so nearly interested* in the Consequences of an *Indian* War, as the other, middle Colonies were.

> *Anglia quid rides? Mutato nomine de te*
> *Fabula narratur.*

THEREFORE, my *European* Fellow-Subjects, if *Great-Britain* or *Ireland* should at any Time have a *European** Quarrel on their Hands, you know

---

* The Instances, which Mr. BURKE has brought at Page 46, to prove that the Colonies, or rather that a few out of the many Colonies, have been liberal in their Grants to *Great-Britain*, during the Continuance of a *privateering, smuggling, trucking,* and *huckstering American Sea-War*, in which they were sure to be the greatest Gainers; shall be particularly considered in an ensuing Treatise, An Address to the landed Interest of *Great-Britain* and *Ireland*.

already, what Assistance you are to expect from the Fellow-Feelings of your benevolent Fellow-Subjects in *America*.

HOWEVER, had we been destitute of Governor FRANKLIN's Testimony of the Refusal of the Colonies to contribute any Thing towards the Relief of others, *where their own Interests are not immediately concerned*; we might have been supplied, even out of your own Stores, with very strong and cogent Reasons against depending on such *voluntary* Grants from our dutiful Sons of *North-America*. For you, Sir, according to your usual *Flow of heaped-up Plenty, bursting from the Weight of your own rich Luxuriance, ever running in a most copious Stream*; — you, Sir, in plain *English*, are continually furnishing me with Plenty of Arguments against yourself. You have, for Example, taken uncommon Pains to expose and confute the System of Lord NORTH for obtaining an *American* Revenue, by obliging each Province to furnish its Contingent; which you very humorously describe by the Idea of setting up a State-Auction in the Anti-Chamber of the Premier. And I do freely acknowledge, that the Objections you have started against this Mode of Taxation, seem to me unanswerable. [Though, I trust, you will have more Generosity, than to tell the Prime Minister, *that this is my Opinion*; least he should deny me a Bishoprick, which you say I am aiming at; and which certainly is not likely to be obtained by this Manner of Proceeding.] But alas! while you were so eager in demolishing the ministerial Citadel for *compelling* an *American* Taxation,—you forgot, that by the very same Means, you were undermining your own Edifice for a *gratuitous* Revenue.

FOR 1st.—It plainly appears, that even your own Plan for obtaining a gratuitous Revenue, *from such a People* as you have described, cannot succeed, in *Fact*, without both an Auction-Room, and an Auctioneering-Hammer. Indeed you yourself are so conscious of the Truth of this Observation, that, at Page 59, you do not scruple to represent the Matter in a Point of View still more dishonourable and base, by borrowing the Idea of a Set of Gamblers crouding round a gaming Table. "The Parties are the Gamesters; but Government keeps the Table and is sure to win at last." Now, which of these two delicate Similes, the Auction-Room, or the gaming Table, you choose to prefer, in order to do Honour to your *American* Friends and *Patrons*, is a Matter of Indifference to me. But one Thing is certain, that if any Revenue, in any Shape, or on any Terms, is to be obtained from such honourable Assemblies, as you have here described; those who *harangue*, and *lead*, and *govern* in each Assembly must be *bought off*:—Or as you elegantly phrase it, on a similar

Occasion, "They must be won by great Honours and great Emoluments [all at the Expence of *Old England*] to the Service of the State; otherwise they will prove very formidable Adversaries to Government:. They will grow stubborn and litigious; become prompt in Attack, ready in Defence, and full of Resources." And therefore it must undoubtedly follow, that the more free and unrestrained these patriotic, gaming, or auctioneering Demagogues shall become, the more they will pride themselves on their own Importance, and the higher will be the Price, which they will demand for their Services to *Great-Britain*.

BUT, 2dly.—You bring another Objection against Lord NORTH's Scheme at P. 55, which militates much more strongly against your own. Your Words are, "Suppose the Colonies were to lay the Duties which furnished *their Contingent*, upon the Importation of your Manufactures; you know you would never suffer such a Tax to be laid. You know too, that you would not suffer many other Modes of Taxation." Now, if instead of the Word *Contingent*, which is Lord NORTH's, we insert *Free-Gift*, which is yours; I ask any Man of plain, common Sense, whether the Objection is not at least equally strong against your Plan, as against his?— In Fact it is much stronger. For as there would not be that *legal* and *constitutional* Call for making voluntary *Presents*, as for furnishing necessary *Contingents*; the Consequence would be, that both the Provincial Representatives, and their Constituents would naturally say, if the *rich English* Nation will expect *Presents* from us *poor Americans*, we must raise them by laying Taxes on their own Manufactures;—And then, whatever such Imposts may amount to, they will in the Event promote the Industry and Manufactures of our own Country:—I say, this is the natural Language, which most Men would hold on such an Occasion, and more especially *Americans*. But you, Sir, I own, have a very different Idea of Men, and Things. You say at Page 60, "My Hold of the Colonies is in the close Affection, which grows from *common Names*, from kindred Blood, from similar Privileges, and equal Protection. These are Ties, which, though light as Air, are as strong as LINKS OF IRON." Alas! dear Sir, *England* has already to its Cost, found all these Ties and Connections, to be, indeed, light as Air! Yes, I say,—*England* has experimentally found them to be *no Links* at all, if put into Competition with *present Interest*; much less to be *Links of Iron*:—She has, I repeat and insist upon it, made this unwelcome Discovery concerning Colony-Gratitude, even from the Moment that each Infant-Colony could stand alone, without the Assistance of the Parent-State.

IN short, there is something astonishingly absurd in the very Supposition, that a People so addicted to Chicane, as you have painted these *Americans* to be; and who most undoubtedly have devised many disingenuous Artifices against paying their just Debts to their *English* Creditors;—should all on a sudden, by the mere Magic of your enchanting Metaphors, be so changed and altered, as not only to become very honest, very exact, and punctual in their Dealings; but also very liberal, geneorus, and munificent. And here again, I willingly submit to be ranked in the Number of those poor, ignorant Beings, whom you condescend to mention at Page 61. "All this I know well enough, will sound *wild* and *chimerical* to the PROFANE HERD of those vulgar and mechanical Politicians, who have no Place among us [in the House of Commons;] a Sort of People, who think that nothing exists but what is gross and material; and who, therefore, far from being qualified to be Directors of the great Movement of Empire are not fit to turn a Wheel in the Machine."

Now, Mr. Director of the great Movement of Empire! Will you permit (and it is the only Boon I ask) an obscure Person, whose Province it is to turn only one of the inferior Wheels,—I say, will you permit me to appear in your Presence, whilst you are personating a great Minister of State in this new-intended patriotic Administration?

> *O Diva, gratum quæ regis Antium,*
> *Presens vel imo tollere gradu*
> *Mortale corpus, vel superbos*
> *Vertere funeribus triumphos!*

THE first Act of your Directorship will undoubtedly be

> ————————*Superbos*
> *Vertere funeribus triumphos!*

That is, to turn out the present Set of Ministerial Blunderers, *that profane Herd of vulgar and mechanical Politicians*, who fancy, that Officers are necessary to collect a Revenue, and Laws to enforce the Payment;—then to repeal every penal Statute for compelling the good People of *England* to pay Taxes *against their own Consent*;—to discharge, of Course, those gross and material Beings, called Custom-House Officers, Excise-Men, &c. &c. &c. and to trust entirely to the copious Revenue which shall arise from the *voluntary Flow of heaped-up Plenty, bursting from the Weight of its own rich Luxuriance*, FREE GIFTS AND VOLUNTARY DONATIONS. Methinks, Sir, I see you acting your grand ministerial Part, with great Dignity and Propriety in this new and busy Scene. Methinks I see vast Crouds around you, all pressing forwards, all joyfully pouring forth their *free-will Offerings* for the Service of the State, in the *exuberant Plenty* of rich Luxuriance.   And I too, who never was at a ministerial Levee but three Times in my Life, and that about twenty Years ago,— I also wish most ardently to attend on such an Occasion.   And that I may not come empty-handed, for we shall all be *Givers*, and no *Receivers*, I will humbly beg Leave to bring this Pamphlet with me, and to lay it at your Feet, in Token of that Duty, Gratitude, and Respect, with which I have the Honour to be,

Great and worthy Sir!

Your most devoted, and

Most obedient humble Servant,

JOSIAH TUCKER.

A TREATISE CONCERNING CIVIL GOVERNMENT

EDITORIAL NOTE

Part III of the *Treatise* is not included in this reprint. A list of *errata*, prefixed to the original, is omitted, and the corrections are made in the text.

A

TREATISE

CONCERNING

CIVIL GOVERNMENT,

IN

THREE PARTS.

PART I.

THE NOTIONS OF MR. LOCKE AND HIS FOLLOWERS, CONCERNING THE ORIGIN, EXTENT, AND END OF CIVIL GOVERNMENT, EXAMINED AND CON- FUTED.

PART II.

THE TRUE BASIS OF CIVIL GOVERNMENT SET FORTH AND ASCERTAINED; ALSO OBJECTIONS ANSWERED; DIFFERENT FORMS COMPARED: AND IMPROVEMENTS SUGGESTED.

PART III.

ENGLAND'S FORMER GOTHIC CONSTITUTION CEN- SURED AND EXPOSED; CAVILS REFUTED; AND AUTHORITIES PRODUCED: ALSO THE SCRIPTURE DOCTRINE CONCERNING THE OBEDIENCE DUE TO GOVERNORS VINDICATED AND ILLUSTRATED.

BY JOSIAH TUCKER, D. D.

DEAN OF GLOCESTER.

LONDON:

PRINTED FOR T. CADELL, IN THE STRAND.

M.DCC.LXXXI.

THE

PREFACE.

THE long preliminary Discourse, which I had printed in the Specimen dispersed among my Friends, is now totally suppressed. It was their Opinion, that such an Enumeration of Errors, as were there collected together out of Mr. LOCKE's Writings, was needless at present; because the Degree of Infallibility, which had been ascribed to his Name and Works, is now greatly lessened. They likewise thought, that such a Catalogue of Mistakes might be made Use of by a subtle Adversary, as an Handle to divert the Attention of the Reader from the main Point, to that which was foreign to the principal Design. I am persuaded of the Justice of these Remarks; and I do hereby request my worthy Friends to accept of my grateful Acknowledgments.

My present Design is to speak to another Subject. Some there are, who think it impossible, that such a Man as Mr. LOCKE, ever meant to patronize those dangerous Consequences, which his Followers, and particularly Mr. Molineux, and Dr. Price, have deduced from his Principles. They wish, therefore, that all the Censure might fall on the Disciples, and not on the Master. In Reply to this, I submit to them and the Public the following Considerations.

1st. — That Mr. MOLINEUX was Mr. LOCKE's Acquaintance, Correspondent, and bosom Friend; that he sent him his famous Book, the Case of Ireland, as a Present; — that he desired his Opinion thereon; which though Mr. LOCKE declined, or rather deferred to give; — yet he never once hinted, that Mr. MOLINEUX had mistaken his Principles, and had ascribed Consequences to him, which he must disavow. [See the whole Correspondence carried on between them in Mr. LOCKE's Works.] Moreover, I desire it may be taken Notice, that Mr. LOCKE survived Mr. MOLINEUX several Years; — during which Time the Protestants of Ireland were worked up into intemperate Heats by those very Notions of unalienable Rights and Independence, which Mr. LOCKE's and Mr. MOLINEUX's Writings had infused into them, and which they have since adopted in so decisive a Manner; yet during all this Time Mr. LOCKE was silent, and made no Remonstrance against such Proceedings. He never intimated to any one, as far as I can learn, that they were mistaken in their Inferences; nor did he retort upon them, by saying, that if they thought they had a Right to deduce such Consequences from his Principles, — the Papists of *Ireland* [the original Natives of the Country and the vastly greater Majority of the People] had a much stronger and clearer Right to shake off the Protestant Yoke, and to assert their native Independence, and unalienable Birth-right.   This he probably would, or at least this he *ought* to have done, had he really thought, that Mr. MOLINEUX and the *Irish* deduced such Conclusions from his Premises, as it was incumbent on him to disavow.

2dly.   GRANTING for Argument's Sake, that the DEAN of *Glocester* is either so illiterate, or so blinded with Prejudice, that he cannot see the obvious Meaning of the plainest Propositions in Mr. LOCKE's Work, — yet what shall we say of Dr. PRICE, his warmest Advocate, and professed Admirer?   Is he too in the same Situation with the DEAN of *Glocester?* All the World must allow, that Dr. PRICE is a very learned Man, and a clear Writer: And if his Prejudices *for* Mr. LOCKE, and the DEAN of *Glocester's* Prejudices *against* him, should make them agree in the same Opinions; it must at least be allowed, that such a Clashing of opposite Prejudices hath produced that marvellous Effect, which opposite Prejudices never produced before.   The Doctor and I see Mr. LOCKE's Principles with the same Eyes; we understand them in the same Sense; and all the Difference between us, is, That he admires them, and *glories* in the Consequences of them, which I do not, and think them to be extremely dangerous to the Peace and Happiness of all Societies.

BUT *3dly*, And to end this Controversy at once: Let some Friend to Truth, blessed with greater Discernment than the DEAN of *Glocester*, or even than Dr. PRICE, take Mr. LOCKE's Book in hand, and shew from the natural Construction of the Words, and the Scope and Tenor of the Context, that both of us [and indeed, that all in general, Admirers, and Non-Admirers] have hitherto mistaken Mr. LOCKE's true Sense and Meaning: And in the next Place, let this happy Interpreter or clear-sighted Commentator point out, how such and such Passages ought to have been understood; and what Consequences ought to have been deduced from his Writings, different from all these, which have been deduced before.

THIS would be coming to the Point; and when *satisfactorily* performed, a most useful Work it will be. — I, for my Part, shall be exceeding glad to have it proved, that I was mistaken.   [For I never wish to find Fault without great and urgent Cause]   Therefore if this Point can be satisfactorily proved, I do hereby pledge myself to make a public Recantation.

This I promise to do, because I think it to be no Manner of Disgrace to the Character of an honest, fallible, well-meaning Man to say, I am now convinced that *I was in an Error*; *and I ask Pardon*.

Two Things more I shall beg Leave to add and these I borrow from Mr. LOCKE's own Preface to this very Book on Government.

"FIRST, that cavilling here and there, at some Expression, or little Incident of my Discourse, is not an Answer to my Book.

"SECONDLY, That I shall not take Railing for Arguments; nor think either of these worth my Notice: — Though I shall always look on myself as bound to give Satisfaction to any one, who shall appear to be conscientiously scrupulous in the Point, and shall shew any just Grounds for his Scruples."

THE

NOTIONS

OF

Mr. LOCKE, &c.

CHAP. I.

The only true Foundation of Civil Government, according to Mr. LOCKE and his Disciples:—All Governments whatever being so many Encroachments on, and Violations of, the unalienable Rights of Mankind, if not founded on this Hypothesis.

I N ORDER to shorten this Controversy as much as possible, and to strike every Thing out of it foreign to the Subject, I shall first shew wherein I agree with Mr. LOCKE and his Followers, and 2dly wherein I differ from them.

FIRST then I agree with him, and his Disciples, that there is a Sense, in which it may be said, that no Man is born the *political* Subject of another. Infants the Moment they are born, are the natural Subjects of their Parents: They are also entitled by the Law of Nature, as well as by human Laws, to the Protection and Guardianship of that State, within whose Jurisdiction they are born [nay, indeed they are entitled to Protection whilst in Embrio] though they neither did, nor could enter into any Contract with the State for that Purpose. Therefore in this Sense, they are justly deemed the *natural-born* Subjects of such a Country. This is the Language of all Laws, and of every Government. But in a *metaphysical* Sense, a Man cannot be a Subject before he is a Moral Agent; for it is Moral Agency alone, which renders him amenable, or subject to any Law, or Government. However, as he is born with the Instincts and Dispositions of a social Creature, he necessarily becomes a Member of some Society or other, as soon as he has an Opportunity, by the very Impulse of his Nature, if there are any human Beings within his Reach to associate with. But whether this Association must always be formed by Means of an *express mutual Compact*, Engagement, and Stipulation, or whether it *cannot* be formed [I mean *justly* and *rightly* formed] any other Way, is the important Question now to be determined.

411

2dly.   LET the Mode of entering into this Society be what it may, whether by express Covenant, or otherwise, I perfectly agree with Mr. LOCKE and his Disciples, that the Government and Direction of such a Society is a Matter of public *Trust,* and not of private *Property:* — a Trust to be executed for the Good of the whole, and not for the private Advantage of the Governors and Directors; — any otherwise, than as they themselves will find their own Account in promoting the Prosperity of the Community.

3dly.   I VERY readily allow, that if these Trustees should so far forget the Nature of their Office, as to act directly contrary thereunto in the general Tenor of their Administration; — and if neither humble Petition, nor decent Remonstrance can reclaim, and bring them to a Sense of their Duty;—then Recourse must be had to the only Expedient still remaining, *Force of Arms:* — And I add further, that the critical Moment for the Application of such a desperate Remedy, seems to be, — when the Evils suffered are grown so great and intolerable, without any reasonable Prospect of Amendment, that, according to the most impartial Calculation, they evidently over-balance those which would be brought on by resisting such evil Governors.

ALL these Points being previously settled, there can be no Controversy between Mr. LOCKE's Disciples and me about the patriarchal Scheme in any of its Branches, or indeed about any Sort of an indefeasible hereditary Right whatever: — Much less about unlimited passive Obedience, and Non-resistance.   For I think we are all perfectly agreed, that neither Kings, nor Senators, neither Patrician-Republics, nor Plebean-Republics, neither hereditary, nor elective Governors can, in the Words of the great Poet,

Have any Right *divine* to govern *wrong.*

And if Sovereigns have no Right to do wrong, the Subjects must certainly have a Right to prevent them from doing it.   For it is clear, that in such a Case the People cannot offend against the righteous Laws of God, or the just Laws of Man, in defending their own Rights.

THE Question, therefore, the *sole* Question now to be decided, is simply this, "Whether THAT Government is to be justly deemed an USURPATION, which is not founded on the *express* mutual Compact of all the Parties interested therein, or belonging thereunto?"   *Usurpation* is a Word of a most odious Sound; and Usurpations and Robberies are Things so detestably bad, that no honest, or good Man can wish them Prosperity, or even Existence.   It is therefore to be hoped for the Honour of human

Nature, and the Good of Mankind, that some Governments or other, besides those of Mr. LOCKE's modelling, or approving, may be found in the World, which deserve a better Fate, than that which is *due* to Robberies and Usurpations.

BUT let us now hear the Opinion of this great Man himself, and of the most eminent of his Followers, concerning the Origin, and only true Foundation, of Civil Government, according to their System.

QUOTATIONS *from Mr.* LOCKE.

Mr. LOCKE, in his 2d. Treatise concerning Government, Chap. viii. *of the Beginning of political Societies*, delivers himself in these Words:

"§ 95. MEN being, as hath been said, [in the former Chapters] all free, equal, and independent, — *no one* can be put out of this Estate, and subjected to the political Power of another, *without his own Consent*. The only Way, whereby any one divests himself of his natural Liberty, and puts on the Bonds of Civil Society, is by *agreeing* with other Men to join and unite in a Community, for their comfortable, safe, and peaceable Living one among another, in a secure Enjoyment of their Properties, and a greater Security against any that are not of it.   This any Number of Men may do, because it injures not the Freedom of the rest: They are left as they were, in the *Liberty* of a *State* of *Nature*.   When any Number of Men have so consented to make one Community, or Government, they are thereby presently *incorporated*, and made one Body politic, wherein the *Majority have a Right to act*.

"§ 98. AND thus, that which begins, and actually concludes any political Society, is nothing but the Consent of a Number of *free* Men, capable of a Majority to unite, and incorporate into such a Society.   And this is that and *that only*, which did, or COULD give Beginning to *any lawful* Government in the World.

"§ 116. 'TIS true, that whatever Engagements or Promises any one has made for himself, he is under the Obligation of them, but cannot by any Compact whatever *bind* his *Children*, or *Posterity*.   For his Son, when a Man, being altogether as free as the Father, any Act of the Father can no more give away the Liberty of the Son, than it can of any Body else.   He may indeed annex such Conditions to the *Land* he *enjoyed*, as a Subject of any Common-Wealth, as may oblige his Son to be of that Community, if he will enjoy those Possessions, which were his Father's:— Because that Estate being his Father's Property, he may *dispose*, or *settle* it as he pleases.

"§ 119. EVERY Man being, as hath been shewn, naturally free, and nothing being able to put him into Subjection to any earthly Power, but his *own Consent*, it is to be considered, what shall be understood to be a sufficient Declaration of a Man's Consent to make him subject to the Laws of any Government.   There is a common Distinction of an *express*, and a *tacit* Consent, which will concern our present Case.   Nobody doubts, but an express Consent of any Man entering into any Society, makes him a perfect Member of that Society, a Subject of that Government.   The difficulty is, what ought to be looked upon as a *tacit Consent*, and how far it binds; *i. e.* how far any one shall be looked on to have consented, and thereby submitted to any Government, where he has made no Expressions of it at all.   And to this I say, that every Man, that hath any Possession or Enjoyment of any Part of the Dominions of any Government, doth thereby give his tacit Consent, and is as far forth obliged to Obedience to the Laws of that Government, during such Enjoyment, as any one under it, whether this his Possession be of Land to him, and his Heirs for ever; — or a Lodging only for a Week, or whether it be barely travelling freely on the High Way: And it in Effect reaches as far as the very being of any one within the Territories of that Government.

"§ 120. To understand this the better; — Whosoever therefore from thenceforth by Inheritance, Purchase, Permission, or other ways, enjoys any Part of the Land so annexed to, and under the Government of that Common-Wealth, must take it with the Condition it is under; that is, of submitting to the Government of the Common-Wealth, under whose Jurisdiction it is, as far forth as any Subject of it.

"§ 121. But since the Government has a *direct* Jurisdiction *only* over the Land, and reaches the Possessor of it (before he has *actually* incorporated himself in the Society) *only* as he dwells upon, and enjoys that, the Obligation any one is under by Virtue of such Enjoyment, to submit to the Government, begins and ends with the Enjoyment: So that whenever the Owner, who has given nothing but such *tacit* Consent to the Government, will by Donation, Sale, or otherways quit the said Possession, he is at Liberty to go, and incorporate himself into any other Common-Wealth, or to agree with others, to begin a new one in *vacuis locis*, in any Part of the World they can find free, and unpossessed.

"§ 122. But *submitting* to the Laws of any Country, living *quietly*, and enjoying *Privileges* and *Protection* under them, ☞ makes not a Man a Member of that Society: — Nothing can make a Man so, but his ☞ actually entering into it by *positive* Engagements, and *express* Promise and Compact.

CHAP. IX. *Of the Ends of Political Society and Government.*

"§ 123. IF Man in a State of Nature be so free, as hath been said: If he be *absolute Lord* of his own *Person* and Possessions, *equal* to the greatest, and SUBJECT TO NO BODY, why will he part with his Freedom, why will he give up this Empire, and subject himself to the Dominion and Controul of any other Power? To which it is obvious to answer, that tho' in the State of Nature he hath such a Right, yet the Enjoyment of it is very uncertain, and constantly exposed to the Invasion of others. For all being Kings as much as he, every Man his equal, and the greater Part no strict Observers of Equity and Justice, the Enjoyment of the Property he has in this State is very unsafe, very insecure. ☞ This makes him willing to quit his Condition; which however free, is full of Fears, and continual Dangers.

"§ 127. THUS Mankind, notwithstanding all the Privileges of the State of Nature, being but in an ill Condition, while they remain in it, are quickly *driven* into Society.

CHAP. XI. *Of the Extent of the Legislative Power.*

"§ 138. THE supreme Power [the Legislature] cannot [lawfully, or rightly] take from *any Man* any Part of his Property without his own Consent.

"§ 140. 'TIS true, Governments cannot be supported without great Charge; and 'tis fit every one who enjoys his Share of the Protection, should pay out of his Estate his Proportion for the Maintenance of it. But still it must be with his own Consent, *i. e.* with the Consent of the Majority, giving it either by themselves, or by their Representatives *chosen* by them.

CHAP. XVII. *Of Usurpation.*

"§ 198. WHOEVER gets into the Exercise of any Part of the Power [of governing] by other Ways than what the Laws of the Community have prescribed, hath no Right to be obeyed, tho' the Form of the Common-Wealth be still preserved: Since he is not the Person the Laws have appointed, and consequently not the Person the People have consented to. Nor can such an Usurper, or *any* deriving from him, EVER have a Title 'till the People are both at Liberty to consent, and have actually consented to allow, and confirm him in the Power he hath till then *usurped.*"

Extracts from Mr. MOLYNEUX'S *Case of* Ireland *being bound by Acts of Parliament in* England.   Dublin, *printed* 1698, *and dedicated to King* WILLIAM: *And lately reprinted by Mr.* ALMON, *with a long Preface, exciting the* Irish *to rebel, and promising full Liberty, and Security to the Papists, if they will join in this good Work.*

"*Page* 18. IF a Villain with a Pistol at my Breast, makes me convey my Estate to him, no one will say, that this gives him any Right.   And yet just such a Title as this has an unjust Conqueror, who with a Sword at my Throat forces me into Submission; that is, forces me to part with my natural Estate and Birth-right, of being governed *only* by Laws, to which I give my *Consent*, and not by his Will,—or the Will of any other.

"*P*. 26 *and* 27. FROM what has been said, I presume it pretty clearly appears, that an unjust Conquest gives no Title at all; — that a just Conquest gives Power only over the *Lives*, and *Liberties* of the actual Opposers, — but not over their *Posterity* and *Estates*; — and not at all over those that did *not concur* in the Opposition.

"THEY that desire a more full Disquisition of this Matter, may find it at large in an INCOMPARABLE Treatise concerning the true Original, Extent, and End of Civil Government, Chap. xvi.   This Discourse is said to be written by my excellent Friend JOHN LOCKE, Esq.

"*Page* 113. I shall venture to assert, that the Right of being subject ONLY to such Laws, to which Men give their *own* Consent, is so *inherent* in *all* Mankind, and founded on such *immutable* Laws of Nature and Reason, that 'tis not to be aliened, or given up by any Body of Men whatever.

"*Page* 150. ALL Men are by Nature in a State of Equality, in respect of Jurisdiction or Dominion. — On this Equality of Nature is founded that Right, which ALL Men claim of being free from *all* Subjection to positive Laws, 'till by their *own Consent*, they give up their Freedom by entering into Civil Societies for the common Benefit of all the Members thereof. ☞ And on this Consent depends the Obligation of all human Laws.

"*Page* 169. I HAVE no other Notion of *Slavery*; but being bound by a Law, to which I do not consent.

"*Page* 170. IF *one* Law may be imposed without Consent, *any other Law whatever* may be imposed on us without our Consent.   This will naturally introduce taxing us without our Consent.   And this as necessarily destroys our Property.   I have no other Notion of Property, but a Power of disposing of my Goods *as I please*, and not as another shall command. Whatever another may *rightly* take from me, I have certainly no Property in. To *tax* me without Consent is little better, if at all, than down-right *robbing me.*

Extracts from Dr. PRIESTLY'S *Essay on the first Principles of Government. Second Edition.* London, *printed for* J. JOHNSON, 1771.

SECTION I. *Of the first Principles of Government, and the different Kinds of Liberty.*

"*Page* 6. To begin with first Principles, we must for the Sake of gaining clear Ideas on the Subject, do what almost all political Writers have done before us, that is, We must suppose a Number of People existing, who experience the Inconvenience of living independent and *unconnected:* Who are exposed without Redress, to Insults and Wrongs of every Kind, and are too weak to procure to themselves many of the Advantages, *which they are sensible might easily be compassed by united Strength.* These People, if they would engage the Protection of the whole Body, and join their Forces in Enterprizes and Undertakings calculated for their common Good, must voluntarily resign some Part of their natural Liberty, and submit their Conduct to the Direction of the Community: For without these Concessions, such an Alliance, attended with such Advantages, could not be formed.

"WERE these People few in Number and living within a small Distance of one another, it might be easy for them to assemble upon every Occasion, in which the whole Body was concerned; and every thing might be determined by the Votes of the Majority. ☞ Provided they had *previously* agreed that the Votes of a Majority should be decisive. But were the Society numerous, their Habitations remote, and the Occasions on which the whole Body must interpose frequent, it would be absolutely impossible that all the Members of the State should assemble, or give their Attention to public Business. In this Case, though, with ROUS-SEAU, *it being a giving up of their Liberty*, there must be Deputies or Public Officers appointed to act in the Name of the whole Body: And in a State of very great Extent, where all the People could never be assembled, the whole Power of the Community must necessarily, and almost irreversibly, be lodged in the Hands of these Deputies. In *England*, the King, the hereditary Lords, and the Electors of the House of Commons are these *standing* Deputies: And the Members of the House of Commons are again the *temporary* Deputies of this last Order of the State.

SECTION II. *Of Political Liberty.*

"11. IN Countries, where every Member of the Society enjoys an equal Power of arriving at the supreme Offices, and consequently of directing the Strength and the Sentiments of the whole Community, there is a State of the most perfect political Liberty. On the other Hand, in Countries where a Man is, by his Birth or Fortune, excluded from these Offices, or from a Power of voting for proper Persons to fill them; that Man, whatever be the Form of the Government, or whatever Civil Liberty, or Power over his own Actions he may have, has no Power over those of another; he has no Share in the Government, and therefore has *no political Liberty at all*. Nay his own Conduct, as far as the Society does interfere, is, in all Cases, directed by others.

"IT may be said, that no Society on Earth was ever formed in the Manner represented above. I answer, it is true; because all Governments whatever have been, in some Measure, compulsory, tyrannical, and oppressive in their Origin. But the Method I have described must be allowed to be the ONLY equitable and fair Method of forming a Society. And since every Man retains, and can never be deprived of, his natural Right (founded on a Regard to the general Good) of relieving himself from all Oppression, that is, ☞ from every Thing that has been imposed upon him without his own Consent, this must be the only true and proper Foundation of all the Governments subsisting in the World, and that to which the People who compose them ☞ have an unalienable Right to bring them back.

"*Page* 40. THE Sum of what hath been advanced upon this Head, is a Maxim, than which nothing is more true, that every Government, in its original Principles, and antecedent to its present Form, is an *equal Republic*; and consequently, that *every* Man, when he comes to be sensible of his natural Rights, and to feel his own Importance, will consider himself as fully equal to any other Person whatever. The Consideration of Riches and Power, however acquired, must be entirely set aside, when we come to these first Principles. The very Idea of Property, or Right of *any Kind*, is founded upon a Regard to the general Good of the Society, under whose Protection it is enjoyed; and nothing is properly a *Man's own*, but what general Rules, which have for their Object the Good of the whole, give to him. To whomsoever the Society delegates its Power, it is delegated to them for the more easy Management of public Affairs, and in order to make the more effectual Provision for the Happiness of the whole. Whosoever enjoys Property, or Riches in the State, enjoys them for the Good of the State, as well as for himself: And whenever those Powers, Riches, or Rights of *any Kind* are abused to the Injury of the whole, that awful and ultimate Tribunal, in which every Citizen hath an equal Voice, may demand the Resignation of them: And in Circumstances, where *regular Commissions* from this abused Public cannot be had, EVERY MAN, who has Power, and who is actuated with the Sentiments of the Public, may *assume a public Character*, and bravely redress public Wrongs. In such dismal and critical Circumstances, the stifled Voice of an oppressed Country is a loud Call upon every Man, possessed with a Spirit of Patriotism, to exert himself. And whenever that Voice shall be at Liberty, it will ratify and applaud the Action, which it could not formally authorise.

Extracts from Dr. PRICE's *famous Treatise, Observations on the Nature of Civil Liberty, &c. a new Edition,* 12mo. *corrected by the Author, Price Three-Pence, or One Guinea per Hundred.*

PREFACE *to the* FIFTH EDITION.

"THE Principles on which I have argued, form the Foundation of every State, as *far as it is free;* and are the same with those taught by Mr. LOCKE.

"*Page* 1. OUR Colonies in *North-America* appear to be now determined to risque, and suffer every Thing, under the Persuasion, that *Great-Britain* is attempting to *rob* them of that Liberty, to which *every Member* of Society, and all civil Communities, have a *natural*, and an UNALIENABLE Right.

SECTION I. *Of the Nature of Liberty in general.*

"*Page* 1. IN order to obtain a more distinct and accurate View of the Nature of Liberty as such, it will be useful to consider it under the four following general Divisions.

[IT is hard to say, what could have been the Doctor's Motive for dividing Human Liberty into four Parts; for, in reality, there are either not so many Sorts of Liberty, or a great many more. "Physical Liberty, which is the Foundation of the rest, is, as the Doctor well observes, that Principle of *Spontaneity,* or *Self-Determination*, which constitutes us *Agents*; or which gives us a Command over our Actions, rendering them properly *ours*, and not Effects of the Operation of any *foreign* Cause." Therefore possessing, or enjoying this Power within ourselves, we apply it to various Purposes, according as *Duty*, *Interest*, or *Inclination* — call it forth: Consequently if every distinct, or possible Application of it is to be considered as the Exertion of a distinct Species of Liberty, we may be said to have Sorts without Number. But the Doctor himself, as will be seen below, joins Religious and Civil Liberty in the same Class. And he also observes, that there is one general Idea that runs through them all, the Idea of Self-Direction, or Self-Government.]

"First, Physical Liberty, — Secondly, Moral Liberty, — Thirdly, Religious Liberty, — and, Fourthly, Civil Liberty.

"*Page 3.* As far as in any Instance, the Operation of any Power comes in to restrain the Power of Self-Government, so far *Slavery* is introduced: Nor do I think that a preciser Idea than this of *Liberty*, and *Slavery*, can be given.

Section II. *Of Civil Liberty, and the Principles of Government.*

"*Page 4.* In every free State *every Man* is his *own Legislator.* — All Taxes are *free Gifts* for public Services. — All Laws are particular Provisions or Regulations established by common Consent for gaining Protection and Safety.

"From hence it is obvious, that Civil Liberty, in its *most perfect* Degree, can be enjoyed only in *small States*, where every Member is capable of giving his Suffrage in *Person*; and of being chosen into public Offices. When a State becomes so numerous, or when the different Parts of it are removed to such Distances from one another, as to render this impracticable, a *Diminution* of Liberty necessarily arises. — Though all the Members of a State should not be capable of giving their Suffrages on public Measures *individually* and *personally*, they may do this by the Appointment of *Substitutes* or *Representatives*.

"*Page 7.* In general, to be *free* is to be guided by one's own Will; and to be guided by the Will of another is the Characteristic of Servitude. This is particularly applicable to political Liberty.

Section III. *Of the Authority of one Country over another.*

"*Page 15.* As no People [either individually, or collectively] can lawfully surrender their religious Liberty, by giving up their Right of *judging* for themselves in Religion, or by allowing any human Being to *prescribe* to them, what *Faith* they shall *embrace* or what *Mode* of *Worship* they shall *practice*; so neither can any civil Societies [* either individually, or collectively] lawfully surrender their civil Liberty, by giving up to any extraneous Jurisdiction their Power of legislating for themselves, and disposing of their Property. Such a Cession, being inconsistent with the unalienable Rights of Human Nature, would either not bind at all, or bind only the Individuals who made it. This is a Blessing, which no Generation of Men can give up for another; and which, when lost, a People have always *a Right to resume.*

OBSERVATIONS *on the foregoing* EXTRACTS.

THUS I have finished my Extracts from Mr. LOCKE, and some of the most *eminent* of his Disciples; — Men, whose Writings, (we charitably hope, not intentionally, or maliciously; — though *actually*) have laid a Foundation for such Disturbances and Dissentions, such mutual Jealousies and Animosities, as Ages to come will not be able to settle, or compose. Many more Passages might have been added from other celebrated Writers on the same Side; but surely these are full enough to explain their Meaning. And therefore from the following may be collected.

I. THAT Mankind do not spontaneously, and, as it were, *imperceptibly* slide into a Distinction of Orders, and a Difference of Ranks, by living and conversing together, as Neighbours and social Beings: — But on the contrary, that they naturally shew an Aversion, and a Repugnance to every Kind of Subordination, 'till dire Necessity compells them to enter into a solemn Compact, and to join their Forces together for the Sake of Self-Preservation. Dr. PRIESTLY, the fairest, the most open, and ingenuous of all Mr. LOCKE's Disciples, excepting honest, undissembling ROUSSEAU, has expressed himself so clearly and fully on this Head, that I shall beg Leave to quote his Words again, tho' I had mentioned them before.

"To begin with first Principles, we must, for the Sake of gaining clear Ideas on the Subject, do what almost all political Writers have done before us, that is, we must suppose a Number of People existing, who

---

* I have added the Words *individually, or collectively*, as being Terms absolutely necessary for making the Cases of Religious, and Civil Liberty to tally with each other, according to the Doctor's System. In the Concerns of Religion, every Man must act for himself, and not by a Deputy: He has a Conscience *of his own*, which he cannot delegate to, or entrust with any Proxy or Representative whatsoever. If therefore the Cases are parallel, as the Doctor supposes them, there can be no such Thing allowed as *Representatives* in Parliament; but every Voter must attend in Person. — This is an important Point; therefore more of this hereafter.

experience the Inconvenience of living independent and unconnected; who are exposed without Redress, to Insults and Wrongs of *every Kind*, and are too weak to procure to themselves many of the Advantages, which they are *sensible* might easily be compassed by united Strength. These People, if they would engage the Protection of the whole Body, and join their Forces in Enterprizes and Undertakings calculated for their common Good, must *voluntarily resign* some Part of their natural Liberty, and submit their Conduct to the Direction of the Community: For without these *Concessions*, an Alliance cannot be formed.''

HERE it is very observable, that the Author supposes Government to be so entirely the Work of *Art*, that *Nature* had no Share at all in forming it; or rather in *predisposing* and *inclining* Mankind to form it.   The Instincts of Nature, it seems, had nothing to do in such a complicated Business of Chicane and Artifice, where every Man was for driving the best Bargain he could; and where all in general, both the future Governors and Governed, were to be on the catch as much as possible.   For this Author plainly supposes, that his first Race of Men had not any innate Propensity to have lived otherwise, than as so many *independent, unconnected* Beings, if they could have lived with tolerable Safety in such a State: In short, they did not feel any Instincts within themselves kindly leading them towards associating, or incorporating with each other; though (what is rather strange) Providence had ordained, that this Way of Life was to be so essentially necessary towards their Happiness, that they must be miserable without it: — Nay, they were driven by Necessity, and not drawn by Inclination to seek for *any Sort* of Civil Government whatever. And what is stranger still, it seems they were sensible, that this Kind of Institution, called Government, to which they had no natural Inclination, but rather an Aversion, and whose good or bad Effects they had *not* experienced, might easily procure Advantages which they then wanted, and protect them from many Dangers, to which they were continually exposed, in their independent, unconnected State.   All these Things, I own, are strange Paradoxes to me: I cannot comprehend them.   However, fact it is, that almost all the Writers on the republican Side of the Question, with Mr. LOCKE at the Head of them, seem to represent Civil Government at the best, rather as a *necessary* Evil, than a *positive* Good; — an Evil to which Mankind are obliged to submit, in order to avoid a greater.

BUT if Mr. LOCKE and his Followers have not granted much to human Nature in one Respect, they have resolved to make abundant Amends for this Deficiency in another.   For tho' they have not allowed human

Nature to have any innate Propensities towards the first Formation of civil Society; — yet they do most strenuously insist, that *every Man*, every Individual of the human Species hath an unalienable Right to chuse, or refuse, whether he will be a Member of this, or that particular Government, or of none at all.

THIS was to be my second Observation: And a material one it is. For Mr. LOCKE and his Followers have extended the Privilege of voting, or of giving *actual* Consent, in all the Affairs of Government and Legislation, beyond what was ever dreamt of before in this, or in any other civilized Country; — Nay, according to their leading Principles, it ought to be extended still much farther, than even they themselves have done.

BEFORE this new System had made its Appearance among us, the Right of voting was not supposed to be an unalienable Right, which belonged to *all* Mankind *indiscriminately:* But it was considered as a Privilege, which was confined to those few Persons who were in Possession of a certain Quantity of Land, to Persons enjoying certain Franchises, (of which there are various Kinds) and to Persons of a certain Condition, Age, and Sex. Perhaps all these Numbers put together may make about the Fortieth *Part* of the Inhabitants of *Great-Britain:* They certainly cannot make much more, if an actual Survey and Enumeration were to be made. Whereas the great Mass of the People, who do not come within this Description, are,* and ever have been, excluded by the *English* Constitution from voting at Elections for Members of Parliament, &c. &c. And heavy Penalties are to be levied on them, if they should attempt to vote. Now, according to the Principles of Mr. LOCKE and his Followers, all this is totally wrong; for the Right of voting is not annexed to Land, or Franchises, to Condition, Age, or Sex; but to human Nature itself, and to moral Agency: Therefore, wherever human Nature, and moral Agency do exist together, be the Subject rich or poor, old or young, male or female, it must follow from these Principles, that the Right of voting must exist with it: For whosoever is a moral Agent is a *Person;* and *Personality* is the only Foundation of the Right of voting. To *suppose* the contrary, we have been lately told by a Right Reverend Editor of Mr. LOCKE, is *gross Ignorance*, or something worse: And to *act on* such restraining Principles, by depriving the Mass of the People of their Birth-Rights, is downright Robbery and Usurpation.

III. IF all Mankind indiscriminately have a Right to vote in any

---

* See an express Dissertation towards the Close of this Work on the three Orders of Men formerly in *England*, Slaves, — Tradesmen, — and Gentlemen.

Society, they have, for the very same Reason, a Right to reject the Proceedings of the Government of that Society to which they belong, and to
separate from it, whenever they shall think fit.   For it has been incul-
cated into us over and over, that every Man's Consent ought first to be
obtained, before any Law whatever can be deemed to be valid, and of full
Force. — We have been also assured, that all, and every Kind of Taxes
are merely *Free-Gifts:* Which therefore no Individual Giver is obliged
to pay, unless he has previously consented to the Payment of it.   From
these Premises it undoubtedly follows, that every individual Member of
the State is at full Liberty either to submit, or to refuse Submission to
any, and to every Regulation of it, according as he had predetermined in
his own Mind.   For being his own Legislator, his own Governor, and
Director in every Thing, no Man has a Right to prescribe to him, what
he ought to do.   Others may advise, but he alone is to dictate, respecting his own Actions.   For in short, he is to obey no other Will *but his
own.*

THESE are surely very strange Positions; and yet they are evidently
deduceable, and do naturally result from the Extracts given in this
Chapter.   Nay, there are several others equally paradoxical, and equally
repugnant to every Species of Government, which hath ever yet existed
in the World.   Such Paradoxes therefore deserve a distinct and particular
discussion.

CHAP. II.

*Several very gross Errors and Absurdities chargeable on the Lockian
System.*

The First Species of Error, with its Subdivisions.

THAT Species of false Reasoning, which the Logicians term *a
dicto secundum quid ad dictum simpliciter*, or that which proceeds
from a few Particulars to general Conclusions is so common in
Practice, and steals into the Mind so imperceptibly, that Men can hardly
be too much on their Guard against it. — Considered in its own Nature,
nothing can be more obvious than that a Proposition, which may be
true in a particular Instance, may not be so invariably: And that therefore two such Propositions should never be confounded together, as if
they were synonimous. — Yet the Identity of Words and Sounds often
leads Men to suppose, unless they are very watchful, that there is also
an Identity of Sense.   Many Cases might be given to corroborate and
illustrate this Observation; but perhaps there is no Instance whatever,

which confirms it more strongly than that now before us, the Lockian Principle of the indefeasible Right of private Judgment.

MR. LOCKE in his early Days was a Witness to grievous Persecutions inflicted on the Score of Religion. He saw the Rights of private Judgment exposed to continual Vexations; and he saw likewise, that the Interests of the State were not at all concerned in maintaining that rigid, universal Conformity in Religion, for which the Bigots of those Times so fiercely contended; — nay, that the Principles of Humanity, Justice, and Truth, as well as the Suggestions of sound Policy, plainly required a more extended Plan of religious Liberty: All this he clearly saw: And hence he inferred, and very justly, that every Man had a Right not only to think, but even to act for himself, in all such religious Matters as did not oppose, or clash with the Interests of civil Society. And had he stopt there, and gone no farther, all would have been right; nay, he would have truly deserved the Thanks of Mankind for pleading their Cause so well.

BUT, alas! he extended those Ideas, which were true only in what concerns Religion, to Matters of a mere civil Nature, and even to the Origin of civil Government itself; — as if there had been the same Plea for Liberty of Conscience in disobeying the civil Laws of one's Country, as for not conforming to a Church Establishment, or an Ecclesiastical Institution; — and that the Rights of private Judgment [I mean the open and public Exercise of those Rights] were equally unalienable and indefeasible in both Respects. Indeed it must be confessed, that, had the Cases been truly parallel, a Non-conformist in the one Case ought to have been tolerated equally with a Non-conformist in the other: And I will add, that the whole Merits of the Question depend on the single Point, whether the Cases are parallel, or not.

THUS, for Example, no Man, not even the supreme Magistrate, has a Right to molest me for worshipping God according to the Dictates of my own Conscience, provided I do nothing in that Respect, which can *fairly* be construed to hurt the Property of another Man, or disturb the Peace of Society. Therefore I may be a Papist, as well as a Protestant in my speculative Opinions, and yet do nothing, which can, when justly interpreted, be accounted to be injurious to others: Nay I will not scruple to declare, that I may be a Jew, or a Mahometan, a Gentoo, or a Confucian, and yet be a loyal Subject to my Prince, an honest Man, and an useful Member of the Community. Therefore, if *Toleration were ever

---

* Matters of strict Right are undoubtedly very different from Matters merely prudential; and in the Reason of Things a Line ought always to be drawn between them.

to be extended as far as in Reason, and Justice, and good Policy it ought to go, it ought to be so large as to comprehend every religious Sect whatever, whose Doctrines, or rather whose Practice [for 'tis chiefly by Men's Practice that we ought to determine, whether any Sect deserves to be tolerated, or not; — therefore I say, whose *Practice*] proves them worthy to enjoy the Protection of the State. And there is a very particular, and a most important Reason to be given, why this Liberty of Conscience in religious Matters ought to be extended as far as ever the Safety of the State will permit: It is, because in the Affairs of Conscience no Man can act, or be supposed to act as Proxy for another; no Man can be a Deputy, Substitute, or Representative in such a Case; but every Man must think, and act personally for himself. This is the Fact; and in this Sense it is very true, that the Rights of private Judgment are absolutely unalienable: — but why unalienable? — It is because they are *untransferable:* And therefore every Man must of Necessity, after having used the best Lights and Helps he can obtain, be his own Legislator, (under God) his own Governor, and his own Director in the Affairs of Religion.

APPLY now these Ideas to the Case of Civil Government; and then see, what strange Consequences will arise.

1. IN the first Place, if the same Train of Reasoning is to be admitted in both Cases, then it is evident, that none, no, not Women nor Children, ought to be excluded from the Right of voting on every political Question that may occur; unless indeed you can prove beforehand, that those, whom you exclude, have no Conscience at all, and have no Sense whatever of Right and Wrong: — And you must prove likewise that they are incapable of judging in this Respect, not only to the Satisfaction of others (which perhaps would not be difficult) but also of themselves; — which it is humbly apprehended, will be a most arduous Task: Yet, I say, you

---

Every peaceable and useful Subject has a Right to the Protection of the State under which he lives, in order to enjoy the Fruits of his Industry. And it would be an Act of flagrant Injustice to debar him of that Protection either in whole, or in Part. But he cannot have the same just Pretensions to demand to be created a Magistrate or Judge, or to be raised to Posts of Honour, Power, or Profit of any Kind; because these Offices do not belong to him of *Right*, in the mere Capacity of a Subject. Therefore as they are Matters of a prudential Nature, they must be disposed of according to the Discretion of the ruling Powers in every State, and not according to the Ambition, or Expectation of the Candidates. There may be many Things, in respect of Capacity, Education, outward Circumstances, Party-Attachments, &c. &c. which may disqualify from certain Offices those, who, in other Respects, are useful Subjects, and therefore entitled to Protection. It belongs ultimately to the Prudence of the Legislature to settle the Boundaries.

must prove it, otherwise you will exclude those from voting, who have just Cause to think, on your State of the Case, that their Right is as unalienable as your own; and you will act diametrically opposite to the grand fundamental Principle of your Founder by excluding them. In short, to use your own Language, you yourself will be an Usurper and a Robber. Therefore draw the Line, if you can, between the promiscuous Admission, or Exclusion of such Voters as these, according to the Lockian System.

2dly. IF the Cases are parallel, then the unalienable Rights of private Judgment are not to be set aside by the Determination of any Majority whatever. For as a Plurality of Votes is no Evidence of Infallibility, a Man's inward Conviction may not be altered by his being overpowered by Numbers. What then is he to do in such a Case? The Answer is obvious: He must follow the Dictates of his own Conscience; and he has an *unalienable* Right so to do. Well, but Mr. LOCKE himself acknowledges, that were this to be allowed, that is, were the Minority to be permitted to act contrary to the Sense of the Majority, civil Government itself could not subsist. True: He makes such an acknowledgement: And by so doing he reduces himself to the Dilemma, either of giving up his whole System, that no Man is bound to obey those Laws, which have been imposed upon him without his own Consent; — or he must shew that a Man doth consent, and doth not consent, at the same Time, and in the same Respect. Indeed it is evident, that he found himself greatly perplexed, when he came to touch on this Point; and that he seemed to be like a Man got into a dangerous Pass, full of Precipices, which he wished not to see, in passing through, by not looking about him. Dr. PRIESTLY is more open and ingenuous. He did not attempt to shun the Difficulty, which he saw was unavoidable, but prepared to encounter it, as well as he could. — For after having observed [see the Quotation, P. 14] that every thing in a small Society might be determined by the *personal* Votes of the Majority present, he prudently adds, "provided they had *previously* agreed, that the Votes of the Majority should be decisive." Such a Conduct of the Doctor's is commendable; though the Argument he made use of is weak and trifling: Weak it is, because, 1st. It is impossible for the Doctor to prove, that previous Meetings were held in every, or perhaps in any State whatever, in which it had been *unanimously* determined, that the Votes of the Majority should be decisive; — and trifling, because, 2dly. were it even possible to prove the Fact, it could be of no Service to the Doctor's Cause; inasmuch as an *unalienable* Right is of such a Nature, that it cannot be surrendered to a Majority: And even if this were attempted, "such a Cession, (to adopt the Words of Dr. PRICE,) would either bind not at all, or bind only the Individuals, who made it." And so could be of no Continuance. Therefore in every View, it is strictly demonstrable, that according to the Lockian System, nothing less than *Unanimity* in every Measure can keep such a Society as this from the Danger of breaking to Pieces every Moment; for a single *dissentient Voice*, like the VETO's of the republican Tyrants of *Poland*, is sufficient to throw the whole Constitution of the State into Chaos and Confusion. In short, strange as it may seem, the unalienable Right of one single refractory Member of the Diet destroys, or annuls the unalienable Rights of the whole: Nor is there any other effectual Remedy to be applied in this desperate Disorder, but that of a Sabre held over the Dissentient's Head, with a Threat of cleaving him down, if he should persist in the Exercise of his unalienable Right. This indeed has been known to have produced *Unanimity*, when other Motives could not prevail. What infatuated Politics are these! And to what Mazes of Error, and Absurdity, do Men run, when they stray from the Paths of common Sense! But

Thirdly. FOR the very same Reason, that the Members of a Lockian Republic cannot surrender their unalienable Rights to a Majority, be it small or great, they cannot likewise *transfer* their unalienable Right of voting to Deputies or Representatives to act and vote for them. For this in Fact comes to the same Thing with the former. They must therefore all vote in Person or not at all. Now this is a direct Inference, which necessarily follows from the foregoing Premises. And it is an Inference, which Dr. PRICE is so far from disavowing, when applied to the Case of the *Americans*, that he glories in, and greatly exults upon it. "As no People (says he) [see the Quotation, Page 21] can lawfully surrender their religious Liberty, by giving up their Right of judging for themselves in Religion, or by allowing any human Being to prescribe to them, what Faith they shall embrace, or what Mode of Worship they shall practice; so neither can any civil Societies lawfully surrender their civil Liberty, by giving up to any extraneous Jurisdiction their Power of legislating for themselves, and disposing of their Property. Such a Cession being inconsistent with the *unalienable Rights* of human Nature would either bind not at all, or bind only the Individuals who made it. This is a Blessing, which no Generation of Men can give up for another; and which, when lost, a People have always a *Right to resume*."

THE Doctor's Aim in this Paragraph, we plainly see, was to defend his beloved *Americans* against the supposed Usurpation of the *English* over their unalienable Rights. Be it so: But was he aware, that the very same Argument holds equally strong against the Appointment of Assemblies of Representatives in *America*, and of an House of Commons in *England*, as against the *English* Legislature ruling over the *American?* Was he, I say, aware of this? And yet nothing can be more evident than that the same Argument concludes equally strong in both Cases, if it concludes at all. For Example, "No People, says the Doctor, can lawfully surrender their Religious Liberty, by giving up their Right of judging for themselves in Religion, or by allowing any human Being to prescribe to them, what Faith they shall embrace, or what Mode of Worship they shall practice." I agree with him most heartily on that Head: — But then I add [and I am sure, what I add in this Case, Dr. PRICE will readily allow] that no one Individual can depute another to judge for him, what Faith he shall embrace, or what Mode of Worship he shall practice. — And then what is the Consequence? Necessarily this, That if the Cases between Religion and Civil Government be similar, as the Doctor supposes them to be, no one Individual can appoint another to judge for him, what Laws shall be propounded, what Taxes shall be raised, or what is to be done at Home or Abroad, in Peace, or in War: — But every Person, who has this indefeasible, this unalienable, incommunicable, and untransferable Right of voting, judging, and *fighting*, must vote, judge, and *fight* for himself. — This I say is a necessary Consequence from the Premises: And I defy the acutest Logician to deduce any other Inference from the above Hypothesis.

HONEST, undissembling ROUSSEAU clearly saw, where the Lockian Hypothesis must necessarily end. And as he was a Man who never boggled at Consequences, however extravagant or absurd, he declared with his usual Frankness, that the People could not transfer their indefeasible Right of voting for themselves to any others; and that the very Notion of their choosing Persons to represent them in these Respects, was a Species of Contradiction. According to him, a Transmutation of Persons could not be a greater Impossibility than a Translation of those Rights, which were absolutely incommunicable. And therefore he adds [See his Social Compact, Chap. 15. Of Deputies or Representatives] "The *English* imagine, they are a free People: They are however mistaken: They are only such during the Election of Members of Parliament. When these are chosen, they become *Slaves* again." The Doctors PRIESTLY and PRICE do not indeed absolutely join ROUSSEAU in condemning the Use of national Representatives; but it is plain, that they admit them with a very ill Grace, and, with great Reluctance. Nay, they are so far consistent with themselves as to declare very freely, that

the Admission of them is an *Infringement* on Liberty, more or less: —
even on that Liberty, which they proclaim aloud, every Man has an unalienable Right to *resume, as soon as ever he can*.   Moreover, they accord
with ROUSSEAU in another general Position; that true, genuine Liberty
can only be enjoyed in a State so very small, [undoubtedly they must
mean some paultry Village, consisting of a few thatched Cottages]
that the People can personally attend on all Occasions. — Much more
might have been added: But surely we have now had enough, and to
spare, of this Kind of Reasoning *a dicto secundum quid ad dictum simpliciter*.   And the Upshot of the whole is this, That if Men will jumble those
Ideas together, which ought to be kept separate, they must fall into palpable Errors, and be guilty of great Absurdities in the Course of their
Reasoning.

The second Species of Errors, with its Subdivisions.

THOUGH I have observed before, yet I must repeat again, that according to the Lockian System, civil Government is not *natural* to Man.
It seems, the Seeds of it were not originally implanted in our Constitutions by the Hand of Providence.   For had that been the Case, we might
reasonably have expected, that they would have sprouted up, and germ-
inated of their own Accord, at least in some Degree; without dating the
Origin of Government from the jealous Efforts of political Contrivance,
mutual Compacts, and reciprocal Stipulations.   We might, I say, have
naturally supposed, that Government and Mankind were, in a Manner,
coeval; and that they had grown up together from small Beginnings, or a
Kind of infant State, 'till they had arrived at a maturer Age; in regard to
which we might further have supposed, that they became more, or less
polished and improved, according as they had received different Cultures
from human Art and Industry.   All this, I say, we might have naturally
supposed; but all these Supposition we must entirely lay aside, in order
to adopt another Mode of accounting for the Origin of civil Government.
For according to the Lockian System, Mankind had no natural Inclination towards any Government whatever: But having found the Evils of
Anarchy to be quite intolerable, they resolved at last to submit to the
Evil of Government, as the lesser of the two.   But in order that they
might guard against the Dangers to be feared on this Side, as well as felt
on the former, they determined not to part with their precious natural
Liberty, 'till Security had been given, that such a Cession should not be
turned to their Disadvantage.   Therefore they solemnly stipulated,

that in case their new Lords and Masters should not please them, they might return again to their dear State of Nature, and begin the Work of Government *de novo*, if they chose so to do, or remain as they were, all equal, all free, and independent.   And thus it came to pass, that they, who were under no Sort of Subjection one Moment, became the Subjects of a regular Government the next: And from being no Ways connected with any Body politic whatever, they were transformed, all on a sudden, by the Magic of the *original* social Contract into most profound Politicians.   The Lockians have not yet vouchsafed to tell us, where any one single Copy of this famous original Contract is to be found, — in what Language it was written, — in whose Hands deposited, — who were the Witnesses,—nor in what Archives we are to search for it.   But nevertheless they have taken Care to supply us very amply with Inferences and Deductions resulting from it; — as if it had been a Thing, which had been already proved and admitted, and concerning whose Existence no further Questions ought to be asked.   We must therefore, as we cannot be favoured with a Sight of the Contract itself, attend to those Inferences and Deductions, which they say, are derived from it.

THE first Inference is, that no Man ought to be deemed a Member of a State Politic 'till he has enrolled himself among the Number of its Citizens by some express and positive Engagement.   "For, says Mr. LOCKE, [See the Quotation, Page 9.] submitting to the Laws of any Country, living quietly, and enjoying Privileges and Protections under them, makes not a Man a Member of that Society; — nothing can make a Man so, but his actually entering into it by positive Engagement, and express Promise and Compact."   And again: "Whatever Engagements or Promises any one has made for himself, he is under the Obligation of them, but cannot by any Compact whatever bind his Children or Posterity.   For his Son, when a Man, being altogether as free as his Father, any Act of the Father can no more give away the Liberty of the Son, than it can of any Body else."   [See the Quotation, Page 9.]

ALL this is certainly agreeable to the Nature of the original Contract here supposed.   For if we can believe the one to have existed, and to have been the only Foundation of Civil Government, we must allow, that the other ought to have followed.   Here therefore let us suppose a Case. — A Man, tho' born in *England*, and of *English* Parents, yet, it seems, is not by Birth an *Englishman;* that is, he is not a Subject of this Realm, 'till he has made himself so, by some express Covenant and Stipulation. This methinks, appears a little strange: But stranger Things will soon follow.   For, after having weighed all Circumstances, and considered the Matter pro. and con. he at last consents to become a *British* Subject, and gets his Name enrolled among the Number of its Citizens.   Then he marries, and has a Family; and by living under the Protection of the *English* Constitution, where every Man is safe in the Enjoyment of the Fruits of his Industry, [not to mention those honourable, and *lucrative* Imployments he obtained under the Government.]   He grows rich and wealthy, leaving seven Sons behind him, all grown up to Man's Estate: To the six younger he gives ample Fortunes in moveable Goods and Chattles, and to the eldest a large Estate in Land.   The Question therefore is, Among what Species of political Beings are these seven Children to be classed?   And are they the Subjects of *Great-Britain*, or are they not, before they have entered into an express Covenant or Treaty with the State for that Purpose?

ACCORDING to Mr. LOCKE's leading Idea, he ought to say, that they are the Subjects of no Government upon Earth; but that they are all in the original State of Nature, perfectly free from any political Laws or Connection whatever, entire Masters of themselves, and absolutely independent Beings.—Consequently, that they ought to be allowed to do as they pleased relative to *Great-Britain* [*Great-Britain* I say, which *had enriched their Father, had nursed them up, and protected them* from their very Infancy to mature Estate] and that if they chose to forsake her in any particular Period of her Distress, she ought not to stop their Emigration, or to hinder them from carrying all their *moveable* Goods and rich Effects with them [their *Immoveables*, no Thanks to them, they could not carry] much less ought she to demand the Assistance either of their *Persons*, or of their *Purses*, as a Matter of *strict Right*, if they should *not* be disposed to grant it.   This I say, is the true Lockian Principle without Exaggeration: And let the impartial World be the Judge, whether it be consistent with common Sense, or common Honesty. Indeed Mr. LOCKE himself seems to have been aware, that he had carried this Point too far: For he allows, that one of these Sons, suppose the eldest, that is, the Landholder, might be obliged, by the Nature of his *Tenure*, to defend that State, within which his Lands lay, and to make some Recompence to it for the long Protection and many Blessings he had enjoyed.   Yet, that he might never lose Sight of his darling Ideas of Consent, or Contract, he calls the Accepting of the Estate on these Terms, a *tacit Consent*.   And then he adds: "He [the Father] may indeed annex such Conditions to the Land he enjoyed, as a Subject of any Common-Wealth, as may *oblige* his Son to be of that Community, if he will enjoy those Possessions, which were his Father's; because the Estate

being the Father's Property, he may dispose, or settle it *as he pleases.*"
And thus Reader, at last we seem to have gotten one of these Sons, the
Landholder, back again into the Service of his Country, in order to defend
it in Times of Danger. But let us not be too sure: For this Lockian
Principle is of such a changeable Nature, and is endowed with so much
Versatility, that it will often give us the Slip, when we think we have the
firmest hold of it.

HERE therefore let it be asked, — If a Man hath a Right to annex what
Conditions he pleases to the Possession of his Landed Estate after his
Decease, — By what Law did he acquire that Right? And who gave
him that Authority? Surely in a *mere State of Nature* he could have
had no such Right; — because the Land could be no longer *his*, than
whilst he himself was using and occupying it; — which 'tis plain, he
could not do after he was dead. Granting therefore, that in a State of
Nature he had a Right, during his Life-Time, to appropriate to himself
a certain Portion of Land for his own Sustentation, [which yet ROUSSEAU
with great Shew of Reason positively denies.] Still that Land must
revert to the Public, and become *common* again after his Decease. But
if it should be said, that he derived the Right of bequething Land, and of
annexing various Conditions to the Bequest, from the positive Laws of
civil Society (which is the Truth of the Case, and which Mr. LOCKE
himself is obliged to allow, by stiling this Father a Subject of some
Commonwealth) Then I ask, Why could not the Commonwealth, if it so
pleased, exercise the same Right itself, which it had empowered the
Father to exercise? Why could not the State oblige the other six Sons,
as well as the eldest, to perform the several Offices, and discharge the
Duties, civil and military, of loyal Subjects, if the Exigencies of the State
should so require? Or if there be any essential Difference between the
two Cases of moveable Property, and immoveable, respecting the Duty
and Allegiance due to Government; — shew the Difference if you can.
In short, what is it, about which we have been so long disputing? For,
after all it is plain to a Demonstration, that we must allow at last, what
ought to have been allowed at first; *viz.* That Protection and Allegiance,
between Prince and People, are reciprocal Ties, and that the one necessarily infers the other, without the Formality of an express personal
Covenant, or positive Stipulation; so that if the Duty of Protection be
performed on the one Side, that of Allegiance ought to be observed on the
other, and *vice versa.* An Author, not inferior to Mr. LOCKE, or any of
his Disciples, in the Defence of *true* Liberty, both Civil and Religious, and
who is acknowledged to be an excellent Judge of the *English* Constitution,

thus expresses himself on this important Subject. "Natural Allegiance is founded in the Relation every Man standeth in to the Crown, considered as the Head of that Society whereof he is *born a Member*; and on the peculiar Privileges he deriveth from that Relation, which are with great Propriety called his *Birthright*. This Birthright nothing but his own Demerit can deprive him of; it is *indefeasible* and *perpetual*. And consequently the Duty of Allegiance which ariseth out of it, and is *inseparably* connected with it, is in Consideration of Law likewise *unalienable* and perpetual." [*See* FOSTER'S *Reports. Introduction to the Discourse on High Treason.*]

2dly. The Assertion, that Taxes are a Free Gift, and not a Debt due to the Public, is another strange Inference resulting from Mr. LOCKE'S Idea of an original Contract. Indeed had Government been that vague, unsettled, and precarious Thing, which the Lockian System represents it to be; without any better Foundation to rest upon, than the Breath and Caprice of each Individual; — then it would have been very true, that those, who supported it by their voluntary Contributions, were the *Givers*, or *Donors* of their respective Sums. But doth the Idea of such a Benefaction at all accord with the Idea of a Tax? Surely no: For a Tax in the very Nature of it, implies something compulsory, and not discretionary; something, which is not in our own free Choice, but is imposed by an Authority superior to our own: Whereas a mere Gift, or free-will Offering implies just the contrary. However, as I said before, it is not the Inference itself, which is here to blame; for had the Premises been true, the Inference would have been just enough; and therefore we must trace the Error higher up. Here then be it observed, that it can never be true, that Providence hath left Mankind in a State of such total Indifference respecting Government, that it should depend on their own Option, whether they will have any Government, or none at all. I say, this can never be true of the Species in general; whatever particular Exceptions there might be of here and there a wayward Individual, who ought to be regarded as a Monster deviating from the common Course of Nature. In fact, the Instincts and Propensities of Mankind towards social* Life, are in a Manner so irresistible, that I might almost say, Men will as naturally seek to enjoy the Blessings of Society, as they do to obtain their daily Food. In the one Case it is not left to their own Choice, whether they will eat or not eat, drink or not drink (for

---

* It will be distinctly shewn in the first Chapter of the second Part, that a social State among such Creatures as *Men* must necessarily produce a Government of some Kind or other.

kind Nature has determined that Point for them); but it is left to themselves to judge and to choose, in many Instances, what Kinds of Food, and of Liquids they will use, how they will have them prepared, and whether they will make a proper, or improper Use of these Destinations of Providence. Just so, or nearly so, in my Opinion, is the State of human Nature respecting Government. For Providence seems to have determined for them, that there shall be *a Government* of some Sort or other; and then to have left it, for the most Part, to themselves to fix on the Form or Mode, and to regulate the several Appendages belonging to it, according to their own good Liking, Judgment, and Discretion. Now, if this be the Case, that is, if there must be a Government of some Sort, or in some Shape or other; it then necessarily follows, that certain *Means* must be found out for the Support of such an *End*. What, therefore, it may be asked, are these Means? And which are the best, the least burthensome, and the most unexceptionable? [For in this Respect likewise, as well as in the former, a great deal is left to the Prudence and Sagacity of Mankind to weigh and consider, and provide for themselves.] The Answer to which Question is the following, That there can be devised but three Ways for the Support of any Government whatever, viz. Personal Service, — Crown Lands, — or public Taxes; — and each of these Methods (such are the Imperfections of human Nature) is attended with Conveniences and Inconveniences not a few.

AND (first) as to *personal Service.* — In the Infancy of a very small State, and before the Arts of Civilization had sufficiently taken Place, personal Service seems to have been the first, and indeed the only Idea, which would occur. For when Men had nothing else to pay, towards that Government which protected them, *they must have paid that*; — paid it, I mean, as a Matter of Duty, Debt, or Obligation, and not as the Lockians suppose, a free-will Offering, or voluntary Service. But it is easy to see, that such a Tribute as this would soon appear to be very burthensome for the Subject to discharge, and not at all convenient for the Prince to receive. In respect to the Subject, were he to be obliged to leave his own private Affairs, in order to attend the Public on all Occasions, civil, military, legislative, and judicial; — there would be hardly any Time left, which he could call his own: His Fields must lie neglected, his Manufacture and his Shop be deserted, and all Business, both in the Way of Agriculture, and of Commerce, by Land and by Sea, be in a Manner at a Stand. In respect to the Prince, the State, or the Public, such a promiscuous Attendance of Persons of all Ranks, Ages, and Professions would be found to be a very great Nusance, and to be productive of many

Evils of various Kinds, without sufficient Benefits to counter-balance them. Add to this, that as the Bounds of the State became extended, the Attendance of Persons living at a great Distance, would become more and more impracticable: So that in every View, this Kind of Tribute, though the Source of all others, must soon be laid aside, and be exchanged for something more useful, and less inconvenient. — Only thus much of this primeval Idea ought always to be retained, that in Times of universal Danger, we must again recur to the original Use of personal Service.   For in such a Case, the Principle of Self-Preservation authorizes every State to summon all its Inhabitants capable of bearing Arms, to be ready to appear in its Defence.   Nor, I trow, would the Lockian Plea of Exemption in such a Case be regarded in any other Light, than as proceeding either from the Fears of an arrant Coward, or from the Schemes and Conspiracies of a Traitor.   In either Light it would certainly meet with its deserved Punishment.   Indeed the very Recital of such a Plea carries so strong a Confutation in it, that nothing stronger can be added: "Gentlemen, though I was born and bred in this Country, and have submitted to its Laws, [when that was attended with some Advantage, and no Danger;] and though I have lived quietly, and enjoyed Privileges and Protection under them; — moreover, tho' the Invader is making great Strides to subdue you, and HANNIBAL is in a Manner at the Gates; — yet I must at present beg Leave to be excused from opposing him: For as I never did actually enter into any positive Engagement, and express Promise and Compact to defend this Country, I am not legally obliged to defend it.   In Fact, I am not a Member of your Society, and therefore you have no Right to press me into its Service." — Thus much for this Part of the Lockian Scheme, that Taxes, alias personal Services, are *free Gifts*. And let all Mankind from the highest to the lowest, from the greatest to the meanest Capacities, be the Judges, what Epithets such a Scheme deserves.

ONCE more; the Case of pressing Sailors for the Sea-Service, is a Confirmation of every Thing which hath been advanced concerning the Necessity of retaining the original Idea of serving the State in Person, and not by Substitutes. For Sailors are a Body of Men, whose Service cannot be performed by any but Sailors; and therefore they are, and, from the Nature of Things, ever must be, liable to serve in Person. Now, were you to call *Pressing* a free Gift, or the voluntary Offer of personal Service on the Part of the poor Sailor that is pressed, what would the World think of you, but that you were either *insane* yourself, or that you esteemed all others to be mere Ideots?   However, your Plea perhaps may be, that tho' the personal Service of Sailors at present is, generally speaking, very far from voluntary; — yet it might have been rendered more desirable, and consequently voluntary [rather *less-involuntary*] were a proper Mode adopted for inviting Sailors to inlist of their own Accord. This I will suppose is your Plea: And the Meaning of it is, — to recommend a *national Register for Seamen*. Great Things have been said of late Years in Praise of such an Institution; but they have been chiefly said by those, who least understood what is meant and implied by it. I myself once thought it a fine Thing; but ever since the Year 1748 (when I had the first Opportunity of examining it on the Spot) I have been thoroughly convinced, that a Register doth not deserve a tenth Part of the Praises, which our modern Patriotic Pamphleteers, and ignorant News-Writers have bestowed upon it. For it is a very operose and intricate Business, not at all calculated for the Dispatch of Trade, and Freedom of Navigation; moreover, it is loaded, in its Consequences, with such an Expence, as renders Freight in *France** excessively dear:—These are the Evils attending it even in Times of Peace; and yet it is of little or no Efficacy in Times of War. For when the Sailors, who have been registered, will not appear to their Summons at their respective Ports, or will not voluntarily surrender themselves up at the Ports where they may happen to be; — the last Resource is *Violence* and *Compulsion*. Now I ask, what is there in this boasted Method, which is a Whit preferable to our own? For we always begin with *Bounties* and *Invitations*; and seldom or never have Recourse to *Pressing*, till the gentler Methods are found

---

* This Circumstance of the Dearness of the French Freight [more than 30 per Cent. dearer than the English] renders the Conduct of the French Court, in supporting the Independency of *America*, and granting a Freedom of Navigation (at least in part) between *Old France*, the *French Islands*, and the *American Continent*, one of the most impolitic Measures that ever that Nation adopted. For, as the very *Forté* of the *Americans* consists in the Cheapness of their Navigation, and as they are a People more addicted to Chicane of every Kind, to Quirks and Quibbles in the Law, and have greater *Invention* that Way, than any People upon Earth (even according to the Confession of their best Friends); they, with the Assistance of their new Allies, the *French* Planters of *Martinico, Guadaloupe, &c. all united in one common Interest*, will evade the restraining Laws of *Old France*, in Spite of every Effort of a French Ministry to the contrary. This, I will venture to predict, will be the Consequence in Process of Time. And then the *Americans* will engross almost the whole of that Carrying-Trade to themselves, which used to be the best Nursery of Seamen for the *French* Navy. What Infatuation is this! But I forbear — The silly groundless Notion, that the Separation of *America* would be the Ruin of *England*, hath done more to advance the real Interests of *England*, than we could, or, at least, would have done for ourselves. May we profit by these Blunders of others, and see our own real Interests, before it be too late!

to fail. So that, after all, we are much on a Par with the *French* in Times of War, and feel none of the Inconveniencies of their Registers in Times of Peace. The late ALEXANDER HUME, Esq; Member of Parliament for *Southwark*, spent many Years in framing a Bill for a national Register of Seamen; and as he was a Man of strong natural Parts, and had had long Experience in nautical Affairs, it was natural for him to conclude, that he had succeeded in correcting the many Evils and Imperfections of the *French* Register. This Bill, I think, was once read in the House of Commons, and ordered to be printed. At Mr. HUME's Request I got it laid before the Society of Merchant Adventurers in *Bristol*, in order to have their Opinion; and I received for Answer, that, bad as the Mode of pressing was, both Merchants and Seamen, and all Parties concerned, would prefer it to the Cloggs and Shackles, and various restrictive Clauses contained in the registering Bill of Mr. HUME. It seems, the Idea of a Register is revived again; and great Expectations are founded on some promising Scheme of that Nature. My sincere Wish is, that what has appeared so plausible to several Gentlemen in Theory, may become as favourable to Liberty, as beneficial to Commerce, and as practicable in Fact as they themselves expect, or desire. But in the mean Time, and 'till that happy Period shall arrive, when a sufficient Number of Sailors shall be induced by some inviting Scheme or other [call it a Register, or call it what you please] to enlist of their own Accord; the Mode of Pressing (there is no Help for it) must be retained. — And need I add, that the Man, who is pressed, is not a *Volunteer?* Need I go about to prove that he is not his own Legislator? and that he is neither self-governed, nor self-directed?

2dly. A second Mode of supporting Government is by Crown Lands, or large Domains. Now this is another Species of personal Service, together with the Addition of some Part of the Produce of such Lands either to be taken in kind, or to be exchanged for Rent. How such vast Tracts of Country came into the Possession of the respective *Regents* in Society (which we know was antiently the Case, at least all over Europe) is a Matter not to be easily explained. Probably these immense Estates were principally owing to two very different Causes, viz. The patriarchal Rights, — and the Rights of Conquest. The Patriarchs, or the Progenitors of Nations, it is natural to suppose, took Care to secure vast Tracts of the most commodious Land to their own Use: — and very probably they divided the Remainder, as Mankind encreased and multiplied, among the Subaltern Heads of Families; — subject nevertheless to such Restrictions and Conditions, and to such personal Duties and

Services, as were judged to be necessary, whether civil, military, or servile, in the infant State of Society. The Histories of the Beginning of all Clans and Tribes, and Hords of People sprung from the same Original, seem to confirm this Hypothesis. But it ought to be observed, that the strict, patriarchal Plan could not have obtained here in *Britain*, ever since the Invasion of the *Saxons*, *Danes*, and *Normans* (and possibly of the *Romans*) whatever it might have done in the more antient Times of the *Britons*, the primeval Natives of the Country.

ANOTHER Origin of Domain Lands is, — *That of Conquest:* For when a Country was conquered by any of the barbarous Nations, the Commander in Chief, and his Subalterns, *alias* his Comites, Earls, Thanes, or Generals, divided the Territory into two Shares or Lots: — The one was reserved, and generally speaking it was a very large one, for the Use of the Commander in Chief, in order to support the Dignity of his Station, to entertain his numerous Vassals and Dependants, and likewise to raise, feed, and cloathe a considerable Body of Troops at his own Expence, and out of the Tenants on his own Domain, without calling for further Assistance. The rest of the Country was divided and subdivided among the several Chieftains, according to their respective Ranks and Stations, their military Merit, the Number of their Followers, the Favour of the Prince, and other Circumstances. In this Allotment each Chieftain had, for the most Part, the same Jurisdiction, both civil and military, over his respective Tenants, as the Prince had over those on his own Domain; — each Chieftain had also the same Right to demand the personal Services of those who held under him, whether military, or servile, as the Prince himself: — But each Chieftain was likewise obliged to do Suit and Service at the Court of the Sovereign, and to attend him in his Wars, in the same Manner, and almost in the same Form, as his military Tenants were obliged to do Suit and Service to him. This, therefore, together with Escheats and Forfeitures, Compositions and Confiscations, and the Perquisites arising from Escuage, Reliefs, Heriots, Alienations, Wards and Liveries, Pre-emptions, Purveyances, Prisages, Butlerages, &c. &c. constituted the main Branches of the Gothic Revenues and Prerogatives. Now I ask, is there any one Thing in all this Catalogue, which in the least resembles the Idea of a Free-Gift, and voluntary Donation? On the contrary, is it not evident, that the very best, and most innocent, of these Prerogatives were *compulsory* in some Degree, and that the most of them were arbitrary and tyrannical in a shocking Degree? In Fact, there hardly ever was a *civil* Constitution more productive of Slavery and Oppression on the one Extreme, — or of Tumults, Insurrections, and Rebellions on the other, than the Gothic. Indeed it ill deserved the Name of a *civil* Constitution: For it partook much more of a *military*, than of a civil Nature; being little better than the Idea of an Encampment, or rather of a Cantonment of Forces extending far and wide, according to the Dimensions of the Country; and subject to such Alterations, as these great Distances and Dispersions made necessary. One Thing is certain, that true civil Liberty was a Stranger to every Country, where the Gothic Constitution was introduced; — and that what was called Liberty in those Days, and what our modern Patriots so much boast of in ours, as the Glory of *Old England*, was the Liberty which one Baron took of making War on, and plundering the Estates, and murdering the Vassals of another — and tyrannizing over his own: — And that when Half a Score of these petty Tyrants could band together, and make a common Cause, they were a Match for the King himself, who otherwise would have been a Tyrant over them. Now this was the boasted Liberty of the Gothic Constitution: And because that in *France* and *Spain*, *Sweden* and *Denmark*, and perhaps in some other Countries, this Power of the Barons of doing Mischief, and of being a Plague to each other, to their own Vassals, and to all around them, has been much curtailed, if not totally abolished; — therefore we are told by very great and grave Historians, that these Countries, have lost their Liberties.* Indeed I grant, that the Kings of each of these Countries

---

* Of a like Nature is that other Assertion of our modern Patriots, that in former Times, there was no such Thing as a Standing-Army; but that this is a modern Invention, to enslave Mankind. Indeed, if they meant to say, that the Term itself was not in use in former Times, they are right; for the Word *Standing-Armies* is of modern Date. But if they wish to propagate a Notion, (which they certainly do) that the Thing itself, the *Substance*, was not in Being 'till very lately, they are guilty of a wilful Misrepresentation; for they *do* know, that the Gothic Constitution necessarily created a Standing-Army in *Fact*, tho' not in *Name*, in every Kingdom, wherever it prevailed. They know also, that the essential Difference between antient and modern Standing-Armies consists in this, that ours are paid in *Money*, and the *Gothic* Troops were paid in *Land:* And that consequently their Forces were much more dispersed, much worse disciplined, much more subject to the Wills and Caprice of their respective Generals and subaltern Officers, *alias* the Barons, and Lords of Manors; and, in short, in every View much more unfavourable to civil Liberty than ours are. — Not many Miles distant from the Place where I now write, the two great Barons, Lord BERKELEY and Lord LISLE, fought a bloody Battle on *Nibley Common*, *Anno*. 1470 [*See* ATKYNS's *Hist. Glocestershire, Page* 577] with 400 Men on a Side, raised in less than 48 Hours, from among their respective Vassals and Dependants. The famous Battle of *Chevy Chace*, is still a more extraordinary Circumstance, according to the antient Song: For in that we are told, that Earl PERCY had made a Vow, that he would be the Aggressor

have risen in Power in Proportion as the Nobles have sunk; but nevertheless I do aver it for a solemn Truth, that the common People have been Gainers likewise. For though they have not *acquired* as much Liberty, as they ought to have, and what is their Right to have, — yet they have obtained a much greater Degree of it every where, *even in Denmark itself*, than ever they enjoyed before.

BUT to pursue this Subject no further: — Be it observed, that the Crown Lands or Royal Domains in antient Times were so very extensive, as to contain a fifth Part of the Lands of *England*, and that the several Rents, and Profits, and Services arising from them, and from the other Branches of the feudal System, were judged to be fully sufficient, without further Aid, to answer all the common Expences of Government*. Nay, it has been computed, that had all the Lands of antient Demesne borne a Rack-Rent according to the present Standard, the Sum total would have been not much short of 6,000,000l. Sterling. And what seems to confirm this Calculation is, that it is pretty well known, that the Estates belonging to what is called the Duchy of *Lancaster* [which

---

in breaking the Peace between the two Kingdoms, by hunting in a Wood that belonged to the House of DOUGLAS. Yet rash and unjustifiable as such a Vow was, the Event shews, that his Pleasure alone was a sufficient Reason for the very Flower of his Vassals and Dependants to attend him in that frantic bravading Expedition. Now here I ask, Were any two modern great Men, any two Dukes, Earls, or Barons, or any two Generals, or Colonels, in the Army, to have a Quarrel with, and to send Challenges to each other (as we are assured was the Case between the Lords BERKELEY and LISLE, and the Earls PERCY and DOUGLAS) would they be able to prevail on any of their Tenants to take up Arms in such a Quarrel? and could they engage, I do not say a Regiment on a Side, but even a single Troop, or Company, to draw a Sword, or fire a Musket in their Defence? Surely no: Yet we are told, that these were the Days in which our brave Fore-fathers enjoyed that glorious Liberty of thinking and acting for themselves, which we, their degenerate Sons, have lost!

* See a very ingenious and instructive Pamphlet, intituled, The Rights of the *British* Legislature to tax the *American* Colonies vindicated, printed for T. BECKET. I differ from this Author in nothing very materially, but in his Calculation of the present Rental of *England*, which he seems to me to have set a great deal too low. Had he attended to the vast Improvements in Agriculture throughout *England* and *Wales*, partly by Skill and good Husbandry, partly by the Enclosure of common Fields, and by the enclosing and cultivating of above a Million of Acres of Commons, Wastes, Forests, Chases, Mountains, Moors, Fens, Marshes, &c. &c. And above all by the prodigious Encrease of Buildings in *London, Bristol, Bath, Birmingham, Liverpool, Manchester*, and in almost every manufacturing Town and District whatever, for these last 40 Years: I say, had he duly attended to the Advance of Rents on these, and on other Accounts, he would have found that the Rack-Rental of *England* and *Wales*, independently of *Scotland*, cannot be so little as 30,000,000l. a Year; a Fifth of which is 6,000,000l.

were little more than the confiscated Estates of four great Barons] would not have been much short of 1,000,000l. Sterling of annual Rent; — supposing, that the several Manors, Hundreds, Parishes, Precincts, Streets, and Houses in *London*, and throughout *England* and *Wales*, which formerly did belong to the Duchy of *Lancaster*; [many of which now claim those Privileges, and Exemptions, which the Dukes and Earls of *Lancaster* once granted to their Tenants;] — I say, supposing that all these Estates were at present in the Hands of one Person, and that he were to receive a Rent for each proportionably to the present Standard, — then, and in that Case, it has been computed, that the Amount of the whole would be little less than 1,000,000l. Sterling.

BUT be this Calculation erroneous, or not, the Fact is certain, that even as low down as the Reign of EDWARD the Fourth, the Crown-Lands, together with the feudal hereditary Revenue, were judged to be adequate to the common Expences of Government.   Indeed, this is not much to be wondered at, when we consider, that the Charges of the Navy, together with the several Appendages of Docks, Yards, Magazines, Fortifications, Victualing and Admiralty Offices, &c. &c. (so expensive at present) scarcely had an Existence in those Days: and that the military Tenures then supplied the Place of a standing Army.   Therefore, as the Crown could support itself, without the Aid of Parliament, it is obvious to any reflecting Mind, that the real and rational Liberty of the Subject could hardly have been enjoyed during all that long Period: — I say, the real and rational, to distinguish it from the *mad, fanatical* Liberty of a *Polish* VETO, which our modern Republicans seem to wish to introduce among us.   In short, when the hereditary Revenue of the Prince, and his hereditary Prerogatives, were so excessively great, as to set him above Controul, by making him independent of the Parliament, what Remedy was to be applied, in Case he abused his Power? — None that I can think of but that one, which is almost as bad as the Disease, and to the common People it was certainly worse; — the Remedy I mean, was that of the great Barons forming a League against him. — I have not scrupled to say, that such a Remedy was worse to the common People than the Disease itself: For there cannot be a clearer, and a more evident Proposition, than that it is far better to be a Subject under the absolute Monarchies of *France* or *Denmark*, than to be a Vassal to a Grandee of *Poland*, or, what is nearly the same Thing, a Slave to a Planter in *Jamaica*.   [But more of this hereafter.]

HOWEVER, as Providence is always bringing Good out of Evil, so it happened, that partly thro' the Profusion of our former Princes, and partly through the Contempt which Queen ELIZABETH had entertained of her Successor, JAMES the First, the Crown-Lands were so dissipated and alienated (notwithstanding the common Law Maxim of *Nullum Tempus occurrit Regi*) that it was impossible for Government even with the utmost Oeconomy, to subsist on the small Pittance of these Lands still remaining. This was the Case when the STUART Family mounted the Throne. And JAMES the First, by his thoughtless, and childish Extravagance, soon made bad to become worse. What then was to be done in such a Situation? — Two Things, and only two, seem to have occurred. The first was, to *command* the Parliament to supply the Place of the former Domain by some Kind of Tax; and in Case the Parliament should refuse, then to have Recourse to the Prerogative itself for raising Money without their Consent: The second was, to yield to the Times with a good Grace, and to sue for that as a *Favour* which, in a certain Sense, could not be strictly and legally demanded as a *Right*. Unhappily for them, they chose the former Method, which begat a long civil War, and ended at last in the total Expulsion of the Family.

Now as this brings us to the Revolution, I will here observe, that it may likewise suggest to our Thoughts, a

3d. MODE of supporting civil Government, viz. by Means of *Taxes*. For tho' Taxes were in Being Ages before, yet the proper Uses and Advantages of them never began to be understood 'till after that Period: Nor indeed are they yet understood so well, and so thoroughly, as the Nature of such a Subject, and its great Importance really deserve.

Two Uses may be made of Taxes, a Primary, and a Secondary; — the primary Use is to support Government, and to defray the several Expences military and civil incurred, or to be incurred thereby: The Secondary is to provide for these Expences in such a Manner, as shall render the Subjects in general the more industrious, and consequently the richer, and not the poorer by such a Mode of Taxation, And I do aver, that every judicious Tax tends to promote the latter of these Uses, as well as the former; — as shall be distinctly shewn in its proper Place. Now as we have already exposed the great Inconveniences, and the many Dangers attending the Allotments of Crown Lands, or public Domains for the Support of Government; — and as we have likewise sufficiently proved, that the requiring of personal Services is a still greater Hardship, and a much sorer Infringement on personal Liberty; — What have we yet left, but *Taxes*, *Duties*, or *Impositions* to descant upon? For in Fact we have no other Choice remaining: — And therefore if we will, or must submit to have Government at all, we must submit to have Taxes;— there being no other Resource.

BUT say the Lockians, Taxes are the Free-Gift of the People: — Nay, they are the Free-Gift of each Individual among the People: "For even the Supreme Power [the Legislature] cannot [lawfully or justly] take from *any Man* any Part of his Property without his own Consent." This is Mr. LOCKE's own Declaration. And Mr. MOLINEUX corroborates it by another still stronger, viz. "To tax me without my own Consent is little better, if at all, than down-right *robbing* me." In short all the Lockians hold one and the same Language on this Head: And therefore you must take their favourite Maxim for *granted*, or you will incur their high Displeasure: "You are an Advocate for Despotism, if you do not acquiesce in this Maxim: You attempt to defend what is down-right Robbery; you are a ministerial Hireling, a dirty Tool, &c. &c."

Now, as there is no answering such Arguments as these, I shall very contentedly let them pass; in order to proceed to some others, which really deserve to be properly stated, and clearly explained.

THEREFORE in the first Place, we must distinguish between *Power* and *Right:* For without this we do nothing. The People in their collective, as well as every Individual in his private Capacity, may have the *Power* of doing many things, which ought not to be done. *Power* therefore doth not in all Cases confer *Right*. This I lay down as a fundamental Maxim: And if I am wrong in this, I shall be wrong in all the rest. In the next Place I observe, that a free Gift implies in the very Idea of it, a Matter of mere *Favour*, and not a Matter of strict *Right:* — Consequently the with-holding of a Favour is not the with-holding of a Right. Being advanced thus far, I have yet to add, that Government itself may be considered in a two-fold View: 1st. As it is in its own Nature, abstracted from the Consideration of this, or that particular Set of Administrators, or of this, or that particular Mode or Form of administering it: And 2dly, as it comprehends the latter as well as the former, being relative to some certain Person or Persons presiding in the State, and to some particular Mode or Form of Government. And then I do assert, that Taxes never ought to be considered as *Free-Gifts*, or Acts of mere Favour, or voluntary Generosity respecting the former; — because Mankind have no *Right* to say, we will have no Government at all; and therefore we will have no Taxes for the Support of it; But respecting the latter, they may have a Right to say in certain Cases, and on particular Emergencies, we will have this, and not that Man to reign over us; — or we do prefer this Form or Mode of Government, and do reject that. Therefore at the *original Settling* of such a Constitution, they may have a Right to consider such special Designations, as particular Free Gifts, or spontaneous Options.

BUT lest I should be misunderstood by the careless and inattentive, or be misrepresented by the malevolent on this Head, I will endeavour to illustrate the Subject by a familiar Example, taken from the Case of the *Americans* themselves, and to confute my Opponents by their own Arguments.

HERE then I will wave my Opinion, that the *Americans* are, and indeed that they ever were, as far as they dared to shew themselves, a most ungrateful, ungovernable, and rebellious People; — I say, I will wave this Notion, and for the present adopt theirs; viz. That the Cruelties and Oppressions, the Miseries and Slavery, which the poor, plundered, ruined and famished *Americans* had long suffered under the tyrannical Yoke of the *English*, were at last become so many, so great, and intolerable, that it was high Time to throw off such a galling Yoke, and assert their native Freedom. Well: They have thrown off the *English* Yoke, and have set up what they are pleased to call *American* Independency. [Would to God they had done so fifty Years ago.] But in what Manner did they set up this Independence? And what did they do on this Occasion? — Did they, for Example, attempt to live in an absolutely independent State, without Order, or Controul, or Subordination of any Sort? No: Did they even pretend to say, that they had a *Right* to live after that Manner, if they saw fit? No; They did not. On the contrary, their own Conduct plainly intimated, that they thought themselves *bound* to have some Government, or other: — And therefore, the only Point which they had to determine [for they did not pretend to determine any other] was, Who should govern, *Americans* or *Englishmen?* — And after what Manner? — Now their Conduct in this Affair clears up all the Difficulty at once, by shewing, that in one Respect, Taxes are a Debt due to the Public for the Support of Government, — and that in another, they are the free Gifts of the People towards a particular Set of Men, to whom they have entrusted the Administration of the Common-Wealth. For though Government was to be supported, and Taxes to be raised, as the best and most eligible Means of supporting it; — yet it did not follow from thence, that Messrs. HANCOCK and ADAMS, WASHINGTON and LAURENS, &c. &c. &c. were, by an unalienable hereditary Right, or indeed by any *legal* Right whatever, ['till after they were chosen] to be the Administrators, or Conductors of it. In one Word, from this View of Things, it evidently follows, that Government itself, or in its own Nature, is INDEFEASIBLE: Though the several Forms of it may undergo various Changes and Alterations, and the old Administrators of it may be set aside, and others chosen in their room, according as certain pressing Exigencies, or very great Emergencies shall require.

AND what has been observed relative to the present Revolution in *America*, is also applicable [supposing the *Americans* to have *Right*, as well as *Power* on their Side] to the Case of the Revolution here in *England*, in 1688. For in that Case, as well as in this, there was evidently a Line drawn, and a Distinction made, between the *Indefectibility* of Government, and the *Defectibility* of the Governors; — Inasmuch as the Convention-Parliament never presumed to start the Question, — Whether there should be any Government, or none at all. — Probably because Mr. LOCKE's System, or rather the Consequences of his System, had not then so far prevailed over the Understanding of Mankind, as to extinguish the Feelings of Common Sense.

BUT nevertheless, tho' the Lockians are, I should think, fairly beaten out of this Hold, which they used to consider as one of their strongest, — they will not, I am persuaded, give up the Cause for lost, seeing they have one Fortress more to retire to, which is built on the express Words of all Acts of Parliament, where Taxes are to be laid, and Money to be raised on the People. The Stile of such Acts being the following, WE GIVE AND GRANT; or Words of a like Import.

NOW in order to go to the Bottom of this Affair, we must return to the Case of Crown Lands, or Royal Domains. For when these, together with the feudal, hereditary Revenues, were sufficient to answer all the ordinary Expences of Government, what Right or Pretence could the Prince have, in a common Way, to ask for more? — And if more was granted him, in what Shape, or under what Denomination, could it be granted but as a *Free-Gift?* — that is, as a Matter of *Favour*, and not of *Right?* Indeed the very Uses, for which these public Benevolences were asked, and to which they were generally applied, is a plain Proof, that they were not understood by either the Givers, or the royal Receiver, as intended to defray the ordinary Charges of Government, but to make Provision for some extraordinary Festivities or Rejoicings:— such as a royal Tilt or Tournament, a Repetition of the Ceremony of Coronation [a favourite Entertainment in those Days;] the making of the King's eldest Son a Knight, the Marriage of a Daughter; &c. &c.; — all of them Matters of public Festivity and Diversion in which Spectacles the great Families of the Kingdom bore a principal Part, — and therefore made the less Objection against such Kinds of Free-Gifts.

HENCE therefore the Propriety of the Expression *give* and *grant*, considered with a View to such Things as these; — or indeed to any others, which are of a similar Nature, where the Parade, and external Grandeur of Government, and not the Vitals or Essentials of it, are concerned.

HOWEVER the Language *give* and *grant* being once introduced, continued to be the Stile of Parliament ever after. — So that in fact, it hath come to pass in this, as well as in many other Cases, that certain Words and Phrases, Usages or Customs, which owed their Originals to particular Causes, have been retained long after the Causes themselves have ceased, and been forgotten, — to the great Confusion of Ideas, and Increase of Error.

IN short, if Stile alone is to govern our Opinions, then we must conclude, that the King of *Great-Britain*, is also King of *France:* An Inference this, which I think no Man in his Senses can make at present; whatever might have been the Case formerly. — And if the Stile *give* and *grant*, can revoke at Pleasure the public Faith solemnly pledged, by turning Matters of *strict Debt* into Matters of *mere Favour*, then our Lockian Politicians have discovered a more expeditious Method of discharging the National Debt, than any of our plodding Projectors had thought of before. For it is only to tell the *public Creditors*, that the Parliament will give and grant *no longer*, and then, — What? — Then these Creditors can have no Right to complain of any Injury or Injustice done them: — Because they ought to have known, that all Taxes are absolutely free Gifts: And therefore it was a Matter of mere Indulgence, (for which they ought to have been very thankful) to have these Gifts and Grants continued to them as long as they were. This happy Discovery will, no Doubt, administer great Consolation to all the national Creditors, both Foreigners and Natives, who have vested their Property, on the Security of Parliament, in our public Funds. And therefore I would humbly recommend it to Dr. PRICE, and his Friends, the *American* Congress, to try to borrow Money on these Terms, towards defraying the Expence of their glorious War.

BUT to pursue such Absurdities no farther, be it observed in general, that the Root, from which these Evils spring, is, that strange Notion so stiffly maintained by all the *Lockians*, — That the Father's being a Subject to any Government, lays no Sort of Obligation on the Son to be a Subject likewise; notwithstanding that he was born under its Jurisdiction, bred and educated under its Protection, and had enjoyed all its Privileges and Advantages from his helpless Infancy 'till he arrived at Man's Estate: Yet, for all this, it seems the State has no Right to consider such a Person as a *Subject:* — She has no just Pretentions to suppose, that he is bound in Duty and Conscience to be obedient to her Laws, to assist her with his Person, or his Purse, or to bear any Part of her Burdens. — On the contrary, she ought to allow, that he has a just, and an *unalienable* Right to refuse to contribute a single Farthing towards any of these Things, unless he had actually given his previous Consent thereunto.   And if you should be curious to know, how such an extravagant Notion as this ever came to enter into the Heads of Men of sober Sense, it is, because they esteem civil Government, even in its best Estate, to be a Kind of unnatural Restraint on the native Freedom of Man: — It is an Evil which he must bear, because he cannot help himself; — but yet which he is continually endeavouring to shake off, in order to become totally free and independent.

So much as to the *primary* Use of Taxes: And the Reader must now determine for himself, whether he will consider them, — I mean, in all Cases *essential* to Government, — to be real Debts due to the Public, as a Compensation for the Enjoyment of its Benefits and Protection, — or to be mere Free-Gifts and voluntary Donations, which every Man has a Right to chuse, or to refuse to pay, as it seemeth best.

THE *secondary* Use of Taxes comes next to be spoken to: But in respect to this I must be very brief, partly on account of having been obliged to be so copious and diffusive in regard to the former Article; and partly because this is itself a Digression from the main Subject, tho' an useful one.   Suffice it therefore for the present just to observe, that I set out on the Strength of two Propositions, which necessarily infer each other, viz. That the Hand of the diligent maketh rich, — and that the Hand of the idle maketh poor.   Therefore all Taxes whatever are to be denominated either good or bad, in Proportion as they promote Industry, or discourage it.   Now were a Survey to be taken of our present System of Taxation, according to this Rule, it would be found, that many of our Taxes are very good ones, — that some are indifferent, partaking of a Kind of neutral State, — and that very few are really bad ones.   Whereas formerly the very Reverse was the true State of the Case; which might easily be made to appear to the Satisfaction of any reasonable, impartial Man, by comparing the whole System of Taxes, Article by Article, as it stands in the present Year 1780, — and as it stood at any Period whatever during the Life-Time of Mr. LOCKE, — or during the golden Days of good Queen BESS, including her Monopolies, — or indeed at any Time, or during any Reign, antecedent to the 8th of GEO. 1, C. 15: — That famous commercial Statute, for which the Authors of it [Sir ROBERT WALPOLE and his Brother] received the most ungrateful Returns from a Set of Mock-Patriots, and from a deluded commercial Nation.

EXPERIENCE plainly tells us (and therefore we must cease to wonder) that the Generality even of intelligent People, do not reason at all, or at least will not reason to the Purpose concerning the Tendency of Taxes: That is, (they will not enquire, whether they tend to promote Idleness or Industry, to transform Drones into Bees, or Bees into Drones. In Fact, that which they mostly attend to, is the Quantity of Money, or the Sum Total produced by any given Tax. If the Sum should be a great one, then they generally pronounce that they are sadly oppressed, and most heavily taxed, and complain most bitterly of their Rulers: In regard to which, they are sure that Mock-Patriots and seditious News-Writers will echo back their Complaints from every Quarter. But if the Sum produced should be a very small one, then they think, that they are not quite so heavily taxed; and therefore they are not altogether so profuse in their Lamentations. Now, nothing can be more fallacious than such Conclusions: Inasmuch as it is strictly demonstrable, that a Tax, which would hardly produce 100,000l. a Year to the Revenue, might yet be more oppressive, more impoverishing, and a much greater Stab to Industry of every Kind, than others which produce TEN MILLIONS. For the Nature of Taxes is such, that they may be compared to the pruning of Fruit-Trees; an Operation, which all will allow to be not only useful, but in some Sense necessary. Now if this should be judiciously performed, the Trees will be much healthier, and bear abundantly the better; but if ignorantly and unskilfully done, the Trees will bear nothing, or next to nothing, and perhaps will sicken, and die away.

HERE therefore let us put a Case: — Suppose, that all the numerous Taxes at this Day subsisting, were to be repealed, and that only one Tax was to be laid on in their Room, viz. A Tax of 20l. a Day on every Plow, when at Work, [or on every Machine performing the Office of a Plow] and the like Sum on every Cart, or Waggon, or any other Machine drawing, or carrying Goods, or Merchandize of any Kind: — And then I ask, What would be the Consequence? — Plainly this; That such a Tax would produce but a very Trifle to the Revenue; because it would stop Labour and Industry to such a Degree, that our Farms in the Country would be deserted, — Grass and Weeds would grow in the Streets of our Towns and Cities; — and the whole Kingdom would in a Manner become a Desert. — Yet the few Beggars who were left in such a desolate Country, would have it to say, that they paid but one single Tax; nay, that they could get drunk on Spirituous Liquors [as small Stills would be set up every where, being light of Carriage, and paying no Tax] Therefore they would have it to say, that they could get drunk for a Halfpenny, and perhaps dead-drunk for a Penny. Happy Times these! whereas their enslaved, oppressed, exhausted, and impoverished Forefathers in the

Year 1780, paid several Hundred different Taxes!   And, what was harder still, they could not enjoy the Blessing of getting drunk under the exorbitant Price of 6d. — Such were the Miseries and Calamities, which poor *Old England* then suffered under the Pressure of a Multitude of Taxes, and of ministerial Excises!!!   And now, Reader, having ended this long Article concerning Taxes, I cannot help exclaiming at the Close of it, in the Words, which I have heard the late Earl of CHESTERFIELD several Times repeat, How much easier is it to *deceive* Mankind, than to *undeceive* them!   But to return.

A third capital Error chargeable on the Lockian Sect, (and to be ranked under this Class of Errors) is that dreadful Notion, propagated by them with a Kind of enthusiastic Ardor, that *their System* of Government is the only true one, in the Nature of Things: — And that all others, not built on this Foundation, are, in Deed and Truth, so many detestable Robberies, and bare-faced Usurpations of the unalienable Rights of Mankind. Now this is in Fact proclaiming War against all the Governments upon Earth, and exciting their Subjects to rebel.   And indeed these new-fangled Republicans do not appear to be shocked at the Imputation of such horrid Consequences, but on the contrary, they admit them with a Kind of Pleasure, and seem to glory in such Deeds.   The Extracts from their Writings already given, are so decisive on this head, that there can be no Need of any further Proof, or Illustration.

BUT that which seems the most unaccountable in this whole Proceeding is, that they have adopted almost every Thing into their own System, which is exceptionable in Sir ROBERT FILMER's, and against which they have raised such tragical Exclamations.

THUS for Example, Sir ROBERT, and all the Patrons of an indefeasible, hereditary Right, declare with one Voice, that no Length of Time can bar the Title of the right Heir.   For whenever he shall see a fit Opportunity of setting up his Claim, every Subject is bound in Duty and Conscience to renounce their Allegiance to the reigning Prince, and to resort to the Standard of the Lord's Anointed: — Just so, *mutatis mutandis*, is the Stile and Declaration of the Lockians: The People are the only right Heirs; or rather, they are the only Persons who have a *Right* to appoint right Heirs; and no Length of Prescription can bar their Title.   For every Settlement of a State, monarchical, or even republican, whose Title is not derived from a popular Election, or doth not exist at present by Virtue of some express, and previous Contract, is a manifest Usurpation of their unalienable Rights; and therefore ought to be subverted and destroyed as soon as possible; — moreover the Authors of so daring an Attempt on the Liberties of a free People deserve to be punished with exemplary Vengeance, and to have their Goods and Estates confiscated for the Benefit of the Public, alias, to reward the Patriots. Now if any one should ask, what that is, which constitutes the People in this Case? or who are those Persons that are invested, *jure divino*, with these extraordinary Powers, these King-creating, and King-deposing Prerogatives? — The Answer I own, in Point of Theory, is attended with very perplexing Difficulties: — But in respect to *Practice*, and as referring to a *Matter of Fact*, it is the easiest Thing imaginable. For the Persons, or the People in this Case, are no other than the first Mob that can be got together, provided they are strong enough to undertake, and execute the work; if not, the next Mob, or the next to that, and so on, *ad infinitum*. For this is a Subject, which, it seems, ought never to be lost Sight of by a true-born Patriot: Though he may allow that the Efforts of the People for regaining their native Rights, may be delayed for a while, or may be *dissembled*, and postponed till he and his Friends shall find a more convenient Season for executing their laudable Designs.

AGAIN: The Notion of Kings de *Facto*, and Kings de *Jure*, that Opprobrium of the Jacobites, is also revived by the Lockians. For whosoever dares to reign without, or in Opposition to the Lockian Title, is only a King *de Facto*: — The rightful King, or the King *de Jure*, being yet in *petto*, and not to be brought forth, 'till the People can assemble together to assert, and exercise their *unalienable* Rights with Safety.

MOREOVER the persecuting and intolerant Spirit of the System of Sir ROBERT FILMER, and of the Jacobites, is another very just Reproach to it: And none inveighed more bitterly, or more justly against it on this Account, than Mr. LOCKE himself, and his Disciples. — Yet such is the Inconsistency of these Men; — that they tell us so plainly, that we cannot mistake their meaning, that they would allow no Government on the Face of the Earth to subsist on any other Title, but their own, had they a *Power* equal to their *Will* in these Cases. For says Dr. PRIESTLY, [and all the Rest join in the same Sentiments] This [the Lockian, or popular Title] must be the *only* true and proper Foundation of *all* Governments subsisting in the World; and *that to which the People have an unalienable Right to bring them back.*" — "This is a Blessing, says Dr. PRICE, which no Generation of Men can give up for another; and which, when lost, the *People have always a Right to resume.*" So that nothing less will content these Men than the universal Establishment of their own Principles, and the Renunciation or Abjuration of all others. Yet these are the Champions who stand up for Liberty of Conscience, and are the only Friends to reconciling Measures, to universal Toleration, to Peace on Earth, and Good-Will among Men.

ONCE more: All Laws made, or to be made by the Authority of *Usurpers*, alias of Kings *de Facto*, are, according to the Doctrine of Sir ROBERT FILMER and the Jacobites, absolutely null and void; 'till they shall have received the Sanction and Confirmation of the rightful King. And so say the Lockians in respect to *their sole* rightful King, — the People.   For here again they have told us so often, that we cannot forget it, that no Law can be valid, unless the people have authorized the making of it: — Nay, they have gone so far as to declare, that the very Essence of Slavery doth consist in being governed by Laws, to which the Governed have not previously consented.   This being the Case, you see plainly, that the Consideration, whether the Law be good or bad in itself; whether it is a Law that is wanted or not wanted; and whether it tends to promote the Liberty of the Subject, or to restrain it, is at present entirely beside the Question: — For the sole Point here to be determined, is simply this. — Had the Makers of such a Law any *Right* to make it, according to the Lockian Ideas of *Right* and *Wrong?*   If they had no such Right, they must be pronounced to be *Usurpers*, be the Law in itself whatever it may; and therefore as they are Usurpers, their Doom is fixed; inasmuch as they cannot expect Mercy for their daring Attempts to alienate the unalienable Rights of Mankind.

BEFORE this Lockian System had been broached, or at least before it had made many Proselytes among us, it used to be considered as no bad Maxim in Politics, — "Not to be very inquisitive concerning the *original Title* of the reigning Powers."   For if the State was actually at Peace, and if every Man sat, or might sit under his own Vine, and his own Fig-Tree; or in plainer English, if the essential Ends of Government were answered both by the Protection of good Subjects, and by the Punishment of bad ones, and also by the Defence of the Community from external Violence; — then it was thought, that this was a sufficient Reason for considering such Powers as ordained of God. — And if ordained of God, the People ought to obey them, under Peril of Damnation. — But now it seems, the World is grown much wiser: For the first Question to be asked is, What is your Title, to be the Governor, or Chief Magistrate of this Country?   And what Proofs do you bring that you have received your Authority from the People, without Fraud on the one Hand, or Violence on the other?   Answer me this, before you can expect, that I should submit to obey you.

FEW Governors, I believe, would like to be catechized after this Manner by their Subjects: And fewer still would be able to answer these

Questions to the Satisfaction of a Lockian Patriot. — Nay, we have been expressly told by one of the chief among them, Dr. PRIESTLY, that there is not a Government on the Face of the Globe, which can stand the Test of such an Enquiry. "For, says he, all Governments *whatever* have been, in some Measure, compulsory, tyrannical, and oppressive in their Origin." Now this being the Case, why will not these benevolent, political Philosophers, erect a Government of their own, for the Good of Mankind; — a Government on their own Plan, and perfectly agreeable to the Lockian Principles; which shall therefore be a Pattern for the Rest of the World to copy after? Nay, why are they always sowing Discords and Dissentions among *us*, instead of establishing a free, and equal, and *harmonious* Republic among *themselves?* Most certainly *Great-Britain* is not the proper Spot for exhibiting Specimens of this Sort: Because, to say the Truth, we have had, and we have felt, too many of these political Experiments already, during the last Century, to wish to have them revived again. — But *America!* — Yes, the interior Parts of *America* is the Country of all others, the fittest for putting every fond Imagination of their Hearts in Practice. For if Fame says true, and if Mr. LOCKE himself is to be credited, there is as yet no Government at all in the inland Parts of those immense Regions: Nor have even the Congress extended their *gentle Sway* beyond the Lakes *Erie* and *Ontario*, if they have gone so far. Thither, therefore, let all our Republican Patriots speedily repair: Time is precious, and the Cause invites: A Passport will undoubtedly be granted them, as soon as applied for: And ample Leave will be obtained to exchange the Slavery of this Country for the Freedom of *America.* Thither, therefore, let them all retire: For there they will live (according to the Prediction of Dr. PRICE) undisturbed by Bishops, Nobles, or Kings; and there likewise they will enjoy all the Blessings which can attend that happy State, where every Member of Society will be his own Law-giver, his own Governor, Judge, and Director.

CHAP. III.

An Enquiry how far either the Revolution in England,—or the Reduction of Ireland,—or the present Proceedings of the Congress in America, can or may be justified according to the leading Principles of Mr. LOCKE, *and his Followers.*

I. *Of the* REVOLUTION *in* England.

IT IS allowed on all Hands, and it has been the continual Boast of the Friends and Admirers of Mr. LOCKE, that he wrote his Essay on Government with a View to justify the Revolution. We have therefore a Right to expect, that his fundamental, political Maxims tend immediately and directly to vindicate this necessary Measure. How great therefore will be our Disappointment, if the quite contrary should appear!

THE grand Objections against King James the Second were, that his Government was tyrannical, and his Proceedings illegal; — that he assumed Powers which the Constitution had expressly denied him; — that he had repeatedly broken his solemn Coronation-Oath, and forfeited his Royal Word; — and that, in short, his Actions proved him to be an Enemy both to Civil Liberty, and to the Protestant Religion.

Now grant these Objections to be well founded (which I think no Man at this Day, even the warmest Friend of the STUART Family, will pretend to deny;) and the Inference is plain, that such a Prince deserved to be deposed, and that the Nation did very right in deposing him. — So far therefore we are all agreed: For Mr. LOCKE's Principles serve admirably well for the Purposes of *Demolition* in any Case whatever, as far as mere Demolition is concerned.   But alas! after we have pulled down, how are we to build up?   For something of this Kind must certainly be done, and that speedily.   The Nation was then in a State of Anarchy and Confusion, without Law, or Government: The Legislative Power could not assemble, according to the prescribed antient Forms of the Constitution: Nor could the Executive legally act for want of being authorised so to do. In such a Situation the Principle of Self-Defence would naturally suggest to a Nation in general, and to every reasonable Man in particular, — *to do the best they could without Loss of Time*, and not to stand upon mere *legal Punctilios*, where the *Essentials* of the Constitution, and the Happiness of Millions were at Stake: Moreover common Prudence and sound Policy would likewise suggest, that as few Innovations of the antient Form of Government should be introduced, and as many of its Laws and Ordinances be retained, as the Good of the whole, and the public Safety would permit.   This, I say, seems to be a fair, and honest, and upright Mode of Procedure; — a Mode which all impartial Men would allow to be reasonable, and every Lover of his Country would approve and justify: — And in short, this was the very Procedure adopted at the Revolution.

Now, let us see, what Methods ought to have been taken according to the System of Mr. LOCKE; — and whether his Plan, and the Revolution Plan, co-incide with each other.

BY the Desertion, or Abdication, or Forfeiture, or Deposition of King JAMES [take which Term you please] the Government was dissolved, and no new one was yet appointed.   So far we are again agreed.   But says a Lockian (if he will reason consistently with his own Principles) this Dissolution of Government set the Nation free from all Ties and Obliga-

tions: So that they were no longer the *Subjects* of a Government, which
itself did not exist: And if they were not the Subjects of an annihilated
Government, they could be under no Obligation to any other.   They
were therefore actually returned back to a State of Nature; — that happy
State, wherein there is a perfect Equality of Rights of all Kinds whatever; and where no one Man can pretend to have a better Claim than
another either to Lands, or Legislations, to Power or Pre-eminence of
any Kind.   Admirable!   CATALINE himself could not have wished for a
more ample Scope, — not only for paying all his own Debts, and those of
his Followers, — but also for coming in for a considerable Share in the
general Scramble, on a new Division of Property.   Nay, his Speech in
Sallust seems to indicate, as if he had some such Notion in his Head,
had his Genius been fertile enough to have drawn it out into Form, and to
have methodized it into a System.

BUT evidently as these Conclusions flow from Mr. LOCKE's fundamental Maxims, I do by no Means allow myself to suppose, that either he or
any of his Followers, with whom I have now Concern, would grant, that
these Conclusions are justly and fairly drawn.   On the contrary, I do
verily believe, that they thought they were serving the Cause of *rational*
Liberty, when they were advancing such Positions, as, if carried into
Execution, would unavoidably introduce the most shocking Scenes of
Despotism on the one Hand, and of Slavery on the other.   [Just as a
rank Antinomian wildly imagines, that he is consulting the Glory of God
and the Good of Mankind, whilst he is instilling such Doctrines, as necessarily derogate from the Supreme Being, by making him the Author of
Sin; and as necessarily turn human Creatures into ravenous Beasts to bite
and devour one another, by destroying all moral Obligation.]

THEREFORE I observe, that though all these shocking Consequences
are justly chargeable on the *Principles* of a Lockian, yet I do not charge
the *Man*, the Individual, with the Guilt of them, provided he declare his
Abhorrence of such Inferences.   Now, taking it for granted that he would
disavow them, were the Question asked, I will charitably suppose, that if
Mr. LOCKE and his Followers, had the Management of an Event similar
to that of the Revolution in 1688, they would not dissolve the Bands of
Society any farther, than was just necessary for compassing their Ends
of a free and general Election, according to their peculiar Ideas of Freedom, and of the *unalienable* Right of human Nature.   I will therefore
suppose also, that they would permit Men to enjoy unmolested their
hereditary Honours and hereditary Estates, and Property of all Kinds,
notwithstanding that their Principles necessarily tend to level every

thing without Distinction, and to bring us back to a State of Nature: Nay, I will suppose, that they would admit a Majority of the Voters present to include not only the Minority present, but also the great Majority, who might happen to be absent: — Though the Lockian Principles have in themselves a very different Tendency; as I have fully made to appear in the preceding Chapter. However, granting all this with a liberal Hand; and granting also for Argument's Sake, that it is consistent with his modern System of *unalienable* Rights, to exclude every Male under twenty-one Years of Age, and Females of every Age, from the unalienable Right of voting: — And then we have still remaining all the Males in *England* of twenty-one Years of Age and upwards, to compose an Assembly of Legislators, Electors, and Directors, according to the Lockian System. A goodly Number truly! All Voters by the unalienable Rights of Nature! All equal, free, and independent! This being the Case, the first Step to be taken is, to summon all these adult male Voters throughout the Kingdom to meet at some certain Place, in order to consult about erecting a new Government, after pulling down the old one: Here therefore I make a Pause; — and ask a Question, Was this done at the Revolution? No. Was it attempted to be done? No. Were there any Meetings appointed in different Parts of the Kingdom, from whence Deputies could be sent up to represent these Meetings, and to act in their Name? No. Was there then, [tho' that at best is a very preposterous Mode of Representation, according to Mr. LOCKE, yet] was there a previous general Election of Members of Parliament, in order that there might be at least a new Parliament to elect a new King? No, not even that, according to any legal, or constitutional Forms. — What then was that great NATIONAL VOTE which established the Revolution? — A few Scores of Noblemen, and a few Hundreds of Gentlemen, together with some of the Aldermen and Common Council of *London*, met at *Westminster*, [but without any Commission from the Body of the People authorising them to meet] and requested (thereby empowering) the Prince and Princess of *Orange* to assume the Royal Prerogative, and to summon a new Parliament. They summoned one accordingly, which was called the Convention Parliament: This Assembly put the Crown on their Heads [the Power of which they had exercised before] The Crown, I say, not only of *England*, but also of *Ireland*, and of all the *English* Dominions throughout every part of the Globe, and this too, not only without asking the Consent, but even without acquainting the People of those other Countries with their Intentions. Now if this Transaction can be said to be carried on agreeably to Mr. LOCKE's Plan, or if it can be justified by his Principles, I own myself the worst Judge of Reason and Argument, and of a plain Matter of Fact, that ever scribbled on Paper.   Nay, I appeal to all the World, whether the whole Business of this famous Revolution, from whence nevertheless we have derived so many national Blessings, ought not to be looked upon as a vile Usurpation, and be chargeable with the Guilt of robbing the good People of *England*, of *Ireland*, and of all the Colonies of their unalienable Rights, if Mr. LOCKE's Principles of Government are the only *true* and *just ones*.   But I ask further, Was the Convention itself unanimous in its Decisions?   No, very far from it.   On the contrary, it is a well-known Fact, that the Members of it [I mean a Majority of the Members] would never have voted the Crown to the Prince of *Orange*, had it not been for his threatening Message, that he would leave them to the Resentment of King JAMES, unless they complied with such a Demand.   So that even a Majority of this very Convention would have acted otherwise than they did, had they remained *unawed*, and *uninfluenced*.   And thus, Reader, it is demonstrated to thee, that this famous Convention [and in them the whole Nation] was self-governed, and self-directed, according to the Lockian Principle, in establishing the glorious Revolution!

II.   *The* REDUCTION *of Ireland.*

THE Reduction of *Ireland* about the Year 1690 is another capital Affair, which is to receive Sentence either of Justification, or Condemnation, at Mr. LOCKE's Tribunal.   For if *Ireland* was reduced, and the Constitution thereof peaceably settled according to the Lockian Plan, the Founder of this Sect and his Followers have certainly a good deal to glory in.   But if the very Reverse should prove to have been the Case, what shall we say? — And with what Front could Mr. MOLINEUX, the Friend of Mr. LOCKE, dedicate his Book on the Independency of *Ireland* to King WILLIAM, if King WILLIAM's own Conduct in the Reduction of that Kingdom was altogether repugnant to the Principles of his Book?   Now it unfortunately happens, that all the *Lockians* have precluded themselves from making Use of the very best Arguments, which could be brought in Justification of this memorable Event: — I say, they have precluded themselves, by chusing to rest the Merits of their Cause on one single Point, — *The Universality of Consent*; — that is to say, the Consent of the People, — at least of the major Part of them, *expressly* obtained, and *freely given*.   For they have solemnly declared over and over, and do continue to declare, that no Title whatever in the reigning Powers can be *valid*, if this be wanting.   MR. MOLINEUX's own Words will best speak his

Sentiments, and those of his Party on this Occasion; which therefore I shall beg Leave to repeat.

"I shall venture to assert, that the Right of being subject *only* to such Laws, to which Men give their *own* Consent, is so inherent in *all* Mankind, and founded on such *immutable* Laws of Nature and Reason, that 'tis not to be *aliened*, or given up by any Body of Men whatever." And a little lower: "I have no Notion of *Slavery*, but being bound by a Law, to which I do not consent. — If one Law may be imposed without Consent, any other Law whatever may be imposed on us without our Consent. This will naturally introduce *Taxing* us without our Consent. And this as necessarily destroys our *Property*. I have no other Notion of Property, but a Power of disposing of my Goods, *as* I *please*, and not as another shall command. Whatever another may *rightfully* take from me, I have certainly no Property in. To tax me without Consent is little better, if at all, than down-right *robbing me*."

AND now, Reader, having just observed, that this Mr. MOLINEUX of *Ireland* was to all Intents and Purposes, the Precursor of the Congress of *America*, let us consider what Right had King WILLIAM to invade *Ireland* at first, and what Pretensions could he have afterwards for establishing a Protestant Constitution in that Popish Country, according to the Principles of Messrs. LOCKE and MOLINEUX.

KING JAMES the Second fled from *England*, and, after having made some Stay in *France*, landed in *Ireland*, and was received by the whole Body of the *Irish* Nation with open Arms. A few Protestants in the North made some Opposition; and at last, being driven to Despair, they made a most surprizing Resistance, under the Conduct of the Rev. Mr. WALKER, Governor of *Londonderry*. But it is their *Number*, as having an unalienable Right to *vote*, — and not their *Courage* or Valour, as *Heroes*, which is the subject Matter of our present Inquiry. Now in respect to this, the Protestants were vastly the Minority of the Natives, and are so still, according to every Mode of Computation. Why therefore if the Votes or Consents of a Majority are to decide the Question, — Why, I say, did these few Protestants resist at all? — Or if a Lockian will not submit to be governed by this Rule of a Majority concluding the Minority [for sometimes he will, and at other Times he will not] Why did not the Handful of Protestants desire Leave to retire peaceably into some other Country, instead of committing Hostilities in *that?* Nay more, why did they send to *England* for Succours, to drive out King JAMES, and establish King WILLIAM? For surely according to the Lockian Hypothesis, that every Man ought to be governed *only* by Laws of his own appointing, —

the great Majority of the *Irish* Nation had at least as good a Right to refuse Obedience to King WILLIAM, as the Minority had to refuse it to King JAMES. But notwithstanding all this, King WILLIAM sailed with a large Reinforcement of Troops to *Ireland*; he landed, and he conquered; and in a short Space of Time the Peace of the Country was settled by the Capitulation and Treaty of *Limeric*.

Now in order to reconcile the Reduction of *Ireland* to the Lockian Standard of Right and Wrong, of just Government, and of Usurpation, we must believe first of all, that this Handful of Protestants, who appeared in Arms at *Inniskillen* and *Londonderry*, were the great Majority of the *Irish* Nation: And when we have digested this Pill, we must believe further that all Things were quite inverted, or in other Words, That the *few* Natives of *Ireland*, who were Papists [not more perhaps than ten to one Protestant] we must believe, I say, that these *few* Papists all voluntarily consented to be governed by the many, who were Protestants: And having proceeded thus far in our Credulity, we must not hesitate at swallowing the rest, viz. That the Papists of *Ireland* sent an Embassy to invite King WILLIAM to come over, and offered to swear Fealty and Allegiance to him at the Battle of the *Boyne*; — yea, and that all the Laws successively made afterwards for disarming them, for taking their Estates from them, for banishing them, for exciting their own Children to rebel against them, and for subjecting them to Fines and Imprisonments, and to Pains and Penalties in Thousands of Instances; — we must believe, I say, that all these Laws were made with the whole Assent, and Consent, Will, and Agreement of the Papists of *Ireland*. O Genius of Popish Legends, confess thou are fairly outdone by Protestant Patriots! O Purgatory of St. PATRICK, hide thy diminished Head!

III. *The Case of the present* CONGRESS *in America*.

IT has been observed at the Beginning of this Treatise, that the Lockian System is an universal Demolisher of all Civil Governments, but not the Builder of any. And it has been distinctly shewn, that this Observation has been found to be remarkably verified in two memorable Instances, [those very Instances which were pretended to correspond the most with the Plan of Mr. LOCKE] the Revolution in *England*, and the Reduction of *Ireland*. Come we now therefore to a 3d Instance, the Revolt of the Colonies in *North America*.

WHEN it is seriously enquired, what were the chief *Grievances* which the Colonies had to complain of against the Mother Country, the Answer is, and must be, that she governed, or attempted to govern them, in such a

Manner as was not agreeable to the Lockian System. For the imposing Laws on them of any Kind, whether good or bad in themselves, and whether for the Purposes of Taxation, or for other Purposes, without their own Consent, is, according to this hypothesis, a most intolerable Grievance! a Robbery! and an Usurpation on the unalienable Rights of Mankind. Nay, we are repeatedly told, that the very Essence of Slavery consists in the being obliged to submit to be governed by such Laws as these. Therefore if you want to know the very Root and Foundation of the present *American* Rebellion, it is this very Principle: And the Fact is so far from being denied, that it is gloried in by Dr. PRICE, and others their warmest Advocates. In short, the brave *Americans* were resolved not to be Slaves; but Slaves, it seems, they must have been (according to the Lockian Idea) had they acknowledged the Right of the Mother Country, even in a single Instance, to make Laws to bind them without their Consent: — I say, even in a *single* Instance; for the Lockian Mode of Reasoning is, that there is no Difference between being vested with discretionary Power, and with despotic Power. "Inasmuch as, if a Government has any Right to rule me without my Consent in *some* Cases, it has a Right to rule me in *every* Case; consequently it has a Right to levy every Kind of Tax, good or bad, reasonable, or exorbitant upon me, and to inflict all Sorts of Punishments whatever."

BUT Dr. PRICE himself, the great Champion of the *Americans*, has so expressly applied this Train of Reasoning to the *American* Cause, that I think myself happy in co-inciding with him in Sentiments on this Occasion. "Our Colonies in *North America*, saith the Doctor, appear to be now* determined to risque, and suffer every Thing under the Persuasion, that *Great-Britain* is attempting to *rob* them of that Liberty, to which *every Member* of Society, and all civil Communities have a natural, and unalienable Right."

HERE therefore the Case is plain: For every Member of Society, as well as the Community at large, hath, according to Dr. PRICE, not only a natural, but an *unalienable* Right to be self-governed, and self-directed. Be it so: And then comes the important Question, "Is this the Case at present with every Member of Society in *North-America*, now groaning

---

* Happy would it have been for *Great Britain*, had the Colonies come to this Determination 50 or 60 Years ago; for then we should have avoided two most expensive and bloody Wars, and, to speak the honest Truth, very *unjust* ones, entered into for their Sakes. But better late, than never. *America* ever was a Mill-Stone hanging on the Neck of this Country; and as we would not cast it off, the *Americans* have done it for us.

under the Dominion of the Congress?" And as Dr. PRICE has taken such Pains to extoll the *American* Mode of Government to the Skies, — a most happy Mode, without Bishops, without Nobles, without Kings! I wish he would return a plain Answer to the plain Question here propounded. In Honour and Conscience he is certainly called upon so to do. But tho' the Doctor loves to set Controversies on Foot, we learn from his own Words, that he loves his Ease too well, to clear up the Objections arising from them. Consequently being deprived of the Doctor's Assistance, unless he should think proper to change his declared Resolution, we must do the best we can without him.

HERE therefore be it observed, that without taking any Advantage from the Arguments that may be deduced from the tarring and feathering of their numerous Mobs; and without insisting on the burning and plundering of the Houses, and destroying the Property of the Loyalists by the *American* Republicans, even before they had openly thrown off the Masque, and set up for Independence; — I say, without bringing these Instances as Proofs that they would not grant that Liberty to others, for which they so strenuously contended for themselves; — let us come to that very Period, when they had established various Civil Governments in their respective Provinces, and had new-modelled their several Constitutions according to their own good Liking: — I ask therefore, Was any one of these Civil Governments at first formed, or is it now administered, and conducted according to the Lockian Plan? And did, or doth any of their Congresses, general or provincial, admit of that fundamental Maxim of Mr. LOCKE, that every Man has an *unalienable* Right to obey no other Laws, but those of his own making? No; no; — so far from it, that there are dreadful Fines and Confiscations, Imprisonments, and even Death made use of, as the only effectual Means for obtaining that Unanimity of Sentiment so much boasted of by these new-fangled Republicans, and so little practiced. In one Word, let the impartial World be the Judge, whether the *Americans*, in all their Contests for Liberty, have even ONCE made use of Mr. LOCKE's System for any other Purpose, but that of *pulling down*, and destroying; and whether, when they came to erect a new Edifice of their own on the Ruins of the former, — they have not abandoned Messrs. LOCKE, MOLINEUX, PRIESTLY, and PRICE, with all their visionary Schemes of universal Freedom, and Liberty of Choice.

CHAP. IV.

*On the Abuse of Words, and the Perversion of Language, chargeable on
the Lockian System.*

THE Importance of this Subject requires a distinct Chapter; but it
need not be a long one; for the chief Point here to be attended to, is
to fix and explain the Meaning of certain Terms and Phrases, and
to guard against Misrepresentation or Mistake.

IT is observeable, that in every Government, from that of a petty
Schoolmaster to that of a mighty Monarch, the respective Rulers must
be invested with two Sorts of Power; the one is that which *may be* fixed
and limited by written and positive Laws; but the other, being unlimit-
able in its Nature, must be left to the Discretion of the Agent.   The
Order and Course of Things require the Use of both these Kinds of Power
in every Instance where *Authority*, properly so called, is to be exercised.
In respect to the first of these, it is unnecessary at present to consider it in
any separate, or independent View; because it is not the Subject now
immediately before us.   But with regard to the second, it is the very
Thing here to be attended to; and by explaining the Nature of this, we
shall eventually explain the other.

WHEN the Founder of a School [and the same Observation, *mutatis
mutandis*, would hold good for Things in a much higher Sphere; — I
say therefore] when the Founder of a School is about to establish Rules
and Constitutions for the Discipline, and good Government thereof; —
he finds himself able to establish certain Statutes and Ordinances in
respect to some Things, but unable in respect to others.   He can, for
Example, fix the Salary of the Master by a positive Law; — he can
limit the Hours of School, and the Hours of Recreation; — he can
ordain, if he think proper, what Authors shall be read in his School,
and may prescribe likewise a Regimen of Diet to be observed by the
Youths, who shall be maintained on his Foundation; — with a few
other Things of the like Nature.   But much farther than this he cannot go, were he ever so desirous.   He cannot, for Instance, lay down
Rules aforehand, how many Periods or Paragraphs *each* Youth is to
learn at *each* Lesson, or how many Lines or Verses he is to get by Heart on
a Repetition Day; and in Cases of Neglect, or Misdemeanor, he cannot
determine the Force or Momentum, with which the Ferula or Rod is to
fall on the offending Culprit; — nor yet can he prescribe, or limit the
Tone of Voice, or Looks, or Gestures of Displeasure, or Words of Reprimand, which are to be used on such Occasions.   For as all these Affairs

are not, and cannot be, subject to any fixt Regulations, the Master must be vested with a *discretionary*, alias an *unlimited* Power in respect to such Things.   [Need I add, that the very Institution of a School is (according to the Lockian System) a Contradiction to the social Compact?   Because, if every one is to be accounted a Slave, who is obliged to submit to Laws not of his own making, — or to Governors not of his own chusing, then School-Boys and Slaves are synonimous Terms: Hard Measures these! And what Inroads are the Doctrines of Passive Obedience, and Non-Resistance daily making in our *English* Schools on *English* Liberty!   But to return] The Powers of this Magistrate, [the School-Master] being thus shewn to be partly circumscribed, and partly indefinite; I here ask, Doth his *indefinite* Power thereby become *infinite?*   Or is he vested with arbitrary and despotic Power, because he is entrusted with that which is *discretionary?*   Surely no: And the very putting such a Question, one would think, is sufficient to confute every Lockian Cavil on this Head. * Yet, strange to tell, the whole Weight of their Arguments rests on this single Point.   For [according to them] if you admit *discretionary* Power, you must admit it to be *arbitrary:* If you allow the Power of your Magistrate to be in any Case *indefinite*, you must allow it to be *infinite*.   Now it so happens, that Experience and common Sense, no bad Judges to appeal to, entirely confute these confident Assertions.   For were the Master of any School to treat his Scholars with wanton Cruelty, to beat them unmercifully, or to inflict any unnecessary Severity upon them, — all the World would soon distinguish such Abuses of Power from necessary Chastisement, and moderate Correction; and they would not hesitate in giving their Opinion, that such a Wretch deserved the severest Punishment.   So much easier it is, to discern the Use of Things from the Abuses of them, after the Fact has happened, than it is to make Laws in *all Cases* aforehand for the Prevention of Abuses.

THE King and both Houses of Parliament, that is, the supreme Legislature of this Country, have a general, unlimited Right to make Laws for binding the People, in *all Cases whatsoever*.   They have this Right, because it is impossible to define exactly in what particular Instances they ought *not* to be entrusted with such a Right, or how far their Power ought to extend in every Case, and every Circumstance, which might occur, and where it ought to be stopped.   I say it is impossible to define these

---

* Dr. PRICE and the Congress ground all their Outcries against the declaratory Law, for binding the Colonies in all Cases whatsoever, on this very Plea, weak and illogical as it is.

Points before-hand, or to draw the Line between *Trust*, and *Distrust* in these Respects.   Yet can any Man in his Senses pretend to say, that the King and the Parliament would be *justifiable*, or even *excusable*, were they to abuse this discretionary Power of *making Laws in all Cases whatsoever;*— I mean wilfully and designedly abuse it, so as to enslave the People by cruel, unjust, and tryannical Laws?   Surely no: For even Sir ROBERT FILMER, and the Jacobites, do not say that such Rulers are at all *excusable*; — nay, they expressly say the contrary; and are as ready at denouncing Hell and Damnation against such *wicked Tyrants*, as the Lockians themselves: — Indeed they protest against any Punishment whatever being inflicted on Tyrants, especially on royal Tyrants, during the present Life, by the Hands of Men: For which ill-judged Tenderness, and mistaken Points of Conscience, they are highly to blame: And therefore their Tenets of *absolute* and *unlimited* Passive Obedience and Non-Resistance are deservedly had in Detestation: But nevertheless they make no wrong Judgment concerning the Nature of, and the Punishment due to, the Crimes of Tyranny; tho' they are so weak as to maintain, that this Punishment ought to be deferred, 'till the Criminals themselves are removed into another World, when the Punishment due to such Offences can be no Terror to those Evil-Doers who survive, and who herefore ought to be deterred by such Examples from attempting to do the like.

CONCLUSION.

UPON the whole, if this new political System of Mr. LOCKE and his Followers hath not received a full and ample Confutation in the preceding Sheets, I must ingenuously acknowledge, that nothing could have prevented it, but the Inability or Incapacity of the Author.   For surely a more pernicious Set of Opinions than the Lockian, — [I mean, with regard to the Peace and Tranquility of the present Life] could hardly be broached by Man.   And it is but small Consolation to reflect, that probably the original Author, and several of his Disciples never meant to draw Conclusions so horrid in their Nature, and so full of *wanton* Treason and Rebellion, as the Congresses have actually drawn from it in *America*, and as the Republican Factions are daily endeavouring to draw from it here in *England*, had they Power equal to their Will.

MOREOVER what greatly aggravates the Crime of every Attempt of this Nature, and renders it utterly inexcusable, is, that there is no Manner of Need of having Recourse to such Measures, or to such Principles, for the Sake of confuting either the patriarchal Scheme of Sir R. FILMER, or the *absolutely* passive Obedience Creed of the Jacobites; Insomuch as both these erroneous Systems may be, at least, as fully and effectually confuted without Mr. LOCKE's Principles, as with them. Nay, if the Lockians had been content with their own Set of Opinions, and had left others undisturbed in the quiet Enjoyment of theirs, something might have been pleaded in their Favour. For though one may easily see, that theirs is an impracticable Scheme in any Society whatever, great or small; yet, if they think otherwise, and are firmly persuaded that the Affair is of such Importance as to merit a fair and open Trial; — Let a fair Trial be given it; and let those unpeopled Regions of *America*, those *vacua loca*, mentioned by Mr. LOCKE, be the Theatre for exhibiting this curious Phœnomenon, a LOCKIAN REPUBLIC! Where all Taxes are to be *Free-Gifts!* and every Man is to obey *no farther*, and no *otherwise*, than he himself *chuses* to obey! In such a Case, inconsiderable as I am, I will venture to promise [or to use the Language of an Arch-Patriot, I will pledge myself to the Public] that all the Sons and Daughters of *genuine* Freedom shall be at Liberty to remove thither as soon as they please; — and that Thousands and Tens of Thousands of their Fellow-Citizens will be heartily glad of their Departure.

BUT if not content with this Liberty for themselves, they will be indefatigable in disturbing the Repose of others, and will incessantly excite the Subjects of every State to rebel, under the shameful Pretence, that their Governors are *Usurpers* of their *unalienable* Rights; — they must expect to have their Sophistry detected, and themselves exposed in their proper Colours. Indeed, happy it is for *them*; — happy it is for *us all* [notwithstanding some petty Inconveniencies] that we live in such an Age, and such a Country, where Men may dare to say and do such Things with Impunity. I own, the very Contemplation of this Circumstance always gives me Pleasure: For rejoice to find, that on every Comparison between the Liberty pretended to be enjoyed under the patriotic Congress in *America*, and the Slavery, which it seems, we daily suffer here in *England*, every Instance is a Demonstration that *English* Slavery is infinitely preferable to *American* Liberty: So that in short, while I find, that here in *England*, a Man may say or do, may write or print, a thousand Things with the utmost Security, for which his Liberty and Property, and even his Life itself would be in the most imminent Danger, were he to do the like in *America*. I want no other Proofs, that *Englishmen* are still a Nation of *Freemen*, and not of *Slaves*. Sorry I am, that any of my Fellow-Subjects should misapply so great a Blessing as Liberty is, both civil and religious: But at the same Time, I am sincerely glad that they themselves are such undeniable Evidences of the Existence of Liberty among us by the Security they enjoy in their manifold Abuses of it. May they grow wiser and better every Day; But may we, on our Parts, never attempt to weed out these Tares from among the Wheat, lest by so doing, we should root out the Wheat also.

PART II.

CONTAINING

THE TRUE BASIS

OF

CIVIL GOVERNMENT,

In OPPOSITION to the SYSTEM of

Mr. LOCKE and his FOLLOWERS,

By JOSIAH TUCKER, D. D.

DEAN of GLOCESTER.

THE

PREFACE

TO THE

SECOND PART.

*T*HE *Author imagines, that he has confuted the* Lockian *System in the fore-going Part of this Work. And he is supported in this Opinion by the Judgment of many Persons, not only distinguished for their Learning and good Sense, but also for their zealous Attachment to the Civil, and Religious Liberties of this Country. If this be the Case, that is, if he has really confuted* Mr. LOCKE, *he may now, he hopes, with some Propriety, venture to submit to Public Consideration, a System of his own; which he is inclined to think, may serve as a Basis for every Species of Civil Government to stand upon. — At the same Time he is well aware, that it doth not follow, that his must be true, because* Mr. LOCKE'S *may have been proved to be false: He is also very sensible, that it is much easier to pull down, than to build up; and that many a Man can demolish the System of another, who cannot defend his own.*

For these Reasons he is the more desirous of proceeding with due Reserve and Caution; — not expecting, that this Plan should be adopted, as soon as proposed, nor yet supposing, that it will be totally rejected, before it shall have undergone some Kind of Examination. In order to give it a fair Trial, he has added a Series of Objections, partly as they occurred to himself, in reasoning on the Case, and partly as they were suggested to him in the Conversation he had with others. In respect to all which it will be readily allowed, that not one Objection has lost any of it's Force and Weight in passing through his Hands: And as to their respective Answers, every Reader will judge for himself.

He is very willing to allow, that some Parts of his System are weaker than others: For this must happen more or less, to all human Compositions. Therefore he doth not pretend to lay before the Public a faultless Piece, *free from all Objections, but only such a Plan for a political Edifice, as may serve all the good Purposes of real and rational Liberty, and at the same Time be more practicable, and better accommodated to the State of Mankind in every Age and Country, than* MR. LOCKE'S *is confessed to be.*

469

The Author doth not build much on the Authority of great Names, — not that he rejects human Authority, when it can be properly introduced in Matters of doubtful *Disputation; but because he cannot find that the* Point *was ever brought into Controversy 'till of late, whether the Inclinations of Mankind are* naturally *and* spontaneously *turned towards Society and the Subordinations of Civil Government, or towards living in a State of perfect Equality, and Independence. Therefore it is in vain to look for long Argumentations in the Works of political Writers of former Times, relative to this Question, either pro or con, before the Question itself was supposed to exist.*

However, as it may be a Satisfaction to some Persons to know, What were the genuine *Opinions of the Sages of Antiquity on this Subject, before the Arts of Sophistry, and the Rage of Party-Disputes, had blinded Men's Eyes, and corrupted their natural good Sense; — such Persons will, I hope, be sufficiently gratified, when they come to peruse the third Part of the ensuing Treatise. They will also there find the judicious* HOOKER *now rescued out of the disagreeable Company of Modern Republicans, with whom he has been made to associate for some Time past, much against his Will, and restored to his true Friends both in Church and State.*

THE
TRUE BASIS
OF
CIVIL GOVERNMENT, &c.

CHAP. I.

Concerning those Principles in Human Nature, which may serve as a Basis for any Species of Civil Government to stand upon, without the actual Choice, or personal Election of every Member of the Community either towards the first Erection, or the Continuation of such a Government.

AS MR. LOCKE, and his Followers have objected to our deducing Kingly Government, or indeed any Kind of Civil Government from the Authority of Parents over their Children [though the Out-Lines, and first Rudiments of all Governments had probably no other Origin,] and have taken such Pains to shew the Disparity of the Cases; we will gratify them to their Hearts' Content in this particular: For we will endeavour to shew, that were Numbers of the Human Species to be brought together, (tho' no otherwise connected than by being of the same Species) they would soon fall into some Kind of Subordination among themselves, and consequently into some Kind of Government; — and that too without that personal, and particular Election, for which Mr. LOCKE and his Followers have so strenuously contended.

IN order therefore to keep at a sufficient Distance from the *Patriarchal System*, and the *indefeasible Right Lined Monarchy* of Sir ROBERT FILMER; — Let us suppose, that, instead of one Pair, an Hundred Pair of Men and Women were at first created: And let us contemplate the various Instincts, Qualities, and Propensities (as far as the present Subject is concerned) with which this Tribe of Animals would be found to be endowed; — supposing them to be made of the same Sort of Materials, which we see Mankind to be of, at present.

AND as we are now setting out on our Inquiries, be it carefully remembered, that the *first* Difference between the Lockians, and others seems to be this; — The Lockians maintain, that Mankind have a *Capacity* for becoming Members of a Civil Society; — but no *natural* Desire, or Inclina-

471

tion for entering into such a State of Life: [Indeed they do not say the latter in express Terms, but they do by necessary Consequences:] Whereas we maintain, that Human Nature is endowed with both Capacity, and Inclination: — And that the natural *Instinct* precedes the *Capacity*, much in the same Manner, tho' not with the same Strength, or in the same Degree, as the innate Instincts of Individuals towards Food, or of the Species towards each other, precede the *Arts* of Cookery, and Brewery, of Marriage-Ceremonies, and Marriage-Settlements.

THIS therefore being the Question, we are now to endeavour to find out, how far *Nature* herself hath led the Way towards the Formation of Civil Government by means of various Instincts, Biasses, and Propensities implanted in Mankind before *Art* was introduced either to mend or mar her Handywork.

1. THEREFORE, the first Thing observable in the Class of Animals above-mentioned [the hundred Pair of adult Men and Women] is, That they are formed by Nature to be of the *gregarious* Kind. For most certainly the Individuals of the Human Species are so far from seeking Solitude, as their *natural* State, that such a Course of Life would be one of the sorest Punishments which could be inflicted on them: And nothing can be a clearer Proof of a contrary Bias in Nature, than the strong Desire which not only Children manifest to associate together, but which adult Persons feel, to be acquainted even with Strangers, differing from themselves in Language, Manners, and in almost every Thing, excepting their being of the same Species, *rather than not to enjoy any Company at all.* Now this Disposition in Human Creatures to associate with their *Like*, is a leading Step towards Civil Society; because no Animals whatever, but the *gregarious*, can be *fit* to form a Community, or a Common-Wealth.

2. A SECOND Thing observable is, That there is a prodigious Variety even in the *natural* Endowments, both of Body and Mind belonging to the several Individuals of the human Species: So that probably no two among them are altogether, and in every Respect alike. Far therefore, very far it is from being true, that all Mankind are naturally equal, or on a *Par*, respecting their several Endowments either mental, or corporeal. Indeed had this been the Case, it is hard to say, how any Kind of Subordination, and consequently Government, could have been introduced among such a Tribe of equal, independent, unconnected Beings: Wherefore

3. A THIRD Observation is, that these Differences of Genius and Talents, these several Excellencies and Defects, these Capacities and Incapacities are found, for the most Part, to be relative and reciprocal;

so that wheresoever one abounds, another is defective, and vice versa: By which Means all these Animals stand in Need of each other's Assistance in some Respect, or in one Degree or other: — Surely this is another plain Proof, that they were not framed by Nature for an equal, independent, unconnected State of Life.

4. A FOURTH Remark is, That *as* these Animals mutually want each other's Help and Assistance; *so* are they naturally endowed with a Power of making known their Wants to each other, and their mutual Willingness to relieve them. Now, as this is a Fact, which cannot be controverted, it is very immaterial to decide, whether the Manner of making known such mutual Wants, or Intentions, was at first by Means of dumb Signs and Gestures, and inarticulate Sounds, or thro' the Medium of some primæval Language infused in, or communicated to them at the Time of their Creation. Therefore be that as it may, it is more material to observe in the

5th and last Place, That each of these human Animals feels, generally speaking, a strong Instinct to succour and relieve the Wants and Distresses of his Fellow-Creatures: — Inasmuch as, next to providing what is necessary for his own Preservation, and removing Pain from his own Person, he is prompted and spurred on to do the like good Offices for others. And he finds, that he receives great Pleasure both in the immediate Gratification of this benevolent, sympathizing Instinct, and in his subsequent Reflections on it.

Now from a Contemplation of this Sketch, or Out-line, if I may speak, of the Portrait of Human Nature, it is, I think, not very difficult to determine, what would be the probable Result of an Assemblage of an Hundred Pair of such Animals as these, after a short Acquaintance, respecting Society and Civil Government. For

1. THEY would not be long before they endeavoured to gratify the first, and the quickest in Succession, of all the Calls of Nature, the Appetites of *Hunger* and *Thirst*; and that too without having any distinct Knowledge, perhaps without the least Idea, that such a Gratification was necessary for the Preservation of the Individual. Nay, it is highly probable, that Nature at the first Creation of the Human Pairs, proceeded much farther in her instinctive Instructions, than she need do at present. For at the first, Men were not only impelled by the Appetites of Hunger and Thirst to seek for Meat and Drink, but were also taught, either by some Guardian Angel sent on purpose to instruct them, or were led by some extraordinary Impulse to discover and chuse what were proper Eatables and Drinkables in their peculiar Situation. — To suppose the contrary, would

be to suppose, that this Hundred Pair of adult Men and Women, were left to themselves to make Experiments, as they could, on every thing around them, — by endeavouring to swallow perhaps Sand or Gravel, instead of Water, towards quenching Thirst, and to gnaw a Stone, or a Stick, instead of chewing a Root, a Fruit, or a Berry for appeasing Hunger. It cannot therefore reasonably be doubted, but that the first Race of Men were taught by Nature, or rather by Nature's God, to distinguish, without the tedious Process of uncertain Experiments, the proper from the improper, the wholesome from the unwholseome in such a Situation.

[As to the Instinct between the Sexes for the Renovation of the Species (as the former was for the Preservation of the Individual) suffice it just to put the Reader in Mind, that as we have supposed the Creation to have been made in *Conjugal Pairs*, we have thereby avoided, at least for the present, all the Difficulties, that might otherwise have arisen in the Choice and Preference of Objects; — only this much is necessary to observe on this Head, as well as on the former, that 'till they had been taught by Experience, it was impossibe for the wisest of them to have guessed what would have been the Consequence, at the Expiration of a certain Term, of such an Intercourse of one Sex with the other.]

2dly. THESE human Animals, when herding together, and beginning to eat and drink, would soon discover a vast Superiority, and Inferiority of *Talents* among themselves, in respect of making Provision for satisfying the Cravings of Thirst and Hunger. For some would be found to be much more ingenious, and perhaps more industrious and provident than others, either in the gathering of Viands, and the procuring and portage of drinkable Liquids; — or in storing them up, and preserving them sweet and wholesome. This Man would excel either in turning the Ground in search after Roots, or in climing Trees for Fruit; — another in swimming and diving for Fish, or in the Pursuit of Game;—a third in the taming certain Beasts and Birds for domestic Use, or in the planting of such Vegetables, as were found to be good for Food, and so quick of Growth as soon to come to Maturity; — whilst a fourth perhaps would display a Dexterity and Genius in the Preparation of several Kinds of Victuals, and in the first Rudiments of the Arts of Cookery. Now in all these Cases, it is obvious to conceive, That the less ingenious, or adventurous, the less provident and frugal would naturally become, without any formal Contract, dependent on, and subservient to their Instructors and Benefactors, in one Degree or other.

3dly. THE like Superiority of Parts and Talents would necessarily appear, tho' at somewhat a later Period, in the Cases of procuring Rayment, and of constructing Habitations. For no Man can pretend that all the Human Species are endowed with equal Powers, or equal Capacities in these Respects. And therefore in Proportion as the less adroit, or less provident, felt themselves incommoded by the Extremes either of Heat, or of Cold, and wished to free themselves from their Evils; — in nearly the same Proportion would they become the Ministers of those, who could, and would relieve them from their Distresses. For here it must be remembered once for all, that in such a Situation as we are now describing, and before Commerce and Money were introduced, the Person who felt himself inferior in any of these Respects, could make no other Compensation to his Superior, but by some Kind of *personal Service*.

4th. THE Advantage arising from a peculiar Genius to abridge Labour by Means of Machines, — or to divide, and subdivide it into distinct Parts, or Portions for the Sake of greater Ease, Expertness, and Expedition, is another Cause, why some Men must rise in Society, without any Compact, or Election, and others as naturally sink; — and consequently, why Subordination at first, and Government afterwards, must take Place. For had there been no Difference of natural Genius between Man and Man;—and no Distinction of Talents and Powers both mental, and corporeal, between Males and Famales, — it is hardly possible to conceive, how there could have existed any Distinction of Trades, or Diversity of Employments. And without them a regular Plan of Government cannot be supported.

To illustrate this Matter, be it observed, that tho' Horses, and horned Cattle naturally herd together, as well as Men, being all of the *gregarious* Kind; — yet as none of these Individuals display any Genius either to abridge Labour, or to divide it into separate Parts or Portions, — so there is nothing approaching towards a Distinction of Trades, or a Diversity of Imployments to be found among them; — consequently they are total Strangers to any Forms of Government, Republican, or Monarchical; and they know nothing of the Rules of Justice or Equity, or of any Laws, but those of brutal Force. Whereas Bees, Ants, and Beavers, who are remarkable for dividing the Labour of the *Whole* into distinct Portions, assigning to each Individual a proper Share, become of Course a regular Community among themselves, wherein some preside, and others must obey. All Authors, who have favoured us with the natural History of these three Tribes of Animals, speak with Raptures of their admirable Police, Discipline, and Œconomy. Yet not one Writer, that I know of, hath once suggested the most distant Thought, that these Things are owing to any social Compact, or popular Form of Government: — No, not one hath hitherto dared to maintain, that each Bee, Ant, or Beaver is his own Law-giver, Governor, and Director.

[THERE are other Causes which might be mentioned, as greatly contributing towards the first Formation of Government, without any explicit Compact, or mutual Stipulation. And these are the *Power of Language*, — and the *Power of saving*, or *protecting* from impending Dangers. In regard to Language, some striking Observations might have been made, had we the Time, and Abilities to have done Justice to the Subject: — Suffice it for the present just to declare my Opinion, That at the first Creation of the human Kind, the Adams and Eves, spoke some certain Language (whatever it was) by mere *Instinct*, without any previous Teaching (excepting the instantaneous Teaching of Nature) and without Education, or Instruction. I know indeed, that the contrary is the prevailing Opinion, That all Words, and the Meaning of all Words were originally settled by mutual Consent, and at some certain Congress held for that Purpose. But here I should be glad to know, what particular Language was spoken by Adam and Eve, and their Sons and Daughters, — or by this hundred Pair of Adams and Eves, *before* they met in Congress? — In what Language or Dialect were they summoned to meet? — And even after they had met, how came they to understand one another so readily before they had learnt to speak? — And how came they to speak at all, to define, and to agree about the Meaning of certain Words, before these, or any Words whatever had been known among them? — Away therefore with this absurd Notion: And let us believe, as we ought to do, that Nature was more benevolent to her Children at their first Appearance on the Theatre of the World, than this and such like Schemes represent her to be. She certainly *infused* the first Rudiments of Language, — she *instilled* the first Knowledge of Things proper for Meats and Drinks, — and she *implanted* the constituent Principles of Government into Mankind, without any previous Care or Thought on their Parts. But having done this, she left the rest to themselves; in order that they might cultivate and improve her Gifts and Blessings in the best Manner they could.

As to the Power of protecting from impending Danger, if that should mean only the Power of rescuing, or preserving from the Injuries of the Weather, from the Attacks of wild Beasts, or from some other natural Evils, it is included, at least in Part, under some of the former Heads. — But if it is to signify a Power of protecting the Weak from the intended Violence of the Strong, it will include likewise the Right of Retaliation and Reprisal, — and in its Consequences, the Right of Conquest.

Therefore if this should be the Thing meant, I shall not insist on such a Subject at present; — because I wish to shew, That Government can date its Origin from other Causes, besides those of popular Elections, or popular Defeats; — and because a Government founded on Conquest, however justifiable the Occasion of it might have been, is at first very odious, and requires a Length of Time to reconcile Men to it.]

LASTLY, there is yet another Consideration, which when properly developed, greatly corroborates all the former. And that is this, That there is found to exist in Human Nature a certain Ascendency in some, and a Kind of submissive Acquiescence in others. The Fact itself, however unaccountable, is nevertheless so notorious, that it is observable in all Stations and Ranks of Life, and almost in every Company. For even in the most paltry Country Village, there is, generally speaking, what the French very expressively term, *Le Coque de Village;* — A Man, who takes the Lead, and becomes a Kind of Dictator to the rest. Now, whether this arises from a Consciousness of greater Courage, or Capacity, — or from a certain overbearing Temper, which assumes Authority to dictate and command, — or from a greater Address, that is, from a Kind of instinctive Insight into the Weaknesses, and blind Sides of others, — or from whatever Cause, or Causes, it matters not. For the Fact itself, as I said before, is undeniable, however difficult it may be to account for it. And therefore here again is another Instance of great Inequalities in the original Powers and Faculties of Mankind: — Consequently this natural Subordination (if I may so speak) is another distinct Proof, that there was a Foundation deeply laid in Human Nature for the political Edifices of Government to be built upon; — without recurring to, what never existed but in Theory, universal, social Compacts, and unanimous Elections.

HERE therefore I will fix my Foot, and rest the Merits of the Cause. An hundred Pair of Adams and Eves are supposed (for the Sake of Argument in this Debate) to have been created at once, and to have been endowed with the various Instincts and Inclinations above described, all tending in one Degree or other, to the Formation of Civil Government. As soon as they see each other, they associate and converse. [*N.B.* Infants and Children do still the same in their Way.] The next Step they take, is to gratify those Desires and Inclinations towards which *Nature has most powerfully incited them. But they find almost instan-

---

* The Appetite between the Sexes can have no Place in this Question; because it is not of that Sort, or Kind, which renders Mankind *gregarious.* Indeed it is observable, that the most solitary Animals, which are not fond of *herding* together, yet, at certain Periods, converse in *Pairs.*

taneously, that they are hardly able to satisfy any one of these Desires without the Help and Assistance of others of their Kind.   And they feel also, that in whatsoever Sort of Talents, Geniuses, or Capacities they are deficient, others are generally abounding, and vice versa: — They perceive likewise that in receiving good Offices from others, there is a certain pleasing Temper of Mind excited, now called *Gratitude*, — and that in conferring good Offices, there is another very pleasing Sensation raised, now termed *Benevolence*.   And thus it came to pass, that a mutual Dependence and a mutual Connection were originally made by the wise Creator of all Things to pervade the Whole: — Yet with this remarkable Diversity, that the Power and Talents of winning and obliging, of influencing, persuading, or commanding, were imparted to some in a much greater Degree than they were to others.

SURELY therefore in such Circumstances as these, every human Creature would fall into that Rank in Society, and that Station in Life, to which his Talents and his Genius spontaneously led him, — as *naturally*, I had almost said, as Water finds its Level.   And be it ever remembered, that distinct Ranks and different Stations, would produce a Civil Government, of some Kind or other, in a *new* World much sooner than they could in an *old* one. — I said MUCH SOONER; because in a new World, there could be no Complaints made against former Mismanagements, no Fears about the Incroachments of Power on the one Hand, or the Intrigues and Declamation of Faction on the other, and consequently no *Distrust* arising from the Abuses either of former Governors, or of former Demagogues.   In short, as in such a World there could be no Manner of Experience, there could hardly be any such Things as Caution and Reserve; and therefore all the Disputes of later Times about social Compacts, Contracts, and Conventions, about positive Stipulations, reciprocal Engagements, and Reservations of Rights, would have been probably as little understood at that Juncture, as the Terms of Art in Cookery, before Cookery became an Art, or the Orders in Building, before a single Building was erected.   In short, and to sum up all in one Word, where *Nature* alone was the Guide, the Terms of *Art*, and the Additions, or Alterations of subsequent Times, whether for the better, or for the worse, must have been absolutely unknown, and consequently could not have been attended to, at the first Formation of Civil Government.

BUT after all, perhaps some will say, "We do not differ from you in real Sentiments, tho' we express ourselves somewhat differently.   We mean to say, that no Part of the human Species, has a Right to enslave the other; and we mean no more."   Very well, be it so, and we are agreed:

But let us first know, what do you mean by *Slavery?* And what Ideas do you include under that Term? — For if you mean to say, that every Man is a *Slave*, who has not the Power of electing his own Law-giver, his own Magistrate, his Colonel, Captain, or Judge, I deny the Position, and call on you to prove it by better Arguments, than your own bare Assertion. But if you only meant to say, that bad Laws, if any, ought to be repealed, and good Laws enacted, and faithfully and impartially executed; — and that when Governors shall abuse their Power to the Detriment of the People, they ought to be stopped in their Career, and even to be called to an Account for their Misconduct, in Proportion to the Detriment received. — If this be all you meant to say, when you talked about original, unalienable Rights, social Compacts, &c. &c. we are agreed again: But surely, surely, this is a very odd, and intricate Way of expressing the plainest, and most obvious Truths imaginable.

MOREOVER, if you intended to say, that tho' Government in *general* did not derive its Existence from any *personal* Contract between Prince and People, between the Governors and the Governed; — yet, that it hath so much of what a Civilian would term a *Quasi-Contract* in the Nature of it, that the Duties and Obligations on both Sides of the Relation, are altogether to the same Effect, as if a particular Contract, and a positive Engagement had been entered into; — If this be your Meaning, we are ready to joint Issue with you once more; — and this the rather, because the Ideas of a *Quasi-Contract* contain our own on this Head, and those of every Constitutional Whig throughout the Kingdom.

HOWEVER, though we are ready to grant you all these Things, yet it is plain, that you meant a great deal more; — else, why do you cavil at the Phrases, *implicit Consent, tacit Agreement, implied Covenant, virtual Representation*, and the like? — All which naturally and necessarily imply the Idea of a *Quasi-Contract.* Moreover why so loud in your Exclamations, and bitter in your Invectives against supposing, that a Government may be good and lawful in itself, tho' the People are not represented in it, according to your Mode of Representation? Recollect the several Extracts from Messrs. LOCKE, MOLINEUX, PRIESTLY, and PRICE, already produced in the former Part of this Work: And then you must maintain, in Conformity to the leading Principles of your Sect, — That throughout this whole Dispute, your grand Objection lies not so much against the mere Laws themselves, or against any supposed Culpability in the Manner of administering them, — as against the Right, Title, or Authority to make, or to execute any Laws at all, be they in themselves good, or bad. In one Word, according to your Doctrine, *that*

Man is a *Slave*, who is obliged to submit to the best Laws that ever were made, and to the mildest Government, that ever existed, if he did not give his previous Consent towards establishing the one, and enacting the other: And that Man is FREE, who submits to no other Government but that which he himself hath chosen, and obeys no other Laws, but those, which he himself hath helped to make; tho' they should be in themselves as tyrannical and cruel, as unjust, and unreasonable, as can be conceived.   So that the great Good of political Liberty, and the intolerable Evil of political Slavery, are according to this blessed Doctrine, resolved at last into the single Words — CONSENT, or NOT CONSENT, What astonishing Absurdities are these! — And yet, alas! how prevalent, and contagious!

THE Idea of a *Quasi-Contract*, instead of an *actual* Contract [which never existed] between any Sovereigns, and *all*, or even the *major Part* of their Subjects, would have prevented Men of good Intentions, and honest Minds, from falling into these gross Absurdities, and dangerous Mistakes. Therefore as the Term itself *Quasi-Contract* may be new to some Readers, tho' the Sense is obvious to every one, when properly explained, I will beg Leave to bestow some Words upon it, before I conclude this Chapter.

IN all human *Trusts* whatever, from the highest to the lowest, where there is a *Duty* to be performed, which is not actually expressed, specified, or contracted for, — but nevertheless is strongly implied in the Nature of the Trust; — the Obligation to perform that implied Duty, is of the Nature of a *Quasi-Contract;* — a Contract as binding in the Reason of Things, and in the Court of Conscience, as the most solemn Covenant that was ever made.   This I think is a plain Case; at least I cannot make it plainer, and therefore tho' I might illustrate this Matter by appealing to the Proceedings of the Courts of Equity, which are little more than the inforcing of the Performance of *Quasi-Contracts*, yet I will confine myself to Subjects, that are altogether political; — because I wish to meet the Lockians on their own Ground, and to confute them by their favourite Principles.

BE it therefore allowed, for Argument's Sake, that there is an *actual*, and not a *Quasi-Contract*, this Day subsisting in *Great-Britain* between Prince and People.   The Question then is, When was this Contract made?   And the Answer must be [for no other can be given] that it was made at his Majesty's Coronation, when he took a solemn Oath to govern his People according to Law; and when they on their Parts expressed their Consent to his Accession to the Throne by loud Huzzas, and Shouts of Joy. — Well: To take no Advantage of one material Omission among many, that the Spectators on this Occasion were *not a thousandth* Part of the People of *Great Britain* and *Ireland* [not to say a Word about the Colonies.] Let it be granted, that this was a good Contract, fair, valid, and reciprocal. — Yet the difficulty is still to come, — What was the Case *before* this Contract was made? And how stood Matters during the long Interval, which elapsed between his Accession, and Coronation? Or suppose, that he had not yet been crowned, Was the Prince in that Case, and during these nineteen Years of his Reign, not obliged to govern his People according to Law? Or were the People, on their Parts, not obliged to become his dutiful and loyal Subjects, 'till they had shouted and huzzaed at his Coronation? Resolve this Difficulty, if you can, on the Lockian Principle of an *actual* Contract: But if you will admit of a *Quasi-Contract*, the Difficulty vanishes at once: So that Reason and Common Sense, and the *known Laws* of the Land all co-incide in perfect Harmony: I said the *known* Laws of the Land, because it is notorious to all the World, that there was not one political Duty incumbent on either Prince, or People, *after* the solemnity of a Coronation, but was equally incumbent *before* that Ceremony was performed.

AGAIN: The Lockians stiffly maintain, that every Civil Government must be an Usurpation of unalienable Rights, if the People are neither permitted to assemble together in their personal Capacities, for the Purposes of making Laws, for seeing them executed, and the like, —* nor allowed to elect Deputies to represent them, and to act as their Attornies or Proxies. Well: Be this Position admitted for the present: — Nay, be it likewise admitted, that whenever the Freeholders or Freemen of any County, City, or Borough do appoint such Parliamentary *Attornies*, they have a Right to insist on their renouncing their own private Judgment (at least in Practice) in order to act in Conformity to the Instructions of their Constituents, and not according to the Dictates of their own Consciences. Such a Contract as this [for a Contract it must be of the Lockian Principle, if it be any thing at all] methinks, sounds a little *odd*, — especially when considered as the discriminating Characteristic of the professed Friends of Liberty! But let it pass at present among other *odd* Things. — And then comes the main Question to be resolved: — What Contract or Covenant have these Electors made with the other Members of Parliament, chosen by other Freemen or Freeholders, and for other Places, where they have no Concern, and no Right to interfere,

---

* The proper Use, and great Advantages of Deputies from, or Representatives of the People, will be set forth at large in the 4th Chapter of the ensuing Work.

— who nevertheless make Laws to bind *them?* — "Laws to bind them!"
Yes to bind them *in all* [reasonable] *Cases whatsoever,* as much as the
Members of their own electing. "Surely this is strange to tell:" And
yet not more strange than true. — Therefore I ask again, What express
Covenant or Stipulations have Mess. PRIESTLY, or PRICE, made with the
rest of the Members of Parliament, — perhaps not so few as 550 in Number, whom they did *not* elect, — and for whom they had *no Votes* to
give?—I ask this Question even on a Supposition, that they had expressly
covenanted with their own Members to act agreeably to those Instructions, which from Time to Time they were to have received from them?
— Or do they indeed pretend to have an Authority to instruct *all* the
Representatives of the united Kingdom, as well as their own?

BUT to return to the principal Subject. On the whole, and turn which
Way you will, the Upshot of the Matter must come to this, that Civil
Government is *natural* to Man; and that at the Beginning, before the
Human Heart was corrupted by the Tyranny of Princes or the Madness
and Giddiness of the People, by the Ambition of the Great, or the Crafts
and Wiles of scheming Politicians, Civil Government as naturally took
Place among Mankind, according to their respective Talents and Qualifications, as the Marriage Union between Adam and Eve so elegantly
described by MILTON.

In after Times we will readily allow, That the Scenes were greatly
changed in both Cases: — But to argue from the present State of Things,
occasioned either by the Mal-Administration of Governors on one Side, or
by the false Pretensions of Demagogues on the other, or by the still
greater Evils which the Public suffers by the Struggles and Conflicts,
and Counter-Machinations of both; — to argue, I say, from these Corruptions and Adulterations to the Origin of Civil Government in its pure
and uncorrupted State, — would be just as preposterous, as it would be
to maintain, that Adam and Eve did not begin their domestic Government till the Marriage Portion was fixt and ascertained, till the Marriage-
Articles were signed and sealed, the Jointure, Dowry, Pin-Money, &c. &c.
all previously settled, and Trustees appointed for the due Execution of
these several Contracts.

THEREFORE, to sum up all in one Word, let a thousand Revolutions
happen in the Forms or Modes of Government, and ever so many
Changes take Place in the Persons or Families of the Regents of the
State, still Civil Government itself is no other than a PUBLIC TRUST, in
whatever Shape it may appear, or in whose Hands soever it may be
placed. In some few Instances [very few indeed] the Terms and Condi-

tions of this important Trust may perhaps be ascertained and specified: But in Multitudes of others they cannot, tho' of the highest Concern: Yet wherever they cannot, they are *implied:* And this Implication may be very justly termed a QUASI-CONTRACT.

CHAP. II.

OBJECTIONS ANSWERED.

HAVING in the preceding Chapter humbly submitted to the Consideration of the Public, my own Opinion concerning the Origin of Civil Government, in Opposition to the Notion of Mr. LOCKE and his Followers, I esteem it my Duty in the next Place to endeavour to answer such Objections, as seem to militate the strongest against what has been advanced.

OBJECTION I.

"ACCORDING to the foregoing Hypothesis, the higher Powers in every Country should be Heroes of the first Magnitude; — or if not Heroes in War, they should at least be endowed with the greatest Genius, the most distinguished and useful Talents in the Arts of Peace. For we are told, that it is their Superiority of natural Endowments, which, like Water finding its Level, laid the Foundation of Civil Government. Whereas, were we to turn from this ideal Perfection, to the plain, simple Fact, we shall find that few of the ruling Powers, especially crowned Heads, are wiser, or better, or braver, or more usefully employed than other Mortals. Moreover, according to the foregoing Representation of the Matter it should also follow, That on the Demise of any of these super-eminent, exalted Beings, a Kind of Dissolution, or at least a Suspension of Government ought to ensue, 'till another *Non-pareil* could be found out, in order to fill [worthily and properly] the vacant Throne."

ANSWER.

THIS Objection, smart and plausible as it may appear, is wholly grounded on a Mistake, which being removed, the Objection vanishes. The Mistake is this, That what was necessary, or expedient at first, must continue to be necessary, or expedient ever after. Whereas the Course of Nature in almost every Instance plainly proves the contrary.

SIR ISAAC NEWTON and Mr. BOYLE had most extraordinary natural Talents and Sagacities in their respective Provinces; which they improved by almost incessant Industry and Application.   Their Discoveries in Astronomy, Mathematics, Optics, Natural Philosophy, Mechanics, Chemistry, &c. &c. &c. are wonderfully great and curious. But doth it follow, that every Man must have the Genius of a BOYLE, a NEWTON, in order to be benefited, or enlightened by their Discoveries? And now, that they have led the Way, may not Men of very moderate Capacities, be able to tread in their Steps?   Nay I will go farther, and even ask, may not an illiterate Mechanic [illiterate, comparatively speaking] by Dint of mere Use and Practice, and by the Advantage of having good Models before his Eyes; — may not even such an one be able to construct, or to manage some of their most curious Machines in a much better Manner than the great Philosophers themselves could have done, had they been alive?   Surely he may: For nothing can be more obvious, than that the Man, who cannot invent, may nevertheless by Means of daily Use, and Habit, be able to improve on a former Invention, greatly to his own Advantage, and that of others.

THE Case in Politics is much the same; or rather it is a still stronger Confirmation of the foregoing Remark.   For tho' it may be necessary to have an Hero to found an Empire; or [to come still nearer to the Plan of the preceding Chapter] tho' it may at first require some extraordinary Efforts of an uncommon Genius, to form an Hundred Pair of independent Savages into a regular Community, and to bind them together with the Bonds of Civil Society, — yet when this is once done, and good Order and Harmony well established, — Things will then go on, in a Manner, of their own accord, if common Prudence be not wanting.   Nay, what is still more to our present Purpose, it is observeable, that great Geniuses are likely to do more Harm than Good, if there should happen to be a Succession of them in the same Government, for two, or three Generations.   The active Spirits of such Men, and their eccentric Dispositions will not suffer them to remain in a neutral State; so that they will certainly be employed either for the better, or for the worse.   And as Ambition, and the Lust of Power are the reigning Vices of the Great, it is therefore but too probable, that they will become bad Neighbours to other States, in Proportion, as they shall have less Occasion for exerting their Abilities at Home: Or if they should confine their Attention chiefly to their own Territories; — can it be a Doubt which Course they will take, Whether to encrease, or diminish the Privileges of their own Subjects? — In short, Woe be to the Country, which happens to be cursed with a successive Race of Heroes: Long Experience hath too fatally confirmed this Observation.   And the Misfortune is, that the Subjects of these victorious Princes, are, generally speaking, so blinded with the Glare of Glory, and so intoxicated with the Fumes of Conquest, that they will be content to be enslaved themselves, provided they shall be so happy as to be employed in the glorious Work of enslaving others. — It must, I think, be allowed, that a ROMULUS was necessary to found *Rome*, and to bring that Set of Banditti, which he first drew together, into some Degree of Order and Regularity, by obliging them to submit to the Rules of Justice among themselves, and the Laws of Civil Government. — But after those good Ends were in Part accomplished, the mild, pacific Disposition, and the steady and temperate Conduct of a NUMA, were much fitter to constitute a Successor, than the dangerous Abilities of another ROMULUS.

OBJECTION II.

"THE Account given in the preceding Chapter of the Origin of Civil, or Political Government, must be liable to great Exceptions, because it confounds those Ideas, which ought always to be kept distinct and separate. Thus for Example, there is a Society, which may be called *natural*, and there is another which is *political*. And tho' Man is formed by Nature to become a Member of both Societies; yet it is a very great Mistake to say, that he has the same Inducement, or that he is influenced by the same Motives in both Cases. As a gregarious Animal, he loves to associate with his like, and to herd with them. This is mere *natural* Society, and cannot be called *political*. And even after it had been perceived, that there are many Inequalities between the respective Powers, Talents, and Capacities of the several Members which compose this Society: — Perhaps indeed so great as would necessarily introduce some Kind of Difference, or Distinction among them; still it doth not follow, that these Distinctions should change natural Society into political. For no mere Meeting together, or Assemblage of the People, no Contiguity of Habitation, or Vicinage of Inhabitants ought to be allowed to constitute a State politic, till *Legislation* hath been actually introduced, and *Jurisdiction* exercised among them: — Which it is apprehended, could not be done without common Consent, or at least the Consent of the major Part.

"IN Fact, the Motives for entering into these two distinct Societies, the *natural* and the *political*, are not only different, but in a Manner *opposite*. For if Men are drawn to herd together as gregarious Animals, by a Kind of *instinctive Love;* — they may be justly said to be compelled to form political Associations by a Sort of *instinctive Fear:* That is, dreading the Approach of some alarming Danger, or desirious of retaliating some Injury received; — they collect their scattered Forces together, and put them under the Direction of one Man, or of one Set of Men, in order to be employed for the public Good and Safety. Now this being the proper Cause or Motive, and therefore the only true Origin of *political Union*, it is plain, that the very Description of it implies both universal Caution, and mutual Distrust. For in this Case, every Man acts from a Principle of Self-Interest, or Self-Preservation. And therefore it is *not credible*, that any Number of Men, in order to guard against one Danger, would rush headlong into another: It is not, it cannot be supposed, That rational Creatures would surrender up their natural Liberty and Independence, and with it, in some Sense, their Lives and Fortunes, without demanding any Security for the right Use and faithful Application of so great a Trust."

ANSWER.

WHEN Mr. LOCKE was a very young Man, it was the Custom of the Pastors of his Time to make the junior Part of their Congregations to undergo the following strange Examination, "At what Day or Hour did you feel the Influxes of Saving Grace, and receive the Seal of your Election and Justification?" Something like the same Question is couched under this Objection, founded on Mr. LOCKE's System, relating to the [supposed] Time of our first Entrance into a political Union, or Confederacy with the State, under which we live. For it seems, there cannot be any such Thing as a *natural-born* Subject: It is, according to the Lockian Doctrine, a Solecism in Language, and a Contradiction to common Sense. Surely therefore we have a Right to ask a Lockian this plain Question: As you say you are not a *natural-born Subject*, tho' born and bred here in *England*, be pleased to tell us, Are you *now* a Member of the *British* Constitution? Or are you not? — And if you are, When? Or from what Day or Hour did your Membership commence? Moreover what Ceremony of Adoption, Admission, Matriculation, or whatever else you will please to call it, was used by you, or by others on that solemn Occasion? The Answer to these Questions, it is apprehended, would be rather embarrassing; and might draw on Consequences, which a prudent Man would willingly avoid.

INDEED the whole Objection, tho' seemingly a new one, is nothing more than a Position of Mr. LOCKE and his Followers already considered and confuted. However, as it is here revived, and appears in something like a new Dress, let us bestow a Remark or two upon it.

"THE Incredibility of sliding *insensibly*, and *without any previous Contract*, from that Society, which is merely natural, into that which is political!" But why, I pray, is this incredible?— "Because [says a Lockian] the Motives, or Inducements are not only different in themselves, but even contradictory. Inasmuch as the Inducement to form the one is instinctive Love, but to create the other is evidently Caution, Apprehension, or the Fear of Danger." Now this is taking that very Thing for granted, which ought to be proved. And indeed it is one of those Arguments, which destroys itself. For if Caution is supposed to operate so strongly as to prevent the Formation of political Society, till Men had previously settled the Terms of this intended Association, — and had given, and received Securities for reposing a Trust and Confidence in each other; — it ought to operate still more strongly for the Prevention of natural Society, lest the *strongest*, or the most *vicious* of these *ungoverned* Human Animals, when herding together, should bite, or kick, should seize on his Prey, and devour the *Weakest:* — A Circumstance this, which we must allow, might *possibly* happen. Therefore, according to this System, neither the Society which is called *natural*, nor that which is *political* can exist at all, till there has been a previous Contract entered into for the Safety and Preservation of all Parties. And yet methinks, it is rather difficult to conceive, how a Connection could be formed, how Terms could be settled, and a solemn Contract entered into, for binding all Parties, before Men had once met together, or indeed before they could *prudently*, or *safely* trust themselves in the Company of each other for this, or any other Purpose.

THE Thing to be proved was this, that there must be some certain Period in each Person's Life, when he or she first commenced a Member of political Society. — A Period, when he or she surrendered up those Liberties, and that Independence which belonged to him or her, in a State of Nature, in order to receive from the Government of the Country, that Protection, and those Advantages, which result from Civil Society. Now such a Covenant as this, so peculiarly marked and circumstanced, could not easily have been forgotten, if it had ever happened. And therefore we must call upon the Lockians once more [each to answer separately for him or herself] to name the Year, Month, Week, Day, or Hour, when this Contract was made between the Government of *Great-Britain* on the one Part, and A. B. or C. D. or E. F., on the other.

IN the mean Time [as they will not be in Haste to inform us on this Head] let us endeavour to trace this, as well as other dangerous Errors of modern Republicanism, to their proper Source, in order to put the

Friends of real and constitutional Liberty on their Guard against such Delusions.

THE arguing from particular Exigences to general Practice, and from extraordinary Events to the usual, and (for the most Part) uninterrupted Course of Things, seems to have been the *Ignis fatuus*, which misled Mr. LOCKE, and all his Followers. Thus, for Instance, if there happened at any Time to be so much Discord, and such a Dissention between Sovereign and Subject, Prince and People, as could not be healed, without the Help of a written Compact, and a formal Treaty between Party and Party: — Then this *eccentric* Emergence is urged as a proper Precedent for requiring the constant Use of formal Compacts in all Cases, and at all Times and Seasons whatsoever. Now this Reasoning is just as sound and judicious, as it would be to maintain, that if a most violent Remedy was deemed necessary to be prescribed in the last Stage of a most acute Disease, it would be right to prescribe the same Remedy in all Cases, and in every Circumstance that could happen, let a Person be sick, or well, and whatever his Complaint might be, or even if he had no Complaint at all.

AGAIN, when any Number of independent Persons are incorporated into one Society by Means of a parliamentary Law, or of a Royal Charter; it would be a very easy Matter not only to tell the Year, the Month, and the Day of such a *new* Incorporation, but also to assign the public Reasons or Motives for establishing such a Body Politic: — Nay more, it is apprehended, that it would be no very difficult Task, even to point out the respective Views of Self-Interest and private Advantage, which some at least of these independent Persons proposed to themselves, by giving up their natural Independency, and putting on the Shackles (if they must be so called) of political Concatenation and Dependence. But in the Name of common Sense, what have such Cases as these to do with Civil Government at large? And what Affinity hath any political Institution of this Sort, where the Act of Incorporation is in a Manner *instantaneous*, with that *progressive* Course of Civil Society, which like the infant State of Man, [*moral* and *intellectual* as well as natural] grows up gradually from small Beginnings to Maturity? — As well might you pretend to define, where the Night ends, and the Day begins, as to assign the exact Period when that Society which is *natural*, puts on the Dress and assumes the Form of the *political*. — Besides, if it hath been already shewn in the first Chapter, that Mankind would insensibly slide into some Kind of Subordination or other, in Consequence of the Difference between their respective Talents, Genius, and Capacities; — I would here ask, How could they stop at any given Point of natural Society, and proceed no farther? — How indeed, when 'tis also considered, that at the first Creation of the above-mentioned hundred Pair of Patriarchs, those Members of natural Society would be entire Strangers to every Kind of Fear and Jealousy, and to all that Apprehension of Danger, which the *Experience* of after Ages hath suggested to Mankind.

To make this Matter still plainer, if possible, I would here observe, That in the Infancy of States and Empires, political Societies were not formed at once, as Guilds of Trades, or Companies of mercantile Adventurers, or Bodies Politic are formed at present, by Means of Paper, Parchment, and Wax, Signing and Sealing. But Civil Societies grew up by Degrees from small, and in a Manner, imperceptible Beginnings, according as the Numbers of Mankind encreased, or as their Wants and Exigencies required. Nay, it is exceedingly probable, that neither the first Governors, nor the first Governed [or if you please, neither the Men of superior Qualifications, nor those of inferior] had conceived the whole of the Plan, which they were afterwards to pursue through the rest of their Lives. But they were like Men groping in the dark, and feeling their Way by little and little. As new Lights broke in upon them, they still advanced: But it is very absurd to suppose that at first, they saw clearly into those Consequences or Relations of Things, which the present Science of Politics, raised on the Experience of Ages, hath discovered to us. Indeed, whenever new Cases did arise, it is natural to suppose, that such new Powers, both of Legislation and Jurisdiction, would be exerted, as those Cases required: But certainly the Society itself had an Existence before the Exertion of those Powers, or even before it could be known that they were wanted. So that in Fact, and in every View, this second Objection must be deemed to be as groundless as the former.

THAT which the Lockians ought to have said, is probably to this Effect, That tho' it be absurd to suppose, that Civil Government *in general* took its Rise from previous Conventions, and mutual Stipulations *actually* entered into between Party and Party; — and tho', whenever such a Contract as here supposed did take Place, *at some very extraordinary Conjuncture*, — [a Contract, by the by, which could only bind the *contracting Parties*:]— Yet as Civil Government in general is in Reality a *Public Trust*, be the Origin, and the Form of it whatever they may;— there must be some Covenant or other *supposed* or *implied* as a Condition necessarily annexed to every Degree of Discretionary Power, whether expressed or not.—Had they said only this, they would have said the *Truth*; and their Doctrine would have exactly coincided with

the Ideas of a *Quasi-Contract* before mentioned.   Nay more, they would
have avoided all those Paradoxes, which attend their present System,
and render it one of the most mischievous, as well as ridiculous Schemes
that ever disgraced the reasoning Faculties of human Nature.

OBJECTION III.

"WHATEVER Difficulties in Theory may be supposed to attend the
Idea of a Contract *actually* [not *virtually*] subsisting between Prince and
People; the Fact itself is so decisive in Favour of an *actual Contract*, that
the bare mentioning of it, with its concomitant Circumstances, is enough
to silence any Plea, or Pretence to the contrary.   For Example,—even
among the most unenlightened Nations, whether ancient, or modern;
it is remarkable, that the Powers and Prerogatives of their Kings and
Leaders were very limited, and circumscribed.—Sometimes extending
little farther, than was just necessary for the carrying on a War, or
conducting an Expedition with Secrecy and Success;—at other Times
consisting of but little more than a bare Sufficiency to act the Part
of powerful Judges and Mediators in civil Disputes;—and at all Times,
so balanced by counteracting Powers, as never to be, in a *legal* Sense,
unlimited, or despotic.   The Case of the antient *Gauls*, as described
by CÆSAR, and of the *Germans* by TACITUS, strongly confirms what is
here advanced.   To which we may add that amazing Uniformity of
Government so visible in the Feudal System of the barbarous Nations,
which overspread all Europe, and exhibited every where a *limited*
Constitution.   If we wanted historical Examples of this Sort, our own
Country might furnish enough.   For surely the Mode of obtaining the
famous Magna Charta here in *England*, and the History of the Wars
between the Houses of STUART and DOUGLASS in *Scotland*, afford such
flagrant Instances of a limited Monarchy, and a *conventional Constitution* (if I may use the Term) that more could not possibly be desired,
or expected."

ANSWER.

THESE Objectors are very unfortunate in appealing to the Example,
or Practice of *unenlightened* Nations for Proofs of actual [not virtual]
Contracts subsisting between Prince and People, if by actual they suppose
written Contracts.   For it is hard to conceive, how written Contracts
could have been in Use among Barbarians, before they had learnt to read
and write.   But if by *actual* the Objectors mean *verbal* Contracts, the
Difficulty is indeed removed in one Respect, and as much increased in

another. For it exceeds even the Powers of Credulity itself to believe, That the Prince of any Country entered into a *verbal*, and *personal* Contract with every one of his Subjects,—or even with the thousandth Part of them, if his Territories were at all populous and extended. And yet there certainly is such a Thing as an *implied* Covenant [I say implied, not expressed] between every Prince, and every Subject throughout his Dominions, be the People many, or few in Number, and his Empire great or small. For every Trust implies a Covenant, or Condition of some Kind, or other, according to the Nature of the Case; and therefore these Trusts may with great Propriety be termed *Quasi Contracts*. So much as to *this* Part of the Objection. — Need any Thing more be added?

THE other Part of the Objection is, "That all the Kingdoms in Europe, erected on the Basis of the Feudal System, were limited Monarchies." Granted: For the Fact was really so.—But what Inference can be deduced from this Circumstance?—Not surely, that these Limitations arose either from *written* Contracts, or from *verbal* Covenants, and *personal* Conferences made with each Individual, or even with the Majority of the Individuals of any of these States; [because these Things have been proved already to be impossible:]—But they arose from the aristocratical Power of the Heads of Tribes, or the Chieftains of Clans and Families, who in their military Expeditions, acted a Part more like that of Allies and Confederates with the Commander in Chief, than as his own proper Subjects: And who therefore, on the Division of the conquered Country, got so much Territory, and such Royalties and Jurisdictions to be allotted to themselves, that they were all a Species of little Kings, each on his own Domain.

GRANTING therefore to these Objections every Thing they ask;—nay granting much more;—granting, I say, that the Heads of Tribes, and Chiefs of Clans of all the barbarous Nations of Antiquity, and more especially of *Gaul* and *Germany*, elected their Kings by *unanimous* Consent;—and that they bound them down to what Terms they pleased;—still the Question will return, Who elected these Heads and Chiefs? And what Right of *fair* and *unconstrained Delegation* had they to act for others, as well as for themselves?— In fact, if the Chiefs of each Tribe, or Clan were not elected by *unanimous* Consent, —nay if they were not elected at all, What have we gained, by proving, That the Heads of these little Societies took great Care, that they themselves should be the only Tyrants? — Now, there is, I believe, not the least Vestige either in CÆSAR, or TACITUS, or any other ancient Author, that the Individuals of each Tribe, or Clan, met together for Election of an Head, or Chief, in

Case of a Vacancy.—No; these Chieftains acted on a quite contrary Principle respecting their own Power;—inasmuch as they considered, that they had an *inherent* and a *natural* Right to rule over their own Tribes, Clans, or Vassals, tho' none had such a Right to rule over them.— Consequently all the Parade about the Restraints and Limitations laid on the Power of Kings, according to the Gothic Constitution, and during the Continuance of the Feudal System, ends at last in this, *That the Kings were bound, but the Nobles were free.* — A Sample and Illustration of which Kind of regal Submission, and of Aristocratical Exaltation, we have, or lately had, in the Gothic Constitution of that fertile but unhappy Kingdom of *Poland.* Nay more, the History of Magna-Charta itself is a striking Proof, and Confirmation of this Point. For the Barons of *England,* in that Struggle with King JOHN, did not fight in Defence of the general Liberties of the People of *England,* but for the particular Preservation and Continuance of their own Domination over their Vassals. And at the last, what little was granted to the People in, and by that Charter, [little, I mean, in Comparison to the Liberties they have since enjoyed] was obtained by the King himself, not only without the Assistance, but even contrary to the Good-Will and Approbation of his Barons. For when he saw himself in danger of being stript of so much feudal Power, which of course would strengthen his Enemies in Proportion as it weakened himself,* he obliged them to part with some of their exorbitant Claims, in Favour of their Vassals, according as they had compelled him to do the like in Favour of themselves. The Motives of his Action, it must be confessed, were not the purest, nor the most patriotic. But nevertheless the People in general reaped the Benefit. And thus it came to pass, that the Mass of the People of England, by

---

* It was a great Mistake in a late noble Author to assert, That the Army of the Barons at Running-Mead was an Assembly of the People, demanding a Restitution of their Rights from a tyrannical Prince. — No: The Fact was just the contrary. For it was this tyrannical Prince, who took the People's Part, even whilst they themselves were ignorant of the Matter, in order to raise a Power towards counter-balancing the Aristocracy of his great Barons. — I am credibly informed, That there is a Copy now extant of the very Magna-Charta, which the Barons intended should have passed, had their Plan succeeded in all Respects, in which there are none, or next to none of those great Advantages in Favour of the Bulk of the People, which the real Magna-Charta now contains. But it was hardly possible for them to withstand the Force of that Argument urged by the Royal Party, [and that too in the Presence of their own Vassals, then in Arms for their Sakes,] which was to this Effect: —"As you, who are the Vassals of the Crown, demand such and such Concessions from your Prince, you must grant the like Concessions to your own Vassals, to be inserted in the same Magna-Charta." — See particularly the 69th Clause of Magna-Charta.

a lucky Concurrence of Circumstances, and without any intentional Efforts of their own, got considerably by that famous Struggle, and thereby laid the happy Foundation of their future Greatness.

Now after having said so much in regard to England, we may be allowed to be very brief in respect to Scotland: For most undoubtedly, neither the great House of DOUGLAS, in all their Civil Wars with the Crown, nor any of the Lords in the Lowlands, nor Chieftains in the Highlands harboured so much as a Wish to have their Power abridged over their respective Clans, Vassals, and Dependents, by their Attempts to abridge the Power of the Crown over themselves. As soon therefore should I believe that the late Mr. BECKFORD of famous, and patriotic Memory, in his Vociferation for Liberty, intended to set the wretched Slaves on his numerous Plantations in Jamaica free, as I could suppose, that a Gothic Baron meant to part with his Power over his own Vassals and Dependents, when he contended to abridge the regal Power over himself, and his Fellow Barons. And were the Planters in Jamaica to imitate their Brethren on the Continent, by setting up an intire Independence [Would to God, that not only they but all the Leeward-Islands were to do the like!—And that England had the Wisdom and good Sense to permit them to do it!] Were, I say, these Planters, to set up an independent Government, and to elect a King of their own,—there is no Doubt to be made, but that they would tie up his Majesty's Hands as much as possible, and make him little more than a Cypher;—at the same Time, that they would expect to be at full Liberty themselves to whip and scourge, and torture their poor Negroes, according to their own brutal Will and Pleasure. Nay, it is very observable, that the most eminent Republican Writers, such as LOCKE, FLETCHER of *Saltown*, and ROUSSEAU himself, pretend to justify the making Slaves of others, whilst they are pleading so warmly for Liberty for themselves. And what is still more extraordinary, the greatest *American* Champions for the unalienable Right of Mankind, one the Generalissimo of the Republican Army, and the other lately the President of the Congress, have shewn by their own Example, that they have no Objections against Slavery, provided they shall be free themselves, and have the Power of enslaving others: For Mr. WASHINGTON, I am credibly informed, has several Slaves now on his Plantations, and Mr. LAWRENS got his Fortune by acting as a Kind of Broker in the Slave Trade, buying and selling his Fellow-Creatures on Commission.

OBJECTION IV.

"ONE plain Matter of Fact is better than a thousand Arguments spun out of the Cobwebs of Metaphysics. And therefore the surest Way, in all Cases of Dispute, is to recur to the Fountain-Head, if we can; which in the present Case we may easily do, by appealing to an established Custom among the Savages of *America*. For it is an historical Fact, universally acknowledged, that the Individuals in each of their Tribes live in a State of absolute Freedom and Equality among themselves, in Times of Peace, without Subordination, Jurisdiction, or Legislation of any Kind: And that they only act in Concert, and submit to some Kind of Authority during a War. When that is over, the Power of their Chief, or Leader ceases of Course; and each returns to his original Equality and Independence. Here therefore we have the fullest Proof, and the clearest Illustration of the distinct Existence of the two Societies above-mentioned, namely, of that natural Society which is founded ont he Attractions of instinctive Love, and of that political Union, which arises from Fear, which operates by Consent, and is grounded on *actual* Compact."

ANSWER.

Is it fair, just, or reasonable, That any of the peculiar Customs of this savage People, [with whose History natural, moral, or political we are very little acquainted] should be urged in the present Debate, as Patterns of, or Examples to, the rest of Mankind? Before *America* was ever discovered, we had the Customs and Manners of almost all *Europe*, *Asia*, and *Africa*, to descant upon;—a Field, one would have thought, large enough for every Theory of Government, and for all possible Investigations of Civil Society, without having Recourse to another Part of the World, which was discovered but as Yesterday. And now it is in* Part discovered, we have the Mortification to find, that the original

---

* See Dr. ROBERTSON's excellent and impartial History of *America*, Vol. I. Book IV. viz. Condition and Character of the *Americans*, Pages 281–409. I myself have heard Mons. CONDAMINE at *Paris* confirming almost all the Particulars mentioned in these Pages. He added likewise one Circumstance, which I ought not to omit: Speaking of the Indians in the Empires of *Mexico* and *Peru*, whom the *Spaniards* had converted to Christianity for several Generations past. "They make, says he, excellent Catholics; for they are charmed with the Pomp and Ceremonies of Religion, and *never think*. Indeed it appears to me, that they are incapable of much Thought: For they are Children all their Lives. —*Toujours Enfans*."

Natives, far from being the Ornament, are almost universally the Disgrace of Human Nature;—as having many Defects and Vices peculiar to themselves, with few, or no Virtues and Excellencies to counterbalance them. Surely then, our modern Patriots, and zealot Republicans might have spared both themselves and us the Trouble of going into this Part of the World in Search after *Models* of Government worthy of Imitation.

BUT nevertheless, as our Adversaries, after having been defeated every where else, have chosen to entrench themselves on this Spot, and to set us at Defiance, let us not avoid the Combat even on their own Ground, and let us not despair of being able to wrest the *Tomahoc*, their favourite Weapon, out of their Hands.

Now all that we know of *America*, relative to the present Subject, seems to be this, That the far greater Part of the Native Indians [Indians I mean, as they were formerly, before their Subjection, or those at present, who are not in Subjection to any European Power] may be divided into three different Ranks, or Classes, *mere Savages,—half Savages*, —and *almost civilized*. I do not mention these Distinctions, or Classes, as accurate Definitions, according to logical Rules, but as Descriptions of Men, and Manners sufficiently exact for our present Purpose.

To begin therefore with those in the most perfect State of *American* Society, whom I call ALMOST CIVILIZED. The Reason of giving them this Denomination is, because they had a permanent Government, Legislation, and Jurisdiction of their own before the *Spanish* Conquests, and enjoyed many Blessings to which the rest of the Natives of that vast Country were almost Strangers. These were the Subjects of the two great Empires of *Mexico* and *Peru*. The Question therefore is, How were these Empires formed? Did they arise from the actual and express Consent [I do not say, each Individual but even of] the Majority of the Individuals, who composed them? Or were these Empires owing to some other Cause or Causes?—The Empire of *Mexico*, it must be owned, before MONTEZUMA'S Usurpation, was a *limited* Constitution: and therefore here, if any where, we may expect to find that solemn League and Covenant between the Sovereign and all his Subjects, which we have been so long searching after. But alas! here likewise we must be prepared to meet with a Disappointment. For the Restraints and Limitations laid upon the Emperors did not arise from any Compact solemnly entered into between the Sovereign and the People, or the Mass of the People, or even any Representatives chosen by the People,—but from the Aristocratical Power of the Nobles, or Princes of the Empire;—who, like the Barons of the *Gothic* Constitution in *Europe*, chose to have no other Tyrants than themselves: And that their *Tyranny was very great is beyond a Doubt. Granting therefore, for Argument's Sake, that some solemn Convention had passed between the Emperor and the mighty Princes of his Empire, whereby he was bound to observe certain Conditions stipulated between them,—still the Question returns again, Who elected these Princes, alias great *Mexican* Barons?   And what *social Compact* had they to shew for exercising any Authority whatever, much less despotic Authority, over their respective Slaves, and numerous Dependents?   Or, are we to suppose, that these Slaves and Vassals first met to elect their respective Masters, and then told them, "We prescribe such and such Terms to you; and then you may, if you please, prescribe the like to your Master the Emperor?"   Something like this must certainly be made to appear, before these Cases can be allowed to be any Kind of Confirmation of the Lockian System.   In the mean Time, I will bring a Case in Point, which is a decisive Proof of the contrary in similar Circumstances.   The King of *Bohemia*, for Example, and the Marquess of *Brandenburgh* (at War with each other in the Year 1777) are the two greatest Electors in the *German* Empire; the former of whom was likewise chosen Emperor a few Years before; and the latter is better known by the Stile and Title of the King of *Prussia*.   Now there are extant Volumes of Imperial Bulls and Capitulars, which plainly shew, that the Electors have reduced the Powers and Prerogatives of the Emperor to little more than a Shadow.   But what Benefits or Advantage can the oppressed Subjects of *Brandenburgh*, and of *Bohemia*, derive from these Limitations?   And do the poor *Peasants*, and other Vassals of either of these great Princes dare to say, "You have no Right to reign over us, but what we voluntarily gave you by such and such Acts of our Assemblies?   And therefore we will limit your Power over us, in the same Manner, as you limit the Power of the Emperor over you?" Dare they say these Things?   Or indeed can they say with Truth, that either the *Bohemians*, or the *Brandenburghers* did ever elect the Houses of *Austria*, or *Brandenburgh* to be their respective Sovereign Lords and Masters?

BUT to return: The great Empire of *Peru* comes the next under our Consideration.   And we read, that MANCO CAPAC, and his Consort MAMA OCOLLO, were the Founders of it, by making the People believe, that they were the Children of the Sun: Which illustrious Pedigree, and

---

* See ROBERTSON's History of *America*, Vol. I. Book 7, concerning the State of the *Mexican* Empire before the Invasion of the *Spaniards*. — See also the same concerning the State of the Empire of *Peru*.

imperial Title, the *Incas*, their Successors, laid Claim to ever after. Now a rank Republican may, if he pleases, spy out a social Compact even here: For he may assert, with his usual Confidence, that the *Peruvians* first met together in Congress, and after solemn Debate, and impartially scrutinizing the Matter, allowed the Proofs to be valid, which MANCO and his Consort there exhibited of their lineal Descent from that glorious Luminary; and recognized their Title to the Empire. For my Part, I can discern nothing like a social Contract between equal, and independent Beings, in the Formation of this Empire: But I can see plainly enough, that MANCO used, what may be called a *pious Fraud*, as MINOS, NUMA and LYCURGUS had done before him, in the like Circumstances. All which Examples evidently prove, that these Legislators were conscious to themselves, that their Plans even of doing Good, and of being of Service to Mankind, would have miscarried, had they trusted only to the Consent of the People, convened together *a la Monsieur* LOCKE, and had they not had Recourse to Measures of a very different Nature, by availing themselves of the popular Ignorance and Superstition.

So much as to the first Class of original *Americans*, the *almost civilized*.

THE next is, the *half Savages*. Now these People may be so termed, because they were in a Kind of Medium State, between the more refined Inhabitants of the great Empires of *Mexico*, and *Peru*, and the gross Savages of the Woods and Deserts. They had a Property in Lands and Goods, and consequently some Sort of Industry, together with a Species of Legislation and Jurisdiction within themselves. The Countries, in which they principally dwelt, were *Florida*, and along the Banks of *Mississippi*, some Part of the great Continent, and particularly a District called *Bagota, Hispaniola, Cuba*, and all the greater Islands: Of whom in general one striking Observation may be made; that they had noble Families among them, who enjoyed *hereditary Honours*, and were possessed of ample Patrimonies, Dignities, and Prerogatives, which they transmitted from Father to Son, without any actual Consent, or Election of the People. Now whether these distinguished Personages [Some of whom claimed also to be descended from the Sun, like the *Incas* of *Peru*] Whether, I say, these great Personages, and Heads of their respective Tribes, Clans, or Vassals, ought to be called Chieftains, or Princes, or Kings, is very immaterial, and nothing to the Purpose. Evident enough it is, let them be called by what Name you please, that neither they, nor the People over whom they presided, ever dreamt of a social Compact, as the Foundation of their hereditary Power and Pre-eminence. Whether therefore their Fore-fathers acquired this Ascendency, and these Prerogatives, by Means of a certain Superiority of natural Endowments [according to the Supposition of the foregoing Chapter] which elevated them above the rest of their Species,— Or whether by Virtue of a patriarchal, regular Descent, or by what other unknown Means, is not worth the Inquiry; since it is obvious, that the Merits of the Cause cannot turn on these Points, that all of them are equally repugnant to the Lockian Hypothesis of Contracts and Conventions.

However, we may from hence take Occasion to make one very useful Remark, that the Antiquity of some Families, and the Respect and Veneration *every where* shewn them, is another distinct Proof, that Mr. LOCKE and his Followers had not sufficiently studied human Nature, when they ascribed [at least their Arguments, and Train of Reasoning tend to ascribe] the general Pre-eminence of some Families over others to Contracts, Covenants, and Conventions. For it is not consistent with any Degree of common Sense to suppose, that the Dignity and Elevation of some Families, and the servile Condition and mean Estate of others, ever were, or ever could be settled by the mutual Consent of all Parties concerned, who met together in Congress for that Purpose;—each of them equal to, and all independent one of another. Moreover, what makes this Affair still the more extraordinary is, that such Respect paid to Family-Antiquity is greatest, by far, in those Countries, whose Inhabitants are the least removed from the original State of Nature. In rich Countries, for Example, such as *England* and *Holland*, the Honour of a long Pedigree is much lessened to what it formerly was, in Proportion as Riches and Opulence have encreased among the People: In *Scotland* and *Ireland* it still retains its Influence in the *poorer* Parts, but is evidently losing Ground in the *richer*, according as Manufactures and Commerce have begun to spread. In *France*, the Influence of Family is still considerable; in *Germany* much more, and in *Hungary, Poland, Moscovy,* &c. the most of all.

Now, what shall we say to these Things? For the Fact is really so, reason how you please upon it: And therefore, whether this Notion of *antient Blood* is well, or ill supported in *particular* Cases, still as it is generally so prevalent throughout the World, we ought, I think, to conclude, that it hath its Foundation in human Nature; Providence graciously intending to stimulate us to great and good Actions, and to prevent us from doing any Thing base and unworthy of our Ancestors. At the same Time, as such a Predilection in Favour of what is not properly our own, is liable to great Abuse, we ought to be the more watchful in guarding against the Abuses and Perversions of it.

HAVING said thus much, I leave it to every Reader to determine, towards which Extreme, that of paying too great,—or too little a Deference to the Antiquity of Family, and the Notions of high Blood, we of this Age and Country are leaning most at present.— For my own Part, I make no Secret of declaring, that had I now the Option, whether I would chuse to obey the Powers that be, or those that *wish to be*, I should have a mortal Aversion against submitting to the upstart Sway of an ADAMS, or a LAURENS, or of any other of that Tribe. And Experience hath taught us long ago, that such Sort of newly exalted Beings grow to be the most insolent of Men, and prove the worst of Tyrants.

BUT to return: It is said, that besides these Aristocratical, or Patriarchal Governments in *America*, there were others subsisting [that of the *Thlascallans* in particular] which bore a nearer Resemblance to a Republic, than to any other Form. But even of Republics, there are so many different Species, that it is hard to say, to which of our *European* Common-Wealths, the *American* could be supposed to bear the nearest Resemblance. Suffice it therefore to observe once for all, that neither in the old, nor in the new world, in antient, or in modern Times, was there ever, as far as appears, any one Republic, which was literally *democratical*, in the Lockian Sense of the Word, For even at *Geneva*, the most popular of all Governments, which I can think of, a Moiety at least of the Male and adult Inhabitants [not to mention Females, and Male Youths] are excluded from giving Suffrages by the Constitution of the Place:—None but *Citizens* being permitted to enjoy that Privilege; mere *Commorantes*, and *Sojourners*, though of ever so long standing, and Natives of the Place, being all excluded. And were we to mount up into high Antiquity, and ransack the most celebrated Republics of *Greece*, for Proofs and Illustrations of this Matter, we should find that their Exclusions and Rejections were still greater.

HAVING now, it is to be hoped, had tolerable Success in this Part of our *American* Warfare, let us at last have the Courage to face that fell Monster himself with his Scalping Knife; the MERE SAVAGE;—of whom we have heard so much from Mr. LOCKE, and all his Followers, that in Times of Peace he bravely disdains all Subordination, because he is duly sensible of his natural Rights, and (to use Dr. PRIESTLY's emphatic Words) feeling his own Importance, he considers himself as fully equal to any other Person whatever.

WELL: The Scalping Knife, if you please, we will here lay aside, as having nothing to do with such an Instrument in this Dispute: Nor yet need we describe the canibal Feasts which these celebrated, independent Beings used to make on their Prisoners, after having roasted them alive.   For as Mr. LOCKE and all his Followers not only allow but even insist, that the Savages generally elect a Chief, and submit to his Authority during a War, but return to their original Equality after it is over,—our Business is to find out, if we can, how it comes to pass, that they live in a State of absolute Independance, and without the Controul of Authority in Times of Peace;—those very Times, when the Advantages arising from Government and Law would have been productive of the most Good, and the least Evil, both to themselves, and others.

Now, in order to prosecute this Inquiry in such a Manner as would bring us the nearest to the Truth, we ought to compare these human Beings with others of their Kind, in every Point, which can give us any Light.   For by so doing we have a better Chance of discovering the real Cause of this surprising Phænomenon, this grand Omission of a Civil Government for Ages upon Ages;—after the rest of the World, all Nations, People, and Languages, had established one everywhere, of some Kind, or other.   If, for Example, this capital Defect is, in a great Measure, owing to some radical Weakness, or Imbecility in the corporeal and mental Powers, or moral Tempers of this singular People,—it is a Disease the more difficult to be cured, in Proportion as it proceeds from those natural Imperfections, which human Art and Instruction may correct in some Degree, but cannot totally remove.   But then, if this be the Case, surely the LOCKIANS have not dealt very ingenuously by us, in holding forth this defective Race, as a Sample of the Progenitors of other Men in their original State of Nature: And the Inferences and Conclusion, which they draw from this Instance of the *American* Savages, must pass for nothing.

1st. BODILY CONSTITUTIONS: We will begin with these, because all Men, as well as ROUSSEAU, are led almost naturally to suppose, that a Savage is a brawny Creature, healthy, vigorous, and long lived.   His simple Diet, his Way of Life, and continual Exercise in the open Air;— and above all his happy Ignorance of the Delicacies, Luxuries, and Debaucheries of populous Towns and Cities, seem to indicate, that he must have a Constitution such, or nearly such as here described.   How great therefore is our Disappointment, when we are informed by the united Voice of History, that the Savages of *America* are in general, a loose-jointed, and weakly Race of Men, frequently afflicted with various Kinds of Diseases, and the least capable of under-going any Degree of *hard*, and *constant* Labour, of any Human Creatures upon Earth: And moreover, that they are, in general, very far from being long-lived.   Add to this, that their *beardless* Faces, and smooth Skins betray evident Symptoms of a cold Habit, and a lax Frame; inasmuch as they are destitute of the usual Signs and Characteristics of Vigour and Robustness in other Men. All this is surely ominous at first setting out: And yet every Tittle of it is true. Multitudes of Authorities might here be adduced to corroborate these Points. But I shall content myself with two, both of which for their Singularity, and for the Opening they give to various Speculations, eclipse all the rest.

THE first is, the total Ineptitude of the Savages in general for Labour and Toil.

EVERY *European* Nation, which in their Wars with the native *Indians* has taken any of them Prisoners, hath attempted to make them work; but to very little Purpose. For after repeated Trials, and after using them smoothly, as well as roughly, it has been found, that the weakly Frame of an *Indian* would sink under that Portion of Labour, which was no more than Exercise to another Man. An old Planter from *South Carolina* told me about 35 Years ago, that the *Carolinians* being at War with a Tribe of *Indians*, had made the Experiment on some of their Prisoners; and found this Observation to be strictly true. "It appears to me, said he, that the *Indians* have the Agility of a Beast of Prey, but not the Strength of a Beast of Burden. They are light and nimble, and can march at a vast Rate for two or three Days; provided they have no heavy Burdens to carry: They can also subsist without Victuals for as many Days, and perhaps longer, by drawing their Belts closer and closer. But here ends all their Excellence. For when you take them out of this sauntring Life, and put them to any Kind of Labour, their Spirits droop, and they soon die." Now, this strange Debility of Body was the very Circumstance, which gave rise to that most inhuman Custom of making Slaves of the Negroes of *Africa*, in order to spare the *Americans:*—of which detestible Practice the *English*, those professed Patrons, and Guardians of the unalienable Rights of Mankind, are, alas! more guilty than any Nation under Heaven: For they carry on a greater Slave-Trade than any others.

LAS CASAS, the *Dominican* Missionary, afterwards Bishop of *Chiapa*, was the first who began this Practice. And what is really astonishing, he began it from a good Motive. Shocked at the prodigious Numbers of native *Americans*, who were falling Victims to the Cruelty of the *Spaniards* in *Mexico* and *Peru*, by being made to work beyond their Strength, he conceived a Plan for hiring robust Labourers from *Old Spain*. But the Landed Interest both of the new, and the old World violently opposed this Scheme, through different Motives;—the former, lest their Country should be drained of its useful Hands by such prodigious Emigrations; and the latter, lest they should be obliged to give up that Power over the Natives, which they had so unjustly usurped, and of which they had made an Use barbarous, and cruel beyond Example. Being therefore defeated in this Project, he conceived another, in which he had none of his former Antagonists to oppose him:—Nay, unhappily for Mankind, he found them ready enough to join him; as soon as they perceived that his Scheme was practicable, and attended with much Profit and Advantage: That was, To purchase Slaves on the Coast of *Africa*, and to transport them to *America*.   And thus it came to pass, that this misguided Zealot became the Author of that very Slavery, of those innumerable Murders, and Calamities to Millions and Millions of his Fellow-Creatures born on one Part of the Globe, which he was endeavouring to prevent, and exclaiming against, in another.—As if the black Inhabitants of *Africa* had not as good a Title to Life, and Liberty, as the copper-coloured Natives of *America*, or even the Whites of *Europe*.

THE other Thing remarkable is the *sickly Habit* of these *Indians*. Indeed a sickly Habit, and a weak and tender Frame, are very often both the Cause and Effect of each other.   But, to pass over this, let it be observed, that there were various Disorders to which the Savages were subject from their Mode of Living.   For not having that constant Supply of Food, which is to be found in a civilized State, by Means of Agriculture, and regular Markets; but depending altogether on the precarious Events of their Fishing, and Hunting Expeditions, they sometimes abounded, and then they gorged most voraciously, eating their Fish and Meat almost raw: At other Times they suffered great Want, and were forced to fast for several Days.   Hence Palsies, Pleurisies, Consumptions, and all other Diseases, which date their Origin from Indigestions, Repletions, and Inanitions, were very rife among them.   Not to mention that terrible Malady, which once was peculiar to *America*, but now is diffused over every Part of the Globe, to the farthest Part of *Siberia*, and *Tartary*.   [See the Abbé CHAPPE's Account of this Journey into *Siberia*].   But, what is stranger still, these Diseases, and others of the same Stock, continued to make Havock among several of them, even after they had altered their former Modes of Living (at least in Part) by their Conversion to Christianity, thro' the indefatigable Zeal of the *Jesuit* Missionaries of *Paraguay*.

MURATORI* is the Author to whom I appeal on this Occasion: And

---

* MURATORI'S Relation of the Missions of *Paraguay*.   The *English* Translation printed for J. MARMADUKE, 1759.   P. 101–102.

his Testimony is the more to be depended on, as he is reputed not only a very faithful and exact Historian, but also as he particularly endeavoured in this Treatise, to set forth the Contrast in the strongest Point of Light, between the *Indians* of *Paraguay* in their converted, and unconverted State. His Words are these: "Hitherto it has been impossible to moderate their ravenous Appetites. Custom, and a craving Stomach, which has a great Power over them, have *prevailed constantly* against all the Instructions they have had, with regard to the Advantages for the Preservation of Health: And so they continue to eat without Moderation.—This Irregularity is the Cause of many *Infirmities*, that descend from Father to Son. What is worse, the *Indians*, when indisposed, cannot take the least Care of themselves. A Reduction [This is a Name given to a Number of Savages converted to Christianity by the Missionaries, and incorporated in one Politico-Ecclesiastical Community] of seven or eight Thousand Souls is esteemed very happy, that has only two Hundred sick at once, or reduced to keep their Beds." Now, I say, this Circumstance is a very strange one, and not to be accounted for according to the common Vicissitudes of Health, and Sickness here in *Europe*. For even in those Sinks of Vice, Debauchery, and Disease, *London* and *Paris*, there hardly ever is an Instance, unless during the Violence of some epidemical Distemper, that out of a Parish consisting of seven or eight Thousand Souls, two Hundred of them, at an Average, are always sick, and obliged to keep their Beds. And were we to compare this *American* Account, with the Bills of Health of our large and populous Parishes in Country Towns and Villages, we should find that there are not sixty Persons always sick, out of eight Thousand, taking the whole Year together. Thus much as to the *Bodily Constitutions* of these poor miserable People.

IN respect to the INTELLECTUAL POWERS of these Savages,—very narrow and confined they are, according to the Relation of all Historians. MURATORI observes, "That the Indians, before they were taught Christianity, had no Word to signify any Number above four: If they would signify five, they held up one Hand, if ten, both: To express twenty, they pointed to both hands and feet: Any number above twenty was expressed by a generical Word, that signified many. They could not distinguish a Number of Years, Persons, or Things, that should be told exactly. But now they learn Arithmetic from their Infancy. Nor is this all: On *Sundays*, after Divine-Service, the Numeration-Table is repeated to the People in the Church, that the Indians may retain better what they learned in their Infancy."—Surely, a more convincing Proof need not be given of a slow and dull Understanding, than what is here mentioned.   Indeed Dr. ROBERTSON takes Notice, that the very Negroes consider themselves as a Race of Men much superior to the Indians in Point of mental Endowments; and therefore treat them with no small Scorn on that Account.   In short the original Natives can hardly be said to discover either a fertile Genius, or a solid Judgment, in any thing they either say or do:—At the same Time, that they are remarkable for Patience, and Perseverence almost invincible in prosecuting such things, as they have undertaken to accomplish, be they what they may. But the worst Part of their Character is yet to come,—Namely,

1st,—*Their Want of Tenderness, Sympathy, and Affection;*
2dly,—*Their astonishing Laziness and Improvidence;*
And 3dly,—*Their Gloominess, Sullenness, and Taciturnity.*

With respect to the first Class of these bad Qualities, all Historians agree, without one Exception, that the Savages in general are very cruel and vindictive, full of Spite and Malice; and that they have little, or no Fellow-feeling for the Distresses even of a Brother of the same Tribe,— and none at all, no not a Spark of Benevolence towards the distressed Members of an hostile Tribe.   But the Missionaries, to their eternal Praise be it spoken, have converted these blood-thirsty, unfeeling Animals, into a very different Sort of Beings: So that if the Accounts given of them are true, or even near the Truth, there can be hardly a more humane and benevolent People upon Earth, than the *Indian* Converts of *Paraguay.*

BUT in Regard to the second Class, namely, Their Indolence, Laziness, and astonishing Improvidence,—here alas! it may be asked, Can the Ethiopian change his Skin, or the Leopard his Spots?   For with respect to these Evils, the Missionaries, with all their Zeal and Emulation, with all their Arts of alluring the Passions, and captivating the Imaginations of an ignorant, and simple People, have not been able to work a radical Cure;—if indeed it can be called any Cure at all.   MURATORI's Observations are very striking on this Head; and after him I will refer to others.

"AFTER having assigned, says he, (Page 141,) a Parcel of Land, more than sufficient to maintain each Family, they [the Missionaries] distribute among them the Quantity of Grain that is necessary to sow their Ground, but on this Condition, that after Harvest, they shall bring to the public Stores as much Grain as they have received, that the common Fund of Seed-Grain may be always kept up.   ☞ Without this Precaution the Indians would certainly eat all their Grain, and leave themselves even without Hopes of another Harvest.

"EVERY Family has a Pair, or two of Oxen *lent* them for their Husbandry. ☞ If they were the *Property* of the *Indians*, the poor Animals would soon be passed all Service. For it has often happened, that some *Indians*, to spare themselves the daily Trouble of putting the Yoke on their Cattle, never took it off. Others would knock them down, and soon eat them up, without giving any Reason, but that they were hungry. Now indeed they are more careful of them, as they are *obliged* at the Expiration of a certain Term, to restore them in good Plight. Whatever Care is taken, Provisions are wanted by many about the *Middle* of the Year, either through Sickness, or some private Misfortune they have suffered; or it is owing to their *imprudent Profusion*, — To fence against these Inconveniencies, they [the Missionaries] take this Method. Besides the Lands assigned to Particulars, there is a considerable Extent of Ground, the best, and most fruitful that they can find, which the *Indians* call *Tupambae*, that is, the *Possession of God*. The Management is committed to some understanding laborious *Indians*. This is cultivated under their Direction, by the Children of the Reduction, who to the Age of fifteen are employed in this Work, and who supply by their Numbers, what they want in Strength—All Grains, Fruit, and Cotton gathered from the *Tupambae*, are deposited in the public Granaries and Store-Houses, in order to be distributed in the Course of the Year to the Sick, the Orphans, the Handicraft's Men, who have no Profit from their Labour but being fed and maintained at the public Cost; in a Word to all such as are any Ways *dispensed* from Tillage by their Imployment and Business, and even to those, who thro' their *own Negligence*, or some Casualty reach the End of their Provisions before that of the Year.

"KEEPING the Indians in Clothes does not require less Attention. Were this left to them [the converted Indians] *they would soon go naked like the Savages*." Pages 143, 144, 145. Thus far MURATORI: To whom we might add Abundance of other Authorities, were we not apprehensive of having been too tedious already. Suffice it therefore, briefly to observe, from Dr. ROBERTSON, and other Historians, that this inbred Laziness, and unaccountable Indolence, so visible throughout all the original Natives of America, do not arise from the Want of *Mementoes* of every Kind, were this Class of Men but wise enough to take the proper Warning. Thus for Example, the *Indians* dwelling in the higher Latitudes both in *North* and *South America*, feel the Colds, and Frosts, and Snows of Winter, as sensible as any People whatever: Indeed perhaps more so, as their smooth Skins are evident Symptoms of a cold Constitution: Yet all this is not enough to teach them to get a Stock of *warm Cloathing* in Readiness, against the Approach of cold Weather. The same Observations may be made with respect to *Dwelling*. For the return of every Autumn might put them in Mind, that *that* is the Season for them to repair their Cabins, and to make them strong, warm, and comfortable, before the Rains, and Snows fall, and Frost sets in;—yet the lazy Indian puts off these necessary Repairs from Day to Day, 'till it becomes too late, or at least so late in the Season, that he cannot do it effectually, if he would. In short, he seems to be incapable of using any Forecast: For even the Example of the provident, and industrious Beaver, in a like Situation, tho' continually before his Eyes, is lost upon him. Lastly, if any Teaching could suffice, respecting Food, one would think that the voracious Stomach of an *Indian*, and his frequent Disappointments, might tell him, that it would be much better to cultivate some Spots of Ground near his Cabin, and to tame some Animals for domestic Use (which he might do by Way of Amusement and Recreation) than to depend on the uncertain Events of Fishing and Hunting, which he knows must cease at some Seasons of the Year, and which so often fail, that hundreds of *Indians* are annually obliged to live on the bad Food of wild Roots, Plants, and Berries, and even of the most nauseous Reptiles, for a considerable Time, till Death itself puts an End to their Misery.—Yet alas! plain, and instructive as this Voice of Nature is, it is ineffectual to work a *practical* Conviction on the Minds of this stupid, and unthinking People. Nay more; the Missionaries themselves, who according to the Faith of the converted *Indians*, are invested with the Keys both of Heaven and Hell, and can dispense either Happiness or Misery both in this Life and the next;—these Missionaries, I say, who have civilized the Savages, and have wrought great, and happy Changes in them in several Respects; who are therefore beloved almost to Adoration—yet even they are not able to work any tolerable Reformation respecting the capital Points of Laziness and Improvidence, so deeply rooted in the Constitution of an Indian: So that the utmost they can do, is to palliate an unhappy, hereditary Disorder, instead of performing a radical Cure.

HENCE therefore it comes to pass, that when the Savages in their natural State, are destitute of the Benefit of such faithful Monitors, such wise and able Governors, as the Missionaries have proved themselves to be, they frequently kill their infant Children, because they are not provided with the Means of rearing them up. Thus for Instance, if a Mother should die before her Child is weaned, the Child must be destroyed, there being no Nurse for it: And then it is buried in the same Grave with its Mother. A like Circumstance happens, when a Woman is delivered of Twins; for one, or other of these Innocents must be put to Death, because she cannot rear them both. And as she receives no Assistance from her Consort, or next to none, towards the Support of their common Offspring [he on the contrary always using her as his Drudge, and expecting, when he kills the Game, even at the Distance of several Miles from their Cabin, that his Squaw should go to fetch it Home.] She herself frequently procures Abortion, in order to be freed from the excessive Fatigue of rearing up Children, and of providing for their Sustenance by her own Toil. Nay, we are informed, that there have been Instances of Mothers having murdered their female Infants, through mere Tenderness, foreseeing the perpetual Misery to which they would be exposed, after they were grown up. For this, and for other Reasons it is observable, that savage Nations ☞ never increase, and multiply like other Men. Nay more, MURATORI, and all the Historians agree, that when the Savages have been unsuccessful in their hunting Expeditions, and are extremely pinched with Hunger, they hunt, kill, and eat one another. See particularly the Lord Bishop of *Oxford* [SECKER'S] Sermon preached before the Society for propagating the Gospel. A. D. 1740-1. Page 8.

Now, as one Evil follows another, all these horrid Consequences, and perhaps many more, derive their Origin from that almost unconquerable Aversion to Labour, which prevails so universally in this defective Race. For were they but frugal, and industrious, even in a moderate Degree, they might not only prevent those Calamities, with which they are often so grievously afflicted, but also abound in all the Necessaries, and in many of the Conveniencies, and Elegancies of Life. But alas! industrious, and provident they will not be: Indeed their very Natures seem to be repugnant to it: For we find, that the Missionaries themselves would have failed of Success, had they urged no other than *rational* Motives to induce the Indians to Labour; and then had they left it to their own Choice, whether they would work, or not, without using any Sort of Compulsion.

THIS being the Case, can we want a Reason, why Civil Government is not introduced among the Tribes of Savage *Indians?*—Yea rather, might it not be very properly asked, How can it be introduced among such a Sort of People?—that is, How can the Expences of Government be supported by a Race of Men, who will not work enough to support themselves? Besides; Of what Use, would it be to them? For as to

*Property, that great Source of Litigation among other Men.   They
have nothing to contend about; because they have no Labour, which
is the Foundation of Riches: So that they are all equal, because
equally poor.   Having therefore no special Right to Lands, Woods,
or Waters, one more than another, there can be no Disputes concerning
them.   And as to their Wives and Children, the mere Savages seem to
be quite careless and indifferent about such Sorts of Chattels.   In
short, their general Mode of Life is this: They fish, and hunt wherever they think it most likely for them to get Plenty of Fish, or Game:
Then they greedily devour what they have caught: After this they
sleep; and when they are hungry, they fish, or hunt again; giving
themselves little, or no Concern, what is to become of them, or
how they are to subsist, when these Resources shall fail.   Now, whilst
they remain in this Situation, and follow such a Course of Life,
Civil Government must be almost, if not altogether an *useless Thing:*—
In fact, it never can be of any real Service, unless it causes them to forsake their savage Manner of living, and to become civilized.   Then,
indeed, notwithstanding the Ravings of ROUSSEAU, if must be owned
that it would be of signal Advantage to them, and a great Blessing.   But
in order to accomplish these good Ends, there are very great Difficulties
to be encountered.   For first, you must either change and alter the
whole Frame of their Constitutions, if I may so speak, in order to render

---

* The Savage *Indians* occupy no Lands in *severalty:* Therefore there is neither Tillage, nor Planting among them; except perhaps what their Wives may do in little Spots
near their Cabins.   In fact, as the whole Country lies open before them, in the Nature
of a great COMMON, they hunt and fish wherever they please.   But tho' these Lands,
Woods, and Waters are considered as common to all the Individuals of the same Tribe;
— yet, in their public Capacity, or as a collective Body, they claim an *exclusive Right*
to vast Tracts of Country against other Tribes.   In this respect they are so greedy,
that perhaps an Extent of *Wastes, Forests,* and *Deserts* as large as *England,* is hardly
judged sufficient for a few Hundreds of these Vagabonds to roam about.   And it is
the Invasion of this [supposed] *public Property,* which furnishes them with Pretences
for their frequent, bloody, and scalping Wars: For the better Management of which,
they elect a Chief, or Governor.   Hence therefore we see, even from this imperfect
State of Things, that wherever the Idea of Property prevails, Government must
follow, as a necessary Consequence for the Preservation of it.   N.B. Since their Commerce with the *Europeans,* the *Indians* have begun to use Horses, not for the Purposes
of Husbandry, but for their Journies.   They treat these Creatures with shocking Inhumanity; and indeed they seem to exhibit very little Fondness or Affection for any
Sort of Beings whatever, but for SELF.   In this they are quite the Reverse of the wild
Arabs, who are as remarkable for their Kindness and Attachment to all their domestic
Animals, and particularly to their Horses, as the *Indians* are for the contrary.

them fitter for receiving a good and liberal Plan of Civil Government: Or, 2dly. You must oblige them to submit to those Terms which you shall prescribe, by the mere Dint of *absolute Power*, according to the fundamental Maxims of the great Empires of *Mexico*, and *Peru:*—Or 3dly. You must win them to co-operate with your Measures, by such Combinations of Force and Persuasion, happily blended together, as the Jesuit Missionaries have devised and practiced in the Countries of *Paraguay*. The first of these is, I think, beyond the Reach of any human Power to effect.—The second is certainly no actual Compact, voluntarily entered into between equal and independent Beings;—the Lockians themselves being Judges: And as to the third,—If these enlightened, and benevolent Philosophers will undertake the Province of Missionaries to *Paraguay*, or to any other *American* Country, now the *Jesuits* are expelled, may good Success attend them! And may no one detract from the Merits of their Labours!

IN the mean Time, and 'till they shall have returned from this Expedition, let them learn a little Modesty here at Home; and not boast of Victories, which they never won. Let them in short, be silent for the future, on this Topic: And let them not din our Ears with the Examples of the Savages of *America*, as being any Proofs and Illustrations of their Hypothesis;—which, when thoroughly discussed, and accurately examined, prove and illustrate just the contrary.

RESPECTING the third Class of *bad* Qualities, their native Sullenness and Taciturnity;—It has been frequently observed by Travellers, that the Savages of *North-America* are, in general, a joyless Race, seldom discovering any Symptoms of Gladness, unless when exulting over a vanquished Foe, and contriving to inflict some new Torture. Moreover, it has been noted, that they are such Strangers to the Pleasantries of Conversation, and so sparing of Speech, [except, when haranguing in Public, in order to prepare for, or to give an Account of, some hostile Expedition] that they will spend whole Days without uttering a Word, contenting themselves with dumb Signs and Nods.

SURELY, surely Mr. LOCKE and his Followers either did not know what they were about, when they ventured to produce these unhappy, defective Beings, as the Prototypes of Mankind in all other Countries;— or they must have acted a very disingenuous Part, if they knew better, and yet wished to serve their Cause at the Expence of Truth.

CHAP. III.

A Comparison of the different Forms of Government with each other,
A Preference given to the Mixt, and the Reasons why,—The Republics
of Sparta, Athens, *and* Rome, *proved to be improper Models for a*
Commercial State,—The supposed unalienable Right of each In-
dividual to be self-governed in the Affairs of Legislation, examined,
and refuted.

ACCORDING to the Lockian System there ought to be no other Legislators but the People themselves,—or those at least whom the People had expressly commissioned for that Purpose;—nor ought there to be any Magistrates, Judges, Justices of the Peace, civil or military Officers, or any executive Powers whatever, but such only, as either mediately or immediately receive their Commissions from the People.   Every other Species of Legislation or of Government is, it seems, a manifest *Usurpation* of the *unalienable* Rights of Mankind, let the Antiquity of it be ever so remote, or the System and Administration of it ever so productive of public Peace and Happiness.

It is to be hoped, that these idle Notions have received a full and satisfactory Confutation in the former Part of this Work.   However, though we must reject the absurd Doctrine of personal Contracts between Prince and People, as a Thing which never existed in any State, and which never can (except perhaps in a very small Village for a few Days, or rather Hours) yet as all Governments whatever are so many public Trusts for the Good of the Governed;—therefore there is a Contract *implied*, though not exprest, a *quasi*, tho' not an *actual* Contract always subsisting between all Sovereigns, and every one of their Subjects.   The Consequence of which is, as hath been afore observed, That these *Quasi-Contractors* ought to be made responsible to each other, for the due Performance of their respective Engagements.

This being the Case, we are now to consider which is the best Method of *obliging* these reciprocal Contractors to perform their respective Duties; —the best I mean, as being the safest and easiest, as well as the most effectual.

In respect to one Side of the Obligation, viz. The Duty and Obedience of the People,—the Rulers themselves are to enforce this Part of the Covenant, and no others.   For as they are to enact the Laws, and as they likewise, or their Deputies, are to put them in Execution, it is their Duty, as well as their Interest, to see, that none but good Laws are made, and when made, that they are impartially and universally obeyed.   Therefore, if they should permit the People wantonly to trample upon legal Authority, and to transgress with Impunity, the Blame must rest upon themselves. For Lenity in such a Case is only another Name for Timidity; and Timidity and Government, where the public Good is concerned, are inconsistent Things. Only let me add, that those Laws are the readiest obeyed, and therefore the easiest to be executed, which are plain and simple, and obviously calculated for the general Good,—not to serve a present Turn, or gratify a Faction. Therefore great Care should be taken to enact such only as will stand the Test, and bear to be examined by this Rule. For when any of the Laws in being are of such a Nature, that it would be better to connive at their Infraction, than to enforce their Observance, it is high Time that such Laws should be repealed. Indeed every Plea or Pretence for their Continuance, is only so many Evidences, that Mankind had much rather find out Excuses to gloss over that System, which they know they cannot defend, than ingenuously to acknowledge themselves in the wrong, and alter their Conduct. Thus much as to the *Governing* Part in all Societies, let the Form of the Government be whatever it may.

WE are now to turn to the opposite Side, the Case and Circumstance of the *Governed*.—Here therefore we must set out with this Inquiry, How shall the People receive a *reasonable* Security, that the Powers, wherewith their Governors are entrusted for their Good, both in making Laws, and in executing them, shall not be misapplied?—That there is a Danger of Misapplication is, alas! a Case too apparent to admit of any Doubt. And therefore the Question comes to this;—First, What is to be done, in order to prevent, as far as human Foresight can reach, the Misapplication of such a Trust? And 2dly. What Methods should be taken to cure those Evils, or redress those Abuses, which either were not, or could not be prevented at the first, so that Government in general may be restored to its original Ends and Uses, the Good of the Governed?

To solve these Questions in any Manner, that can bear some Proportion to the Importance of the Subject, several Points ought to be previously considered:

As 1*st*. What are those essential Principles, on which every Government must be founded, and by Virtue of which it doth actually subsist?

2*dly*. WHAT are those Forms, or exterior Modes of Administration, which give distinct Denominations to different Governments?

AND 3*dly*. Which Form affords the best, and most reasonable Security to the People, that they shall be well and happily governed?

WITH respect to the first Branch of the Inquiry, there must be *Power*,

Wisdom, and *Goodness*, subsisting in one Degree or other, in every Government worthy to be so called, let the exterior Form of it be whatever it may.

FOR Example, without *Power* the very Idea of Government is annihilated; and there are no Traces of it left.

WITHOUT *Wisdom* to conduct this Power towards some certain End, or Object, the Thing itself would not be *Power*, in a *moral* Sense, but blind Impulse, or mechanic Force.

AND without *Goodness* to influence and incline the Operations both of Wisdom and Power towards some benevolent Uses, conducive to public Happiness, the Efforts of Wisdom would in effect be Knavery, Trick, and Cunning; and the Display of Power mere Tyranny and Oppression.   There must therefore be a Coalition, or Cooperation of all three, in order to form a Government fit to rule over such a Creature as *Man*.

SECONDLY, as to the several *Forms*, or external Modes of Government, they are almost as complicated and various, and their Origins as different, as the Degrees of parental Authority may be supposed to vary in different Cases,—or as the Skill and Foresight of discerning and good Men may be found to be greater or less in others,—or as the Caprice and Humour of the giddy Populace,—or lastly, as the Intrigues, Wiles, and Address of popular Leaders, or daring Usurpers, may happen to prevail. But notwithstanding this great Variety, and these different Origins, all Sorts of Governments may be reduced to four Classes,—the Monarchical, —the Aristocratical,—the Democratical, and the Mixt.   Let us therefore endeavour to investigate the *Quasi-Contracts* contained or implied in each of these Forms, in order to discover their respective Excellencies or Imperfections.

Now this very Attempt will usher in the third grand Inquiry, namely, which of the several Modes of Government affords to the People the best and most reasonable Security against the Misapplication of the Trust reposed in the Governors for the Sake of the Governed.

I. MONARCHY.

OF all the Forms of Government, *Monarchy*, according to all History sacred and profane, is the most antient: It is likewise the most extensive and universal, for a very obvious Reason.   For as it is neither clogged in its Motions, nor counteracted in its Schemes by rival Factions, it can exert more Power both offensively and defensively, and with greater Ease and Expedition, than either of the other Forms.   Consequently it would be the very *best*, were there a Certainty, that it would be endowed with *Wisdom* and *Goodness* proportionably to the Advantages it receives from united Strength and combined Power.   But here, alas! lies the great and incurable Imperfection of all human Monarchies.   An earthly Monarch cannot see every Thing with his own Eyes, nor hear with his own Ears, even were he ever so well disposed to do what is right, and to make his People happy.   Moreover he is continually subject to strong Temptations to abuse his Power through various Motives, some of them of a pitiable Nature, and others highly blameable.   Add to this, That the very Persons, who ought to inform him better, and dissuade him from pursuing wrong Courses, are, generally speaking, the most intent in keeping him ignorant of what is right, and to divert his Thoughts from the real Welfare of his People.   Hence it is, that they study his Weaknesses with a View to flatter his Vanity, gratify his Vices, inflame his Passions, and to instigate him to divert that very Power towards accomplishing some By-ends of their own, which ought to have been consecrated to the Promotion of public Happiness.   For these Reasons an absolute Monarchy in the Hands of such a frail, imperfect, and peccable Creature as *Man*, is by no Means a desirable Species of Government.

II. On ARISTOCRACY.

Nor is an *hereditary* Aristocracy much more preferable than an absolute Monarchy.   For it is subject to several of the same Inconveniences, without that Glare of Glory, which surrounds a Throne, and which, by amusing the Bulk of Mankind, captivates their Imaginations, and attaches them strongly to that Form of Government.   However, it must be allowed, that there are Advantages attending an Aristocracy, *provided it be a numerous one*, which serve to mitigate some of its greatest Evils, and to provide an Antidote against others.   For its very Numbers, which occasion so much Faction and Contention, serve as a preventive Remedy against their conniving at each other's Tyranny and Oppression: So that out of mere Spite to each other, they become a mutual Check on the Conduct of Individuals.   Likewise they often enflame each other with an Emulation of doing Good: Hence therefore it is, that in Matters of mere civil Concern, where the Disputes are only between Man and Man in private Life, there we find, that Justice is administered under an Aristocratical Government impartially enough, and that Life, Liberty, and Property, are as well secured under that Form, as under any other. Indeed it must be confessed, that wherever the Aristocratical Power is supposed to interfere with some particular Branch of the People's

Rights, there the whole Body of the *Nobles* will immediately oppose the Demands or Expectations of the *Commons*, and act as one Man in keeping them still in Subjection. [Moreover, wherever the Lords have such a personal Jurisdiction over their Vassals, as is distinct and separate from the general Jurisdiction of the State (which is still the unhappy Case in *Poland*) there Despotism and Tyranny prevail to a shocking Degree, without the Hopes of any Thing to counter-balance, mitigate, or correct them. And I will add, that there cannot be a worse Constitution upon Earth than an Aristocracy of Barons tyrannising over their Vassals;—or, what comes to nearly the same Thing, of Planters amusing themselves with the infernal Pleasure of whipping and slashing their Slaves.]

THEREFORE, were it to be asked in general, what Degree of *Power*, *Wisdom*, and *Goodness*, naturally belong to an Aristocratic Government, —I think it would not be difficult to give an Answer clear and satisfactory enough.

FOR as to Power, it is *externally* very weak, even on the *defensive* Side, where it ought to have been the strongest, being hardly able to protect itself against Invaders. This Weakness is owing to its numerous Factions and Divisions caballing against, and thwarting each other:—The secret Springs of which are more frequently to be ascribed to foreign Gold successfully applied to the pretended patriotic Leaders of each Party, than to any other Cause. But *internally* all those Factions and Divisions cease; inasmuch as the poor Subjects are destitute of the Means of making the like Application. Moreover, as they have no Persons particularly appointed to represent them in this Form of Government, they have none to stand forth as their Guardians and Protectors, being left in a Manner without Defence. Here therefore an Aristocracy is the strongest: Because the Nobles will of Course unite against the Plebeians, in maintaining, and perhaps extending, the Dignity and *Power* of their own Order.

As to the *Wisdom*, which may be supposed to be contained in this Institution, it has certainly some Advantages over a Government merely monarchical, or merely popular. For all the Members, of which it is composed, are by their Education, their Rank in Life, and other Circumstances, better qualified than most others, to enact Laws with Judgment, with Prudence, and a Knowledge of the Subject. The Independence of their Station, and Distance from mercantile Connections, prevent them from making Laws respecting Trade and Commerce with a View to some present dirty monopolizing Job: And being Sovereigns themselves, they are not compellable to submit to the arbitrary Will of an ignorant or absurd Tyrant, nor yet to obey the imperious Dictates of a foolish, head-strong, conceited Populace,* who are almost universally bent on gratifying some present destructive Whim, at the Expence of their future Happiness. Moreover as to the executive Part of an Aristocratical State, that, as I observed before, is tolerably free from very gross Abuses;—because it is under little Temptation to act amiss, except in those unfortunate Cases, where the peculiar Interests, Honour, or Dignity of the Patrician Order happen to interfere with the general Welfare of the People.—There indeed, it is much to be feared, that the *Quasi-Contract*, on the Part of the Nobles, would be made a Sacrifice to their Lust of Power, their Pride, and Ambition.

HAVING said thus much as to the *Power* and *Wisdom* of an Aristocracy, the Reader will of his own Accord suggest to himself every Idea that is necessary, concerning the *Goodness* or *Benevolence* of such an Institution.

III. *A* MERE DEMOCRACY.

THE third Class of Civil Government is the *Democratical*.—I mean, a Democracy literally such, unmixt with any other Form: Where therefore all the adult *Males* [and why the adult *Females* should be excluded, is impossible to say] are supposed to assemble together, whenever they will, in order to deliberate and vote on all public Affairs, to change and

* During an attentive Observation, and the Experience of 50 Years, sorry I am to say, but Truth obliges me to do it, that I hardly ever knew an unpopular Measure to be in itself a bad one, or a popular one to be truly salutary. *Internally* the People violently opposed the best of all Schemes for a commercial Nation, — That of ware-housing Goods on Importation, and paying the Duties by Degrees. They were also as bitterly averse to the making of Turnpike Roads, to the Use of Broadwheel Waggons, to the enclosing and improving of Lands, to the Freedom of Trade in Cities and Towns corporate, to the Introduction of Machines for abridging Labour, and also to the Admission of industrious Foreigners to settle among them. Nay, they very lately were so absurd as to raise loud Clamours against the Execution of the Act for preserving the public Coin, and their own Property from Debasement and Adulteration. *Externally*, they are perpetually calling out for new Wars (though against their best Customers) on the most frivolous or unjustifiable Pretences. Moreover, if there was any Convention or Treaty to be broken through or disregarded, (the Observance of which would have restored Peace or prevented Bloodshed) or if there was any new Colony to be planted in a desart Country, or Conquest to be undertaken in a populous one, even in the most distant Part of the Globe. — All these Measures, though totally opposite to a Spirit of Industry at Home, and though the Bane of a commercial Nation, were sure to receive the Applauses and Huzzas of the unthinking Multitude. Such was the *Vox Populi* for 50 Years last past, which some Persons blasphemously stile Vox DEI.

alter, to pull down, and build up, without Controul, and as often as they please.—Consequently, where every adult Individual is to consider himself as his own Legislator, his own Governor, and Director in every Thing. —Happily for Mankind, this wild and visionary Plan of a *free* and *equal* Republic is absolutely impracticable in any District of larger Extent than a common Country Parish! And happily again, even there it could not subsist for any Length of Time, but must be transformed either into a petty Sovereignty or Aristocracy, or at least into an Oligarchy, much after the same Manner, and for the same Reasons, that the Business of populous and extensive Parishes here in *England*, devolves at last into the Hands of a *few*, and is managed by a *select* Vestry.

BUT waving all Considerations respecting the several Changes it may probably undergo;—let us, since so much Stress is laid upon it by our modern Republicans,—let us, I say, consider it in its own Nature, as either abounding, or deficient in the three Qualities afore mentioned, of *Power*, *Wisdom*, and *Goodness*;—Qualities, so essential for the Formation and Establishment of all Civil Governments, that none can subsist without them in one Degree or other.

AND 1st as to *Power*;—Scanty indeed must the Pittance of Power be, which is to result from the Union of 40, 50, or even 100 Savages, issuing forth from their Dens and Caverns, and assembled together *for the first Time*, in order to constitute a *Body Politic*. We will not now enquire, *Who* among this Herd of equal and independent Sovereigns had the Right of appointing the Time and Place of Rendezvous for the rest of his brother Sovereigns to meet at and *consult* together: Nor will we presume so much as to ask, *How* or *Why* such a Superiority came to be vested in him alone, or how long this extraordinary exclusive Privilege was to last:—Or what *corporal* Punishment [it being to be presumed that they could not be *fined* in their *Goods* and *Chattels*, before *meum* and *tuum* was established.] Therefore, I say, what *corporal* Punishment was to be inflicted on those independent Sovereigns, who either would not, or did not obey the Summons. But not to boggle at little Matters, let us suppose all these Difficulties happily got over:—And then the first Question at this first Meeting is, What are they to do? And wherefore were they called together?—Perhaps the very Appearance of such a Body of Savages might be sufficient to fray away a few Eagles, or Vultures, Wolves, or Tygers, if they were too near them: But most certainly it would not be adequate to the Purposes even of a *defensive*, not to say an offensive War, if this *genuine* Republic should happen to exist in the Neighbourhood of any State, whose Union was more perfect, and consequently whose Skill and

Dexterity were superior to their own. Therefore this Insect Common-wealth, this Grub of a free, equal, and Sovereign Republic would be swallowed up, as soon as hatched, by some devouring political Animal of a firmer Texture, and stronger Stamina;—unless these lately independent Sovereigns would condescend either to fly away to remote Woods and Deserts, or to submit to the Terms which their Conquerors should think fit to impose upon them.

AFTER this Specimen of the *Power*, it will be unnecessary to say a Word about the *Wisdom* or *Goodness* of such a reptile, democratical Institution. But here, methinks, some of the enthusiastic Admirers of Antiquity will be apt to say, "What? Do you compare the famous Repub-lics of *Greece* and *Rome* to Insects, Grubs, and Reptiles? Do you dare to say, That either of these were of short Continuance? Or that they were at all remarkable for the Want of Power, Wisdom, or Goodness?"

To this smart Objection I have the following Reply to make:

1st. THAT neither of the Common Wealths above mentioned, were pure Democracies in the Sense here set forth:—For they had other Magi-strates, and other Institutions besides those which were merely popular;—and even in respect to the most popular Part of their Government, they excluded much greater Numbers from enjoying a Share in the Privileges and governing Part of the Constitution than they admitted: So that this whole Objection falls to the Ground.

2dly. THE Subjects of these Republican Governments were so far from enjoying greater Liberty than the Subjects of other States, that they were known to be more oppressed, and more enslaved, than any others: So that no Proofs can be drawn from hence concerning the *Wisdom* and *Goodness*, that is, the Justice and Benevolence, of such Republics, what-ever may be said of their great Power, and despotic Sway.

BUT 3dly, Granting more than can be required, even granting [what is absolutely false in Fact] that each of these Republics were modelled and administered, according to the Heart's Desire of a true Disciple of Mr. LOCKE, had he been then in being.—Still even on this Supposition, there was nothing so inviting in the *fundamental* Maxims, and *distinguish-ing* Practices of either of these Institutions, to make us so much in love with it, as to wish to copy it into our own.

The SPARTAN REPUBLIC.

THE fundamental and distinguishing Maxim of SPARTA was, to lead a military Life in the City, as well as in the Camp, and never to enjoy any of those Comforts and Conveniences which Peace and Plenty naturally bestow. Consequently, the Police of their *Legislator was, to forbid Improvements of every Kind (excepting in the Science of War) to banish all Trades and Manufactures whatsoever, which related to the Arts of Peace, to proscribe every Part of a learned and ingenuous Education, and more particularly, and above all the rest, to expel the Use of Gold and Silver from the State of *Lacedemon*. But as these military Heroes must eat, as well as fight, it was contrived that they should have Slaves [the *Helotes*] for the Purposes of Agriculture, and other menial Offices, whom they used much worse, and with more *wanton* Cruelty, than the Planters do the Negroes in the *West-Indies:*—And that is saying a great deal. Now I ask, are these Measures proper to be adopted in *Great-Britain?* And is this the Plan of a Republic, which some future patriotic Congress is to set up, in order to correct the Evils of our present unhappy Constitution?

The ATHENIAN REPUBLIC.

THE distinguishing Practice of *Athens*, or at least, that which made the Conduct of the *Athenians* to appear different from that of most other States, was the Use of the *Ostracism*. Nothing could have been better calculated for gratifying the Caprice and Licentiousness of a Mob, or for indulging the Spleen and Jealousy of a Rival, or for concealing the Wiles and Intrigues of a pretended Patriot, than this very Project. For by Virtue thereof, any Man, even the best and most deserving in the State, was liable to be banished for ten Years, whenever the Citizens should have a public Assembly (which they often had) consisting of 6000 Suffrages and upwards;—and when any one of this Number should write,

---

* Quere, — Whether this famous Legislator was not guilty of a gross Equivocation in the very Act of making his social Contract with the People of *Lacedemon?* It is said, that he bound them by an Oath to observe his Laws and Regulations, till he should return from a Voyage to *Crete*, where he then purposed to go. He went, but never returned: And lest they should bring back his Bones after his Death, and thereby suppose themselves released from the Obligation he had laid them under, he ordered his Body to be thrown into the Sea. Few Moralists, I believe, would judge such a fraudulent Contract as this, to be good and valid. And no Court of Equity upon Earth would pronounce such a palpable Deception to be binding in any other Case. The learned Reader is requested to consult XENOPHON's Account of the Policy of the *Lacedemonians* in the Original. He will there find, that many of the Institutions of LYCURGUS were very whimsical and absurd, (notwithstanding XENOPHON's Endeavours to gloss them over) that some of them were very criminal, others obscene, that few were worthy to be adopted into that benevolent and liberal Plan of Government, where *true national Liberty* was to be the Basis.

or cause to be written on a Shell, or a Leaf, the Name of the Person he chose to doom to destruction, then this upright, sagacious, and impartial Sentence immediately took Place: And the *accused* [if that Person can be called *accused*, against whom no Crime was alledged] was not permitted to say a Word in his Defence, or to expostulate on the Hardships of his Case, but must go instantly into Banishment, there to remain 'till the ten Years were expired.

By Means of a Condemnation of this Sort, ARISTIDES, who had borne some of the highest Offices in the Common-wealth, and who had obtained the Surname of the *Just*, from his great Integrity and inflexible Honour,— even this ARISTIDES was banished from his native Country, and dearest Connections, and was reduced to such abject Poverty, that his only *Daughter was maintained by public Charity after his Death. The Story of this unhappy Victim to democratical Insolence well deserves to be repeated as a Memento to the present Times.—On a Day of public Assembly he was accosted by a Citizen, whom he did not know, desiring him to write the Name of ARISTIDES on his Shell. ARISTIDES, sur-prized at such a Request, asked him whether he knew ARISTIDES, and whether he had ever offended him? No, says the other, I should not know him, were I to meet him. But I hear such an universal good Char-acter of him, that I am resolved to banish him, if I can, from the ATHENIAN State. ARISTIDES wrote his Name on the Shell as the Patriot had de-sired: And as there happened to be no other Names than his then proposed to be proscribed, he was banished of Course, according to the fundamental Law of this celebrated Republic. The Truth is, [and this explains the Matter] ARISTIDES was a remarkably *just Man*, by much too honest to cajole the Populace, and to gratify their Follies at the Expence of their own Interest; therefore he was not popular; as indeed few honest Men really are: **Whereas PERICLES, who laid the Foundation of their Ruin, and deserved Banishment an hundred Times, was the Idol of the Athenians.

---

* PLUTARCH doth not mention this Circumstance of the Daughter of ARISTIDES, exactly after this Manner, but other Authors do.

** The most unpopular Man in all *France* in his Day, was the Duke de SULLY; the most popular the Duke de GUISE: The most unpopular Ministers in *England*, were the Earl of CLARENDON, and Sir ROBERT WALPOLE, during their respective Administrations; the former a true, a steady, and equal Friend to a limited Monarchy, and the just *civil* Rights of the People; and the latter the best commercial Minister this Country ever had, and the greatest Promoter of its real Interests: — The most popular in their Turns, were Mr. PULTENEY, and Mr. PITT. *Sed Opinionum Commenta delet Dies.*

ANOTHER Instance of the great Sagacity of this People as *Politicians*, and Benevolence as *Men*, is observeable in the Methods they took for narrowing and contracting the Foundations of their Republic, instead of making them broader and firmer.   For in the *Times of their Prosperity*, they shut up every Avenue against the rich, or ingenious, the industrious, deserving, or oppressed of other Countries, from partaking in the common Rights of Citizens of Athens.   No Invitations, or general Naturalizations were so much as thought of: But on the contrary, the whole Tenor of their Laws ran in a different Strain.   [See particularly POTTER'S Greek Antiquities, and TAYLOR on Civil Law] Nay, they contrived to exclude as many as they could, even of their own natural-born Subjects, from enjoying the common Rights and Privileges of Citizens.   And as to their Slaves, tho' almost twenty in number to one free Man, they were excluded of Course.   So that in Fact, had this People been always successful in their Wars, and had they made great and extended Conquests, or had their State been of very long Duration, their Republic would have become an *hereditary Aristocracy*, similar to that of Venice; for it was strongly verging that Way.

INDEED in Times of universal Calamity, when their Losses by Sea and Land were so great, that they were in Danger of being annihilated, *as a People*, then they naturalized Foreigners, and manumitted Slaves. But it was their Necessity that compelled them, and not their Benevolence, Penetration, or Wisdom, which prompted them to adopt such patriotic Measures.

BUT above all, the Probity and Rectitude of this celebrated People will be displayed in the strongest Light, by setting before the Reader their Mode of dispensing Justice.   In order to do this, let us suppose a parallel Case existing in our own Times.   The present Livery-Men of *London* answer very nearly, if not altogether, to the Idea of the antient [ANDRES ATHENAIOI] the MEN OF ATHENS.   Let us therefore imagine, that these select Citizens, were the only Legislators in the State;—not only making Laws for themselves and for *Great-Britain*, but also for *Ireland*, and for all our Colonies and Settlements abroad.   This is something; but what is to come, is still more extraordinary: For we are to suppose farther, That these *Law-giving* Liverymen, are also the *supreme Judges* both of Law and Equity, constituting the *only* sovereign Court of Judicature for all the Provinces of the British State.   Hence it becomes necessary for every Suitor to this High Court of Justice,—*every Suitor*, I say, whether *English*, *Scotch*, or *Irish*, whether *American*, *West*, or *East-Indian*, to flatter and cajole all the Members thereof, as much as he can,—bowing and scraping to the highest, and *taking the meanest by the Hand*, as he is entering Guildhall to hear the Cause, and to pronounce the final Sentence. The Court being now assembled, let us attend also to some of the Pleadings of the Council on such an Occasion.

Gentlemen of the Livery,

"My Client is a rich and generous Man. If you will decree for him, he shall treat his Judges with splendid Entertainments at *Ranelagh, Vauxhall*, and *Sadler's Wells*, and at other Places of Diversion. Moreover he will give you Tickets to go for several Nights to both the Theatres, &c. &c. &c."

Now what shall we say to such an Oration? The Parallel here supposed, is either just or unjust in the *principal Features*, for there can be no Medium. I am therefore content, that the learned Reader should sit in Judgment on me relative to this Point. Only let me add, that I would have produced the very Passages from the original Authors, as Vouchers for the general Truth and Justness of the Parallel, [*mutatis mutandis,*] if I had had the Convenience of *Greek* Types at the Place where I am printing. One Thing more, I must beg Leave to suggest, namely, that every Man of Learning must be sensible, that, so far from exaggerating Matters,—I have taken the Words of XENEPHON concerning the *Athenian* Polity, in the most advantageous Sense, of which they are capable. For I have allowed him to say, that the supreme Court of *Athens* was a Court of Appeal from inferior Jurisdictions; whereas his Words, and the Context strongly imply, that the *Athenians* would not suffer any Court whatever, to exist in any Part of their Empire but their own. Nay, XENEPHON expressly declares, that the Allies of the *Athenians*, or their Auxiliaries, or Fellow Soldiers, or Colonies, or by whatever Name you will please to call them [SYMMACHOI is the Term in the original] were *enslaved* by the *Athenians* by these Means. Many other curious Observations might yet be made; and some of them of Importance to *Great-Britain*, by Way of *Caution*.—But surely enough has been said already, to give every true Friend to Liberty an Abhorrence of the Idea of an *Athenian* Common-Wealth.

The ROMAN REPUBLIC.

COME we now to the *Roman State*, whose Citizens were the great Masters of the World. But here an unlucky Observation arises at first setting out, viz. That the *Roman* Citizens, for the most Part, were not Tradesmen: For Trades of all Kinds were held at *Rome* in sovereign

Contempt.   Therefore its Tradesmen and Mechanics, its Shop-keepers and Retailers of all Sorts, were almost all either actual Slaves, or Slaves, lately made free, or the very Scum of the People.   This was the original State of Things.   But in the Time of CICERO, the Condition of Tradesmen, and the Idea affixed to Trade were a good Deal advanced in Reputation.   Yet even he represents the Matter in such a Light, as would make, I should think, those consummate Politicians, the learned Liverymen of *London*, not very desirous of seeing a Return of such Times. CICERO expresses himself to this Effect: "That according to antient Tradition, and as far as he can learn, Trades and the Gains thereof may be distinguished into the reputable and disreputable, after the following Manner.   In the first Place, these Professions must be reckoned infamous, which are odious to Mankind, such as the Business of Toll Gatherers, at the Ports and Gates of Cities, also of Usurers, or Pawn-Brokers.   In the next Place, all those Persons should be considered as a base and servile People who work for Hire, or Wages, because they are paid for their *Labour*, and not for their Skill or Ingenuity.   For the very receiving of Wages is a Badge of Servitude.   Those also who buy of the Merchants to sell again directly, must be ranked in a dishonourable Class; for they can get nothing thereby unless they cheat and lye abominably; and nothing can be baser than cheating.   Moreover all Artificers whatever are a base Order of Men: Indeed it is hardly possible, that a Shop and Work-House should have any Thing of an ingenuous Nature belonging to them: And least of all, are those Professions to be approved of, which are subservient to Luxury, such as the Trades of Fish-mongers, Butchers, Cooks, Pastry-Cooks, and Fishermen: To whom you may add, if you please, Perfumers, Dancers, and Tumblers, and the whole Tribe of such, who administer to gaming.

"BUT those Arts, which require much Study and Knowledge, are of great Use to Mankind, such as Medicine, Architecture, and teaching the liberal Sciences, these, if exercised by Men of a *certain Rank*, [that is under the Degree of Patricians] do not dishonour their Profession.   As to Merchandize, if in a little low Way, it is mean; but if great and extensive, importing Goods from various Countries, and dealing them out again to various Persons, without Fraud, *it is not altogether to be discommended*.   Nay, if the Persons who follow it, could be satiated, or rather be content with their Profits, *not making long Voyages*, but *returning speedily to their Farms*, and landed Estates, they would deserve to be rather commended.   But after all, in Things of this Nature, nothing is better, more profitable, more pleasant, or more *honourable* than the Cultivation of Land."

WHAT a strange Jumble of Things is here! And how little did this great Man understand the Nature of the Subject, about which he was writing! But leaving our City Patriots to censure CICERO, and to settle the Points of Precedency, and the Punctilios of Honour between the different Companies of Trades, as they shall think proper, I hasten to observe

2dly. That there is another essential Difference between the Freemen of *Rome*, and the Freemen of *London*. For the Freemen of *Rome* voted very often by Classes, Tribes, or Companies; which I am well persuaded the Freemen or Livery-men of *London* would consider as a manifest Infringement of their Rights and Privileges. And indeed very little can be said in Defence of such a Practice. For if one Tribe, or Company should have 1000 Voices, and the other not a tenth Part of the Number, it seems very unreasonable, that the larger Tribe should be deprived of nine-tenths of its Suffrages, [which it is in Effect by this Mode of voting] merely because the smaller Tribe had not an equal Number.—However such was the Practice of those Lords of the World, the Citizens of *Rome*.

A 3d capital Difference between their Case and ours, consisted in their Method of enacting or repealing Laws. For when a Law was propounded to the whole Body of the People in their public Assemblies, to be either confirmed, or repealed, they had not the Choice of mending, or altering any Part, by correcting this, or rejecting that, by adding any thing to it, or subtracting from it, but were obliged either to approve all, or refuse all. This was a very great Defect in the Constitution of the *Roman* Common-wealth, but it was unavoidable in their Situation. For as the People did not send Deputies from certain Districts, or particular Classes, to represent them in the Senate, similar to our Members of Parliament, they could no otherwise transact the Business of the State, in their numerous and tumultuous Assemblies [convened together for a few Hours] than by a simple Affirmation, or Negation. Therefore the only Part, which this Mob of Voters had to act, or could act, in the grand Affair of Legislation, wherein the *Majestas Populi Romani* was so immediately concerned, was to pronounce a single YES or NO. [The *sovereign* Council, that is the Body of Citizens, at *Geneva*, do the same at this Day.] A mighty Matter truly, and greatly to be envied by us *Britons!*

BUT 4thly, and above all, the Propensity of the *Romans* for War, and their Aversion to any lasting Peace, constituted, or ought to constitute the most direct Opposition between their Conduct and ours. A Nation, whose only Trade was to conquer and subdue, might with some Propriety, or at least with no Inconsistency, seek every Occasion of following their destructive, bloody Occupation. But how a commercial Nation, such as ours, whose continual Aim it should be to increase the Number of its Friends, and to attract Customers from every Part of the Globe, by promoting the mutual Interests of Mankind, and by giving no just Alarms to their Fears and Jealousies:—I say, how such a Nation should entertain that Fondness for War, and should espouse so many Quarrels as the *English* have eagerly done for almost half a Century last past, is, I own, beyond my Comprehension.   Nor can I find, even if we had come off Conquerors in every Engagement, which we had, or* wished to have, whether by Sea or Land, and had triumphed over all the People upon Earth, that these shining Victories would have reduced the Price of our Manufactures, or have rendered them one Jot the better, or cheaper, or fitter to be exported to foreign Markets.   In fact, there is something so preposterous, and indeed so ridiculous in the Farce, were any Shop-keeper to try to *bully* all his Customers in order to compel them to deal with him against their own Interest and Inclination, that one can hardly treat it in a serious Manner.   Yet alas! *mutato nomine de te Fabula narratur.* [See the Case of going to War for the Sake of Trade among my *American* Tracts, printed for CADEL.]   Moreover our affecting the Dominion of the Ocean, in the Manner we do, greatly prejudices all Mankind against us.   For the Ocean, and all open Seas, are the bountiful Gifts of Providence, like the Winds and Atmosphere, wherein all the World have a COMMON RIGHT; and ought to enjoy it unmolested.

I HAVE now, I think, cleared off a great deal of those vast Heaps of Rubbish, which lay in my Way; and therefore might proceed to erect a Super-Structure on the Foundation already laid.   But there is one Objection still remaining, which though a very false one, and supported by no Proof, is yet of so popular, and plausible a Nature, that it must not be passed over unnoticed.

---

* One Time the People were very clamorous for assisting the Queen of Hungary; and nothing else could content them.—Then the Tide turned, and they were equally clamorous to assist the King of *Prussia*.   At one Time that miserable Island *Corsica* was the favourite Object, at another a Set of Rocks, absolutely barren, in the midst of a most inhospitable Sea, and in a most wretched Climate, called *Falkland Island*, engrossed their Attention.   In short, any Thing, and every Thing, excepting that one Thing the most needful for a Commercial State, To *study to be quiet, and do our own Business.*

The OBJECTION is this:

"The People, that is, every individual moral Agent among the People," [for it must mean this, if it means any Thing, it being impossible to admit some, and refuse others the Right of Voting, with any Face of Justice, where all have an equal, indefeasible Right: Therefore the Objection means, that] "every individual Moral Agent among the People has an *unalienable Right* to be *self-governed*, that is to chuse his own Legislator, Governor, and Director. Consequently to take from, or to deny any of them the free Exercise of this natural and fundamental Right, is to act the Tyrant, and to be guilty of the worst Kind of Robbery that can be committed. It is such an atrocious Violation of the just Rights of Mankind, as will authorise every Man to use the most speedy and efficacious Methods in his Power, to assert and recover his native Freedom, by redressing his Wrongs, and *punishing* the Tyrants and Usurpers."

Now, if the Case be really such, as is here supposed, all that we have hitherto said, must pass for nothing. And therefore we must first examine into these strange Pretensions of our modern patriotic Objectors, which tend to unhinge all Society, before we can propose any Scheme for regulating the Mode of electing Deputies or Representatives.

THERE are two Kinds of Rights, and only two belonging to human Nature which are strictly and properly *unalienable*. These are the Functions of Nature, and the Duties of Religion. And they are in no other Sense unalienable, but because they are *inseparable* from the Subject to which they belong, and cannot be transferred to another.

A Man, for Instance, must perform his animal Functions for himself alone; there being no such Thing as Eating and Drinking by Means of a Proxy, or Deputation. Neither can one Man discharge the Duties of Religion in another's Stead: For these are personal Acts, which become null and void the Moment that one Man shall pretend to give, or another undertake to execute a Commission to act for him. In short, no Man can believe for another: Every Man do this for himself. And no Man can substitute another to repent, or obey in his Stead: For the Repentance and Obedience must be his own, otherwise it will not be valid. So far the Cases are clear: Indeed they are self evident.

BUT will any Man dare to affirm, that the Affairs of Government and Legislation, and all the Concerns of Civil Society relative both to Peace and War, are under the same Predicament, and incapable of being performed by Proxies or Deputations? Surely no: Nothing less than Insanity could excuse the uttering of such a Paradox. Indeed the Lockians themselves, to give them their Dues, are conscious that the Cases are not parallel: They are obliged to make this Confession, notwithstanding all their Parade about their unalienable Rights to be *self-governed* (as Dr. PRICE phrases it) that is, to elect their own Legislators, Governors, and Directors. For all of them [except honest ROUSSEAU, who is generally consistent, whether in Truth, or Error, and *perhaps* also except Dr. PRIESTLY;—I say, all of them] scruple not to maintain, that the Minority ought, for the most Part, to be concluded by the Majority; and that it is their Duty to acquiesce under such Determinations, tho' those Decrees may happen to be very contrary to their own private Judgments. Now this is a Thing impossible to be complied with in the Functions of Animal Life: For no Man can, even if he would, consign over his own Privilege of eating and drinking; or depute another to act in his Stead: In this Respect the Minority cannot compliment the Majority with their unalienable Rights. Moreover as to the Affairs of Religion, and the Performance of moral Duties,—in these Cases also the Rights of Conscience cannot be transferred either from the few to the many, or from the many to the few, by any Covenant or Compact whatsoever: Because they are truly and literally unalienable. Therefore no Majority of Votes can bind in these Cases.—

WHAT then becomes of this boasted Demonstration, this unanswerable Argument, whereby the Lockians have undertaken to prove, That all the Governments and Legislatures upon Earth are so many Robberies and Usurpations, (yea too, and all their Subjects *Slaves*) such only excepted, if any such there be, as are administered according to the Lockian System?—Why truly, this same Confidence of boasting, when sifted to the Bottom, dwindles into nothing: And the Mountain in Labour is brought forth of a Mouse. However, one Thing must be acknowledged on their Part, That this very Argument of *unalienable Rights*, weak and trifling as it is, may nevertheless become a formidable Weapon, in the Hands of desperate *Catalinarian* Men, for establishing a real and cruel Tyranny of their own (according to the Example which the *American* Rebels have already set) instead of that harmless, imaginary Tyranny, of which they so bitterly complain at present.

CHAP. IV.

Of a limited Monarchy, and mixt Government. Its component Parts, Monarchy, Aristocracy, and Democracy. Of the comparative Influence of each:—On which Side the greatest Danger is now to be apprehended.—The Remedy proposed, and proper Regulations.

HAVING at last, it is to be hoped, got over every *material* Difficulty, let us return to the main Point, from which we have been detained so long.—Deputies from, or Representatives of the People, though not *absolutely* necessary to the very Being and Existence of *every legitimate* Government, might nevertheless be of great Use and Benefit to them all. For though we dare not join with that unhappy Principle which denounces open War, or meditates Conspiracies and Assassinations against all who should presume to govern without an *actual* Election, Nomination, or Consent of the People;—yet we would by no means derogate from the singular Advantage, which might arise from a proper Choice of Representatives, to act as their Trustees and Guardians. But above all, be it ever acknowledged, and for ever gloried in, that the Election of Persons to represent the People of *Great-Britain* in Parliament, is a fundamental Part of the *British* Constitution. Here in *Britain*, the important Distinctions, so often mentioned, of actual Contracts and of Quasi-Contracts, enter into the very Essence of our Government. For every Voter or Elector, by giving his Vote, makes himself an *actual* Contractor: And every Non-Voter, whether Male of Female, young or old, by living peaceably and securely amongst us, and enjoying the Protection of the State, is a *Quasi*-Contractor. By means of that actual Contract, which is made between the Representatives in Parliament, and a certain Number of Electors or Voters in *every District*, the Abuse of delegated Power may be in a great Measure guarded against;—perhaps as effectually as can be expected in the present imperfect State of Things. And by means of that Quasi-Contract, which always subsists between the Governing Powers of a State, and the whole Body of the People, and every Individual thereof; the Evils of democratical Anarchy and Confusion are prevented, and Government itself is rendered an useful, practicable Thing, instead of being either a visionary Scheme, or an Engine of the blind Fury of a mad Populace.

TOWARDS the Beginning of the former Chapter, we set out with he following Enquiry, "How shall the People receive a reasonable Security, that the Powers wherewith their Governors are entrusted, both in making Laws, and in executing them, shall not be misapplied?" And in the

Progress of the Work, we examined into those constitutional Principles [*Wisdom, Power,* and *Goodness*] on the Exercise of which, in one Degree or other, all moral and civil Governments must depend.—In the next Place, we took a View of those several Forms, or exterior Modes of Administration, which give distinct Denominations to different Governments, the Monarchical, the Aristocratical, and the Democratical. The chief Defects and Imperfections of each of which were then endeavoured to be pointed out. [And besides this, particular Exceptions were made to the Governments of *Sparta, Athens,* and *Rome,* as being altogether improper for our Case and Circumstances, and indeed very repugnant to that Provision for general Safety, and social Happiness, which ought to be the End and Aim of every political Institution.]

FROM this Survey of Things, it evidently follows, That as neither of the above Forms is desirable in itself, a Government compounded of all three, and partaking of so much of the Nature of each, as shall make every Part be a Check and Counter-balance to the others, [without impeding the Motion of the whole] seems to be the *best:* It is indeed the fittest to give a reasonable Security to the People, that they shall be well governed. And such a Constitution, Thanks to kind Providence, is that under which we now live;—did we but attend properly to it, by correcting those few Errors, which Time has introduced; and did we but improve every Circumstance belonging to it to the most Advantage.

Now, as the *British* Government is compounded of three distinct Parts, the Regal, Aristocratical, and Popular; the first Inquiry should be, which of these wants rectifying the most? Or, in other Words, Which of them seems to preponderate so much at present, as to threaten Destruction to the other two?

IT hath been a Practice of many Years standing with those Gentlemen who chuse the Road of Opposition, (instead of pursuing other Methods) for obtaining Honours, Places, and Preferments, to alarm and terrify well-meaning People with incessant Cries, that the *Constitution is in Danger,* through the corrupt Influence of the Crown:—And that *they* are the only Persons who can save a sinking State.—This was the Watch-Word always made use of during a very long Contest against Sir ROBERT WALPOLE. But no sooner were these uncorrupt Patriots got into Power, and had gratified their Ambition and Revenge, than they changed their Note. They then happily discovered, what was hid from their Eyes before, that each of the component Parts of a mixt Government, ought to have a certain Influence on the others;—and that the Influence of the Regal on the Aristocratical and Democratical Branches, was neither more, nor greater than it ought to be. Nay, these new-enlighted quondam Demagogues then deigned to instruct us in their celebrated Treatise, *Faction detected by the Evidence of Facts*, in how many several Respects the ancient feudal Prerogative had been abridged and curtailed, and how much greater Security we enjoy for the Preservation of our Liberties, than our Fore-Fathers had before us. There is no Doubt to be made, were our present Race of Patriots ever to become victorious, either by the Subversion of the Ministry, or the Subversion of the State, and the Erection of a Common-Wealth, but that they too would wish to mimic their Predecessors in displaying the vast Advantage which their Country have reaped from their Labours for the public Good.—The plain *English* of which is, That *they ought to be well paid*. In the mean Time, as this Event is perhaps not so near its Accomplishment as they could wish;— and as neither the *Inns* nor the *Outs* are to be relied upon for giving a fair and impartial State of the present Influence of the Crown [neither Side being willing to discover the real Truth:] It is not impossible but that a Person of infinitely less Abilities than those who have undertaken to give an Account of this Matter, may succeed better; because he is enlisted under no Man's Banners, has no Party to serve, has nothing but the Truth in View, none to fear, and none to flatter.

WHAT is generally understood by the Influence of the Crown, must arise either from an open and avowed Exertion of some undoubted Prerogative of the Crown;—or from some secret Artifice, not authorised by Law, and therefore not to be justified, which the Crown is supposed to make use of, in order to obtain some certain End.

IF the former is here meant by the Assertion, that the Influence of the Crown has rapidly encreased of late Years;—it is saying in other Words, that the legal or constitutional Prerogative of the Crown has been *extended*, instead of being curtailed,—has been enlarged instead of being abridged;—and that the Power of the Prince is more absolute and unrestrained, and less confined by Law since the Revolution, than it was before. Will any Man in his sober Senses dare to maintain such a Paradox?—

BUT if the Term *Influence* is to be taken in the latter Sense; that is, if by it is meant such clandestine Practices as the Law condemns, and therefore would punish, if legally detected;—this is an Accusation, which must first be proved before Sentence can be past on the Offenders. For tho' it is very probable, that the best of human Governors have, in all Ages, shewn themselves not much averse to the Use of bad Means for the attaining such Ends as they wish to accomplish, and not other ways attainable;—yet it is much to be questioned, whether the particular Vices of *Bribery* and *Corruption*, [I mean in the gross Sense of the Word] have been practiced by the Agents of the Crown, to a greater Extent of late Years than they used to be.—Far therefore from suggesting a Thought, that our present Ministers, any more than their Predecessors, are perfectly immaculate;—I only say, that it has not yet appeared, that they are worse in this Respect than former Ministers;—much less has it been proved, that *Bribery* and *Corruption* have of late Years made such a rapid and alarming Progress, as to deserve a peculiar Stigma. My Reasons are the following: First, in the greatest Electioneering Contests, which perhaps this Country ever saw, when every Species of undue Influence was put in Practice, with shameful Notoriety:—Yet it was not so much as attempted to be proved, that the public Treasury had been opened to bribe the Electors in any of those Disputes.—For the Truth of this, I appeal to those, who remember all, or any of the most violent Contests which have been raised within the last 30 Years;—particularly the three great ones at *Bristol* within that Period,—the great Contest in *Oxfordshire*, at *Northampton*,— in *Cumberland*,—and lately in *Glocestershire*. In all which there can hardly be a Suspicion, much less a direct Proof, that the Bribery and Corruption, (but too much practiced) whether in Money, or by other Means, were owing to the Sums issued from the Treasury. My second Reason is, That by means of that quick Vicissitude of Things, to which perhaps this Country is more subject than any other, it has often happened that many of the *Outs* have come *in*, and many of the *Ins* have gone out;— yet no Side, notwithstanding their mutual Rancour, hath impeached the other, when they had the Books of the Treasury in their own Hands, of having been guilty of those Mal-Practices, and of that Bribery and Corruption which are here surmised.— Now this they most probably would have done, had any such Proofs been upon Record;—or even could they have brought any Thing suspicious from the Minutes in the Treasury-Books, of such a Misapplication of public Money.—Thirdly, the Sums generally spent at such contested Elections, is another strong Evidence, that Place-Men and Pensioners are not the principal Actors in these modern Tragedies. A Place-Man [or, if you please, a Pensioner] has perhaps 1000l. or 1500l. or even 2000l. a Year: This is accounted to be his *Summum Bonum*, his Conscience, his Country, and his God. Now, can it be imagined, that such a Man, who is thus characterized to have no Regard to any Thing but his own Interest, would spend, if *he could*, 10,000l.—perhaps 20,000l. nay,

30,000l.—or even more, for obtaining a Seat in Parliament to secure his Place, or his Pension? No: The Supposition is foolish and absurd: It confutes itself. Any Book of Calculations may suffice to inform us, that such *precarious* Things as Places or Pensions, are not worth a tenth Part of such Purchase-Money.—Lastly, in almost all vehement Electioneering Struggles, where vast Sums are expended, the Ground of the Contest is seldom or never about any national Affair:—But about the important Question,—Who shall be uppermost?—Whether this great Family, or that, in such a County, or such a Borough?—What Party Connection, or Party Colour shall have the Ascendent? And whether this Leader, or that Leader, this Club, or that, in such a County, City, or Borough, shall poll the most Votes?—Points, which concern the Public, or even the Minister for the Time being, just as much as the Big-endians, or Little-endians of the facetious Dean SWIFT.

WELL then; if the great Influence of the Crown, that *dangerous* Influence, which is every Day encreasing, and ought to be diminished, doth not arise from such Causes as these, at least in any considerable Degree;—from what doth it arise? and how is the Growth of it to be prevented?—The Causes of this encreasing Influence, are the vast Territories abroad, and those ruinous Wars, and immense Expences which they occasion; and ever will occasion whilst we are connected with them, under one Pretence of other. Can any Man make a Doubt of this?— If he doth, let him try, even in Thought and Imagination, to substitute a System for the Government, or Reduction of such remote Countries, which would stand clear of those Evils, which we now feel, and continually deplore. Suppose, for Example, a certain Event, which most probably is approaching with hasty Strides; viz. That the *English* settled in *Bengal*, and in the other Provinces of the Indian Empire, should take it into their Heads, that they too have unalienable Rights as well as the *Americans;*— and that, like them, now they are freed from the Apprehensions of a *French* Domination, they will no longer receive Laws from a little, paultry Spot in *Europe*, distant by Sea almost 10,000 Miles. Fired therefore with the glorious Thought of native Freedom, the Birth-right of every *Englishman* [though not of other Men; for by the by, the most zealous of our *English* Independents, are the least inclined to make other Men independent: And therefore I say] fired with the glorious Thought of their own Independence, and of Self-Government, they bravely defy not only the Gentlemen and *Ladies* of *Leaden-Hall* Assembly, but also the King,

---

* The Ladies have Votes at the *East-India House.*—Let the Lockians give a Reason consistently with their Principles, if they can, — Why Women are debarred from voting for *Directors* in Parliament, and yet allowed to vote for Directors at the *India House.*

Lords, and Commons of *Great-Britain* in Parliament assembled. Now here I ask, How is this Rebellion to be suppressed? And who is to have the Appointment, and the Payment of all the Troops, and of all the Squadrons, Transports, &c.; also of the several Officers, Commanders, Contractors, Purveyors, Surveyors, Examiners, Store-keepers, Deputies, Clerks, and of numberless other Beings to be employed for the Suppression of it? The Crown undoubtedly,—for it is the undoubted Prerogative of the Crown,—as the supreme executive Power: Otherwise there will be TWO Supremes within the same State;—a Solecism this, which even our modern political Refiners have not yet attempted to propose. This being the Case, how will you prevent the Crown from gaining a prodigious Influence by the Creation of such a Multitude of new Appointments, and by the annual Expenditure of the many Millions which will be wanted for the Payment of them? How will you prevent it, I say, whilst it has such gainful Things to give;—even supposing (which no Man in his Senses can suppose) that not a single Place would be created, nor a Farthing expended, beyond what the Nature of the Case required? Yet, even on this Supposition, and without Jobs or Embezzlements of any Kind, so many lucrative Places and Employments, [all necessarily in the Disposal of the Crown] must create a Dependence, call it by what Name you please, as long as human Nature shall continue to be what it has ever been since Government began. And this is the very Influence which now too much preponderates in our public Councils. Here then the Secret is out at last. The legal and constitutional Prerogative of the Crown is not to be blamed: But our distant, unwieldly Colonies, and our ruinous Wars for their Sakes are the real Causes of all our Complaints.—It is these which involve us in thousands of Distresses, of which we should have been happily ignorant, had it not been for such Connections. They therefore, and they only, are the Authors of our present Misfortunes; and will involve us in still greater, if we shall obstinately persist in retaining these remote, unmanageable Possessions:—

☞ For the Governing of which, I will be bold to say, the *English* Constitution was not calculated, and *is not fit*. This is so plain a Case, that no Man of Reason will pretend to deny it, or undertake to prove the contrary. How then comes it to pass, that neither Ministers, nor Anti-Ministers have ever assigned the true Cause of those Evils, which we daily feel, and of which we are perpetually complaining?—The Reason is this, Neither Ministers, nor their Opponents ever meant to serve the Public, at the Risque of their own Interest.—The uttering of disagreeable, unpopular Truths might be attended with certain Consequences to themselves which they wish to avoid: And therefore they desire to be excused.

SHOULD, for Example, the Minister for the Time being, have the Honesty and Sincerity openly to declare, that extended Commerce, and extended Territorial Acquisitions are repugnant to each other: That Industry, Probity, and Frugality are much more serviceable to the Promotion of Agriculture and Manufactures than all the Glare of War and military Glory;—and that the Boast of conquering *America* in *Germany*, or anywhere else, was, an improper, idle, Bravado, fitter to raise the Resentment of other Nations, than to serve ourselves.   Should, I say, a Minister have the Honesty and Sincerity openly to avow these unpopular Truths, and venture to declare, that the proper Way of diminishing *that Influence* of the Crown which is really dangerous, would be to diminish our Expences,—by renouncing all foreign Possessions, and cultivating the Arts of Peace in the two fruitful Islands of *Great-Britain* and *Ireland:* Should any ostensible Minister have the Courage to utter these honest, unwelcome Truths;—Who would support him?—Who would thank him?—Who would not persecute him.

AGAIN, Were any of our Demagogues to tell their best Friends, the Mob, that *Gibraltar* and *Portmahon* are very expensive, and very useless Things;—that the Ocean is the great *Common of Nature*, which belongs to no Nation, Language, or People, in any exclusive Sense; but ought to be free, like the Air, for the Use of all; and that the keeping up any Pretensions to the contrary, is as impolitic, as it is unjust; serving no other End, but to irritate all the World against us:—Also should he observe, that Colonies of every Sort or Kind are, and ever were, a *Drain* to, and an *Incumbrance* on the *Mother-Country*, requiring perpetual and expensive Nursing in their Infancy;—and becoming headstrong and ungovernable, in Proportion as they grow up,—and never failing to revolt, as soon as they shall find that they do not want our Assistance:—And that even at the best, those commercial Advantages, which are vulgarly supposed to arise from them, are more imaginary than real;—because it is impossible to compel distant Settlements to trade with the parent State, to any great Degree beyond what their own Interest would prompt them to: [And Self-Interest needs no Compulsion.]—Moreover, should any Orator of this Stamp proceed to shew, that since the Laws for governing the Colonies, have from the Beginning proved nugatory and vain, attended with vast Expence, and no proportionable Profit;—therefore should he propose a total Separation, and recommend the shaking them entirely off;—in Consequence of which Multitudes of Places would be abolished, Jobbs and Contracts effectually prevented, Millions of Money saved, universal Industry encouraged, and the Influence of the Crown reduced to that Mediocrity it ought to have:—Should, I say, any of our modern Demagogues dare to recommend these salutary Truths, what would his Brother-Demagogues say to him?—Would they assist him in this good Work?—No; they would not,—though conscious to themselves, that nothing better, or more seasonable, could be recommended.—On the contrary, they would open in full Cry against such an *Apostate* from the common Cause, —would persecute him in every Shape, and excite the Populace to pour forth the bitterest Execrations against him;—if not to proceed to still greater Extremities.

WHAT Course is he then to take? And how is he to act, in order that he may *seem* to aim at a national Reformation, and a Redress of Grievances, without intending any Thing real? The public Good requires one Conduct: But Popularity and Party another. Pressed by this Dilemma, it is but too obvious which his Choice would be. Such a Man would warmly recommend a Reform in the K—g's Kitchen, in his Cellar, in his Household Servants, and his Household Furniture;—nay, I had almost said, in his Dog-Kennel.—In short, he would propose to save and to retrench in every Article, except that grand one, a Separation from the Colonies, which is worth a thousand of the rest.—So that in order to gratify the perverse Humours of these unhappy Times, Majesty must be sacrificed to a republican Faction, and the Power of the Prince in the Management of his own private Concerns, be reduced to a Condition much more abject than that of any of his Subjects.

As long as the Temper and Intellects of Mankind shall remain in this wretched and disordered State, nothing truly good is likely to be done. We must therefore wait with Patience for better Times; hoping, that kind Providence will inspire one Part of the Community with sounder Understandings, and the other with better Hearts.

§. *The Aristocratical Part of the Constitution.*

RESPECTING this Branch very little need be said. For the present Aristocracy is very far from being formidable. Indeed it can hardly be said to have Weight enough in the political Scale, so as to maintain a proper Balance between the two other great Powers of the Constitution. —'Tis true, the Baronage in former Times was a dreadful Engine of Tyranny and Oppression. A few great Lords combining together, often shook the Throne, often trampled on Law and Justice, and oppressed the common People at their Pleasure. But these Times are no more:

A Peer of the Realm has no Jurisdiction annexed to his Barony; he is entitled to no Privilege or Prerogative authorising him to treat his Tenants, as Slaves and Vassals; but is as amenable to the regular Courts of Law, as any private Subject. Moreover as to the landed Estates of Peers, they being as divisible into small Shares as the Estates of Commoners; therefore the Power of the Peerage is so far from encreasing, that it is greatly on the Decline, if compared with what we find on Record in former Times.

§. *The Democratical Part of the Constitution;—wherein the Power of electing Deputies to represent the People is particularly considered.*

THAT Government was ordained for the Good of the People; and that this is the great Object which ought always to be attended to in every political Institution, are Points, which I shall take for granted. The only Matter worthy our present Inquiry is, How shall this public Good be most effectually promoted? And, if divers Means should be proposed, which is the Best?—Deputies from, and Representatives of the People, not only bid the fairest of any others, for this Purpose; but are likewise made an essential Branch of the British Constitution. Therefore the Benefits and Advantages thence arising, are the Subjects which come next to be considered.

THE best of human Institutions cannot be supposed to be so absolutely perfect, as to want no Correction or Amendment. Nay, Time, and an Alteration of Circumstances will introduce some Disorders into the best, and point out Defects, which could not be foreseen at first. This is the Case with Respect to the democratical Part of our Government. Disorders undoubtedly there are, and Defects not a few, which call aloud for a Remedy; if any can be found, which will not increase the Disease, instead of curing it, or will not introduce new, and worse Evils, by attempting to remove the old ones.

THE Remedies which have been of late Years most warmly proposed by those Gentlemen, who glory in the Title of being the Disciples of Mr. LOCKE, are the following:

1st, THAT there shall be a more equal Representation of the People, respecting their *Numbers:*

2ndly, THAT there shall be a more equal Representation of them, respecting their *Property*.

AND 3dly, THAT these Representatives shall not continue longer than one Year, or at most than three Years, without a new Election.

LET us begin with the first of the Remedies here proposed for the Cure of our political Disorders. This Notion of the Necessity of an equal Representation, is grounded on that Lockian Idea of the *unalienable Right of each Individual to be Self-governed*; Notions, which I hope, have been sufficiently confuted. However, as Truth will bear to be seen in various Lights, and what is wrong never can become right, I will now pursue this Deception, through a new Disguise, and endeavour to present the Reader with a second Confutation of it.

THEREFORE in Conformity to the Lockian Plan of equal Representation, I will state the following Case: [A Case sufficiently exact for our present Purpose] Let us suppose that the Island of *Great-Britain* contains seventy Millions of Acres, and seven Millions of Inhabitants;—and that it is proposed by the Lockian Politicians, [something similar to which is done almost every Day] That these seven Millions of Inhabitants ought to send nearly seven hundred Deputies to represent them in Parliament: So that each Million shall elect an hundred Representatives. So far the Scheme looks plausible; but mark the Consequences:—One Million out of the seven are crowded together, inhabiting a small Spot, perhaps not more than twenty thousand Acres; whilst the remaining six Millions are scattered over the Face of the Country; also several Millions of Acres lie waste, without any Inhabitants at all. Now this *central* Million, as it may be called, [alias *London, Westminster, Southwark*, and their Environs] with an hundred Deputies, all of their own electing, and continually under their Influence, and always ready at Hand, will be an over-match for the Rest of the Kindgom in every Contest, and become every Day more and more predominant.—Can any Man doubt of this?—He cannot, if he either knows, what human Nature is in general, when armed with Power;—or can reflect on the many Monopolies and Exclusions, which *London* in particular hath already obtained both by Sea and Land. For even at present, when *London, Westminster*, and *Southwark*, have but eight Representatives, they have encroached on the Liberties and Trade of their Fellow-Subjects in Hundreds of Instances, have had the Appropriation of vast Sums of the public Money, for building of Bridges, &c. &c. and have engrossed several Advantages, which ought to have been left common to all. Now, if the Metropolis has the Balance of Power already so much in its Favour, would you wish to make it preponderate upwards of twelve Times more than it doth?

AGAIN: All over-grown Cities are formidable in another View, and therefore ought not to be encouraged by new Privileges, to grow still more dangerous; for they are, and ever were, the Seats of Faction and

Sedition, and the Nurseries of Anarchy and Confusion. A daring, and desperate Leader, in any great Metropolis, at the Head of a numerous Mob, is terrible to the Peace of Society, even in the most despotic Governments:—But in *London*, where the People are the most licentious upon Earth,—In *London*, where the Populace are daily taught, that they have an unalienable Right to be self-governed:—and that their Rulers are no other than their Servants:—In *London*, where nothing is held sacred, but the Will of the People [blasphemously called, the *Voice of God*] what are you to expect from an Addition of Privilege and Power, but an Encrease of the most daring Outrages, and the Subversion of Law and Government? The audacious Villanies recently committed in *June*, 1780, are sufficient, one would think, to give any Man a Surfeit of the very Idea of adding still greater Influence and Power to a *London* Mob.

ONCE more, If a Man has any Sense of Rectitude and good Morals, or has a Spark of Goodness and Humanity remaining, he cannot wish to entice men into great Cities by fresh Allurements. Such Places are already become the Bane of Mankind in every Sense, in their Healths, their Fortunes, their Morals, Religion, &c. &c. &c. And it is observable of *London* in particular, that were no fresh Recruits, Male and Female, to come out of the Country, to supply those Devastations which Vice, Intemperance, Brothels, and the Gallows are continually making, the whole human Species in that City would be soon exhausted: For the Number of Deaths exceed the Births by at least 7000 every Year.— So much as to the 1st Remedy proposed by the Lockians for the Cure of our political Disorders.

THE 2d is, That there shall be a more equal Representation of the Inhabitants of this Island respecting their *Property*.

Mr. LOCKE himself strongly leans towards the Doctrine of representing *Property*;—and many of his Followers directly maintain it.—Though the Notion itself is little less than a Contradiction to their favourite grand Principle of unalienable Rights belonging to each Individual, whether poor or rich. For if such Rights do belong to any Beings whatever, they must belong to *Person*, not to *Property*. Moreover, according to this Doctrine, every Man, who has *no Property*, ought to have *no Vote*, notwithstanding the supposed unalienable Rights of his Nature. And a rich Man, with large and extensive Property, ought to have many Votes in Proportion to his Riches. Consequently the Grand *Turk*, and every other Despot, who is the only rich Man, being the Proprietor and Lord of all, is justly entitled to every Vote within his Dominions:—

Or rather, he is the only rightful Voter, and therefore represents all Property in his own Person. What a Revolution is this! For hence it comes to pass, that the *Ottoman* Empire, the very Quintessence of Tyranny, is all of a sudden transformed into a mild, just, and equitable Government; exhibiting a most perfect Model of fair Representation.

THE last Remedy proposed for the Cure of our political Disorders, is the Frequency of general Elections, which it seems ought to be triennial, —if not annual: And then all would be well. Never did Mountebank Doctor puff off his sophisticated Drugs with more rhetorical Flourishes, than our State Doctors have celebrated the Virtues of their *infallible Nostrum* of annual or triennial Parliaments. Nay, they have assured the Populace in some of their Harangues, that they have an unalienable Right to require us to swallow this Prescription.—But let us enquire a little before we swallow.—The first Benefit, we are told, which is to accrue from annual General Elections, is, "That we shall be restored to our antient Constitution of annual Parliaments." What? Doth not the Parliament now meet annually? And hath it ever failed to meet annually since the Revolution? "Oh, no: It meets, 'tis true: But it is not a *new* Parliament, [a *new* House of Commons] which meets; but only a Continuation of the old one; whereas there ought to have been a new House of Commons every Time that there is a new Sessions of Parliament. And the People have an unalienable Right to demand a Restoration of their antient Privileges."—How doth it appear, that annual General Elections ever were an antient Privilege of the People?—And what Authority do you produce in support of this extraordinary Assertion?— "There was a Law made the 4th of EDWARD III. C. 14.—which enacts, that Parliaments shall be held once a Year, or more often, if need be: This Law was confirmed in the 36th Year of the same Prince, and still remains unrepealed. Therefore"—Therefore what?—"Therefore, the holding of a Parliament once every Year, or more often if need be,— signifies the same Thing, [in patriotic Language] as that there shall be a General Election of the House of Commons once every Year, or oftener." —Surely the candid and impartial Reader doth not expect a formal Confutation of so wild an Argument.—Taking therefore for granted, that the holding of a Parliament, and a General Election of the Commons, are *not synonymous Terms*, I will endeavour to employ the Reader's Time and my own to better Purposes, by stating the Fact, from which this strange Notion of the constitutional Right of annual General Election seems to have taken its Rise.—When the Commons of *England* were excessively poor, and when the Members of the House of Representatives were, almost to a Man, either the Tenants of the Crown, or the Vassals, Dependents, and Retainers of the great Barons [there being hardly such a Person then existing, as what we now call an *independent Country Gentleman*] two Things were deemed great Favours at that Juncture, which would be looked upon in these Times in a very different Light. The one was, The excusing of the poorer Boroughs (especially the Tenants of the Crown) from sending Members to Parliament: And this was so frequent a Practice, that even the Sheriffs would sometimes make Returns, that this or that Borough was in such a pauper State, as not to be able to bear the Expence of sending Representatives. The other was, That the Elected themselves [for small Cities and Towns Corporate] did not consider the Office of a Member of Parliament in that high and honourable Light in which it stands at present. Men, who have not much to give, and no Favours to bestow, and who stand more in need of the Protection of others, than others do of them, are not much courted and caressed at any Time. Now this was the very Case with the Representatives in Parliament, I mean for small Cities and Borough-Towns, during all the Reigns of the *Plantagenets*, and the TUDORS; [as shall be more fully made to appear in the ensuing Chapter] therefore many, if not most of such Members, thought it a greater Favour to be excused from serving a burthensome Office, than to be elected to it. As to the Wages they received from their Constituents, every one must know, that at any Time, and according to the most frugal Mode of Living, the Sums received could not be sufficient for defraying the Expences incurred. Hence therefore it was natural for them to consider the Dissolution of the House at the End of every Sessions as a Matter of Grace and Favour; in order that they might have a Chance of not being elected a second Time. So that from this Circumstance we may trace the true Cause, how it came to pass, that at the End of every Sessions of Parliament, the House of Commons was generally dissolved:—I say *generally:* For there were some Exceptions: And most assuredly the Prince was not then under the Obligation of any *positive Statute Law* [as he now is] for dissolving it at any particular given Time. It was wholly at his own Option, when to do it. The *Irish* House of Commons, copied from the *English* Model, puts this Affair beyond Dispute. For in that Kindgom, when an House of Representatives was elected, at the Accession of a new King, it was to remain undissolved ['till the late octennial Act altered the Case] during the Life of the reigning Prince, if he thought proper:—If not, he might dissolve it as often as he pleased, and command new Elections to be made.—So much as to the boasted constitutional Rights of annual Elections.

HOWEVER, though our Modern-Patriots have failed most egregiously in this Point; yet, if they can make it appear, that annual or triennial Elections would be productive of more Good than Evil, every real Patriot will wish Success to their Endeavours, whatever may have been their Motives.

AND 1*st*. They assure us, "that annual Elections would put an End to all Bribery and Corruption." Good News indeed! But are you *really* sure of that? "We are; for when General Elections were annual, there was no Bribery."—Probable enough; and if you intend to reduce the Power of the House of Commons to the like *insignificant State* it was in during the Reigns of the *Plantagenets* and the *Tudors*, that very Insignificance would effectually remove all the Evils of which you now complain. As a Proof of this, take the following Example in modern Times.—The Clergy are no longer taxed by their Representatives in Convocation, but by Laymen in the House of Commons.—And what is the Consequence?—The Election of Convocation-Men is now become one of the most peaceable Things in Nature. No Bribery, no Corruption are even suspected, not a Treat, not an Intrigue is heard of, and Calumny herself is dumb. Now do you really wish to have our State-Diseases cured, and our political Complaints removed after the same Manner? and is this one of those *infallible Nostrums*, of which such Boastings have been lately made?—However, let us hear what you have further to propose.

2*dly*. YOU say "Were Elections to become annual, Bribery would cease; because it would be worth no Man's while to bribe so often, as every Year." To this I answer, that there is an Ambiguity in the Phrase *worth no Man's while*, which must be first explained: And then the Merits of the Cause will soon appear. Among the many Motives which induce Men to stand Candidates for a Seat in Parliament, some good, and some bad, two of the most predominant are, AVARICE, and AMBITION. Now, as far as *mere Avarice* or the Thirst of Gain is concerned, no Man in his sober Senses would think it worth his while to give 20,000l.—or 10,000l.—or 5000l.—or 2000l.—or even 1000l. annually, in Bribes, in order to procure a Place, or a Pension of 1000l.—2000l.—or at the most 3000l.—without any Security of holding it a Day:—I say, no Man in his Senses would think it worth his while to risque such a certain Sum on such an Uncertainty. And so far I agree most cordially with you. But remember that I have already proved [Page 247.] that no Man doth act after this senseless Manner, even at present. But as to AMBITION, and Vain-Glory, and the Lust of Power, the Stings of Envy, Hopes of Revenge, Religious Bigotry, and Party-Rage, &c. &c. &c.—are these Evils to be cured by having Recourse to annual Elections? No, no: You cannot suppose any Thing so foolish and absurd. As soon might you undertake to quench Fire with Oil, as to cool and moderate the Passions of Mankind, by keeping them in a perpetual State of Strife, Jealousy, and Rancour. It has ever been the Advice of medical People, to keep sore Places from being fretted;—but it seems, our modern State-Doctors prescribe the Use of continual fretting, as an infallible Means of Cure.

BESIDES, if Experience is to be our Guide, let the Experience of former Times decide the Question. During the long Contest between the Houses of *Lancaster* and *York*, annual Elections were, according to this Hypothesis, the constant Practice. Whether that was the Case, or not, is immaterial. If it was, what Good did these annual Elections then produce? And how much of the Fury and Madness of the Combatants did they restrain?—If annual Elections were then set aside, what was their Efficacy, if not used, when most wanted?—That Parliament upon Parliaments were held during those troublesome Times, is an undoubted Fact:—And therefore if annual Elections are such a sovereign Remedy, as here supposed, this was the Time for them to have produced their salutary Effects. Yet alas! the only Effect which we can learn from History, was, That the victorious Side always reversed what the vanquished had enacted, and added new Confiscations, and Attainders of their own. —Could any Thing better have been expected from the annual Revivals of Civil Discords?

BUT above all, if you will view the Matter in a commercial Light, you must acknowledge, that annual, or even triennial Appeals to the whole Mass of the People, [each of whom, it seems, hath an equal and an indefeasible Right to be represented, and to be self-governed, &c.] would bring swift Ruin and Destruction on all our Trade and Manufactures. The Clubs and Combinations of Tradesmen to raise the Price of Goods, and of Journeymen to raise their Wages, have a bad Effect on national Commerce even at present:—judge therefore what would be the Consequences, were every Tradesman, and every Journeyman, to be annually *authorised* [as he would be in effect] to make his own Terms with the Candidate, before he would promise him his Vote! Most undoubtedly *Birmingham* and *Manchester*, *Leeds*, and *Halifax*, and many other populous Towns and manufacturing Places would soon be reduced to mere Villages, when blessed with equal Representations, and frequent Elections: And the Trade and Manufactures, the Shipping and Navigation of *England* would soon migrate into *Scotland*:—Into *Scotland*, I say, where the common People have no Concern in County Elections, and not much in most of their Cities and Boroughs; and therefore they suffer but very little from the Drunkenness and Intemperance, the Idleness and Dissipation, and other Vices, which generally prevail in Consequence of contested Elections.

BUT be that as it may, enough hath surely now been said to prove the Inefficacy of the Remedies hitherto proposed. And if what I have to offer in their Room should be found on Examination to be equally defective, I can only say that these Defects must be charged either on the Nature of the Disease, which will not admit of a Cure,—or on the Incapacity of the Author, who cannot discover one. [For as to Care and Attention in considering, and reconsidering the Subject, nothing has been wanting in that Respect]. If therefore the Disease is really incurable, Patience and Resignation is the only Prescription. But if a great Part of the Evils now complained of, might be rectified, and others so far redressed as to be of small Importance,—it is to be hoped that some happy Genius may yet arise, who will propose a Plan more efficacious in itself, and free from those Difficulties, which perhaps may be objected to what I have now to offer.

HAVING premised thus much, I would now beg Leave to observe, that the following Points appear to me of such Consequence, that every Man, who would propose any Remedy either for removing, or palliating the present Evils, ought to have them constantly in View, as the Scope and End of all his Endeavours.

1st. TRUE Policy requires, that every Part of a compact [middle-sized] State, such as *Great-Britain*, ought to be well cultivated, and fully settled; —Therefore every Scheme, Plan, or System, which has a contrary Tendency, ought to be discouraged and opposed, as much as possible.

2dly. TRUE Policy requires, that in the well peopling of a Country, Abundance of single Farm-Houses and Cottages, numerous Country Seats, Villages, and Towns, and not a few Cities of a moderate Size are much preferable to large, unwieldy Capitals in, or near the Centre, with Wastes and Deserts, or Districts thinly inhabited, at or near the Extremities:—Consequently every good and really patriotic Scheme should have an Eye towards promoting the former, and checking the Encrease of the latter, as much as the Nature of the Case will permit.

3dly. THOUGH it would be highly absurd, to admit indiscriminately every individual Moral-Agent to be a Voter, yet true Policy requires that the Voters should be so numerous, and their Qualifications respecting Property be so circumstanced, that the actual Voters could not combine against the Non-Voters, without combining against themselves, against their nearest Friends, Acquaintance, and Relations.

4thly. GOOD Policy also requires, that in the Matter of electing Representatives, of sending Deputies to the great Council of the Nation, the general and particular, the national and personal Interests both of the Electors, and of the Elected, should be made to harmonize as much as possible.

LASTLY, it also requires, that the proposed Alterations from the present System, should deviate as little as may be, from the present Forms of Government, and cause no *remarkable* Changes in the external Police, and long established Customs of the *English* Nation.

ON these Positions, which I hope the candid, and judicious Reader will *readily* allow, I will venture to proceed in my intended Scheme of Amendment or Improvement.

The QUALIFICATIONS of VOTERS.

LET me therefore previously remark, that the Qualification for voting both as Freemen, and as Freeholders, ought to be raised a little. The public Good, as well as private Happiness, calls aloud for a Reformation in this Point; and none can reasonably object to such a Measure, but those who maintain the absurd, and often confuted Notion of the unalienable Rights of each Individual to be his own Legislator, and his own Director. But, I would beg Leave to observe, that this Qualification ought to be placed in such a Mediocrity of Condition, between the two Extremes of great Riches, and of wretched Poverty, that no sober, diligent, and frugal Man could well fail of raising himself by his Industry, in *a Course of* Years to the honourable Distinction of a Voter; — and that almost every idle, vicious, and abandoned Spendthrift would be in Danger of sinking beneath, and of being degraded from the Privilege of voting. How different from this is the Case at present!

1st. THEN, the Qualification for voting as a Freeholder for the County should still be no more *nominally* than that of Forty Shillings a Year above all Reprisals. But in order that this Qualification might not be subject to any Fraud or Collusion, it would be necessary to insist that the Voter, or intended Voter should be assessed to the Taxes both of King and Poor, for no less a Valuation of the Premises, than the whole Sum of forty Shillings; — and that he himself ought to be in full Possession of them, and to have paid the Tax or Taxes arising from such Assessments, [Reference being had to the Books of the Collectors] a full Year before he could be entitled to give his Vote. This single Regulation would cut off three-fourths of the bad Votes usually obtruded on Sheriffs at contested Elections; — nay, it would put an End to the whole Trade of splitting Freeholds on such Occasions.

2dly. THOUGH all Persons ought to be free as to the Exercise of any handycraft Trade, or Calling, both in Town and Country [and all Laws, and Byc-Laws to the contrary ought to be repealed] yet none but *Residents* in Cities and Borough Towns ought to be allowed to vote at Elections as *Freemen.* And the legal Qualification of a *Resident*, to entitle him to be considered as a *voting* Freeman, ought to be the having paid *Scot* and *Lot* in such Town or City in his own Person, and for his own Property, [Reference being had to the Collectors Book] for one clear Year, preceding the Time on which he tenders his Vote. Nevertheless all Men, free or not free, resident, or Absentees, who have *Freeholds* within the Precincts, Liberties, or Boundaries of such Cities, or Borough Towns, ought likewise to be entitled to the Privilege of voting for Representatives in Parliament; — provided that their Freeholds come within the Description of the full Sum of forty Shillings above-mentioned: — It being very evident that the Interest of such Freeholder, generally speaking, is more permanent, and local, than that of a mere Freeman paying *Scot* and *Lot*. Now here again, the whole System of electioneering Bribes, and of Borough-Brokage, would in a Manner be annihilated by this single Regulation; — and the remaining Evils be so very few in Comparison, as hardly to deserve our Notice. — So much as to the Qualification of Voters.

The QUALIFICATION of CANDIDATES.

RESPECTING the Gentlemen to be elected Representatives, their Interest, it is presumed, would best be connected with that of the Public in general, and of their Constituents in particular, by the following Arrangement.

1st. LET the Person offering himself a Candidate for a County, cause to be delivered to the Sheriff, or returning Officer, ten Days at least before the Commencement of the Poll, a List, or Schedule of his *landed* Qualification, — Shewing, that he has *not less* than 1,000 Acres of Land in such a Parish, or Parishes, according as the Lands may lie contiguous, or dispersed, within the said County; on which are erected ten Dwelling Houses *at least*, which are, and which have been for 12 Months last past inhabited by ten distinct Families; and that he himself hath enjoyed the said Estate in his own full Right, and hath been the Landlord of the said Tenants for at least twelve Months preceding, having paid, either by himself, or by them, every Kind of Tax, which hath been legally charged upon the same. Moreover, he should be obliged to cause a printed Copy of the said List or Schedule to be affixed on the Market-House, Sessions-House, Town-Hall, Church Doors, and every other public Building of, and in every Market-Town within the said County: — And should also cause Duplicates of the same to be inserted twice, or oftener, in the Journals or News-Papers of the said County, if any such shall be published; — if not, of some neighbouring County or City, the most read by, and circulated among the Electors.

2dly. The Candidates for Cities, or Boroughs, should be obliged to deliver similar Lists, or Schedules, and to give equally long Notice to their respective returning Officers, and indeed to all the Inhabitants of such Cities, or Boroughs, by causing printed Copies to be affixed on the Market-Houses, and on every public Building whatsoever, ten Days at least before the Poll begins: Nor should the Insertion of such List or Schedules in the public Papers (as related in the former Article) ever be omitted; in order that Freeholders at a Distance, as well as Freemen on the Spot, may be made perfectly well acquainted with the Pretensions, and landed Qualifications of each intended Candidate: — Only respecting the *Quantum* of the Qualification, it may be necessary, [in order to approach nearer to the present Law] that no more Acres should be required than 500, — and five Dwelling Houses, occupied or inhabited by five distinct Families. But nevertheless, that this Qualification may be a real one, and not pretended, or a borrowed, [which alas! is too often the Case at present] it may be necessary to insist, that *no Part* of this landed Estate should be thirty Miles distant from the City, or Borough, for which he offers himself a Candidate, so that many of the Inhabitants might be able to detect the Cheats if any should be attempted: — The Miles to be measured along the King's Highway, and public Roads, and not as the Crow flies. But it is immaterial in what County or Counties the Estate itself should happen to be situated, the Vicinity being the main Point to be regarded.

3dly. The Penalties or Forfeitures for contravening, or not duly performing any of the above Rules and Conditions, should be the following.

[*1st.*] Though it would not be right to debar the accused, before his Guilt is legally proved, the Liberty of standing a Candidate; — yet as soon as the Election was ended, and for nine Months afterwards, it might be lawful for any Person whatever to prosecute him in the King's-Bench for the [supposed] Breach of this intended Law; — provided, that the Plaintiff previously gave Security for paying 1000l. Damages in the Case of a County Election, and 500l. in that of a City or Borough, to the Defendant, if he did not, according to the Verdict of a Jury, make good his Charge: — But in Case he did, then the Defendant should forfeit the Sum of 1000l. for a County, and 500l. for a City or Borough, with treble Costs to the Plaintiff; and the *Onus probandi*, that he was actually and *bona Fide* possessed of such an Estate, and that he had performed all the Conditions required by this intended Law, should rest on the Defendant, because it would always be in his Power to prove his Innocence, if he was falsely accused.

[*2dly.*] IN Case the Defendant should be cast, then, if he was returned Member, his Seat should be declared vacant, *ipso facto*, and a Writ be made out for a new Election: — But he himself should be rendered incapable of standing a Candidate for that, or for any other County, or Place, for at least three Years to come.

[*3dly.*] IF any Thing else can be supposed yet to be wanting towards putting a total End to the numerous Frauds and Forgeries of *unqualified* Candidates, [now, alas! so very common] and of their Adherents, Coadjutors, or Abettors, — It may be thus supplied: — Let every Person who can be proved to have been an Accomplice, or Assistant in making up false Accounts, or publishing the same, (knowing them to be false) respecting the Property of, or Title to the Lands, — the Quantity of Acres which they contain, — the Number of Dwelling Houses erected on them, — the Families actually inhabiting them, — the Length of Time, in which the Candidate may have been in the Possession of them in his own Right; — I say, let every such convicted Accomplice, Agent, or Assistant, be judged by this intended Law to have incurred the same Guilt as a Principal, and be subject to the like Penalties, and Disqualifications in every Respect whatever.

HAVING laid down these several Regulations for ascertaining the Qualifications both of those, who are to *elect*, and of the Candidates to be *elected;* it is humbly conceived, that, were they duly executed, they would prove such a sufficient Guard to the Freedom of Elections, and such a preventive Remedy against almost every Kind of Fraud and Imposition, that more, or greater need not be required.   Indeed, it may be questioned, whether in the present State of Things, more or greater would not embarrass the main Design, instead of promoting it.   Let us therefore take a View of the whole Plan, as it lies before us. — Supposing, that it was fairly set in Motion, and when all the Parts are co-operating with each other.

BUT in order to do this, I must premise, that such an important Bill ought not to be attempted to be introduced into Parliament, at or near the Dissolution of an old one, but about the beginning of a new one. Those, who know any Thing of the Spirit of Electioneering, which is ready to burst forth, as a Flood, when a Parliament is drawing near the Time of its Dissolution, and of the vile Arts and Stratagems usually practised on such Occasions, to inflame the Populace with Names, and Noise, and Nonsense, can easily comprehend my Meaning.

This being premised, I am therefore to observe,

FIRST of all, That when such a regulating Bill shall have passed into a Law, — even the lowest of the People, and those, who perhaps might be deprived thereby of their present Privilege of voting [a Privilege alas! which is now their greatest Misfortune] would soon find, that they would be Gainers by it in Reality, instead of Losers; — *Gainers*, I say, unless the Removal of the Power of doing Mischief to others, and of ruining themselves, can be called a *Loss*. In fact, all the great Blessings of Society, Life, Liberty, and Property, would be as much ensured to them under this Circumstance, as to any Set of Men whatever.

NAY 2*dly*, They would also soon find, that the Honor or Privilege of becoming a BRITISH VOTER [it would then indeed be a *real* Honour, and a great Privilege] lay within their own Reach to obtain; — provided they were so much their own Friends, as to live a Life of Industry, Sobriety, and Frugality for a few Years; — I say, for a *few* Years; it being almost demonstrable that any common Day-Labourer, or common Mechanic, acting uniformly on a Plan of Industry, and Œconomy, might raise himself [unless particularly unfortunate] to the Degree of a Voter, before he arrived at the middle Stage of Life; — Yes, he might raise himself to it by his own good Conduct, without applying to any one for Interest, or using any Sort of Solicitations. — Now, when the Road to public Prosperity, and to private Happiness, to external Honours, and to internal Virtue, is thus made straight and easy, without any Turnings or Labyrinths whatsoever, — What can any People upon Earth reasonably desire more?

3*dly*. THOSE, who should feel themselves either elevated to, or confirmed in the Rank of VOTERS, by Means of these new Regulations, would prize this Privilege so much the more, and contend for it with the greater Zeal, in Proportion, as they found that it would be an *honourable Distinction*, not conferred indiscriminately, as at present, on the very Dregs of the People, or the most worthless of Mankind; but bestowed on the more deserving, both as a Reward for their own exemplary Conduct, and also as an Incitement held forth to others to copy after. Men in such a Situation will value that Constitution, which distinguishes them from others, so much to their Credit and Reputation, for the same Reason that they love and value themselves. And the Lockian Doctrine of *unalienable Rights* will necessarily fall to the Ground.

4thly. WHEN the Time of electing Representatives shall draw near, the Electors for Cities and Towns, as well as for Counties, will be tolerably well secured by these new Regulations from the Solicitations of those bribing Mushroom Candidates, who always mean to *sell*, having no Chance to succeed, unless they *buy*. Therefore, generally speaking, neither the Plunderers of the *East*, nor the Slave-Drivers of the *West*, nor the Privateering, trading Buccaneers of the *American* Continent, nor our *English Newmarket* Jockeys, nor *London* Gamblers, nor *Change-Alley* Bulls and Bears, &c. &c. will be able to shew their Heads, when such *terra firma* Qualifications shall be required, before they offer themselves as Candidates. Yet these landed Qualifications are so low and moderate in themselves, and the Time required to be in Possession of them so very reasonable, that no Man in the Neighbourhood, who has any Title to the Character of a Gentleman, would be excluded from being a Candidate, if he pleased.

HENCE therefore *5thly*, it is very apparent that all Candidates for Boroughs, answering to this Description, would have a real Interest in the Welfare of the Neighbourhood of the Place they intended to represent. A Circumstance this, in which our present System is too often very defective: For when an Adventurer of the former Stamp, (as mentioned in the *3d.* Article) whose Wealth lies in far distant Countries, or in the Funds (if indeed it is any where) happens to be elected, he has no personal Motive to concern himself at all in the Prosperity of the Borough, or in the Improvement of the Estates, situated in its Neighbourhood. Nay, indeed it may so happen, that his own private Interest as a Planter, a Monopolizer, a Jobber, or Contractor, &c. &c. may be directly opposite to the true Interest of that Place, or District, which he represents in Parliament: And therefore, if he can attach to his electioneering Views two, or three leading Men of the Borough, either by pecuniary Bribes, or by the Promise of Places to them, their Relations, or Dependents, — his End is answered, and he looks no farther; — unless it be to assist these dirty Tools to oppress and harrass those, their fellow Burgesses, who should dare to oppose them.

6thly. When the general and particular Interest both of the Electors, and Elected, of the Constituents, and of their Representatives, are thus made to con-center, Parliament-Men become in fact, what they are always supposed to be in Theory, and Speculation, both *Guardians*, and *Guarantees:* Guardians of the Rights of the People, and of their own Property against the Encroachments or Innovations either of the Crown, or of the Aristocracy — if any should be attempted; — and *Guarantees* to both the Crown and the Nobility, that the People shall not abuse the Liberty they enjoy, by aiming at too much, so as to overturn the Constitutional Balance; which indeed would sooner or later prove their own Ruin: — For a turbulent, factious Democracy is quickly, and easily converted into the Tyranny of a single Despot.

IT has been often said by certain Writers on Politics, that Wealth and Power naturally, and even necessarily infer each other. In a qualified Sense this may prove true, but not universally. It would be true, were none but Persons of some Property in Counties, Cities, and in Borough-Towns, [that is, were *substantial* Freeholders, and all Persons paying *Scot* and *Lot*, and not the lowest of Mankind, though frequently a Majority as to Numbers] were those, I say, and *none but those* to elect their own Representatives, and to empower them to act in their Stead. In such a Case the Wealth of Individuals thus confederated together under proper Heads to direct and govern the whole, would become its Strength; — And Strength so circumstanced would be only another Name for Wealth. — Suppose, therefore, that in the Vicissitudes of human Affairs, our Body Politic should be threatened with such a violent Shock as would greatly disorder it: — As soon as the Danger was perceived, every Voter or Elector, every Freeman, and Freeholder, would immediately unite with their respective Representatives to guard against the approaching Evils, and repel the Blow. All little Divisions and Animosities would then be forgot: The general Solicitude would swallow up every inferior Consideration, and unite all Parties in the common Cause. Suppose again, that thro' Want of Attention in some, and from a much worse Cause in others, the Blow was actually given, and that the Wound was almost mortal; — yet even then, as long as Life remained, and any Hopes were left, the whole Mass of the [voting] People, as well as their Representatives, would struggle hard to get the better of this dangerous Convulsion, and to restore the Body-Politic to its antient Vigour. These Efforts they would certainly make, because they would then directly feel, that the Loss of such a Constitution as ours, would be their own Loss, and that they themselves could never be of so much Importance, either in their private, or their public Capacity, under any other Form of Government, as they are under the present.

HERE therefore, it may be highly necessary to observe, that the democratical Branch of our Constitution has more to fear from its own internal

Tendency, than from any external Cause whatever. — I have, I hope, already proved, that neither the Crown nor the Peerage, according to the present State of Things, could either attack or undermine the Liberties of the People, with any Prospect of Success. We may therefore consider ourselves as safe on that Side. But I own, I am not without Apprehensions, that the People themselves are strongly inclined to do those Things, which would in the Event prove a *Felo de se*. Too many among them are alwayd disposed to think, that because Liberty is a good Thing, *therefore they can never have too much of that good Thing*. — This fatal Mistake has been the Ruin of every free Government, both in antient, and modern Times; and will, if persisted in, prove the Ruin of ours. The new Regulations here proposed, bid the fairest of any that I know of [consistently I mean, with the Spirit of our Constitution, and a due Regard to *real* Liberty] to check that strange Propensity so observable in our common People towards *Levelling*, and *Licentiousness*, and to give their Minds a better and more reasonable Turn. It is indeed a melancholy Reflection, that in most Cities, and Borough-Towns, and perhaps in Counties, the far greater Number of Voters are such, whose Circumstances lead them to wish for a new Division of Property, because they have little, or nothing to lose, but may have much to get in Times fo Confusion, and by a general Scramble. Therefore every Rule of sound Policy, not to say Religion and Morality, suggests the Necessity of raising the Qualification of voting to such a Mediocrity of Condition, as would make it the Interest of the Majority of Electors, to assist in the Support and Preservation of Order and good Government, and not to wish their Overthrow.

7thly and *lastly*. THE new Regulations here proposed, if carried into Execution, would cause every Part of the Kingdom, the Extremities, and intermediate Places, [as well as the Centre, or Seat of Government] to be better represented than they are at present. The Complaint usually brought against *Cornwall* and *Wiltshire*, is, that they return too many Members in Proportion to the rest of the Kingdom: Whereas these Counties might justly retort the Accusation, by saying, that though they have *nominally* more Members than *London*, *Westminster*, and *Southwark*, yet in *Reality* they have fewer. For most of the Members for the *Cornish* and *Wiltshire* Boroughs have their chief Residence in the Metropolis, with Country-Seats perhaps in its Environs: — None of which Villas, generally speaking, are at a greater Distance than 20 or 30 Miles from it: — And what is still worse, most of such Members have not a Foot of Land *in*, or any where *near* the Places for which they were elected: So that having no personal Interest in the Premises, they might with much greater Propriety, be stiled the Representatives of *London*, *Westminster*, and *Southwark*, and of the several Districts in that Neighbourhood [where their Estates and Fortunes are supposed to be] than the Representatives of the Boroughs in *Wiltshire* and *Cornwall*, where they have no Property at all.

WHEN Men are determined to support a favourite Hypothesis, it is curious to observe, what Pains they take, to make every Thing, however discordant in its Nature, to bend and ply towards their beloved System. The Boroughs of the two Counties just mentioned return more Members to Parliament than any others: This is a Fact which cannot be denied. But how is it to be accounted for? The Disciples of Mr. LOCKE, who maintain, that all Persons have an unalienable Right to choose their own Legislators, Governors, and Directors, gravely tell us, that these Boroughs, now fallen into Decay, were once very large, and extremely populous, and the Seats of various extensive Manufactures: — And then the short Inference is, that as the Trade is gone, and the Inhabitants become very few, the Right of sending Members to Parliament ought to be transferred to more populous and flourishing Towns. [*Birmingham, Manchester, Leeds, Halifax, Stroud, Bradford, Trowbridge*, and many such like Places, would not think themselves at all obliged to the Author of such a Proposal, and would certainly remonstrate strongly against it] But waving that Matter, let us, if we can, trace the real Origin of this Difference between the State of Representation of the Boroughs in the two Counties of *Wilts* and *Cornwall*, if compared with those of other Counties. *Wiltshire* was long the Residence of the Kings of the *West-Saxons*, who in Process of Time conquered all the rest. Now where the Royal Residence was, there of Course would be the chief Domain: For the stated Revenue of our antient Princes, both *Saxon* and *Norman*, consisted chiefly in Landed Estates, that is, in Castles, with their Territories, Manors and Honours, and Towns and Villages, held by various Services, some of them military or noble, and others base and servile. *Cornwall* was in like Manner, and for the same Ends and Purposes the Domains of the Earls and Dukes of *Cornwall*. Hence therefore it naturally followed, that as the great Tenants of the Crown were obliged to attend *in Person* at the Courts of their Sovereign [thereby constituting an House of Peers] so the smaller Tenants, and inferior Vassals, were to do the same by Deputation; which Circumstance gave the first Idea of an House of Commons. Indeed there was a stronger Reason for the Attendance of the Deputies from those Towns and Villages, which belonged to the

Crown, *if their Poverty did not prevent them;* — I say, there was a stronger Reason for their Attendance in some Respects, than for that of others; — because the Quantum of those Acknowledgments, Services, and Quit-Rents, which they were to pay to their great Landlord, the Crown, as well as their Free-Gifts and Benevolences, if they were disposed to make any, were to be fixed and apportioned at such Meeting.   Moreover, when the Duchy of *Cornwall* escheated to the King, the Tenants, and Borough-Towns, and Villages of the Duke became a Part of the Royal Patrimony; in consequence of which, they were obliged to do the same Suits and Services at the King's Courts, which they had done before to their ducal Masters, or great feudal Lords.   I own indeed, that several of the *Cornish* Boroughs were not *chartered* to send Members to the General 'Parliament of the Realm 'till the Reign of King JAMES I. — But nevertheless they were such Places as were supposed to have sent Deputies to the Courts of the Earls, or Dukes of *Cornwall*, and therefore were considered as having a Kind of *equitable* Right to send Members to the General Council of the Nation, now that their own particular Courts were suppressed, or rather swallowed up.   Therefore, to return: —

SURELY there is nothing forced, or unnatural in this Account of the Matter; — nothing, but what is perfectly analogous to the Customs and Manners of antient Times, and correspondent to the Genius of the Gothic System.   Why therefore should we have Recourse to an imaginary Hypothesis of the great Commerce, great Population, and extensive Manufactures of these two single Counties of *Wilts* and *Cornwall*, to the Prejudice of all the rest of *England*, without any Foundation in History for such a Supposition?— Why indeed, when it is farther considered, that such an Hypothesis can answer no other End, than to confirm, by forged Accounts, that false Notion of every Man having an unalienable Right to be self-governed; — a Notion which was not so much as dreamed of in those Times?

THERE is but one Objection, as far as I can perceive, which can be made to the Account here given of the Reason, why a greater Number of Members are sent by the *Wiltshire* and *Cornish* Boroughs, than by the Towns and Villages of other Counties: — And that is this; "Were the Case as here stated, it would be natural to expect from the Analogy of the Thing, that the Dutchy of *Lancaster*, now united to the Crown, would have furnished Examples similar to those of the Dutchy of *Cornwall:* — But it doth not." — This Objection, it must be owned, looks plausible at first Sight: — But the whole Force of it is built on a Mistake. — The Dutchy of *Lancaster* is, and ever was a scattered Thing, composed out of the forfeited Estates of four great Barons, besides other Accessions, which lay dispersed in almost every County both of *England* and of *Wales*. It was therefore impossible, that the same Phœnomenon could have occurred in the one Case, as in the other. Had indeed those forfeited Estates been situated altogether in *Lancashire*, or in any one single County, there is hardly a Doubt to be made, but that the same, or nearly the same Circumstance would have taken Place, on the Union of that Dutchy with the Crown. — And if it had, what ill Consequences would have ensued, — supposing, I mean, that the Regulations here proposed, had been adopted, as a Part of the System? — For my Part, I can see none: — Nay, I will not scruple to declare, that it would be a much more rational Plan, that the Deputies from *Cornwall*, or *Westmoreland, Cumberland*, or *Northumberland*, — or, if you please, from *Sutherland* and *Caithness*, (now these Kingdoms are united) should out-number those of *London, Westminster, Southwark*, and the adjacent Parts, than that these latter should be more numerous than the former: — Because the Centre and the Residence of the Legislative, and executive Powers; — or in one Word, the Metropolis will never fail to take Care of itself: — Not so, *vice versa*.

BIBLIOGRAPHY

THE BOOKS AND PAMPHLETS OF JOSIAH TUCKER

In the following chronological list of Tucker's writings the titles, in most cases, are not reproduced in full. The author's name is omitted, as are the names of printer and bookseller, and Arabic numerals are substituted for Roman in the date of publication. The list does not include letters and articles which Tucker contributed to newspapers and magazines. The titles of some of these can be found in the Bibliography appended to Professor Walter Ernest Clark's *Josiah Tucker: Economist.*

A Brief History of the Principles of Methodism. Oxford, 1742.

A Calm Address to All Parties in Religion concerning Disaffection to the Present Government.

> Published anonymously in 1745. Republished, "corrected and enlarged," as Appendix to Part II of *Reflections on the Expediency of a Law for the Naturalization of Foreign Protestants.*

Hospitals and Infirmaries, Considered as Schools of Christian Education for the Adult Poor and as Means Conducive towards a National Reformation in the Common People. London, 1746.

> Reprinted in *Six Sermons* and in *Seventeen Sermons.*

Two Dissertations on Certain Passages of Holy Scripture. London, 1749.

A Brief Essay on the Advantages and Disadvantages Which Respectively Attend France and Great Britain with Regard to Trade. London, 1749.

> This went through several editions. The author's name first appears on the title page of the third edition (London, 1753), which contains a long appendix.

An Impartial Inquiry into the Benefits and Damages Arising to the Nation from the Present Very Great Use of Low Priced Spirituous Liquors. London, 1751.

Reflections on the Expediency of a Law for the Naturalization of Foreign Protestants. Part I. London, 1751.

Reflections on the Expediency of a Law for the Naturalization of Foreign Protestants. Part II. London, 1752.

An Earnest and Affectionate Address to the Common People of England
    on their Barbarous Custom of Cock-Throwing on Shrove Tuesday.
    Probably published in 1752 or 1753.   Advertised in *A Letter to a Friend
    concerning Naturalizations*, second edition.   A second edition was pub-
    lished in 1787.

Reflections on the Expediency of Opening the Trade to Turkey.   London,
    1753.
    A second edition, containing an appendix, was published in 1755.

A Letter to a Friend concerning Naturalizations.   London, 1753.
    A second edition, with corrections, was published in the same year.

A Second Letter to a Friend concerning Naturalizations.   London, 1753.

The Important Question concerning Invasions.   London, 1755.
    Published anonymously.   See Clark, *Josiah Tucker*, 245.

The Elements of Commerce and Theory of Taxes.
    Privately printed, 1755.   Published for the first time in the present
    volume.

The Case of the Importation of Bar Iron from Our Own Colonies of
    North America.   London, 1756.

A Short and Familiar Way of Explaining the Important Doctrine of
    Justification and the Points Dependent on It, Agreeably to Scrip-
    ture and the Church of England.
    Published before 1757.

Instructions for Travellers.   Dublin, 1758.

The Manifold Causes of the Increase of the Poor.
    The "advertisement" is signed by Tucker and dated May 26, 1760.

The Case of Going to War for the Sake of Procuring, Enlarging or Secur-
    ing of Trade, Considered in a New Light.   London, 1763.
    Reprinted as Tract II of *Four Tracts*.

A Sermon Preached in the Parish Church of Christ Church, London, on
    Wednesday, May the 7th, 1766.   London, 1766.

A Letter from a Merchant in London to His Nephew in North America,
    Relative to the Present Posture of Affairs in the Colonies.   London,
    1766.
    Reprinted as Tract III of *Four Tracts*.

Six Sermons on Important Subjects.   Bristol, 1772.
    Republished in *Seventeen Sermons*.

An Apology for the Present Church of England, as by Law Established. Gloucester, 1772.

A second edition was published in the same year.

Sermons on Important Occasions, Principally Relating to the Quinquarticular Controversy.

Advertised in *Letters to Dr. Kippis*.

Letters to the Rev. Dr. Kippis. Gloucester, 1773.

The True Interest of Great Britain Set Forth in Regard to the Colonies. Norfolk, 1774.

Reprinted as Tract IV of *Four Tracts*.

Four Tracts Together with Two Sermons. Gloucester, 1774.

A second edition was published in 1774 and a third in 1776.

Religious Intolerance No Part of the General Plan either of the Mosaic or Christian Dispensation. Gloucester, 1774.

A Brief and Dispassionate View of the Difficulties Attending the Trinitarian, Arian and Socinian Systems. Gloucester, 1774.

Republished as an appendix to *Seventeen Sermons*.

A Review of Lord Vis. Clare's Conduct as Representative of Bristol. Gloucester, 1775.

Tract V. The Respective Pleas and Arguments of the Mother Country and of the Colonies. Gloucester, 1775.

A Letter to Edmund Burke. Gloucester, 1775.

A second edition was published in the same year.

An Humble Address and Earnest Appeal. Gloucester, 1775.

A second edition was published in the same year, and a third in 1776.

A Series of Answers to Certain Popular Objections against Separating from the Rebellious Colonies. Gloucester, 1776.

Seventeen Sermons. London, 1776.

The Notions of Mr. Locke and His Followers.

Privately printed, 1778.

A Treatise concerning Civil Government. London, 1781.

Cui Bono? Gloucester, 1781.

A second and third edition were published in 1782.

Reflections on the Present Low Price of Coarse Wools. London, 1782.

Four Letters on Important National Subjects. London, 1783.

A second edition was published in the same year.

A Sequel to Sir William Jones' Pamphlet on the Principles of Government. Gloucester, 1784.

Reflections on the Present Matters in Dispute between Great Britain and Ireland. Dublin, 1785.

Arguments for and against an Union between Great Britain and Ireland Considered; to Which is Prefixed a Proposal on the Same Subject, by Josiah Tucker. London, 1798.

Union or Separation, Written Some Years Since by the Rev. Dr. Tucker . . . . . and Now First Published in This Tract upon the Same Subject. By the Rev. Dr. Clarke. London, 1799.

INDEX

Aber, William, license granted to, 187

Aberystwith, Wales, Tucker raised near: Jacobites and Hanoverians in, 5

Absolution, judicial, 272

Act of Parliament. *See* Parliament

Admiralty, commissioners of, conference with shipwrights, excerpt of resolutions, 118–20

Agents in foreign ports, 86, 88, 162, 163

Agrarian laws, 249; Roman, 288

Agriculture. *See* Husbandry

Alien duty, 86

Allegiance, duty of, 433

All Saints' Church, Bristol, T. appointed vicar of, 8; parishioners in, 11

Alumni Oxonienses, record of T. in, 6

Ambassadors, payment of, by exclusive companies, 160, 161

Ambrose, Earl of Warwick, patent granted to, 188

America, Lockian republic in, suggested, 453, 465

American colonists, 11, 30, 35, 419, 428, 445, 526; trade of, 30, 34, 35, 301, 315, 321, 334, 359–62, 385, 388, 437n; character and disposition, 35, 319, 322, 345, 376, 377, 385, 388, 389, 390, 437n; Benjamin Franklin's attitude in relation to, 297, 376; discontent, 305, 333; taxation without representation, 306–14, 337; as English subjects, 307; charters, 307, 336; favored by Parliament, 314; case of the Stamp Tax, 316, 337, 342, 351; wealth and luxury of, 317; aid enemies of England, 320, 376, 396; laws confining trade of, to mother country, 321n, 334; subordination to England, 322, 342; non-payment of debts, 323, 326, 334, 336, 366, 387; desire to throw off British yoke, 323, 376; proposals for dealing with, 324, 339; by military power, 324, 355; by

procrastinating compulsion, 326, 340; by separating from: effects of separation, 37–39, 327–29, 358–69; history of their insubordinations, 333, 376, 395; statute confining trials for, to English courts, 334; evasions of law, 334, 336, 390, 395; penalties for evasion, 335; effect of reduction of Canada upon, 337; provocation of: of France: of Spain, 338; assemblies called House of Commons, 341, 343; usurp legal rights of England, 341; begin framework of democracies: representation in Parliament proposed for, 343; scheme of representation and self-government, 344–55; quartering troops in, 349, 390; efforts to start manufactures, 356; proposal to make them seat of empire, 358; danger of possession of, by France, 362; emigration to, 364, 366, 386n; inducements to emigrants, 365; persecution of Church of England, 368; Edmund Burke's speech on, 372, 375; T.'s reply to, with quotations from Burke, 375–401; spirit of liberty and its sources, 376, 377; descent of: first emigrants, 377; religion, 380–82; republican tendencies, 380, 381; slavery, 382, 501; education, 384; lawyers and law-suits in, 384, 388; amount spent in defence of, 386n; struggles between governments of and England over non-payment of debts, 387; attitude toward "every idea of taxation," 390; effect of population and expansion upon, 393; effect of distance from England upon, 394; Burke's theory of a voluntary revenue for, 394, 398; grants of money: difficulties over sharing expenses of public burdens, 396; Lord North's system for obtaining revenue, 398, 399; freedom of naviga-

COLUMBIA UNIVERSITY PRESS

COLUMBIA UNIVERSITY

NEW YORK

———

FOREIGN AGENT

OXFORD UNIVERSITY PRESS

HUMPHREY MILFORD

AMEN HOUSE, LONDON, E. C.